# New York City 2010

A SELECTION
OF RESTAURANTS
& HOTELS

**Manufacture française des pneumatiques Michelin**
Société en commandite par actions au capital de 304 000 000 EUR
Place des Carmes-Déchaux – 63000 Clermont-Ferrand (France)
R.C.S. Clermont-Fd B 855 200 507



Dépot légal Octobre 2009

Made in Canada

Published in 2009



MICHELIN
A better way forward

**Please send your comments to :**

Michelin North America, Inc.
One Parkway South
Greenville, SC 29615 USA
www.michelintravel.com
Michelin.guides@us.michelin.com

# Dear Reader

*We are thrilled to present the fifth edition of our Michelin Guide to New York City.*

*Our energetic team has spent this year updating our selection to fully reflect the rich diversity of New York's restaurants and hotels. As part of our meticulous and highly confidential evaluation process, our inspectors have anonymously and methodically eaten through all five boroughs to compile the finest in each category for your enjoyment. While these inspectors are highly trained food industry professionals, we remain consumer driven: our goal is to provide comprehensive choices to accommodate your comfort, tastes, and budget. Our inspectors dine, drink, and lodge as 'regular' customers to evaluate the same level of service you would experience as a guest.*

*Furthermore, we have expanded our criteria to reflect some of the more current and unique elements of New York dining. "Small Plates" is a new category introduced to highlight establishments with a distinct style of service, setting, and menu than previously included in our selection. Additionally, new symbols have been created to showcase those restaurants with notable specialty cocktail or sake lists—these offerings have grown to be increasingly more impressive over the last five years.*

*Our company's two founders, Édouard and André Michelin, published the first Michelin Guide in 1900, to provide motorists with practical information about where they could service and repair their cars, find quality accommodations, and a good meal. Later in 1926, the star-rating system for outstanding restaurants was introduced, and over the decades we have developed many new improvements to our guides. The local team here in New York enthusiastically carries on these traditions.*

*We sincerely hope that the Michelin Guide will remain your preferred reference to the city's restaurants and hotels.*

# Contents

Peter L. Wrenn / MICHELIN

John Peden

Contents

# The Michelin Guide

"*This volume was created at the turn of the century and will last at least as long".*

This foreword to the very first edition of the MICHELIN Guide, written in 1900, has become famous over the years and the Guide has lived up to the prediction. It is read across the world and the key to its popularity is the consistency in its commitment to its readers, which is based on the following promises.

## → Anonymous Inspections

Our inspectors make anonymous visits to hotels and restaurants to gauge the quality offered to the ordinary customer. They pay their own bill and make no indication of their presence. These visits are supplemented by comprehensive monitoring of information—our readers' comments are one valuable source, and are always taken into consideration.

## → Independence

Our choice of establishments is a completely independent one, made for the benefit of our readers alone. Decisions are discussed by the inspectors and the editor, with the most important decided at the global level. Inclusion in the guide is always free of charge.

## → The Selection

The Guide offers a selection of the best hotels and restaurants in each category of comfort and price. Inclusion in the guides is a commendable award in itself, and defines the establishment among the "best of the best."

# How the MICHELIN Guide Works

## → Annual Updates

All practical information, the classifications, and awards, are revised and updated every year to ensure the most reliable information possible.

## → Consistency & Classifications

The criteria for the classifications are the same in all countries covered by the Michelin Guides. Our system is used worldwide and is easy to apply when choosing a restaurant or hotel.

## → The Classifications

We classify our establishments using XXXXX-X and 🏨🏨🏨-🏨 to indicate the level of comfort. The ✿✿✿-✿ specifically designates an award for cuisine, unique from the classification. For hotels and restaurants, a symbol in red suggests a particularly charming spot with unique décor or ambiance.

## → Our Aim

As part of Michelin's ongoing commitment to improving travel and mobility, we do everything possible to make vacations and eating out a pleasure.

# How to Use This Guide

## Where to **Eat**

### Restaurant Classifications by Comfort

More pleasant if in red

| | |
|---|---|
| ✗ | Quite comfortable |
| ✗✗ | Comfortable |
| ✗✗✗ | Very comfortable |
| ✗✗✗✗ | Top class comfortable |
| ✗✗✗✗✗ | Luxury in the traditional style |
| ▤ | Small plates |

### The Michelin Distinctions for Good Cuisine

**Stars for good cuisine**

| | |
|---|---|
| ✿✿✿ | Exceptional cuisine, worth a special journey |
| ✿✿ | Excellent cuisine, worth a detour |
| ✿ | Very good cuisine in its category |

**☺ Bib Gourmand**
Inspectors' favorites for good value

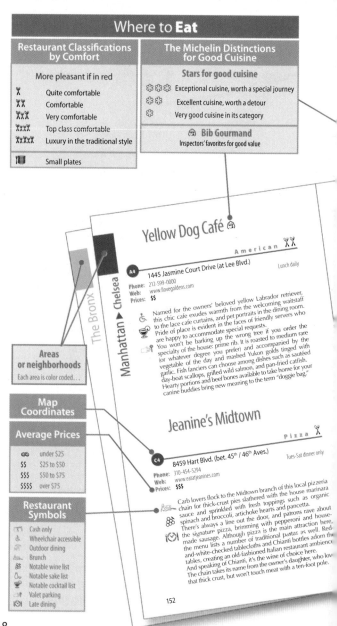

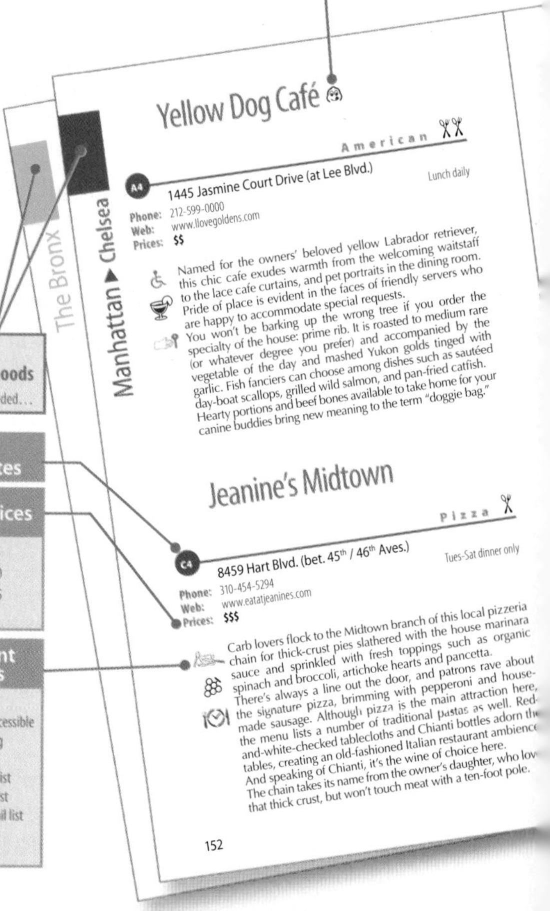

### Areas or neighborhoods
Each area is color coded…

### Map Coordinates

### Average Prices

| | |
|---|---|
| ⊛ | under $25 |
| $$ | $25 to $50 |
| $$$ | $50 to $75 |
| $$$$ | over $75 |

### Restaurant Symbols

| | |
|---|---|
| 🖅 | Cash only |
| ♿ | Wheelchair accessible |
| ✿ | Outdoor dining |
| ⚘ | Brunch |
| 🍷 | Notable wine list |
| 🍶 | Notable sake list |
| 🍸 | Notable cocktail list |
| 🗝 | Valet parking |
| 🕙 | Late dining |

---

## Yellow Dog Café ☺

American ✗✗

**A4** 1445 Jasmine Court Drive (at Lee Blvd.)          Lunch daily

Phone: 212-599-0000
Web: www.ilovegoldens.com
Prices: $$

Named for the owners' beloved yellow Labrador retriever, this chic cafe exudes warmth from the welcoming waitstaff to the lace cafe curtains, and pet portraits in the dining room. Pride of place is evident in the faces of friendly servers who are happy to accommodate special requests.

You won't be barking up the wrong tree if you order the specialty of the house: prime rib. It is roasted to medium rare (or whatever degree you prefer) and accompanied by the vegetable of the day and mashed Yukon golds tinged with garlic. Fish fanciers can choose among dishes such as sautéed day-boat scallops, grilled wild salmon, and pan-fried catfish. Hearty portions and beef bones available to take home for your canine buddies bring new meaning to the term "doggie bag."

## Jeanine's Midtown

Pizza ✗

**C4** 8459 Hart Blvd. (bet. 45th / 46th Aves.)          Tues-Sat dinner only

Phone: 310-454-5294
Web: www.eatatjeanines.com
Prices: $$$

Carb lovers flock to the Midtown branch of this local pizzeria chain for thick-crust pies slathered with the house marinara sauce and sprinkled with fresh toppings such as organic spinach and broccoli, artichoke hearts and pancetta. There's always a line out the door, and patrons rave about the signature pizza, brimming with pepperoni and house-made sausage. Although pizza is the main attraction here, the menu lists a number of traditional pastas as well. Red-and-white-checked tablecloths and Chianti bottles adorn the tables, creating an old-fashioned Italian restaurant ambience. And speaking of Chianti, it's the wine of choice here. The chain takes its name from the owner's daughter, who loves that thick crust, but won't touch meat with a ten-foot pole.

152

How to Use This Guide

# Where to **Stay**

## Average Prices

Prices do not include applicable taxes

| | |
|---|---|
| $ | under $200 |
| $$ | $200 to $300 |
| $$$ | $300 to $400 |
| $$$$ | over $400 |

## Hotel Symbols

| | |
|---|---|
| 149 rooms | Number of rooms & suites |
| ♿ | Wheelchair accessible |
| | Exercise room |
| Spa | Spa |
| | Swimming pool |
| | Conference room |
| | Pet friendly |

## Hotel Classifications by Comfort

More pleasant if in red

- Quite comfortable
- Comfortable
- Very comfortable
- Top class comfortable
- Luxury in the traditional style

## Map Coordinates

's Palace

italian

ner Place (at 30th Street)

Dinner daily

9

fabulouspalace.com

Manhattan ▸ Chelsea

David Buffington/Getty Images

ome cooked Italian never tasted so good than at this npretentious little place. The simple décor claims no big-name designers, and while the Murano glass light fixtures are chic and the velveteen-covered chairs are comfortable, this isn't a restaurant where millions of dollars were spent on the interior.

Instead, food is the focus here. The restaurant's name may not be Italian, but it nonetheless serves some of the best pasta in the city, made fresh in-house. Dishes follow the seasons, thus ravioli may be stuffed with fresh ricotta and herbs in summer, and pumpkin in fall. Most everything is liberally dusted with Parmigiano Reggiano, a favorite ingredient of the chef.

For dessert, you'll have to deliberate between the likes of creamy tiramisu, ricotta cheesecake, and homemade gelato. One thing's for sure: you'll never miss your *nonna's* cooking when you eat at Sonya's.

153

The Fan Inn

D1

135 Shanghai Road, Oakland

Phone: 650-345-1440 or 888-222-2424
Fax: 650-397-2408
Web: www.superfaninnoakland.com
Prices: $$

45 Rooms
5 Suites

John A. Rizzo/Getty Images

Housed in an Art Deco-era building, the venerable Fan Inn recently underwent a complete facelift. The hotel now fits in with the new generation of sleekly understated hotels offering a Zen-inspired aesthetic, despite its 1930s origins. soothing neutral palette runs throughout the property, ctuated with exotic woods, bamboo, and fine fabrics. the lobby, the sultry lounge makes a relaxing place for a mixed cocktail or a glass of wine.

linens and down pillows cater to your comfort, while een TVs, DVD players with iPod docking stations, ireless Internet access satisfy the need for modern es. For business travelers, nightstands convert to tables and credenzas morph into flip-out desks. printer, fax or scanner? It's just a phone call away. uest, the hotel will even provide office supplies. half of the accommodations here are suites, where factor ratchets up with marble baths, spacious , and fully equipped kitchens. Although the inn a restaurant, the nearby blocks hold nearly ou could want in terms of food, from soup haute cuisine.

Manhattan ▸ Chelsea

419

How to Use This Guide

# Where to Eat

Peter L. Wrenn / MICHELIN

# Manhattan

# Chelsea

Restaurants in this entertaining neighborhood—the hub of New York's gallery scene—feature flavors from around the globe, encompassing everything from French bistros to sushi bars and the contemporary Spanish fare at **Socarrat Paella**. Old World Puerto Rican luncheonettes on and around 9th Avenue—where patrons are accommodated in English or Spanish, and the *café* con leche packs a heady wallop—provide a striking contrast to the mega-hip places that punctuate Chelsea today. For heavenly Italian, try the much-hyped pizza joint, **Company**, home to iconoclast Jim Lahey's blistered and crispy pies. The Chef/owner and founder of Sullivan Street Bakery, fires his pizza in a wood-burning oven imported from Modena, and the lines of folks eager to taste them stretch out the door. If that's not hip enough, there's always the scene at **Buddakan**, that tried and trendy temple of modern Asian fare, brought to New York by Philadelphia restaurateur wunderkind Stephen Starr.

In the burgeoning area known as the West Club District, patrons of nightspots like Mansion, Guest House, Home, and Marquee are grateful for all-night restaurants like the **Punjabi Food Junction**, offering a delish self-serve Indian buffet. Also in the open-late category, the quintessential New York spot **The Half King** dishes up good all-American grub. Named for an 18th century Seneca Indian chief, Half King also sponsors book readings on Monday nights, thanks to owner and writer Sebastian Junger, author of *The Perfect Storm: A True Story of Men Against the Sea.*

No food-finding excursion to this area would be complete without a visit to the **Chelsea Market**. The 1898 Nabisco factory—where the Oreo cookie was first made in 1912—was reopened in 1997 as an urban food market. Interspersed throughout its brick-lined arcades with stores selling flowers, meats, cheeses, artisan-made breads, and other gourmet essentials are cafés, bakeries, and eateries. Drop by to peruse the wares, stock your pantry, and have a bite to eat while you're at it. Treat yourself to organic farm-fresh cuisine and biodynamic wines at **The Green Table** at The Cleaver Co. You can even buy an artisanal potpie here to take home for dinner. And speaking of take-out, seafood lovers can pick up a luscious lobster roll or some freshly steamed lobsters at **The Lobster Place**, New York's leading purveyor of these sea creatures. If you have kids in tow, a stop at **L'Arte del Gelato** is a must. No matter your preference, a trip to the market will nourish you for hours of gallery-hopping among the more than 350 art galleries that fill garages and lofts on the district's western flank.

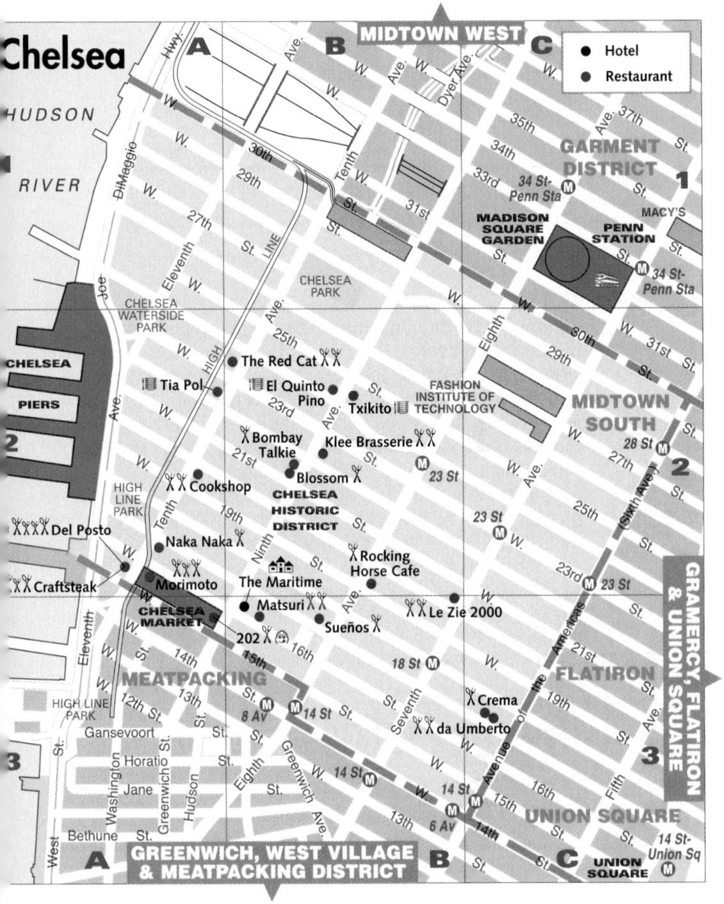


Upstairs, the Chelsea Market pavilion houses the studios and test kitchens for the Food Network. Once off-limits to the public, these facilities were recently opened for 45-minute tours. To catch your favorite TV chefs in action, call the ticket hotline or visit the Food Network Shop at Chelsea Market Baskets.

And while you're in the neighborhood, consider dining with a view of Lady Liberty and the island of Manhattan on one of the dinner cruises that departs from Chelsea Piers, an ever-evolving recreational waterfront area located along the West Side Highway between 17th and 23rd streets. Comprising four historic piers along the Hudson River, the complex now houses state-of-the-art sports facilities, including a spa, ice skating rink, and bowling alley. It's also the home of Silver Screen Studios, where the long-running television series *Law and Order* is produced.

# Blossom

B2 — **Vegan**

187 Ninth Ave. (bet. 21st & 22nd Sts.)

**Subway:** 23 St (Eighth Ave.) — Lunch Fri – Sun
**Phone:** 212-627-1144 — Dinner nightly
**Web:** www.blossomnyc.com
**Prices:** **$$**

Serving dynamic, inventive cuisine to vegans and open-minded omnivores, Blossom is a fantastic restaurant. Convivial yet calm, intimate but not claustrophobic, and deliciously satisfying while strictly vegetarian, this eatery is a favorable study in balance. Candles and votives illuminate diners enjoying conversations above soft background music, including some celebrated reggae beats.

Menu items feature bright flavors, bold spices, and are so pleasantly rich that they almost seem meaty. Offerings include spinach-filled ravioli with cashew cream, or seitan *scaloppine* in a white wine, lemon, and caper sauce. Be sure to save room for the wonderfully smooth desserts; and make a reservation early—evidence of its popularity is its tendency to fill quickly.

# Bombay Talkie

B2 — **Indian**

189 Ninth Ave. (bet. 21st & 22nd Sts.)

**Subway:** 23 St (Eighth Ave.) — Dinner nightly
**Phone:** 212-242-1900
**Web:** www.bombaytalkie.com
**Prices:** **$$**

As a nod to India's movie craze, owner Sunitha Ramaiah credits her inspiration for Bombay Talkie to a 1970s film of the same name. The Thomas Juul-Hansen designed space followed her lead creating mural paintings of Indian movie stars in the hip room, styled after an Indian tea house. Bollywood films are looped above the downstairs bar, serving a mesmerizing blend of East-meets-West cocktails.

Eat family style at the communal table with friends and enjoy varied "Street Bites," such as Bombay *Bhel*, assorted wheat flour chips, and rice puffs tossed with green mango salsa and mint chutney. "Dinner by the Roadside" and "Curbside" menus include generous servings of more classic regional dishes, permeated with spices and drizzled with cooling sauces.

# Cookshop

American XX

A2

156 Tenth Ave. (at 20th St.)

**Subway:** 23 St (Eighth Ave.) Lunch & dinner daily
**Phone:** 212-924-4440
**Web:** www.cookshopny.com
**Prices:** $$

Owner Vicki Freeman and husband, Chef Marc Meyer have made an enduring commitment to a philosophy of locally procured ingredients. Whenever possible, they create menus that read as lessons in terroir—with Hudson Valley rabbit and venison, and Vermont lamb. For the herbivores, a large chalkboard highlights the produce—apples, herbs, and squash—that change with the seasons. This is not cookie cutter food simply following the latest green trend. Their food is prepared with pride and their diligence is apparent in every nibble. Be patient because food this thoughtful can only be handcrafted.

The room is airy and softly lit during dinner and floods with natural light at lunchtime. Order a cocktail or quartino of wine and relax in the room decked in the season's bounty.

# Craftsteak

Steakhouse XXX

A2

85 Tenth Ave. (at 15th St.)

**Subway:** 14 St - 8 Av Dinner nightly
**Phone:** 212-400-6699
**Web:** www.craftrestaurant.com
**Prices:** $$$$

There are wine snobs and cheese dorks, but most figure a steak is just a steak. It's all in how you cook that sucker, right?

No, says Tom Colicchio, with his gorgeous, see-and-be-seen modern steakhouse. The enormous menu (rounded out by a beautiful raw bar) takes readers on a dizzying cattle odyssey that may include corn-fed steaks from California; a few grass-fed Bessie's from Hawaii and Oregon; or Texan Wagyu. Sweet freaks should save room for seasonal desserts like a moist pumpkin cheesecake on crumbled gingerbread, with toasted pumpkin seeds and crème fraîche ice cream.

Diners looking for a taste of the action without the eye-popping bill can hit Halfsteak, the newly designated front room, for a $14 half-steak and tangle of fries.

# Crema

**C3**

Mexican ✗

**111 W. 17th St. (bet. Sixth & Seventh Aves.)**

**Subway:** 18 St                                    Lunch & dinner daily
**Phone:** 212-691-4477
**Web:** www.cremarestaurante.com
**Prices:** $$

Serving equal parts casual and upscale, the bright décor and upbeat Latin music are pure Mexican oasis, while the vibrant presentation of dishes showcase Chef Julieta Ballesteros' penchant for dramatic flair. Crema's rather artistic, regional Mexican cuisine perfectly complements its crowd. A long, narrow room with colorful walls, a white marble bar, and a cactus garden are all brought to life by the buzzing and visible kitchen. Lovely glass jars filled with a variety of sangrias sit on the bar.

Appealing dishes offer strong visual impressions, balanced flavors, and a great hint of heat. A $19 prix-fixe lunch menu may feature the *sopa del dia*; entrées like grilled quesadillas with "Huitlacoche Negro" (Mexican black truffles); a side dish; and soft drink.

# da Umberto

**C3**

Italian ✗✗

**107 W. 17th St. (bet. Sixth & Seventh Aves.)**

**Subway:** 18 St                                    Lunch Mon – Fri
**Phone:** 212-989-0303                              Dinner Mon – Sat
**Web:** N/A
**Prices:** $$$

"Happy families are all alike," begins Tolstoy's most famous novel, and the same might be said of good Italian food. Not so at Da Umberto, which raises the bar with their exacting attention to detail. The payoff for this sort of type-A behavior is creamy, perfectly-cooked risotto; fork-tender rabbit, stewed in a fragrant Sicilian sauce; and seductively sweet ricotta cheesecake, poured into a buttery crust and studded with candied fruit.

Unfortunately, the restaurant's prices are right in step with the sharply dressed businessmen and lunching ladies that fill its sophisticated dining room. And yet, everything is relative—as menu prices across the city have climbed, the questionable numbers gracing da Umberto's menu seem to have returned to market value.

# Del Posto ✿

Italian XXXX

A2

85 Tenth Ave. (bet. 15th & 16th Sts.)

**Subway:** 14 St - 8 Av
**Phone:** 212-497-8090
**Web:** www.delposto.com
**Prices:** $$$$

Lunch Wed – Fri
Dinner nightly

Lydia Gould Bessler

Mario Batali's most formal restaurant is as grand as an opera house—with a sexy, over-the-top theatrical interior fitted out with swirling verandas, wrought-iron balconies, and dripping chandeliers. It's a stark difference from its windy west Meatpacking District location, on Tenth Avenue's all-star chef's restaurant row.

The rustic Italian menu, conceived by Batali and partner Lidia Bastianich, reads deceptively simple, but layers intense flavors into dishes like a soft pile of fresh *caramelle*—a type of pasta wrapped to look like its namesake sweet—filled with rich, creamy *Robiola*, and gently bathed in silky black truffle butter; or a seasonal Italian-style crêpe that arrives perfectly caramelized and loosely folded over sweet, earthy roasted pumpkin, then laced with smoked apple purée and a touch of whipped crème fraîche.

There are two ways to lighten the bill: Sample two or three pastas between your table or hit the *enoteca* for a scaled-back menu—a smattering of delicious, but simpler, fare. Italian grapehounds will want to linger over Del Posto's never-ending wine list, teeming with regional Italian producers and varietals, not to mention an ample Champagne selection.

# El Quinto Pino

B2 — Spanish

401 W. 24th St. (bet. Ninth & Tenth Aves.)

**Subway:** 23 St (Eighth Ave.) — Dinner nightly
**Phone:** 212-206-5900
**Web:** www.elquintopinonyc.com
**Prices:** ⊜

Chelsea has enough tapas joints to give the Basque region a run for its money, but its newest kid on the block, El Quinto Pino, is worth breaking out those dancing shoes for one last time. Brought to you by the threesome that opened nearby Tia Pol (the original tapas it-girl), the Lilliputian Pino aims to bring tapas back to its original concept—as a quick snack rather than a sit-down meal.

And despite there being no real tables, the bar in this warm, narrow space has been mobbed since its 2008 debut. Credit goes to the chef de cuisine—Amorette Casaus—who offers up creative tapas like a fresh uni panini, squeezed into bread slathered with Korean mustard oil; or a plate of smoky eggplant with honey and bonito flakes.

# Klee Brasserie

B2 — Contemporary

200 Ninth Ave. (bet. 22nd & 23rd Sts.)

**Subway:** 23 St (Eighth Ave.) — Lunch Tue – Sun
**Phone:** 212-633-8033 — Dinner nightly
**Web:** www.kleebrasserie.com
**Prices:** $$

It's the little details that make this Chelsea steady stand out from the neighborhood's ample restaurant competition. Guests melt into the soft, toffee-colored banquettes, flanked by bare brick walls and soothing blonde wood, and people-watch from the huge windows that line the façade.

Meanwhile, the sharp-as-a-tack staff quietly slides out plate after plate of Chef Daniel Angerer's innovative cuisine. A velvety bowl of chilled five-color carrot soup arrives lined with crispy dried corn kernels and studded with organic cherry tomatoes, micro chives, and shaved *Idiazábal* cheese; a nutty apple strudel is flanked by a housemade Tahitian vanilla gelato, and paired with crunchy caramelized walnuts, warm apple butter, and a soft, sweet lingonberry sauce.

Peter L. Wrenn/MICHELIN

# Le Zie 2000

B3 **Italian** XX

172 Seventh Ave. (bet. 20th & 21st Sts.)

**Subway:** 23 St (Seventh Ave.) Lunch & dinner daily
**Phone:** 212-206-8686
**Web:** www.lezie.com
**Prices:** **$$**

Italy's Veneto culinary region stars in the pastel dining room, where Le Zie 2000 continues to embody wholesome Italian cuisine. Begin your meal sharing the antipasti sampling—*cicchetti*—which includes several Venetian savory classics and is served with the region's signature starch, grilled polenta. Among several fine *paste* and *secondi piatti* offerings are Venetian-style calf's liver and hearty homemade pastas. Around the corner on 20th Street, Le Zie lounge offers light tasting and cocktail menus. All wines from Le Zie's extensive list, which cites some 200 labels representing all of Italy's viticultural regions, are available in the lounge.
Outside, Le Zie's small patio remains a fine place to while away the sunny days.

# Matsuri

B3 **Japanese** XX

369 W. 16th St. (bet. Eighth & Ninth Aves.)

**Subway:** 14 St - 8 Av Dinner nightly
**Phone:** 212-243-6400
**Web:** www.themaritimehotel.com
**Prices:** **$$**

Matsuri deserves the hiss of surprise that its jaw-dropping interior provokes—but unlike some Trojan Horses in this town, it has the food to back it up. Step inside the cavernous dining room, with its enormous curved ceiling, extensive sake collection lining the wall, and beautiful misshapen paper lanterns, and soak in the grandeur (the acoustics here rival some of the more prominent concert halls around this city).
When your jaw snaps back into place, settle in for some decadent Japanese fare, which might include a silky, red miso soup, infused with scallion and ginger, and with a single tender claw of lobster floating elegantly in its center; or a fresh young sea bass, deep fried with ponzu-*momiji* sauce.

# Morimoto

Fusion XXX

A2

88 Tenth Ave. (at 16th St.)

**Subway:** 14 St - 8 Av
**Phone:** 212-989-8883
**Web:** www.morimotonyc.com
**Prices:** $$$

Lunch Mon – Fri
Dinner nightly

Located in the super-trendy Western nook of Chelsea, Morimoto has been packing them in on nights when even its most famous neighbors are a quarter-full. The draw? A starkly sexy interior with a cuisine bold enough to match it. Sail past Morimoto's billowing curtains and into the sultry cement-and-metal filled space, and you'll be greeted by more beautiful people than you can shake a Blahnik at.

Back on your plate, you'll find upscale Japanese fusion (heavy on the fusion, light on the Japanese) courtesy of the great Masaharu Morimoto. Try the delicate lamb carpaccio, perfectly sliced on the bias and garnished with a creamy lemon-kissed sauce, ginger, and scallions; or curried beef points wrapped in rice paper and breadcrumbs, then tossed in curry.

# Naka Naka

Japanese X

A2

458 W. 17th St. (at Tenth Ave.)

**Subway:** 14 St - 8 Av
**Phone:** 212-929-8544
**Web:** N/A
**Prices:** $$$

Dinner Tue – Sun

Like a mouse bucking a tsunami, little Naka Naka has stayed put while everything around it has caved to the ever-changing landscape where Chelsea borders the Meatpacking District. The winning concept of this homespun Japanese restaurant is simple—a small, pretty room tucked into a timeworn tenement building on 10th Avenue, where you'll discover a low-slung, horseshoe-shaped bar and a few well-spaced tables.

Save for the servers kneeling to take your order or ferrying food back and forth, the only commotion in this little haven is on the plate, where you might discover a perfectly-charred Spanish mackerel in sake paste, paired with a fried green horn pepper and roasted cherry tomato; or a fresh lobe of creamy uni, with Japanese pickles and grated radish.

# The Red Cat

B2 — American

227 Tenth Ave. (bet. 23rd & 24th Sts.)

**Subway:** 23 St (Eighth Ave.)
**Phone:** 212-242-1122
**Web:** www.redcatrestaurants.com
**Prices:** $$

Lunch Tue – Sat
Dinner nightly

Filled with bold, rich colors as vivid as its innovative cuisine, The Red Cat recreates classic seafood and contemporary dishes. Menus are designed according to seasonal availability and are worth return visits. Enjoy starters like grilled peaches with fresh ricotta, baby greens, and grilled ham, before an entrée of juicy double-cut pork chops. The bar also offers the full menu—a fine option for diners who need prompt service, or for those dining alone.

The décor features a jovial banquette extending the wall opposite a bar that dominates the dining room, lavish with flower arrangements and Moroccan-inspired lanterns. White-washed pine walls are adorned with fine art worthy of the artists and patrons who frequent this popular Chelsea establishment.

# Rocking Horse Cafe

B2 — Mexican

182 Eighth Ave. (bet. 19th & 20th Sts.)

**Subway:** 14 St - 8 Av
**Phone:** 212-463-9511
**Web:** www.rockinghorsecafe.com
**Prices:** $$

Lunch & dinner daily

Head to Rocking Horse for great Mexican dishes in sophisticated surroundings. The flavors are as vivid as the tangerine and apple-red hues in the hip, contemporary space. Start your meal with handmade tortillas and crispy chips accompanied by a creamy, chunky jalapeño-laced salsa. Soups of the day may include marvelous bowlfuls of warm zucchini thickened with potatoes, and cooled with cilantro and cream. The entrées are myriad and include *budin Azteca*—tortillas layered with tender, free-range chicken breast, Chihuahua cheese, and *salsa verde*. The bar also boasts a serious offering of tequila, mixed in margaritas or served straight up.

Red garage-type doors open to the sidewalk, where a handful of outdoor tables are available for warm-weather dining.

# Sueños

Mexican

B3

311 W. 17th St. (bet. Eighth & Ninth Aves.)

**Subway:** 14 St - 8 Av
**Phone:** 212-243-1333
**Web:** www.suenosnyc.com
**Prices:** $$

Dinner nightly

Sueños isn't the easiest place to access—you'll need to duck down an alley and walk something like a maritime plank to enter—and its interior won't be winning any design awards anytime soon. But this little Mexican charmer is more than a step above the mom-and-pop ethnic eateries that dot the Latin neighborhoods of East Harlem and Queens.

It's the little touches, like the fresh tortillas being churned out by hand in the rear of the dining room, or the criminally fresh guacamole, made to order with ripe chunks of avocado and bright tomato, and paired with a basket of salty, housemade chips. For dinner, try the empanadas—stuffed with rich, sweet plantain and tart chunks of goat cheese—each warm bite is a delicious study in contrasts.

# 202

Contemporary

A3

75 Ninth Ave. (bet. 15th & 16th Sts.)

**Subway:** 14 St - 8 Av
**Phone:** 646-638-1173
**Web:** N/A
**Prices:** $$

Lunch daily
Dinner Tue – Sun

Quietly tucked into the Nicole Farhi boutique in Chelsea Market, 202 may be the perfect spot to luxuriate in a handcrafted cocktail while trying to decide which body-hugging dress to try on next. Although high-end shopping opportunities abound, this unique café and restaurant remains welcoming, low-key, and very dedicated to presenting high quality, well-prepared cuisine. The silky, tender, juicy, and flavor-packed lamb burger, topped with a melting goat cheese medallion, and served with chick pea fries, is considered one of the best in town. British chef, Annie Wayte's menu also includes crisp seasonal salads and fish tacos.

A $35 prix-fixe Sunday brunch menu includes an appetizer, main course, and dessert—a perfect ruse to continue shopping.

# Tia Pol

Spanish

A2

205 Tenth Ave. (bet. 22nd & 23rd Sts.)

**Subway:** 23 St (Eighth Ave.)
**Phone:** 212-675-8805
**Web:** www.tiapol.com
**Prices:**

Lunch Tue – Sun
Dinner nightly

On its surface, this tapas joint of much buzz is nothing more than a narrow, characterless space with a whirring fan and a horse sculpture, tucked behind a steel-patch door on Tenth Avenue.

So why all the fuss? Location, for starters: if you want a good bite along this stretch, the really good eats tend to be super high-end, like Del Posto or Craftsteak. Then there's the clever, affordable Spanish wine list, and the always-buzzing crowd, happily packed around Tia Pol's bar. But mostly, they come for the delicious tapas, a mouthwatering roster that might include tender lamb skewers; seasonal whitebait; cod done every which way but Friday; plus cheese and charcuterie platters loaded with silky hams and garlicky chorizos.

# Txikito

Spanish

B2

240 Ninth Ave. (bet. 24th & 25th Sts.)

**Subway:** 23 St (Eighth Ave.)
**Phone:** 212-242-4730
**Web:** www.txikitonyc.com
**Prices:** $$

Lunch Tue – Fri
Dinner Tue – Sun

The rise of the tapas movement in the United States is a fascinating one: what began as a concept on loan from Spain—a smattering of small plates paired with alcohol—has gotten so popular that people are willing to shell out as much cash as they would a proper meal.

Good thing the tiny little Txikito offers so many reasons to unload your wallet, with a knowledgeable wait staff, proper silverware (though fingers and forks are just fine for tapas), and a simple, if slightly grim, décor where Chef Alex Raij, who hails from venerable tapas neighbor, Tia Pol, whips out mouthwatering small plates like meatballs pooled in shellfish broth; and *boquerónes* (marinated white anchovies), smoky eggplant purée, red peppers, and a fan of boiled egg.

# Chinatown & Little Italy

As different as chow mein and chicken cacciatore, these two districts are nonetheless neighbors, though in recent years, their borders have become blurred with Chinatown voraciously gulping up most of Little Italy.

## Chinatown

The end of California's Gold Rush brought the arrival of New York's first Chinese in the 1870s. The immigrant influx arrived energetically, setting up garment factories, markets, and restaurants in the quarter, which has inexorably spread into Little Italy and the Lower East Side. It is documented that New York cradles the maximum number of Chinese immigrants in the country and specifically, Queens, followed by Manhattan, holds one of the largest Chinese communities outside Asia. Immigrants from Hong Kong and mainland China (most recently Fujian province) populate the Manhattan Chinatown, each bringing their distinct regional cuisines.

Chowing in Chinatown can be both scrumptious and delightfully affordable. Elbow your way through the crowded streets and find a flurry of food markets, bubble tea cafés, bakeries, and eateries large and small. Feast on freshly pulled noodles; duck into an ice cream parlor for a scoop of avocado or black sesame; or breeze past a market window and spy the crocodile meat and frogs on display (with claws). Haggle aggressively over the freshest fish and produce at the storefronts and then sneak under the Manhattan Bridge for a *banh mi*.

Klezmer meets Cantonese at the Egg Rolls and Egg Creams Festival, an annual summer street celebration honoring the neighboring Chinese and Jewish communities of Chinatown and the Lower East Side. Partygoers pack the streets for Chinese New Year (the first full moon after January 19th), with dragons dancing down the avenues accompanied by costumed revelers and fireworks.

## Little Italy

The Little Italy of Scorcese's gritty, authentic *Mean Streets* is slowly vanishing into what may now be more aptly called Micro Italy. The onetime stronghold of a large Italian-American population (once spanning from Canal Street north to Houston, and from Lafayette to the Bowery) has dwindled to a mere corridor—Mulberry Street between Canal and Broome streets. Chinatown is quickly devouring Mulberry Street, the main drag and the tenacious heart of the area.

But the spirit of the origins still pulses in century-old, family-run markets, delis, gelato shops, and mom-and-pop trattorias. Established in 1892, **Alleva Dairy** (known for their homemade ricotta) is the oldest

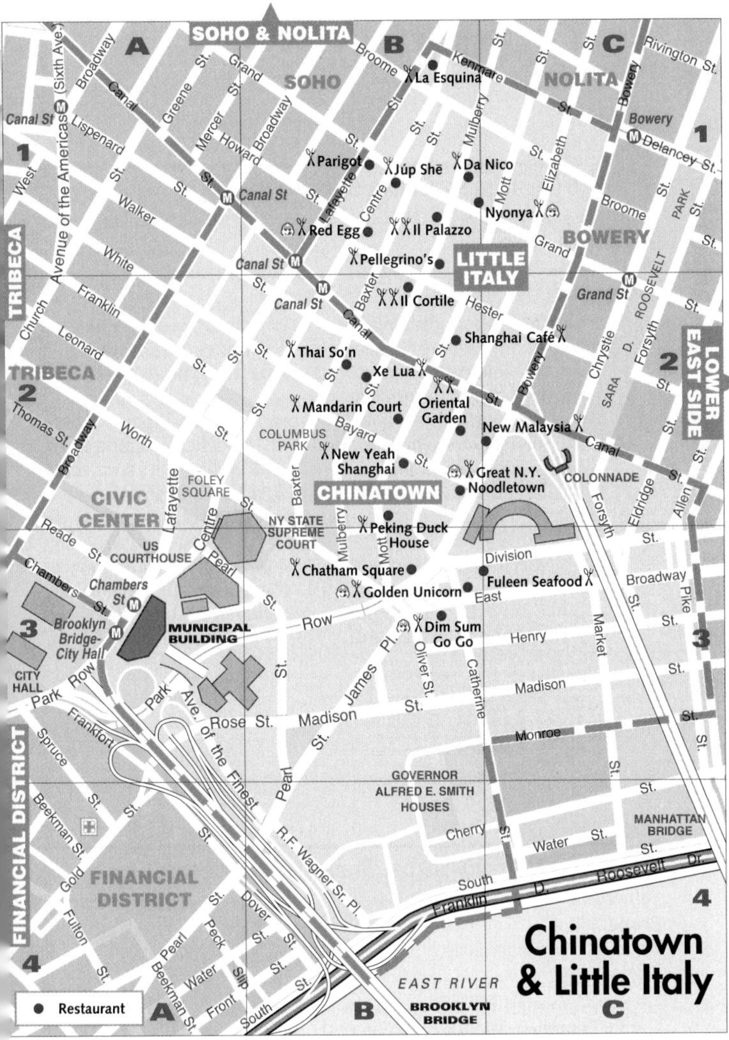


Italian cheese store in the U.S.; a few doors down at **DiPalo's Fine Foods** find imported sopressata and *salumi*. Renowned for its Italian pastries and strong espresso, devotees frequent the beloved **Ferrara's Bakery and Café** on Grand Street.

On weekends from May to mid-October, Mulberry Street is a pedestrian zone, creating one big alfresco party—the Feast of San Gennaro in September is particularly raucous. While these days you get better Italian food elsewhere, tourists still gather to treasure and bathe in the nostalgia of Mulberry Street.

# Chatham Square

B3 **Chinese**

## 6 Chatham Sq. (at East Broadway)

**Subway:** Canal St (Lafayette St.) Lunch & dinner daily
**Phone:** 212-587-8800
**Web:** N/A
**Prices:** ⓢⓢ

Situated on a thriving stretch of the Bowery known as "Chatham Square," this lively, well-priced spot draws a mostly Chinese crowd for its fantastic daytime dim sum and evening classic Cantonese.

Large round tables line the colorful dining space where friendly servers wheel around carts of delicious dumplings, puffs, buns, and soups at lunch. The rolling dim sum show has become a rarity so sidle up next to some strangers at a shared table and indulge in savory steamed dumplings—with at least ten varieties of fillings—or baked puffs surrounding a savory mound of shredded roast pork. Sticky rice, congee, and dumpling soups provide some warmth. Feeling the funk? Brave the durain puffs-cigar-shaped pastries filled with a sweet and fruity custard.

# Da Nico

B1 **Italian**

## 164 Mulberry St. (bet. Broome & Grand Sts.)

**Subway:** Canal St (Lafayette St.) Lunch & dinner daily
**Phone:** 212-343-1212
**Web:** www.danicorest.com
**Prices:** $$

Although Da Nico's (of the Luizza family's Mulberry Street empire) interior was recently refitted, the place to sit—weather permitting—is on the back patio. This enclosed outdoor terrace nearly doubles the restaurant's seating space in the summer and provides a countryside ambience, seemingly far from the commotion of Little Italy's commercial thoroughfare.

The Italian-American menu features dishes that celebrate garlic, tomatoes, and the traditional flavors typically associated with this culture—and neighborhood. From the coal-fired oven comes a variety of pizzas, all made using a crust recipe that has been passed down through generations of the Luizza family. The copious entrée selections may range from veal saltimbocca to house-made gnocchi.

# Dim Sum Go Go

Chinese

B3

5 East Broadway (at Chatham Sq.)

**Subway:** Canal St (Lafayette St.)

Lunch & dinner daily

**Phone:** 212-732-0797

**Web:** N/A

**Prices:**

There are none of those cute little dim sum carts at Dim Sum Go Go, nor, despite the devil-may-care moniker, are there any scantily clad go-go dancers. There is, however, a most excellent selection of dim sum at this bright, funky Chinatown restaurant—loads of it, in fact, with over 24 varieties of the light plates to choose from, even well into the evening (dim sum is traditionally served at lunch). One might gather that owner and French-American food writer, Colette Rossant, has a taste for the stuff, but then there's also the fabulous, often-overlooked, Cantonese cooking to marvel over.

Don't miss the sautéed Chinese chives—studded with Chinese celery and crunchy, candied walnuts—the dish offers a divine intermission from the dumpling parade.

# Fuleen Seafood

Chinese

C3

11 Division St. (bet. Catherine & Market Sts. )

**Subway:** Canal St (Lafayette St.)

Lunch & dinner daily

**Phone:** 212-941-6888

**Web:** N/A

**Prices:**

This Chinatown mainstay's wall of fully stocked tanks calls out to fans of fish and the like. The attractive dining room is outfitted with large round tables routinely occupied by gregarious groups indulging in revolving platters of well-prepared food. If unsure of what to order, the polite staff will graciously guide you through the menu and make helpful recommendations. Whole fish are presented at the table for approval and then re-emerge steamed with soy, ginger, and scallions. Cantonese-style lobster and harbor-style crabs sautéed with dried shrimp and chilies are but a few of the tasty preparations offered.

For those who shy away from the sea, there are plenty of options on the sizeable menu, notably the house rendition of Peking duck.

# Golden Unicorn

B3 Chinese

18 East Broadway (at Catherine St.)

**Subway:** Canal St (Lafayette St.) Lunch & dinner daily
**Phone:** 212-941-0911
**Web:** N/A
**Prices:** $$

Golden Unicorn has recently hung a new sign on the building housing its multi-story restaurant. Not that it was required as the restaurant is popular enough, especially during weekend brunch when waits are long. The crowds pack in for good reason—delicious dim sum from carts rolling around the lively rooms of families and friends.

It takes a little perseverance and a lot of appetite to truly enjoy Golden Unicorn. Swiftly, you must win the attention of the woman wheeling the cart of goods you're interested in. Post-victory, it takes a prolific appetite to consume the variety of dim sum you've acquired, hopefully including steamed shrimp and snow pea shoot dumplings or barbequed pork buns.

# Great N.Y. Noodletown

B2 Chinese

28 Bowery (at Bayard St.)

**Subway:** Canal St (Lafayette St.) Lunch & dinner daily
**Phone:** 212-349-0923
**Web:** N/A
**Prices:**

At first glance, this unassuming corner spot's no-frills décor, menus displayed under glass-topped tables, and lack of alcohol may seem unimpressive. Luckily, appearances are deceiving, for what makes this place special is its reasonably priced, quality food served to a devoted following.

Foodies and cognoscenti focus on the house specialties: sweet and salty morsels of barbecued or roasted meats served over plates of rice, and the selection of salt-baked seafood. When available, the salt-baked soft-shell crabs are highly recommended and of course, given the name, the noodles aren't too shabby.

Open from 9:00 A.M. until 4:00 A.M., Great N.Y. Noodletown is available to satisfy your cravings at almost any hour and at a superbly reasonable rate.

# Il Cortile

Italian XX

B2

125 Mulberry St. (bet. Canal & Hester Sts.)

**Subway:** Canal St (Lafayette St) — Lunch & dinner daily
**Phone:** 212-226-6060
**Web:** www.ilcortile.com
**Prices:** **$$**

Beyond this quaint and charming façade lies one of Little Italy's cherished mainstays. This expansive restaurant features a series of unique dining rooms, each with its own Mediterranean ambience, but the most celebrated is the pleasant, airy garden room (*il cortile* is Italian for "courtyard"), which seems more like an atrium with its glass-paneled ceiling, brick walls, and abundant greenery.

Chef Michael DeGeorgio presents a wide array of meat and seafood dishes; as well as a range of pasta specialties, such as house-made ravioli stuffed with crab and grilled endive, sautéed in butter and sage. More than 30 years of sharing family recipes has earned Il Cortile a longtime following and holds a special place in the heart of this city.

# Il Palazzo

Italian XX

B1

151 Mulberry St. (bet. Grand & Hester Sts.)

**Subway:** Canal St (Lafayette St.) — Lunch & dinner daily
**Phone:** 212-343-7000
**Web:** N/A
**Prices:** **$$**

For a good, traditional Italian-American meal, head to this "palace" on Little Italy's celebrated Mulberry Street. A tuxedo-clad host ushers guests into a long room lined with stucco walls and linen-draped tables. Beyond, the sunken dining room recalls a winter garden of lush greenery and natural light.

Repasts begin with a basket of focaccia accompanied by spiced olive oil. Lunchtime frittata specials represent especially good value. Old World dishes reign here, as in *pollo ai carciofi* (a pan-fried breast of chicken crowned with artichokes and moistened with tomato sauce); or a grilled *bistecca*—a prime aged Porterhouse. For dessert, tiramisu is both innovative and satisfying, as a round of espresso-soaked ladyfingers topped with creamy mascarpone mousse.

# La Esquina

B1

Mexican

106 Kenmare St. (bet. Cleveland Pl. & Mulberry St.)

**Subway:** Spring St (Lafayette St.) Lunch & dinner daily
**Phone:** 646-613-7100
**Web:** N/A
**Prices:** $$

This fun and sultry spot offers its cool clientele three distinct dining sections, each sharing the same kitchen preparing simple yet tremendously flavorful Mexican cuisine. The first dining space is a storefront with sidewalk seating, takeout, and a small counter; the second a mellow, cozy corner café (no reservations); and the third a stylish subterranean dinner-only room—look for the unmarked entrance and a doorman checking reservations, which must be made well in advance.

After opening to buzzing fanfare, La Esquina has calmed a bit, but just enough to let the food finally take center stage, where it deserves to be. Flavors from the kitchen are bright, balanced, and may be best enjoyed alongside signature cocktails, perfectly classic with subtle flair.

# Júp Shē

B1

Korean

171 Grand St. (at Baxter St.)

**Subway:** Canal St (Lafayette St.) Lunch & dinner daily
**Phone:** 212-343-0090
**Web:** N/A
**Prices:** 

This appealing establishment graciously serves heartwarming Korean favorites like spicy, bubbling hot stews, and various permutations of the rice casserole, *bibimbab*, served in hot stone bowls. The heat of the bowl continues to cook the rice as it sits, resulting in a layer of golden crusty goodness. The dumplings, known as *mandoo* in Korean, are an especially fine start; this is no surprise, as these owners are also behind Mandoo Bar. Salads, grilled and marinated meats, as well as a list of inexpensive lunch box specials augment the menu.

The understated corner location, far away from the sensory overload of midtown's Koreatown, features a simple décor of pale walls, wood furnishings, and pretty touches like panels of graphically scribbled red flowers.

# Mandarin Court

B2 — Chinese

61 Mott St. (bet. Bayard & Canal Sts.)

**Subway:** Canal St (Lafayette St.) — Lunch & dinner daily
**Phone:** 212-608-3838
**Web:** N/A
**Prices:** ⊜

Dim sum is not just for weekend brunch anymore. At Mandarin Court, dim sum is served every day from 8:00 A.M. to 4:00 P.M. The presentation is Hong Kong-style; the waitresses roll carts full of dumplings, buns, wontons, and other savories past your table so you can take your pick. There's even sweet dim sum for dessert (egg custard; coconut-flavored gelatin; and sesame balls).

If you're really hungry, try one of the entrées, which include steaming bowls of broth brimming with noodles, vegetables, meat, or seafood. The dining room may not look like much, and it may be a bit noisy with your neighbors a little too close for comfort, but the regulars don't come here for the atmosphere. They're attracted by good Cantonese fare at reasonable prices.

# New Malaysia

C2 — Malaysian

46-48 Bowery (bet. Bayard & Canal Sts.)

**Subway:** Canal St (Lafayette St.) — Lunch & dinner daily
**Phone:** 212-964-0284
**Web:** N/A
**Prices:** ⊜

Hidden in the Chinatown arcade accessed from either Bowery or Elizabeth, New Malaysia is the spot to go to in Manhattan for regional Malaysian. Some dishes are better than others, so reserve stomach space for the kitchen's strengths.

*Asam laksa* is a bowl of soupy, funky heaven, and the fried anchovies are a glorious and addictive could-be bar snack. *Roti canai* comes with a masterful coconut curry so delish you'll want to drink it up; and the fried *belacan* lady finger with shrimp is a complex, haunting stir fry. *Nasi lemak* and *beef rendang* are also killer but don't expect the skinny jeans to fit after all that coconut.

Insulin levels will spike with one of the Malaysian beverages, or colorful sweet shaved ices that bring sugary to a whole new level.

# New Yeah Shanghai

Chinese

B2

65 Bayard St. (at Mott St.)

**Subway:** Canal St (Lafayette St.)
**Phone:** 212-566-4884
**Web:** N/A
**Prices:** ¢¢

Lunch Mon – Fri
Dinner nightly

Just off the bustle of Bayard Street in the heart of Chinatown, New Yeah Shanghai offers a taste of its namesake city. Live plants, arched ceilings, and Asian decorative accents lend a cave-like, Pacific Rim feel to this otherwise casual restaurant. Decision-making may be difficult here, where an extensive menu features Shanghai favorites, dumplings galore, all sorts of noodles, and many daily specials; as well as seasonal items created specifically for holidays throughout the year. The carefully cooked food is served as promptly as it is prepared by the capable staff, and the large portions are ideal for family-style gatherings (with leftovers to go).

New Yeah Shanghai's loyal crowd of regulars, locals, and tourists feel equally at home here.

# Nyonya

Malaysian

C1

194 Grand St. (bet. Mott & Mulberry Sts.)

**Subway:** Canal St (Lafayette St.)
**Phone:** 212-334-3669
**Web:** N/A
**Prices:** ¢¢

Lunch & dinner daily

Beyond the bowlfuls of *"arrabbiata,"* Nyonya's multi-layered Malaysian cuisine is spicing up Little Italy. Look past the framed accolades adorning the front of the gold-toned dining room and peer into the windowed kitchen, where chefs are preparing *roti canai*—a favorite dish of flaky roti served with coconut chicken curry—and allow yourself to be lured inside. Here, turmeric, chilies, and shrimp paste are skillfully combined in a warming array of satays, curries, noodles, and clay pot casseroles. More unique house specials include tender slices of pork belly mixing dark, rich flavors with mild sweetness.

The restaurant's moniker often refers to early Chinese brides, forced to intermarry with Malaysians to strengthen trade ties between the countries.

# Oriental Garden

Chinese XX

B2

14 Elizabeth St. (bet. Bayard & Canal Sts.)

**Subway:** Canal St (Lafayette St.) — Lunch & dinner daily
**Phone:** 212-619-0085
**Web:** N/A
**Prices:** ¢¢

Located in the bustling heart of Chinatown, Oriental Garden's mid-block location is easily spotted by the large gold lettering on its stone façade. Inside, the slender windows make the dining room feel decidedly tucked away, amid pale walls simply lined with framed Chinese characters and gold dragons. Towards the front, tanks brimming with fish illustrate the expansive menu's orientation toward seafood in dishes like braised abalone with oyster sauce, drunken live prawns, and sautéed cuttlefish with black bean and green pepper.

During the day, there is a hearty selection of dim sum; and you will always find a wide range of stir fries, as well as mounds of delish noodles and vibrant vegetable and tofu dishes.

# Parigot

French X

B1

155 Grand St. (at Lafayette St.)

**Subway:** Canal St (Lafayette St.) — Lunch & dinner daily
**Phone:** 212-274-8859
**Web:** www.parigotnyc.com
**Prices:** $$

Straddling a bright corner between Little Italy and SoHo, Parigot works because it does a little bit of everything right. The food is good, but the unending hospitality of Chef/owner Michel Pombet leaves an indelible impression; the cozy bistro atmosphere, covered in black and white nudes, is lovely without being gauche; and the staff is loose and friendly, but efficient.

The restaurant's name is slang for a person born and raised in Paris, and the menu covers said territory by touching all the croque-monsieur-and-ox-tail-terrine bases. Kick things off with a French onion soup, bubbling with hot, stringy cheese over soft chunks of bread; and then move on to a plate of crispy, pan-fried trout in a silky sauce of butter, capers, chives, and tomato.

# Peking Duck House

Chinese

B2

28 Mott St. (bet. Chatham Sq. & Pell St.)

**Subway:** Canal St (Lafayette St) Lunch & dinner daily
**Phone:** 212-227-1810
**Web:** www.pekingduckhousenyc.com
**Prices:** $$

Only rookies open the menu at Peter Luger steakhouse—and the same ought to apply to any restaurant named after a menu item. So while you may stumble onto a few gems like the fragrant wonton soup, the bird is the word at this group-friendly Chinatown joint.

Despite its boorish name, the Peking Duck House is a touch classier than her Chinatown sisters, with a contemporary polish that won't frighten your Midwestern cousin. Service may slow down at the more elegant midtown location, but both locations wheel out the golden brown duck with proper flare, and carve it into mouthwatering slices. Your job is easy: Fold the freshly carved meat into fresh pancakes, sprinkle with scallion, cucumbers, and a dash of hoisin sauce—then devour.

# Pellegrino's

Italian

B1

138 Mulberry St. (bet. Grand & Hester Sts.)

**Subway:** Canal St (Lafayette St) Lunch & dinner daily
**Phone:** 212-226-3177
**Web:** N/A
**Prices:** $$

On a warm summer day, the view from one of Pellegrino's sidewalk tables takes in the heart of Little Italy. You're likely to find a good number of tourists here, since the long, narrow dining room is attractive, the umbrella-shaded outdoor tables are inviting, and the service is courteous. Children are welcome at Pellegrino's; in fact, the restaurant offers half-portions for smaller appetites.

The food, which stays true to its roots in sunny Italy, includes a balanced selection of pasta, meat, and fish. Linguini alla Sinatra, the signature dish named for the beloved crooner, abounds with lobster, shrimp, clams, mushrooms, and pine nuts in red sauce. Large portions of tasty food make Pellegrino's a good value in this frequented destination.

# Red Egg

Chinese

B1

202 Centre St. (bet. Grand & Hester Sts.)

**Subway:** Canal St (Lafayette St) — Lunch & dinner daily
**Phone:** 212-966-1123
**Web:** www.redeggnyc.com
**Prices:** ⊖⊖

Where are the grandchildren of Chinese immigrants eating? As Chinatown creeps north of Canal Street, fast approaching micro Italy's turf, a stretch of newer Chinese restaurants angled to a younger crowd arrives.

One of the best and brightest of the new pack is Red Egg, a modish restaurant with an imitation Sex and the City décor: think SoHo style with less fancy cocktails but much better food. By day, there's a massive dim sum menu where you check off boxes until a wealth of goodies start piling up on your table. The dinner menu features a shorter choice of dim sum, plus a ton of great Cantonese and Latin-Cantonese fusion options. Don't miss the stir-fried radish cake, topped with crispy shredded duck; or the terrific pan-fried pork dumplings.

# Shanghai Café

Chinese

B2

100 Mott St. (bet. Canal & Hester Sts.)

**Subway:** Canal St (Lafayette St.) — Lunch & dinner daily
**Phone:** 212-966-3988
**Web:** N/A
**Prices:** ⊖⊖

Head to this contemporary Chinatown spot when the craving hits for good Shanghai-style cuisine at a fair price. Dumpling assemblers beckon diners in from the front window, assembling the tiny, succulent juicy buns, and adding them to massive steamers. Filled with crabmeat and/or pork, these juicy little jewels explode with flavor in your mouth. A hands-down favorite, "steamed tiny buns," as the menu calls them, appear on nearly every occupied table, sometimes in multiple orders.

In addition, the enormous menu cites a decision-defying array of Shanghai classics including cold and hot starters, soups, and seafood and noodle dishes.

Have a taste and you'll agree that Shanghai Café ranks a bun above the usual Chinese fare on this stretch of Mott Street.

# Thai So'n

Vietnamese

B2

89 Baxter St. (bet. Bayard & Canal Sts.)

**Subway:** Canal St (Lafayette St.) — Lunch & dinner daily
**Phone:** 212-732-2822
**Web:** N/A
**Prices:** ⊜

Set on busy Baxter Street, Thai So'n is a neighborhood standout for high-quality Vietnamese fare at tremendous value. The atmosphere may feel like a catering hall with minimal focus on comfort, but this does not dissuade the droves from nearby City Hall, seeking the authentic Vietnamese offerings from this huge menu of fresh, fiery, and flavorful cuisine. Ignore the Chinese selections in favor of steaming bowls of *pho*, comforting bowls of rice noodles and delicate slices of raw beef that instantly cook when the scalding broth is poured over top. Garnish this with ample condiments for a traditional (and delicious) experience.

This casual spot is a prime choice for groups or families dining with children; takeout and delivery are also available.

# Xe Lua

Vietnamese

B2

86 Mulberry St. (bet. Bayard & Canal Sts.)

**Subway:** Canal St (Lafayette St) — Lunch & dinner daily
**Phone:** 212-577-8887
**Web:** www.xeluanewyork.com
**Prices:** ⊜

A cheery orange sign splashed in yellow, blue, and green blazons this lovely spot's name in both English and Vietnamese, while tropical themes outfit the interior in royal blue, bamboo, and a floor-to-ceiling mural of boats, sea, and sky.

The expansive menu features a flavorful assortment of appetizers, stir fries, clay pots, noodles, and rice dishes, with headings like "Porky," "Froggy Style," and "Chicken Little" to express their quirky humor. Dive into one of fourteen varieties of *pho*—these steaming bowls of rice noodle soup are all under seven dollars. Heartier appetites are satisfied with the *pho xe lua*, a massive bowl of noodles, brisket, tendon, tripe, and meatballs swimming in a rich beef broth. The staff is pleasant, quick, and efficient.

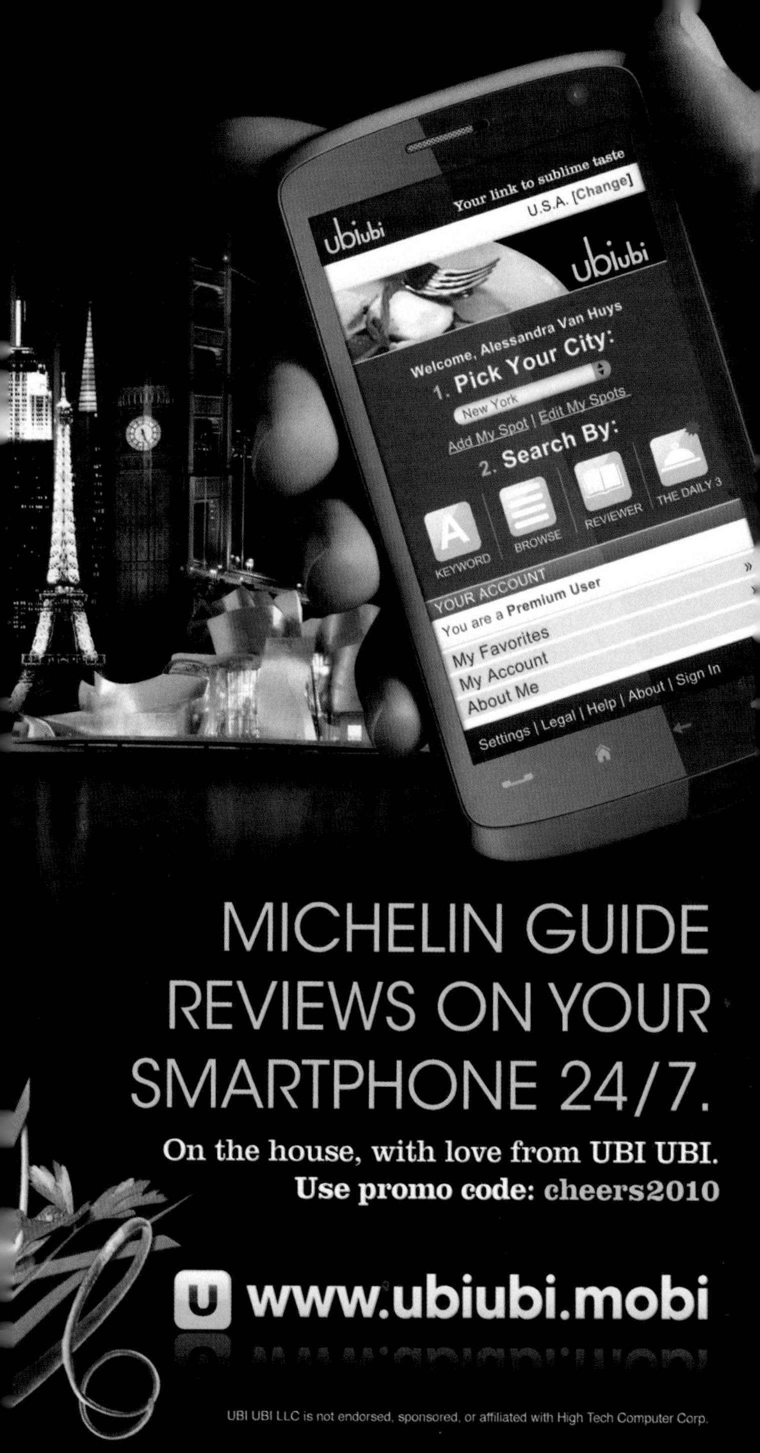
Your link to sublime taste
U.S.A. [Change]
ubiubi
Welcome, Alessandra Van Huys
1. Pick Your City:
New York
Add My Spot | Edit My Spots
2. Search By:
KEYWORD
BROWSE
REVIEWER
THE DAILY 3
YOUR ACCOUNT
You are a Premium User
My Favorites
My Account
About Me
Settings | Legal | Help | About | Sign In
MICHELIN GUIDE REVIEWS ON YOUR SMARTPHONE 24/7.
On the house, with love from UBI UBI.
Use promo code: cheers2010
www.ubiubi.mobi
UBI UBI LLC is not endorsed, sponsored, or affiliated with High Tech Computer Corp.

# East Village

This storied bohemia is no longer rampant with riots, rockers, and radical zeitgeist, but remains crowned as Manhattan's uncompromising capital of counter-culture. East Villagers may seem tamer now that CBGB is closed, but they are no less creative, casual, and undeniably cool.

The neighborhood's bars and eateries exhibit the same edge, and denizens craving a cheap, nightly nosh have plenty to choose from. **Una Pizza Napoletana**, a sparse, chic boutique pizzeria with a menu limited to four pies, is open four nights a week from 5:00 P.M. 'til the dough runs out. **Momofuku Bakery & Milk Bar** (of the local empire), turns out a head scratching assortment of delectable baked goods and soft serve ice cream in flavors like "sour gummy" till midnight. A cone of crispy Belgian fries from the walk-up window at **Pomme Frites** is heightened by sauces like curry-ketchup and smoked-eggplant mayo. For burgers, **Paul's Palace** may have the best in town. **Crif Dogs**—open until 4:00 A.M. on weekends—deep fries their dogs for the perfect post-pub-crawl snack. Many inexpensive eateries, cafés, second-hand shops, and outdoor vendors line these blocks with specialties ranging from macaroni & cheese **(S'mac)** to pork **(Porchetta)** in a distinctly East Village way.

Perhaps most spirited, and in keeping with the kitschy downtown feel, is Japantown—a decidedly downmarket, infinitely groovier "Harajuku" version of its Midtown East sibling. Along St. Marks Place look for the red paper lanterns of hip yakitori spots like **Taisho**, or smell the *takoyaki* frying and sizzling *okonomiyaki* at **Otafuku**; and explore the fun, divey izakayas, such as **Go** or **Village Yokocho**. Among the area's sultry sake dens, few can rival subterranean **Decibel**—serving an outrageous selection of sake and shochu in its hideaway setting.

While Japantown may tuck its lounges down a nondescript stairway, everything along the "Curry Row" stretch of East Sixth Street smacks of festivities, with spices as bold as the strings of neon lights that decorate the awnings. These spots may cater to NYU students seeking low prices, but there are indeed places serving great Bangladeshi or Indian food, like **Angon on the Sixth**. Still, devout bargain-hunters journey east of First Avenue into Alphabet City, teeming with fantastic taquerias, bodegas, and bars.

For a bit of old-world flavor, an afternoon at **Veniero's Pasticceria & Caffè** is in order. Established in 1894, this friendly staple has stood the test of time, drawing long lines (especially around

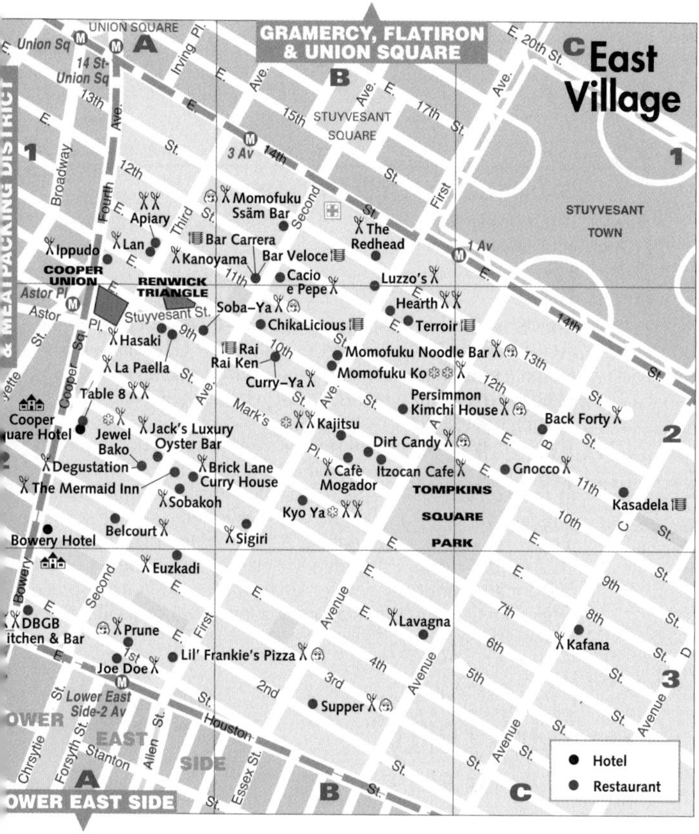


holiday time) for its traditional Italian baked goods. The ever-popular, family-run **Veselka** has been serving Ukrainian specialties for over 50 years, representing the area's former Eastern European population. For specialty items, **East Village Cheese** is one of the city's premier vendors—find an ample selection here, minus the mark-up of many gourmet emporiums.

It goes without saying that liquor flows freely in the East Village. There are an abundance of dive bars, but those with a more urbane palate will be happy that this neighborhood is at the nexus of cutting-edge mixology. **Angel's Share**, (hidden in a Japanese restaurant on Stuyvesant Street); **PDT**, or Please Don't Tell (accessed through Crif Dogs); and **Death & Co.** on East Sixth Street all take an epicurean approach to cocktail service garnering them accolades.

Whole Foods and Chipotle may have moved in but there's no taking the culinary edge off this vibrant edible quarter with its youthful, international vibe.

# Apiary

Contemporary XX

A1

60 Third Ave. (bet. 10th & 11th Sts.)

**Subway:** 14 St - Union Sq  
Dinner nightly  
**Phone:** 212-254-0888  
**Web:** www.apiarynyc.com  
**Prices:** **$$**

Chef Scott Bryan's new post is at this sleek yet comfortable establishment designed and furnished by Ligne Roset. The intimate and slender dining room is outfitted with generously sized espresso-hued tables, crimson Luca chairs, and modish lighting treatments.

The straightforward menu's skilled production, global accents, and clean presentation are a fitting complement to the contemporary space. Specials display a nod toward seasonality as in a fillet of wild-harvested salmon served atop a bundle of sweet ramps. A bowl of the orzo mac and cheese, bathed in a decadently rich sauce, is a perfect side dish for just about any entrée. Apiary's wine program displays a broad reach and offers a large listing of wines available as a "taste" or a "glass".

# Back Forty

Contemporary X

C2

190 Ave. B (at 12th St.)

**Subway:** 1 Av  
Lunch Sat – Sun  
**Phone:** 212-388-1990  
Dinner nightly  
**Web:** www.backfortynyc.com  
**Prices:** **$$**

The folks behind Savoy bring straightforward cooking and simple charm to this East Village newcomer. The mostly unadorned room is spare yet comfortable, with a gently lit mural at the long bar and bare-wood tables topped with brown-paper placemats that double as menus.

Start with a perfect Orchard Manhattan, substituting apple brandy for the traditional rye, and dig into the farm-stand inspired fare. Seasonal assortments of locally grown side dishes from "The Garden" menu, such as a chilled green wheat salad of grains dressed with fresh herbs, lemon, and a thick dollop of yogurt; accompany "The Core" selections, including spice-rubbed rotisserie chicken and grass-fed burgers with homemade ketchup.

# Bar Carrera

Spanish

B1

175 Second Ave. (bet. 11th & 12th Sts.)

**Subway:** 1 Av

Dinner nightly

**Phone:** 212-375-1555

**Web:** www.barcarrera.com

**Prices:** $$

Perfectly focused and deliciously simple, the owners of beloved Bar Veloce (next door) have erected this culinary temple to Spain. The dark and intimate room brims with regulars, from bankers to scenesters, sipping a lovely selection of Spanish wines and lingering over tapas. With both traditional and modern options, these small plates offer unique authenticity and skill—as in the *albondigas*, simmered so slowly in rich tomato sauce that the meatballs develop deep, savory flavors beyond expectation. A testament to quality is the *jamón serrano*, available in a variety of ages, with each one more decadent and gamey than the last. Chorizo fans will be equally enthused by the offerings.
A second (slightly larger, if less ambient) location is in SoHo.

# Bar Veloce

Italian

B1

175 Second Ave. (bet. 11th & 12th Sts.)

**Subway:** 1 Av

Dinner nightly

**Phone:** 212-260-3200

**Web:** www.barveloce.com

**Prices:** $$

Veloce was one of the pioneers in the wine bar craze long before they became repeat cases of banal food and overpriced glasses of wine. A long, stylish strip of spot in the East Village, often marked by a Vespa in front, Veloce makes up for in personality what it lacks in space.
The *vini, aperitivi,* and *digestivi* are mostly Italian and very well-chosen, and the gracious bar team can easily guide you the right direction. Panini are divine, made with an expert hand on the press, and a select assortment along with some *bruchette* and *formaggi* will happily accompany a few glasses of wine.
Veloce now has locations in Chelsea and SoHo, both with more seating and a few tables in larger spaces but neither with the modern, charismatic charm of the original.

# Belcourt

A2 **Mediterranean**

84 E. 4th St. (at Second Ave.)

**Subway:** Astor Pl — Lunch & dinner daily
**Phone:** 212-979-2034
**Web:** www.belcourtnyc.com
**Prices:** $$

With antiqued mirror panels, vintage French signs, and mix-and-match tables furnished with simple wooden chairs, this newcomer devises the well-worn ambiance of a time-honored neighborhood favorite. An intimate bar mixes innovative cocktails, such as the namesake's blending of champagne and elderflower nectar, which adds to the convivial setting and bistro-inspired fare.

With the promise that "everything that can be made in-house, is," the kitchen turns out the likes of coffee barbecue-braised brisket with soft organic polenta; Persian spice-roasted organic chicken sided with fingerling potatoes and pancetta; and burgers of beef or lamb cradled in a house-made bun. Come lunch, Belcourt offers a scaled-back listing of salads and sandwiches.

# Brick Lane Curry House

A2 **Indian**

306-308 E. 6th St. (bet. First & Second Aves.)

**Subway:** Astor Pl — Lunch & dinner daily
**Phone:** 212-979-2900
**Web:** www.bricklanecurryhouse.com
**Prices:** $$

This East Village curry house sets itself apart from the Sixth Street crowd by offering curry devotees an establishment inspired by those found along Brick Lane, London's historic Curry Row. Northern Indian fare is the focus here, served in an attractive dining room that features brick walls and a bar serving a selection of perfectly tapped and poured brews, sure to warm any Anglophile's heart.

The kitchen allows guests to mix and match ingredients in classic preparations. For instance, creamy, saffron-accented korma is available with a choice of chicken, lamb, goat, or paneer. Tandoor prepared dishes and vegetarian specialties complete the menu.

Cool and creamy lassi provides a refreshing finish to the sometimes fiery, always flavorful cuisine.

# Cacio e Pepe

Italian

B1

182 Second Ave. (bet. 11th & 12th Sts.)

**Subway:** 3 Av — Dinner nightly
**Phone:** 212-505-5931
**Web:** www.cacioepepe.com
**Prices:** $$

With its low-key temper and genuinely gracious service, this charmingly rustic Italian can be trusted to satisfy. The menu of traditional Roman dishes features a house specialty from which the establishment takes its name: house-made *tonnarelli* tossed with pasta water, olive oil, cracked black pepper, and a plethora of pecorino cheese. Likewise, the kitchen features a number of creative flourishes, such as a starter of bacon-wrapped shrimp in a pool of eggplant purée. Reserve aside, embark on dessert—cannoli filled with lemon-flavored ricotta—and wind up in heaven.

The wine list is short but carefully selected to highlight less-familiar producers in the most notable Italian regions. In warm weather, the backyard garden makes a lovely dining area.

# Café Mogador

Moroccan

B2

101 St. Mark's Pl. (bet. First Ave. & Ave. A)

**Subway:** 1 Av — Lunch & dinner daily
**Phone:** 212-677-2226
**Web:** www.cafemogador.com
**Prices:** ⚭

This family-run, neighborhood favorite serves breakfast, lunch, and dinner daily while exuding an inviting coffee-house vibe. Moorish lanterns, jars of spices, and black-and-white photographs of Morocco impart an air of exoticism. Mediterranean small plates like hummus and tabouli make a fine start leading up to the warm and fluffy house specialty: couscous, offered here with vegetables, lamb, or spicy *merguez* sausage. Traditional *bastilla* fills layers of crispy filo with shredded chicken, eggs, almonds, and cinnamon while the mildly sweet-spicy, simmering tagines are moist, tender, and always popular.

Open since 1983, reasonable prices and affable service should ensure Café Mogador's continued longevity.

# ChikaLicious

Contemporary

B2

203 E. 10th St. (bet. First & Second Aves.)

**Subway:** Astor Pl — Dinner nightly
**Phone:** 212-995-9511
**Web:** www.chikalicious.com
**Prices:** $$

Named for Pastry Chef/owner Chika Tillman, this sweet spot presents an all-encompassing dessert experience that somehow manages to impress without overkill. The chic white space offers counter seating overlooking a lab-clean kitchen where the team prepares elegant jewels that start as butter, sugar, and chocolate. À la carte is offered, but the best way to appreciate this dessert bar is to select the prix-fixe menu. Feasts here may begin with an *amuse-bouche* of Darjeeling tea gelée with milk sorbet, followed by a mascarpone *semifreddo* topped with espresso granita, then finish with the pillowy cubes of coconut-marshmallow petits fours.

Dessert Club across the street tempts with cookies, cupcakes, and shaved ice for a grab-and-go fix.

# Curry-Ya

Japanese

B2

214 E. 10th St. (bet. First & Second Aves.)

**Subway:** Astor Pl — Lunch & dinner daily
**Phone:** 866-602-8779
**Web:** www.nycurry-ya.com
**Prices:** $$

From the co-owner of Soba-Ya, comes this tasty newcomer, specializing in Japan's unique version of curry—*yoshoku*. This culinary icon belongs in the repertoire of Western style dishes that have become a part of the Japanese palate. Characterized by a mild sweetness and restrained heat, Curry-Ya's rich sauce is garnished with pickled vegetables, short grain rice, and is available with a selection of accompaniments like *panko*-crusted Berkshire pork cutlet, organic chicken, and grilled hamburger. The small menu also offers inspiring starters like a salad of *yuba* and snow peas with green olive dressing.

The bright space, warmed by pale pink walls and blond wood stools, offers seating for 14 at a marble counter set in front of the white tiled kitchen.

# DBGB Kitchen & Bar

A3 French

299 Bowery (bet. First & Houston Sts.)

**Subway:** Lower East Side - 2 Av
**Phone:** 212-933-5300
**Web:** www.danielnyc.com
**Prices:** $$

Lunch Tue – Sun
Dinner nightly

Chef Daniel Boulud's take on casual dining features a front windowed café/bar followed by a grey and brown shaded dining room designed to evoke the Bowery's past as a hub for restaurant supplies. Shelves are stocked with dry goods and crockery, while a wrap-around exposed kitchen displays gleaming steel surfaces and the bright whites of an eager brigade.

The chef's gilded approach to burgers takes a fun, new direction here with offerings like the "piggie" topped with pulled pork served on a cheddar-cornbread bun. Burgers aside, the menu also includes a lengthy selection of charcuterie and sausages supplemented by fish and meats in classically French preparations. For dessert, a listing of ice cream sundaes illustrates the playful spirit here.

# Degustation

A2 Spanish

239 E. 5th St. (bet. Second & Third Aves.)

**Subway:** Astor Pl
**Phone:** 212-979-1012
**Web:** N/A
**Prices:** $$

Dinner Mon – Sat

This intimate East Village tapas bar from Jack and Grace Lamb, the proprietors of Jewel Bako located next door, bears the chic vibe New Yorkers would expect from this stylish couple. Dark slate-tiled walls, red leather placemats, and sleek place settings make the dimly lit space feel elegant. Similar to a sushi bar, seating is arranged on a counter facing the open kitchen, where small plates are artfully prepared by this fresh-faced and well-trained team. Offerings may include crunchy and creamy *croquetas*, or caramelized bread pudding served on frozen pink grapefruit segments.

The knowledgeable and smartly attired staff ensures care is given to each guest, often guiding them through the menu and making suggestions from the all-Spanish wine list.

# Dirt Candy

Vegetarian

B2

430 E. 9th St. (bet. First Ave. & Ave. A)

**Subway:** 1 Av
Dinner Tue – Sat
**Phone:** 212-228-7732
**Web:** www.dirtcandynyc.com
**Prices:** $$

Accommodating less than twenty in a boutique-sized space, Chef/owner Amanda Cohen keeps a watchful eye on each and every diner as she skillfully crafts vegetarian fare from the tiny rear kitchen. Certified by the Green Restaurant Association, the bright room has glass paneled walls and closely packed tables furnished with Arne Jacobsen chairs.

Both devotees and skeptics alike are impressed by this menu of unique items featuring such preparations as portobello mousse with truffle-oil-slicked toast and pickled pear compote; or golden crisped blocks of semi-firm tofu draped with kaffir lime beurre blanc. Yield to temptation with desserts like light and spongy zucchini-ginger cake served à la mode with deliciously smooth cream cheese ice cream.

# Euzkadi

Basque

A3

108 E. 4th St. (bet. First & Second Aves.)

**Subway:** Lower East Side - 2 Av
Dinner nightly
**Phone:** 212-982-9788
**Web:** www.euzkadirestaurant.com
**Prices:** $$

Haven't heard of Euzkadi? Maybe you've been living in a cave. While some restaurants dish out great food but disappoint in the décor department, this one-of-a-kind place delivers both. With textured, exposed walls painted with prehistoric-style cave drawings, thick, velvet curtains shutting out all sunlight, and soft, low lighting, diners can be cave dwellers—even if just for the evening. This cocoon-like restaurant is a great find, despite its cramped quarters.

Of course, no caveman ever ate this well. The menu covers all the bases of traditional Basque cooking, including tapas and the house specialty, *paella mariscos*. Loaded with fish and shellfish, and redolent of saffron, the paella comes sized for two in a traditional cast-iron pan.

# Gnocco

C2 — Italian

## 337 E. 10th St. (bet. Aves. A & B)

**Subway:** 1 Av
**Phone:** 212-677-1913
**Web:** www.gnocco.com
**Prices:** $$

Lunch Sat – Sun
Dinner nightly

The bohemian vibe of this quaint Alphabet City Italian makes it a favored neighborhood hangout. Large windows look out to the colorful cast of characters that populate Tompkins Square Park; inside, the dining room's rustic charm is accented by rough hewn plank flooring and exposed brick. In summer, the shady back terrace with vine-covered walls and pretty mural, is a great place to enjoy the namesake specialty, *gnocco*: crispy, deep-fried pillows of dough served with thin slices of prosciutto di Parma and salami.

Enjoyably straightforward pastas, thin-crusted pizzas, and a well-prepared list of meat and fish dishes comprise the tasty offerings here, served by an attentive and gracious staff. The fluffy and creamy white chocolate and coffee *semifreddo* is a pleasant finish.

# Hasaki

A2 — Japanese

## 210 E. 9th St. (bet. Second & Third Aves.)

**Subway:** Astor Pl
**Phone:** 212-473-3327
**Web:** www.hasakinyc.com
**Prices:** $$$

Lunch Wed – Sun
Dinner nightly

Opened in 1984 and still going strong, this unassuming spot on a tree-lined stretch of the East Village is quietly housed just below street level. The dapper dining room has a clean and spare look, with seating available at a number of honey-toned wood tables, or the generously sized counter manned by a personable chef.

Hasaki's longevity is attributed to the high quality of its product. Skillfully prepared, delicately sliced sushi and sashimi share the spotlight with silky noodle soups and crisp tempura, at prices that won't break the bank. The menu is supplemented by a listing of fascinating daily specials that do tend to sell out quickly. Hasaki's "Twilight" menu offered before 6:30 P.M. is cherished, both for its quality and quantity.

# Hearth

Mediterranean XX

B2

403 E. 12th St. (at First Ave.)

**Subway:** 1 Av
Dinner nightly
**Phone:** 646-602-1300
**Web:** www.restauranthearth.com
**Prices:** $$$

Guests are warmly greeted and introduced to the comfort and charm of this Mediterranean-inspired restaurant. A candlelit dining room features simple wooden tables and walls lined with copper pots and bookshelves.

Pure, contemporary flavors with a rustic edge are captured by a meticulous kitchen. The menu may feature starters such as grilled quail, its meat rich and smoky, served with farro, tomato salad, and poached quail egg. Entrées may feature a moist, firm monkfish with caramelized speck, on a bed of heirloom beans, with juniper and sage. A five-course tasting menu, which changes with seasonal availability, can be paired with well-chosen wines.

Watch the chefs work their magic at one of the kitchen-facing counter seats.

# Ippudo

Japanese X

A1

65 Fourth Ave. (bet. 9th & 10th Sts.)

**Subway:** 14 St - Union Sq
Lunch & dinner daily
**Phone:** 212-388-0088
**Web:** www.ippudo.com/ny
**Prices:** ©©

A wall covered in soup bowls is your first indication of what to order at this stateside outpost of the popular Japanese chain. Ramen-hungry diners are given a boisterous welcome from the youthful staff upon entering; the same can be said for the farewell. With most seating arranged at communal oak-topped tables and prominently displayed open kitchen, Ippudo feels laid-back and fun. The classic *shiromaru* ramen is a deeply satisfying bowl of rich pork broth and slender, fresh-made noodles garnished with sliced pork and cabbage.

In addition, you'll also find miso and *shoyu* (soy sauce flavored) ramen. If left with a bowlful of extra broth, simply tell your server *"kae-dama"* and for a small charge you'll receive an additional bowl of noodles.

# Itzocan Cafe

Mexican

B2

438 E. 9th St. (bet. First Ave. & Ave. A)

**Subway:** 1 Av

Lunch & dinner daily

**Phone:** 212-677-5856

**Web:** www.itzocanrestaurant.com

**Prices:** **$$**

With seating for less than 16, Itzocan is *muy pequeño*, but its menu of bold Mexican fare is certainly big on flavor. Quality ingredients abound in a lunchtime listing of quesadillas and burritos, as well as at dinner when a full menu is offered. The *queso fundido*, a molten cheese dip spiked with poblano peppers and chorizo, is so rich you'll need assistance to finish. The short list of entrées displays dashes of creativity as in the hearty serving of plump, jumbo shrimp sautéed with a flavor-packed sauce of tequila, lime, and *guajillo* chile. Desserts include a cheesecake-dense yogurt flan, dressed with chocolate sauce and candied almond slices.

The predominantly grey interior is brightened with colorfully painted tables and glazed flowerpots.

# Jack's Luxury Oyster Bar

Seafood

A2

101 Second Ave. (bet. 5th & 6th Sts.)

**Subway:** Lower East Side - 2 Av

Dinner Mon – Sat

**Phone:** 212-253-7848

**Web:** N/A

**Prices:** **$$$**

Tucked away on a busy Second Avenue block, this oyster bar may be tiny in stature but does not fall short of personality thanks to owners Jack and Grace Lamb. You'll find a tempting raw bar menu that includes oysters, peel-and-eat shrimp, and chilled lobster tail as well as confident cooking evident in the substantial listing of small plates. These may include tuna paillard, crispy sweetbreads, and braised short rib rounded out by a cheese selection and small dessert menu. The dining counter overlooking the open kitchen is always a popular seating option but upfront, there are cozy wood topped tables.

The intimate space has a romantic glow with red and white plaid walls, red painted wainscoting, and red glass votive holders.

# Jewel Bako ✿

Japanese

A2

239 E. 5th St. (bet. Second & Third Aves.)

**Subway:** Astor Pl

Dinner Mon – Sat

**Phone:** 212-979-1012

**Web:** N/A

**Prices:** **$$$**

Swee Phuah

Jack and Grace Lamb, the incredibly talented husband-and-wife restaurateur team that helped define East Village fine dining, often get things right—but they especially get it right at their beloved flagship, Jewel Bako: a lovely, gilded sushi den hidden behind an otherwise unassuming façade in New York's perennial Bohemian enclave.

The proof is in the ever-packed house, run by an understated, but incredibly sharp, waitstaff and a kitchen that—despite a rotating roster of sushi chefs—manages to throw their full attention into every detail.

Though a full omakase is offered, the sushi and sashimi omakase is where it's at—the long, gorgeous affair best enjoyed at the counter, where you can watch the chefs kick off a meal that might start with Japanese red snapper steamed in banana leaf; proceed to bright sashimi like tender octopus, king salmon, and sweet shrimp; and then move on to a never-ending array of fresh sushi like tuna with ginger, Tasmanian ocean trout, or golden eye snapper. Sake and wine lovers should steal a moment to chat up the knowledgeable waitstaff, many of whom take a connoisseur's pleasure in parsing the myriad differences between the house's bottles.

# Joe Doe

A3 **Contemporary**

45 E. 1st St. (bet. First & Second Aves.)

**Subway:** Lower East Side - 2 Av
**Phone:** 212-780-0262
**Web:** www.chefjoedoe.com
**Prices:** $$

Lunch Sat – Sun
Dinner nightly

The intimate setting of this East Village newcomer from Chef/partner Joe Dobias has an appealing ruggedness to its quaint ambience. Exposed brick and vintage décor strewn throughout complement the assortment of dark wood chairs and salvaged church pews. Seating is bolstered by the bar that doubles as a comfortable dining counter.

The chef's concise, highly enjoyable menu emerges from the closet-sized open kitchen and displays a vibrant personality. These inspired creations may include a sea scallop cured in Veev (*acai* berry-based spirit) and garnished with jalapeño mayonnaise; or braised *cabrito* (goat) sauced with tortilla soup. Save room for dessert: the sundae of vanilla ice cream, chocolate chip-studded banana bread, and "bananas Foster" sauce.

# Kafana

C3 **Eastern European**

116 Ave. C (bet. 7th & 8th Sts.)

**Subway:** 1 Av
**Phone:** 212-353-8000
**Web:** www.kafananyc.com
**Prices:** $$

Lunch Sat – Sun
Dinner nightly

Translating to "café" in Serbian, Kafana has a heartwarming ambience that beckons one to stay for a while. Exposed brick walls decorated with mirrors, vintage photographs, rough-hewn wood tables topped with votives and flowers, and boldly patterned banquettes outfit the intimate space, attended by a genuinely friendly staff. In one corner sits the small bar, with a charmingly low-tech antique cash register.

Kafana offers worldly diners an exotic cuisine not often found in Manhattan. The list of hearty Serbian specialties includes a phyllo pie filled with cow's milk feta and spinach, grilled meats, or slow-cooked stews prepared with large, tender white beans perfumed with garlic and paprika, topped with slices of smoky peasant sausage.

# Kajitsu ✿

Japanese XX

B2

414 E. 9th St. (bet. First Ave. & Ave. A)

**Subway:** Astor Pl
Dinner Tue – Sun
**Phone:** 212-228-4873
**Web:** www.kajitsunyc.com
**Prices:** $$$

Kajitsu

Billions of Buddhist monks can't be wrong. An understated sliding door off East 9th Street leads to a serene, slate and wood-soaked room bathed in natural light and an elegant, minimalist décor featuring a smattering of tables and a dining counter.

This is Kajitsu—an authentic new Japanese restaurant that specializes in Shojin cuisine, a seasonal vegetarian style developed in Buddhist monasteries. Under the guiding principles of the ancient tradition, no meat or fish is used; only fresh, in season vegetables, grains, and the like. Every detail from the incense to the greenery is of the utmost importance here.

After a ten year stint at Kitcho in Kyoto, Chef Masato Nishihara brings his understanding of the craft west, spinning fresh ingredients into nightly four- or eight-course productions that rotate seasonally, but might include a wildly clear broth bobbing with fiddlehead ferns and fresh spring mountain yams filled with *Yomogi* paste; a soft tangle of chilled homemade soba noodles topped with a flutter of fresh scallions and paired with an irresistible dipping sauce; or fresh bamboo shoots flown in from Kyoto, cooked to perfection and paired with vegetable tempura and fried fu.

# Kanoyama

Japanese

B1

175 Second Ave. (at 11th St.)

**Subway:** 3 Av
**Phone:** 212-777-5266
**Web:** www.kanoyama.com
**Prices:** $$

Dinner nightly

Positive energy emanates from this tiny sushi spot where the amiable young staff caters to a clientele that is fanatical about their *nigiri*, sashimi, and maki. In pleasant contrast to the power-scene sometimes experienced uptown, petite Kanoyama adeptly holds its own chill, downtown vibe. Take a seat at the counter for a view of the chefs' amazing knife work and warm banter.

Daily fish specials display incredible variety and the menu supplements with even more choice. Kanoyama offers good value considering the quality. It's really how much buttery toro or creamy uni you consume that determines the final tab.

Kanoyama does not accept reservations on Friday and Saturday nights but there are plenty of lively bars nearby for a drink in case there's a wait.

# Kasadela

Japanese

C2

647 E. 11th St. (bet. Aves. B & C)

**Subway:** 1 Av
**Phone:** 212-777-1582
**Web:** www.kasadela.com
**Prices:** ⊜

Dinner nightly

This simply furnished, low-key *izakaya* offers an array of traditional Japanese snacks best washed down with an iced cold beer or sake; just remember that here, your glass of sake can be embellished with gold leaf for a small fee, said to promote better health.

Located in Alphabet City, the space is often quieter early in the evening and stays open late enough to satisfy the cravings of the neighborhood's nocturnal scenesters. Patrons arrive here seeking honest, good-valued satisfaction, in the likes of creamy and smooth Japanese-style potato salad; addictively sweet and salty glazed chicken wings; or the classic fare of *tori kawa*: charred skewers of rich chicken skin. Finish with a crème caramel that would do any talented pastry chef proud.

# Kyo Ya ✿

Japanese XX

B2

94 E. 7th St. (bet First Ave. & Ave. A)

**Subway:** Astor Pl Dinner Tue – Sun
**Phone:** 212-982-4140
**Web:** N/A
**Prices:** **$$$**

Kimiko Ukaji/Kyo Ya

Tucked into the basement of a comfy residential building in the East Village's blossoming den of Japanese joints, Chikara Sono's Kyo Ya doesn't look like much from the outside. But that's just how this gorgeous little *kaiseki* lair likes to kick it: On the down low (they intentionally don't advertise), with all heads focused squarely on the food.

Of course, they didn't skimp on the interior either. Duck down those unmarked slate steps, and you'll find a surprisingly elegant, wood-kissed atmosphere, smartly dressed in clean, Zen lines that—despite the obvious spatial confines—manages to exude a light, sexy air.

*Kaiseki* is a series of haute cuisine small plates traditionally served with Japanese tea, and the chef's tasting menu here requires two days notice. Still, drop-ins can breathe easy: The à la carte menu is no-miss, with rotating, seasonal goodies like a beautiful white mousse of bamboo shoots, poached in a fragrant broth of kelp and peppery mountain plant; or grilled Spanish mackerel in a green tea glaze, a fine layer of custardy egg tucked in between; or a small hot pot, fragrant with duck, kelp, turnips, and carrots, and paired with grilled *mochi*, a Japanese rice cake.

# Lan

A1 Japanese

56 Third Ave. (bet. 10th & 11th Sts.)

**Subway:** 3 Av — Dinner nightly
**Phone:** 212-254-1959
**Web:** www.lan-nyc.com
**Prices:** $$

The name translates as orchid, and with its exposed brick walls, white linen-covered tables, and warm candlelight, Lan offers an elegant and refined setting that is a fitting compliment to both its namesake and creative menu. In addition to the rear sushi counter's array of tempting offerings, cooked items are especially well-represented here with appetizers like handmade tofu steamed with sea urchin; egg custard *chawanmushi* with lobster bisque; and entrées like roasted Long Island duck breast with yuzu, dashi, and soy. The kitchen also takes great pride in its meat dishes, serving various cuts of top-quality steak.

The concise wine list is well chosen and bolstered by a large selection of sake and *shochu.*

# La Paella

A2 Spanish

214 E. 9th St. (bet. Second & Third Aves.)

**Subway:** Astor Pl — Lunch & dinner daily
**Phone:** 212-598-4321
**Web:** www.lapaellanyc.com
**Prices:** $$

La Paella recalls the charm of an old-world Iberian inn with rustic furnishings, wooden ceiling beams draped with bundles of dried flowers, and wrought iron accents. A fresco of a picador on the parchment-colored wall further illustrates the point. Well suited to groups, the aptly prepared menu encourages sharing with its sizable choice of vegetable, seafood, and meat tapas as well as the house specialty: paella. Several variations of this namesake dish include the Catalana with chorizo, chicken, and sausage or the Negra with squid and squid ink.

The paella is sized for two and the cozy, dimly lit space makes a tasty date spot... for couples who don't mind the spirited sounds of merrymaking fueled by fruity sangria or a bottle from the Spanish wine list.

# Lavagna

Italian

B3

545 E. 5th St. (bet. Aves. A & B)

**Subway:** Lower East Side - 2 Av
**Phone:** 212-979-1005
**Web:** www.lavagnanyc.com
**Prices:** $$

Lunch Sat – Sun
Dinner nightly

The steady stream of regulars who frequent this charmingly low-key trattoria is immediately evident at Lavagna. The caring staff often greets guests by name, but this same courteous attention is given to those visiting for the first time. This warm service is enhanced by the cozy dining room, featuring an exposed brick wall hung with framed mirrors, pressed-tin ceiling, and a wood-burning oven in the visible kitchen. The Italian menu may highlight thin, tender ribbons of fresh *pappardelle* tossed in a hearty sauce of shredded, braised rabbit with whole black olives, or individual apple *crostata* topped with an excellent dark caramel sauce and vanilla ice cream.

Sunday nights feature a reasonably priced three-course set menu from 5:00-7:00 P.M.

# Lil' Frankie's Pizza

Italian

A3

19 First Ave. (bet. 1st & 2nd Sts.)

**Subway:** Lower East Side - 2 Av
**Phone:** 212-420-4900
**Web:** www.lilfrankies.com
**Prices:**

Lunch & dinner daily

This offshoot of the ever-popular Frank Restaurant features a multi-room setting that includes a greenery-adorned dining room and a bar area given the nickname of owner Frank Prisinzano's father, "Big Cheech". The classic East Village space is furnished with a combination of wood and marble topped tables, colorful vinyl benches, and brick walls with black and white portraits.

Naples-style pizza stars on a menu supported by an impressive lineup of antipasto and pastas. Cooked to crispy perfection in a wood-burning oven, Lil' Frankie's ten variations include pies topped with homemade sausage and wild fennel, or Sicilian salted anchovies, capers, and olives.

Come with a crowd or expect to wait, reservations are accepted only for parties of six or more.

# Luzzo's

Pizza

B1

211-13 First Ave. (bet. 12th & 13th Sts.)

**Subway:** 1 Av — Lunch & dinner Tue – Sun
**Phone:** 212-473-7447
**Web:** www.luzzomania.com
**Prices:** ©©

These days, it seems that New Yorkers can't do anything without breaking some sort of code. There's no smoking or dancing in bars, and the city no longer issues permits for coal-burning ovens. Has all the fun, and taste, left the city? Not at Luzzo's, a former-bakery-turned-Italian-restaurant complete with a coal-burning oven that has been grandfathered. Thank heaven for small miracles and head straight for this rustic, tavern-style spot with its lip-smacking-good pizza.

Choose from 18 varieties, all with a light, chewy crust and a pleasingly charred flavor. Luzzo's also features a large selection of antipasti and pasta. Desserts are as delicious as they are whimsical, as in two menu specials: chocolate "salami" and nutella "pizza."

# The Mermaid Inn

Seafood

A2

96 Second Ave. (bet. 5th & 6th Sts.)

**Subway:** Astor Pl — Dinner nightly
**Phone:** 212-674-5870
**Web:** www.themermaidnyc.com
**Prices:** $$

When schedules won't permit a sojurn to the sandy shores of Cape Cod, the Mermaid Inn offers a polished take on those familiar sea-sprayed fish shacks. Dark wood furnishings, walls decorated with nautical maps, and a quaint backyard dining area give the setting an undeniable charm. The concise menu begins with a first-rate raw bar and continues with deftly prepared entrées like grilled mahi mahi with orange chervil emulsion or pan-roasted cod with beets and horseradish cream. Their addictive crunchy, golden, Old Bay fries are an essential side dish. A complimentary demitasse of creamy pudding ends things sweetly.

West Siders take note—the Upper West Side location serves a similarly themed menu as well as weekend brunch.

# Momofuku Ko ✿✿

B2 **Contemporary**

163 First Ave. (bet. 10th & 11th Sts.)

**Subway:** 1 Av — Lunch Fri – Sun
**Web:** www.momofuku.com — Dinner nightly
**Prices:** **$$$$**

Noah Kalina/Momofuku Ko

Getting into David Chang's Momofuku Ko is hard. Excruciatingly, throw-things-at-your-computer-monitor hard. Reservations can only be made a week in advance by logging onto their website at 10:00 A.M., but the restaurant's 12 backless stools fill up in seconds. Once you do snag a seat, there is no formal service, no printed menu, and you'll have to show i.d. at the door like a blushing freshman.

So what is the upside to this circus? A lot—not only has Chang gifted New York's elite culinary scene with a rare egalitarian process, in which Obama himself couldn't score an inside ticket, but this multi-course extravaganza is a relative steal at around a hundred bucks a pop.

And here's the kicker. This sense-jogging trip through the strange hollows of David Chang's mind is...mind-blowing... with an endless parade of dishes you're likely to have never encountered before—like a small bowl of fresh, hand-torn pasta, pocked with savory snail sausage, pecorino, and crispy chicken skin; or a fresh bullet of fluke, dusted with crunchy poppy seeds and pooled in whipped buttermilk; or top-grade foie gras, grated like falling snow over a sweet mélange of lychee, Riesling gelée, and pine nut brittle.

# Momofuku Noodle Bar

Asian

B2

171 First Ave. (bet. 10th & 11th Sts.)

**Subway:** 1 Av
Lunch & dinner daily
**Phone:** 212-475-7899
**Web:** www.momofuku.com
**Prices:** ⊜

Chef David Chang's popular destination, and its hoards of hungry fans, recently moved into bigger digs but is still a "lucky peach" of a restaurant (the name's Japanese translation). Momofuku's gutsy menu is fashioned with Asian street food in mind. Iowa Berkshire pork enveloped in steamed buns, topped with thin, cool cucumbers are offered alongside large bowls of chewy Ramen noodles in rich, flavorful broth. Dense soft serve ice cream in flavors like pistachio and cannoli twist may not be Asian but ends meals with a fun and awesome twist.

Whether sitting at one of two counters or select a spot at one of the communal tables, join the devotees slurping noodles elbow-to-elbow and watching the chefs' sleight of hand in the open kitchen.

# Momofuku Ssäm Bar

Contemporary

B1

207 Second Ave. (at 13th St.)

**Subway:** 3 Av
Lunch & dinner daily
**Phone:** 212-254-3500
**Web:** www.momofuku.com
**Prices:** $$

Restless Chef David Chang somehow always manages to wow to taste buds of even the most jaded foodies. At this culinary playground, he offers a contemporary menu so far-reaching that it somehow all makes sense; rest assured Chang and his team only serve dishes that they themselves are sure to find delicious.

The signature steamed pork buns are praiseworthy; raw bar items are brilliantly dressed; a selection of hams showcase the best Southern smokehouses; fried chicken is reinvented as a block of battered, boneless white and dark meat accompanied by slow-cooked egg and pickled ramps; and mad-scientist desserts have included the likes of corn cereal ice cream pie. Loud and crowded, the chicly minimalist space is often mobbed by a sophisticated crowd.

# Persimmon Kimchi House

B2

Korean

277 E. 10th St. (bet. First Ave. & Ave. A)

**Subway:** 1 Av
**Phone:** 212-260-9080
**Web:** www.persimmoncuisine.com
**Prices:** $$

Lunch Wed – Sat
Dinner Mon – Sat

Opened by a graphic designer-cum chef and restaurant owner, this "kimchi house" features a spare aesthetic befitting an artist's studio and is simply furnished with a blonde wood communal table that seats twenty. For diners seeking more intimacy, there is a small counter in front of the tidy open kitchen.

The best way to experience Persimmon's contemporary Korean cuisine is to choose one of the reasonable prix-fixe menus. Each offers a progression of small dishes, or *banchan*, followed by a main course and dessert. Fried, housemade fishcakes and sweet potato glass noodles sautéed with vegetables are some of the starters one may experience leading up to a concise selection of hearty stews or perhaps bubbling rice cake soup with chicken dumplings.

# Prune

A3

Contemporary

54 E. 1st St. (bet. First & Second Aves.)

**Subway:** Lower East Side - 2 Av
**Phone:** 212-677-6221
**Web:** www.prunerestaurant.com
**Prices:** $$

Lunch & dinner daily

This East Village favorite radiates the warm glow of a beloved neighborhood bistro, although it may seem perpetually packed with enthusiasts trekking from afar to enjoy talented Chef/owner Gabrielle Hamilton's straightforward cooking. Prune's mosaic tile floor, paper-topped tables, and swirling ceiling fans create a charming setting in which to converse with a neighboring table, or watch the open kitchen. The diminutive room means scoring a table can be difficult, but dishes like stewed pork shoulder with *salsa verde* or soupy rice with lobster and squid more than compensate for the struggle.

Lunch is served daily, and the weekend brunch menu includes a fluffy Dutch-style pancake served warm from the oven as well as a creative Bloody Mary menu.

# Rai Rai Ken

Japanese

B2

214 E. 10th St. (bet. First & Second Aves.)

**Subway:** Astor Pl — Lunch & dinner daily
**Phone:** 212-477-7030
**Web:** N/A
**Prices:** ⊜

This sliver of a spot specializes in slurp-inducing, soul-satisfying ramen that stands out among the city's recent proliferation. The setting is barebones and unembellished: 14 low stools are situated at the busy counter overlooking a narrow kitchen lined with bubbling pots. Besides the caddies of chopsticks and paper napkins, there's just room enough for a deep brimming bowl at each setting.

The menu shines in its concise listing of near-addictive, complex broth variations such as *shio*, *shoyu*, miso, and curry. Each is chock-full of garnishes, like fishcakes or roasted pork, and nests of fresh, springy noodles. Before leaving, be sure to grab a business card; Rai Rai Ken rewards frequent diners with a complimentary bowlful after ten visits.

# The Redhead

Gastropub

B1

349 E. 13th St. (bet. First & Second Aves.)

**Subway:** 1 Av — Dinner Mon – Sat
**Phone:** 212-533-6212
**Web:** www.theredheadnyc.com
**Prices:** $$

A stocked bar and a substantial list of well-poured libations hint at the distinctly Southern origins of this popular East Village addition. Stop here for a creative cocktail, best enjoyed with the near-addictive bacon peanut brittle—a snack so popular that the restaurant now sells it online. Then, continue on to the comfortable rear dining area complemented by exposed brick walls and a red velvet banquette.

The menu's Southern accent is appetizingly evident in the kitchen's preparations that feature shrimp and grits spiced with slices of andouille sausage, and buttermilk fried chicken served with cornbread. A dessert called the "car bomb" hot chocolate embellished with Guiness, whiskey, and Bailey's marshmallows cleverly unites "gastro" and "pub".

# Sigiri

B2 — Sri Lankan

## 91 First Ave. (bet. 5th & 6th Sts.)

**Subway:** 1 Av — Lunch & dinner daily
**Phone:** 212-614-9333
**Web:** www.sigirinyc.com
**Prices:** 💲💲

The unique flavors of Sri Lankan cuisine set Sigiri apart from the Indian and Bangladeshi cooking that dominates East 6th Street's Curry Row. The second floor dining room is decorated with cinnamon-colored walls, festive table linens, and stylish furnishings. This is a lovely spot to feel worldly on a budget. The reasonably priced menu displays an intermingling of global influences—primarily Dutch, Portuguese, and Indian—that has resulted in such enticing specialties as chicken *lamprais* (baked rice studded with chicken, fish, plantain, and egg, spiced with whole peppercorns, cinnamon bark, and cardamom).

Fruit-based, non-alcoholic drinks—mango cordial and apple iced tea—are refreshing. Sigiri doesn't serve liquor.

# Sobakoh

A2 — Japanese

## 309 E. 5th St. (bet. First & Second Aves.)

**Subway:** Lower East Side - 2 Av — Lunch & dinner daily
**Phone:** 212-254-2244
**Web:** N/A
**Prices:** 💲💲

While approaching Sobakoh, stop to see Chef Hiromi Takahashi forming layers of organic, locally grown buckwheat flour dough into impressively uniform noodles—in his diminutive, glass-walled booth. This ritual creation of the mildly nutty, tender noodles is done several times a day; the chef's smiling face is a warming welcome. Steaming pots of richly flavored wild mushroom soba warm wintry evenings just as their chilled, refreshing bowlfuls of noodles and broth topped with sea urchin and salmon roe can thwart a sultry summer night. This is a delightful spot anytime. Many bowls are accompanied with golden, lightly-crisp tempura.

Creative variations such as soba risotto and soba gnocchi prove that noodles are not the grain's only guise.

# Soba-Ya

A2

Japanese

229 E. 9th St. (bet. Second & Third Aves.)

**Subway:** Astor Pl — Lunch & dinner daily
**Phone:** 212-533-6966
**Web:** www.sobaya-nyc.com
**Prices:**

Students from nearby NYU frequent this place for its Zen-like minimalist ambience and its hearty and inexpensive noodle dishes. Soba are made on the premises each morning by the chef, and then presented along with your hot or cold broth and an array of garnishes and ingredients. You can substitute the chewier udon, or wheat noodles (which some say taste more like traditional pasta), if you prefer. Seasonal sashimi or "country-style" soft tofu with edamame sauce are other options.

There's a good selection of Japanese beer and sake to pair with your meal. Made by the owner's wife, ice cream boasts unusual flavors like honey wasabi. Soba-Ya is open seven days a week, but the restaurant doesn't take reservations.

# Supper

B3

Italian

156 E. 2nd St. (bet. Aves. A & B)

**Subway:** 1 Av — Lunch & dinner daily
**Phone:** 212-477-7600
**Web:** www.supperrestaurant.com
**Prices:** $$

This is the rare Italian restaurant that reminds us of how simple pleasure can be: straightforward cuisine; an energetic, unfussy setting; reasonable prices; and perfectly low lighting to make everything and everyone look even better. Sure, neither credit cards nor reservations are accepted (see the chilly masses lining up for outdoor tables even in colder months), but this is worth it.

Impressive, classic cooking emerges from the tiny open kitchen as tagliatelle fashioned from ribbons of zucchini, dressed with olive oil, and toasted almonds; and a spot-on *spaghetti cacio e pepe*. Supper's wine program is interesting and features a unique "wine by consumption" service.

While away the wait time at lovely sibling, Sugo Bar, located next door.

# Table 8

A2 — Contemporary XX

25 Cooper Sq. (bet. 5th & 6th Sts.)

**Subway:** Astor Pl — Lunch Sat
**Phone:** 212-475-5700 — Dinner nightly
**Web:** www.table8la.com
**Prices:** $$

Chef Govind Armstrong's Table 8 concept has arrived in NYC and taken up residence at the Cooper Square hotel. The chocolate- and cognac-toned room, complete with secluded garden dining, has the requisite downtown chic that attracts a young and pretty clientele.

The cuisine favors Mediterranean flavors, and those who prefer to graze when dining out will be especially pleased by the multi-tiered menu. As small plates, slices of rabbit sausage are sprinkled with grains of black truffle salt; and an appetizer of torn pasta is studded with black pepper-spiked pieces of crunchy fried sweetbreads. Heartier fare may include a flattened and grilled baby chicken, partnered with short rib hash and dressed with *cipollini* jus.

# Terroir

B2 — Italian

413 E. 12th St. (bet. First Ave. & Ave. A)

**Subway:** Astor Pl — Dinner nightly
**Web:** www.wineisterroir.com
**Prices:** $$

How many wine bars does one town need? Probably about ten less than the city currently has, but when Marco Canora and Paul Grieco—the partners behind Hearth and Insieme—get in the game, people take notice. As it turns out, Terroir ought to be the prototype: a cozy little 24-seat nook with exposed brick walls, a long communal table, and a habit of getting packed to the gills by 7:00P.M.

Those lucky enough to snag a seat, however, will find a very clever lineup of by-the-glass choices, and a straight-up delicious Italian small plates menu featuring plump white anchovies with pickled onions; delicately fried beet risotto balls with gorgonzola cheese; savory chicken liver served with toasted sour-dough; and lamb sausage-stuffed sage leaves.

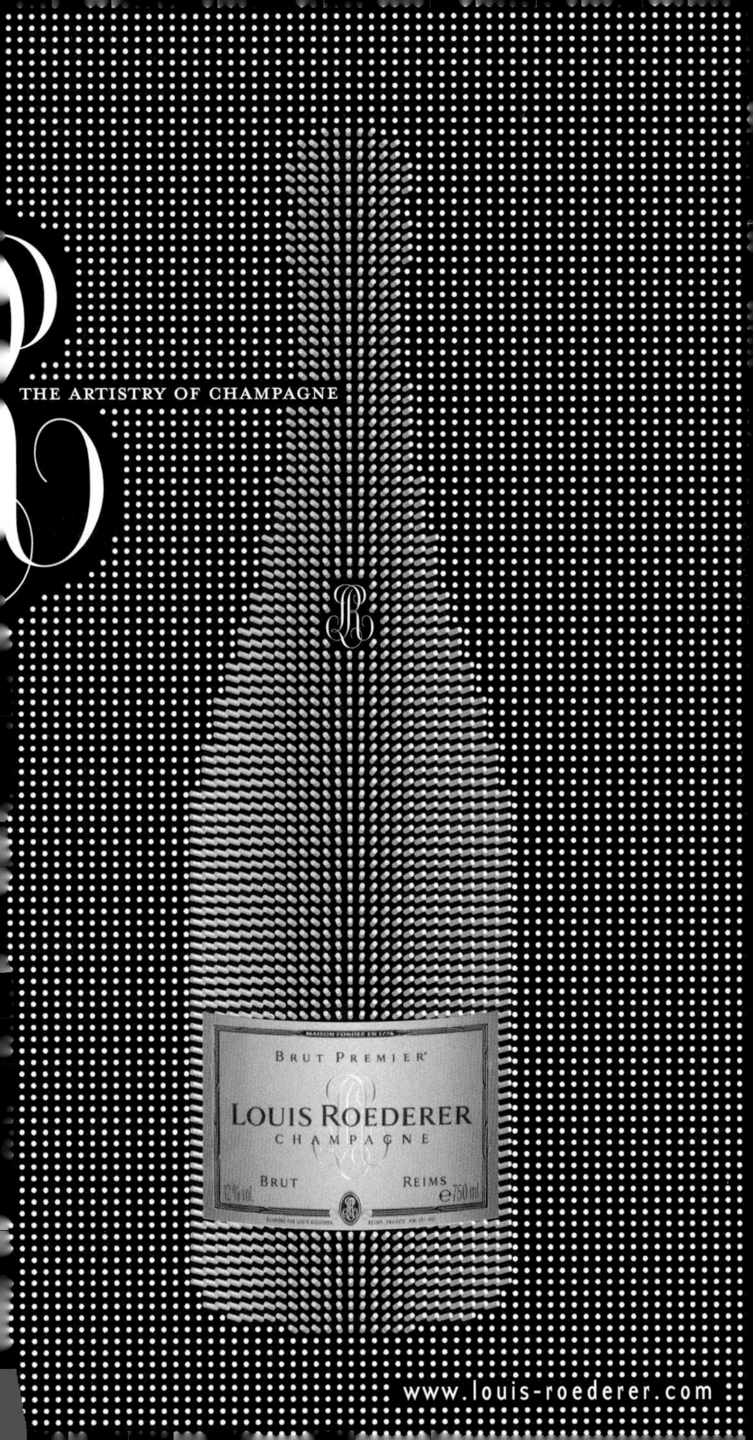
THE ARTISTRY OF CHAMPAGNE
BRUT PREMIER
LOUIS ROEDERER
CHAMPAGNE
BRUT
REIMS
e750 ml
www.louis-roederer.com

# Financial District

Widely considered the financial center of the world, the southern tip of Manhattan is populated by hard-driving Wall Street types. When it's time to eat, they love a hefty steak, especially when expense accounts are paying the bill. And though expense accounts around here may be shrinking these days, bigger is still better at stalwarts like **Delmonicos**, which opened in 1837 as America's first fine-dining restaurant. The restaurant that introduced diners to now-classic dishes such as Eggs Benedict, Lobster Newburg, and Baked Alaska, continues to pack 'em in for the signature Angus boneless ribeye, aka the Delmonico steak.

New is replacing old as the publicly owned Tin Building and New Market Building—home to the former Fulton Fish Market—may soon house tenants in the form of **The New Amsterdam Market**, a year-round indoor marketplace where butchers, grocers, fishmongers, artisan cheese producers, and other vendors hope to create a regional food system. With a stated mission "to reinvent the indoor public market as a civic institution in the City of New York," this non-profit organization dedicates itself to promoting sustainable agriculture and regionally sourced food, while offering space for independent purveyors to sell on behalf of farmers and food producers. Check their website, www.newamsterdampublic.org, for market dates.

One of the district's largest tourist draws, South Street Seaport is surrounded by a host of eateries from family-friendly Irish pubs to the historic **Fraunces Tavern**. Innkeeper Samuel Fraunces purchased this three-story, 18th century brick mansion at the corner of Pearl and Broad streets in 1762.

The Financial District has traditionally catered to power-lunchers by day and business travelers by night. However, that's all changing as the neighborhood becomes increasingly residential. What you will discover is a smorgasbord of bars, restaurants, and food services catering to the local population. These blossoming culinary delights incite buttoned-up Wall Street suits to loosen their collars and chill out over, say, a plate of steak frites at **Les Halles Downtown**—the brasserie affiliated with bad boy chef and Travel Channel celebrity Anthony Bourdain.

Front Street has attracted a surprising spate of Italian eateries counting **Il Brigante**, with its dough-spinning *pizzaiolo* who belongs to the United States Pizza Team, among their number. Another newbie, **Barbarini Alimentari** raises the bar with gourmet grocery items and an equally upscale menu of Italian fare.

The ultimate in express lunch, New York's famous food-carts are hugely popular in the Financial District. For a

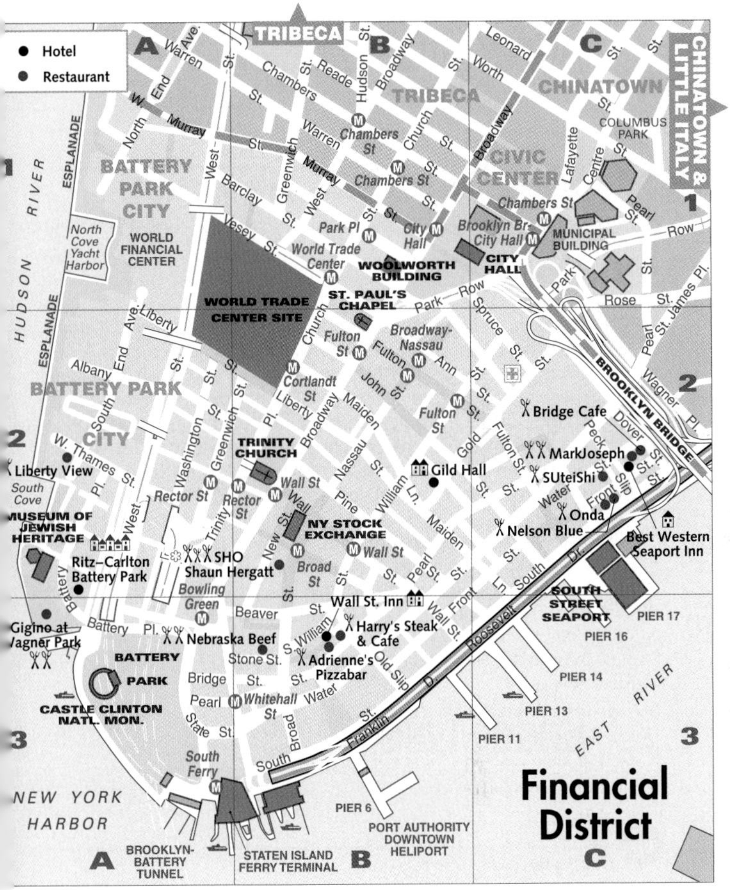


quick nosh at a bargain price, follow your nose to **Alan's Falafel Cart** on Cedar Street. Then for something sweet, head to **Financier Patisserie** on charming cobblestoned Stone Street, one of the narrow, sinuous streets laid out in the 17th century by New York's Dutch settlers. Wash it all down with an espresso at **Zibetto's** on Fulton Street.

Despite the economic downturn, restaurants downtown are as busy as ever, with former Wall Street wonders drowning their worries in martinis and Manhattans, and reviewing their portfolios over burgers and beer. Events such as the Stone Street Oyster Festival, sponsored by the same folks who operate Financier Patisserie and Ulysses pub, play to the area's strengths. What better way to lift spirits and celebrate the local Blue Point harvest in September than by slurping oysters and swilling libations outdoors on Stone Street?

# Adrienne's Pizzabar

B3 — Pizza

## 54 Stone St. (bet. Coenties Alley & S. William St.)

**Subway:** Bowling Green — Lunch & dinner daily
**Phone:** 212-248-3838
**Web:** www.adriennespizzabar.com
**Prices:** ☺☺

At noon, Adrienne's is abuzz—its Financial District setting attracts hordes of business types for delectable pizzas. With their thin crusts, slightly chunky sauce, and fresh toppings, these pies are a true classic on all fronts (except for the square shape). Come evening, the restaurant calms, as diners notice the custom-made oak paneling and upscale touches. This is also when the menu adds a list of baked dishes such as thinly sliced, roasted eggplant *rollatini* stuffed with creamy ricotta; as well as a 10-inch round pizza to the square pie selection. Likewise, the servers are more engaging at dinner, when less pressed by diners rushing back to work.
Adrienne's owners, the Poulakakos family, recently opened Inatteso Pizzabar Casano in Battery Park City.

# Bridge Cafe

C2 — American

## 279 Water St. (at Dover St.)

**Subway:** Fulton St — Lunch Sun – Fri
**Phone:** 212-227-3344 — Dinner nightly
**Web:** www.bridgecafenyc.com
**Prices:** $$

Opened in 1794 as a grocery in a wooden structure on the East River's bank, the Bridge Cafe is now hailed as "New York's oldest drinking establishment." Over the years, this colorfully historic building has housed a restaurant, brothel, boardinghouse, and saloon before it was finally christened the Bridge Cafe in 1979.
Find upscale American food in this cozy setting, embellished by creaky, sloping floors, paintings of the bridge, and an old New York patina. Corn and red onion fritters in jalapeño cheddar sauce, or steamed P.E.I. mussels in a spicy tomato broth are featured alongside lunchtime lush sandwiches or more refined dinner entrées. A stop here is de rigueur for any malt or scotch lover visiting NYC. Go Sunday for the popular Bridge Brunch.

# Gigino at Wagner Park

Italian XX

A3

20 Battery Pl. (in Wagner Park)

**Subway:** Bowling Green — Lunch & dinner daily
**Phone:** 212-528-2228
**Web:** www.gigino-wagnerpark.com
**Prices:** $$

After a long day of downtown sightseeing or a cruise to the Statue of Liberty, this unpretentious Italian restaurant is a welcome, calming oasis. Sister to Gigino Trattoria in TriBeCa, this Gigino is tucked into the ground floor of a wedge-shaped building in Wagner Park.

The best seats are on the raised outdoor terrace where harbor views abound—call ahead to reserve these. Gracious service is assured throughout. The dining room has a pleasant air with its palette of creamy whites and large windows.

Select from the well-prepared antipasti before moving to heartier fare, such as the succulent, perfectly grilled veal chop with sweet, smoky red onions. In the colder months, a prix-fixe menu offers good value, and a children's menu keeps picky palates happy.

# Harry's Steak & Cafe

American X

B3

1 Hanover Sq. (bet. Pearl & Stone Sts.)

**Subway:** Wall St (William St.) — Lunch & dinner Mon – Sat
**Phone:** 212-785-9200
**Web:** www.harrysnyc.com
**Prices:** $$

The ground floor of the historic Hanover Bank building is home to two distinct and equally gratifying experiences from a single kitchen. Both are accessible from entrances on Pearl Street and Hanover Square, though navigating between them may seem mazelike. Those in the mood for a Kobe beef hotdog should make their way to Harry's Cafe. For serious lamb or steak, outstanding pasta specials, and one of New York's better cheesecakes, we suggest the well-ensconced Harry's Steak.

The café's unencumbered bar area is clearly the place where Wall Street types blow off steam after work. The whitewashed alcoves and private dining at the steakhouse are where politicians come to broker deals. The wine list includes some great vintages and well-priced offerings.

# Liberty View

A2 — Chinese

21 South End Ave. (below W. Thames St.)

**Subway:** Rector St (Greenwich St.) — Lunch & dinner daily
**Phone:** 212-786-1888
**Web:** N/A
**Prices:** **$$**

You'll probably get better Chinese food in Chinatown but you aren't going to get this gorgeous peep show of the Hudson River, Ellis Island, and the Statue of Liberty. This upscale Chinese restaurant holds true to its name, offering killer views of the original gray lady from its prime ground floor location (with outdoor seating) at the tip of Battery Park City.

So how's the grub? It pays to be choosy—the chef is from Shanghai, which offers a clue as to the direction you might want to take. No one would kick the lo mein out of bed for eating crackers, but the crab and pork soup dumplings are a better bet. And despite sounding heavy by design, the Shanghai-fried rice, diced with Chinese sausage, shrimp, and peas, is perfectly delicate and sweet.

# MarkJoseph

C2 — Steakhouse

261 Water St. (bet. Peck Slip & Dover St.)

**Subway:** Fulton St — Lunch Mon – Fri
**Phone:** 212-277-0020 — Dinner Mon – Sat
**Web:** www.markjosephsteakhouse.com
**Prices:** **$$$**

Nestled in the shadow of the Brooklyn Bridge in the South Street Seaport Historic District, MarkJoseph's caters to financiers, Wall Street wunderkinds, and tourists with deep pockets. The cozy dining room is a notch above the standard steakhouse design, with art-glass vases and pastoral photographs of the wine country adding sleek notes.

At lunch, regulars devour hefty half-pound burgers (there's even a turkey variety). At dinnertime, prime dry-aged Porterhouse takes center stage, accompanied by salads and favorite sides like creamed spinach, caramelized onions, and hash browns, along with less guilt-inducing steamed vegetables. And what better to wash your steak down with than one of the selections on the generous list of red wines?

# Nebraska Beef

Steakhouse XX

B3

## 15 Stone St. (bet. Broad & Whitehall Sts.)

**Subway:** Bowling Green
**Phone:** 212-952-0620
**Web:** N/A
**Prices:** $$$

Lunch Mon – Fri
Dinner Mon – Sat

It's easy to miss the door that marks the entrance to this beloved Financial District watering hole-cum-steakhouse (look for the red and gold sign out front), but not the raucous happy hour crowd that floods the narrow bar leading to the restaurant. Smile and squeeze through, though, and you'll find a much calmer scene on the flip side: A dark, wood-paneled dining room with a clubby, in-the-know vibe.

This is one Wall Street oasis where the recession's on hold—the martinis flow free, the garlic bread melts in your mouth, and the hand-picked, 28-day, dry-aged ribeye still arrives sizzling, perfectly charred, and juicy as sin. If you're short on time or looking for lunch options, you can also grab a steak sandwich, Caesar salad, or burger on the fly.

# Nelson Blue

New Zealand X

C2

## 233-235 Front St. (at Peck Slip)

**Subway:** Fulton St
**Phone:** 212-346-9090
**Web:** www.nelsonblue.com
**Prices:** $$

Lunch & dinner daily

The Kiwi culture comes alive at this casual downtown restaurant, a few short blocks from South Street Seaport. Smartly decorated with Maori designs, artifacts, and a long carved wood bar, this airy pub exudes Down Under flair.

Enjoy generous and outstanding dishes of fresh roasted squid, served warm with fennel, cucumber, and carrots; or a perfectly traditional curried lamb pot pie, crispy, golden, tender, and spicy all at once. Green-lipped mussels, venison, and lamb—natch'—are flown in from New Zealand. Even the selections on the wine list hail from the Southern Hemisphere, and New Zealand-brewed Steinlager beer is on tap at the bar. A warm, lively ambience, and communal table foster gatherings of families, friends, and colleagues.

# Onda

C2 — Latin American

229 Front St. (bet. Beekman St. & Peck Slip)

**Subway:** Fulton St
**Phone:** 212-513-0770
**Web:** www.ondanyc.com
**Prices:** $$$

Lunch & dinner daily

Front Street's bustling restaurant scene gets a spicy pick-me-up from this South American newcomer, with delicious fare courtesy of Guyana-born chef, Raymond Mohan. The space is Latin-bright in all the right ways with Moorish blue-and-white tiles, funky colored industrial bulbs, and chicken wire cabinets behind the bar. So who could blame people for getting a little loud after work? This is like liquid sunshine.
Try a plate of seductively smoky lamb belly, sliced and laced with jerk sauce and surrounded by roasted red peppers dressed in olive oil and garlic; or a pearly-white fillet of mahi mahi wrapped in crunchy coconut flakes, resting on a silky mound of Rioja-braised oxtail; or warm basil crema ice cream, topped with a pumpkin seed praline.

# SUteiShi

C2 — Japanese

24 Peck Slip (at Front St.)

**Subway:** Fulton St
**Phone:** 212-766-2344
**Web:** www.suteishi.com
**Prices:** $$

Lunch Mon – Fri
Dinner nightly

Red lacquer, black leather, and backlit bonsai trees behind the bar paint a sleek picture at this corner sushi bar. The clientele of young financial types and tourists seem unfased by the occasional service flaws; they concentrate instead on the inventive maki. Try the Happy Lobster Roll, with sweet chunks of meat, tucked with mayonaise and delicate greens into warm, perfectly seasoned sushi rice, topped with crunchy, red flying fish roe. Desserts continue this focus on innovation, with offerings such as creamy and nutty black sesame brûlée.
At lunch, the bento box combination lets diners sample a range of fare. In nice weather, the restaurant opens sidewalk seating onto this quiet cobblestoned street, surrounded by Federal-style buildings.

# SHO Shaun Hergatt ✿

Contemporary XXX

B2

40 Broad St. (bet. Beaver St. & Exchange Pl.)

**Subway:** Broad St — Lunch Mon – Fri
**Phone:** 212-809-3993 — Dinner Mon – Sat
**Web:** www.shoshaunhergatt.com
**Prices:** $$$

Lucy Schaeffer

The staid Financial District restaurant scene gets a sexy kick in the pants from this impressive new restaurant showcasing the myriad talents of Chef Shaun Hergatt - a talented Aussie and stone cold veteran of the Ritz-Carlton's legendary Dining Room restaurants. With his newest menu, Hergatt plays off his classical training, pulling notes from his Australian heritage and infusing a wealth of Asian accents (think kaffir lime, galangal, and lychee) into his cooking.

Located on the second floor of the Setai New York, every last inch of the sleek, enormous space—which features an infinity pool, a wine gallery, and a smattering of private dining rooms—is impeccably appointed.

The restaurant serves breakfast, lunch, and dinner—the last available in a two- or three-course prix-fixe option that might include a spiced double duck consommé bobbing with one delicate chicken *raviolo* wrapped in threads of black truffle and scallion greens; a fresh hunk of slow-poached halibut, topped with black truffle-flecked celeriac purée and laid over a bed of tender white asparagus spears and salsify; or milk-fed veal tenderloin, surrounded by crispy *pomme almondine* and a bright mix of glossy vegetables.

# Gramercy, Flatiron & Union Square

Gramercy Park, anchoring its namesake neighborhood, is steeped in history, old-world beauty, and tranquility; but its extreme exclusivity is the stuff of legends among life-long New Yorkers, few of whom have set foot on its pretty yet private paths. This may be where tourists have an advantage, because outside of the residents whose home address faces the square, Gramercy Park Hotel guests are among the few permitted entrance. The staff accompanies guests to the daunting cast-iron gate, allows them in, and reminds of the number to call when they wish to be let out again, perhaps to explore this lovely enclave filled with charming cafés and brownstones.

Still this is New York, so walk a few blocks in any direction to discover the neighborhoods' diverse offerings. North of the park find Gramercy's very own "Curry Hill" with an array of satisfying, budget-friendly restaurants. Enthusiasts should visit **Kalustyan's**—a spice-scented emporium specializing in a wealth of exotic products ranging from orange blossom water, to thirty varieties of dried whole chilies. Just next door is **Rice**, an inexpensive café serving flavorful stews and curries accompanied by myriad preparations of the grain.

A few blocks to the west, find the very open and welcoming Madison Square Park, which boasts its own unique history and vibe. This was the home of the city's first community Christmas tree in 1912, the original location of Madison Square Garden arena, and site of New York's very first baseball club, the Knickerbockers of 1845. It is therefore only fitting that greeting park visitors is the original **Shake Shack**, serving its signature upscale fast food from an ivy-covered kiosk. Burgers and Chicago-style dogs are popular, but the house-made custard has its cultish followers checking the online "custard calendar" weekly for their favorite flavors, like red-velvet or salted caramel. Barbecue fans should time their visits here with the Big Apple Barbecue Block Party held in June. This weekend-long event features celebrity pit masters displaying and serving their talents to throngs of hungry aficionados.

However, this neighborhood's most famous, familiar, and remarkable feature is actually its namesake building, the Flatiron. Measuring an impossibly narrow six feet across at its acute northern edge, the view of this 22 story landmark has been immortalized on countless films, shows, and postcards.

Nearby Union Square may be known as an historic downtown park with playgrounds and tiered plazas that occasionally host political protests and rallies, but today the square is best known for its year-round **Greenmarket**. Despite the park's ongoing renovations,

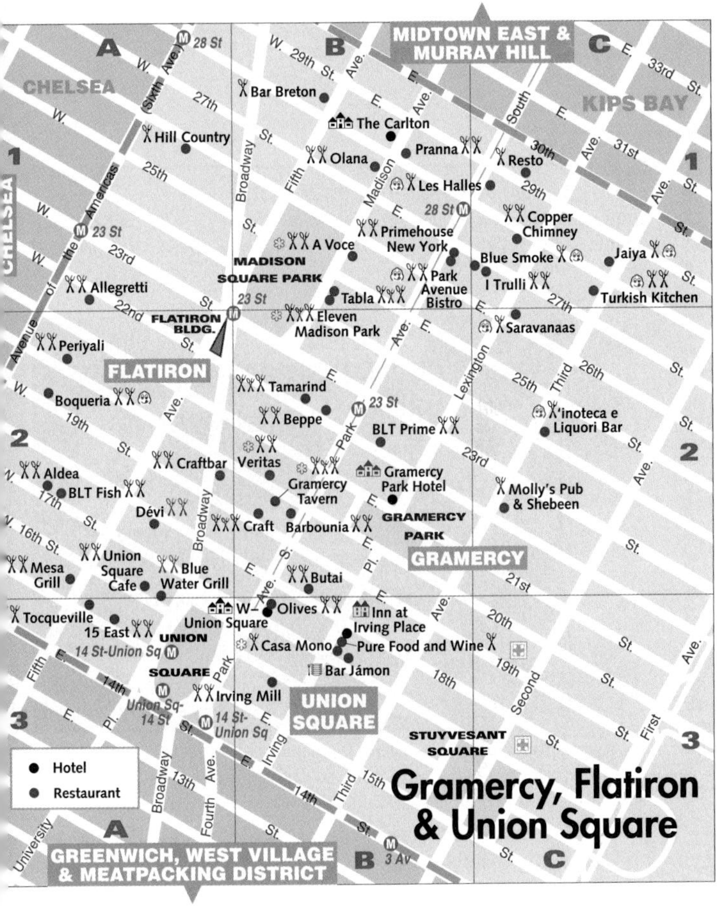


its beautiful array of seasonal produce, baked goods, fresh meat, seafood, dairy, plants, and flowers are still available every Monday, Wednesday, Friday, and Saturday. Early in the day, it is not uncommon to spot chefs dressed in their whites selecting the day's supplies. During Christmastime, the Union Square Holiday Market features stalls of candles, shirts, knit caps, and decorations for gift shopping in a festive atmosphere.

Beyond the market's borders, find a nice bottle of wine to complement that farm-to-table meal from the comprehensive **Union Square Wines and Spirits**, or the regionally-specific **Italian Wine Merchants**. Further testament to Union Square's reputation as the center of Manhattan food shopping is the presence of **Whole Foods** and the city's very first **Trader Joe's**, all within blocks of one another.

# A Voce

B1

Italian

41 Madison Ave. (enter on 26th St.)

**Subway:** 28 St (Park Ave. South)

**Phone:** 212-545-8555

**Web:** www.avocerestaurant.com

**Prices:** $$$

Lunch Mon – Fri
Dinner Mon – Sat

Evan Sung

In the wake of Andrew Carmellini's departure, Chef Missy Robbins—who held the executive chef post at Chicago's esteemed Spiaggia—takes the wheel at A Voce.

The restaurant's name means "word of mouth," and the buzz on Robbins is that, while she certainly reflects her predecessor's taste for regional Italian cooking, she also arrives with a new bag of tricks—sashaying into deeper pockets of the peninsula, turning out deliciously restrained fare like pristine, thinly-sliced Nantucket bay scallops laced with olive oil, sea salt, orange zest, and chiles; a soft tangle of *taglierini* tossed with *bottarga*, lemon zest, and pecorino; tender, roasted chicken breast topped with grilled lemon and served over thinly-sliced potato; or an exceptionally light vanilla panna cotta studded with roasted figs and drizzled in acacia honey.

Though the crowd seems more subdued these days, the stylish space still packs the requisite slick-and-hip city punch, with a gorgeous, ornately-carved dark wood door leading to a cool, modern interior where diners linger over the impressive Italian-dominated wine list. Oh, and midtowners—rejoice. The owners are opening a second location in the Time Warner Center.

# Aldea

Mediterranean XX

A2

31 W. 17th St. (bet. Fifth & Sixth Aves.)

**Subway:** 14 St - 6 Av
Dinner Mon – Sat
**Phone:** 212-675-7223
**Web:** www.aldearestaurant.com
**Prices:** $$

Portuguese-American chef, George Mendes, bounced around the kitchens of many great chefs—including David Bouley, Alain Ducasse, and Kurt Gutenbrunner—before finding his own voice with Aldea (which means *village* in Portuguese). The intimate dining space evokes a sun-bleached coastal setting, and the chef's counter is a nice surprise for solo diners—set so closely to the kitchen that you feel like you could touch the chefs toiling just beyond the glass partition.

The tight little menu might offer two sardines cooked *a la plancha*, paired with bread, almonds, and bitter almond milk; or a crumbly little rice pudding tart sporting a crunchy brûléed hat, a smear of vanilla bean-flecked caramel sauce, and lovely quenelle of chamomile sorbet.

# Allegretti

Mediterranean XX

A1

46 W. 22nd St. (bet. Fifth & Sixth Aves.)

**Subway:** 23 St (Broadway)
Lunch Mon – Fri
**Phone:** 212-206-0555
Dinner Mon – Sat
**Web:** www.allegrettinyc.com
**Prices:** $$$

Chef Alain Allegretti's solo venture has a confidently understated mien where light wood flooring, navy-blue furnishings, and pale walls hung with mirrored panels frame the good-looking crowd enjoying this French-Mediterranean inspired menu. The chef's native Provence is fully explored in flavorful preparations like leek fondant accompanied by a breaded poached egg and sauce *gribiche*; chestnut purée-filled *cappelletti* with tender, flavorful duck ragout; and John Dory accompanied by octopus and shrimp in fennel-saffron broth.

The setting and cuisine are complemented by an impressively focused, smartly dressed service team. The chef's charm and personality extend beyond the menu, into the simply elegant dining room, where he enjoys checking on his patrons.

# Barbounia

B2 — Mediterranean

250 Park Ave. South (at 20th St.)

**Subway:** 23 St (Park Ave. South) — Lunch & dinner daily
**Phone:** 212-995-0242
**Web:** www.barbounia.com
**Prices:** **$$**

Favored by the nearby business crowd and residents alike, this sprawling space boasts exotic touches throughout. Fat columns and arched openings abate the room's scale, while pillow-lined banquettes, a knobby-wood communal table, and open kitchen equipped with a wood-burning oven allude to the menu's rustic Mediterranean theme.
A recent chef change has resulted in a revamped menu that continues to serve the sunny flavors of the region. Start with the selection of spreads accompanied by a slab of addictive, freshly baked flatbread. Then branch out to explore a tempting array of meze, oven-roasted whole fish, or house specialties like lamb terracotta—a stew perfumed with sweet spices, covered with a crusty bread lid, and baked in an earthenware dish.

# Bar Breton

B1 — French

254 Fifth Ave. (bet. 28th & 29th Sts.)

**Subway:** 28 St (Broadway) — Lunch & dinner daily
**Phone:** 212-213-4999
**Web:** www.chefpiano.com/bar-breton
**Prices:** **$$**

After closing his lovely one-starred Fleur de Sel, Chef Cyril Renaud decided to focus the cuisine of this latest venture even more on his native Brittany. Here, he offers a hearty listing of organic buckwheat crêpes (or *galettes*) filled with the likes of wild smoked salmon, horseradish crème, and chives; or Black Forest ham, Gruyère, and a sunny-side-up egg. The rotating selections of daily specials and entrées clearly display the touch of a talented professional, as in the rosy slices of velvety duck breast sauced with a savory, orange-scented reduction.
Open from breakfast through dinner daily, this unassuming location features a petite, zinc-topped bar serving draught beers and ciders, as well as a casually adorned dining room in back.

# Bar Jamón

Spanish

B3

125 E. 17th St. (at Irving Pl.)

**Subway:** 14 St - Union Sq
**Phone:** 212-253-2773
**Web:** www.barjamonnyc.com
**Prices:** $$

Lunch Sat – Sun
Dinner nightly

Is Andy Nusser the unsung hero of the Batali empire? A nibble at Casa Mono's next door neighbor and sister wine bar, Bar Jamón—with its brilliant by-the-glass selection of Spanish wines and freshly crafted tapas—could convince you. It takes a Midas touch to turn out such delicious fare in a restaurant the size of a newsstand, but Nusser, raised in Spain, does so with panache.

No dish is bigger than your fist, but Nusser breaks the tired tapas mold so creatively it packs a big culinary punch—try the soft boiled egg with tangy *romesco*; stewed pork shoulder and chorizo, pressed into a terrine and served with *pan con tomate*; or the house specialty, a ham-and-aged-goat-cheese *bocadillo* so tasty you'll want to cheat on your deli guy.

# Beppe

Italian

B2

45 E. 22nd St. (bet. Broadway & Park Ave. South)

**Subway:** 23 St (Park Ave. South)
**Phone:** 212-982-8422
**Web:** www.beppenyc.com
**Prices:** $$$

Lunch Mon – Fri
Dinner Mon – Sat

With its orange plastered façade, Beppe is easy to spot. Chef Cesare Casella has moved on, but the Tuscan-inspired farmhouse continues to burn bright without his firebrand talent at the helm. The hearty and imaginative cuisine still draws crowds, keeping the room abuzz day and night. Warm and inviting, the terracotta-tiled space features sunny colors and a commanding, wood-burning fireplace topped with potted greenery.

Whittling down the expansive menu can be challenging when faced with antipasti such as grilled handmade sausage served with stewed beans; and pastas that may include a luscious pesto-dressed pasta *verde* with raw tomatoes and slender string beans. Before your departure, savor dessert—house-made cannoli—it redefines the standard.

# BLT Fish

A2 — Seafood XX

21 W. 17th St. (bet. Fifth & Sixth Aves.)

**Subway:** 14 St - 6 Av — Lunch Mon – Fri
**Phone:** 212-691-8888 — Dinner nightly
**Web:** www.bltfish.com
**Prices:** **$$$**

BLT Fish presents two options to hungry seafood fans. On the ground floor, the Fish Shack offers an extensive raw bar, beachfront-worthy lobster rolls, and fish and chips. Or, choose the upstairs dining room that bears all the hallmarks of BLT's casual elegance: dark wood furnishings, mocha color schemes, and a wine list to be pondered. There's more! The sightly space is equipped with a glass roof and white-tiled open kitchen.

Exceptionally fresh shellfish or line-caught, hand-cut fish may be simply brushed with olive oil and grilled; but the menu also boasts more ingenious offerings, like the semi-smoked King salmon with avocado hollandaise. Thoughtful extras throughout the meal enhance the experience.

Lunch is served daily at the Fish Shack.

# BLT Prime

B2 — Steakhouse XX

111 E. 22nd St. (bet. Lexington Ave. & Park Ave. South)

**Subway:** 23 St (Park Ave. South) — Dinner nightly
**Phone:** 212-995-8500
**Web:** www.bltprime.com
**Prices:** **$$$**

In a city that offers a world of dining options, sometimes there's nothing wrong with meat and potatoes. In fact, there's something very right about BLT Prime, where cuts of USDA prime and certified black Angus are dry-aged in house, served sizzling hot in a cast iron pan, and topped with a slowly melting sheen of herbed butter. To further adorn your steak, choose from an array of homemade sauces and the hearty listing of sides that elevate the humble potato: creamy home fries, blue cheese tater tots, and leek hashbrowns. The Gruyère popovers start meals with a warm and tasty welcome.

The handsome room and bar area, popular with local professionals, is done in rich tones of butterscotch and mocha, and furnished with sleek zebrawood tables.

# Blue Smoke

**American** ✗

**C1**

### 116 E. 27th St. (bet. Lexington Ave. & Park Ave. South)

**Subway:** 28 St (Park Ave. South)　　　　　　　Lunch & dinner daily
**Phone:** 212-447-7733
**Web:** www.bluesmoke.com
**Prices:** $$

Jazz and barbecue are a winning combination, and nowhere more so in the city than at Blue Smoke, where hickory and applewood are used to flavor the "low and slow" smoked meats. Sharing is encouraged since hearty portions are the rule, as in the pulled pork platter served with pit beans, slaw, and homemade white bread; and the rib sampler featuring three styles of BBQ—Kansas City, Memphis, and Texas on one hefty plate. Difficult no doubt, but try to save room for the fab sides and old-fashioned desserts. The wine list features small producers and is impressive for a barbecue joint.

You can enjoy the same food downstairs at Jazz Standard while you listen to live jazz and blues. Owner Danny Meyer stamps the restaurant with his signature brand of service.

# Blue Water Grill

**Contemporary** ✗✗

**A2·3**

### 31 Union Sq. West (at 16th St.)

**Subway:** 14 St - Union Sq　　　　　　　　　　Lunch & dinner daily
**Phone:** 212-675-9500
**Web:** www.brguestrestaurants.com
**Prices:** $$

Facing the Union Square Greenmarket, Blue Water Grill is housed in a former bank that dates back to the turn of the last century. The dining room bustles with eager guests and a well-trained service team, yet retains a stately air with its soaring molded ceiling, gleaming marble, and large windows overlooking the terraced dining area, ideal for warmer weather.

The crowd-pleasing menu offers a raw bar and selection of sushi or maki. Entrées focus on seafood either simply grilled or accented with international flavors, as in the ginger-soy lacquered Chilean sea bass. Live jazz is served up nightly in the downstairs lounge; and private group dining is available in the Vault Room, a former repository for gold bullion.

# Boqueria

A2 — Spanish XX

53 W. 19th St. (bet. Fifth & Sixth Aves.)

**Subway:** 18 St (Seventh Ave.) — Lunch & dinner daily
**Phone:** 212-255-4160
**Web:** www.boquerianyc.com
**Prices:** **$$**

At this Flatiron favorite, partners Yann de Rochefort and Chef Seamus Mullen offer their deliciously urbane take on the humble little restaurants lining Barcelona's famed market, from which this establishment takes its name.

The pleasing space features a white marble dining counter lit overhead by clear glass light bulbs, and a dining area comprised of leather banquettes matching the height of the tall communal tables. The décor's creamy shades create a sophisticated and snug atmosphere.

The restaurant dishes up a dizzying array of authentic offerings, sized from tiny (*pinxto*) to plates for sharing (*compartir*); and at lunch, hot and cold sandwiches (*bocatas*) simply adds to the mélange.

A recently opened SoHo location offers a comparable menu.

# Butai

B2 — Japanese XX

115 E. 18th St. (bet. Irving Pl. & Park Ave. South)

**Subway:** 14 St - Union Sq — Lunch Mon – Fri, Dinner nightly
**Phone:** 212-228-5716
**Web:** www.butai.us
**Prices:** **$$**

Butai's sleek bi-level space, accented with gorgeous marble and dark wood, is an attractive setting in which to enjoy contemporary Japanese cuisine. Quieter at lunch, the space comes alive when the sun sets and the lively lounge area fills with young professionals from nearby offices.

Attractive presentations of sushi are nicely done here, but Butai is best known for its *robata* grill offerings, which are only available in the evening. As one of the few Japanese restaurants in the city to offer *robata*-style cuisine, you'll find such delights as charcoal-grilled organic chicken with sea salt; *kalbi*; jumbo prawns; and squid with ginger-soy sauce on a menu that also offers classic starters such as *agedashi* tofu and various *sunomono*.

# Casa Mono ✿

Spanish

B3

52 Irving Pl. (at 17th St.)

**Subway:** 14 St - Union Sq — Lunch & dinner daily
**Phone:** 212-253-2773
**Web:** www.casamononyc.com
**Prices:** $$

Casa Mono

If you were wandering through this lovely pocket of Gramercy Park—just steps from bustling Union Square—you couldn't miss Casa Mono. With big, glossy doors that swing out into pretty, tree-lined Irving Place when the weather's right, the pleasant thump of music and irresistible smell of meat done *a la plancha*, Andy Nusser's corner of Barcelona delights would be a hit even if the guy wasn't a culinary genius.

Opened with backing from partners Mario Batali and Joseph Bastianich, Casa Mono's rustic interior can read a bit cramped, the kind of place where the bar might prove more comfortable than the Lilliputian tables. A trifling inconvenience, nonetheless, when that ruby-red glass of Spanish wine hits your palm, and those amazing *raciones* start flying out of the kitchen.

Try the fresh seared octopus, served over a shaved fennel salad laced with parsley, garlic, and olive oil, and dented with grapefruit segments; cornmeal-crusted lamb's tongue, fried to crispy perfection and sliced over a mint aïoli; homemade chorizo served with crunchy *manchego*; or tender razor clams, cooked *a la plancha* and hit with a healthy shake of bright parsley and fragrant garlic.

# Copper Chimney

C1 **Indian** XX

126 E. 28th St. (bet. Lexington Ave. & Park Ave. South)

**Subway:** 28 St (Park Ave. South) Lunch & dinner daily
**Phone:** 212-213-5742
**Web:** www.copperchimneynyc.com
**Prices:** ©©

Copper Chimney's impressive Indian fare offers plenty to satisfy, in this attractive room with a hip décor and fun vibe. A meal here begins with a small plate of mini-*pappadums* drizzled with mint and tamarind chutney, surrounding a neat mound of minced tomato, onion, and pepper. The appetizer selection includes tandoori samosas and fried cauliflower florets with honey and garlic. Main courses incorporate a wide range of traditional ingredients, while emphasizing refined preparation and elegant presentation. Non-meat eaters will be happy with the ample selection of flavorful vegetarian items.

Copper Chimney's youthful ambience is further accentuated by a second floor lounge area.

# Craft

B2 **American** XXX

43 E. 19th St. (bet. Broadway & Park Ave. South)

**Subway:** 14 St - Union Sq Dinner nightly
**Phone:** 212-780-0880
**Web:** www.craftrestaurant.com
**Prices:** $$$$

As host of the popular Bravo reality show, *Top Chef*, Tom Colicchio is a Hollywood natural. But years ago, he shot to fame on his home turf—the New York food scene—by ushering in a new, albeit simple, way of thinking about haute cuisine: let fresh, local, organic ingredients do the work, and let customers design their own plates. At Craft, diners can tailor their meals ingredient by ingredient to suit them perfectly, choosing from a basic lineup of seafood, charcuterie, roasted meats, salad, or vegetables. That they can do it in a beautiful Flatiron space with leather-paneled walls, brick-covered columns, and dramatic filament bulbs dripping from the ceiling, takes the cake.

Speaking of, don't miss the to-die-for desserts.

# Craftbar

Contemporary XX

A2

## 900 Broadway (bet. 19th & 20th Sts.)

**Subway:** 14 St - Union Sq
Lunch & dinner daily
**Phone:** 212-461-4300
**Web:** www.craftrestaurant.com
**Prices:** $$

Craftbar offers a toned-down setting and simpler menu structure than at Chef Tom Colicchio's first-born, Craft. The lofty space outfitted with brown paper-topped tables, exposed duct work, and chic lighting portrays the casual elegance expected from the acclaimed chef.

Modern American style with Mediterranean flair and a focus on seasonality typify Craftbar's bill of fare, the majority of which is conventionally arranged by course, but also features a selection of tidbits accompanied by oysters, cheeses, and charcuterie. Dishes may include house-made *cavatelli* Bolognese; day boat scallops with roasted lemon risotto; or plum and blueberry crisp with vanilla bean-speckled ice cream.

Revel in the boundless wine list, with many selections by the glass.

# Dévi

Indian XX

A2

## 8 E. 18th St. (bet. Broadway & Fifth Ave.)

**Subway:** 14 St - Union Sq
Lunch Mon – Fri
**Phone:** 212-691-1300
Dinner nightly
**Web:** www.devinyc.com
**Prices:** $$$

Cookbook author Suvir Saran and tandoor master Hemant Mathur oversee this sultry spot and lucky for aficionados of regional Indian cooking, the cuisine here honors it's roots while receiving a modern spin from these very talented chefs.

The sumptuous setting is indeed fit for the Hindu mother goddess who inspired the restaurant's name. Gauzy jewel-tone fabrics swathe the walls; banquettes covered in patchwork of chocolate, gold, and saffron tones provide cozy seating; and colored glass lanterns light the transporting room.

A mouthwatering choice of vegetarian dishes like yam dumplings in an aromatic onion-tomato gravy will appeal to some, while others may prefer the likes of Tandoori prawns with eggplant chutney and crispy okra salad.

# Eleven Madison Park ✿

B1 — Contemporary XXX

11 Madison Ave. (at 24th St.)

**Subway:** 23 St (Park Ave. South) — Lunch Mon – Fri
**Phone:** 212-889-0905 — Dinner Mon – Sat
**Web:** www.elevenmadisonpark.com
**Prices:** **$$$**

Robyn Lehr

Tucked into one of the city's most beloved buildings, the MetLife Insurance tower overlooking Madison Square Park, Danny Meyer's most elegant restaurant is flat-out gorgeous—with jumbo windows flooding natural light into an enormous dining room featuring soaring ceilings, glossy marble floors, and ethereally pale walls and white linens broken up by the bright pop of deep-shaded roses.

Back in the kitchen, Swiss Chef Daniel Humm spins impeccably fresh, seasonal ingredients into creative contemporary fare like a smartly updated braised oxtail dish topped by a savory layer of potato purée and elegant bordelaise sauce, and accompanied by a bright pile of baby brussel sprouts studded with grilled pancetta; or a mind-blowingly good New England cranberry pastille with ivoire chocolate crémeux, pocked with juicy little segments of Satsuma tangerine.

Those looking to steal a meal at a fraction of the usual cost should check out the $28 lunch option, which offers a choose-your-own 2-course tasting menu. While the real stellar meal is to be had only at dinner, pause before flipping out over their excellent wine list and cocktail offerings—or you might not make it back to work.

# 15 East

**Japanese** XX

A3

## 15 E. 15th St. (bet. Fifth Ave. & Union Sq. West)

**Subway:** 14 St - Union Sq — Lunch Mon – Fri
**Phone:** 212-647-0015 — Dinner Mon – Sat
**Web:** www.15eastrestaurant.com
**Prices:** $$$

Steps from bustling Union Square, this sleek little sushi den is nestled into a charming four-story building overlooking 15th Street. Inside, you'll find a modest, but beautifully detailed interior decked out in gauzy white curtains, lush gray walls, and dangling geometric lanterns.

Chef Masato Shimizu apprenticed in Japan for seven years—a training that comes to light in a gorgeous display of a dozen different seaweeds, each trimmed in different ways (one has a drizzle of sesame, another is sprinkled with grated lemon zest); a beautiful ceramic tile sporting a bright array of supremely fresh sashimi; or creamy almond-flavored tofu topped with plum wine sorbet, resting in a pool of sweet sake syrup and flanked by fresh strawberries.

# Hill Country

**Barbecue** X

A1

## 30 W. 26th St. (bet. Broadway & Sixth Ave.)

**Subway:** 28 St (Sixth Ave.) — Lunch & dinner daily
**Phone:** 212-255-4544
**Web:** www.hillcountryny.com
**Prices:** $$

This Texas-size roadhouse has won over the hearts and stomachs of smoked brisket deprived New Yorkers. Always a rollicking good time, Hill Country's food and atmosphere set it apart from the competition resulting from a recent barbecue boom.

A lower level stage fills the space with live country music (a nod to its Austin roots), making this a festive spot for groups and families alike.

Cords of oak fuel massive smokers to recreate a truly Texan Hill Country experience. Flintstone-size ribs are sold by the pound. Kreuz sausages, straight from Lockhart, are sold by the link. Have your meal ticket stamped and head over to the trimmings counter for authentic home-style sides. Takeout and delivery are good options for those who prefer a more subdued setting.

# Gramercy Tavern ✿

Contemporary XXX

B2

42 E. 20th St. (bet. Broadway & Park Ave. South)

**Subway:** 23 St (Park Ave. South) — Lunch & dinner daily
**Phone:** 212-477-0777
**Web:** www.gramercytavern.com
**Prices:** $$$

Bill Bettencourt

With its dramatic wood beams, charming period portraits, and heavenly smells of drifting wood-smoke, Danny Meyer's famed Gramercy Tavern somehow manages to capture both the genuine and ironic sides of Americana. Imagine an elegantly appointed country tavern as seen through the eyes of a clever city slicker, and you start to get the whimsi-cozy feel of the place.

The whole thing works beautifully, of course. To prove it, look around: After fifteen years and counting, the house is still packed most nights of the week. It helps that the kitchen received a delicious kick into straightforward American culinary territory from Chef Michael Anthony, who earned his greenmarket stripes at the two Blue Hill restaurants before taking the Tavern's reigns a few years back.

All that locavore training might appear in a small bowl of perfectly-cooked squid ink tagliatelle, tossed with tender pieces of squid, plump mussels, and savory chorizo; or a velvety smoked trout carrying the faintest hint of smoked wood, set atop a sweet purée of *cipollini* and pickled onion rings; or a warm and fluffy chocolate bread pudding, paired with a creamy scoop of vanilla ice cream studded with crunchy cocoa nibs.

# 'inoteca e Liquori Bar

Italian ✗

**C2**

### 323 Third Ave. (at 24th St.)

**Subway:** 23 St (Park Ave. South)  
**Phone:** 212-683-3035  
**Web:** www.inotecanyc.com  
**Prices:** $$

Lunch & dinner daily

Dressier than her downtown sister, 'inoteca e Liquori Bar brings a beloved menu of small plates to Gramercy. Awash in a warm glow, the chic space is decorated with an earthy rainbow of marble slabs paneling one side of the room. The bar features a bright corner setting with large windows and white marble-topped tables—it is here that owners Jason and Joe Denton have decided to truly elaborate on the 'inoteca theme. The cocktail menu lists more than thirty-five masterly crafted classic and vintage libations, heightened with fresh juices and infusions, and chilled with crystal clear blocks of ice.

Besides antipasti and panini, a selection of pasta includes a decadent baked rigatoni with creamy cauliflower and the crunch of herbed breadcrumbs.

# Irving Mill

Contemporary ✗✗

**B3**

### 116 E. 16th St. (bet. Irving Pl. & Union Sq. East)

**Subway:** 14 St - Union Sq  
**Phone:** 212-254-1600  
**Web:** www.irvingmill.com  
**Prices:** $$

Dinner nightly

In a warm and comfortable setting, this popular dining room continues to serve its distinct brand of enjoyable and unpretentious cuisine that is as equally focused on small plates as it is on the more substantial fare.

The casual front area styles a New England tap room, where a zinc-topped bar dispenses local brews to a thirsty crowd. The back room is pleasantly subdued, offering a formal vibe to complement the rustic atmosphere.

The seasonal menu begins with a lengthy assortment of starters like charred spring bean bruschetta with ricotta. From here, offerings continue with homemade pasta and a short list of entrées that may include a roulade of roasted chicken dressed with Camembert sauce and finished with a crostini of chicken liver mousse.

# I Trulli

C1 — Italian XX

122 E. 27th St. (bet. Lexington Ave. & Park Ave. South)

**Subway:** 28 St (Park Ave. South) — Lunch Mon – Fri
**Phone:** 212-481-7372 — Dinner nightly
**Web:** www.itrulli.com
**Prices:** $$$

This Gramercy Italian celebrates Puglia, homeland of owner Nicola Marzovilla, in its setting and cuisine; the restaurant even has its own label of olive oil harvested and bottled in Italy. The dining room's fireplace, open kitchen, and wood-burning oven evoke the countryside, as does an appetizing bill of fare that features an array of snacks to begin your meal like handmade *grissini* and creamy *burrata* served with bitter greens. The impressive pastas are made in-house by "mama"—Dora Marzovilla, and a selection of hearty entrées display a skillful hand.

During warmer months, the covered terrace is to be enjoyed; and attached to the restaurant is a wine bar called Enoteca I Trulli. Across the street—Vino—sells Italian wines and spirits.

# Jaiya

C1 — Thai X

396 Third Ave. (bet. 28th & 29th Sts.)

**Subway:** 28 St (Park Ave. South) — Lunch & dinner daily
**Phone:** 212-889-1330
**Web:** www.jaiya.com
**Prices:**

Whether it's dinner with your sweetie, the whole family or a group of friends, Jaiya is comfortable for all. Portions are generous, ideal for sharing, and the prices are reasonable. Skip the popular pad Thai and satay because a foray into the large number of curries and chef's specialties is bound to delight your palate with the true taste of Thailand—shrimp with glass noodles and bean sprouts; pork with ground pepper and garlic; and roast duck with red curry. Since the kitchen here does not Americanize the traditional Thai spice levels, ordering a dish "medium spicy" may well yield a more fiery taste than you bargained for.

The waitstaff is efficient and strives to be helpful by talking diners down from their spice requests.

# Les Halles

French

C1

411 Park Ave. South (bet. 28th & 29th Sts.)

**Subway:** 28 St (Park Ave. South) Lunch & dinner daily
**Phone:** 212-679-4111
**Web:** www.leshalles.net
**Prices:** $$

Everyone's favorite bad boy chef, Anthony Bourdain, may have put this well-worn brasserie on the map (this is his alma mater, though an offshoot now resides in the Financial District), but let's get this straight—it's the simple, unfussy French cooking that continues to pack this joint nightly. Why? Because sometimes a fresh-off-the-boat bundle of mussels served with crackling pommes frites, or soft, delicate crêpes, flambéed tableside, can bring a tear to the eye of even the most jaded foodie; and also because certain French classics are best left untouched—not mucked up or modernized. Add that to a budget-friendly wine list, and you've got a recipe for longevity.

# Mesa Grill

Southwestern

A2

102 Fifth Ave. (bet. 15th & 16th Sts.)

**Subway:** 14 St - Union Sq Lunch & dinner daily
**Phone:** 212-807-7400
**Web:** www.mesagrill.com
**Prices:** $$$

As part of the original Food Network rat pack, the French Culinary Institute-trained Bobby Flay was dishing edgy, high-end southwestern fare before Rachael Ray could spell E.V.O.O. The triple-threat star (television, cookbooks, and restaurants) can hardly be expected to man his own grill these days, but the food at Mesa Grill—if a bit wobbly on the master's technique from time to time—still packs Flay's signature spicy punch.

Start with a tender blue corncake, fat with moist, smoky, shredded barbecued duck and surrounded by a vibrant-orange swirl of zesty, habanero chile-star anise sauce. Come for drinks, come for fun—but don't come looking for an intimate hideaway. Like the redhead himself, Mesa Grill is bold, colorful, and boisterous.

# Molly's Pub & Shebeen

Gastropub

C2

287 Third Ave. (bet. 22nd & 23rd Sts.)

**Subway:** 23 St (Park Ave. South)
Lunch & dinner daily
**Phone:** 212-889-3361
**Web:** www.mollysshebeen.com
**Prices:** ©©

Molly's is as traditional a pub as you're likely to find in New York. Even the exterior screams "Ireland" with its white stucco façade against dark wood beams, and its carved wooden sign. Inside, low ceilings, dark walls, and sawdust floors are warmed by the wood-burning fireplace—a great place to defrost any winter chills.

The pub draws patrons of all stripes, from twenty-somethings to seasoned regulars, minus the boisterous happy-hour set. An ideal watering hole for a pint and an awesome burger, Molly's also serves corned beef and cabbage, fish and chips, and Shepherd's pie.

You may have to wait for a table here, but if so, the bar staff will take good care of you, and the friendly regulars usually have a few good stories to share.

# Olana

Contemporary

B1

72 Madison Ave. (bet. 27th & 28th Sts.)

**Subway:** 28 St (Park Ave. South)
Lunch Mon – Fri
**Phone:** 212-725-4900
Dinner Mon – Sat
**Web:** www.olananyc.com
**Prices:** $$

Named after the Hudson River Valley estate of 19th century landscape painter Frederic Church, this stately establishment near Madison Square Park serves a menu that draws inspiration from the seasons. The dining room is outfitted with striking backlit murals of nature scenes, hefty red-velvet seating, and generous woodwork. The front bar is comfortably spacious, and the organized service staff attends to its patrons in earnest.

Detect an enjoyable Italian accent in a listing of pastas that may include mint *tacconi* with housemade lamb sausage ragù; preparations like slow-roasted halibut display a skilled hand. Desserts are equally impressive with a list of treats that may include rhubarb strudel with *pain d'epices* (gingerbread) ice cream.

# Olives

Contemporary XX

B3

201 Park Ave. South (at 17th St.)

**Subway:** 14 St - Union Sq
Lunch & dinner daily
**Phone:** 212-353-8345
**Web:** www.toddenglish.com
**Prices:** $$$

Despite the usual disdain for the large, commercial dining affairs, Chef Todd English's Olives restaurant, located on the first floor of the W Hotel-Union Square, offers a serious culinary experience.

The contemporary setting is divided into a popular lounge area and high-ceilinged dining room with comfortable furnishings and warm colors. The ample space is equipped with an open kitchen fronted by a curved dining counter.

English's rendering of Mediterranean cuisine is on display in items like escargot flatbread with Montrachet goat cheese; king crab pappardelle with preserved lemon; and lamb Porterhouse with pistachio vinaigrette.

The prix-fixe lunch menu emphasizes ingredients sourced from the nearby Greenmarket and is certainly meritable.

# Park Avenue Bistro

French XX

B1

377 Park Ave South (bet. 26th & 27th Sts.)

**Subway:** 28 St (Park Ave. South)
Lunch Mon – Fri
**Phone:** 212-689-1360
Dinner Mon – Sat
**Web:** www.parkavenuebistronyc.com
**Prices:** $$

Park Bistro is finally back and proving worth the wait. A new name, location, and look have transformed this venerable restaurant. Airy and inviting, it now has an elegant European feel, much calmer than the stretch of Park Avenue South on which it lies. Still, a scattering of sidewalk tables is prime real estate in warm weather for those interested in remaining part of the fray.

Bistro fare remains the heart of this menu, with some contemporary dishes. The signature *petatou* (warm fingerling potatoes with shallots and Niçoise olives, topped with a golden layer of goat cheese) is a wonderful starter. Follow this with any of the main courses—just be sure to order a side of the fantastic pommes frites.

The three-course prix-fixe lunch offers terrific value.

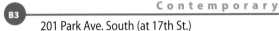

# Periyali

Greek XX

A2

35 W. 20th St. (bet. Fifth & Sixth Aves.)

**Subway:** 23 St (Sixth Ave.) Lunch Mon – Fri
**Phone:** 212-463-7890 Dinner nightly
**Web:** www.periyali.com
**Prices:** $$$

In a city that prides itself on offering what's new and what's next, the owners of Periyali deserve credit for their sincere dedication to what works—serving their brand of lovely Greek fare in a sophisticated setting since 1987. The freshly done interior's white-washed walls, billowing swathes of fabric, and shimmering fish-shaped accents transport diners to a light and breezy Mediterranean locale.

The gracious staff attends to a crowd of devoted regulars who know that the strength of Periyali's kitchen is in such solid and tempting preparations as oven-cooked *gigante* beans brightened with fresh thyme; skillfully charred yet tender marinated octopus; and hearty rabbit stew cloaked in a rich sauce redolent of tomato, red wine, and vibrant herbs.

# Pranna

Asian XX

B1

79 Madison Ave. (at 28th St.)

**Subway:** 28 St (Park Ave. South) Dinner Mon – Sat
**Phone:** 212-696-5700
**Web:** www.prannarestaurant.com
**Prices:** $$

Pranna offers exotic cuisine in a soaring, glitzy, three-level setting. Dark bamboo flooring, metallic tile work, and a rich scheme of brown and gold embellish the lounge area and dining counter overlooking the satay grill station. The stately dining room, awash in ivory and grey, offers a more formal experience.

Served family-style, the attractive dishes of Pranna's Indian-born chef are influenced by his travels around Southeast Asia and feature the likes of red curry chicken satay accompanied by a quartet of dipping sauces; cubes of homemade *paneer* sauced with tomato and ground almonds; and braised goat with fruit *rojak* and coconut scented basmati.

Groups seeking seclusion can enjoy Pranna's tasty cuisine in a number of private dining rooms.

# Primehouse New York

Steakhouse XX

B1

381 Park Ave. South (at 27th St.)

**Subway:** 28 St (Park Ave. South) — Lunch & dinner daily
**Phone:** 212-824-2600
**Web:** www.brguestrestaurants.com
**Prices:** $$$

Primehouse New York fashions a grand ambience that sets it apart from the recognizable herd of traditional steakhouses. Here, glossy multi-room spaces sport walls covered in pale marble and ebony tiles, sleek furnishings, and an impressively stocked smoke-glass-walled wine cellar. However, style does not trump substance.

Well-prepared cuts of prime Black Angus beef are aged in-house and supported by a tempting selection of "ocean meats" or raw bar combinations like the "Chrysler" and "Empire" seafood towers. Attentive servers wheel trolleys throughout the room, ladling smooth, flavorful soups and preparing traditional Caesar salads tableside—just remember to order that dessert soufflé in advance. The sexy bar lounge is a chic stop for an after-work cocktail.

# Pure Food and Wine

Vegan X

B3

54 Irving Pl. (bet. 17th & 18th Sts.)

**Subway:** 14 St - Union Sq — Dinner nightly
**Phone:** 212-477-1010
**Web:** www.purefoodandwine.com
**Prices:** $$

Carnivores beware: this restaurant's name means what it says. A disciple of the raw-food movement, Pure Food and Wine serves only raw vegan dishes. This means that to preserve vitamins, enzymes, minerals, and flavors in the food, nothing is heated above 118°F.

Dishes like a compressed heirloom tomato, fennel, and avocado salad, or a Lapsang-smoked Portabello mushroom with caper potato salad don't just taste good, they're good for you—especially if you buy into the purported health benefits. Regardless, the kitchen uses only the freshest organic produce and there is no sense of deprivation with desserts like a deceptively decadent non-dairy ice cream sundae.

During the summer, seating spills out to the backyard dining space ringed with greenery.

# Resto

C1 — **Belgian**

111 E. 29th St. (bet. Lexington Ave. & Park Ave. South)

**Subway:** 28 St (Park Ave. South) — Lunch & dinner daily
**Phone:** 212-685-5585
**Web:** www.restonyc.com
**Prices:** $$

Culinary soulmates, *moules frites* are represented in top form, as steaming pots of plump bivalves and flavorful broth cover wooden tables alongside plates of crisp, golden fries. Resto remains true to its Belgian inspiration by accompanying these with rich mayonnaise, vibrantly enhanced with sweet chile sauce or tart lime pickle. Starters like a *boudin noir* tart with cheddar crumble and apple purée, and desserts of dense Liege-style waffles flecked with crunchy sugar are delicious book-ends to any meal. Peruse their expansive selection of beer to find the perfect accompaniment to this hearty fare, which is no slight to the wine list.

This chicly spare room features a marble-topped bar, tin ceiling, and exposed brick, designed to exude warmth.

# Saravanaas

C2 — **Indian**

81 Lexington Ave. (at 26th St.)

**Subway:** 28 St (Park Ave. South) — Lunch & dinner daily
**Phone:** 212-679-0204
**Web:** www.saravanabhavan.com
**Prices:** ⊜

Set smack in the midst of Curry Row, Saravanaas stands out with its simple, clean contemporary décor. Pastel-hued walls, colorful votives, and gleaming aluminum serving pieces brighten the dining room.

The menu embraces a contemporary reflection of time-honored Southern Indian dishes. *Thalis*, a selection of different foods served with appropriate condiments, come in small or large sizes for a set price. *Dosas*, made with rice and lentils, are a specialty here. You can order these wonderfully thin pancakes plain or with your choice of vegetarian fillings. The *dosas* are so enormous, it's easy to make a meal of just one—for less than $10. And the veggie fillings are so tasty and satisfying, you'll never miss the meat.

# Tabla

Contemporary XXX

B1

## 11 Madison Ave. (at 25th St.)

**Subway:** 23 St (Park Ave. South) — Lunch Mon – Fri
**Phone:** 212-889-0667 — Dinner nightly
**Web:** www.tablany.com
**Prices:** $$$

Steps away from Madison Square Park, Tabla is housed in an art deco space done in shades of green and persimmon orange. A vibrant mosaic of tropical fruit lends an exotic air to the grand two-story setting. The boisterous street-level Bread Bar is topped by the more formal upstairs dining room.

Polished service displays the trademark of Danny Meyer's Union Square Hospitality Group. Executive Chef, partner, and Mumbai native Floyd Cardoz has been at the helm since the restaurant's beginning more than 10 years ago, skillfully fusing contemporary American cuisine with flavorful Indian accents. Fresh ingredients combine in fresh and unexpected ways, as in the pumpkin *rasam* soup, warmed by ginger and other spices providing a pleasant depth of flavor.

# Tamarind

Indian XXX

B2

## 41-43 E. 22nd St. (bet. Broadway & Park Ave. South)

**Subway:** 23 St (Park Ave. South) — Lunch & dinner daily
**Phone:** 212-674-7400
**Web:** www.tamarinde22.com
**Prices:** $$

At Tamarind, the gusto of Indian cuisine is tempered by an elegant milieu featuring courteous, alert service, and an enchantingly appointed room in a sophisticatedly restrained palette.

The hefty menu offers a regional tour through the country with flavorful bites from Goa, Punjab, Madras, and Calcutta. Airy and flocculent breads, smoky tandoori dishes, piquant curries, and delectable vegetarian specialties are prepared by an ardent brigade of cooks. A peek inside the dining room's glassed-in kitchen is sure to stimulate your taste buds.

At lunch, Tamarind offers a decent fixed-price menu.

For a casual bite, try the petite Tea Room located next door for its lighter *carte* of sweets and treats, each paired on the menu with a recommended tea.

# Tocqueville

Contemporary XX

A3

1 E. 15th St. (bet. Fifth Ave. & Union Sq. West)

**Subway:** 14 St - Union Sq — Lunch & dinner Mon – Sat
**Phone:** 212-647-1515
**Web:** www.tocquevillerestaurant.com
**Prices:** $$

Chef/owner Marco Moreira and his wife Jo-Ann Makovitsky named their popular labor of love after the 19th-century French writer Alexis de Tocqueville. Lush fabrics, vintage mirrors, and bold art fashion an elegant décor—a soothing respite in which to enjoy the menu's contemporary French-accented creations.

Located just one block from the Union Square Greenmarket, the restaurant displays a creative approach to seasonal cuisine in a salad of caramelized figs with local cheddar; *schmaltz* roasted country chicken; and coconut *tres leches* cake. During the summer months, three-course lunch and dinner menus showcase the market's bounty. The 300-label wine list features selections from little-known regions around the world as well as a number of sakes.

# Turkish Kitchen

Turkish XX

C1

386 Third Ave. (bet. 27th & 28th Sts.)

**Subway:** 28 St (Park Ave. South) — Lunch Sun – Fri, Dinner nightly
**Phone:** 212-679-6633
**Web:** www.turkishkitchen.com
**Prices:** $$

This longtime neighborhood fixture is a worthy destination for unique Turkish cuisine. The attractive setting is accented with jewel tones of ruby and sapphire, enhanced by an air of formality from the proper yet personable service team. At the bar, colorfully filled martini glasses stand at the ready for the festivities to begin.

The bountiful appetizer selection makes for a tasty starting point with dishes like pan-fried zucchini pancakes and *manti*, savory beef-filled dumplings served with yogurt sauce. Well-prepared meat and seafood entrées follow suit with fresh flavors. At lunch, Turkish Kitchen offers a reasonably priced four-course prixe-fixe, and on weekends, the buffet brunch adds pastries and omelets to the tasty delights.

# Union Square Cafe

American XX

A2

21 E. 16th St. (bet. Fifth Ave. & Union Sq. West)

**Subway:** 14 St - Union Sq
Lunch & dinner daily
**Phone:** 212-243-4020
**Web:** www.unionsquarecafe.com
**Prices:** **$$$**

With its comfortable bistro décor, winning service, and excellent modern American cooking, Union Square Café is the definition of casual elegance. Opened back in 1985, New Yorkers hold a special place in their hearts for this ever-popular institution that launched the careers of noted restaurateur Danny Meyer and Chef/partner Michael Romano.

Do as the regulars do, arrive before the crowds and grab a seat at the comfortable bar for a great burger or a three-course meal and a sampling of the café's wines by the glass. The Union Square Greenmarket next door figures largely into the planning of the menu that is supplemented by daily and weekly specials.

Worth a mention is the tremendous wine list, which is diverse, special, and reasonably priced.

Hotels and restaurants change every year, so change your Michelin Guide every year!

# Veritas ✿

**Contemporary** ✗✗

B2

43 E. 20th St. (bet. Broadway & Park Ave. South)

**Subway:** 23 St (Park Ave South) Dinner nightly
**Phone:** 212-353-3700
**Web:** www.veritas-nyc.com
**Prices:** $$$$

Veritas

A tiny "V" marks the discreet entrance to Veritas—an oenophile's dream of a restaurant tucked into a stately gray stone building along East 20th Street, just steps from the beautiful gated gardens of Gramercy Park. With literally thousands of bottles from all regions of the world lining the restaurant's shelves, many of the rarer vintages arrive courtesy of private collector, Park B. Smith, and carry eye-popping price tags—but grapehound's looking to pinch pennies will find some steals as well.

With all that concentration on the vino, how does the food stack up? Exceptionally well, thanks to the careful kitchen craft of Chef Grégory Pugin, who took the wheel in 2008. The three prix-fixe dinner menus spin seasonally, but might include an irresistibly frothy lobster *nage*, flooded with pearls of rutabaga, chestnuts, butternut squash, and celery root; or tender roasted halibut in a fragrant *barigoule*, served with a vibrant mound of pan-glazed root vegetables.

With food and drink this good, it's easy to sink into the soft banquettes, and let the clean, cool room—with its pale walls, polished wood panels, and soft, halogen lighting—envelope you for the evening.

# Greenwich, West Village & Meatpacking District

Artistic, poetic, and edgy: these ideals are the Village's identity. Thank the Beat Generation for this, because fifty years later, many still seek out this neighborhood for its beloved street cafés brimming with struggling artists, philosophical meanderings, and revolutionary convictions. Perhaps due to the prominence of New York University, local residents still embrace the liberal, intellectual, bohemian spirit that, in many ways, is the heart of this city.

Nevertheless, the belly of this area is equally worthy of attention and praise; even the humble **Peanut Butter and Co. Sandwich Shop** flaunts its creative side with peanut-buttery concoctions like the Elvis, which is grilled with bananas and honey (bacon is optional). Or, pick up a jar to-go, flavored with the likes of maple syrup, white chocolate, or chili powder. Nearby, **Mamoun's** has been feeding NYU students some of the best falafel in town for generations; topping one with their killer hot sauce is a must. In Washington Square Park, savvy students and foodies stand shoulder-to-shoulder in line for **N.Y. Dosas**, wrapped in delicate rice and lentil flour crêpes, served with character and flair.

## Bleecker Street

Peer into the assortment of old-time Italian bakeries and shops along Bleecker Street, where **Faicco's Pork Store** has been offering its specialties for over 100 years—take home a sampling of their fresh and perfectly seasoned sausages or a tray of *arancini* (fried risotto balls), though etiquette dictates that one must be eaten warm, before leaving the store. Yet the neighborhood's most noteworthy storefront may be **Murray's Cheese Shop**. This is Manhattan's definitive cheesemonger, run by a deeply informed staff, happy to initiate hungry neophytes into the art and understanding of their countless varieties (enthusiasts note that classes are also available, exploring the meaning of terroir or cheese-pairing fundamentals).

If seeking a more lowbrow spot, try **Dirty Bird** for fried or rotisserie chicken. Rest assured that these birds are locally sourced from an Amish farm, and are free-range, vegetarian fed, and anti-biotic free—all necessary qualifications for any self-respecting takeout joint in downtown bohemia.

Of course, no Village jaunt is complete without pizza—with some of the finest to be found coal-fired and crisp, only by the pie, at the original **John's**. For a quick slice, stop by Joe's for traditional thin-crust, or **Famous Ray's**, but be prepared to use a fork here. A visit to Cones is equally enticing, where uniquely textured Argentine ice cream is available in both expected and unforeseen flavor combinations.

## West Village

For a nearly royal treat, stop by **Tea and Sympathy**, offering tea-time snacks or full Sunday dinners of roast beef and Yorkshire pudding. The storefront also sells prized English wares, ranging from teas to pots to jars of clotted cream.

No matter where you grab your picnic, one of the best places to enjoy it is Hudson River Park, watching the urban vista of roller skaters, marathoners, and an ever-colorful parade of passersby, set against a backdrop of departing cruise ships and the setting sun. Pier 45 is a particularly lovely spot, decorated with benches and patches of grass at the end of Christopher Street, across the Westside Highway.

While strolling back through chic boutiques and camera-ready brownstones, peek down quaint Perry Street for yet another very NY moment: a glimpse at where Carrie Bradshaw (of *Sex in the City*) "lived." Then, let the overpowering aromas of butter and sugar carry you further west on Bleeker to **Magnolia Bakery**. Filled with pretty little pastel-flowered cupcakes and prettier couples donning Jimmy Choo shoes, this is the Village's official date night finale. Another sweet spot is **Li-Lac**, dispensing chocolate-covered treats, caramel squares, fruit-flavored creams, marshmallow bars, and nostalgic confections since 1923.

One of the West Village's most celebrated landmarks may be the **Corner Bistro**, whose pub fare has been at the heart of "Best Burger in Town" debate for decades. Its long mahogany bar, cheap beers, and great jukebox complete this perfectly laid back (and perennially crowded) scene. Another "bar's bar" incarnate that strives to embody everything a cheap beer and retro juke hope to effuse is the **Rusty Knot**. Kick back, hang out, and grab some Po' boys or pickled eggs to go with that pint.

For a more refined late-night scene, expert mixologists can be found creatively pouring "long drinks and fancy cocktails" at **Employees Only**. Likewise, bartenders approach celebrity status at **Little Branch**, where an encyclopedic understanding of the craft brings dizzying and delectable results.

## Meatpacking District

Further north is an area known as the Meatpacking District. Just a short decade ago, its cobblestoned streets were so desolate that only the savviest young Manhattanites knew that its empty warehouses held the city's edgiest clubs. Young hipsters take note: the Meatpacking has already arrived, repopulated, and regrouped with seas of sleekly designed lounges serving pricey cocktails to the fashionable minions, as if in defiance of these cautious times. Luxury hotels have risen, and storied bistros so infamously festive that they once defined the neighborhood have fallen. Completing this picture is the High Line, an abandoned 1934 elevated railway that is currently being transformed into a 19-block long park.

# Greenwich, West Village & Meatpacking District

**A**

**B**

CHELSEA MARKET

Tenth Ave

Eleventh Ave

Ninth Ave

PARK Ave

HIGH LINE

W. 16th St.

**1**

**MEATPACKING DISTRICT**

Standard Grill
The Standard

Little W. 12th St.

Spice Market

Pastis

Paradou

Scarpetta

W. 14th St.

Vento

8

Gansevoort

Gansevoort St.

Fatty Crab

R I V E R

Horatio St.

Jane St.

El Faro

Barbuto

W. 12th St.

Greenwich St.

Cafe Cluny

Eighth Ave

The Pla

4th

**2**

Bethune St.

Bank St.

Spotted Pig

Bleecker St.

11th St.

Wallsé W.

Braeburn

Extra Virg

Perry Street

Perry St.

Hudson St.

August

Mary's Fish Camp

Charles St.

Washington St.

Mexicana Mama

10th St.

L'Artusi

Christopher St.

Sheridan S

West St.

**HISTORIC GREENWICH VILLAGE**

Grove St.

Bedford St.

H U D S O N

**3**

Christopher St.

The Little Owl

Barrow St.

Greenwich St.

Morton St.

Commerce

**WEST VILLAGE**

Seventh Ave

Bleecker St.

Leroy St.

EN Japanese Brasserie

St. Luke's Pl.

Mai Tab

Clarkson St.

Grand Sichuan

Carmine St.

Downin

PIER 40

Blue Ribbon Bakery

Mas

Quir
Qua

Houston St.

Houston St

King St.

**4**

HOLLAND TUNNEL

PIER 34

West St.

Washington St.

Greenwich St.

Charlton St.

Vandam St.

**SOHO**

St.

St.

Spring St.

NEW YORK CITY FIRE MUSEUM

Renwick St.

Hudson St.

Dominick St.

Varick St.

Avenue

Sp

Broome St.

Canal St.

● Hotels

● Restaurants

**A**

**TRIBECA**

**B**

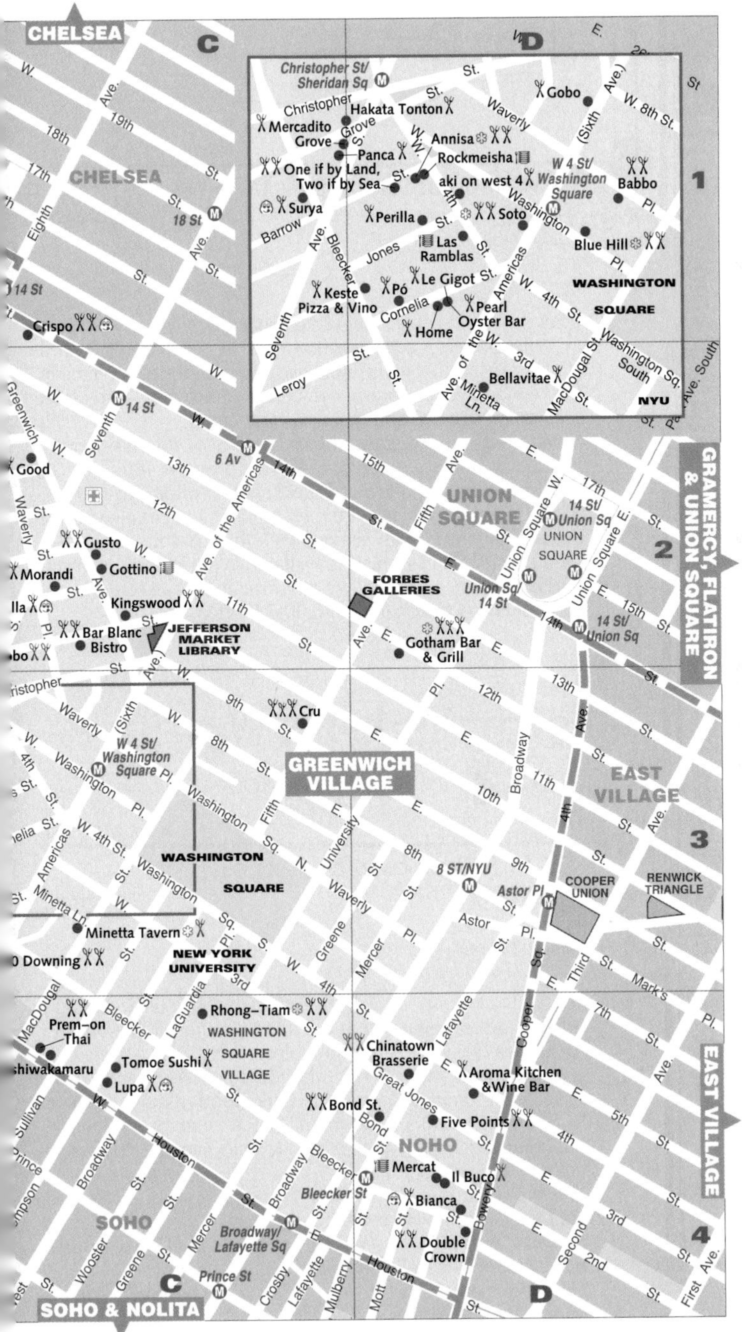
CHELSEA
C
D
1
2
3
4
Christopher St/ Sheridan Sq
Hakata Tonton
Mercadito Grove
Panca
One if by Land, Two if by Sea
Surya
Annisa
Rockmeisha
aki on west 4
W 4 St/ Washington Square
Gobo
Babbo
Perilla
Soto
Las Ramblas
Blue Hill
Keste Pizza & Vino
Pó
Le Gigot
Pearl Oyster Bar
Home
WASHINGTON SQUARE
Bellavitae
NYU
18 St
14 St
Crispo
14 St
6 Av
Good
Gusto
Gottino
Morandi
Kingswood
Bar Blanc Bistro
JEFFERSON MARKET LIBRARY
FORBES GALLERIES
UNION SQUARE
14 St/ Union Sq
Union Sq/ 14 St
Gotham Bar & Grill
GRAMERCY, FLATIRON & UNION SQUARE
Cru
GREENWICH VILLAGE
W 4 St/ Washington Square
EAST VILLAGE
WASHINGTON SQUARE
8 ST/NYU
Astor Pl
COOPER UNION
RENWICK TRIANGLE
Minetta Tavern
Downing
NEW YORK UNIVERSITY
Rhong-Tiam
WASHINGTON SQUARE VILLAGE
Prem-on Thai
Tomoe Sushi
Lupa
Chinatown Brasserie
Aroma Kitchen &Wine Bar
Bond St.
Five Points
NOHO
Mercat
Il Buco
Bleecker St
Bianca
Double Crown
SOHO
Broadway/ Lafayette Sq
Prince St
SOHO & NOLITA
EAST VILLAGE

# aki on west 4

D1 Japanese

181 W. 4th St. (bet. Sixth & Seventh Aves.)

**Subway:** W 4 St - Wash Sq Dinner nightly
**Phone:** 212-989-5440
**Web:** N/A
**Prices:** $$

Chef/owner Shigeaki "Siggy" Nakanishi arrived in New York in 1997, bringing with him flavors of the Caribbean from a stint as private chef to the Japanese Ambassador to Jamaica. In this diminuitive restaurant, two culinary traditions—Jamaican and Japanese—are combined to great effect.
Some of the more extraordinary results of this fusion may include a ramekin of cold, silky uni mousse with *junsai*, topped with yuzu-flavored gelée—perfection in texture, contrast, and creativity. *Satoimo* croquette is a creative fusion of riced taro yam with seafood in a thick dashi soup. A full menu of sushi and sashimi is available to diners seeking more traditional fare. A four-course prix-fixe menu is an economical early dining option between 6:00-7:00 P.M.

# Aroma Kitchen & Wine Bar

D4 Italian

36 E. 4th St. (bet. Bowery & Lafayette St.)

**Subway:** Bleecker St Dinner nightly
**Phone:** 212-375-0100
**Web:** www.aromanyc.com
**Prices:** $$

This welcoming spot, tucked away on the edge of Greenwich Village, radiates an amiable vibe thanks to hospitable owners Alexandra Degiorgio and Vito Polosa. Simply decorated with a warm and rustic aesthetic, the focal point of the intimate, street-level dining room is a dark-wood dining counter. In warmer weather, the room opens onto the sidewalk, providing additional real estate to alleviate the throng of enthusiastic regulars.
This wine bar offers a substantial menu of small plates and appetizers along with expertly prepared pastas and tempting desserts. Available on Mondays only, the chef's five-course tasting menu is a delicious way to start the week.
The unique and fairly priced wine list contains many varietals rarely found outside Italy.

# Annisa ✿

Contemporary XX

D1

13 Barrow St. (bet. Seventh Ave. South & W. 4th St.)

**Subway:** Christopher St - Sheridan Sq — Dinner nightly
**Phone:** 212-741-6699
**Web:** www.annisarestaurant.com
**Prices:** $$$

Annisa

Located on a lovely, tree-lined street in the West Village, the serene, oh-so-pretty Annisa ("women" in Arabic) packs an elegant punch for such an intimate little space. The interior, designed by co-owner and sommelier Jennifer Scism, features hushed pastel accents, soft lighting, and big, glossy windows facing the street.

Chef and co-owner Anita Lo spins out a seasonal, globally-infused menu that draws as much on her culinary days in France as it does her Chinese-American heritage. Asian ingredients like miso, tofu, and soybeans wind their way through a contemporary menu that might feature three gorgeous half-moon soup dumplings filled with fragrant broth and crunchy bits of jicama, paired with tiny little squares of seared foie gras, and a ring of syrupy soy sauce; a tender, juicy pan-roasted chicken with pig's feet, dancing in a sherry and white truffle sauce; or creamy goat cheese cheesecake and juicy citrus segments set atop paper-thin squares of candied beet.

The kitchen suffered from a terrible fire this past summer which burned the walls, but not the spirit of the place. Still standing is the international wine list boasting many labels hailing from female vintners.

# August

B2 — **European** X

359 Bleecker St. (bet. Charles & 10th Sts.)

**Subway:** Christopher St - Sheridan Sq — Lunch & dinner daily
**Phone:** 212-929-8727
**Web:** www.augustny.com
**Prices:** **$$**

This charming establishment located on a boutique-lined stretch of Bleecker Street has the cozy spirit of a rustic trattoria. Distressed walls, wood plank flooring, and simple furnishings are complemented by the appetizing aromas wafting from the wood-burning oven. From here, temptations emerge such as a *tarte flambé* topped with a layer of creamy melted onions and smoky lardons, or oven-roasted whole fish. Brunch may feature a variety of baked eggs *en cocotte*, or cast-iron German pancake.

The young staff is decorously laid back yet courteous in this small dining room, augmented by additional seating in the graceful glassed-in back patio. Despite August's plebeian air, don't be surprised to see a celebrity discreetly ducking in for a bite.

# Babbo

D1 — **Italian** XX

110 Waverly Pl. (bet. MacDougal St. & Sixth Ave.)

**Subway:** W 4 St - Wash Sq — Dinner nightly
**Phone:** 212-777-0303
**Web:** www.babbonyc.com
**Prices:** **$$$**

Packed to the nines most nights of the week, Mario Batali's flagship restaurant manages to please everyone from out-of-towners to downtown foodies. Maybe it's that whole quaint-townhouse thing; or the kitchen's inventive spin on rustic Italian fare. Or maybe it's the rock n' roll wafting through the dining room, just loud enough to make you wonder if that famous ponytail is back there cooking your food himself.

The menu changes seasonally, but might unearth a plate of bright green asparagus tips, lightly poached and sporting a sunny-side-up duck egg and rainfall of freshly grated Parmigiano; or a tangle of smooth orecchiette, laced with a bright tomato, onion, and carrot sauce and pocked with rapini and aged pecorino flown in from Tuscany.

# Bar Blanc Bistro

**Contemporary** XX

C2

142 W. 10th St. (bet. Greenwich Ave. & Waverly Pl.)

**Subway:** 14 St (Seventh Ave.) — Lunch Sun
**Phone:** 212-255-2330 — Dinner daily
**Web:** www.barblanc.com
**Prices:** $$

After a recent kitchen shuffle and the addition of "Bistro" to its name, this enjoyable spot still gives West Villagers good reason to step inside its sleek interior. Brunch is offered on Sundays, drink specials are featured throughout the week, and an expanded bar menu gives one ample cause to park at the white marble bar for a few bites. Its list of snacks features a housemade country terrine; the Blanc burger with Vermont cheddar; and crunchy croquettes of crushed potato, ham, and fontina dressed with smoked paprika aïoli.

Serious dining is to be had as well, with entrées that include a creamy risotto made extra luscious by the addition of a purée of fresh sweet peas, studded with slices of sautéed cremini mushrooms and shards of nutty Parmesan.

# Barbuto

**American** XX

B2

775 Washington St. (at 12th St.)

**Subway:** 14 St - 8 Av — Lunch & dinner daily
**Phone:** 212-924-9700
**Web:** www.barbutonyc.com
**Prices:** $$

Fun, relaxed, rustic, and very inviting, this restaurant is spectacularly located where the West Village borders the Meatpacking District. When the weather is warm, the garage-style doors open to spill tables out onto the front sidewalk; the ambience at Barbuto can be incomparable.

Chef Jonathan Waxman's market-based Italian cuisine hones the best qualities of pristine ingredients to create dishes that seem deceptively and deliciously simple. Among the highly enjoyable classics are *pollo al forno* with salsa verde, perhaps accompanied by *contorni* like sweet mounds of shaved Brussels sprouts with sharp pecorino and toasted walnuts.

The cavernous yet warm space also features an open kitchen and long bar, which is especially packed later in the evening.

# Bellavitae

D2 Italian

24 Minetta Ln. (bet. MacDougal St. & Sixth Ave.)

**Subway:** W 4 St - Wash Sq — Dinner nightly
**Phone:** 212-473-5121
**Web:** www.bellavitae.com
**Prices:** $$

Tucked away on the unique Minetta Lane, this hugely popular charmer is staffed by bustling Italian servers who seem to do everything right. The comprehensive wine list offers a veritable education and includes myriad precious discoveries, with many available by the *quartino* (small carafe) allowing diners to explore the wealth of choices.

Sophisticated comfort food may include a floury fava purée topped with wild dandelion greens over thick toast; or a Bosc pear poached in sangiovese and mulling spices: simple, delicious, and outstanding. Intoxicating scents from an array of pastas fill the smart, atmospheric room, adorned with beams and dark woods that hint of an old wine vault. Devotees may pick up a bottle of olive oil from Bellavitae's pantry.

# Bianca

D4 Italian

5 Bleecker St. (bet. Bowery & Elizabeth St.)

**Subway:** Bleecker St — Dinner nightly
**Phone:** 212-260-4666
**Web:** www.biancanyc.com
**Prices:** $$

Curtained windows lead the way to this charming, unassuming spot, perfect for a date or catching up with friends. Wood plank flooring and walls covered with tile and wallpaper are lined with shelves displaying delicate floral-trimmed china. An open kitchen is tucked in the cozy back. Candlelit tables are set with blue-striped kitchen towels to be used as napkins; Bianca's casual personality extends through to its cuisine.

Grilled radicchio and prosciutto dusted with grated pecorino cheese; homemade tagliatelle with wild mushrooms and fresh herbs; and chocolate chip-studded tiramisu remind guests that simplicity is always satisfying.

Generous portions and a moderately priced Italian-focused wine list naturally result in a large following.

# Blue Hill ✿

American XX

D1

75 Washington Pl. (bet. Sixth Ave. & Washington Sq. Park)

Dinner nightly

**Subway:** W 4 St - Wash Sq
**Phone:** 212-539-1776
**Web:** www.bluehillnyc.com
**Prices:** **$$$**

Thomas Schauer/Blue Hill

When President Obama flew his missus into the Big Apple for a theater date in spring of 2009, what restaurant did he choose? Blue Hill, a ten year old pioneer of the organic-farm-to-urban-table movement and a solid choice by any foodie's standard.

Much of the credit goes to Chef Dan Barber, who is such an avid proponent of utilizing local, seasonal products that he takes the time to forge personal relationships with neighboring farmers. The result is a tightly-knit network of small farms to cull ingredients from, all located within a 250-mile radius of the city. One of them is his very own Stone Barns, a biodynamic farm in Pocantico Hills where you'll find a second outpost of Blue Hill.

Back here in Washington Square, you can sample Barber's goods in an elegant storybook townhouse. Dinner spins to the season, but may include tender half-moons of pasta bursting with ramps and crushed potatoes, atop a flurry of Stone Barns Bordeaux spinach and julienned salami; Rabbi Bob's Veal, a juicy, rosy-pink nod to Barber's butcher served on a bed of chopped snap peas, shiitake mushrooms, and pistachio nuts; or steamed almond bread paired with citrus and homemade Hudson Valley milk caramel.

# Blue Ribbon Bakery

B3 — Contemporary

35 Downing St. (at Bedford St.)

**Subway:** Houston St — Lunch & dinner daily
**Phone:** 212-337-0404
**Web:** www.blueribbonrestaurants.com
**Prices:** $$

This story of this classic New York bistro begins with an abandoned, old-world brick oven that brothers Eric and Bruce Bromberg discovered in the basement of a bodega. This sparked an idea for a bakery, so they hired a master craftsman to rebuild it and in 1998 opened Blue Ribbon Bakery. Today, the downstairs space is carved into charming, exposed-brick rooms; the street-level windows offer a lovely West Village view; and the bar has a casual, jovial vibe.

House-baked breads star on lunchtime sandwiches, like the Blue Ruben, which can objectively be described as "to die for." The brilliant menu features everything from a terrine of foie gras to a turkey burger; each dish is prepared with outstanding ingredients, rich flavor, and impressive skill.

# Bobo

C2 — Contemporary

181 W. 10th St. (at Seventh Ave.)

**Subway:** 14 St (Seventh Ave.) — Lunch & dinner daily
**Phone:** 212-488-2626
**Web:** www.bobonyc.com
**Prices:** $$

This turn-of-the-century brownstone is decorated more like a chic home rather than a hip downtown dining destination, and proves that cool can be comfortable. Bobo's pale blue and white-washed brick dining salon has an eclectic charm, accented with framed pictures, gilded mirrors, book-filled shelves, and beaded lighting. Food is served on a mélange of vintage china, and a patio area completes the convivial setting.

The kitchen is seasonally inspired and uses global accents in items like Gulf shrimp salad with charred *broccolini*, and halibut with Chinese celery, black beans, arugula pistou, and miso. The delightful first floor Den offers an informal menu of light bites, an array of creative cocktails, and board games for your entertainment.

# Bond Street

Japanese XX

D4

6 Bond St. (bet. Broadway & Lafayette St.)

**Subway:** Bleecker St
**Phone:** 212-777-2500
**Web:** N/A
**Prices:** $$$$

Dinner nightly

There is no name to mark the three-story brownstone that houses Bond Street—only a brown dot on a banner. And just like that, you just know you're in for a scene. Always stylish, always hopping—the music starts thumping early at Bond Street, where wealthy hedge funders and leggy beauties converge for high-end sushi that looks as beautiful as it tastes. Take a piece of uni, served in a purple shell, then laced with a necklace of diced cucumber and crowned with a golden leaf. A plating that is guaranteed to drop some jaws, undoubtedly—but with urchin so fresh it's pudding-sweet, Bond Street can afford to flash some bling.

Speaking of, come prepared to flash a little of your own—appetizers start at $16, and prices just go up from there.

# Braeburn

American XX

B2

117 Perry St. (at Greenwich St.)

**Subway:** Christopher St - Sheridan Sq
**Phone:** 212-255-0696
**Web:** www.braeburnrestaurant.com
**Prices:** $$

Lunch Sat – Sun
Dinner nightly

You couldn't find a better home for this hot newcomer than quaint, tree-lined West Village—and Braeburn knows it, proudly straddling the corner of Perry and Greenwich streets, its big, glossy windows offering rubbberneckers a peek into its gorgeous rustic-chic interior, detailed in smoky brown banquettes and reclaimed tobacco shed wood.

Chef Brian Bistrong, who previously headed the kitchen at the Harrison, likes to dabble creatively with freshly-sourced American ingredients. A quail sausage arrives perfectly tender and juicy, licked with a smoky mustard sauce and resting over poached baby white turnips; while a fragrant pair of lavender and lemon cakes are topped with a slowly melting quenelle of ice cream and ringed with a drizzle of honey.

# Cafe Cluny

B2

American

284 W. 12th St. (at W. 4th St.)

**Subway:** 14 St - 8 Av
Lunch & dinner daily
**Phone:** 212-255-6900
**Web:** www.cafecluny.com
**Prices:** $$

With its winsome glow, this quintessential neighborhood restaurant sprinkles Village chic throughout its comfortable multi-room interior. Walls are lined with caricatures of regular celebrities and a wall installation of shadowy bird cutouts comes alive in the candlelit space—the popular corner-set bar continues this motif with a bird-themed diorama alongside mounted antlers. Still attracting a devoted following, the service is affable and able.

Open daily from 8:00 A.M until midnight, the kitchen continually churns out dishes with a classic touch. In the morning, homemade granola or poached eggs with short rib hash keeps you going until it's time to refuel with choice delicacies like pan-roasted Arctic char with braised lentils or coq au vin.

# Chinatown Brasserie

D4

Chinese

380 Lafayette St. (at Great Jones St.)

**Subway:** Bleecker St
Lunch & dinner daily
**Phone:** 212-533-7000
**Web:** www.chinatownbrasserie.com
**Prices:** $$

Dim sum all day is a dreamy concept and though it's not traditional, it's been well-received in a city that shuns rules. Chinatown Brasserie follows no code with its all day menu of dim sum, Cantonese fare, fusion favorites, and creative cocktails in the China-chic cavernous space, traced by glossy columns, floor-to-ceiling silk curtains, and oversize red lanterns. Despite the grown up vibe, it's surely one of the most family-friendly brunches in town.

Modern dim sum, prepared artfully, includes crispy taro root shrimp or lobster cream cheese sticks. A plate of crisp Peking duck is a great way to round out the mix, and salads offer a bit of crunch.

Downstairs, the mod lounge—complete with a koi pond—sets the stage for post-dinner canoodling.

# Commerce

**Contemporary** ✗

**B3**

### 50 Commerce St. (near Barrow St.)

**Subway:** Christopher St - Sheridan Sq
**Phone:** 212-524-2301
**Web:** www.commercerestaurant.com
**Prices:** **$$**

Lunch Sun
Dinner nightly

Nestled into a tiny, curving West Village alleyway so utterly charming, it makes the rest of the city pale in comparison, Commerce surely landed one of Manhattan's sweetest locations. If that means that quarters are bit cramped in this former speakeasy (the building dates back to the early 1900's), then so be it.

Just relax into your Lilliputian table, let one of the crackerjack servers calm your jangled nerves with a basket of warm, freshly-baked bread, and settle in for Chef Harold Moore's ace cooking. A sanguine beef *tataki*, served rare, gets some zip from a mingling of ginger, scallion, and tiny *shiso* leaves; while a lush mound of shredded duck *rillettes*, carrying a hint of nutmeg, surrounds a creamy, buttery lobe of foie gras.

# Crispo

**Italian** ✗✗

**C1**

### 240 W. 14th St. (bet. Seventh & Eighth Aves.)

**Subway:** 14 St (Seventh Ave.)
**Phone:** 212-229-1818
**Web:** www.crisporestaurant.com
**Prices:** **$$**

Dinner nightly

Sometimes a restaurant becomes your go-to spot simply because it does everything from the ambience to the food very, very well—without all the unnecessary pomp and fuss. Such is the case with Crispo, a quiet, brick-walled charmer tucked behind a wrought-iron fence along bustling 14th Street. The restaurant is named after Chef Frank Crispo, who honed his skills at La Côte Basque and Zeppole before taking the wheel himself. The result is a menu littered with classically-prepared, rustic Italian staples. But while the menu reads deceptively simple, more than a few items turn out to be flavor powerhouses, such as the house signature of spaghetti carbonara—a simple dish in concept, but a thing of beauty in the deft hands of Mr. Crispo.

# Cru

C3 **Contemporary** XXX

24 Fifth Ave. (at 9th St.)

**Subway:** 8 St - NYU
**Phone:** 212-529-1700
**Web:** www.cru-nyc.com
**Prices:** $$$$

Dinner Tue – Sat

Straddling a quiet corner of the Village, just two blocks north of spiffed-up Washington Square Park, Cru is home to one of the most mind-boggling wine lists in the city. So enormous, they need two, thick-as-bible leather tomes just to list the 150,000+ bottles drawn from owner Roy Welland's private collection.

Shea Gallante has broken up with his longtime girl and moved on to shack up with the famed David Bouley, but new talent is on the way in to stamp their unique, signature style on the menu, and perhaps will bring some more casual, recession-friendly fare.

The dining room is also up for a makeover that will lend a lighter touch to the serious décor.

# Double Crown

D4 **Fusion** XX

316 Bowery (at Bleecker St.)

**Subway:** Bleecker St
**Phone:** 212-254-0350
**Web:** www.doublecrown-nyc.com
**Prices:** $$$

Lunch Sat – Sun
Dinner nightly

Just when you were thinking—where the heck are all the British colonialism-meets-Far East restaurants in this town? Chef Brad Farmerie, who designed Public's menu, takes the wheel at this deliriously popular new Village restaurant, which aims to tap into the strange in-between cuisine created after Britain invaded Far Eastern countries like India and Singapore in the 19th century.

With a bizarre dada interior (think clocks caged behind metal wall screens and armless mannequins) and a young, sexy crowd with money to burn, the scene tends to trump the food. Still, a few standouts remain: try a plate of tender, gamey lamb meatballs studded with creamy cashews, bobbing in a sweet-and-tart tomato stew, and paired with a fat stack of onion rings.

# El Faro

Spanish

B2

823 Greenwich St. (at Horatio St.)

**Subway:** 14 St - 8 Av
Lunch & Dinner Tue – Sun
**Phone:** 212-929-8210
**Web:** www.elfaronyc.com
**Prices:** $$

Still straddling its original West Village corner spot, El Faro has seen a lot of neighbors come and go since they opened in 1927. Upheld by loyal local regulars and big, celebratory parties, some foodies overlook the dearth of traditional Spanish places left in a city being taken over by tapas joints. So hey, if you have to put up with a bit of crumbling décor and salty service for Spanish seafood this good, then so be it.

The menu boasts an endless lineup of garlicky classics, but the two things not to miss are the paella (in any of its delicious variations), and any dish offered in El Faro's lip-smacking green sauce. Most of the entrées come with a bright green salad sporting a house dressing so addictive they now sell it by the bottle.

# EN Japanese Brasserie

Japanese

B3

435 Hudson St. (at Leroy St.)

**Subway:** Houston St
Dinner nightly
**Phone:** 212-647-9196
**Web:** www.enjb.com
**Prices:** $$$

How's this for fresh? The silky tofu is made four times an evening at EN Japanese Brasserie. *Yuba* is the name of the game, and those uninitiated to the delicate little sheets (created by heating soy milk) will never dismiss the subject lightly again. Housed in an old furniture shop near the Meatpacking District, the spacious, modern restaurant boasts lofty ceilings, mesmerizingly intricate woodwork, and a vast, open kitchen spinning out great Japanese pub fare a few steps up from the typical *izakaya*.

Don't let the word "pub" fool you: expert culinary attention is given to the seasonal omakase dinners (and lo and behold, the service matches), with pristine, high-quality products marking each plate. In particular, the *yuba* sashimi is a milky-sweet revelation.

# Extra Virgin

B2 **Mediterranean**

259 W. 4th St. (at Perry St.)

**Subway:** Christopher St - Sheridan Sq
**Phone:** 212-691-9359
**Web:** www.extravirginrestaurant.com
**Prices:** **$$**

Lunch Tue – Sun
Dinner nightly

Casual yet classy, Extra Virgin is staffed by charming, beautiful people serving fine Mediterranean fare in a pleasant and relaxed environment; every neighborhood should have an oasis like this.

In the spirit of its name, diners are offered a choice from a parade of top-notch olive oils to sample. The menu features creative yet comforting dishes, such as delicate halibut with tomato carpaccio, anointed with pristine olive oil and deeply flavored herbs; or a goat cheese salad with roasted beets and crisp endive dressed in an apple-based vinaigrette that verges on addictive. Seasonal flower arrangements on the bar set the mood of the cheery and rustic space. Booming rock music pouring from speakers does not detract diners from their food or conversation.

# Fatty Crab

B2 **Malaysian**

643 Hudson St. (bet. Gansevoort & Horatio Sts.)

**Subway:** 14 St - 8 Av
**Phone:** 212-352-3592
**Web:** www.fattycrab.com
**Prices:** **$$**

Lunch & dinner daily

For bold Malaysian cooking, check out this eclectically Asian dining room, with dark wood tables, antique Chinese chairs, and red lacquer accents. Sidewalk seating in fair weather offers a welcomed expansion to the small space.

Chef Zak Pellacio's specialties reflect his time spent in Malaysia and include chili crab, a fun, messy bowl of large segments of Dungeness crab in a spicy-sweet, tomato chili sauce; or the Fatty Duck brined, steamed, fried, and brushed with a sticky soy-chili glaze. Dishes are served family style; be forewarned that larger parties run the risk of overwhelming their tables.

Enjoy a range of beers from Saigon to Singha to soften the wait at this hugely popular spot; or head to the equally delightful outpost on the Upper West Side.

# Five Points

American

D4

31 Great Jones St. (bet. Bowery & Lafayette St.)

**Subway:** Bleecker St — Lunch & dinner daily
**Phone:** 212-253-5700
**Web:** www.fivepointsrestaurant.com
**Prices:** $$

Still going strong after all these years, Five Points has a universal quality that appeals to almost everyone. Perhaps it's the timeless urban décor, with just the right balance between casual and high design. Perhaps it's the happy-hour specials, the family-friendly attitude, or the reasonably priced American menu that pulls in influences from everywhere. Whatever that special quality is, Five Points has it in spades.
Seasonality drives Chef/owner Marc Meyer to pair pan-seared day-boat halibut with cucumber gazpacho in summer; and to couple house-made ricotta *cavatelli* with pancetta, toasted garlic, caramelized onions, and an organic egg when it's cold outside. The clutch of customers who pack the place on weekends between 11:30 A.M. and 3:00 P.M. will testify to the terrific brunch.

# Gobo

Vegetarian

D1

401 Sixth Ave. (bet. 8th St. & Waverly Pl. )

**Subway:** W 4 St - Wash Sq — Lunch & dinner daily
**Phone:** 212-255-3902
**Web:** www.goborestaurant.com
**Prices:** ©

In keeping with the restaurant's Zen philosophy, the space is dressed in muted tranquil colors, soft lighting, and caters to vegetarian and omnivore diners alike with well-prepared and tasteful "food for the five senses." Start by sipping through the "healthy beverage menu," offering organic fruit and vegetable smoothies, teas, and seltzer tonics. Larger plates may include toothsome green tea noodles with vegan Bolognese, melding Asian ingredients with an Italian classic for rich flavors and silky textures in a truly unique dish.
Light wood shelves contrast with dark plank floors, framing the simple and comfortable furnishings. The energetic staff is stylishly attired in purple polos, jeans, with aprons de rigueur; while sweet, service can be haphazard.

# Good

C2 American

89 Greenwich Ave. (bet. Bank & 12th Sts.)

**Subway:** 14 St - 8 Av
**Phone:** 212-691-8080
**Web:** www.goodrestaurantnyc.com
**Prices:** $$

Lunch Tue – Sun
Dinner nightly

This Village mainstay lives up to its simply stated name by offering a pleasantly familiar appeal and a comforting menu that features a sprinkling of global influences to the American menu of Chef/owner Stephen Picker—romaine salad with *ricotta salata* and green goddess dressing; house-smoked pulled pork with crisp polenta; and macaroni and cheese spiced with green chilies topped with a tortilla crumb crust. Weekdays, the inexpensive lunch special includes a cup of soup and a cookie with any salad or sandwich and brunch features the likes of a breakfast burrito filled with housemade chorizo, and banana cream cheese stuffed French toast. Good's "brunch punch" or "morning martini" flavored with chilled espresso gets the weekend off to a rosy start.

# Gottino

C2 Italian

52 Greenwich Ave. (bet. Charles & Perry Sts.)

**Subway:** Christopher St - Sheridan Sq
**Phone:** 212-633-2590
**Web:** www.ilovegottino.com
**Prices:** ⊜

Lunch & dinner daily

This charming *enoteca* offers a lovely setting to sit and savor a glass of wine and a snack (or three). Intimate and sophisticated, the space uses knobby wood, exposed brick, and a marble dining counter to conjure that requisite chic rusticity that draws the Village crowds. Still, the setting is genuinely welcoming and warm, with baskets of nuts strewn throughout for guests to enjoy while perusing the blackboard listing of wine specials.

Chef Jody Williams offers a slender, thoughtful menu of small plates which gracefully emerge from a white-tiled work space doubling as the bar. The likes of creamy, house-cured *baccala* and delicate *crespelle* filled with prosciutto and fontina are featured alongside a selection of meats, cheeses, and pastas.

# Gotham Bar and Grill ✿

Contemporary XXX

D2

12 E. 12th St. (bet. Fifth Ave. & University Pl.)

**Subway:** 14 St - Union Sq
**Phone:** 212-620-4020
**Web:** www.gothambarandgrill.com
**Prices:** $$$

Lunch Mon – Fri
Dinner nightly

Gotham Bar and Grill

How do you make a perfect tuna tartare? If you have to ask, then you haven't tried Gotham Bar and Grill's—a soft, ruby-red pile of diced yellowfin tuna, kissed with ginger-soy vinaigrette and ringed in crunchy Japanese cucumber. It's often imitated, but rarely duplicated, and the same could be said of the restaurant itself—a 25 year-old Village mainstay set along lovely East 12th Street, just south of Union Square.

Happy hour finds singles buzzing into Gotham post-work, soaking in the live jazz before heading to the tables to sample Chef Alfred Portale's New American cuisine. Save room for the chef's gifted seasonal risottos, like one boasting a cluster of savory wild mushrooms and tender, braised baby artichokes tossed in creamy porcini foam; and playful pastries, like a frozen dark chocolate whiskey parfait, with a side of caramelized banana and a malted milk shake.

No one's endorsing hooky but if you can manage to sneak an afternoon off—the three-course lunch paired with wine is not only a great bargain, but a gorgeous way to while away an afternoon, soaking up the natural light streaming through the restaurant's enormous windows and watching the endless parade of passersbys.

# Grand Sichuan

B3 — Chinese

15 Seventh Ave. South (bet. Camine & Leroy Sts.)

**Subway:** Houston St — Lunch & dinner daily
**Phone:** 212-645-0222
**Web:** www.thegrandsichuan.com
**Prices:** ⊜

This latest outpost of the well-run chain strives to offer a more healthy Chinese option in this Sichuan-focused menu. The enjoyable, delicious fare includes excellent shredded chicken with sour cabbage; chewy *dan dan* noodles layered with spicy minced pork; and a mouthwatering braised whole fish with hot bean sauce. In addition to the expansive "American Chinese," "Classic Sichuan," and "Latest" sections of menu offerings, dining here features a thoughtful touch—both small- and large-sized portions are offered, allowing guests to feast without fear of over doing it.

The pleasant room may be restrained in its décor, but boasts large windows overlooking a stretch of Seventh Avenue and is graciously attended to by the polite, uniformed staff.

# Gusto

C2 — Italian

60 Greenwich Ave. (at Perry St.)

**Subway:** 14 St (Seventh Ave.) — Lunch & dinner daily
**Phone:** 212-924-8000
**Web:** www.gustonyc.com
**Prices:** $$

Although Gusto's kitchen has been a revolving door of notable talent, this sleek and sexy Village Italian continues to serve impressively prepared trattoria-inspired provender. The antipasti selection rekindles an appreciation for fried foods such as seafood *fritto misto*, fried artichokes, and beignets of Parmigiano Reggiano with prosciutto *cotto*. Many of the enticing pastas are made in-house, and a generous listing of fish and meat courses round out the menu. Don't say *basta*, until you've tried the gelato of the day. When available, the fresh fig is not to be missed.

With its whitewashed walls, velvet banquettes, Viennese crystal chandelier, and Missoni upholstered bar stools, Gusto's black-and-white setting recalls an elegant by-gone era.

# Hakata Tonton

Japanese

D1

61 Grove St. (bet. Bleecker St. & Seventh Ave. )

**Subway:** Christopher St - Sheridan Sq — Dinner nightly
**Phone:** 212-242-3699
**Web:** www.tontonnyc.com
**Prices:** $$

A new cuisine has taken root in New York. Enter this tiny red and yellow dining room to be educated in this other facet of the Japanese culinary repertoire: *tonsoku* (pigs' feet, ears, and the like).

Varied *tonsoku* dishes may include a luxurious slow roasted pork, or *oreilles du cochon*—French in name only—which are an explosion of crunchy, cool, creamy, sweet, sticky, and vinegary flavors. Truer to its Italian roots, *Tonsoku* carbonara is made with smoky bacon and is a good choice for wary newbies. A "rare cheesecake" of piped cheese and sour cream is a very smart and completely delicious take on the traditional dessert.

The plain-Jane décor sits in stark contrast to the rich and porky fare that diners will come rushing back for.

# Home

Contemporary

D1

20 Cornelia St. (bet. Bleecker & W. 4th Sts.)

**Subway:** W 4 St - Wash Sq — Lunch & dinner daily
**Phone:** 212-243-9579
**Web:** www.homerestaurantnyc.com
**Prices:** $$

The menu's tagline promises "farm-to-table" fare, and Chef/partner Ross Gill is true to this philosophy with seasonal cuisine offered as small and large plates in a charming setting. With a focus on comfort, preparations may include the likes of grilled trout with lentils, macaroni and cheese with overnight tomatoes, and butterscotch pudding topped with lightly whipped cream. The wine list focuses on local producers and appropriately includes several labels from Barbara and David Shinn's current endeavour, Shinn Estate Vineyards, the couple who opened Home back in 1993.

This pleasant, slender space features a small bar upfront, colorful artwork hung on white painted brick walls, denim-blue banquettes, and a discreet open kitchen tucked into the back.

# Il Buco

D4 **Italian**

47 Bond St. (bet. Bowery & Lafayette St.)

**Subway:** Bleecker St
**Phone:** 212-533-1932
**Web:** www.ilbuco.com
**Prices:** $$

Lunch Tue – Sat
Dinner nightly

It's a classic New York story. Fifteen years ago, an independent filmmaker, Donna Lennard, partnered with an old friend, Alberto Avalle, to take over an artist's studio space in the then-burgeoning NoHo neighborhood. Their original intent was to form a countrified antiques store. But while quirky chandeliers and antiques remain in this adorable farmhouse-style restaurant, the food has long since taken center stage at Il Buco.

Though recent years have seen the food become a bit less even, the ever-changing menu continues to push out seasonal, innovative Mediterranean small plates like flaky, baked empanadas, plump with beef tenderloin and caramelized onion; or a succulent pork sausage, accompanied by a quince *mostarda* and *risina* beans.

# Keste Pizza & Vino

D1 **Pizza**

271 Bleecker St. (bet. Cornelia & Jones Sts.)

**Subway:** W 4 St - Wash Sq
**Phone:** 212-243-1500
**Web:** www.kestepizzeria.com
**Prices:** ©©

Lunch & dinner daily

Co-owner Roberto Caporuscio was born and raised near Naples, is a former mozzarella producer, and is the current American-chapter president of the *Associazione Pizzaiuoli Napoletani*. When it comes to creating authentic Neopolitan-style pizza, he knows what he's doing.

A list of salads are offered as a starting point for the main event—distinctively charred, crusty, tender pies scented with wood smoke and baked on a layer of volcanic stone. Fashioned from mostly imported ingredients (flour, tomatoes, cheese, and olive oil) there are eighteen varieties of pizza with a specific combination of toppings (the menu states no changes allowed). The *salsiccia* is crowned with local basil and sweet, meaty crumbles procured from across the street at Faicco's.

# Kingswood

**Contemporary** XX

C2

121 W. 10th St. (bet. Greenwich & Sixth Aves.)

**Subway:** 14 St (Seventh Ave.) — Lunch Sat – Sun
**Phone:** 212-645-0044 — Dinner nightly
**Web:** N/A
**Prices:** **$$**

Young, hip, and fresh on the scene, Kingswood has that of-the-moment cachet that restaurateurs dream about, with more beautiful people clamoring to get in than space allows. What can you do? Plan on catching a little attitude at the door, and then get over yourself—because the woodsy, whimsically-decorated Kingswood is pure fun, with a vibrant bar scene that stays open late, and a meat-and-potatoes menu that turns pub food on its head. Three lovely bone-in lamb chops come sealed in an excellent, charred crust, but stay perfectly baby pink within, and arrive with a rich, creamy tomato orzo finished with a little shaved *fiore sardo*.

A short, focused wine list pays homage to the owners' homeland Down Under, Australia.

# L'Artusi

**Italian** XX

B3

228 W. 10th St. (bet. Bleecker & Hudson Sts.)

**Subway:** Christopher St - Sheridan Sq — Dinner nightly
**Phone:** 212-255-5757
**Web:** www.lartusinyc.com
**Prices:** **$$**

L'Artusi's façade may be demure, but this attractive dining room offers a buzz-worthy vibe to accompany an upscale rendition of Italian-rooted fare, anchored by small plates. The large space, done in gray and ivory, offers three dining counters, table service, and a quieter mezzanine dining area. An open kitchen adds to the lively air.

The impressive, all-Italian wine list, complete with maps, is laid out with a gravitas that demands attention. The well-versed staff is pleased to suggest the best pairings to compliment the mushroom bruschetta slathered with *Robiola*, or the dense and chewy *cavatelli* studded with black kale and "rice beans." A perfect finale is the airy coconut *semifreddo* set atop almond cake and drizzled with dark chocolate sauce.

# Las Ramblas

D1 **Spanish**

170 W. 4th St. (bet. Cornelia & Jones Sts.)

**Subway:** Christopher St - Sheridan Sq
**Phone:** 646-415-7924
**Web:** www.lasramblasnyc.com
**Prices:** ©©

Lunch Sat – Sun
Dinner nightly

Serving quality tapas packed with flavor, Las Ramblas' small yet imaginative space complements its cuisine. The restaurant, named for Barcelona's historic commercial thoroughfare, also impresses with its smooth, well-informed, and impeccably timed service.

Pleasantly while away time in this beautifully compact bar, where attention to detail is evident in flower arrangements balancing on a tiny shelf; the water fountain embedded in a brick wall; and a banquette that cozies up against the front windows.

This traditional bar food makes a satisfying meal. Go in groups to fully explore the menu. Such small plates as *patatas bravas* (garlicky potatoes with aïoli) and grilled sardines *en escabeche*, arrive on an array of colorful crockery and delicate porcelain.

# Le Gigot

D1 **French**

18 Cornelia St. (bet. Bleecker & W. 4th Sts.)

**Subway:** W 4 St - Wash Sq
**Phone:** 212-627-3737
**Web:** www.legigotrestaurant.com
**Prices:** $$

Lunch & dinner Tue – Sun

Look for a tiny, cheery, apricot-colored façade with a cast iron sign to find this perfectly quaint restaurant nestled into Cornelia Street. Inside, the immaculate and cozy design closely resembles the landmark Left Bank bistro, Polidor, with parquet floors and banquettes lining mirrored walls with wood crisscrossing.

The friendly and professional staff warmly greets regulars by name and are dedicated to creating a lovely dining experience.

Chef Alione Ndiaye serves meticulously prepared cuisine with products of the utmost freshness. Offerings may include a perfectly sweet, briny, and flaky jumbo lump crabcake with baby greens; or daily vegetables bursting with flavor, like blanched sweet peas, leeks, and carrots lightly seasoned with thyme.

# The Little Owl

Contemporary

B3

90 Bedford St. (at Grove St.)

**Subway:** Christopher St - Sheridan Sq — Lunch & dinner daily
**Phone:** 212-741-4695
**Web:** www.thelittleowlnyc.com
**Prices:** $$

Nesting on the corner of Bedford and Grove streets, The Little Owl puts the pleasure back into dining out. Since its opening, this West Village favorite has been perfecting hospitality with a comforting tone that pervades the staff and even diners—all of whom leave any attitude at the door.

Inside, natural light flows in through the two large windows framing the small corner room. The menu is focused on what it does very well; the kitchen crew creates earthy, carefully crafted, and intensely flavorful dishes. The meatball "sliders" appetizer and utterly satisfying pork chop with Parmesan butter beans and wild dandelion greens both elicit "oohs" and "aahs" from regulars. Indeed, this is the kind of restaurant that makes people want to dine out every day.

# Lupa

Italian

C4

170 Thompson St. (bet. Bleecker & Houston Sts.)

**Subway:** W 4 St - Wash Sq — Lunch & dinner daily
**Phone:** 212-982-5089
**Web:** www.luparestaurant.com
**Prices:** $$

Lupa's principals represent a league of culinary maestros who have forged a profound impact on Italian dining in New York City. Their Roman trattoria setting continues to attract masses just as ardently as when it first opened in 1999. While the consistent cuisine is due much of the credit, Lupa's casual excellence and convivial attitude also contribute to its appeal.

Snack at the bar on house made *salumi* and a carafe of vino from the all-Italian wine list, or dive into deep bowls of *bucatini all'amatriciana*, sample spoon-tender pork shoulder with radicchio and balsamic, and indulge in bocce ball-sized *tartufo*.

Closely arranged wooden tables, a ceramic tile floor, and sienna-toned plaster walls bestow warmth to Lupa's buzzing dining room.

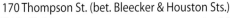

# Market Table

B3 — American

54 Carmine St. (at Bedford St.)

**Subway:** W 4 St - Wash Sq — Lunch & dinner daily
**Phone:** 212-255-2100
**Web:** www.markettablenyc.com
**Prices:** $$

Can Joey Campanaro—the man behind the perpetually-booked downtown darling, The Little Owl—do no wrong? Not when he has tapped the talents of former Mermaid Inn chef, Mike Price, to create a fresh, unpretentious menu with a fantastic staff and rustic décor to match.

Straddling a sunny corner of the West Village, Market Table is part-restaurant, with reclaimed beams and hardwood floors, and part-market, where you can purchase Price's top-of-the-line ingredients. Some critics wish they'd opted for more tables instead—for that's where you'll find fat pockets of fresh lamb ravioli, tumbling with farm-fresh vegetables and soft, crumbled goat cheese; or a luscious, otherworldly cheesecake, oozing with moist chocolate.

# Mary's Fish Camp

B2 — Seafood

64 Charles St. (at W. 4th St.)

**Subway:** Christopher St - Sheridan Sq — Lunch & dinner Mon – Sat
**Phone:** 646-486-2185
**Web:** www.marysfishcamp.com
**Prices:** $$

Mary Redding opened this tiny Florida-style seafood joint in a West Village brownstone in 2000 and has been enjoying wild success ever since. Her lobster rolls overflow with succulent chunks of meat, slathered in mayonnaise and piled on a buttered hotdog bun—they might be messy, but they sure are good! Other selections such as conch chowder and conch fritters recall Key West cuisine; while lobster potpie and pan-seared diver scallops pay homage to the bounty of New England waters. Old Bay fries, steamed spinach, and grilled corn on the cob accompany the delicious, fresh preparations.

Bear in mind that Mary's only serves seafood and the restaurant doesn't accept reservations, but the counter couldn't be better for dining on your own.

# Mas

Contemporary XXX

B3

39 Downing St. (bet. Bedford & Varick Sts.)

**Subway:** Houston St
Dinner nightly
**Phone:** 212-255-1790
**Web:** www.masfarmhouse.com
**Prices:** $$$

This tasteful jewel box of a restaurant sits on a lovely West Village block, hidden behind an unassuming façade. Behind the worn wood and glass exterior, Mas is reminiscent of a Provençal farmhouse, with weathered wood beams and a bar made of piled sandstones. Then, upscale and modern details—from the warm and well-orchestrated staff, to the Prouvé chairs—are perfect contrasts for the chic clientele.

The seasonal menu changes daily, and plays off the natural sweetness of organic and locally-sourced ingredients. An heirloom tomato tart is "marinated" in its own juices, or tender Flying Pigs farm pork belly is braised to perfection. Dishes are rustic without the drama or pretense.

The bar is an intimate spot for a creative and expertly concocted libation.

# Mercadito Grove

Mexican X

C1

100 Seventh Ave. South (at Grove St.)

**Subway:** Christopher St - Sheridan Sq
Lunch Sat – Sun
**Phone:** 212-647-0830
Dinner nightly
**Web:** www.mercaditorestaurants.com
**Prices:** $$

Largest in the Mercadito chainlet, Grove has a devoted following filling its pastel-painted chairs and corner sidewalk dining area nightly. Starters range from a small list of fresh ceviches to flautas filled with chicken and black beans. The tacos, prepared from homemade tortillas, are certainly recommended as are any of the *platos fuertes* that make up the menu's concise selection, like the shrimp-filled enchiladas *rojas*, draped with a creamy, tangy, sweet sauce seasoned with *guajillo* and *arbol* chiles.

In the East Village, Mercadito Cantina serves a mouthwatering menu of tacos and guacamoles daily for lunch and dinner. Hungry night owls should note that all three of their locations offer an all-you-can eat taco special late in the evening.

# Mercat

**Spanish**

D4

## 45 Bond St. (bet. Bowery & Lafayette St.)

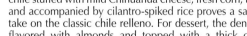

**Subway:** Bleecker St — Dinner nightly
**Phone:** 212-529-8600
**Web:** www.mercatnyc.com
**Prices:** $$

Brick walls, white subway tiles, and plank wood flooring line this hip restaurant and tapas den, whose name translates to "market" in Catalan. Owner Jaime Reixach hails from Barcelona, and the two American chefs he hired have both spent extensive time in the area, giving the cooking an authentic leg up on the endless string of Spanish tapas bars that have popped up across the city in recent years.

But don't take our word for it. Taste for yourself in decadent little plates like, cold octopus salad with salsa verde; deep fried artichokes with fennel aïoli; and *fideua negrea amb allioli*—noodles with sepia and black ink, topped with spicy and succulent squid. The Spanish wine list sports cavas, sherries, and seasonal sangrías.

# Mexicana Mama

**Mexican**

B2

## 525 Hudson St. (bet. Charles & 10th Sts.)

**Subway:** Christopher St - Sheridan Sq — Lunch & dinner Tue – Sun
**Phone:** 212-924-4119
**Web:** N/A
**Prices:** ⊜

A tiny restaurant with a big heart, Mexicana Mama stands out for its well-executed and authentic cuisine. A cup of earthy black bean soup warmed with a bit of jalapeño will brighten any chilly day; while a roasted, perfectly skinned poblano chile stuffed with mild Chihuahua cheese, fresh corn, tomato, and accompanied by cilantro-spiked rice proves a satisfying take on the classic chile relleno. For dessert, the dense flan, flavored with almonds and topped with a thick caramel sauce and whole almonds, hazelnuts, and cashews, ranks tiers above the run-of-the-mill custard.

The décor is colorful, spare, curious, funky—and completely beside the point. Here the service is unhurried; for less than $25, take your time eating deliciously and well.

# Minetta Tavern ✿

Gastropub

C3

113 MacDougal St. (at Minetta Ln.)

**Subway:** W 4 St - Wash Sq — Dinner nightly
**Phone:** 212-475-3850
**Web:** www.minettatavernny.com
**Prices:** $$$

Ngoc Minh Ngo

There are two ways to get into Keith McNally's much-buzzed-about new bistro: make advance (very, very advance) reservations or duck past the old sign marking the corner entrance, smile at the gorgeous, but blasé hostess, and pray for the best.

The good news is that once you do make it into this lair of cool, you'll find a charming, knowledgeable wait staff; a surprisingly serious kitchen; and an irresistibly fun atmosphere in the newly revamped space. The building dates back to 1937 and the designers were clever enough to leave all the good stuff—black-and-white checkered floors and funny old wall caricatures—intact when they took over.

The gastropub menu turns out spot-on versions of the classic bistro staples, and the burger and steak are two of the more popular items (along with the soufflé) for good reason. Both arrive freshly-sourced, impeccably seasoned, and sizzling to rosy-pink perfection. But why stop there when the kitchen is pushing out all kinds of delicious goodies like tender, stuffed calamari; gorgeous veal chops, paired with sautéed sweetbreads and mushrooms in demi-glace; and an *aligot* so brilliantly executed you'll think you've died and gone to *Auvergne*.

# Morandi

Italian

C2

211 Waverly Pl. (bet. Charles St. & Seventh Ave. South)

**Subway:** 14 St (Seventh Ave.) Lunch & dinner daily
**Phone:** 212-627-7575
**Web:** www.morandiny.com
**Prices:** $$$

This prominent newcomer appears to be both an Italian cantina and farmhouse, with its antique-tiled floor, weather-beaten wood, Italian-speaking waiters, and straw-covered Chianti bottles displayed on shelves, recalling Tuscany with all its glorious clichés. The menu, too, respects its Italian roots, offering dishes such as *polpettini alla siciliana* (meatballs with pine nuts and raisins); *baccalà con ceci* (salt cod with chickpeas, tomatoes, and peppers); and the ever-popular tender, deep-fried artichokes, with outer leaves that crunch like potato chips, served with wedges of lemon on classic butcher paper.

Those who know Gucci better than gnocchi may pack this place, but this Italian comfort food doesn't miss a stiletto-heeled step.

# One if by Land, Two if by Sea

Contemporary

D1

17 Barrow St. (bet. Seventh Ave. South & W. 4th St.)

**Subway:** Christopher St - Sheridan Sq Lunch Sun
**Phone:** 212-255-8649 Dinner nightly
**Web:** www.oneifbyland.com
**Prices:** $$$

New York City claims more than its fair share of great date restaurants, but only a select few can be counted on for bringing so many men to their knees with offers of marriage. One if by Land, Two if by Sea is one of them.

Housed in an 18th-century carriage house infused with old-world sophistication, this lovely brick building fosters romance with four fireplaces, glittering brass chandeliers, tapers, and fresh roses on each table. Live piano music mellows the mood.

Contrasting the setting, an updated bill of fare offers the likes of roasted breast of duck with fregola, hearts of palm, and blueberry purée. Despite the modernized menu, long-time fans will be happy that the signature filet of beef Wellington is still available.

# Panca

Peruvian

C1

92 Seventh Ave. South (bet. Bleecker & Grove Sts.)

**Subway:** Christopher St - Sheridan Sq — Lunch & dinner daily
**Phone:** 212-488-3900
**Web:** N/A
**Prices:** $$

The exciting flavors of Peru are served in a contemporary space with cool citron walls, a stacked-stone fronted bar lined with bottles of *pisco*, and a sidewalk dining area set along the hubbub of Seventh Avenue.

Discreetly tucked into the dining room's corner is the ceviche station, where ocean-fresh seafood is given a bold dressing up—the *tiradito mixte* is a sampling of sashimi-style ceviche sparked with tart lime juice, chopped garlic, and slivers of red chilies. Cooked options include hearty soups like *aguadito de pollo* (cilantro-flavored chicken soup stocked with yucca and potato, served as an entrée). Specialties like grilled skirt steak with *tacu tacu* (a mixture of mashed beans and rice vibrant with *aji amarillo*) assure no one leaves hungry.

# Paradou

French

B1

8 Little W. 12th St. (bet. Greenwich & Washington Sts.)

**Subway:** 14 St - 8 Av — Lunch Sat – Sun
**Phone:** 212-463-8345 — Dinner nightly
**Web:** www.paradounyc.com
**Prices:** $$

Paradou is a welcome respite from the spate of gargantuan over-the-top-posh restaurants that have lately opened in the Meatpacking District. Here, a strictly casual crowd shares a carefree French spirit while relaxing over crisp, vivacious glasses of champagne, and bowls of plump, tender mussels Provençal, in a tomato broth heady with thyme.

The whimsical covered "magical garden" tent offers winter enchantment with heat lamps warming the space during colder evenings, but comes down in spring and summer. Enjoy unlimited champagne cocktails, truly al fresco, during their weekend brunch. Live music and "Paradou Happenings" are scheduled regularly.

The all-French wine menu offers some reasonably priced selections to complement the classic and rustic bistro menu.

# Pastis

B1 — French

9 Ninth Ave. (at Little W. 12th St.)

**Subway:** 14 St - 8 Av — Lunch & dinner daily
**Phone:** 212-929-4844
**Web:** www.pastisny.com
**Prices:** **$$**

With the closing of Florent, the first success story of the then-nascent Meatpacking District, Pastis can now be considered the last holdout of its kind in the neighborhood. Even now it remains a trendy and popular place, which squeezes in a fashionable flock from breakfast through dinner. Expect celebrity sightings in this stylish boîte, where the timeless bistro décor (decorative mirrors, long zinc bar, walls lined with vintage Pastis ads) has that hip, informal charm so difficult to replicate.

The menu is good and satisfying, focusing on neighborhood favorites: *moules frites au Pernod*; a seared tuna Niçoise salad; and roasted *poussin*. The cocktail list, as expected, leans heavily on the anise-flavored aperitif from which the restaurant takes its name.

# Pearl Oyster Bar

D1 — Seafood

18 Cornelia St. (bet. Bleecker & W. 4th Sts.)

**Subway:** W 4 St - Wash Sq — Lunch Mon – Fri
**Phone:** 212-691-8211 — Dinner Mon – Sat
**Web:** www.pearloysterbar.com
**Prices:** **$$**

In 1997, Chef/owner Rebecca Charles opened Pearl Oyster Bar in memory of her grandmother and the childhood summers they spent in Maine. Today, she is serving a slice of New England to the heart of Manhattan. This beloved eatery has a small dining room, a classic counter handling a brisk business for shellfish aficionados, an accompanying cookbook, and long lines out the door.

The classic New England menu offers small and large plates of pristine seafood: fried oysters, P.E.I. mussels, and the celebrated lobster roll—chunks of fresh lobster moistened with seasoned mayonnaise. Wash this down with one of their beers on tap or a glass of Rebecca's carefully selected wines. Save room for the blueberry crumble pie, another Down East staple, for dessert.

# Perilla

Contemporary

D1

9 Jones St. (bet. Bleecker & W. 4th Sts.)

**Subway:** W 4 St - Wash Sq — Lunch Sat – Sun
**Phone:** 212-929-6868 — Dinner nightly
**Web:** www.perillanyc.com
**Prices:** $$$

This casually elegant Village fave, with its unaffected vibe, showcases the talents of partners Chef Harold Dieterle and General Manager Alicia Nosenzo. He is a CIA graduate and premier winner of the reality television hit "Top Chef"; and she is a San Francisco native who has honed her front of the house skills at impressive establishments on both coasts.
Upfront is an inviting bar and the rear dining room, with its zebrawood tables and warm lighting, is attended to by an eager staff, forthcoming with suggestions on the seasonally respectful menu. Reflecting global influences, the chef spices a beautifully prepared snapper crudo with pickled radish and *tom yum* broth, and transforms game hen into bacon-wrapped roulades sauced with pomegranate molasses.

# The Place

Contemporary

B2

310 W. 4th St. (bet. Bank & 12th Sts.)

**Subway:** 14 St - 8 Av — Lunch Sat – Sun
**Phone:** 212-924-2711 — Dinner nightly
**Web:** www.theplaceny.com
**Prices:** $$

Tucked deep into the West Village, The Place is the kind of cozy, grotto-style dining that makes people want to up and move to the big city. Rendezvous-like, guests duck below street level to find a small bar with lots of flickering votive candles and a few tables with a view of the bustling sidewalk. Wander back a bit, and you'll find low, rustic beams, and white tablecloth seating; behind that, two outdoor terraces beckon in summer.
Even the food seems designed to comfort, like a piping-hot roasted tomato soup, drizzled with chive oil, and pocked with pecorino-baked croutons; or seared duck mu shu pancakes, drizzled with sweet tamarind. With a kitchen that employs only fresh, organic ingredients, diners are taken on a surprising gastronomic tour.

# Perry Street ✿

Contemporary XXX

B2

176 Perry St. (at West St.)

**Subway:** Christopher St - Sheridan Sq

Lunch & dinner daily

**Phone:** 212-352-1900

**Web:** www.jean-georges.com

**Prices:** **$$$**

Jean Georges Management, LLC

Still one of the most glamorous places to dine in New York City, Jean-Georges Vongerichten's casual ode to modern fusion food, Perry Street, aims to be as cool as its gorgeous, jet-setting clientele. It hits the mark with an icy-clean, cutting-edge interior tucked into the bottom floor of a striking Richard Meier glass tower overlooking the Hudson River.

The young, stylish professionals that frequent Perry Street set the dress code here—casual but sexy, with guests arriving in everything from tailored suits to designer jeans. Look closely around the dining room—an airy, Zen-like space bathed in light from the floor-to-ceiling picture windows, and dotted with uncluttered, polished wood tables and supple leather banquettes—and you might even spot a celebrity or two.

With this globe-trotting menu, Vongerichten pulls inspiration from America, Europe, and Asia to craft dishes like a wildly fresh peekytoe crab salad dancing in a light honey vinaigrette; tender skate, roasted in a *beurre noisette* and served over a clean fennel salad; or an exotic passion fruit mousse served with a delicious mango coulis. At lunchtime, you'll find a simpler menu offering good value for the money.

# Pó

Italian

D1

31 Cornelia St. (bet. Bleecker & W. 4th Sts.)

**Subway:** W 4 St - Wash Sq — Lunch Wed – Sun
**Phone:** 212-645-2189 — Dinner nightly
**Web:** www.porestaurant.com
**Prices:** $$

It's no wonder reservations at this longstanding neighborhood gem still fill up a week in advance. A devoted following is attracted to Pó's cozy and romantic ambience, well-run front of the house, and its fine, freshly prepared fare.

The satisfying menu may include a cured tuna appetizer, beautifully flavored with white beans, raw crunchy baby artichokes, and spicy yet cool chili-mint vinaigrette. As a twist on the typical presentation, the linguini *vongole* is served with crispy pancetta; and a tasting menu is offered at both lunch and dinner. For a delightful and surprisingly light end to the meal, Vermont maple syrup sauce is poured over a delicate round of flan-like ricotta cheesecake.

Brooklyn now has a Pó of its own—located in Carroll Gardens.

# Prem-on Thai

Thai

C4

138 Houston St. (bet. MacDougal & Sullivan Sts.)

**Subway:** Spring St (Sixth Ave.) — Lunch Mon – Fri
**Phone:** 212-353-2338 — Dinner nightly
**Web:** www.prem-on.com
**Prices:** $$

Pioneering Chef Prakit Prem-on opened his first Manhattan restaurant in 1979, and dining at his eponymous West Village location proves why Thai cuisine now dominates the city's dining landscape. The sleek and gracious dining room is outfitted with deep-toned wood and generously sized, white marble-topped tables, warmed by burgundy and orange upholstered banquettes, and flickering candlelight. The upbeat playlist fashions a lounge-like aspect.

Concerned and creative cooking exceeds the typical, with flavor-packed dishes like spicy and tangy jungle curry; crisped basil duck; and banana-leaf roasted rice. Decorative carving of vegetables and garnishes emphasize an appetizing use of color and balance.

The two-course lunch menu is a great value.

# Quinto Quarto

Italian

B3

14 Bedford St. (bet. Downing & Houston Sts.)

**Subway:** Houston St — Lunch & dinner daily
**Phone:** 212-675-9080
**Web:** www.quintoquarto.com
**Prices:** $$

This newly opened *"osteria Romana"* is named after a neighborhood that once served as Rome's Meatpacking District. Its enticingly rustic menu is served in an intimate setting that beams warmth; the dark-wood furnishings, exposed brick walls, and friendly service offer a charmingly heavy Italian accent.

The adept kitchen paves the way to the Eternal City with a listing of regional specialties that include a luscious *bucatini all'amatriciana*, a tangle of perfectly cooked strands dressed with carrot and onion sweetened tomato sauce, bacon, and pecorino cheese. Entrées may include roasted bone-in pieces of tender rabbit wildly fragrant with rosemary, sage, and accompanied by crisped potatoes. Dessert offers a short listing of jam-filled *crostatas*.

# Rockmeisha

Japanese

D1

11 Barrow St. (bet. Seventh Ave. South & W. 4th St.)

**Subway:** Christopher St - Sheridan Sq — Dinner Tue – Sun
**Phone:** 212-675-7775
**Web:** N/A
**Prices:** $$

New York City's fascination with *izakayas*—those fabulous little Japanese drinking joints where they take the small plates as seriously as they do the sake—has reached a fever pitch. Enter Rockmeisha: an intimate little West Village restaurant where kitschy memorabilia (think poison warning signs) and curious little cartoon drawings line the walls.

Regional specialties are the way to go on Rockmeisha's menu, especially those hailing from Kyūshū, a large island in Japan and the chef's hometown. The house is known for its ramen, and a thick tangle of noodles flown in from Hakata and laced with barbecued pork easily backs that claim. Items like deep bowls of barbecued beef; fluffy leek omelettes; and succulent yakitori pork skewers round out the menu.

# Rhong-Tiam ✿

Thai XX

C4

541 LaGuardia Pl. (bet. Bleecker & 3rd Sts.)

**Subway:** W 4 St - Wash Sq — Lunch Mon – Sat
**Phone:** 212-477-0600 — Dinner nightly
**Web:** www.rhong-tiam.com
**Prices:** $$

Cui Meng/Erik Cheah

We know, we know. You've been told you have to roll out to some far-flung Queens spot to get good Thai food. Maybe not—take a stroll down leafy, tree-lined Laguardia Place in Greenwich Village, and make your way over to Rhong-Tiam, a deservedly clucked-over newcomer that's set critics' tongues a-wagging since it first swung open its doors.

What's all the fuss? This is hardcore, real-deal Thai—no fusion, no babying around. The secret lies in Rhong-Tiam's kitchen, which has a serious talent for concocting fresh, made-to-order curry pastes (the backbone of good Thai food) by hand in a mortar and pestle, filling the pleasant little room with delicious, exotic scents.

The kitchen shows a studied knowledge of regional Thai fare, dancing effortlessly between the best dishes the country has to offer, including some numbers rarely seen outside the various borders. Try the *moo-na-rok*, also known as pork on fire, a divine creation that elicits the slow, slightly sadistic burn known to visitors and natives of Northern Thailand; or the unusual Southern-style chicken, minced into tasty, tiny little morsels, and then thumped with a freshly-mixed curry paste and crunchy fried basil leaves.

# Scarpetta

Italian XX

B1

355 W. 14th St. (bet. Eighth & Ninth Aves.)

**Subway:** 14 St - 8 Ave — Dinner nightly
**Phone:** 212-691-0555
**Web:** www.scarpettanyc.com
**Prices:** **$$$$**

Stuffed between a diner and a comedy club on bustling West 14th Street, Scarpetta is in the wrong place to merit attention from serious eaters in this town. Yet merit it does—due to revered Chef/owner Scott Conant. Throw in an accomplished staff and a neophyte-friendly wine list—and you'll start to see why this restaurant packs them in nightly.
The dining room, designed by S. Russell Groves, is perfectly slick and pretty—but the bar area, with its thick marble and jumbo people-watching windows, is a real draw. No matter where you sit, you'll soon find out what put Conant on the map—wildly good pastas like a soft pile of black macaroni studded with fresh seafood and sea urchin, laced with bright tomato sauce and mint breadcrumbs.

# Sevilla

Spanish X

C2

62 Charles St. (at W. 4th St.)

**Subway:** Christopher St - Sheridan Sq — Lunch & dinner daily
**Phone:** 212-929-3189
**Web:** www.sevillarestaurantandbar.com
**Prices:** **$$**

Having been around since 1941, Sevilla retains a warm patina in its *taberna*-style interior, and continues to stand above its neighboring West Village Spanish restaurants.
While the atmosphere is convivial and fun, tradition reigns here, starting with the hospitable and attentive cadre of waiters. The well-priced menu offers a slice of Spain in its delightful paellas, seafood, and meat dishes. Refreshing, fruity sangria makes the perfect accompaniment to Spanish favorites, all authentically fragrant and garlicky—the heaping portions confirm that this is no place for tapas.
Try dining here during the week when it might be a bit quieter, and ask for a table by the windows, which look out onto one of the most charming blocks in the West Village.

# Soto ✿

D1 Japanese

357 Sixth Ave. (bet. Washington Pl. & W. 4th St.)

**Subway:** W 4 St - Wash Sq — Dinner Mon – Sat
**Phone:** 212-414-3088
**Web:** N/A
**Prices:** **$$$**

Soto

Insist on omakase at Soto, and the well-meaning staff may try to talk you out of it. Hold your ground—because with a pristine raw fish omakase starting at $45 (the regular version begins at $120), this is easily one of the best bargains in town.

It's easy to rush past the little restaurant's discreet entrance along this grungy section of lower Sixth Avenue, but what a shame. For then you would miss the decadent Japanese stylings of Atlanta-transplant, Chef Sotohiro Kosugi. The simple, spotless interior, designed by Hiro Tsuruta (who also designed Momofuku Noodle Bar), is small and modern—the whitewashed landscape dotted with traditional pottery and sleek white china.

Service can be slow, but it's worth the wait for a mind-blowing omakase experience that might include minute-steamed tai sashimi, boasting perfectly-torched skin and kissed with thin slices of ginger and scallion; or a silky sliver of Long Island fluke puddled in a spot-on ponzu sauce and topped with ginger shoots, *shiso* leaves, and chives. If you must go à la carte, don't miss the chef's star ingredient, uni, which finds its way into dishes like a truffle oil mousse wrapped in crunchy lotus root with steamed lobster.

# Spice Market

Asian XX

B1

403 W. 13th St. (at Ninth Ave.)

**Subway:** 14 St - 8 Av — Lunch & dinner daily
**Phone:** 212-675-2322
**Web:** www.spicemarketnewyork.com
**Prices:** **$$**

Now a Meatpacking mainstay, Spice Market continues to attract its fair share of the area's well-dressed scenesters, where they come to graze on Chef Jean-Georges Vongerichten's skillful homage to Southeast Asian street food.

This 12,000 square-foot former warehouse realized by Jacques Garcia sexes up marketplace stalls with deep shades of red, violet, and gold; a large teak pagoda takes center stage, while wooden arches divide the seating areas. Eat-with-your-eyes first, as you take in the packaging of this trend-setting spot that can also claim impressive cuisine to its credit.

The chef's trademark style is evident in such vibrant creations as black pepper shrimp with sun-dried pineapple; onion and chili-crusted short ribs; and Ovaltine *kulfi*.

# Standard Grill

Contemporary XX

B1

848 Washington St. (bet. Little W. 12th & 13th Sts.)

**Subway:** 14 St - 8 Av — Dinner nightly
**Phone:** 212-645-4100
**Web:** www.thestandardgrill.com
**Prices:** **$$**

Perched beneath phase one of the Highline, The Standard Grill offers myriad options to this crowd-drawing neighborhood. There is a front outdoor space, bright and airy bar room, and knockout dining room that bears the shine of boutique hotelier André Balazs: rich-toned wood accents play up red leather furnishings, an ivory-tiled ceiling, and a whimsical floor completely covered with pennies. The open kitchen is fronted by white-washed brick and has glossy teal blue walls.

Chef Dan Silverman has been recruited to prepare a delicious, contemporary menu that may include a cool and creamy almond soup drizzled with gazpacho; and flash-seared lamb chops smeared with fluffy mint purée. Accompany this with the hotelier's private label Long Island rosé.

# Spotted Pig

Gastropub

B2

314 W. 11th St. (at Greenwich St.)

**Subway:** Christopher St - Sheridan Sq — Lunch & dinner daily
**Phone:** 212-620-0393
**Web:** www.thespottedpig.com
**Prices:** $$

The Spotted Pig

The bad news first: you may be greeted at the corner entrance of April Bloomfield's wildly popular gastropub with an army of hosts touting an insanely long wait time. Unfortunately, they're often correct. And once you do get piped into a table, you may find yourself precariously teetering on a stool, hunched over a Lilliputian table.

But the good news—no, the great news—is that one bite of Bloomfield's breathtakingly simple, but brilliant, upscale pub grub will erase all of that unfortunate business from your mind: grilled calf's liver laced with balsamic-roasted *cipollini* and crispy pancetta; seasonal summer eggplant roasted with garlic, cumin, and turmeric, then topped with a soft pile of sheep's milk ricotta; silky flourless chocolate cake sprinkled with powdered sugar sided with tangy whipped cream. Need we go on?

There's more: go on an off-hour (before 8:00 P.M. or lunch hour is ideal), or command a cozy seat at the bar, and you'll miss all the chaos. Without that, there's not a lot to go wrong at this lively two-story pub other than Jay-Z, ordering the last plate of *gnudi*—Bloomfield's naked sheep's milk ricotta dumplings that are often imitated, but never duplicated.

# Surya

Indian

C1

302 Bleecker St. (bet. Grove St. & Seventh Ave. South)

**Subway:** Christopher St - Sheridan Sq — Lunch & dinner daily
**Phone:** 212-807-7770
**Web:** www.suryany.com
**Prices:** $$

The sun truly does shine upon this little West Village restaurant, whose name means "sun" in Tamil. Vibrant colors fashion a sleek, dimly-lit interior, attended by a superb kitchen and service staff. Surya's menu boasts an array of regional Indian fare to please both vegetarians and meat lovers. Start with the hot, crisp aloo *tikkiyas* of spiced, crushed potato in a tamarind sauce that runs the gamut of fresh herbs and tangy flavors, accompanied by blistered, fresh naan, topped with clarified butter. Tandoor dishes, as well as *saag gosht* of lamb cooked in spinach purée, are among the high recommendations.
Budget-conscious diners should be sure to take advantage of the weekday lunch specials, where all items (except dessert) are offered at half price.

# 10 Downing

Contemporary

C3

10 Downing St. (bet. Bleecker & Hudson Sts.)

**Subway:** Houston St — Lunch Sat – Sun
**Phone:** 212-255-0300 — Dinner nightly
**Web:** N/A
**Prices:** $$

This well-run hotspot is for anyone seeking a most sensational and inspirational dining experience, with a cheeky slice of Muppetmania.
While the menu may display quotes from Miss Piggy, it shows talent with the likes of fresh squid ink *agnolotti* with peekytoe crab, or just-baked molten chocolate cake. The sophisticated crowd's good looks further enhance the chicly spare setting of pale walls, bold artwork, and warm lighting. But look to the white marble bar and notice a pair of antlers hung upside down; this calculated assortment of eclectic accents shows focus on the hipster aesthetic, yet does not detract from the fact that this is a serious restaurant, serving impressive food. In warmer months, French doors open to a sidewalk seating area.

# Tomoe Sushi

C4 Japanese

172 Thompson St. (bet. Bleecker & Houston Sts.)

**Subway:** Spring St (Sixth Ave.) Lunch Tue – Sat
**Phone:** 212-777-9346 Dinner nightly
**Web:** N/A
**Prices:** ⊜

Diners come here in droves for the high-quality sushi and sashimi, which is cut in large pieces as if indicative of this menu's focus on great value. Ample dishes of cooked seafood round out the offerings. Do remember to save room for dessert, as Tomoe's creamy version of cheesecake is scented with green tea and served with a red fruit coulis.

Through the packed room, it is almost difficult to notice the Spartan décor, which consists of a small sushi bar, bare pine tables, and specials scrawled on pieces of paper.

The downside to dining here is that long waits followed by rushed service can be a drag. Patience is clearly a necessary virtue if planning a dinner at Tomoe Sushi, where the wait in the evening can range up to an hour or more.

# Ushiwakamaru

C4 Japanese

136 Houston St. (Bet MacDougal & Sullivan Sts.)

**Subway:** B'way - Lafayette St Dinner Mon – Sat
**Phone:** 212-228-4181
**Web:** N/A
**Prices:** **$$$$**

Manhattan's sushiphiles rejoice for a taste of Chef Hideo Kuribara's outrageously fresh, authentically prepared Japanese food.

Most nights of the week, the place is packed with its loyal Japanese clientele, and the passing plates explain the reason: artfully-arranged *sayori* (needlefish) topped with glistening salmon roe; blow-torched *anago* (salt water eel), delicately licked with sweet sauce; shrimp heads rolled in fluffy tempura batter; and tiny glassy eels, so transparent you might mistake them for gelatin. Their good selection of sake is the perfect complement to a meal here.

Inside, this small, casual, lively, and loud downtown spot is dressed in white linen, paneling, and soothing blond wood tones. Just don't forget to make that reservation.

# Vento

B1 Italian XX

675 Hudson St. (at 14th St.)

**Subway:** 14 St - 8 Av Lunch & dinner daily
**Phone:** 212-699-2400
**Web:** www.brguestrestaurants.com
**Prices:** **$$**

This classic Manhattan space is a New York story unto itself: an S&M club in a seedy neighborhood is now a crowd-pleasing trattoria in a landmarked historic district. With its expansive menu of small plates, wood-fired pizzas, homemade pastas, and a revolving list of daily specials, Vento satisfies less carnal appetites and fuels the fashionable masses flocking to this prime Meatpacking corner. When temperatures rise, the wrap-around sidewalk dining area is highly coveted.

Exposed brick and wood beams accent the comfortably understated two-story space, spotlighting the beautiful people within. Enjoy the upbeat scene with a cocktail at the popular front bar before heading into the more relaxed dining area where service is vigilant and knowledgeable.

Hotels and restaurants change every year, so change your Michelin Guide every year!

# Wallsé ✿

Austrian XX

B2

344 W. 11th St. (at Washington St.)

**Subway:** Christopher St - Sheridan Sq

**Phone:** 212-352-2300

**Web:** www.wallse.com

**Prices:** $$$

Lunch Sat – Sun
Dinner nightly

Maike Paul

Tucked into one of Greenwich Village's loveliest pockets—where the narrow cobblestoned streets are lined in storybook brownstones and that legendary Manhattan clip slows to a more reasonable Sunday crawl—the sun-drenched Wallsé undoubtedly gets a leg up from its location.

But neighborhood charisma alone can't create this loyal a following—what really catapults Wallsé into the upper echelon is Chef Kurt Gutenbrunner's careful, unfussy cuisine, which manages to be every bit as fresh and innovative as the art that graces the walls. And the artist? Stellar creator—Julian Schnabel.

Named for the Austrian town Gutenbrunner was born in, Wallsé takes guests on a sophisticated culinary tour of the chef's homeland with plates of crispy ravioli—plump with goose confit, foie gras, and cracklings—bobbing in a crystal-clear pool of consommé pocked with diced carrots, potatoes, and chives; or tender pheasant, tucked between delicate sheets of white cabbage and strudel, and set atop creamy potato and vanilla-scented apple purée. Save room for a divine seasonal dessert like the warm pear strudel paired with a fluffy pile of house-made *schlag* and a creamy scoop of roasted walnut ice cream.

# Harlem, Morningside & Washington Heights

Flanked by Riverside and Morningside parks and home to stately Columbia University, Morningside Heights is a lovely quarter of the city... and known for some of the best breakfast spots around. Sandwich shops and small eateries line these avenues, where quick, inexpensive meals are a collegiate necessity. Resident academics and Ivy leaguers are found darting to and from class or lounging at the **Hungarian Pastry Shop** with a sweet and cup of tea. Considered a landmark, this old-world bakery has been open for more than three decades and is a focal point for students and gatherings. Across the street, Saint John the Divine, a gorgeous Gothic revival and a formidable presence on Amsterdam Avenue offers beauty, history, and wonderful community outreach programs. Special occasions call for an evening at Butler Hall's **Terrace In the Sky**. Rather than be misled by the plain building in which it's housed, prepare yourself for the expansive views of the city and fine continental fare. In the summer, enjoy a drink in the breeze on the alluring outdoor terrace.

To the north is Harlem—a true feast for the stomach and soul. Fifth Avenue divides the neighborhood into two very unique areas: West Harlem, an epicenter of African-American culture; and East Harlem, a diverse Latin quarter affectionately known as "El Barrio."

West Harlem still retains a kind of sassy edge as it gives way to slow, welcomed gentrification—one of its most visible borders is at **Fairway**, a Tri-State area staple that lures shoppers off the West Side Highway for their mind

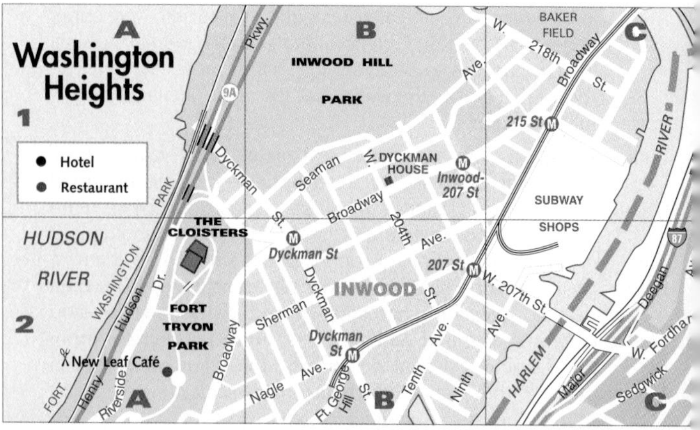

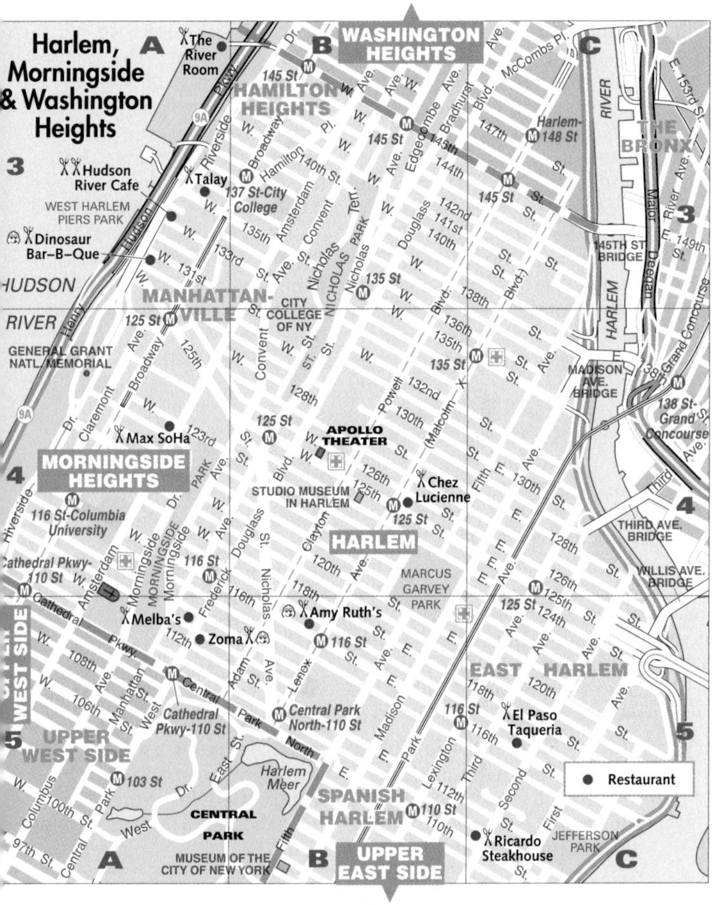


boggling product offering and sensational produce. For a taste of the area's rich history, sift through the impressive literary collection at The Schomburg Center for Research in Black Culture on Lenox Avenue, or spend a sunny afternoon among the beautiful row houses in the historic districts of Sugar Hill and Hamilton Heights. In the evening, slip into famed 60-year old **Lenox Lounge** for jazz and drinks and grab a seat at one of the banquettes. Harlem Week, an annual festival celebrating its 35th year, features art, music, and food each August. While there, cool off with a cone of red velvet cake ice cream if the natural ice cream stand is around.

Food factors heavily into Harlem culture—both east and west of Fifth Avenue—and the choices are as diverse as the neighborhood itself. From Mexican to Caribbean to West African, the culinary delights abound. Locals line up around the block at **Famous Fish Market** for deep fried favorites such as fish and chips or baskets of crispy shrimp. For dangerously spiced Senegalese food, head into **Afrika Kine** restaurant; or shop around **Darou Salam Market** for West African groceries. **Carrot Top Pastries** entices locals with sweet potato pies, while **Raw Soul**, a health-focused Harlem spot, offers a menu of vegan "living foods" and ongoing cooking classes designed to educate seekers of well-being. **The DEN** (Dining Entertainment and Nightlife), a happening restaurant and lounge with a downtown feel, is worth a visit for the menu titles alone. Few can resist these feasts of "Slapsumbadi Shrimp" or "Weezies Crabcakes." Then, head to the bar for a "Lick Ya Lips" cocktail and night of live rhythm and blues.

Classy **Harlem Tea Room** on Madison Avenue offers a three-course afternoon tea and evenings of spoken word, while **Amor Cubano's** tradional suckling pig—or *lechon*—is savored amidst a vibrant atmosphere of live Cuban music. For a sampling of Caribbean fare stop into **Sisters** for a taste of the islands. Or peruse the taco trucks and taquerias along the Little Mexico strip of East 116th Street in the heart of one of New York's many Mexican communities.

A remnant of the former Italian population of East Harlem, **Rao's** is a New York institution. Run out of a small basement and frequented by the likes of Donald Trump and Nicole Kidman, Rao's is one of the most difficult tables to get in all of Manhattan. The original patrons have exclusive rights to a seat here and hand off their reservations like rent-controlled apartments. Better try to get in good with the owner if you can. Bid farewell to **Morrone & Sons Italian Bakery** which closed it's doors after fifty-one years but **Patsy's** is still holding strong in Harlem, burning it's coal oven and sometimes its pizza.

The Tony award-winning musical *In The Heights* pays loving tribute to the energetic, ebullient Washington Heights neighborhood where Dominican and Puerto Rican communities have taken root in Manhattan's northern tip. Latin beats blast through the air and bright, refreshing Puerto Rican piragua carts can be found on almost every corner selling shaved ice soaked in a rainbow of tropical flavors. Try *jugos naturales*—juices made from cane sugar and fresh fruits like pineapple and orange—for a healthful and refreshing treat. Great fish markets and Dominican butcher shops dot the streets, and less than ten bucks will get you a delicious plate of pernil with rice and beans at any number of eateries. Duck into **La Rosa Fine Foods**, a wonderful Latin gourmet market, for fresh fish, meat, and produce; or **Nelly's Bakery** for a creamy cup of *café con leche* and a *guayaba con queso* (guava and cheese pastry).

**Piper's Kilt**, a standing relic in Inwood, represents the former Irish and German population of the area. Settle into a booth at the lively "Kilt" with some Irish nachos and a perfect pint.

# Amy Ruth's

Southern

B5

113 W. 116th St. (at Lenox Ave.)

**Subway:** 116 St (Lenox Ave.) Lunch & dinner daily
**Phone:** 212-280-8779
**Web:** www.amyruthsharlem.com
**Prices:** ⊜

Established in 1998, this Harlem darling is named for the owner's grandmother—a fine Southern lady, good cook, and toast of NY's soul-food loving minions. Connoisseurs of honest, down-home, Southern food, all know to head to the famed Amy Ruth's.

Seek out the smoker parked out front on 116th and rest assured that it is no prop. Nearby barrels are filled with firewood used to smoke the delectable and tender barbecue ribs. The place is always brimming with locals, tourists, and the occasional celebrity hungering for this outstanding cooking. From freshly prepared waffles for breakfast, to succulent, crackling (yet non-greasy) fried chicken with a side of mac' and cheese for dinner, one of the best memories New York City can offer is a visit to Amy Ruth's.

# Chez Lucienne

French

B4

308 Lenox Ave. (bet. 125th & 126th Sts.)

**Subway:** 125 St (Lenox Ave.) Lunch & dinner daily
**Phone:** 212-289-5555
**Web:** www.chezlucienne.com
**Prices:** $$

French drifts between patron and staff at this refreshing addition to Central Harlem, overlooking historic Lenox Avenue. Turquoise banquettes and brick walls line the lovely, narrow space, where servers don the typical Parisian bistro uniform (black bowties, white aprons) and present well-made French fare from the semi-open kitchen.

The menu focuses on the homey simplicity inherent to great food, as in the *pâté de maison*, wonderfully textured and served with a sweet reduction and delicate chutney. The talented founders, Jerome Bougherdani and Chef Matthew Tivy (both of Daniel), have created a classic bistro in an unlikely area—and are succeeding. Note the location is very convenient to the subway, which is sure to draw foodies from across the city.

# Dinosaur Bar-B-Que

A3 **Barbecue**

646 W. 131st St. (at Twelfth Ave.)

**Subway:** 125 St (Broadway) — Lunch & dinner daily
**Phone:** 212-694-1777
**Web:** www.dinosaurbarbque.com
**Prices:** $$

The sumptuous smell of smoking meat carries beyond the block, beckoning barbecue lovers for miles. With a roadhouse-style vibe similar to its Syracuse counterpart, this upbeat, unpretentious eatery sports a casual, family-friendly setting with large tables, a lively bar, and fantastic food. Dinosaur Bar-B-Que's monstrous menu demands a colossal appetite—options are as delicious as they are plentiful.

For a starter, try the Jumbo BBQ chicken wings, smoked in-house, and doused with your choice of sauce (go for the Wango Tango), complete with bleu cheese dressing. Next, order up the ribs and half chicken combo served with honey hush cornbread and a choice of two sides. After your mammoth meal, buy a bottle of Dino BBQ sauce to take home.

# El Paso Taqueria

C5 **Mexican**

237 E. 116th St. (bet. Second & Third Aves.)

**Subway:** 116 St (Lexington Ave.) — Lunch & dinner daily
**Phone:** 212-860-4875
**Web:** N/A
**Prices:** 

Manhattan may be a hotbed of Latin restaurants these days, but the soul of the city's Mexican population lies along East 116th Street in Harlem. Enter El Paso Taqueria, a Harlem jewel that stands out for its charming, immaculate space, friendly waitstaff, and authentic, affordable Mexican cuisine. Dishes are all worthy of savoring, and include a fluffy corn tamale oozing with fragrant, tender pork, presented with swirls of *crema* and salsa verde. Plates of enchiladas rally the tastebuds, from tart and spicy corn tortillas to chipotle-tinged sauces to the *cojita* cheese sprinkled on top. The sweet, fizzy house-made sangria uses just the right amount of seasonal fruit and proves the perfect complement to a meal.

# Hudson River Cafe

American XX

A3

697 W. 133rd St. (at Twelfth Ave.)

**Subway:** 125 St (Broadway) — Lunch Sat – Sun
**Phone:** 212-491-9111 — Dinner nightly
**Web:** www.hudsonrivercafe.com
**Prices:** $$

In an area of Harlem that's prime for development, this bustling café is a welcome addition to the neighborhood.

It's all about fun here, between the strong cocktails, the live music on weekends, and the big flavors in American dishes—such as deep-fried crab cakes served with a tart remoulade sauce; and a refreshing salad of greens, fennel, orange segments, and grapefruit-juice reduction. For dessert, pistachio ice cream plays a cool foil to a warm flourless chocolate cake.

The overall ambience is sleek and modern, with black molded chairs standing out against stark white walls. Outside, the bi-level patio, surrounded by gated walls and greenery, is a fabulous spot to wash away the day's worries with a mango *mojito* or a Harlem sidecar.

# Max SoHa

Italian X

A4

1274 Amsterdam Ave. (at 123rd St.)

**Subway:** 125 St (Broadway) — Lunch & dinner daily
**Phone:** 212-531-2221
**Web:** www.maxsoha.com
**Prices:** $$

Set on a corner in Morningside Heights in the shadow of prestigious Columbia University, Max SoHa rates as a great neighborhood find. Wide sidewalks here make room for outdoor seating, and a good opportunity to observe the avalanche of change that is currently transforming Harlem.

Entrées run from breaded chicken cutlet to grilled flank steak. However, the true reason to dine here is the decadent, well-prepared, satisfying pasta. Tender chunks of lamb in a deeply aromatic sauce drenching the housemade spaghetti *chitarra al ragù d'agnello* make, quite simply, a great plate of pasta. Gnocchi, fusilli, and lasagna dishes consistently touch all the right rustic notes. To complete your meal, sip a fragrant glass of Italian wine from the well-priced list.

# Melba's

A5 — **Southern**

300 W. 114th St. (at Frederick Douglass Blvd.)

**Subway:** 116 St (Frederick Douglass Blvd.) — Lunch & dinner daily
**Phone:** 212-864-7777
**Web:** www.melbasrestaurant.com
**Prices:** $$

This popular Morningside Heights joint stays elbow-to-elbow most nights of the week despite small digs, loud music, and a molasses staff. In fact, that's all part of the charm for the regulars that crowd into Melba's to eat, drink, and listen to music.

Set along a rapidly gentrifying street pocked with as many cutesy storefronts as West African mom-and-pop eateries, Melba's bleeds cozy-chic, with custom chandeliers, plush banquettes, and exposed brick. The Southern comfort menu is decadent all around—velvety catfish strips with chipotle mayo are paired with an eggnog waffle lathered in piping-hot strawberry butter; and a heartbreakingly moist coconut layer cake is infused with butter cream and dusted with coconut flakes.

# New Leaf Café

A2 — **American**

1 Margaret Corbin Dr. (Fort Tryon Park)

**Subway:** 190 St — Lunch Tue – Sun
**Phone:** 212-568-5323
**Web:** www.nyrp.org/newleaf
**Prices:** $$

Thanks to the New York Restoration Project and its dedication to reclaim and restore parks, public gardens, and open spaces in forgotten areas of the city, this captivating 1930s stone structure turned over a new leaf in 2001, when it was re-imagined as a café.

Despite its location in an urban center, the dining room wears each season's regalia, the bounty of which is mirrored in the changing menu. Locals as well as visitors to The Cloisters (home to the Metropolitan Museum's world-class collection of Medieval art) favor the restaurant's outdoor terrace on a sunny day. Proceeds from your meal support the upkeep of Fort Tryon Park, in which it sits.

Music lovers will appreciate the live jazz performances every Friday night.

# Ricardo Steakhouse

Steakhouse

C5

2145 Second Ave. (bet. 110th & 111th Sts.)

**Subway:** 110 St (Lexington Ave.) Dinner nightly
**Phone:** 212-289-5895
**Web:** www.ricardosteakhouse.com
**Prices:** $$

In recent years, this East Harlem favorite has become a local hangout among the upscale condo set moving into the neighborhood. One peek inside, and it's certainly easy to see why—weather permitting, there's a cute garden to graze in out back, and inside, you'll find a cozy, exposed brick interior flickering with honeyed light from the votive candles.

True to its moniker, red meat is the name of the game at Ricardo's—a Porterhouse for one arrives perfectly seared, and is paired with a combo of bright *chimichurri* and peppery hot oil. If you can wrangle someone into sharing, kick things off with the Ricardo tasting platter—a smorgasbord of plump steak empanadas, expertly-charred calamari, tender crab cake, and butter-kissed Clams Casino.

# The River Room

Southern

A3

750 W. 145th St. (at Riverside Dr.)

**Subway:** 145 St (Broadway) Lunch Sun
**Phone:** 212-491-1500 Dinner Wed – Sat
**Web:** www.theriverroomofharlem.com
**Prices:** $$

A heavenly wall of floor-to-ceiling windows overlooks the glittering lights of the George Washington Bridge and Hudson River reflecting it below, providing a sensational backdrop to a tranquil evening. The serene space, colorfully lit and outfitted in billowing fabrics and pastel hues, rises to a cathedral-like, angled ceiling creating a calming, airy effect.

Situated inside the Riverbank State Park (most easily reached by car), this popular spot offers Southern-inspired favorites like tender, pan-seared, double-thick pork chops in sweet guava-red wine reduction, and savory sides of braised collard greens with smoked turkey; or macaroni and cheese croquettes. Weekend nights of live jazz and private parties are in high demand, so call in advance.

# Talay

A3 — Thai

701 W. 135th St. (at Twelfth Ave.)

**Subway:** 125 St (Broadway) — Lunch Sun
**Phone:** 212-491-8300 — Dinner nightly
**Web:** www.talayrestaurant.com
**Prices:** $$$

Talay is a recent addition to the hip Harlem stretch along 12th Avenue, informally dubbed Viaduct Valley (or ViVa). Thai for "waterfront," this bustling, bi-level bistro-cum-lounge (formerly a 1920s freight house) ushers guests into its stylish space via an entry way flanked by two massive lion statues. Tasty Thai-Latin cuisine tops the bill of fare, co-created by Kuma Inn's King Phojanakong.

Vivid, distinct flavors define dishes such as crispy shrimp atop creamy plantains served with sweet-chili aïoli; grilled octopus with pickled bamboo shoots; and charred *bistek churrasco* served with three dipping sauces. Service is slow and getting there is a bit of a haul, but the food is well worth it. On weekends, a club scene takes over after hours.

# Zoma

A5 — Ethiopian

2084 Frederick Douglass Blvd. (at 113th St.)

**Subway:** 116th (Frederick Douglass Blvd.) — Lunch Sat – Sun
**Phone:** 212-662-0620 — Dinner nightly
**Web:** www.zomanyc.com
**Prices:**

In terms of Ethiopian joints, this popular Harlem restaurant cuts a particularly cool, sophisticated figure with its spare white interior and beautiful exotic relics. The food is even classier, with ample, delicious portions hovering near the $16 mark—and the mixed crowd of neighborhood locals and budget-minded gourmands are happy to wait their turn for a stab at authentic meat dishes like *doro wett* (a chicken stew redolent with spices and made fiery from berbere).

For two or more, an ideal meal might be a plate of fish or meat, paired with the outstanding vegetarian combination. Mopped up with the tangy, moist *injera* (which doubles as a spoon to scoop the food from the plate to your mouth), and washed down with a sweet glass of honey wine—the result is pure African bliss.

Domaines
Ott

# Lower East Side

Clockwise from the north, this neighborhood is bounded by Houston Street, the East River, Pike Street, and the Bowery. While it has proudly retained the personality of its first wave of hard-working settlers, the area has embraced a steady change to its landscape brought on by artsy entrepreneurs lured to these formerly overlooked parts. A mostly low-lying neighborhood, with the exception of a few high-rise apartments, towering reminders of a recent real estate boom, the Lower East Side feels village-like in its stature with a palpable creative spirit.

## Eastern European Influence

Before checking out the scene as it looks today, visit the Lower East Side Tenement Museum for a glimpse of the past. This restored structure dates back to 1863 and depicts what life was like for the swells of immigrant families, primarily Eastern European Jews that settled here in the early part of the last century fleeing famine and war, making this neighborhood the most densely populated area in the country. For a taste of yore, head to **Russ & Daughters** on Houston Street. Opened in 1914, this beloved institution is a nosher's dream famous for its selection of smoked fish and all things delicious known as "appetizing."

## Orchard Street

Orchard Street, long the retail heart of this nabe was once dominated by the garment trade with stores selling fabrics and notions. Tailors remain in the area, offering inexpensive while-you-wait service; but boutiques selling handmade jewelry, designer skateboards, and handcrafted denim have also moved in. Shoppers looking to cool their heels should drop by **Il Laboratorio del Gelato** for an indulgent scoop. For purchases with a more daily purpose, the **Essex Street Market** houses numerous purveyors of fresh produce, meat, and fish under one roof. The market is truly a gourmet's delight; it features two cheesemongers, a coffee roaster, a chocolatier, and **Shopsin's General Store,** a crazy joint notorious for its encyclopedic menu and cranky owner.

By the 1950s, the melting pot that defined the LES became even more diverse with a new tide of immigrants, this time from Puerto Rico and other parts of Latin America. This population continues to be the dominant force today. For a sampling of home-style Latino fare, like *mofongo* and *pernil*, try **El Castillo de Jagua** on the corner of Essex and Rivington streets.

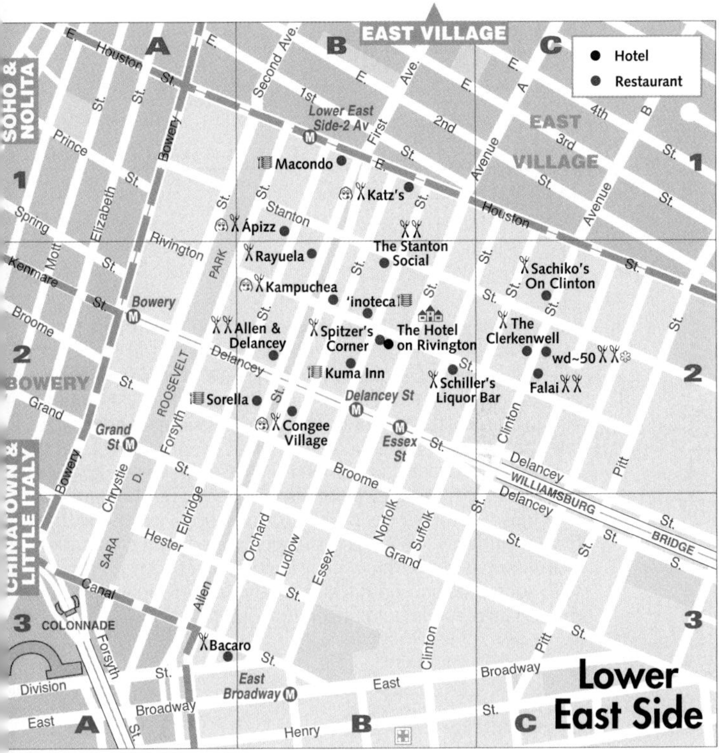


## Rivington Street

Rivington Street embodies this area's hybrid of old and new. Located here is **Streit's Matzo Factory,** in operation since 1925, and **Economy Candy,** an emporium for old-fashioned sweets since 1937. During the day, the mood is pretty chill, perfect for idling in any one of the nearby coffee shops. For a nutritious pick-me-up, **Teany** specializes in vegan vittles served in a café setting. Or, for a stack of what many agree is the city's best stack of pancakes, served all day, stroll over to the always packed **Clinton Street Baking Co**. Come evening, the street fills with meandering groups strolling to and from a number of popular dining spots.

South of Delancey Street, Grand Street is home to well-maintained residential complexes and shops that cater to a cadre of longtime residents. Carb-addicts should be afraid, very afraid; this street is home to **Kossar's Bialys**, several kosher bakeries, and **Doughnut Plant**, where the owner offers an updated take on his grandfather's doughnut recipe in flavors like Valrhona chocolate. For that quintessential deli accent at home, head to **Pickle Guys** on the corner of Essex Street, stocked with barrel upon barrel of ...you guessed it, pickles.

# Allen & Delancey

B2 Contemporary XX

115 Allen St. (at Delancey St.)

**Subway:** Delancey St — Dinner nightly
**Phone:** 212-253-5400
**Web:** www.allenanddelancey.net
**Prices:** $$$

Tucked along a graffiti-strewn stretch of the Lower East Side, there's not a lot to guide you into this sexy little lair—just follow anyone who looks cooler than you and you're probably headed in the right direction. With its bordello-style drapes, curving chocolate leather booths, and flickering candles, the interior is pretty enough to eat.

A recent chef change adds another name to the roster of talent that has blown through these kitchen doors; but hopefully a delicious, seasonal lineup will continue on in creations that have included a sliver of red snapper, paired with cinnamon-braised treviso; or a thick, juicy Colorado lamb chop, served with succulent braised neck meat and tender slices of black truffle-laced Yukon gold fingerling potatoes.

# Ápizz

B1 Italian X

217 Eldridge St. (bet. Rivington & Stanton Sts.)

**Subway:** Lower East Side - 2 Av — Dinner nightly
**Phone:** 212-253-9199
**Web:** www.apizz.com
**Prices:** $$$

In a neighborhood trying to reconcile its past life (think housing projects and homeless shelters) with its glitzy new one (think celebrity sightings and boutique hotels), Apizz is gloriously above the fray. Why? Because its simple, windowless Lower East Side façade hides the kind of cozy, impossibly quaint New York staple you wish there were more of—with warm, fuzzy lighting, good background music, and a young, sexy crowd.

Okay, there is one diva—the fantastic brick-oven that dominates the room (their motto is "one room, one oven"), but it's earned its girth. Try the plump shrimp, roasted in a casuela, and served in a lemony bath of chorizo, toasted breadcrumbs, and herbs; or a warm risotto, humming with mushrooms and freshly shaved Parmesan.

# Bacaro

Italian

A3

136 Division St. (bet. Ludlow & Orchard Sts.)

**Subway:** East Broadway — Dinner Tue – Sun
**Phone:** 212-941-5060
**Web:** www.bacaronyc.com
**Prices:** $$

From Peasant owners Frank de Carlo and his wife Dulcinea Benson, Bacaro takes its name and inspiration from the pub-like wine bars popular throughout Venice. A warm and inviting glow sets Bacaro apart from its edgier surroundings, and features a sexy subterranean dining room. The setting, which once housed a gambling parlor, evokes an ancient cellar with candlelit nooks, weathered plaster walls, salvaged ceiling beams, and brick archways. The marble-topped bar is lit overhead by a blown glass chandelier, making it a lovely spot to enjoy a *crostini di giorno,* or explore the all-Italian wine list.

The menu highlights products of the Veneto region in items like marinated sardines, *baccala mantecato,* and lasagna Treviso with smoked mozzarella and radicchio.

# The Clerkenwell

Gastropub

C2

49 Clinton St. (bet. Rivington & Stanton Sts. )

**Subway:** Delancey St — Lunch Sat – Sun
**Phone:** 212-614-3234 — Dinner Tue – Sun
**Web:** www.clerkenwellnyc.com
**Prices:** $$

The Clerkenwell brings the pub-inspired world of beef pie and mushy peas to Clinton Street's already diverse diningscape. Emanating a warm and comfortable vibe to complement its cuisine, the new pint-sized space features button-tufted banquettes, a visible kitchen in back that provides diners with a bit of a show, and a comfortable, graciously-tended bar. A wine list is offered but a crisp, cold lager on tap is a much more appropriate way to wash down the contemporary pub grub. Offerings include the likes of a pea and leek tart with poached egg; slow-roasted pork belly with parsnip purée; or plump sausages cradled in Yorkshire pudding and topped with red onion marmalade.

The scattering of tables set out front make a great spot to people watch.

# Congee Village

Chinese

B2

100 Allen St. (at Delancey St.)

**Subway:** Delancey St — Lunch & dinner daily
**Phone:** 212-941-1818
**Web:** www.sunsungroup.com/congeevillage
**Prices:**

Porridge for dinner may not sound tempting, but with more than 25 varieties of *congee*, this attractive place is sure to win over even the most wary. This soothing specialty, popular throughout China, is served bubbling hot in an earthenware pot, ready to be seasoned with an assortment of tableside condiments. Besides the namesake signature, you can sample hard-to-find dishes like the sautéed short rib with black-pepper sauce on a sizzling hot plate; cold jellyfish; and rice baked with meat and vegetables in a bamboo vessel.

Located on the fringe of Chinatown, the multilevel space covered in bamboo and stone has a warm ambience. Large tables, a buzzing bar area, and a host of private rooms fill the space with all the revelry of a town square.

# Falai

Italian

C2

68 Clinton St. (bet. Rivington & Stanton Sts.)

**Subway:** Lower East Side - 2 Av — Dinner nightly
**Phone:** 212-253-1960
**Web:** www.falainyc.com
**Prices:** $$

With its concentration of good restaurants, Clinton Street is already a destination for foodies. Falai and its bakery just makes it more so. This sliver of a spot, with its hip lounge ambience, has an airy feel, even though the only window is at the front. During warmer months, diners clamor for a table in the garden out back.

The Italian staff is welcoming and genuinely enthusiastic about the food—and for good reason. Trained as a pastry chef, Ioacopo Falai peppers his menu with sweet notes (cocoa, dates, raisins, apricots) that accent and enhance each dish. It may be a challenge to select between the many *dolci* on a full stomach, but it's worth saving room for the likes of *millefoglie,* or an unexpected savory celery cake with milk gelato.

# 'inoteca

Italian

B2

98 Rivington St. (at Ludlow St.)

**Subway:** Delancey St
**Phone:** 212-614-0473
**Web:** www.inotecanyc.com
**Prices:** ⊜

Lunch & dinner daily

This charmingly rustic wine bar adorned with knobby wood furnishings and wrap-around sidewalk seating has come to be a foodie favorite, and perhaps the definitive dining destination of the Lower East Side. Open all day long, 'inoteca continuously tempts with a menu of lovingly simple yet sophisticated Italian fare in an ambience that beckons guests to stop by anytime.

The offerings may include a quick lunchtime salad of grilled mushrooms with watercress and *Piave vecchio*; an after work respite in a glass of chilled lambrusco and a few slices of *coppa*; or a dinnertime sampling of panini and small plates. The *porchetta*-stuffed *ciabatta* garnished with freshly grated horseradish or polenta with charred ramps and poached egg are all worthy favorites.

# Kampuchea

Asian

B2

78 Rivington St. (at Allen St.)

**Subway:** Lower East Side - 2 Av
**Phone:** 212-529-3901
**Web:** www.kampucheanyc.com
**Prices:** $$

Lunch Fri – Sun
Dinner Tue – Sun

Chef/owner Ratha Chau's tribute to Cambodian street food casts a welcoming glow inside and out. The Allen Street façade is adorned with a giant rooster created by graffiti artist Antonio "Chico" Garcia; while the dining room is beautifully finished with exposed brick walls, pressed tin ceiling, dark wood communal tables, and warm touches of color.

Prepared by a small team dressed in crisp whites, Kampuchea's concise menu emerges from the open kitchen, anchored by a variety of noodle soups (*katiev*) and toasted baguette sandwiches (*num pang*) filled with the likes of house-made pâté, coconut shrimp, or glazed pork. The selection of food samplings, including the omelet-like savory crêpe wrapped in lettuce leaves, makes for an enjoyable starting point.

# Katz's

**B1** Deli

## 205 E. Houston St. (at Ludlow St.)

**Subway:** Lower East Side - 2 Av — Lunch & dinner daily
**Phone:** 212-254-2246
**Web:** www.katzdeli.com
**Prices:** $$

Established in 1888, Katz's is as much a New York institution as the Statue of Liberty. One of the few original Eastern European establishments remaining in the Lower East Side, Katz's attracts out-of-towners, residents, and celebrities alike. In the never-ending debate over who serves the best pastrami in the city, Katz's often tops the list.

For an authentic experience, queue up in front of the salty countermen, collect your meal, and head to a table. What to order? Matzo ball soup and a pastrami sandwich on rye, 'natch, and not toasted, please, with a side of fries.

Just be sure not to lose the ticket you get upon entering. It's your ticket out. If you don't have it, they make such a fuss that you'll want to crawl under a table and hide.

# Kuma Inn

**B2** Asian

## 113 Ludlow St. (bet. Delancey & Rivington Sts.)

**Subway:** Delancey St — Dinner nightly
**Phone:** 212-353-8866
**Web:** www.kumainn.com
**Prices:** $$

Pan-Asian tapas are the theme at this second floor dining room not much bigger than some of the chic boutiques found in this evolving neighborhood. A veteran of Daniel and Jean Georges, New York City born Chef/owner King Phojanakong offers well prepared, flavor-packed fare that reflects the multicultural influences of his Thai-Filipino background. The menu is best suited for grazing so bring reinforcements to ensure you hit all the chef's specialties that include sautéed Chinese sausage with Thai chili-lime sauce; sake-braised beef with Asian root vegetables; and *arroz Valenciana* with chicken, seafood, and sausage.

Genteel service and a background soundtrack of the chef's favorite tracks add to the ambience of the minimally decorated room.

# Macondo

**Latin American**

B1

157 E. Houston St. (bet. Allen & Eldridge Sts.)

**Subway:** Lower East Side - 2 Av
**Phone:** 212-473-9900
**Web:** www.macondonyc.com
**Prices:** $$

Lunch Sat – Sun
Dinner nightly

The vibe at this fun new spot from the owners of Rayuela matches that of its high-traffic location. Weather permitting, the front bar opens onto the street and is abuzz with thirty-somethings sipping *mojitos* sweetened with pure sugarcane juice. Inside, the long, narrow space is accented by shelves of Latin provisions, an open kitchen, rows of communal tables, and low, lounge-like booths towards the back.

Crowds come here to linger over the array of Latin-flavored small plates. Perfect for a group, the menu is divided into a large selection of snacks designed for sharing, such as ceviche, arepas, and empanadas. Their toasty, warm *bocadillos* are popular—the pork, ham, Manchego, and pickle stuffed Cubano is an especially tasty treat.

# Rayuela

**Latin American**

B2

165 Allen St. (bet. Rivington & Stanton Sts.)

**Subway:** Lower East Side - 2 Av
**Phone:** 212-253-8840
**Web:** www.rayuelanyc.com
**Prices:** $$

Dinner Tue – Sun

This inspired "freestyle Latin" cuisine expresses an uninhibited journey through South America and beyond. Cuban-style pork; sugarcane-marinated duck with foie gras topped arepa; and paella infused with coconut milk, lemongrass, and ginger are stops along the way. A fine prelude to your meal is a selection from the lengthy ceviche list; each combines quality seafood and bracing flavors. The cocktail menu is comprised of quenching libations, like the passion-kumquat *mojito* or classic pisco sour.

A slate-tiled bar, exposed brick walls, and iron grating filled with river rock outfit the lofty interior. These hard surfaces are softened by warm candlelight, gauzy fabric panels, hip crowd, and a majestic olive tree that stretches up through the mezzanine.

# Sachiko's On Clinton

C2 — Japanese

25 Clinton St. (bet. Houston & Stanton Sts.)

**Subway:** Delancey St — Dinner Tue – Sun
**Phone:** 212-253-2900
**Web:** www.sachikosonclinton.com
**Prices:** $$

Named after owner, Sachiko Kanami, this comfortable spot draws a loyal clientele who clamor for the range of creative fare and seasonal specials. The attractive dining room has exposed brick accents, orange walls, and is supplemented by a charming garden. In addition to the rich, tender, and consistently fresh raw offerings neatly arranged at the intimate sushi counter, the kitchen team also displays skill in their cooked items like crab cream croquettes and foie gras topped sesame tofu.

House specialty *kushiage* feature morsels of beef, chicken, or vegetables threaded on bamboo sticks, breaded in homemade *panko*, and deep fried. The cocktail menu boasts a Japanese focus with sake making its way into cosmopolitans, margaritas, and *mojitos*.

# Schiller's Liquor Bar

B2 — European

131 Rivington St. (at Norfolk St.)

**Subway:** Delancey St — Lunch & dinner daily
**Phone:** 212-260-4555
**Web:** www.schillersny.com
**Prices:** $$

A Keith McNally restaurant is a lot like the popular girl in high school. She's never the prettiest, smartest, or funniest, but she has just the right combination to pop in a crowd. Schiller's Liquor Bar, like McNally's wildly successful Balthazar and Pastis, touts the same magical mix—though its components are breezy retro-bistro good looks, solid, if not wildly inventive brassiere grub (don't miss the frites); and a prime location straddling a sunny corner of the Lower East Side.

As to how best to describe the atmosphere that draws locals, day trippers, and low-key celebrities alike, we direct you to the cheeky house wine list, categorized into *cheap, decent,* or *good.* A terrific cocktail list rounds out the drink list, including a spot-on Pimm's Cup.

# Sorella

**Italian**

B2

95 Allen St. (bet. Broome & Delancey Sts.)

**Subway:** Delancey St
**Phone:** 212-274-9595
**Web:** www.sorellanyc.com
**Prices:** $$

Lunch Sun
Dinner Tue – Sun

Easily identified by its bulky façade dotted with peepholes, step inside Sorella for a leisurely yet serious offering of small plates.

Seating is available at counters in the narrow, white-washed brick dining area, or at tables in a glass-enclosed back room. The Northern Italian menu is broken down to offer a selection of cheeses, meats, and *qualcosina*, which translates as "a little something." Plates such as marinated anchovies with lemon butter atop their richly flavored flatbread, and a subtly spiced meatball slider with fontina and caramelized onions are both delicious and impressive.

Complement a meal here with a tempting selection from their expansive list of wines by the glass; Sorella's features twenty-five choices, each priced under $15.

# Spitzer's Corner

**Gastropub**

B2

101 Rivington St. (at Ludlow St.)

**Subway:** Delancey St
**Phone:** 212-228-0027
**Web:** www.spitzerscorner.com
**Prices:** ⊖

Lunch & dinner daily

The intentionally grungy gastropub motif gets a slick and modern makeover at the Lower East Side's Spitzer's Corner, where a trendy young crowd piles in despite the no-reservations policy—happy to chill at the bar or settle into a long, sleek waiting bench as long as they can nurse one of the 40 available draft selections, or a glass of wine from the small, but studied, by-the-glass list.

The menu offers a host of delicious salads and sandwiches, but those looking for a proper meal can up the ante with a bowl of perfectly-steamed whitewater mussels, dancing in a white wine broth studded with *piquillo* peppers, chorizo, and parsley; or slow-cooked duck confit salad in pomegranate vinaigrette, paired with a foie gras butter-smeared baguette.

# The Stanton Social

B2 — **Fusion** XX

99 Stanton St. (bet. Ludlow & Orchard Sts.)

**Subway:** Lower East Side - 2 Av
**Phone:** 212-995-0099
**Web:** www.thestantonsocial.com
**Prices:** $$

Lunch Sat – Sun
Dinner nightly

The Stanton Social has a finely tailored décor that pays homage to the haberdashers and seamstress shops that once dotted this trendy neighborhood. Vintage hand mirrors, woven leather straps, and wine shelves laid out in a herringbone pattern outfit the low-lit, dark-wood furnished space.

Choosing from the generous list of ambitious multi-cultural bites executed by Chef/owner Chris Santos is difficult—bring friends to ensure a wholehearted run of the menu. The signature sliders and French onion soup dumplings certainly deserve consideration. This entertaining fare is a perfect pairing with one (or two) of the bar's finely crafted cocktails, or a selection from the well-chosen wine list. The second floor lounge offers the same menu.

Park your car without a problem when you see for valet parking.

# wd~50 ✿

Contemporary XX

C2

50 Clinton St. (bet. Rivington & Stanton Sts.)

**Subway:** Delancey St — Dinner Wed – Sun
**Phone:** 212-477-2900
**Web:** www.wd-50.com
**Prices:** $$$

Robert Polidori

Like a mad scientist who never tires of his own inventions, the culinary wizard of Clinton Street flips yet another year on his wildly successful Lower East Side restaurant, wd~50, and still doesn't miss a beat.

Chef Wylie Dufresne made a name for himself retooling New York's vision of molecular gastronomy with his strange and wonderful concoctions, spinning out dishes that challenge our preconceptions of texture, association, and taste. Witness a warm tangle of noodles cut from fresh shrimp and zucchini, topped with pickled mushroom caps and served over an intense dollop of chamomile yogurt; or tender lamb shoulder adorned with brown bread crumbles, paired with hearts of romaine and pine nuts cooked in the style of baked beans, studded with minced bacon. An exciting dessert menu includes a three- or five-course sweet tasting for an appropriately dramatic finale.

The small, but intense, wine list is curated by Dufresne's father, and offers a clever lineup of bottles from small, intriguing producers. Ask the sommelier and you'll get a story to accompany many of them—all the more reason to linger in the dining room, a simple, clean-lined space broken up by splashes of color.

# Midtown East & Murray Hill

Started by the Vanderbilts in the 19th century, then saved from the wrecking ball with the help of Jacqueline Kennedy Onassis in the 20th century, Grand Central Terminal has somehow become a 21st century foodie haven.

## Grand Central Terminal

A perfect day at the world's largest train station begins with a coffee amid the work-bound masses from either **Oren's** or **Joe's** (choose your camp, because competition between the two is fierce). Lunch options range from the multi-ethnic food court offerings (**Café Spice** for Indian, **Mendy's** for kosher, **Zocalo** for Mexican), to the prized concourse restaurants situated beneath the celestial ceiling murals. Nonetheless, one of Manhattan's most beloved icons, the **Oyster Bar**, has been tucked into the cavernous lower level since 1913. Be sure to first visit the "whispering gallery" located near its entrance, where low, ceramic arches allow whispers to sound like shouts.

Come happy hour, Grand Central continues to inspire with Campbell Apartment—for those who meet the dress code. This 1920s office of railroad mogul John W. Campbell was restored and re-opened as one of the area's swankier stops for a famously dry martini. Those seeking a quiet night of home cooking can simply walk across the concourse to visit the market, for a stunning array of gourmet treats. Fishmongers, produce stands, butchers, bakeries, and possibly the best spices in the city are all found here.

## Local Spots

Grand Central is a perfect microcosm of its eastern Midtown home, because stretching through this neighborhood is the same diversity of shopping and dining. Residents of Beekman and Sutton boast their very own top fishmonger (**Piscayne**), cheese shop (**Ideal Cheese**), butcher (**L. Simchik**), bagel and lox shop (**Tal**), and to complete any dinner party, florist (**Zeze**). One of the area's better-kept secrets is **Dessert Delivery**, specializing in delivering expertly baked treats. Luckily, it is free from the ongoing cupcake war between **Buttercup** and **Bruce's**, with a new **Crumbs** outpost threatening to join the battle. Also find some of the best chocolate in town, from **Richart** to **Teuscher** and **Pierre Marolini**. While **Dag Hammarskjold Greenmarket** may by dwarfed by Union Square, it has just the right amount of everything to satisfy its neighbors.

## Japantown

Within these distinctly commuter, residential, and internationally focused Midtown nooks, is a very sophisticated

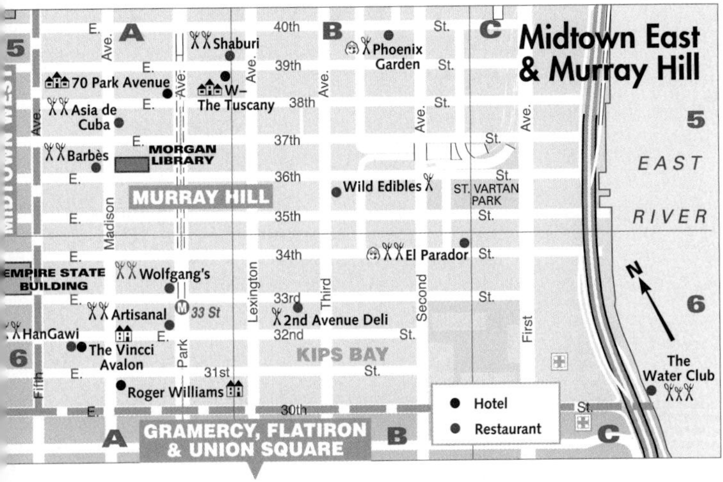


Japantown, with casual izakayas and secreted-away hostess clubs lining the area east of Lexington. For a light lunch or snack, sample *onigiri* at **Oms/b**, or try the modern takeout yakitori, **Kushi-Q**. True Japanophiles should visit the **Japanese Culinary Center** filled with shiny knives and imported delicacies.

## United Nations

Along the neighborhood's eastern border is the United Nations. In the spirit of this landmark, the Delegates Dining Room at the UN sponsors food festivals that spotlight a different cuisine each month. Just remember to make a reservation for this buffet lunch and arrive early, allowing extra time to clear security.

## Murray Hill

Younger and quieter than its northern neighbor, Murray Hill has its own distinct restaurant vibe. Here, faster and casual finds thrive, populated by hungry twenty-somethings seeking a slice of pizza or hearty cheesesteak. Afterwards, they move on to their favored Third Avenue watering holes to hoot and holler with college buddies over Bud Lights while catching the snowboarding championships. This is the Murray Hill of recent college grads spilling out onto sidewalks of **Bar 515** or perhaps **Third and Long**. However, this is only one Murray Hill.

The other Murray Hill rises with the sun over pristine brownstones and apartment towers, awakening young families who gather amid blooming flowers at St. Vartan Park or chat with neighbors over omelets at **Sarge's Deli**. These are the (slightly) senior locals of Murray Hill—they love it here and will remain faithful residents until well-after the frat party has ended.

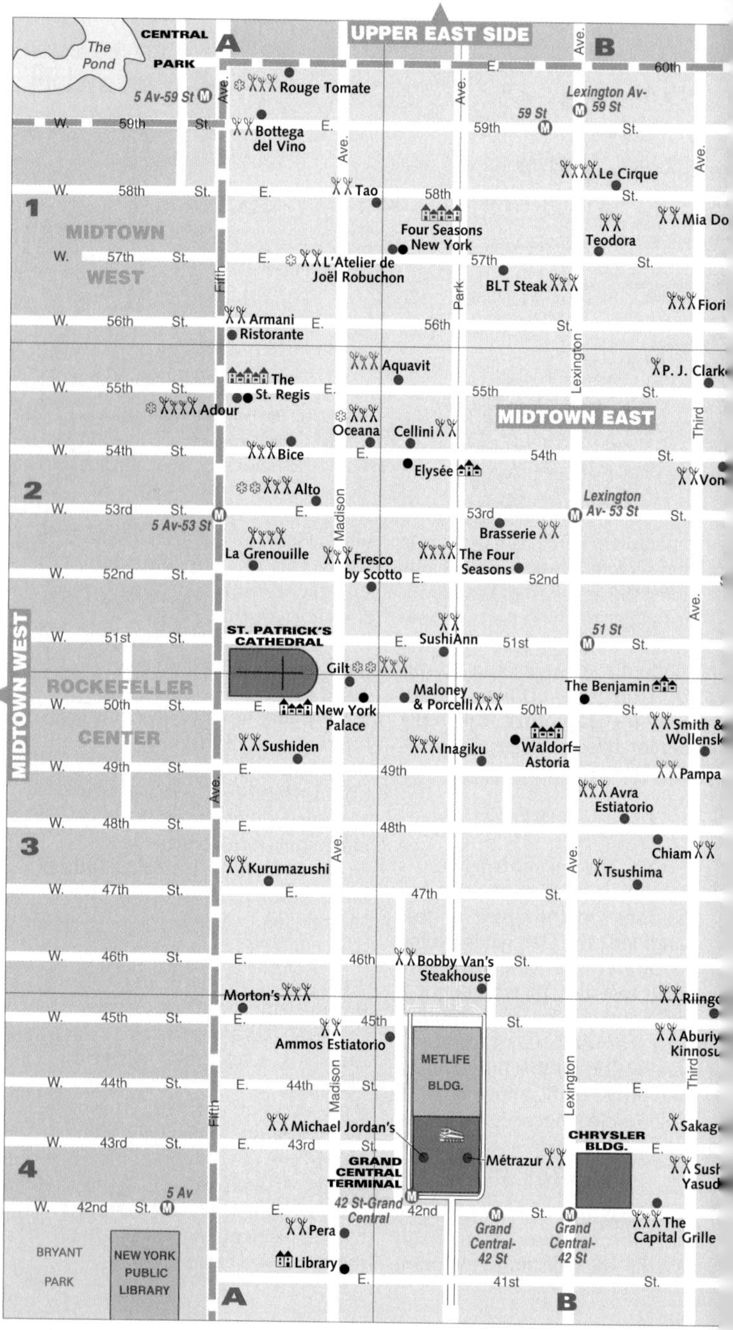
CENTRAL PARK
The Pond
UPPER EAST SIDE
A
B
1
2
3
4
MIDTOWN WEST
MIDTOWN EAST
ROCKEFELLER CENTER
Fifth Ave.
Madison Ave.
Park Ave.
Lexington Ave.
Third Ave.
E. 60th
W. 59th St.
E. 59th St.
W. 58th St.
E. 58th St.
W. 57th St.
E. 57th St.
W. 56th St.
E. 56th St.
W. 55th St.
E. 55th St.
W. 54th St.
E. 54th St.
W. 53rd St.
E. 53rd St.
W. 52nd St.
E. 52nd
W. 51st St.
E. 51st St.
W. 50th St.
E. 50th St.
W. 49th St.
E. 49th
W. 48th St.
E. 48th
W. 47th St.
E. 47th St.
W. 46th St.
E. 46th St.
W. 45th St.
E. 45th St.
W. 44th St.
E. 44th St.
W. 43rd St.
E. 43rd St.
W. 42nd St.
42nd St.
E. 41st St.
5 Av-59 St
Lexington Av-59 St
59 St
5 Av-53 St
Lexington Av-53 St
51 St
5 Av
42 St-Grand Central
Grand Central-42 St
Grand Central-42 St
Rouge Tomate
Bottega del Vino
Tao
Le Cirque
Four Seasons New York
Teodora
Mia Do
L'Atelier de Joël Robuchon
BLT Steak
Fiori
Armani Ristorante
Aquavit
P. J. Clark
The St. Regis
Adour
Oceana
Cellini
Bice
Elysée
Von
Alto
Brasserie
La Grenouille
Fresco by Scotto
The Four Seasons
SushiAnn
ST. PATRICK'S CATHEDRAL
Gilt
The Benjamin
Maloney & Porcelli
New York Palace
Smith & Wollensk
Sushiden
Inagiku
Waldorf=Astoria
Pampa
Avra Estiatorio
Chiam
Kurumazushi
Tsushima
Bobby Van's Steakhouse
Morton's
Riingo
Ammos Estiatorio
Aburiya Kinnosu
METLIFE BLDG.
Michael Jordan's
Sakag
CHRYSLER BLDG.
Métrazur
Sush Yasud
GRAND CENTRAL TERMINAL
The Capital Grille
Pera
Library
BRYANT PARK
NEW YORK PUBLIC LIBRARY

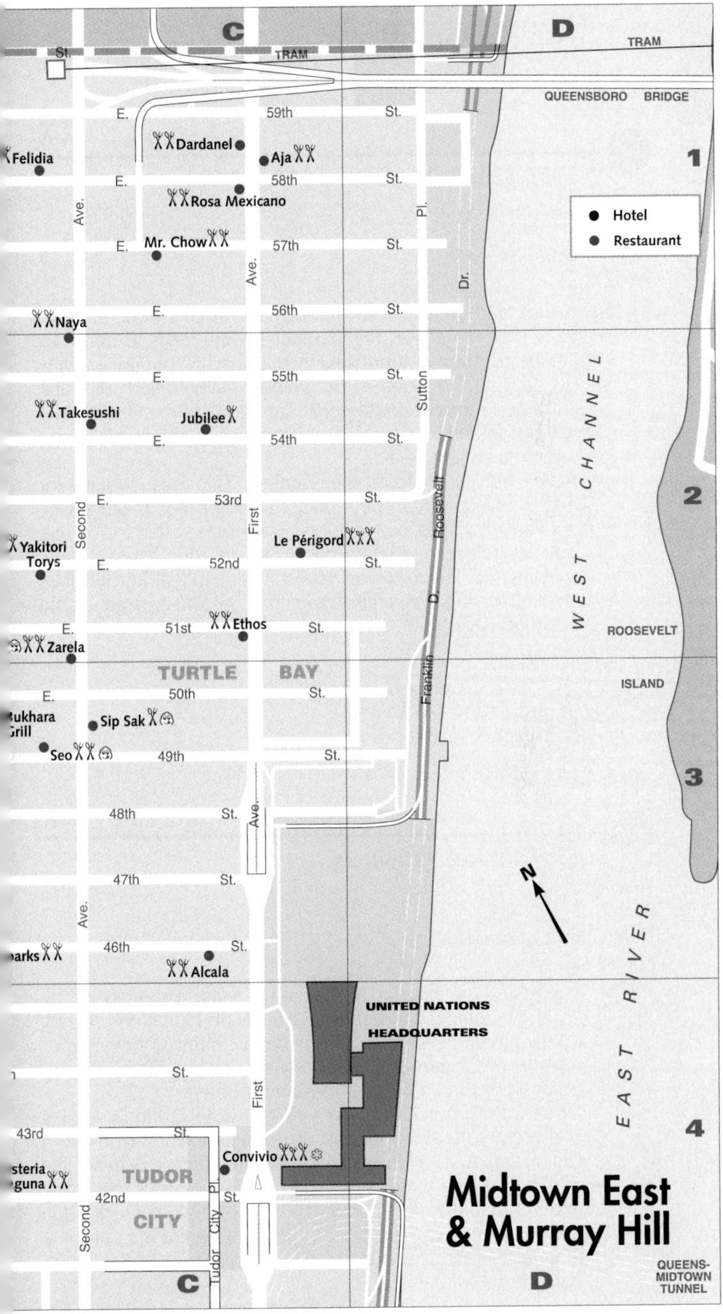
Midtown East & Murray Hill
Hotel
Restaurant
C
D
1
2
3
4
TRAM
QUEENSBORO BRIDGE
E. 59th St.
E. 58th St.
E. 57th St.
E. 56th St.
E. 55th St.
E. 54th St.
E. 53rd St.
E. 52nd St.
E. 51st St.
E. 50th St.
49th St.
48th St.
47th St.
46th St.
43rd St.
42nd St.
Second Ave.
First Ave.
Sutton Pl.
Tudor City Pl.
Franklin D. Roosevelt Dr.
Felidia
Dardanel
Aja
Rosa Mexicano
Mr. Chow
Naya
Takesushi
Jubilee
Yakitori Torys
Le Périgord
Ethos
Zarela
TURTLE BAY
Sip Sak
Seo
Alcala
Convivio
UNITED NATIONS HEADQUARTERS
TUDOR CITY
WEST CHANNEL
ROOSEVELT ISLAND
EAST RIVER
N
QUEENS-MIDTOWN TUNNEL

# Aburiya Kinnosuke

B4 — Japanese XX

213 E. 45th St. (bet. Second & Third Aves.)

**Subway:** Grand Central - 42 St — Lunch Mon – Fri
**Phone:** 212-867-5454 — Dinner nightly
**Web:** www.torysnyc.com
**Prices:** $$

A dark and narrow hallway does not usually bode well for great food—and yet, this particular route leads to delicious Japanese. Aburiya Kinnosuke has a bit of a split personality. By day, it's an upscale bento box haven filled with the chirping sounds of midtowners. Come nighttime, it turns into a lively, intimate *izakaya* to sip Japanese cocktails while you sample the night away.

Action freaks should hit the counter, while those looking for peace and quiet can peel off into one of the small, private nooks with sliding paper doors. The silken sashimi is divine, but don't leave without trying one of the fantastic daily specials or the popular *tsukune*—inexplicably delicious chicken meatloaves, grilled over charcoal and dunked in cold poached eggs.

# Aja

C1 — Asian XX

1068 First Ave. (at 58th St.)

**Subway:** 59 St — Dinner nightly
**Phone:** 212-888-8008
**Web:** www.ajaasiancuisine.com
**Prices:** $$

The plain-Jane exterior of this fusion Asian restaurant at the lip of the Queensborough Bridge (a second location recently opened in Greenwich Village) belies a clubby, trendy interior replete with a giant Buddha, koi pond, and fountain—a turn-on for some, but a bit over-the-top for others.

Either way, Aja packs them in with surprisingly friendly service and a crowd-pleasing lineup of Americanized classics from China, Japan, Thailand, India, and Singapore that read like an Asian dream team. And while the authenticity may have gotten lost in the mix, great ingredients and careful technique make up for it. If there's a wait for a table, guests can bide their time in the tiny lounge which houses a nice selection of Asian beers and wines.

# Adour ✿

Contemporary XXXX

A2

2 E. 55th St. (at Fifth Ave.)

**Subway:** 5 Av - 53 St

Dinner nightly

**Phone:** 212-710-2277

**Web:** www.adour-stregis.com

**Prices:** $$$$

© Bruce Buck

Millions of dollars were poured into creating this Alain Ducasse stunner, and every penny shows. Tucked behind a thick set of beautiful wood doors in the St. Regis New York—a bastion of old-school luxury if there ever was one—the lush interior design features (among other details) exquisite glass moldings, plush seating, and sparkling glass wine cases.

Which leads one to wonder how the food stacks up under all that splendid pomp? Quite nicely, thank you very much—with a silky foie gras terrine amuse-bouche kicking off a most decadent dinner (especially when paired with a bottle off the house's impressive wine list) that might include creamy, melt-in-your-mouth ricotta gnocchi studded with sautéed lettuce, wild mushrooms, and crispy prosciutto; or a tender filet of milk-fed veal, served rosy-pink and paired with glazed baby carrots and a beggar's purse of vibrant green lettuce, finely-chopped vegetables, and sweetbreads.

Between the outstanding décor and the food, is it too much to ask for polished service as well? Some might argue that Adour's is better than before—with a warm, attentive host staff and knowledgeable, professional sommeliers eager to answer questions.

# Alcala

C3 **Spanish** XX

342 E. 46th St. (bet. First & Second Aves.)

**Subway:** Grand Central - 42 St
**Phone:** 212-370-1866
**Web:** www.alcalarestaurant.com
**Prices:** $$$

Lunch Mon – Fri
Dinner nightly

You won't find a lot of the garlic-heavy Spanish staples that Americans have come to know so well at this charming little neighborhood restaurant, located across the street from the United Nations headquarters. Instead, you'll find the rustic, often simple, cuisine found throughout Northern Spain and the Basque region, with a kitchen that is not afraid to bring the pork.

Businessmen, United Nations tourists, and Spanish ex-pats alike pile into Alcala for its cozy-as-home vibe, it's pretty, enclosed garden, and friendly, welcoming staff. Try the *espinacas*, a delicious baked casserole with spinach, pine nuts, raisins, onions, and sheep's milk cheese; or a creamy, decadent *arroz con leche*; and don't leave without sampling one of the mean house sangrias.

# Ammos Estiatorio

B4 **Greek** XX

52 Vanderbilt Ave. (at 45th St.)

**Subway:** Grand Central - 42 St
**Phone:** 212-922-9999
**Web:** www.ammosnewyork.com
**Prices:** $$$

Lunch Mon – Fri
Dinner Mon – Sat

♿ This airy and attractive *estiatorio* occupies a winning spot, directly across from Grand Central Terminal, and adds Greek flair to an area overrun with Italian restaurants and steakhouses. Ammos bustles at lunch, when local business types drop in to grab a quick salad or linger over grilled fish, priced by the pound. Given its location, the restaurant quiets down noticeably at dinnertime. Modern takes on traditional Greek dishes fill the appealing menu, which includes an assortment of appetizers from house-made spreads to *saganaki*.

The modern Mediterranean décor supports the restaurant's name ("sand" in Greek) with natural light, sun-washed colors, blown-glass fishing buoys, and canvas umbrellas.

# Alto ✿✿

Italian XXX

A2

11 E. 53rd St. (bet. Fifth & Madison Aves.)

**Subway:** 5 Av - 53 St
**Phone:** 212-308-1099
**Web:** www.altorestaurant.com
**Prices:** $$$$

Lunch Mon – Fri
Dinner Mon – Sat

Melissa Hom

A 2008 overhaul of this beautiful Upper East Side Italian left only a few remnants of its Austrian influence behind—the name, which pays homage to Alto Adige, a region on the Italian-Austrian border, and an authentic, graffitied chunk of the Berlin Wall placed near the restaurant's entrance.

Other than that, it's a whole new ballgame at Alto—from the décor, which offers a sort of elegant-but-hip business palette of muted browns dotted with lime green chairs, to Chef Michael White's deliciously straightforward Italian menu, bursting with fresh, seasonal ingredients.

The menu happily zigzags between pasta, meat, and seafood, and might include a small bowl of smooth ravioli, folded by hand around tender, braised beef and veal, then garnished with porcini mushrooms; a grilled slice of mackerel, served over silky cauliflower purée and a bed of caramelized onion, dotted with yellow raisins and drizzled with aged balsamic; or a sinfully good seafood risotto, cooked to creamy perfection, and studded with fresh mussels, scallops, and langoustine. Grape hounds won't want to miss the Italian wine list, which offers a healthy by-the-glass selection as well as an impressive display of vintages.

# Aquavit

B2 — Scandinavian XXX

65 E. 55th St. (bet. Madison & Park Aves.)

**Subway:** 5 Av - 53 St — Lunch & dinner daily
**Phone:** 212-307-7311
**Web:** www.aquavit.org
**Prices:** $$$

New York's most famous Swedish restaurant gets a slick new makeover with a gorgeous, if miniaturized, Scandinavian-styled dining room and a front-room café outfitted with clever Arne Jacobson egg swivel chairs.

Up front in the café, you can nosh on lighter, but equally delicious, fare washed down with the restaurant's namesake drink. Those looking for the full story can head back to the dining room to join the beautiful people (you'll want to don a jacket), where the polished staff walks guests through Marcus Samuelsson's elegant menu—a smoked salmon with tart goat cheese ice cream and sour port mustard may kick things off; while a quartet of sweet, delicate pancakes finishes things. Don't miss brunch, which offers a smorgasbord fit for a Swedish prince.

# Armani Ristorante

A1 — Italian XX

717 Fifth Ave. (at 56th St.)

**Subway:** 5 Av - 59 St — Lunch daily, Dinner Mon – Sat
**Phone:** 212-207-1902
**Web:** www.armani5thavenue.com
**Prices:** $$$

As chic, stylish, and dramatic as the legendary fashion designer himself, Giorgio Armani's eponymous new *ristorante*, perched high above 5th Avenue at the top of the Armani store, is a looker—with severe black floors and ceilings and futuristic-looking metal furniture.

The prix-fixe lunch menu is a hit with the Fifth Avenue crowd, and most afternoons find a gaggle of well-heeled ladies picking at bright green salads. After work, a selection of Italian wines draws a dinner crowd looking to tuck into dishes like a rich chard flan with creamy Mahon cheese fondue; herb-crusted Yellowfin tuna fanned over field greens, paired with a nettle sauce; or a creamy, luscious tiramisu, offered a delicious twist from a bright Sicilian orange compote.

# Artisanal

French XX

A6

2 Park Ave. (enter on 32nd St. bet. Madison &

**Subway:** 33 St
Lunch & dinner daily
**Phone:** 212-725-8585
**Web:** www.artisanalbistro.com
**Prices:** $$

Cheese is the focus of this Midtown brasserie, thanks to Chef/owner Terrance Brennan's passion for the stuff (Brennan also runs Picholine). From the house-blend fondue to the retail counter at the back of the restaurant where you can buy wonderful cheeses to take home, Artisanal plays up its strength.

There are other reasons to come here, though, starting with well-prepared French cuisine, such as bouillabaisse, *boudin blanc*, and hanger steak served, of course, with crispy frites. Then there's the prix-fixe lunch, a great bargain at $25 for three courses. And don't forget the thoughtfully chosen wine list; every selection is available by the bottle, the glass, or the taste. If you're not cheesed-out after your meal, try a cheese course instead of dessert.

# Asia de Cuba

Fusion XX

A5

237 Madison Ave. (bet. 37th & 38th Sts.)

**Subway:** Grand Central - 42 St
Lunch Mon – Fri
**Phone:** 212-726-7755
Dinner nightly
**Web:** www.chinagrillmgt.com
**Prices:** $$$

A trendy venue in the Morgans Hotel in residential Murray Hill, Asia de Cuba still packs in a chic crowd, despite the fact that it's no longer new. Designer Philippe Starck fitted the striking bi-level interior with gauzy drapes lining the soaring walls, a 25-foot-high hologram of a flowing waterfall, and a 50-foot-long alabaster communal table running the length of the downstairs room.

Generously sized dishes marry elements of Asian and Latin cuisines in signatures such as *tunapica* (tuna tartare picadillo style), calamari salad, and *ropa vieja* of duck. Don't overlook sides like *panko*-crusted crispy plantains, or Thai coconut sticky rice. Round up a few gorgeous friends who like to share, and order from the family-style menu.

# Avra Estiatorio

B3 **Greek** XXX

141 E. 48th St. (bet. Lexington & Third Aves.)

**Subway:** 51 St — Lunch & dinner daily
**Phone:** 212-759-8550
**Web:** www.avrany.com
**Prices:** $$$

Inviting, from its outdoor terrace to it cavernous dining room, Avra sparkles as a true gem in the heart of midtown. Limestone floors, arched doorways, and colorful crockery suggest a Greek tavern in this always lively space. Billowing fabric laced through the wood ceiling beams brings to mind sailing and the sea, and sets the tone for the seafood-centric menu.

Check out the day's fresh catch, laid out on ice in the front dining room. Fish are grilled whole over charcoal, then drizzled with olive oil and a squeeze of lemon, yieldling simple but delicious results. If you go this route—there are other selections on the menu as well—note that your choice of fish will be priced per pound, so keep this in mind if your eyes are bigger than your budget.

# Barbès

A5 **Mediterranean** XX

21 E. 36th St. (bet. Fifth & Madison Aves.)

**Subway:** 33 St — Lunch & dinner daily
**Phone:** 212-684-0215
**Web:** www.barbesrestaurantnyc.com
**Prices:** $$

Named for a North African neighborhood near Montmartre, this sultry French-Moroccan restaurant draws hustling city slickers in from the dreary gray streets of Midtown with its warm, rustic good looks. Duck past the elaborately carved wooden façade that marks the entrance and you'll find a handsome dining room bathed in burnt orange walls and exposed brick, with a lovely beamed ceiling overhead.

Guests keep sated with zesty, if simple fare, like a smoky, creamy eggplant purée served with toasted pita bread; and tender, charred lamb kebabs paired with a scoop of tangy yogurt sauce. And while the food surely hits the spot, the real draw at Barbès might be the service, which manages to be as warm and polished as the restaurant itself.

# Bice

Italian XXX

A2

7 E. 54th St. (bet. Fifth & Madison Aves.)

**Subway:** 5 Av - 53 St
**Phone:** 212-688-1999
**Web:** www.bicenewyork.com
**Prices:** $$$

Lunch & dinner daily

With over 40 restaurants worldwide, Bice has perfected its formula of preparing upscale Northern Italian cuisine in settings appropriate to each location. What began in Milan has become a success story in New York, with many years spent in its midtown home. Here, they draw a well-dressed crowd to the fashionable dining room, as well as the more casual bar and café.

The menu is wide with extensive choices for each course. Preparations are fairly good and carefully prepared, though not necessarily creative. For this classic cuisine, there is a loyal following of diners who come carrying expense accounts to manage the prices.

The pace of a meal here is relaxed yet efficient—a style long forgotten that is ideal for business or pleasure.

# BLT Steak

Steakhouse XXX

B1

106 E. 57th St. (bet. Lexington & Park Aves.)

**Subway:** 59 St
**Phone:** 212-752-7470
**Web:** www.bltrestaurants.com
**Prices:** $$$$

Lunch Mon – Fri
Dinner Mon – Sat

The en masse belt-tightening hasn't hit BLT Steak—French Chef Laurent Tourondel's vision of an American steakhouse—which still packs them shoulder-to-shoulder despite the crummy economy. Likely because it's easy to forget your troubles in this lively, elegant steakhouse, which not only dishes up beautifully-executed classic cuts alongside Kobe and Wagyu, but a heady dose of daily specials and fresh fish (Tourondel's wheelhouse) as well.

Adding to the abundant spirit are a bunch of delicious, unfussy sides, like towering stacks of crunchy onion rings; clever little complimentary extras like duck mousse; and enormous desserts, big enough to split. Watch for sticker shock on the wine list, though—a better deal can be found glass-by-glass.

# Bobby Van's Steakhouse

Steakhouse XX

B3

230 Park Ave. (at 46th St.)

**Subway:** Grand Central - 42 St
**Phone:** 212-867-5490
**Web:** www.bobbyvans.com
**Prices:** $$$$

Lunch Mon – Fri
Dinner nightly

This scene is so powerful that it intoxicates. New steakhouse concepts may come and go, but a regular flock of brokers and bankers rule this stylish roost, where pricey wines and towering shellfish platters bear witness to the day's important dealings.

Service comes with flourish and perhaps a gruff edge, but with the obvious care required by midtown movers and shakers. As the main attraction, meats are cooked exactly as ordered and carved tableside, with sides served family-style. After work, the bar gets boisterous as well-shaken martinis lift the mood. A separate menu of lighter fare is offered here, and addictive house-made potato chips adorn the bar.

Located in the landmark Helmsley Building, Bobby Van's has three other locations in Manhattan.

# Bottega del Vino

Italian XX

A1

7 E. 59th St. (bet. Fifth & Madison Aves.)

**Subway:** 5 Av - 59 St
**Phone:** 212-223-2724
**Web:** www.bottegadelvinonyc.com
**Prices:** $$$$

Lunch & dinner daily

Owner Severino Barzan picked a primo location just off Fifth Avenue for this charmingly rustic wine tavern. In the alluring sun-colored space, adorned with painted columns, carved dark-wood walls, cozy banquettes, and shelves of wine bottles, a stylish and loyal Euro-crowd gathers to sip wine and revel in authentic Northern Italian fare.

Pasta dishes and house specialties best display the kitchen's talent. Elegant and delicate, housemade ravioli filled with velvety gorgonzola dolce, paired with a nutty pistachio sauce is nothing short of amazing.

Serious contenders from the Veneto and Piemonte regions of Italy are highlights of the blockbuster wine list. Wines are served in hand-blown, lead-free glassware that was custom-made for the restaurant.

# Brasserie

B2 — Contemporary XX

100 E. 53rd St. (bet. Lexington & Park Aves.)

**Subway:** Lexington Av - 53 St — Lunch & dinner daily
**Phone:** 212-751-4840
**Web:** www.rapatina.com/brasserie
**Prices:** $$$

Brasserie creates a 21st-century vision of its French counterpart with retro-modern design and interpreted standards. This dovetails nicely with its location in the basement of the 1958 Seagram Building by Ludwig Mies van der Rohe. Cameras at the catwalk entry connect to a row of TV screens above the bar, so your arrival is on display to the dining room of people-watchers.

Aside from French classics reinvented à la mode, the menu pleases the largely corporate crowds with contemporary offerings like slow-smoked Berkshire pork loin or monkfish over cauliflower purée. Skip the mediocre pommes frites to save room for the decadent yet light and sugary chocolate beignets.

# Bukhara Grill

C3 — Indian XX

217 E. 49th St. (bet. Second & Third Aves.)

**Subway:** 51 St — Lunch & dinner daily
**Phone:** 212-888-2839
**Web:** www.bukharany.com
**Prices:** $$

Tucked into an eastern stretch of midtown called Turtle Bay, Bukhara Grill is a funny little gem. With its wood nymph motif (think waterfalls and tree trunk lounge chairs), sweet but slightly ditzy staff, and enormous wooden menus, a passerby might chalk the place up to a kitschy tourist trap. But what a shame, for then they'd be missing out on some rather delicious upscale Indian food.

The trick here is to stick to the kitchen's wheelhouse—in this case, Northern Indian, and anything cooked in the two tandoor ovens, which push out deliciously high volumes of baked breads and succulent lamb chops. Don't miss the *bhindi bukhara*, a spicy pile of thinly sliced okra, tossed with onions and fresh coriander, and fried to crunchy, addictive perfection.

# The Capital Grille

B4 **Steakhouse** XXX

155 E. 42nd St. (bet. Lexington & Third Aves.)

**Subway:** Grand Central - 42 St
**Phone:** 212-953-2000
**Web:** www.thecapitalgrille.com
**Prices:** **$$$$**

Lunch Mon – Fri
Dinner nightly

Two blocks east of Grand Central Terminal, clubby Capital Grille occupies the ground floor of the complex that includes the famous Chrysler Building. The large space is opulent and elegant, a harmony of comfortable black and red leather chairs, banquettes, mahogany paneling, and gold-framed paintings.

Dry-aged steaks and juicy chops are hand-cut and perfectly grilled to your requested temperature. Given its location, this place stays busy, so book ahead. Also consider that the full menu is also available at the long bar. Professional staff ensures that any wait will be made comfortable.

Of course, a meal here sets guests back more than a few bucks, but the expense-account crowds are too busy brokering deals over lunch and dinner to mind.

# Cellini

B2 **Italian** XX

65 E. 54th St. (bet. Madison & Park Aves.)

**Subway:** Lexington Av - 53 St
**Phone:** 212-751-1555
**Web:** www.cellinirestaurant.com
**Prices:** **$$$**

Lunch Mon – Fri
Dinner nightly

With its pleasant informality, lively atmosphere, fine selection of deliciously simple Italian classics, and efficient service, Cellini appeals to all. Even old school Italian-American standards, such as clams casino, are served with the care and culinary attention often reserved for fancier food. Good flavors and technique are demonstrated in pasta offerings, like spaghetti *frutti di mare*, tossed in olive oil, finished with white wine, tomato, and brimming with shrimp, clams, mussels, and scallops.

A concise, well-chosen wine list featuring Italian labels plus crowd-pleasers from around the world, and a polite waitstaff well-versed in the menu, justify Cellini's popularity. Best to reserve a table in advance, although walk-ins are accomodated.

# Chiam

Chinese XX

B3

160 E. 48th St. (bet. Lexington & Third Aves.)

**Subway:** 51 St — Lunch Sun – Fri
**Phone:** 212-371-2323 — Dinner nightly
**Web:** N/A
**Prices:** $$

Don't confuse Chiam with the neighboring noodle joints. Chiam may not have the neighborhood authenticity of Chinatown, or the star appeal of Mr. Chow, but it continues to win diners over with its serious Chinese cuisine and top-notch service. Think of this place, with its elegant dining room, quality wine list, and well-heeled clientele, as a choice for a special-occasion feast or for an expense-account business dinner.

Presenting Cantonese preparations with flair, the kitchen staff uses excellent products and a refined technique that yields consistently good and well-balanced fare. Dishes, such as the rich Grand Marnier prawns, are intended to be shared; order some steamed or sautéed vegetables to round out the mix.

# Dardanel

Turkish XX

C1

1071 First Ave. (bet. 58th & 59th Sts.)

**Subway:** 59 St — Lunch & dinner daily
**Phone:** 212-888-0809
**Web:** www.dardanelnyc.com
**Prices:** $$

A recent arrival, Dardanel's bright ocean-themed exterior stands out against the rather bleak block on which it sits. Inside, low lighting, mellow tunes, exposed brick, and colorful walls create a lovely atmosphere where a warm and welcoming vibe complement the Mediterranean and Turkish fare.

The house *manti* are reason alone for a visit; these divine micro-versions of the Turkish dumplings are tenderly soaked in a yogurt-garlic sauce. Otherwise, house specialties and starters are the way to go—try the flavorful zucchini pancakes, or shrimp casserole (brick-oven baked with tomatoes, peppers, and mushrooms in a creamy tomato sauce, topped with *kasserie* cheese).

The place hums with a mix of neighborhood locals—a cozy spot for a casual dinner or date.

# Convivio ✿

Italian XXX

C4

45 Tudor City Pl. (bet. 42nd & 43rd Sts.)

**Subway:** Grand Central - 42 St — Lunch Mon – Fri
**Phone:** 212-599-5045 — Dinner nightly
**Web:** www.convivionyc.com
**Prices:** $$$

Melissa Hom

This delicious new ode to Southern Italian food arrives compliments of partners Michael White and Chris Cannon, who dropped the curtain on L'Impero in the summer of 2008 to bestow this gorgeous surprise on Tudor City, a lovely little residential nook overlooking the United Nations that's flown under the radar about as long as it can.

It was a smart gamble. Convivio is unendingly elegant, with a relaxed, sophisticated lounge and a bright mod dining room bathed in oodles of natural light and decked out in luxurious silk drapes, vivid orange banquettes, and slick lacquered walls.

Backed by an impressive Italian wine list, Convivio's regional-specific menu is a gorgeous companion piece to White's menu at nearby Alto—with a recession-proof $59 four-course prix-fixe that might include three perfectly golden *arancini*, filled with creamy, saffron-scented risotto and aged white cheese; fresh ravioli stuffed with a silky blend of potato and salt cod purée, and laced with a bright green sauce of puréed broccoli rabe and sweet sausage; or a tender block of short ribs, soaked in bright red pomodoro and topped with creamy buffalo mozzarella, toasted bread crumbs, and tender black olives.

# El Parador

Mexican XX

B6

325 E. 34th St. (bet. First & Second Aves.)

**Subway:** 33 St — Lunch & dinner daily
**Phone:** 212-679-6812
**Web:** www.elparadorcafe.com
**Prices:** $$

Everything about El Parador is old-fashioned, but in the best possible way. Don't let the windowless façade or the location (near the entrance to the Midtown Tunnel) turn you away; inside, the upbeat Mexican ambience attracts a grown-up crowd who enjoy animated conversation and killer margaritas at the bar.

While the cuisine balances traditional fare with Americanized preparations, all the food bursts with flavor and good-quality ingredients. A line on the bottom of the menu sums up the restaurant's attitude, which is completely focused on the customer: "Please feel free to ask for any old favorite dish that you like." Even if it's not on the menu, they'll make it for you—and that includes special requests for fiery habañero salsa.

# Ethos

Greek XX

C2

905 First Ave. (at 51st St.)

**Subway:** 51 St — Lunch & dinner daily
**Phone:** 212-888-4060
**Web:** N/A
**Prices:** $$

The Murray Hill locals may have hated to part with the beloved, but shabby, Meltemi that used to rent here, but what's emerged in its place might be even better. At once bright, modern and elegant, the stylish new Ethos is bathed in natural light by day; by night, the lights dim and the room fills up with a lively, well-dressed crowd.

The food is solid, not extraordinary, with a menu filled with impossibly lengthy Greek names that evolve into dishes like a smoky roasted eggplant spread with garlic, parsley, olive oil, oregano, and lemon; a country salad with tangy feta, bright red tomatoes, and kalamata olives dancing in a light lemon-olive oil dressing; or a decidedly decadent chicken, baked in a casserole with orzo, tomato, and feta.

# Felidia

C1 — Italian XX

243 E. 58th St. (bet. Second & Third Aves.)

**Subway:** Lexington Av - 59 St
**Phone:** 212-758-1479
**Web:** www.lidiasitaly.com
**Prices:** $$$

Lunch Mon – Fri
Dinner nightly

For the past 25 years, Felidia has consistently attracted a loyal following of well-heeled regulars. TV personality and cookbook author Lidia Bastianich's flagship is housed in a cozy brownstone with a copper-topped bar and seating on two levels. Warm colors and polished wood are used throughout, with wine racks prominently showcasing the restaurant's extensive, mostly Italian list. Although Lidia is no stranger to the kitchen, Sicilian-born Chef Fortunato Nicotra mans the stoves, where he turns out tempting pastas like Istrian "wedding pillows" filled with cheeses, citrus, and raisins; or black and white fettucine with almond pesto; as well as regional fare like quail saltimbocca. Many dishes are elegantly finished in the dining room.

# Fiorini

B1 — Italian XXX

209 E. 56th St. (bet. Second & Third Aves.)

**Subway:** Lexington Av - 53 St
**Phone:** 212-308-0830
**Web:** www.fiorinirestaurant.com
**Prices:** $$$

Lunch Mon – Fri
Dinner Mon – Sat

Lello Arpaia and his son, Dino, are masters at the hospitality trade, and they run their Italian eatery, Fiorini, (which translates to little flower) so tightly that you can't help but leave with a special fondness for the place. Make your way past the elegant front bar, and you'll find an intimate, honey-toned dining room aglow in warm pastels and buzzing with a quietly professional service staff.

Modern, straightforward Italian best describes the menu, where you'll find any number of comfort classics along with a lineup of fresh, silky pastas like a perfectly luscious al dente spaghettini *alla carbonara*, tossed with organic egg, fresh pecorino romano, cracked pepper, and sweet crumbles of bacon. Polished off with the house espresso? *Perfetto*.

# The Four Seasons

American XXXX

B2

99 E. 52nd St. (bet. Lexington & Park Aves.)

**Subway:** 51 St
**Phone:** 212-754-9494
**Web:** www.fourseasonsrestaurant.com
**Prices:** $$$$

Lunch Mon – Fri
Dinner Mon – Sat

There is nothing like a night in the pool room, known as the erstwhile country club of New York's elite. The décor—like the crowd—remains stunningly elegant. With monumental floral arrangements that change with the seasons, the entrance to this landmark building will take your breath away.
The food may be on par with a fancy wedding banquet and the service barely adequate for the undistinguished guest, but a quick glimpse at Henry Kissinger and cronies is worth the staggering price tag for one night among the powerful.
The Grill Room is the spot for lunch, where regulars have had their tables long-assigned on the legendary seating chart.
The bar is an impressive place for a cocktail, and surely worth an early arrival to absorb the scene.

# Fresco by Scotto

Italian XXX

A2

34 E. 52nd St. (bet. Madison & Park Aves.)

**Subway:** 5 Av - 53 St
**Phone:** 212-935-3434
**Web:** www.frescobyscotto.com
**Prices:** $$$

Lunch Mon – Fri
Dinner Mon – Sat

Most folks know the personable Scotto family from their recipe demonstrations on the *Today Show*, so it is no wonder that their restaurant near Rockefeller Center is known to insiders as the "NBC Commissary." Despite a location that draws a crowd on expense accounts, Fresco By Scotto exudes a comfortable yet cosmopolitan aura. This casually elegant dining room offers unobtrusive service and sound Italian-American cuisine. Lunch and dinner menus list rustic and robust appetizers, as well as "Fresco Originals" like penne with chicken and veal Bolognese, a hearty bowl of steaming pasta in a chunky tomato-based meat sauce scented with aromatic root vegetables and finished with a touch of cream.
Stop by Fresco on the go for a quick lunch fix.

# Gilt ✿✿

A3 **Contemporary** XXX

455 Madison Ave. (bet. 50th & 51st Sts.)

**Subway:** 51 St — Dinner Tue – Sat
**Phone:** 212-891-8100
**Web:** www.giltnewyork.com
**Prices:** $$$$

The New York Palace

It's hard not to feel like royalty walking into Gilt—guests stroll past a beautiful, iron-gated courtyard, now populated with dozens of tables before heading up the New York Palace Hotel's historic Villard Mansion's sweeping staircase. And then there's the ornate, renaissance-styled room itself: impossibly opulent, with sparkling mosaic floors, soaring ceilings, and a glossy marble fireplace.

It's a jaw-dropping interior and how could any meal possibly stack up to all this grandeur? But Gilt's most certainly does—largely in part to incoming Chef Justin Bogle, who pushes out perfect little dishes like one of spot prawns dancing in saffron foam, paired with a creamy, dried caper-studded cauliflower purée; or tender, cabbage leaf-wrapped squab breast dressed in a sweet sherry reduction, accompanied by smoked Marcona almond dust, pristine foie gras, and a turnip-pocked parsnip purée.

Guests can put together their own 3-course menu from a list of prix-fixe options for $89, or scale up to the 5-course chef's tasting, or the 7-course grand tasting menu, which clocks in at $140 without wine. Going without the grape is a shame, though, for Gilt has a nice collection of California Cult wines.

# HanGawi

**Korean** XX

A6

12 E. 32nd St. (bet. Fifth & Madison Aves.)

**Subway:** 33 St
Lunch & dinner daily
**Phone:** 212-213-0077
**Web:** www.hangawirestaurant.com
**Prices:** $$

Don't worry about wearing your best shoes to HanGawi; you'll have to take them off at the door before settling in at one of the restaurant's low tables. In the serene space, decorated with Korean artifacts and soothed by meditative music, it's easy to forget you're in Manhattan.

The menu is all vegetarian, in keeping with the restaurant's philosophy of healthy cooking to balance the yin and yang—or *um* and *yang* in Korean. You can quite literally eat like a king here; the emperor's roll and steamboat soup (on the prix-fixe menu) were once cooked in the royal kitchen. Of course, all good things must end, and eventually you'll have to rejoin the rat race outside. Still, it's nice to get away from the pulsing vibe of the city... now and Zen.

# Inagiku

**Japanese** XXX

B3

111 E. 49th St. (bet. Lexington & Park Aves.)

**Subway:** 51 St
Lunch Mon – Fri
**Phone:** 212-355-0440
Dinner nightly
**Web:** www.inagiku.com
**Prices:** $$$

Tucked into a corner of the Waldorf=Astoria, Inagiku may look a bit outdated these days, but the knowledgeable and charming service and top-quality Japanese cuisine more than make up for any fading décor.

The sizeable menu is divided between modern fusion dishes using Western ingredients and techniques, as well as traditional Japanese fare. Stick to the latter and you won't be disappointed. Sushi is expertly prepared and delicate tempura defines the art. Starters are perfectly done: the thin rice crêpes for the uni canapes are generously topped with vibrant uni; *uzaku*, a classic broiled eel salad, is accompanied by fresh cucumber and tossed in a light vinegar dressing. Everything comes elegantly presented with the appropriate garnishes and condiments.

# Jubilee

**French** ✗

**C2**

347 E. 54th St. (bet. First & Second Aves.)

**Subway:** Lexington Av - 53 St
**Phone:** 212-888-3569
**Web:** www.jubileeny.com
**Prices:** $$

Lunch Sun – Fri
Dinner nightly

 Don't tell Turtle Bay, but the secret is out on their beloved neighborhood bistro. With its charming, Old Europe ambience and cozy, close-knit tables, Jubilee was securing two-tops for locals long before the rest of Manhattan decided to horn in on the action. No wonder—the French-Belgian menu is a heady lineup of bistro comfort classics like duck leg confit, escargots, profiteroles, and Prince Edward Island mussels (the house specialty) prepared five different ways.

A warm goat cheese salad arrives brimming with roasted tomatoes and drizzled in a honey and sherry vinaigrette; while a plate of tender mussels is broiled up Provençale-style in garlic and parsley butter, and paired with an addictive stack of crispy frites and a vibrant green salad.

# Kurumazushi

**Japanese** ✗✗

**A3**

7 E. 47th St. (bet. Fifth & Madison Aves.)

**Subway:** 47-50 Sts - Rockefeller Ctr
**Phone:** 212-317-2802
**Web:** N/A
**Prices:** $$$$

Lunch & dinner Mon – Sat

Buried into the second story of a bland midtown office building, there isn't a lot to advertise Kurumazushi other than a few plain letters on a nondescript door. But push past this red herring and head upstairs—there, you'll find a simple, but tidily appointed, sushi den, dressed in a traditional palette of red, white, and black.

Don't let the minimalism fool you. This is the house of Toshihiro Uezu, an omakase master of the first order—and though some loyalists might argue that other chefs behind the counter don't have the master's deft touch, a dinner here is still likely to blow the socks off the uninitiated. Of course, so might the hefty bill—a price you're likely to overlook having sampled otherworldly fish flown in from Japan.

# La Grenouille

French XXXX

A2

3 E. 52nd St. (bet. Fifth & Madison Aves.)

**Subway:** 5 Av - 53 St
**Phone:** 212-752-1495
**Web:** www.la-grenouille.com
**Prices:** $$$$

Lunch Tue – Fri
Dinner Mon – Sat

Opened in 1962 by the Masson family who still oversee the enterprise, La Grenouille has managed to remain the Masson family's bastion of high-priced French cuisine in Midtown—some come for the food, others simply for this traditional experience. A high coffered ceiling, silk wall coverings, and stunning fresh flower arrangements adorn the opulent dining room, which is worthy of a special occasion for those who still prefer to dress for dinner (gentlemen are required to wear jackets).

This classic menu offers the old-world dishes increasingly difficult to find, like quenelles, *rognons*, and of course, les *cuisses de grenouilles Provençale* (sautéed frogs' legs). A lovely Saturday lunch menu offers this rich experience for a fraction of the price.

# Le Cirque

Contemporary XXXX

B1

151 E. 58th St. (bet. Lexington & Third Aves.)

**Subway:** 59 St
**Phone:** 212-644-0202
**Web:** www.lecirque.com
**Prices:** $$$$

Lunch Mon – Fri
Dinner Mon – Sat

Nestled into One Beacon Court's Bloomberg building, the current incarnation of the legendary restaurant, Le Cirque, is dramatic—with huge curving windows, billowing tents draped above the main dining room, and circus motifs gracing the walls.

And yet nothing reads kitschy, least of all Le Cirque's old-money following—a loyal crowd that saunters in nightly, partly for the memories, and partly for the consistently lovely menu where you might find a soft pile of homemade *spaghetti alla chitarra*, laced with a fresh tomato ragù humming with sweet onion, delicate pecorino, and basil; or a paupiette of moist black cod wrapped in crispy, paper-thin slices of potato with a sweet wine reduction, served over braised leeks.

# L'Atelier de Joël Robuchon ✿

B1 **Contemporary** XX

57 E. 57th St. (bet. Madison & Park Aves.)

**Subway:** 5 Av - 59 St Dinner nightly
**Phone:** 212-350-6658
**Web:** www.fourseasons.com/newyork
**Prices:** $$$$

Four Seasons New York

Those familiar with acclaimed French Chef Joël Robuchon's globe-spanning namesake restaurant (there are six locations worldwide) know the drill—expert top-flight haute cuisine dished up in an impeccably sophisticated atmosphere. The mood at his Manhattan outpost, housed in the upstairs lobby of the tony Four Seasons Hotel, leans a bit more subdued than its sister spaces, and the service inconsistent, but still well-heeled business clients and loyal regulars fill in nightly for Chef Xavier Boyer's distinctive fare.

The menu flips to the season but might include perfectly runny soft-poached eggs, served over an eggplant stew that walks and talks like a delicious ratatouille; or a moist, flaky slice of *amadai* (tile fish) served in a refreshing yuzu broth with crunchy bits of lily bulbs, and topped with fried fennel fragments and a dash of edible flowers and herbs.

While those looking for intimate conversation can always huddle in the soothing blond woods that frame the main dining room, others looking for a little more action should hit the beautiful pearwood counter, where they can watch the open kitchen work their culinary magic from a cozy perch at the enormous, u-shaped bar.

# Le Périgord

French XXX

C2

405 E. 52nd St. (off First Ave.)

**Subway:** 51 St
**Phone:** 212-755-6244
**Web:** www.leperigord.com
**Prices:** $$$

Lunch Mon – Fri
Dinner nightly

The best things need not be the most contemporary, and Le Perigord bears witness to that fact. With a classic feel that dates back to the 1960s, this establishment cossets diners at tables with hand-painted Limoges china, crystal stemware, and fresh roses. A coffered ceiling and period chairs upholstered in willow-green fabric add further elegance, as tuxedo-clad waiters proffer formal service to diplomats from the nearby United Nations. This is one of the few places in New York where one still dresses for dinner.

The time-honored French menu is comprised of traditional fare like veal kidneys with mustard sauce, and *loup de mer* with wild mushrooms. For the pièce de résistance, desserts—including tasty seasonal fruit tarts—are wheeled to your table on a cart.

# Maloney & Porcelli

American XXX

B3

37 E. 50th St. (bet. Madison & Park Aves.)

**Subway:** 51 St
**Phone:** 212-750-2233
**Web:** www.maloneyandporcelli.com
**Prices:** $$$

Lunch Mon – Fri
Dinner nightly

This upbeat spot exceeds expectations with its appealing, varied menu, and cheerful waitstaff—a far cry from your run-of-the-mill steakhouse.

One could order the giant, quality Porterhouse, cooked to order and carved tableside, but there are plenty of other enticing choices. Diners who pick a pizza appetizer and pasta main course have no need to envy a neighbor's filet. Sharing is recommended, as starters are entrée-size and sides served family-style. Wine glasses and peppermills are also enormous, supplementing the philosophy that more is more. Know that this is in keeping with the check; prices are anything but petit. Even so, the restaurant is appropriately jammed with an expense-account crowd, and the bar remains a sought after watering hole.

# Métrazur

B4 **American** XX

## Grand Central Terminal

**Subway:** Grand Central - 42 St
**Phone:** 212-687-4600
**Web:** www.charliepalmer.com
**Prices:** $$$

Lunch Mon – Fri
Dinner Mon – Sat

Grand Central Station usually evokes images of passengers dashing for trains. Yet, there is another side to this terminal, best seen from the serene perch at Métrazur (named for a bygone train that traveled the Côte d'Azur en route to Monaco). From its enviable east balcony setting, the restaurant transports diners from the hubbub below, while commanding spectacular views of the station's cavernous main concourse and celestial ceiling.

The food enhances the setting with a variety of contemporary American dishes incorporating premium seasonal ingredients, such as asparagus risotto with rabbit confit and pea leaves; or hand-cut tuna tartare with wasabi cream and ponzu. The bar is a primo spot for cocktails before catching a train.

# Mia Dona

B1 **Italian** XX

## 206 E. 58th St. (bet. Second & Third Aves.)

**Subway:** 59 St
**Phone:** 212-750-8170
**Web:** www.miadona.com
**Prices:** $$$

Lunch Sun – Fri
Dinner nightly

Greek dream team, Michael Psilakis and Donatella Arpaia, have developed a cult following at their Upper West Side restaurants, Kefi and Anthos. With this new eastside charmer, they cross both Central Park—and the Mediterranean—to bring their signature style to a modern, Italian-dominated menu.

Duck inside the beautifully-designed, but unfussy, interior, and let the equally unpretentious staff dole out plate after plate of Psilakis' genius—which might appear in a smartly updated *arancini*, filled with smoked mozzarella and served over an eggplant purée with *cipollini agrodolce*; grilled *branzino* laced with Moroccan olives and a lemon and olive oil pan jus; or scrumptious *zeppole* coated in cinnamon sugar, served with a rich dark chocolate sauce.

# Michael Jordan's

**Steakhouse** XX

**B4**

Grand Central Terminal

**Subway:** Grand Central - 42 St
**Phone:** 212-655-2300
**Web:** www.theglaziergroup.com
**Prices:** **$$$**

Lunch & dinner daily

With Grand Central Terminal's painstakingly restored celestial mural overhead, Michael Jordan's offers dining under the stars anytime of day. Warm colors, wood panelling, and black-and-white photos of sleek locomotives brings glamorous art deco to the lofty mezzanine space.

At dinner, expect generous portions of well-prepared prime Angus beef with warm and attentive, though occasionally flawed service. Sides encompass traditional steakhouse carte, but be sure to save room for the macaroni and cheese, based on a recipe from the basketball star's grandmother. Lunch adds a reasonable pre-fixe menu and selection of lighter fare. The elliptical mahogany bar is an agreeable setting for a happy-hour beverage; while the wine salon is well suited for a cocktail party.

# Morton's

**Steakhouse** XXX

**A4**

551 Fifth Ave. (enter on 45th St. bet Fifth & Madison Aves.)

**Subway:** 5 Av
**Phone:** 212-972-3315
**Web:** www.mortons.com
**Prices:** **$$$**

Lunch Mon – Fri
Dinner nightly

Part of a Chicago-born chain that has mushroomed into a mega-chain with outposts all across the country, Morton's offers a similar experience no matter which location you visit. The Midtown Morton's—one of the older siblings—keeps with the clubby, masculine décor that characterizes so many steakhouses: mahogany paneling, low lighting, deep jewel tones, and imposing chandeliers.

Your server will recite the menu while showing you samples of each main ingredient. A cart bearing baked potatoes, vegetables, and examples of all the cuts of beef offered, is rolled to each table to help you make your selection.

The place has a split personality: during the week, the restaurant and bar both reek of power from the local corporate crowd. Tourists take over on weekends.

# Mr Chow

C1 — Chinese XX

324 E. 57th St. (bet. First & Second Aves.)

**Subway:** 59 St — Dinner nightly
**Phone:** 212-751-9030
**Web:** www.mrchow.com
**Prices:** $$$$

This Mr Chow dates back to 1979 but still lures a high-profile crowd night after night. Actor, artist, restaurateur, and Renaissance man Michael Chow added interior design to his talents in creating this chic black and white dining room accented with a red fabric mobile overhead. The team of white jacketed servers makes closely placed diners feel posh and pampered. Regulars and cognoscenti know not to request the menu; have your waiter order for you (though you may want to include the fried seaweed), and don't be shy about dislikes. Find yourself distracted from your meal when the oft-performed noodle-making demonstration begins. It's impressive, as will be the check.
Downtown residents will appreciate the TriBeCa location.

# Naya

C1 — Lebanese XX

1057 Second Ave. (bet. 55th & 56th Sts.)

**Subway:** Lexington Av - 53 St — Lunch & dinner daily
**Phone:** 212-319-7777
**Web:** www.nayarestaurants.com
**Prices:** $$

In a city starved for good Lebanese food, Naya is a sight for sore eyes. Owner Hady Kfoury, who runs a few restaurants back in Beirut, worked the front-of-house at both Daniel and Payard before bringing in Lebanese chef, Rafic Nehme, to open this tiny, but impeccably sleek space, with its mod, all-white décor and a narrow lineup of glossy, angular booths.
The modern Lebanese menu rounds the usual meze bases before introducing a handful of entrées and a small, but tempting, Lebanese wine list. Try the well-seasoned, crunchy *fattoush*, served with toasted pita; a savory, mint-seasoned kebab of ground lamb, paired with a fluffy stack of Lebanese rice pilaf and grilled vegetables; or a glistening, golden tower of flaky baklava cigars, drizzled with honey.

# Oceana ✿

Seafood XXX

A2

55 E. 54th St. (bet. Madison & Park Aves.)

**Subway:** 5 Av - 53 St
**Phone:** 212-759-5941
**Web:** www.oceanarestaurant.com
**Prices:** **$$$$**

Mon – Fri lunch & dinner
Sat dinner only

Paul Johnson Photography

Consistently serving sensational seafood with international flair, this local favorite has stayed the course over the years. In the kitchen, Chef Ben Pollinger blends superlative ingredients with a display of élan that shines through to the plate. His creativity sparkles in a fillet of flaky, white halibut, wrapped in a crisped ribbon of prosciutto and placed on a bed of pale-green eggplant purée. For dessert, Pastry Chef Jansen Chan's creations are both delicious and surprising, as in the individual browned-butter cheesecake coated with a layer of candied pecan crumbs—the topping becomes almost savory with a mouthwatering hit of salt.

The extensive wine list boasts more than 1,100 global labels, including an impressive selection of white Burgundy. Exclusive pairings are offered with lunch and dinner tasting menus. The affable manager and an attentive brigade of waiters set the tone for professional service.

This fall, Oceana will leave Midtown East and set sail for its new location, at *1221 Avenue of the Americas*. Word has it that in the new expanded space near Rockefeller Center, the restaurant will shed its former cruise-ship interior for a more elegantly nautical theme.

# Osteria Laguna

C4 Italian XX

209 E. 42nd St. (bet. Second & Third Aves.)

**Subway:** Grand Central - 42 St
**Phone:** 212-557-0001
**Web:** www.osteria-laguna.com
**Prices:** $$

Lunch Mon – Fri
Dinner nightly

A primo place for a midtown lunch, Osteria Laguna does a booming midday business and the kitchen fields the crowds with aplomb. Office types and tourists alike appreciate the inviting atmosphere, especially in the rustic front room, which overlooks the street through floor-to-ceiling windows that open onto the sidewalk in summer.

Pizza is a hit any time of day, and if you choose a seat in the back room, you can watch the pies being shoveled in and out of the brick oven. These pizzas are individual size and ring true with Italian ingredients—perhaps prosciutto, artichokes, and black olives; or sweet sausage ragú and porcini. Pasta dishes satisfy too, as in a traditional lasagna Bolognese, baked until it is bubbly and has a crusty layer on top.

# Pampano

B3 Mexican XX

209 E. 49th St. (bet. Second & Third Aves.)

**Subway:** 51 St
**Phone:** 212-751-4545
**Web:** www.modernmexican.com/pampano
**Prices:** $$$

Lunch Mon – Fri
Dinner nightly

This vivid Mexican restaurant is a duet between Mexicateur, Richard Sandoval (who owns sister restaurant, Maya), and legendary tenor, Placido Domingo. The combination hits all the right notes—think coastal Mexican cuisine meets an elegant eastside setting, and you're getting warm. The chic interior, drawn in ivory tones and green palm trees, renders the two-level space open and airy; and there's a great terrace upstairs when the weather plays nice.

The menu's favorites include bowls of ceviche or the *empanadas de camaron* dressed with vibrant salsas, followed by deep entrées like the *pez espada mérida*, a thick fillet of swordfish atop a potato-caper fondue with a fresh pea shoot and Asian pear salad all swimming in a smooth achiote habañero sauce.

# Pera

Turkish XX

A4

303 Madison Ave. (bet. 41st & 42nd Sts.)

**Subway:** Grand Central - 42 St
**Phone:** 212-878-6301
**Web:** www.peranyc.com
**Prices:** $$

Lunch Mon – Fri
Dinner Mon – Sat

Named for an upscale neighborhood in Istanbul, this perennially-packed brasserie pulls in boisterous office groups by day as easily as it does intimate duos come nightfall. No wonder, with Pera's consistently solid kitchen turning out lip-smacking good Turkish fare, like a smoky bowl of whipped, roasted eggplant; or crispy phyllo rolls, stuffed with Turkish cheese and paired with a delicious dunk of *cacik*; or the savory lamb *adana*.

Should the crowds add up to a wait for a table, you can always hang in the lovely lounge area up front, or check out the restaurant's seasoned meats collection, cleverly packaged for takeaway. They cook up almost as well at home—though minus the yummy dipping sauces, they're not nearly as fun.

# Phoenix Garden

Chinese X

B5

242 E. 40th St. (bet. Second & Third Aves.)

**Subway:** Grand Central - 42 St
**Phone:** 212-983-6666
**Web:** www.thephoenixgarden.com
**Prices:**

Lunch & dinner daily

You can take the restaurant out of Chinatown, but you can't take the Cantonese out of this midtown favorite—which serves up authentic dishes at a great value. By day, the midtown office set pours in for quick lunches; by dinner, Phoenix Garden lights up with a fun, diverse crowd looking to check out the mouthwatering daily specials.

While the house's tasty Peking duck is not always on the menu, you can certainly try to request it—a deliciously crispy affair that gets rolled into neat little pancakes with hoisin, scallion, and cucumber. Meanwhile, don't miss the steamed chive dumplings, plump with tender shrimp; the succulent pepper and salty shrimp; or the sautéed snow pea shoots in a lovely crabmeat sauce, with tender mushrooms and snow peas.

# P.J. Clarke's

B2 — Gastropub

915 Third Ave. (at 55th St.)

**Subway:** Lexington Av - 53 St — Lunch & dinner daily
**Phone:** 212-317-1616
**Web:** www.pjclarkes.com
**Prices:** ⊜

Named for Patrick Joseph Clarke, who purchased the place in 1904, this saloon remains a slice of old New York. Pub fare still reigns at this former haunt of Frank Sinatra and Jackie O: big burgers, hearty sandwiches, crispy shoestring fries, a full rawbar, and a long list of beers on tap. The bar scene, usually packed four deep with an agency crowd, is one of the city's best happy hours. Often the throngs of good-looking young professionals there to meet and greet overshadow the charismatic dining room beyond the bar, with its red checkered tablecloths, worn wood walls, and genial service. Through a separate, marked entrance on 55th Street, Sidecar offers a more conversation-friendly dining experience in a speakeasy-like, brick-walled setting.

# Riingo

B4 — Fusion

205 E. 45th St. (bet. Second & Third Aves.)

**Subway:** Grand Central - 42 St — Lunch & dinner daily
**Phone:** 212-867-4200
**Web:** www.riingo.com
**Prices:** $$

Derived from the Japanese word for "apple" (as in the Big Apple), Riingo features celebrity chef, Marcus Samuelsson's interpretation of Japanese and American cuisines. The stylish, contemporary restaurant, just off the lobby of the Alex Hotel, incorporates ebony wood, bamboo floor planks, and thoughtful touches such as custom-made ceramic sake sets. At the front of the restaurant, a small bar, lounge, and a few sidewalk tables offer a pleasant setting for a post-work cocktail or fast business lunch.

In addition to the creative kitchen menu and extensive raw-bar selection, Riingo offers a full range of sushi and maki of impressive quality. Open for all-day dining, Riingo and its original menu rise a cut above your typical hotel restaurant.

# Rosa Mexicano

Mexican

C1

1063 First Ave. (at 58th St.)

**Subway:** 59 St
**Phone:** 212-753-7407
**Web:** www.rosamexicano.com
**Prices:** $$

Dinner nightly

A sure crowd pleaser, Rosa Mexicano promises good food and a good time, and it always delivers. While outposts have popped up in New York and other cities, the East Side original still wins raves on a nightly basis. The place is always packed (reservations essential) with a mix of young and old, families and singles.

With its terrific margaritas and extensive tequila list, the bar is the place to wait for a table or unwind after work. Guacamole made to order tableside, along with authentic entrées like *budin Azteca* (multi-layer tortilla pie), and *crepas de camarón* (corn crêpes filled with shrimp and napped with chile pasilla sauce) keep 'em coming back for more. Appealing desserts are worth saving room for—at least order one to share.

# Sakagura

Japanese

B4

211 E. 43rd St. (bet. Second & Third Aves.)

**Subway:** Grand Central - 42 St
**Phone:** 212-953-7253
**Web:** www.sakagura.com
**Prices:** $$$

Lunch Mon – Fri
Dinner nightly

Oh, Sakagura! You, with your never-ending Japanese delights—where do we begin? With one of the city's best sake lists (over 200 different kinds) and a whole host of yummy Japanese small plates at its disposal, this unassuming little sake den has gotten deservedly popular in the last few years. For those who can find it (hint: it's in the basement by way of the back stairs) this is no boring dinner in midtown, but a swinging night out in Tokyo (especially in a booth).

Though the menu is built to complement the sake list, the food more than merits its own applause—don't miss the killer, sake-marinated fried chicken; out-of-this-world *uzaku* (broiled eel, cucumber, and wakame in tart vinegar); toothsome soba; or pristine sashimi plates.

# Rouge Tomate ✿

A1 **Contemporary** XXX

10 E. 60th St. (bet. Fifth & Madison Aves.)

**Subway:** 5 Av
Lunch & dinner Mon – Sat
**Phone:** 646-237-8977
**Web:** www.rougetomatenyc.com
**Prices:** **$$$**

Katie Sokoler

The philosophy at this stunning new Brussels import is S.P.E., an acronym for "Sanitas Per Escam" (Health Through Food), an idea that rests on three key principles: *sourcing*, selecting ingredients seasonally and locally; *preparation*, using cooking techniques that preserve the food's integrity and nutrition; and *enhancement*, optimizing nutritional value via product combination and menu diversity.

Chef Jeremy Bearman's menu is meant to supply diners with 30% of their daily nutritional intake. Impressive in its science, but can health food be sexy? Rouge Tomate makes a strong argument in favor, with a jaw-dropping, two-level interior fitted out with a floating bridge entrance and a Zen-like décor of varnished unstained wood and red accents.

The menu spins to the season, but might include a wildly fresh ceviche, dressed with ripe green avocado, blood orange, kumquat, jalapeño, and a sprinkling of bright green dill; just-seared Nantucket bay scallops over a silky parsnip purée studded with roasted mushrooms, and paired with pearl onions, baby fall vegetables, and a chervil coulis; or succulent grass-fed N.Y. strip, kissed with a savory beef jus punctuated with mushrooms.

# 2nd Avenue Deli

Deli

B6

162 E. 33rd St. (bet. Lexington & Third Aves.)

**Subway:** 33 St — Lunch & dinner daily
**Phone:** 212-689-9000
**Web:** www.2ndavedeli.com
**Prices:** ⊜

Ignore the kvetching of those who complain that this deli is not the same now that it has moved to midtown. Sure, the décor may be more deli-meets-deco and there's a tad less attitude, but the food is every bit as good as it was on Second Avenue. Get over it already—this is still a true Jewish deli, and one of the best around by far.

What hasn't changed is the menu. It's still meat-only, no-dairy Kosher, with the same phenomenal pastrami, pillowy rye, tangy mustard, and fluffy matzoh balls in fantastic comforting broth. Go for the best of both worlds at lunch with the soup and half-sandwich combination.

In this location the deli also does takeout (popular with the Midtown lunch bunch), and delivery (popular with late-night partyers). Giant platters go equally well for a bris or a brunch.

# Seo

Japanese

C3

249 E. 49th St. (bet. Second & Third Aves.)

**Subway:** 51 St — Lunch & dinner daily
**Phone:** 212-355-7722
**Web:** N/A
**Prices:** $$

This is not your average neighborhood standby, and yet Seo—tucked into a residential street in midtown's booming Japanese culinary scene—draws as many faithful locals as it does weekend adventurers looking for the real deal. Thus, it's best to make reservations early.

The secret lies in Seo's one-two punch of pairing a tranquil dining room and long dining counter with a kitchen staff dedicated to the acumen of traditional Japanese food. Witness a wildly fresh eel and cucumber salad, tossed in a feather-light vinegar sauce; or a perfectly broiled cod, glazed in a spot-on miso sauce, and flanked by Japanese plum and ginger root. Keep an eye out for the popular *chawanmushi*—a silky egg custard that should not be missed if it appears on the daily specials.

# Shaburi

A·B5 **Japanese** XX

125 E. 39th St. (bet. Lexington & Park Aves.)

**Subway:** Grand Central - 42 St
**Phone:** 212-867-6999
**Web:** www.shaburi.com
**Prices:** $$$

Lunch Mon – Fri
Dinner nightly

*Shabu-shabu* and *sukiyaki*, the family-style, do-it-yourself-Asian methods of cooking, are the specialty here at Shaburi. Outfitted with electric burners on each table and at each seat at the sushi bar, this well-kept, contemporary midtown spot is known for its fresh ingredients and pleasant service. Sushi is another popular pick, especially at lunchtime, where the mostly business crowd can be seen tucking into the prix-fixe lunch special or bargain bento box.

Not in the mood to cook, but still craving a cooked meal? The menu offers a variety of alternatives, from starters that may include *goma ae*—steamed spinach bathed in a thick sesame paste—to grilled Kobe beef marinated in sweet miso and *unagi haata*, barbecued eel layered with spinach and mushrooms.

# Sip Sak

C3 **Turkish** X

928 Second Ave. (bet. 49th & 50th Sts.)

**Subway:** 51 St
**Phone:** 212-583-1900
**Web:** www.sip-sak.com
**Prices:** $$

Lunch & dinner daily

Good, authentic Turkish cuisine still holds sway here at Sip Sak and peripatetic founding chef, Orhan Yegen, remains on board. He graces the upbeat dining room nightly with his charismatic persona, and adds to the lively ambience enjoyed by an international crowd of local residents.

The dining room has benefited from some decorative upgrades and now with colorful walls, dark wood tables, and abundant Turkish artifacts, it has a much warmer feel.

House specials like *manti* (aromatic beef dumplings in a yogurt garlic sauce), or stuffed cabbage arrive in abundant portions. Grilled octopus—a frequent daily special—is impeccably prepared, dressed simply in olive oil and herbs. A selection of Turkish wines and beers is offered, a fitting match to a meal here.

# Smith & Wollensky

Steakhouse XX

B3

797 Third Ave. (at 49th St.)

**Subway:** 51 St
**Phone:** 212-753-1530
**Web:** www.smithandwollensky.com
**Prices:** $$$$

Lunch & dinner daily

Long before Manhattan's steakhouse craze reached epic proportions, there was Smith & Wollensky. The New York flagship (they now have restaurants in 9 U.S. cities) opened in 1977, and over 30 years later, the restaurant is still jumping most nights of the week—it's historic green and white façade a welcome beacon to neighborhood power players, families, and tourists alike.

The owners may have plucked the names Smith & Wollensky out of a phone directory, but they were considerably more careful choosing their USDA prime beef, which they dry-age and hand-butcher on premises. The result, paired with heartbreakingly good mashed potatoes, is steakhouse nirvana. Wollensky's Grill serves a late-night menu until 2:00 A.M. to sate the lively bar crowd.

# Sparks

Steakhouse XX

C3

210 E. 46th St. (bet. Second & Third Aves.)

**Subway:** Grand Central - 42 St
**Phone:** 212-687-4855
**Web:** www.sparksnyc.com
**Prices:** $$$$

Lunch Mon – Fri
Dinner Mon – Sat

Phenomenal steaks, exceptional Scotch, frosty martinis, big expense accounts, seating for nearly 700, and carnivorous crowds exuding a raucous, masculine vibe are the fundamentals of Sparks. Service is speedy and efficient, if rough around the edges, throughout the gigantic, bi-level dining space. This is enhanced by large tables and 19th century landscapes of the Hudson River Valley that line the wainscoted walls. There will be time to appreciate the ambience while inevitably waiting for your table among the masses at the bar.

On the menu, go straight to the flavorful, buttery, and perfectly cooked prime sirloin, accompanied by unbeatable creamed spinach. Complete this consistently excellent, powerhouse experience with a bottle of big red wine.

# SushiAnn

B2 — Japanese XX

38 E. 51st St. (bet. Madison & Park Aves.)

**Subway:** 51 St
**Phone:** 212-755-1780
**Web:** www.sushiann.com
**Prices:** $$

Lunch Mon – Fri
Dinner Mon – Sat

Lucky are those who accidentally wander into this midtown sushi den. Nestled into a corporate no man's land along 51st Street, it's hard from the outset to see what separates SushiAnn from the pack of smooth-blonde-wood-and-black-lacquered-tray sushi joints that line this pocket of Manhattan.

Take a seat at the sushi bar (where there is a $30 minimum required to sit down), order the omakase, and wait—incredibly fresh mackerel served with ponzu and minced ginger sauce; fatty blue fin fanned over *shiso* leaf and kelp; smoky, chewy slices of grilled giant clam; rich torched sardine—all of it carefully explained by the attentive, knowledgeable staff. Sure, you can also sit at a table and order à la carte, but where's the fun in that?

# Sushiden

A3 — Japanese XX

19 E. 49th St. (bet. Fifth & Madison Aves.)

**Subway:** 5 Av - 53 St
**Phone:** 212-758-2700
**Web:** www.sushiden.com
**Prices:** $$$

Lunch Mon – Fri
Dinner Sun – Fri

Regardless of recent competition in the form of more modern and stylish spots, Sushiden remains popular for its traditional food and excellent service. The restaurant is an especially big hit with the business lunch crowd that jams the place at midday—so be sure to make reservations.

While the menu offerings have been altered slightly to please the business diners, you can still find high-quality traditional sushi here (perhaps minus the spicy tuna and California rolls). Ask for the omakase, and the skillful sushi chefs will respond with a parade of items, each piece seasoned to enhance its flavor.

Another location of Sushiden feeds the westside business crowd in a larger but less warm setting.

# Sushi Yasuda

Japanese XX

B4

204 E. 43rd St. (bet. Second & Third Aves.)

**Subway:** Grand Central - 42 St
**Phone:** 212-972-1001
**Web:** www.sushiyasuda.com
**Prices:** $$$$

Lunch Mon – Fri
Dinner Mon – Sat

Blond wood furnishings create a Scandinavian feel in this airy, contemporary dining room, which is cached away in an office building in the corridor between Grand Central Terminal and the United Nations. Seating at the counter is best if you want to order the omakase—just remember that counter reservations are limited to 90 minutes.

Everything on the menu is made from scratch and changes constantly according to the market and the whim of Chef/partner Naomichi Yasuda. Turn your attention to the fantastic variety of sushi and sashimi, each item presented on a fresh Hawaiian *ti* leaf. Raw fish here is kept pristine, with no extraneous embellishments or garnishes to detract from the fresh flavors.

Note that if you arrive later than 10 minutes after your reservation time, your spot will be forfeited.

# Takesushi

Japanese XX

C2

1026 Second Ave. (bet. 54th & 55th Sts.)

**Subway:** Lexington Av - 53 St
**Phone:** 212-355-3557
**Web:** www.takesushi.com
**Prices:** $$

Lunch Mon – Fri
Dinner Mon – Sat

Despite the fact that this place seems to change its name and concept on a regular basis (its most recent incarnation was restaurant ON), it has consistently offered good Japanese cuisine. Obviously, a talented team and a well-trained Japanese chef still hold sway here, no matter what they call it.

Takesushi gets jam-packed for weekday lunch, likely owing to the restaurant's proximity to the U.N., as well as its new lunch-menu options. As appealing as they are a good value, set sushi menus and Bento box samplers make the best bargains; and though a bit more pricey, the lunchtime omakase will net you some fine quality fare.

Kimono-clad and sweet as pie, waitresses perform their jobs with genuine hospitality in the small well-maintained space.

# Tao

**A1** Asian XX

42 E. 58th St. (bet. Madison & Park Aves.)

**Subway:** 59 St
**Phone:** 212-888-2288
**Web:** www.taorestaurant.com
**Prices:** $$$

Lunch Mon – Fri
Dinner nightly

This former movie theater is now (literally) a temple of all foods pan-Asian, outfitted with a Chinese scroll draped across the ceiling, and a 16-foot-high statue of Buddha towering over a reflecting pool in the dramatic main dining room. The theater's former balconies now accommodate 300 diners on three levels. The menu spotlights a combination of Hong Kong Chinese, Thai, and Japanese dishes, including sushi and sashimi. Perfect for sharing, a host of small plates offers everything from satay of Chilean sea bass, to Peking duck spring rolls.

While filled with a loyal after-work crowd and business clientele during the week, Manhattan's young and trendy turn out in droves on weekend nights to indulge in libations like the *sake-tini* or *Tao-hito*.

# Teodora

**B1** Italian XX

141 E. 57th St. (bet. Lexington & Third Aves.)

**Subway:** Lexington Av - 59 St
**Phone:** 212-826-7101
**Web:** N/A
**Prices:** $$

Lunch & dinner daily

Conveniently situated on a stretch of 57th Street that draws nearby residential and commercial patrons, Teodora has the comfortable feel of a restaurant that's been around for ages. Two floors offer separate spirits, making it possible to enjoy the same cuisine in two different settings. Dark and lively, the downstairs room has a bit more charm, with more noise and closely spaced tables. Upstairs is quiet and conducive to privacy.

The mostly Italian waitstaff is well-versed in the menu, which emphasizes Northern Italy in its fine array of traditional antipasti, house-made pastas, entrées, and side dishes. Simple means good here; there are no frills to steal attention from the food. Pricey reds, including labels not commonly found, dominate the wine list.

# Tsushima

**Japanese** ✗

**B3**

141 E. 47th St. (bet. Lexington & Third Aves.)

**Subway:** Grand Central - 42 St
**Phone:** 212-207-1938
**Web:** N/A
**Prices:** $$

Lunch Mon – Fri
Dinner Mon – Sat

There are few restaurant secrets left in New York, but Tsushima is one of them. Chances are, you haven't heard of it, but this place stands out among the competition in the thin slice of Midtown jammed with restaurants straight out of Tokyo. It's easy to walk right by Tsushima (it's located a few steps below street level), but once inside, you'll find a sultry décor that contrasts black wood with white leather seating.

Skilled chefs seamlessly juggle the standard table orders with the omakase offerings at the sushi bar, and the kitchen plays backup with an assortment of cooked courses. Though spicy tuna can be had, the chef's choice is the way to go, as Tsushima nets fantastic quality and interesting varieties of fish—all elegantly presented.

# Vong

**Fusion** ✗✗

**B2**

200 E. 54th St. (bet. Second & Third Aves.)

**Subway:** Lexington Av - 53 St
**Phone:** 212-486-9592
**Web:** www.jean-georges.com
**Prices:** $$$

Lunch Mon – Fri
Dinner nightly

♿

Housed at the bottom of the 1986 postmodern tower known as the Lipstick Building, Vong sports a bright scarlet and gold-leaf motif. Jewel-toned Thai silks and bamboo accents contribute to the Oriental aura, while a wooden table between the bar and dining room displays fragrant bowls of whole peppers and spices.

Exotic tastes of Bangkok, Singapore, and Hong Kong marry French technique in the likes of a roasted lemongrass chicken, or peekytoe crab spring rolls. Yet the kitchen misses its mark in other rather pedestrian preparations. With a restaurant empire that stretches around the world, celebrity chef, Jean-Georges Vongerichten cannot possibly attend constantly to all his establishments. Unfortunately, his talented eye seems absent here.

# The Water Club

C6 **Seafood** XXX

E. 30th St. (at the East River)

**Subway:** 33 St — Lunch & dinner daily
**Phone:** 212-683-3333
**Web:** www.thewaterclub.com
**Prices:** **$$$**

For years, birthdays, anniversaries, and engagements have been celebrated at the Water Club, and, indeed, its setting is perfect for special occasions. Set on a barge in the East River, the dining room boasts floor-to-ceiling windows that overlook the river, and water views from every table. Marine signal flags hanging from the ceiling, and a waitstaff dressed as a ship's crew complete the nautical theme.

The menu celebrates American dishes and spotlights seafood such as shrimp cocktail, grilled salmon, and Maine lobster. Meat dishes like Colorado rack of lamb and Long Island duck please landlubbers. Live piano music entertains nightly, and in summer, the Crow's Nest on the restaurant's upper deck offers informal outdoor dining and river breezes.

# Wild Edibles

B5 **Seafood** X

535 Third Ave. (bet. 35th & 36th Sts.)

**Subway:** 33 St — Lunch & dinner daily
**Phone:** 212-213-8552
**Web:** www.wildedibles.com
**Prices:** **$$**

It's a fish market. It's a restaurant. It's an oyster bar. Wild Edibles is all those places rolled into one.

With four other markets in New York, including one in Grand Central Station, Wild Edibles prides itself on netting line-caught fish and organic produce from small farms. In the Third Avenue locale, a retail counter displays the day's catch, while a small bar and a few tables provide seating. A vast array of seafood fills the menu with an appealing mix of light fare and entrées—everything from oyster "flights," (with white wine or beer pairings) to fish cooked your way and accompanied with a choice of seasonings. Cheesecake is the only dessert option, and they don't serve coffee.

At lunch, it feels like you're eating in a fish store, but in the evening candlelight kicks in more atmosphere.

# Wolfgang's

**Steakhouse** XX

A6

4 Park Ave. (at 33rd St.)

**Subway:** 33 St
Lunch & dinner daily
**Phone:** 212-889-3369
**Web:** www.wolfgangssteakhouse.com
**Prices:** $$$$

After 40 years at the esteemed Peter Luger, former headwaiter Wolfgang Zwiener ditched retirement to strike out on his own across the river—a decision that has yielded mouthwatering results. Located in the former Vanderbilt Hotel dining room, this 1912 landmark space showcases a vaulted terra-cotta ceiling by famed architect Rafael Guastavino. The setting is handsome, but the steak's arrival refocuses all attention on the strapping portions of Porterhouse, hand-selected and dry-aged in house. Once the meat is basted with some of its sizzling juices, the feast will begin.

Classic starters and scrumptious sides like shrimp cocktail and creamed spinach are delightful distractions. Be sure to hit the bar for a perfect martini.

# Yakitori Torys

**Japanese** X

C2

248 E. 52nd St. (bet. Second & Third Aves.)

**Subway:** 51 St
Dinner nightly
**Phone:** 212-813-1800
**Web:** www.torysnyc.com
**Prices:** $$

Midtown has its fair share of Tokyo-style restaurants and Torys is no exception. Positioned on the second floor, this tranquil little yakitori house skewers up a remarkable variety of chicken parts and grills them expertly. From livers to tails, poultry rules the roost.

The kitchen's specialty is yakitori, but don't ignore the rest of their vast menu. The chicken soup here easily competes with grandma's version, and do not miss their *gyoza*, a distant relative of the frozen versions found elsewhere.

The attentive staff will present your parade of courses and quenching libations at a relaxed pace; everything is cooked to order and there's surely no rush.

# Zarela

**Mexican** XX

C2

953 Second Ave. (bet. 50th & 51st Sts.)

**Subway:** 51 St
**Phone:** 212-644-6740
**Web:** www.zarela.com
**Prices:** $$

Lunch Mon – Fri
Dinner nightly

Is Zarela Martinez the unsung hero of the city's blazing Mexican food scene? Those who can remember Manhattan's tortilla wasteland of ten years ago would argue yes, because this talented chef and food scholar—who can still be found holding court at her favorite corner table most nights of the week—has been dishing up authentic Mexican fare since the late eighties.

Happy hour finds the bar flooded with a young, spirited crowd chucking back the addictive house margaritas, some of them oblivious to the brilliance passing under their noses. Try a fragrant bowl of rich, smoky posole; a bright chile relleno stuffed with *chicharones* in a tomatillo sauce; or tender baby back ribs and Mexican sausage marinated in lime, garlic, and oregano.

Taking a pet on your holiday? Look for indicating a hotel that will welcome you and your furry friend!

# Midtown West

New York is a city of incomparable diversity, evident in every quiet, tree-lined neighborhood, ethnic enclave, and luxury high-rise. The truth remains, however, that there is only one street in all five boroughs to be boldly hailed Restaurant Row. Consider that its famed location—where celebrity chefs prepare all-you-can-eat pasta alongside promising sushi bars—is in a neighborhood named Hell's Kitchen is further testament to its dedication to great food.

## Everything to Eat

Still, this is an area that insists on reinvention. Hence, Restaurant Row (perhaps due to its uneven reputation) is becoming known as Little Brazil near Sixth Avenue, where samba and street food are celebrated late summer each year on Brazilian Day. A few steps farther west and the city's eclectic identity comes to life again, where a walk down Ninth Avenue offers a world of goods. A wonderful start (or finale) can be found at **Amy's Bread,** whose crusty baguettes supply countless restaurant kitchens, while colorful cakes or cookies tempt passersby. Meanwhile across the avenue, **Poseidon Bakery** is rumored to be the very last place in America to still make its own phyllo dough by hand. Despite this revelation and Food Network feature, it remains grounded in the Old World and has the *spanakopita* to prove it. Regardless of its name, **Sullivan Street Bakery's** one and only retail outlet is actually on 47th, between 10th and 11th (a location so perilously far west in the Manhattan mindset that its success proves its worth in gold). Absolutely anything artisanal and delicious can be found nearby at the **Amish Market**, filled with perfectly fresh produce, meats, and an array of specialty items. A sweet side-trip is the **Little Pie Company**, whose beloved wares are rolled, filled, and baked in its glass-paneled display kitchen.

While this stretch of Hell's Kitchen is rich with markets and restaurants, those highlights are familiar to any theatre-going tourist or Lincoln Tunnel-bound commuter who has been stuck in its traffic, yearning for a burger from the **Film Center Café**. To unearth its hidden treasures, travel south of Port Authority Bus Terminal and visit a string of unassuming storefronts, starting with **Ninth Avenue International Foods**. These olives, spices, and spreads are a serious business, but it is the renowned *taramosalata* (as if prepared by the gods atop Mount Olympus) that finds its way into restaurants throughout the city. Stop by **Giovanni Esposito and Son's** meat market for a sampling of their famed Italian sausages. For sandwiches, **Manganaro's** is the true inventor of the original six-foot Italian-American "hero." These are among the family-owned landmark businesses that have quietly been shaping New York's food scene for the better part of a century.

## Street Eats

While this is an area often choked by traffic and overpopulated with hungry office workers, New Yorkers demand outstanding food, no matter the venue. Under the guidance of the Vendy Awards and the blog (midtownlunch.com), discover a moveable feast of fast, satisfying street-food vendors. Highlights include sausage and schnitzel from **Hallo German Food Stand** (54th and 5th) and the **Treats Truck** (check the web or follow on Twitter for upcoming locales). Those seeking a more stable location to grab a fantastic burger, fries, or milkshake will not be disappointed at **Burger Joint**, quietly tucked inside Le Parker Meridien Hotel. Foodies wanting a rarer treat know to head south to K-town—the type of New York neighborhood that sneaks up and floors you. Its instant, unmistakable Asian vibe owes largely to the prominence of karaoke bars, authentic grocers, and countless spots for fresh tofu or handmade dumplings.

## Shopping and Style

Throughout Midtown West, it is clear that equal attention is paid to cuisine as to arranging storybook holiday mannequins behind the velvet ropes of Saks Fifth Avenue. As if to illustrate the point, the Japanese bakery, **Minamoto Kitchoan**, channels elegance and subtlety in its impossibly beautiful rice cakes, bejeweled with plum wine gelée or golden sprinkles. The exquisite packaging makes these the penultimate hostess gift for any uptown dinner party.

On the other end of the spectrum, **AQ Café** puts every effort into serving three outstanding meals a day to its throngs of midtown devotees (four, if counting the fabulous pastries).

## Time Warner Center

No visit here is complete without tribute to the gargantuan feat that is the AOL Time Warner Center, presiding over Columbus Circle. Here, world-renowned chefs indulge both themselves and their patrons with earth-shaking success. The good news is that the economic downturn has eased demands for reservations (the bad news is the price tag). Still, a range of pleasures can be found here, from **Bouchon Bakery's** classic French *macaron* cookies, to the eye-popping style and sass of Clo Wine Bar. Yet many New Yorkers assert that the crowning glory here is Dizzy's Club Coca Cola. Named for Jazz great Dizzy Gillespie, and launched under the guidance of artistic director Wynton Marsalis, this is where some of America's most talented musicians come to play, hear, and toast this art form.

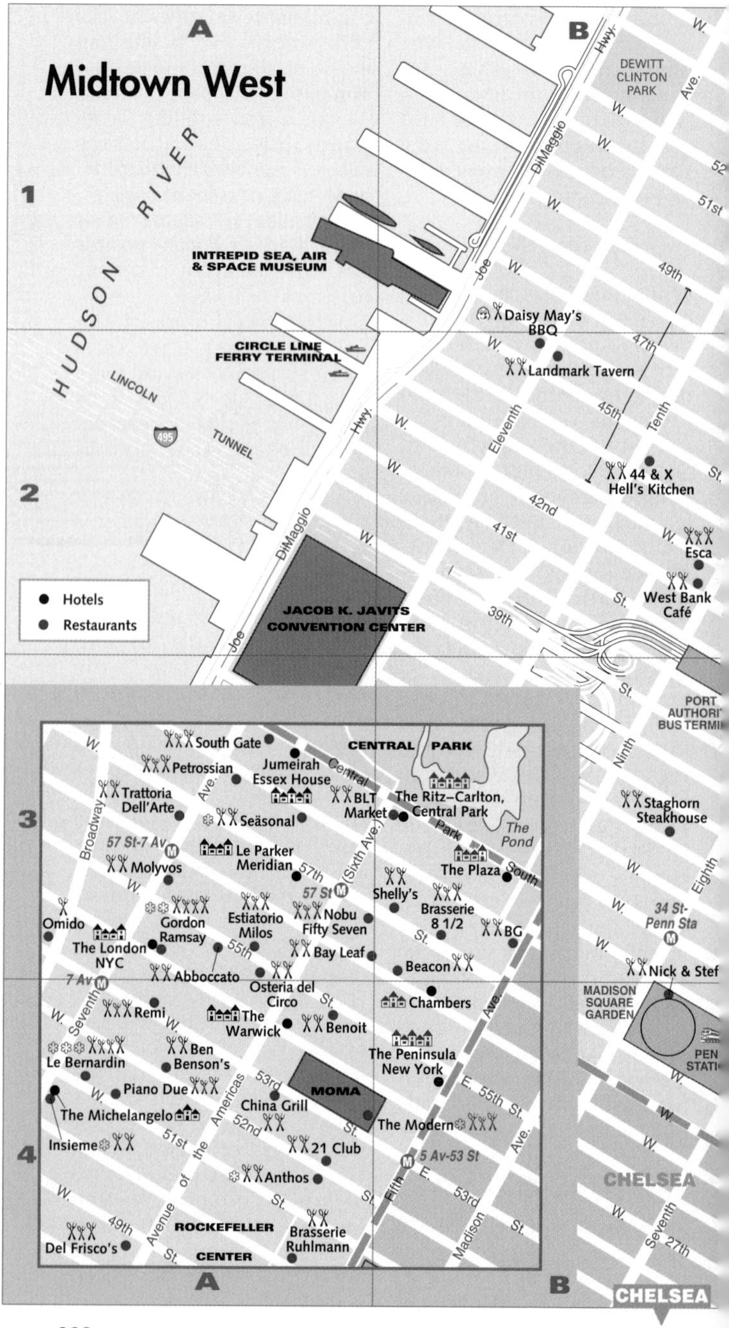

Midtown West
A
B
1
2
3
4
HUDSON RIVER
INTREPID SEA, AIR & SPACE MUSEUM
CIRCLE LINE FERRY TERMINAL
LINCOLN TUNNEL
495
DEWITT CLINTON PARK
Joe DiMaggio Hwy.
Daisy May's BBQ
Landmark Tavern
44 & X Hell's Kitchen
Esca
West Bank Café
JACOB K. JAVITS CONVENTION CENTER
Hotels
Restaurants
PORT AUTHORI BUS TERMI
Staghorn Steakhouse
34 St-Penn Sta
Nick & Stef
MADISON SQUARE GARDEN
PEN STATI
CHELSEA
Eleventh
Tenth
Ninth
Eighth
Seventh
W. 52
51st
49th
47th
45th
42nd
41st
39th
St.
27th
South Gate
Petrossian
Jumeirah Essex House
CENTRAL PARK
Trattoria Dell'Arte
BLT Market
The Ritz–Carlton, Central Park
Seäsonal
57 St-7 Av
Le Parker Meridian
The Pond
Molyvos
The Plaza
57 St
Shelly's
Omido
Gordon Ramsay
Estiatorio Milos
Nobu Fifty Seven
Brasserie 8 1/2
BG
The London NYC
Bay Leaf
Beacon
Abboccato
Osteria del Circo
7 Av
Remi
The Warwick
Chambers
Benoit
Le Bernardin
Ben Benson's
The Peninsula New York
Piano Due
MOMA
The Michelangelo
China Grill
The Modern
Insieme
21 Club
5 Av-53 St
Anthos
Del Frisco's
ROCKEFELLER CENTER
Brasserie Ruhlmann
Broadway
Central Park South
(Sixth Ave.)
Avenue of the Americas
Fifth
Madison
E. 55th St.
E. 53rd St.
57th
55th
53rd
52nd
51st
49th
CHELSEA

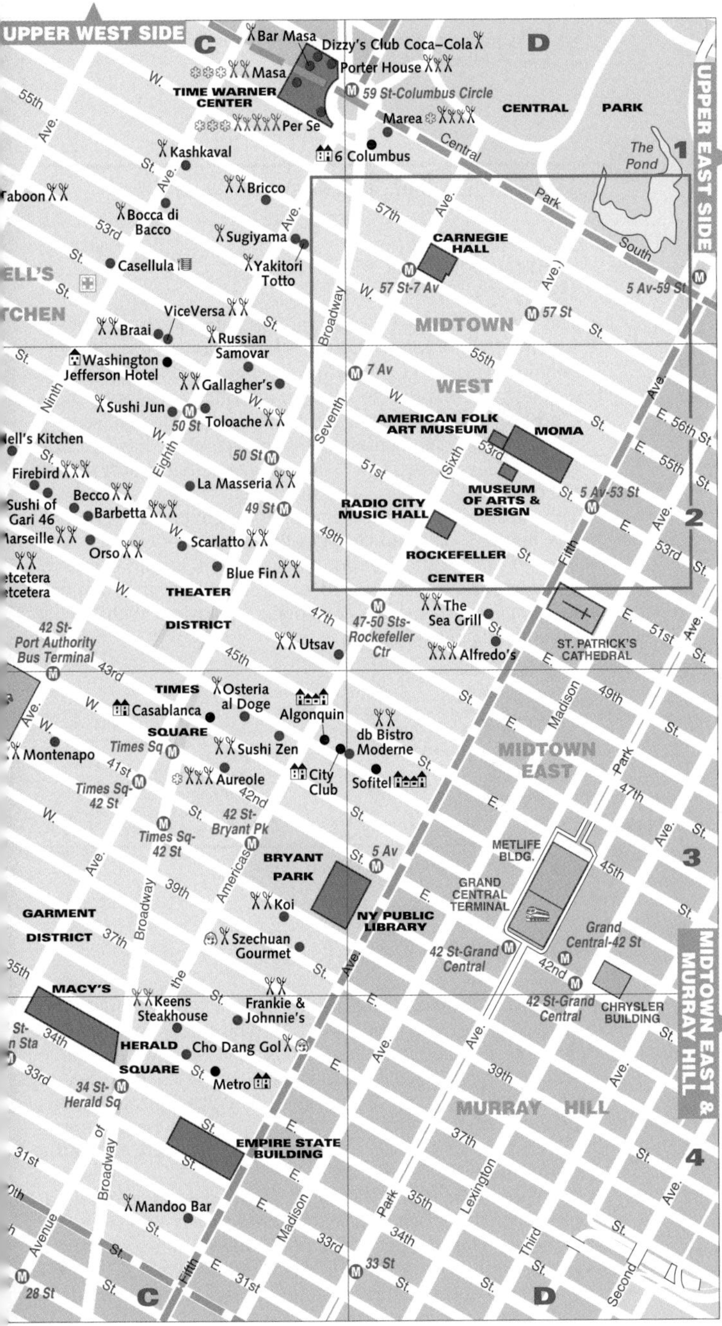
UPPER WEST SIDE
UPPER EAST SIDE
MIDTOWN EAST & MURRAY HILL
Bar Masa
Dizzy's Club Coca-Cola
Porter House
Masa
TIME WARNER CENTER
59 St-Columbus Circle
CENTRAL PARK
Marea
Per Se
Kashkaval
6 Columbus
The Pond
Bricco
Taboon
Bocca di Bacco
Sugiyama
Casellula
Yakitori Totto
CARNEGIE HALL
57 St-7 Av
5 Av-59 St
ViceVersa
Braai
Russian Samovar
MIDTOWN
57 St
Washington Jefferson Hotel
Gallagher's
7 Av
WEST
Sushi Jun
50 St
Toloache
Hell's Kitchen
AMERICAN FOLK ART MUSEUM
MOMA
Firebird
50 St
La Masseria
Becco
Sushi of Gari 46
Barbetta
49 St
MUSEUM OF ARTS & DESIGN
5 Av-53 St
RADIO CITY MUSIC HALL
Marseille
Orso
Scarlatto
ROCKEFELLER CENTER
Etcetera Etcetera
Blue Fin
THEATER DISTRICT
The Sea Grill
47-50 Sts-Rockefeller Ctr
Utsav
Alfredo's
ST. PATRICK'S CATHEDRAL
42 St-Port Authority Bus Terminal
TIMES SQUARE
Osteria al Doge
Casablanca
Algonquin
db Bistro Moderne
Montenapo
Times Sq
Sushi Zen
MIDTOWN EAST
City Club
Aureole
Sofitel
Times Sq-42 St
42 St-Bryant Pk
BRYANT PARK
5 Av
METLIFE BLDG.
GRAND CENTRAL TERMINAL
Koi
NY PUBLIC LIBRARY
Grand Central-42 St
GARMENT DISTRICT
Szechuan Gourmet
42 St-Grand Central
MACY'S
Keens Steakhouse
Frankie & Johnnie's
CHRYSLER BUILDING
HERALD SQUARE
Cho Dang Gol
Metro
34 St-Herald Sq
MURRAY HILL
EMPIRE STATE BUILDING
Mandoo Bar
33 St
28 St
C
D
1
2
3
4

# Abboccato

Italian XX

A3

136 W. 55th St. (bet. Sixth & Seventh Aves.)

**Subway:** 57 St — Lunch Mon – Sat
**Phone:** 212-265-4000 — Dinner nightly
**Web:** www.abboccato.com
**Prices:** $$$

This smartly appointed restaurant operates under the careful watch of the Livanos family—the seasoned restaurateurs behind the popular Oceana and Molyvos. Abboccato, located a stone's throw from the latter on a bustling cross street near the Blakely Hotel, boasts the family's characteristic style—with a sophisticated urban-rustic dining room, a bar area ripe for people watching, and a pretty *terrazza* that almost swings out onto the sidewalk.

The Italian menu meanders all through the old country, offering a virtual map of specialties like a perfectly cooked *bucatini all'amatriciana* doused in a rich, rustic sauce; or a deceptively simple grilled *orata*, topped with a lemony *salmoriglio* and a shake of capers, and paired with a silky mound of spinach.

# Alfredo's

Italian XXX

D2

4 W. 49th St. (bet. Fifth & Sixth Aves.)

**Subway:** 47-50 Sts - Rockefeller Ctr — Lunch & dinner daily
**Phone:** 212-397-0100
**Web:** www.alfredos.com
**Prices:** $$$

Make your way past the hungry 30 Rock tourists that mob Alfredo's, and you'll be rewarded with pizza and pasta so delicious it would make your *Nonna* blush. How can simple lasagna, layered with pasta, ragù, and béchamel, be so heavenly? How can an enormous Valtellina pizza pie—its perfectly crispy, paper-thin crust bursting with fresh toppings like creamy gorgonzola, soft mozzarella, ripe pear, and truffle oil—seem like a revelation?

With a whole lot of love and attention from a polished, professional kitchen—an asset Alfredo's has in spades, no matter how busy it gets. It's a philosophy that extends to the front-of-house as well, with a crackerjack waitstaff familiar with the menu and passionate about the ever-rotating daily specials.

# Anthos ✿

Greek XX

A4

36 W. 52nd St. (bet. Fifth & Sixth Aves.)

**Subway:** 47-50 Sts - Rockefeller Ctr
**Phone:** 212-582-6900
**Web:** www.anthosnyc.com
**Prices:** $$$

Lunch Mon – Fri
Dinner Mon – Sat

Battman/Anthos

Greek food gets the Midas touch at Anthos, the most sophisticated of Michael Psilakis and Donatella Arpaia's growing empire. As head chef and general it-boy-on-the-culinary-circuit, Psilakis shot to fame by reintroducing Manhattan's feta-worn denizens to a more polished vision of his family's food via restaurants like Kefi, the duo's casual, always-packed Upper West Side institution.

The revival may have inspired Anthos' moniker, which means "rebirth" in Greek. Or perhaps it's a nod to the restaurant's ethereal dining room—filled with creamy walls, stone tile floors, and cherry blossom accents—the interior is a decided step into fine dining territory.

But good looks will only get you so far. Anthos' mighty kitchen is the real star here, pushing out plates of tenderly curled smoked octopus, brightened with baby fennel, lemon confit, and earthy mushrooms; or a perfectly-roasted sliver of cod, lined in lemony broth and served on a cool bed of cucumber ribbons, fresh dill, and mint sprigs with briny black olives; or tender, farm raised chicken, poached in fragrant yogurt sauce paired with an apple-cardamom purée. Finished with a sip of Greek coffee, this is the acme of Hellenic dining.

# Aureole ✿

C3 **Contemporary** XXX

135 W. 42nd St. (bet. Broadway & Sixth Ave.)

**Subway:** 42 St - Bryant Pk
**Phone:** 212-319-1660
**Web:** www.charliepalmer.com
**Prices:** $$$$

Lunch Mon – Sat
Dinner nightly

Eric Laignel

Restaurant mogul Charlie Palmer's Upper East Side charmer moves midtown and gets brand new digs near Bryant Park. Tucked into the ground floor of the freshly-opened Bank of America tower, the new Aureole space is really a tale of two dining rooms (each with their own menus): the casual front bar room, a spacious dining area in its own right, with towering ceilings and handsome detailing; and the more formal, intimate, and earthy back room, featuring an eye-catching catwalk lined with wine bottles and an elaborate menu.

Chef Christopher Lee heads the kitchen, overseeing Palmer's vision while bringing his own formidable skills to the table. Witness an impeccably fresh diver sea scallop sandwich, topped with sautéed foie gras and paired with blanched sugar snap peas and a passion fruit and veal reduction sauce; or a duelling plate of butter poached lobster tail with spinach and chanterelle mushrooms pitted against tender braised pork belly in Jura wine sauce with bright summer squash.

Don't leave without talking to the excellent sommelier—a gentleman so on top of his game he might know why one pinot noir would be better suited for milk-fed veal as opposed to grass-fed veal.

# Barbetta

Italian XXX

C2

321 W. 46th St. (bet. Eighth & Ninth Aves.)

**Subway:** 50 St (Eighth Ave.) Lunch & dinner Tue – Sat
**Phone:** 212-246-9171
**Web:** www.barbettarestaurant.com
**Prices:** $$$

Steeped in history, from its landmark décor to a menu that features specialties dating back to 1906, Barbetta proves that old-world glamour will always be fashionable. Still owned by its founding family, the dining room is bedecked with antiques, wood paneling, chandeliers, and potted trees. The Piedmont-influenced menu has offered risotto with wild porcini mushrooms; handmade agnolotti; and *zuppa inglese* since the turn of the twentieth century. The restaurant also boasts that it is the first in America to possess an espresso machine. Pair your meal with one of more than 1,700 different labels on the tremendous wine list.

Scented by gardenia, oleander, and jasmine, the secluded and covered garden is an oasis in the heart of the Theatre District.

# Bar Masa

Japanese X

C1

10 Columbus Circle (in the Time Warner Center)

**Subway:** 59 St - Columbus Circle Lunch & dinner Mon – Sat
**Phone:** 212-823-9800
**Web:** www.masanyc.com
**Prices:** $$$

With its extensive menu and approachable prices, Bar Masa is a proper companion to Chef Masa Takayama's eponymous masterwork next door. Satisfy a yen for first-class fare without jeopardizing your retirement fund, and dig into the seasonal menu's structured listing of sushi offered à la carte; or a variety of grilled, braised, and fried dishes supplemented by rice and noodles. The décor of the slender room is earthy yet refined with pale walls tiled in Japanese limestone and dark wood furnishings. Gauzy fabric panels separate the popular bar area, which offers a well-chosen wine list embellished with several big ticket selections.

More creative offerings may include the house Champagne cocktail made with muddled yuzu zest and rosewater.

# Bay Leaf

A3 — Indian XX

49 W. 56th St. (bet. Fifth & Sixth Aves.)

**Subway:** 57 St — Lunch & dinner daily
**Phone:** 212-957-1818
**Web:** www.bayleafnyc.com
**Prices:** $$

As every Manhattan office bee knows, appearances can be deceiving in midtown. The clichéd Indian font that marks Bay Leaf's façade belies a lovely little Indian restaurant, with a sunlight-soaked dining room and a pretty outdoor patio overlooking 56th Street.

While the business crowd flocks to its ample buffet come lunch hour, nighttime finds a more languid crowd dabbling in Bay Leaf's classic, understated à la carte items, including a wealth of traditional curries and tandoori dishes. Try the smoky, green chili and chicken, laced with curry leaves; the spicy creamed spinach, studded with chickpeas and fragrant with cardamom; or feather-light cheese and semolina fritters, poached in sweetened milk and dusted with pistachio and green cardamom.

# Beacon

B3 — American XX

25 W. 56th St. (bet. Fifth & Sixth Aves.)

**Subway:** 57 St — Lunch Sun – Fri
**Phone:** 212-332-0500 — Dinner nightly
**Web:** www.beaconnyc.com
**Prices:** $$$

Everything—even the succulent little oysters—gets the grill treatment at Chef Waldy Malouf's Beacon. If you don't believe it, you can see for yourself at Beacon's Kitchen Counter, a communal, 6-man table set up to face the kitchen's grill, pizza oven, and rotisserie.

By night, diners can watch everything from suckling pig to rotisserie chicken hit the open flames. But come weekday lunches, the table morphs into the Burger Bar, where Malouf includes a delicious tuna burger made from rough-cut chunks of fresh ruby-red tuna, tucked between two slices of grilled tender bread. Paired with a crispy tangle of shoestring fries and a few other inventive sides, the only thing missing is one of those generous cocktails Beacon is known for.

# Becco

Italian XX

C2

355 W. 46th St. (bet. Eighth & Ninth Aves.)

**Subway:** 42 St - Port Authority Bus Terminal
Lunch & dinner daily
**Phone:** 212-397-7597
**Web:** www.becco-nyc.com
**Prices:** $$

Translated as "nibble" in Italian, Becco is owned by famed food authority Lidia Bastianich and her son, Joseph. This Restaurant Row townhouse has long been a pre-theatre dining favorite, but the well-made, home-style presentations make Becco a destination in its own right. Exposed brick and terra-cotta tiles give the multi-room setting warmth that is brightened by skylights and colorful Italian landscapes on pale walls. Notice little images next to the menu items—these correspond to the specific cookbook in which Lidia's recipe appears—inspiring diners to recreate the experience at home.

Bargain hunters should indulge in the $25 wine selection, $22.95 dinner prix-fixe, or try the *sinfonia di pasta*, an unlimited amount of the chef's three daily pastas.

# Ben Benson's

Steakhouse XX

A4

123 W. 52nd St. (bet. Sixth & Seventh Aves.)

**Subway:** 5 Av - 53 St
Lunch Mon – Fri
**Phone:** 212-581-8888
Dinner nightly
**Web:** www.benbensons.com
**Prices:** $$$

Housed on the ground floor of an office building, Ben Benson's has spent over 25 years serving prime cuts of USDA meats and other classic American fare to its contented business clientele of power brokers and politicians (regulars' names are engraved on brass plaques set in wainscoting). The huge, rotating menu includes perfectly cooked steaks and chops, but southern fried chicken and pot pies are also highlights.

The high-ceilinged dining room, expertly staffed by courteous servers smartly attired in tan jackets, is airier than many of the steakhouses in town. Adding to variations, this New York mainstay remains free from chain ownership. For those who favor alfresco dining, the spacious sidewalk terrace provides a pleasant warm-weather setting.

# Benoit

A4 — French XX

## 60 W. 55th St. (bet. Fifth & Sixth Aves.)

**Subway:** 57 St — Lunch & dinner Mon – Sat
**Phone:** 646-943-7373
**Web:** www.benoitny.com
**Prices:** $$

After opening a New York branch of his beloved bistro, Benoit, in 2008 to a somewhat lukewarm critical reception, renowned Chef Alain Ducasse shuffled his kitchen lineup and reappeared with a new executive chef and partner—Le Cirque veteran, Pierre Schaedelin.

Together, they've reinvented the menu, introducing a host of new items as well as a daily specials list that pulls from Schaedelin's Alsatian origins. Perhaps as a nod to the economy, they've even dropped their prices a bit—all the more reason to dig into tender pig cheeks, served over a frisée and lentil salad laced with mustard-cumin vinaigrette; or a crispy Chatham cod casserole, dusted with fennel pollen and sea salt, and flanked by a bright mix of vegetables and olives.

# BG

B3 — American XX

## 754 Fifth Ave. (at 58th St.)

**Subway:** 5 Av - 59 St — Lunch & dinner daily
**Phone:** 212-872-8977
**Web:** www.bergdorfgoodman.com
**Prices:** $$$

How many Burnettes does it take to feed a group of Bergdorf Blondes? Just one if it's the talented Darryl Burnette—the chef hired by the luxury department store to create an inviting seventh-floor menu for their discerning clientele. Luckily, Burnette comes armed with a heavy-hitting resume (Spice Market and Métrazur, just to name a few), and a knack for spinning out delicate luncheon goodies like tender coins of ahi tuna tartare, layered with ripe avocado and crunchy *tobiko*.

The afternoon tea, served daily, is a perfect fit for the Parisian-styled salon, with its hand-painted wallpaper and 18th century chairs. Those looking for a soup or sandwich, minus the pomp, might want to wander over to Bar III, located in the men's store across the street.

# BLT Market

American XX

B3

1430 Sixth Ave. (at 59th St.)

**Subway:** 5 Av - 59 St — Dinner Tue – Sat
**Phone:** 212-521-6125
**Web:** www.bltrestaurants.com
**Prices:** **$$$**

The BLT empire continues to grow with the addition of Chef Laurent Tourondel's market-themed venture. The focus on seasonal, ingredient-driven cuisine is supported by menus that feature a monthly listing of peak produce and a blackboard of daily specials. Winter may bring spiced orange-glazed duck accompanied by collard greens and bacon. A few months later, this preparation may be updated to duck served two ways with spring onions and red currant jus.

The dining room, housed in the Ritz-Carlton Hotel, is an appealing union of city and country. Reclaimed wood furniture, antique farm tools, and black-and-white portraits of the restaurant's purveyors are complemented by velvet banquettes, colorful artwork, and large windows framing Central Park.

# Blue Fin

Seafood XX

C2

1567 Broadway (at 47th St.)

**Subway:** 49 St — Lunch & dinner daily
**Phone:** 212-918-1400
**Web:** www.brguestrestaurants.com
**Prices:** **$$$**

At first blush, the glass-walled bar that straddles this lively corner of Broadway and 47th Street looks like any other bustling Midtown bar—albeit one hip enough to serve time in the W Times Square Hotel. But hidden behind all that happy hour chatter is the impressive Blue Fin—a two-story restaurant with a winding staircase that leads to a beautiful, serene upstairs dining room filled with soft jazz from the live piano.

The menu tackles seafood and sushi with grace—a slender column of ruby-red tuna is piped with creamy avocado, and capped with wonton crackers and a little spicy *Sriracha*; while a sesame-crusted bigeye tuna gets some oomph from shiitake mushrooms, a scoop of fragrant jasmine rice, and a tangle of carrots and snow peas.

# Bocca di Bacco

C1 **Italian** X

828 Ninth Ave. (bet. 54th & 55th Sts.)

**Subway:** 50 St (Eighth Ave.)
**Phone:** 212-265-8828
**Web:** www.boccadibacconyc.com
**Prices:** $$

Lunch Sat – Sun
Dinner nightly

This chicly rustic wine bar offers a deliciously varied menu, sure to please any mood. The space features heavy woodwork complemented by exposed brick walls, lined with shelves of wine and grappa bottles. Intimate seating is available, but groups or those interested in making new friends should opt for the communal tables, topped with slabs of white marble. Warm and welcoming, the front bar draws crowds of nearby residents and serves more than 40 wines by the glass from an all-Italian list. For a light snack, order a few of the *assagi*, like the chef's selection of cheeses served with fig jam and honey; or the meat-stuffed olives, fried crisp and delicious. More substantial offerings include excellent homemade pastas and simply prepared meat and fish.

# Braai

C1 **South African** XX

329 W. 51st St. (bet. 8th & 9th Sts.)

**Subway:** 50 St (Eighth Ave.)
**Phone:** 212-315-3315
**Web:** www.braainyc.com
**Prices:** $$

Lunch & dinner Tue – Sun

With a menu that includes ostrich, deviled chicken livers, and African road runner, it didn't take long for this South African restaurant to create a buzz. Opened in 2008, Braai has a few service kinks to iron out if it wants to match the popularity of its sister bar, Xai Xai (a South African wine bar located a few hundred feet away at *365 West 51st St*). But for now, the sultry décor—think sexy arched ceilings and gnarled, dark wooden beams—and creative fare more than compensate.

Save room to linger over your wine with a classic South African dessert like the Malva pudding—a soft, springy bread pudding dish of Dutch origin, with caramelized banana and creamy vanilla ice cream that arrives on a thin bed of fragrant *granadilla-amarula* custard.

# Brasserie 8 1/2

Contemporary XXX

B3

9 W. 57th St. (bet. Fifth & Sixth Aves.)

**Subway:** 57 St — Lunch Sun – Fri
**Phone:** 212-829-0812 — Dinner nightly
**Web:** www.brasserie8andahalf.com
**Prices:** $$$

The sweeping, tangerine-colored staircase that delivers you into Brasserie 8 1/2 is probably a bit more theatrical than the restaurant's menu is prepared to live up to, but this Patina group restaurant has a few tricks up its sleeve. Settle into the main dining room—with its eye-popping hues and unique artwork—and you'll find a solid contemporary French menu, with prettily plated items like yellowfin and mackerel tartare, topped with crème fraîche and passion fruit; or a light and springy trio of fruit sorbets.

Though it's clearly designed to impress company, the restaurant also caters well to solo guests, who can head to the handsome, elevated mezzanine for a quick bite; or hunker down at one of the two sleek, sexy bars that anchor the dining room.

# Brasserie Ruhlmann

French XX

A4

45 Rockefeller Plaza (bet. Fifth & Sixth Aves.)

**Subway:** 47-50 Sts - Rockefeller Ctr — Lunch daily
**Phone:** 212-974-2020 — Dinner Mon – Sat
**Web:** www.brasserieruhlmann.com
**Prices:** $$$

Named for the French designer, Emile-Jacques Ruhlmann, this midtown brasserie—with its dark panels, red velvet, and sexy sconces—sweeps you out of touristy Rockefeller Center and into a heady vision of old-school Paris.

A solid and commendable team heads the kitchen, spinning otherwise staid bistro classics into delicious artistry. A poached artichoke vinaigrette arrives tender and succulent, a rémoulade topped with black olive tapenade spooned into its center; while a pristine Dover Sole Meunière is served whole, beautifully browned, and sided with *pommes fondant* and a bright bundle of sautéed spinach. A decadent cookie plate, filled with creamy lemon squares and rich chocolate triangles, almost prepares you for the outside world again.

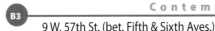

# Bricco

C1 | Italian XX

304 W. 56th St. (bet. Eighth & Ninth Aves.)

**Subway:** 57 St - 7 Av — Lunch Mon – Fri
**Phone:** 212-245-7160 — Dinner nightly
**Web:** www.bricconyc.com
**Prices:** $$

It's a bit of a challenge to spot this cozy space in the swirling hubbub of nearby Columbus Circle, but its well worth keeping your eyes peeled. Romantic little nooks like Bricco don't come easy in this neck of the woods, and smooth-talking owner, Nino Catuogno, knows it—he's got the autographed lipstick kisses that line the ceiling to prove it, not to mention a bevy of female fans who line the wooden bar every evening. Couples can head back to the intimate main room for delicious pizzas (made to order in the dining room); fat ribbons of whole wheat pasta in meaty ragù; or tender filet mignon dancing in brandy and cream, and sprinkled with crunchy peppercorns. Save room for a fragrant dessert of deep purple pears, poached in wine and liqueur.

# Casellula

C1 | American

401 W. 52nd St. (bet. Ninth & Tenth Aves.)

**Subway:** 50 St (Eighth Ave.) — Dinner nightly
**Phone:** 212-247-8137
**Web:** www.casellula.com
**Prices:** ⊜

This charming cheese and wine café arrives courtesy of partners Brian Keyser and Joe Farrell. The former ran the cheese program at The Modern before partnering with Farrell to open this simple, but elegant, space off of Ninth Avenue, where a small bar area and handful of dark wood tables meet simply-adorned exposed-brick walls and rustic rows of wine bottles.

The menu features over 30 varieties of cheese (many recipes include wine or beer), and might include a housemade baguette stuffed with roasted pork butt topped with Fol Epi cheese and bread-and-butter pickles, and served with creamy chipotle aïoli; or a roasted beet salad sprinkled with piles of soft, top-grade buffalo mozzarella, hazelnut, flower pollen, and dressed in red wine vinaigrette.

# China Grill

Asian XX

A4

60 W. 53rd St. (bet. Fifth & Sixth Aves.)

**Subway:** 5 Av - 53 St — Lunch Mon – Sat
**Phone:** 212-333-7788 — Dinner nightly
**Web:** www.chinagrillmgt.com
**Prices:** $$$

Opened more than 20 years ago, this first China Grill continues to be a perennial favorite and serves as the flagship of Jeffrey Chodorow's international restaurant organization. The sprawling interior designed by Jeffrey Beers is housed on the ground floor of the CBS building and features a multi-level dining room of 30-foot ceilings accented with white canopy light fixtures. The long bar area is a popular spot to unwind after a long day at the office; large tables enjoying ample portions of fun cuisine fill the soaring space with good-humored revelry.

Served family style, the Asian-influenced menu shows strength in creativity with items like creamy miso-dressed salad topped with fried calamari, or risotto with edamame and grilled vegetables.

# Cho Dang Gol

Korean X

C4

55 W. 35th St. (bet. Fifth & Sixth Aves.)

**Subway:** 34 St - Herald Sq — Lunch & dinner daily
**Phone:** 212-695-8222
**Web:** www.chodanggolny.com
**Prices:** ⓈⓈ

Let K-town have its barbecue joints. Cho Dang Gol has its own thing going on—namely tofu, that creamy little bean curd that sets hearts a-jumping. The restaurant is named for a South Korean village that's famous for the stuff, and one imagines the locals would stand by this fresh, silky housemade version, which finds its way into menu items like hot and crispy pancakes, filled with ground pork, vegetables, and scallions; or a cast iron pot, loaded with sweet and spicy octopus, oyster mushrooms, and steamed rice.

Looks-wise, Cho Dang Gol cuts a warm and fuzzy figure with its cute Korean artifacts and rustic wooden tables—but don't expect like-minded service. When the house gets packed, servers respond with brusque efficiency.

# Daisy May's BBQ

**Barbecue** ✗

**B2**

### 623 Eleventh Ave. (at 46th St.)

**Subway:** 50 St (Eighth Ave.)
**Phone:** 212-977-1500
**Web:** www.daisymaysbbq.com
**Prices:** ⊜⊜

Lunch & dinner daily

Manhattan's westside cradles some of the best down-home barbecue. This home-style spot (imagine a cross between a barn and cafeteria) is divorced from its location, northwest of Broadway's bright lights. In the spotlight is celebrity chef, Adam Perry Lang (and his vending carts), that can be seen around the city, good weather permitting.

Everyone from bankers to bike messengers frequent Daisy May's for its fantastic food and friendly aura. Order at the counter and receive a tray filled with smoky, tender chicken slathered in rich, sweet barbecue sauce. Bring friends and an appetite to indulge in the whole pig, smoked for eight hours (remember to order this two days in advance). Don't pass on the minty iced tea which will quench any thirst.

# db Bistro Moderne

**Contemporary** ✗✗

**D3**

### 55 W. 44th St. (bet. Fifth & Sixth Aves.)

**Subway:** 5 Av
**Phone:** 212-391-2400
**Web:** www.danielnyc.com
**Prices:** $$$

Lunch Mon – Sat
Dinner nightly

This stylish Daniel Boulud bistro is a big hit with the Chanel-toting theater crowd—the kind of moneyed clientele that looks perfectly at home in the sophisticated space, which is divided into a lively, red-accented front room and a more elegant, refined back room.

Boulud's French-inflected menu showcases the chef's formidable skills in dishes like Moroccan tuna tartare topped with cucumber raita and chickpeas, then ringed with a tasty harissa-infused mayo; *loup de mer en papillote* with ratatouille, artichokes, and fennel purée; or blueberry *mille-feuille* with a corn blini, corn ice cream, and violet meringue. Don't miss the burger—a foie gras and black truffle-laced short rib affair that helped ignite New York's gourmet burger renaissance.

# Del Frisco's

Steakhouse XXX

A4

1221 Sixth Ave. (at 49th St.)

**Subway:** 47-50 Sts - Rockefeller Ctr — Lunch Mon – Fri
**Phone:** 212-575-5129 — Dinner nightly
**Web:** www.delfriscos.com
**Prices:** $$$

Prime, aged, corn-fed beef is the main attraction at this sprawling steakhouse—Manhattan's outpost of the Dallas-based chain. Portions range from a six-ounce lunchtime filet, to the 24-ounce Porterhouse for dinner and will make any Texan proud.

Starters may feature a blue cheese and iceberg wedge salad, or traditional shrimp cocktail. For dessert, the light creamy cheesecake is smooth and delicious.

Complementing its "big business" midtown locale on the ground floor of the McGraw-Hill Building, Del Frisco's showcases a large L-shaped bar with comfortable leather stools and linen-covered tables set against window panels stretching to the second floor. The mezzanine dining area, accessible by a grand sweeping staircase, enjoys a quieter ambience.

# Dizzy's Club Coca-Cola

Southern X

C1

10 Columbus Circle (in the Time Warner Center)

**Subway:** 59 St - Columbus Circle — Dinner nightly
**Phone:** 212-258-9595
**Web:** www.jalc.org
**Prices:** $$

It took legendary jazz man, Wynton Marsalis, plenty of smooth-talking to convince the myriad city officials and developers that the Time Warner Building should permanently house Jazz at Lincoln Center—but the terrific Dizzy's Club Coca-Cola, a jazz hall-cum-restaurant is all the proof needed to greenlight this project.

Housed on the 5th floor of the North tower, at the Frederick P. Rose Hall, this swanky little gem has glossy windows overlooking Central Park, and grub as delicious as the rotating lineup of performers are talented. Dress loosely—the menu features a naughty lineup of southern staples like succulent fried chicken served with creamy mashed potatoes and tender collard greens; and velvety grits studded with plump shrimp.

# Esca

Seafood XXX

B2

402 W. 43rd St. (bet. Ninth & Tenth Aves.)

**Subway:** 42 St - Port Authority Bus Terminal — Lunch Mon – Sat
**Phone:** 212-564-7272 — Dinner nightly
**Web:** www.esca-nyc.com
**Prices:** $$$

For the uninitiated, *crudi* are a type of Italian sashimi—and Esca is the restaurant that put it on New York's culinary map. No wonder, with a triple threat like Mario Batali, Joseph Bastianich, and David Pasternack at the helm. Recently, however, this estimable seafood restaurant has missed its mark on occasion, leaving some to wonder who is steering the ship. But when it's good, it's fantastic—for starters, there are the heavenly Italian-style vegetables from the house table.

And the crackerjack staff seems to have a gift for patiently steering newcomers to the perfect Italian wine. Lastly, there are Esca's undeniable rustic charms. Who cares about a little imperfection when you're bathed in those creamy yellow walls, dark timbers and soft light?

# Estiatorio Milos

Greek XXX

A3

125 W. 55th St. (bet. Sixth & Seventh Aves.)

**Subway:** 57 St — Lunch Mon – Fri
**Phone:** 212-245-7400 — Dinner nightly
**Web:** www.milos.ca
**Prices:** $$$

It's not nice to fool Mother Nature, and at Milos, they don't try—they carefully source organic ingredients, so there's no need to do much to improve on them. The concept here is simple: you choose your fish from the fresh-from-the-sea array displayed at the counter, decide how much you want (it's sold by weight), and specify whether you want it to be charcoal-grilled or baked in sea salt. Soon, it will appear at your table, adorned with olive oil and lemon sauce. The Milos Special is the best starter, and deliriously sweet baklava makes the perfect ending.

The cacophonous dining room melds touches of industrial modern with Greek taverna in a bright setting. Prices can be high, but it's still cheaper than a trip to the Greek Islands.

# etcetera etcetera

Italian XX

C2

352 W. 44th St. (bet. Eighth & Ninth Aves.)

**Subway:** 42 St - Port Authority Bus Terminal
**Phone:** 212-399-4141
**Web:** www.etcrestaurant.com
**Prices:** $$

Lunch Wed & Sun
Dinner Tue – Sun

Brought to you by the talented trio of Italian guys behind Vice Versa, etcetera etcetera finds it's distinctiveness from its sister restaurant in its eye-popping, futuristic décor and its clever Mediterranean-accented Italian fare.

A colorful salad of ripe red tomatoes, cucumbers, onions, and dill fronds gets a shot of tart yogurt dressing; while a trio of moist veal meatballs are cloaked in a chunky tomato sauce, and paired with a thick slab of sour dough bread. The pastas are made in house, and can be ordered in half sizes. All the more reason to sample two—like soft pillows of *amaretti*, veal, and raisin ravioli in butter and sage, studded with salty pancetta; or a tangle of basil-flavored spaghetti, bathed in a garlic-laced tomato sauce.

# Firebird

Russian XXX

C2

365 W. 46th St. (bet. Eighth & Ninth Aves.)

**Subway:** 42 St - Port Authority Bus Terminal
**Phone:** 212-586-0244
**Web:** www.firebirdrestaurant.com
**Prices:** $$$

Lunch Tue – Sat
Dinner Tue – Sun

Firebird celebrates "pre-Revolutionary" Russia in a decadent Theatre District brownstone replete with ornate Russian art, rare books, jewel-toned furnishings, and crystal lighting. This opulent atmosphere is further enriched by the well-orchestrated formal service team.

The menu lists classic Russian specialties such as borscht, chicken Kiev, and an extensive selection of caviar. The comfortable bar area is a lovely spot to sit back and peruse the encyclopedic vodka listing which represents more than 150 labels from such far-flung locales as China, New Zealand, and Scotland. Start your meal on a sweet note with the *tsartini*, made with honey-infused vodka, then end on one again, sipping strong black tea sweetened with preserved cherries.

# 44 & X Hell's Kitchen

American XX

B2

622 Tenth Ave. (at 44th St.)

**Subway:** 42 St - Port Authority Bus Terminal — Lunch & dinner daily
**Phone:** 212-977-1170
**Web:** www.44andx.com
**Prices:** $$

With its jumbo, glossy windows overlooking a prime people-watching corner of 44th Street and Tenth Avenue, this Hell's Kitchen mainstay is a classic choice day or night. Make that any time of year, in fact—on warm summer afternoons, guests queue up for the prime outdoor tables under the big striped awning out front, and come wintertime, the sophisticated, carved wooden bar beckons.

The service staff can read a little flaky on occasion, though it's probably par for the course with waiters sporting cheeky "Heaven" and "Hell" t-shirts. Best to belly up and join the fun, digging into inventive American fare like stacked roasted beets, piped with tangy goat cheese; or moist turkey meat loaf, studded with oyster mushrooms and wrapped in smoky bacon.

# Frankie & Johnnie's

Steakhouse XX

C4

32 W. 37th St. (bet. Fifth & Sixth Aves.)

**Subway:** 34 St - Herald Sq — Lunch Mon – Fri
**Phone:** 212-947-8940 — Dinner Mon – Sat
**Web:** www.frankieandjohnnies.com
**Prices:** $$$

Located in the former home of actor John Drew Barrymore, this renovated town house offers diners a bit of history and a lot of prime, dry-aged steak in the heart of the Garment District—the first Frankie & Johnnie's established in 1926 is just steps away, and the third sibling sits in Rye, NY. The wood-paneled library is now the second floor dining room, featuring a coffered ceiling and original fireplace, enhancing this very comfortable, masculine setting.

Diners with booming voices feel no need to tone down their bonhomie while enjoying choice cuts of prime, dry-aged beef, but no one seems to mind the din. The all-male brigade of waiters is especially helpful; the restaurant even has a limousine service to shuttle guests anywhere in midtown.

# Gallagher's

C2 — Steakhouse XX

228 W. 52nd St. (bet. Broadway & Eighth Ave.)

**Subway:** 50 St (Broadway) — Lunch & dinner daily
**Phone:** 212-245-5336
**Web:** www.gallaghersnysteakhouse.com
**Prices:** **$$$**

Established in 1927 next door to what is now the Neil Simon Theater, this culinary character and true New Yorker satisfies carnivores with beef, beef, and more beef. That focus is brought home when diners enter to see rows of assorted cuts hanging, patiently aging, in the glass-enclosed meat locker. Inside the wood-paneled dining room, charmingly gruff waiters in gold-trimmed blazers efficiently tend red-checked tables, alongside walls lined with nostalgic photographs of Broadway stars, politicians, and athletes.

While meals are not cheap, the beef shows a quality that shines. The traditional Caesar salad and cheesecake are delicious bookends to any meal here. The prix-fixe lunch at under $30 is an excellent option for the budget conscious.

# Hell's Kitchen

C2 — Mexican X

679 Ninth Ave. (bet. 46th & 47th Sts.)

**Subway:** 50 St (Eighth Ave.) — Lunch Tue – Fri
**Phone:** 212-977-1588 — Dinner nightly
**Web:** www.hellskitchen-nyc.com
**Prices:** **$$**

Upscale Mexican food might finally be enjoying its heyday on the city's culinary scene, but Hell's Kitchen was way ahead of the curve. Named for the western midtown neighborhood it calls home, this restaurant has been packing them in from day one—and for good reason. Think delicious, complex Mexican food—spiced to order and lovingly prepared—in a hip, lively, progressive eatery, with great service to boot.

Kick things off with a heaping plate of tender, shredded pork, braised to juicy perfection and folded into soft, warm tortillas, then laced with crème fraîche and chunky guacamole; and wind down with a wickedly good empanada stuffed with warm, gooey sweet banana, and topped with a caramelized bittersweet chocolate sauce.

# Gordon Ramsay at The London ✿✿

A3 **Contemporary** XXXX

151 W. 54th St. (bet. Sixth & Seventh Aves.)

**Subway:** 57 St — Dinner Tue – Sat
**Phone:** 212-468-8888
**Web:** www.gordonramsay.com
**Prices:** **$$$$**

© Tom Shelby

Call him a wild-eyed maniac. Call him a brutal, unrelenting perfectionist who could use a few anger management classes. Call him the devil himself, but there's no denying him this much—when internationally-acclaimed chef and now-infamous reality television star, Gordon Ramsay, decides to bring it, he *brings it*.

Tucked into the posh London NYC, there's nothing particularly crafty about the luxurious, simply-appointed dining room. Think crisp white linens, pale celadon chairs, and muted, unadorned walls and you kind of get the picture—the décor is meant to be effortlessly elegant, with all eyes focused squarely on the food.

Not too difficult a task with a lineup that spins to the season but might include seared Pacific yellowfin tuna and *battera kombu* (pickled kelp) in a yuzu glaze, surrounded by tender little cubes of steamed shiitake mushroom and jicama; or delicious Wisconsin veal rolled in crispy *tramezzini*, accompanied by chilled foie gras and Périgord truffle vinaigrette. Four menu options are offered nightly, but if you can swing an early dinner between 5:30 and 6:30 P.M., a $65 three-course dinner offers a lot of bang for your buck.

# Insieme ✿

Italian XX

A4

777 Seventh Ave. (at 51st St.)

**Subway:** 50 St (Broadway)
**Phone:** 212-582-1310
**Web:** www.restaurantinsieme.com
**Prices:** $$$

Lunch Mon – Fri
Dinner Mon – Sat

Jocelyn Filley/Insieme



Like Noah's Ark, things tend to come in pairs at Insieme. There are the two talented chef and sommelier co-owners, Marco Canora and Paul Grieco. Then there's the restaurant's competing menu, which lists contemporary Italian fare alongside more traditional Old Country plates (the five course tasting menu offers a little of both). Not to mention the polished, good-humored, service staff's knack for wine pairing—no small feat considered the extensive list at hand.

Given all this, is it any surprise that the moniker (pronounced in-see-em-eh) means "together" in Italian? Mercifully, it's a theme that's working, for Insieme—tucked into the Michelangelo hotel, and cut into clean, Scandinavian lines with a soothing palette drawn in shades of earth, wood, and stone—is a seamless operation.

From starters to closers, plates arrive artfully rendered, and taste as good as they look: a beautifully-executed arctic char arrives with crispy skin and a bright, moist center, garnished with tender baby artichoke hearts, glazed fennel, warm black olives, and red grapefruit; while a whipped chocolate custard, presented on delicate cake, is topped with chocolate ganache and bright raspberry *agrodolce*.

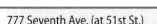

# Kashkaval

C1 — Mediterranean

856 Ninth Ave. (bet. 55th & 56th Sts.)

**Subway:** 50 St (Eighth Ave.) — Lunch & dinner daily
**Phone:** 212-581-8282
**Web:** www.kashkavalfoods.com
**Prices:** **$$**

More often than not, there's a long line to get into this charming little Middle Eastern restaurant, tucked into a food-deprived patch of bustling 9th Avenue. The good news is that there's plenty to busy yourself with while you wait, for the front of house doubles as a grocery store stocked with all kinds of mouthwatering goodies like garlicky spreads, delicious cheeses, and exotic oils.

You're also likely to forget all sense of time when you finally do snag a seat in the rustic little back café, and the delicious food starts hitting the table. Try the *muhammara*, a delicious, peppery Lebanese walnut spread; or flaky little cigars stuffed with spinach and feta and rolled into crispy, spiraled buns; or moist turkey meatballs glistening with tomato.

# Keens Steakhouse

C4 — Steakhouse

72 W. 36th St. (bet. Fifth & Sixth Aves.)

**Subway:** 34 St - Herald Sq — Lunch Mon – Fri
**Phone:** 212-947-3636 — Dinner nightly
**Web:** www.keens.com
**Prices:** **$$$**

A survivor of the erstwhile Herald Square Theater District, this palace of steaks, single-malt, and machismo has been thriving since 1885. A sense of history pervades the restaurant, which enforced a strict men-only rule until 1901, when British actress Lillie Langtry famously (and successfully) challenged this discriminatory policy in court. The restaurant has an impressive collection of long-stemmed clay churchwarden pipes in racks lining the ceiling, a vestige of its men's-club days; and a sublime whiff of smoke imbues the space.

Fresh oysters; iced trays of seafood; and hearty steaks and chops come in portions—and prices—hefty enough to satisfy the hungriest carnivores. A lighter pub menu of salads, burgers, and sandwiches is also available.

# Koi

C3 — Fusion XX

40 W. 40th St. (bet. Fifth & Sixth Aves.)

**Subway:** 42 St - Bryant Pk — Lunch Mon – Fri
**Phone:** 212-921-3330 — Dinner nightly
**Web:** www.koirestaurant.com
**Prices:** $$$

This über-trendy New York offshoot of the West Hollywood flagship is aptly located in the Bryant Park Hotel, packed with the young, hip, and affluent. An enormous lattice canopy dominates the dining room; underneath it, elements of feng shui dictate the eye-popping design, with one exception to the rule—the pulsating music.

The menu is equally fashionable, with a wide array of sushi, sashimi, maki, and original Pan-Asian fare, as in the grilled salmon with yuzu emulsion or soft-shell crabs with spicy cream and ponzu. From the black-clad waitstaff and the chic plating, to the A-list crowd, cool is the operative word at Koi—perhaps replacing warmth from the staff. For a fashionista's night on the town, visit the forever trendy Cellar Bar.

# La Masseria

C2 — Italian XX

235 W. 48th St. (bet. Broadway & Eighth Ave.)

**Subway:** 50 St (Eighth Ave.) — Lunch & dinner daily
**Phone:** 212-582-2111
**Web:** www.lamasserianyc.com
**Prices:** $$

A congenial midtown Italian modeled after the ancient farmhouses of Puglia, La Masseria's décor is portrayed to full effect with exposed wood beams, stucco walls, and generous touches of stone and brick. Despite its scope, the large space retains a hint of intimacy and has a warm, countrified feel that is an interesting contrast to the restaurant's home on the ground floor of a hi-rise apartment tower. The kitchen creates delightfully rustic fare in items like the creamy homemade stuffed fresh mozzarella—simplicity at its very best.

Other offerings highlight a comforting and satisfying, Italian-American spirit, as in rigatoni bathed in a rich, meaty "traditional Sunday grandmother's sauce." This is also a great post-theater spot for an *aperitivo*.

# Landmark Tavern

B2 — American

626 Eleventh Ave. (at 46th St.)

**Subway:** 50 St (Eighth Ave.) — Lunch & dinner daily
**Phone:** 212-247-2562
**Web:** www.thelandmarktavern.org
**Prices:** $$

Originally opened in 1868, this old cat's had more than a few lives. First as an Irish saloon that catered to local dock workers; later as a mediocre restaurant in desperate need of repairs. And repairs it got with its 2005 transformation into the handsome new Landmark Tavern, replete with carved mahogany paneling, shiny beveled mirrors, and a clever new menu to match.

With the exit of the creative chef, Bryce Cole, however, the tavern isn't quite the ambitious foodie operation it was a few years back—but Landmark's commitment to high-minded pub fare is still very much intact with solid fare like the juicy cheeseburger laced with a thick slice of grilled Canadian bacon; or the warm, buttery tart, stuffed with tangy raspberry and crunchy walnuts.

# Mandoo Bar

C4 — Korean

2 W. 32nd St. (at Fifth Ave.)

**Subway:** 34 St - Herald Sq — Lunch & dinner daily
**Phone:** 212-279-3075
**Web:** N/A
**Prices:**

Mandoo is Korean for "dumpling", though you'll find more than that at this Koreatown favorite. Despite its postage stamp dimensions, Mandoo Bar burns through massive amounts of happy customers a day—most likely due to the fresh, unassuming Korean fare, dished out fast enough to keep weekend shoppers on the move.

The bar serves every kind of dumpling you can dream up, along with a host of Korean specialties like *Bulgogi Dolsot Bibimbob*, rice with marinated beef and vegetables in a hot stone pot; or *Yuk Kae Jang*, spicy beef soup with green onion and egg. Noodle lovers will rejoice in countless options, including the spicy, chewy *Joll Noodle* with carrots and boiled egg; or the sautéed clear sweet potato noodles that make up the *Japchae*.

# Le Bernardin ✿✿✿

Seafood XXXX

A4

155 W. 51st St. (bet. Sixth & Seventh Aves.)

**Subway:** 50 St (Broadway) Lunch Mon – Fri
**Phone:** 212-554-1515 Dinner Mon – Sat
**Web:** www.le-bernardin.com
**Prices:** **$$$$**

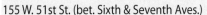

Lyn Hughes

In a town where the reigning fooderati doesn't agree on much, most everyone agrees on Eric Ripert—any way you slice it, the French-born chef of Le Bernardin is the real deal. Having cut his teeth with Joël Robuchon before packing his bags for American soil, Ripert is what you might call a chef's chef—a humble, super-talented guy who still prefers manning his own kitchen to celebrity guest spots.

The authenticity appears to have trickled down to his staff, which is friendly but as on-point as any orchestrated ballet—effortlessly winding through the elegant dining room, tending to the mix of old money clientele and splurging food geeks.

Ripert is a master of seafood, and his understanding of fish combined with his French technique makes for an unforgettable meal. The deceptively simple menu is divvied up into three sections—*almost raw, barely touched,* and *lightly cooked*—and might include fresh hamachi wrapped around a Vietnamese-style imperial roll, laced with a delicate vinaigrette beaded with chili oil and a shake of cilantro; or warm pieces of sweet lobster, topped with shaved heart of palm, micro herbs, and chives, and finished with coarse salt and a splash of orange vinaigrette.

# Marea ✿

Seafood

D1

240 Central Park South (bet. Broadway & Seventh Ave.)

**Subway:** 59 St - Columbus Circle

Lunch & dinner Mon – Sat

**Phone:** 212-582-5100

**Web:** www.marea-nyc.com

**Prices:** $$$$

Daniel Krieger/Marea

Fresh on the heels of wildly successful fine dining ventures, Alto and Convivio, Chef Michael White and partner Chris Cannon swing open the doors on their boldest venture yet—Marea, a stunning new restaurant perched along the southwestern corner of Central Park. But can lightning strike thrice in this economy?

When you're hot, you're hot—and White's menu hits it out of the ballpark once again. Like his other two ventures, Italian themes dominate, but Marea's angle is coastal Italian seafood, with a healthy list of *crudo*, pasta, and meat dishes (hand-picked by the prestigious Pat La Frieda) rounding out the menu. The restaurant itself is tricked out in every way imaginable—stunning backlit walls, impossibly glossy striped wood panels, beet red chandeliers—and one gets the feeling that no expense was spared in the design.

Not the worst place, then, to dip your fork into fresh, bite-sized chunks of sweet, chilled lobster paired with milky *burrata*, pickled eggplant batons, squishy little basil seeds, and a flutter of baby basil leaves; or a perfectly al dente pile of fusilli corkscrews in a velvety tomato sauce floating with tender, red wine-braised octopus and beads of bone marrow.

# Marseille

French XX

C2

630 Ninth Ave. (at 44th St.)

**Subway:** 42 St - Port Authority Bus Terminal Lunch & dinner daily
**Phone:** 212-333-2323
**Web:** www.marseillenyc.com
**Prices:** $$

For all its gussying up, Times Square's commercial food scene can tax the nerves. Who wants to visit the center of the universe only to eat at Applebee's? Enter the lovely Marseille—a bright, sun-streaked brasserie just two blocks west of the ruckus, and a million miles away in charm, with its bright blue floor tiles, apricot-colored walls, and cushy, red banquettes.

The restaurant is named for France's most Arab-influenced city, and the menu zigzags happily around the Mediterranean with fragrant, well-spiced dishes—lamb couscous, crab falafel, and Niçoise salad all make an appearance. For dinner, try the soft gnocchi bathed in a creamy Parmesan and basil sauce; and then move on to a warm apple tart, shot with a zippy line of cranberry sauce.

# Molyvos

Greek XX

A3

871 Seventh Ave. (bet. 55th & 56th Sts.)

**Subway:** 57 St - 7 Av Lunch & dinner daily
**Phone:** 212-582-7500
**Web:** www.molyvos.com
**Prices:** $$

Part of the Livanos family restaurant empire, which boasts Oceana as its crown jewel, and named for the owner's birthplace on the island of Lesvos, Molyvos brings the home-style dishes of Greece to Midtown.

Chef/partner Jim Botsacos, whose signed cookbook is available for purchase, can claim his fair share of the restaurant's success. Dishes such as *paidakia skharas*, smoky grilled lamb chops served alongside the house potato *kefte* and a wood-grilled eggplant salad, are the reasons why.

A block south of Carnegie Hall, Molyvos is well situated for those attending a performance. Order the modestly priced pre- and post-theater menu (available Monday through Saturday before 7:00 P.M. and after 9:30 P.M., and all day Sunday) to get in and out in a jiffy.

# Masa ✿✿✿

C1

Japanese XX

10 Columbus Circle (in the Time Warner Center)

**Subway:** 59 St - Columbus Circle
**Phone:** 212-823-9800
**Web:** www.masanyc.com
**Prices:** **$$$$**

Lunch Tue – Fri
Dinner Mon – Sat

Masa

No, you didn't break a window. That $400 bill is for real. It's outrageous, it's egregious—heck, it's downright irresponsible in this economy. And yet there's good news: if you've got the dough, a taste of Chef Masa Takayama's unparalleled omakase is worth the eye-popping price tag.

Make your way to the 4th floor of the Time Warner Center, and you'll find the legendary sushi chef's namesake restaurant—a beautiful, soothing Zen-like temple of blonde wood and stone, where a smart, but unhurried staff sets the tone for the brilliant parade of otherworldly fish and extraordinary ingredients to come.

The menu changes nightly, but may include a tiny mound of luscious fatty toro, minced and coated with glistening black caviar, then paired with delicate slices of warm brioche; a velvety and heavenly scoop of uni risotto; a warm rice ball rolled in shaved black truffle; or a knock-your-socks-off presentation of the perilous, but milky-white and lovely, fugu, lovingly stacked over a bed of *shiso* blossoms and micro-herbs, and dusted with gold leaf flakes. Real foodies will want to sit at the sushi bar, where they can watch the master and his acolytes go to town mere inches from their nose.

# The Modern ✿

Contemporary XXX

A4

9 W. 53rd St. (bet. Fifth & Sixth Aves.)

**Subway:** 5 Av - 53 St
**Phone:** 212-333-1220
**Web:** www.themodernnyc.com
**Prices:** $$$

Lunch daily
Dinner Mon – Sat

Sara Beth Turner

Even for a big city restaurant impresario, Danny Meyer is one busy guy. With six restaurants in Manhattan, a handful of eateries scattered elsewhere in the city, and a second outpost of Blue Smoke installed in the New York Mets' new ballpark, it's amazing that fine dining establishments like The Modern run so smoothly.

But run smoothly it does, and does so with grace. No one—from the head chef to the coat checker—misses a beat at this airy, sophisticated restaurant, tucked into the Museum of Modern Art and overlooking the Abby Aldrich Rockefeller sculpture garden. It's a fresh, stylish scene, with a pretty, well-heeled clientele to match.

Good thing the food can hold its own. A creamy, magenta-hued risotto is studded with crispy duck and a sprinkle of fried oregano; while a silky fan of *dorade* is dusted with flakes of sea urchin roe, drizzled in green yuzu-parsley vinaigrette, and then offered a shot of color from American caviar and vibrant micro greens. For dessert, try a lemon Napoleon, topped with a bright mélange of diced mango, papaya, kiwi, and pineapple. If you're just looking to soak up a little flavor and people-watch, the Bar Room offers small plates and cocktails.

# Montenapo

C3 **Italian** XXX

## 250 W. 41st St. (bet. Seventh & Eighth Aves.)

**Subway:** 42 St - Port Authority Bus Terminal — Lunch Sun – Fri
**Phone:** 212-764-7663 — Dinner nightly
**Web:** www.montenaporestaurant.com
**Prices:** $$$

Nestled into the bottom floor of the New York Times building, Montenapo cuts a glamorous figure—its sunken dining room boasting soaring ceilings and glass walls overlooking Renzo Piano's birch tree garden. Though not necessarily a bad thing, its sophisticated minimalism can sometimes read a bit corporate, especially at lunch when the power meetings converge.

The kitchen is clearly talented, spinning out a refined Italian menu that might include plump, braised veal cheek *agnolotti* over creamy celery root purée with a veal stock reduction; caper-crusted Alaskan wild salmon, served with sautéed artichokes, white asparagus, and tender spring onions; or warm ricotta cheesecake with Marsala-soaked raisins and a syrupy side of Amarena cherries.

# Nick & Stef's

B4 **Steakhouse** XX

## 9 Penn Plaza (bet. Seventh & Eighth Aves.)

**Subway:** 34 St - Penn Station — Lunch Mon – Fri
**Phone:** 212-563-4444 — Dinner Mon – Sat
**Web:** www.nickandstefs.com
**Prices:** $$$

Adjacent to Madison Square Garden and Penn Station, Nick & Stef's (named for Chef Joachim Splichal's twin sons) is part of his Patina Restaurant Group.

The menu exhibits good variety for a steakhouse; a selection of entrées, including baked halibut, seafood mixed grill, and organic chicken, balance the list of broiled steaks. Meats are served unadorned, so complement your meal with sides of hand-cut sweet potato fries or Brussels sprouts with apple-smoked bacon.

Lunchtime may highlight two burgers, appropriately named "The Nick" with aged cheddar and crisp onion strings; or "The Stef" with Maytag blue cheese and caramelized onions.

A suited clientele regularly fills this contemporary space, featuring angled pine ceilings and warm tones.

# Nobu Fifty Seven

Japanese XXX

A3

40 W. 57th St. (bet. Fifth & Sixth Aves.)

**Subway:** 57 St — Lunch Mon – Fri
**Phone:** 212-757-3000 — Dinner nightly
**Web:** www.noburestaurants.com
**Prices:** $$$$

Chef Nobu Matsuhisa continues to succeed here in midtown. The entrance may be out of view from the hustle and bustle of 57th street, but David Rockwell's sleek interior uses sake jugs above the bar, exotic woods, and rattan wall coverings to fashion a sultry mood—not an easy feat in a place this large and busy.

The restaurant attracts a cosmopolitan, clubbish crowd whose expense accounts can handle the hefty prices. Creative à la carte offerings feature great variety of fresh, well-prepared fish, but the uninhibited gourmand should simply put oneself in this very talented chef's hands and order the omakase. Attractively presented lacquered bento boxes feature tempura, sushi, and signature specialties like black cod with miso, a dish that made Nobu famous.

# Omido

Japanese X

A3

1695 Broadway (bet. 53rd & 54th Sts.)

**Subway:** 50 St (Broadway) — Lunch Mon – Fri
**Phone:** 212-247-8110 — Dinner nightly
**Web:** www.omidonyc.com
**Prices:** $$

David Letterman has tickled your funnybone and now you're hungry. Sushi perhaps? Then head straight to Omido. Next to the Ed Sullivan theatre, this sleek cube of a space, encased in slats of dark wood, features a square counter lit overhead by translucent globes.

The selection of top notch sushi is skillfully prepared before your eyes; and in addition, the menu is bolstered by tempting cold and hot dishes, like a seaweed tasting with sesame ponzu; crisp and delicate tempura; or braised Kobe short ribs. At lunchtime, several bento box options are offered. Now for the punchline: the sake list is well chosen, desserts display talent, and the charming service team ensures satisfaction.

# Orso

C2

Italian XX

322 W. 46th St. (bet. Eighth & Ninth Aves.)

**Subway:** 42 St - Port Authority Bus Terminal  Lunch & dinner daily
**Phone:** 212-489-7212
**Web:** www.orsorestaurant.com
**Prices:** $$

Who says actors don't eat? They certainly have an appetite for Orso, a late-night haunt of Broadway players in search of a post-show meal. It shows off their good taste too, for the food at this intimate little restaurant—with its friendly, easygoing staff and old black and white photos—is heads and shoulders above the Restaurant Row competition.

Occupying the ground floor of a charming brownstone, Orso turns out simple, but delicious, spins on Italian classics like an *insalata caprese*, bursting with colorful tomatoes, bright green basil, and soft pillows of mozzarella; or a spot-on *linguini alle vongole* brimming with fresh clams and toasted bread crumbs. Save room to stargaze over a fluffy cheesecake, topped with plump raisins and maple syrup.

# Osteria al Doge

C3

Italian X

142 W. 44th St. (bet. Broadway & Sixth Ave.)

**Subway:** Times Sq - 42 St  Lunch Mon – Fri
**Phone:** 212-944-3643  Dinner nightly
**Web:** www.osteria-doge.com
**Prices:** $$

Painted in sunny yellow, lit by wrought-iron chandeliers, and decorated with bright Italian ceramics, Osteria al Doge constantly plays to a packed house. The cuisine of Venice takes center stage here, with dishes such as *fegato alla Veneziana* (pan-roasted calves' liver in an onion and red-wine-vinegar sauce), and *brodetto Veneziano* (a mélange of seafood and shellfish braised in broth tinged with pinot grigio) paying homage to Italy's famous canal-laced city.

Set with linen placemats, fresh flowers, and glasses filled with crisp *grissini*, the long bar makes a comfortable perch for solo diners. Tables dress for dinner in the main room; service is attentive and friendly throughout.

# Osteria del Circo

Italian XX

A3

120 W. 55th St. (bet. Sixth & Seventh Aves.)

**Subway:** 57 St — Lunch Mon – Fri
**Phone:** 212-265-3636 — Dinner nightly
**Web:** www.osteriadelcirco.com
**Prices:** $$$

As the name would imply, the Maccioni family's vibrant midtown osteria explodes with exuberance. Overhead, bright, billowing fabric evokes the big top; figurines hang from a trapeze above the bar; and harlequin-patterned fabric covers banquettes and chairs. The service staff is professional and efficient, while maintaining the charm of this family operation.

The large selection of consistently good offerings may include thick chunks of tender octopus, grilled and infused with deliciously smoky flavors; or straightforward homemade pasta dishes like perfectly cooked *tagliolini* in a simple crushed tomato sauce with fresh basil. The day's catch are attractively displayed on ice in the dining room, bolstering the regular menu with seafood specials.

# Petrossian

French XXX

A3

182 W. 58th St. (at Seventh Ave.)

**Subway:** 57 St - 7 Av — Lunch & dinner daily
**Phone:** 212-245-2214
**Web:** www.petrossian.com
**Prices:** $$$

Linger on the sidewalk to marvel at the ornate Renaissance-style 1907 Alwyn Court Building that frames the entrance to Petrossian. Opened in 1984, this is the New York sister to Petrossian Paris, which has been delighting French diners since the 1920s. It was then that the two Petrossian brothers from Armenia made caviar the toast of Paris, and founded the company that now ranks as the premier importer of Russian caviar—the restaurant's specialty.

Located a block from Carnegie Hall, Petrossian showcases ingredients that are as rich as its surroundings, which are adorned with Lalique crystal sconces, etched Erté mirrors, and Limoges china. The contemporary French menu, peppered with caviar and foie gras, is perfect for lunch, brunch, or dinner.

# Per Se ✿✿✿

C1 Contemporary XXXXX

10 Columbus Circle (in the Time Warner Center)

**Subway:** 59 St - Columbus Circle
**Phone:** 212-823-9335
**Web:** www.perseny.com
**Prices:** $$$$

Lunch Fri – Sun
Dinner nightly

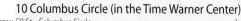

Deborah Jones

Consider Thomas Keller's oyster: He is pristine, just off the overnight shuttle from Duxbury, Massachusetts. Tonight, he'll find itself in the capable hands of one of the most revered chefs in the world—he of French Laundry fame—and be laid upon a bed of silky tapioca pearls, and topped with a soft pile of inky Osetra caviar.

And so begins a dinner at Per Se—a meal that many argue is the finest in the city. Dressed in soothing shades of hazelnut, the restaurant easily transports guests out of the Time Warner Center—the upscale mall that Per Se calls home—and into a world of refined grace. Don your finest (jackets are required for gentlemen) and arrive early to indulge in a glass of champagne in the lounge overlooking Central Park—this night should last as long as possible.

The luxurious dining room offers only three tasting menus—each one a mind-blowing affair that might lead down any number of delicious avenues, like creamy lentil mousse with a buttery vegetable *brunoise*; or tender beef loin over a soft pile of black trumpet mushrooms, kissed with watercress purée; or slips of fresh pasta lined with silky ricotta and spinach, then laced with brown butter and fried sage.

# Piano Due

A4 **Italian** XXX

## 151 W. 51st St. (bet. Sixth & Seventh Aves.)

**Subway:** 49 St — Lunch Mon – Fri
**Phone:** 212-399-9400 — Dinner Mon – Sat
**Web:** www.pianoduenyc.net
**Prices:** $$$

A midtown office courtyard provides access to this restaurant, which encompasses two separate spaces. First, enter through Palio Bar, which showcases Florentine artist Sandro Chia's mural, depicting Sienna's famed Palio horse race, and envelops the large circular bar room in a riot of vibrant color.

An elevator transports diners to Piano Due on the second floor, where red velvet chairs accent the white walls, and natural light reflects off the vaulted ceiling. Glass objets d'art and colorful artwork add to the refined atmosphere.

At dinner the kitchen's ambition shows up in the likes of a peppercorn-crusted filet mignon; and *pappardelle alla cacciatora*, its sauce blending wild game with a hint of cream, Barolo wine, and bitter chocolate.

# Porter House

C1 **Steakhouse** XXX

## 10 Columbus Circle (in the Time Warner Center)

**Subway:** 59 St - Columbus Circle — Lunch & dinner daily
**Phone:** 212-823-9500
**Web:** www.porterhousenewyork.com
**Prices:** $$$

Since the dawn of his newest 'stake'—Porter House—Michael Lomonaco has been delivering the exemplar of great flavors and ingredients, thereby reiterating his dedication to the dignity of American cuisine. Designed by Jeffrey Beers, this gallant roost on the fourth floor of the Time Warner Center, is as sophisticated as its cuisine, and exudes an aura of lavish modern easiness. Much cum laude is bestowed upon the handsome dining room, for its incredible vistas of Columbus Circle and Central Park.

This classic American grill has a solid framework of Porterhouse Cuts and à la carte sides (buttermilk onion rings and creamed spinach with bacon). But a delicious and vibrant selection of seafood and vegetables (crisp corn fried oysters or sautéed mushrooms), is as enticing.

# Remi

A4 — Italian XXX

145 W. 53rd St. (bet. Sixth & Seventh Aves.)

**Subway:** 7 Av — Lunch & dinner daily
**Phone:** 212-581-4242
**Web:** www.remi-ny.com
**Prices:** $$

There's always a convivial buzz winding through the various rooms of this Italian restaurant, from the thumping party room in back to its atrium-enclosed shop, pushing out gourmet food to-go. At the center of the party is Remi's main room—with its whimsical flying buttress archways, murals and mirrors, and Venetian glass chandeliers.

It's hard to remember the place has a delicious menu in this well-orchestrated production, but indeed it does—grabbing specialties from the Veneto region and coupling them with easygoing, rustic Italian basics. Try the fresh pasta, in a rich lamb ragù studded with meatballs and Parmesan; or a coffee-flavored panna cotta, laced with a supple hazelnut salsa, and carrying hints of vanilla bean.

# Russian Samovar

C2 — Russian X

256 W. 52nd St. (bet. Broadway & Eighth Ave.)

**Subway:** 50 St (Broadway) — Dinner nightly
**Phone:** 212-757-0168
**Web:** www.russiansamovar.com
**Prices:** $$

It's no surprise that Russian Samovar borders the Theater District; this restaurant, with its flashy mix of Russian celebrities, bigwigs, and hockey players, provides enough entertainment to rival Broadway. The crowd is raucous and the vodka is strong; guests can sample many varieties of the house-infused spirit available by the shot, the carafe, or the bottle. Though the décor is one part Old World and one part Russian grandmother, this place shows diners a good time.

The staff can seem standoffish but are helpful even so. Authentic favorites, like crisp chicken Kiev; beef Stroganoff; hearty *pelmeni* (ground veal and beef dumplings in a light chicken broth); and the perfectly prepared blini, provide a taste of Moscow in the middle of Manhattan.

# Scarlatto

Italian XX

C2

250 W. 47th St. (bet. Broadway & Eighth Ave.)

**Subway:** 50 St (Eighth Ave.) Lunch & dinner daily
**Phone:** 212-730-4535
**Web:** www.scarlattonyc.com
**Prices:** **$$**

Enjoyable cooking abounds at this conveniently located Theatre district favorite. Passersby, locals, and show-goers seeking fine Italian dining are all tempted by Chef Roberto Passon's vast, hearty selections of antipasti, salads, pastas, and meat courses bolstered by a lengthy list of specials. Offerings may include creamy buffalo mozzarella with ripe tomatoes and balsamic vinaigrette; or pappardelle enriched with tender, braised venison—all served by a polite, attentive staff.

The room is light and airy with pale stone accents, linen-covered tables, ivory leather seats, and exposed brick walls, featuring movie stills from the film *Roman Holiday*. The brick fireplace adds warmth, decorated with copper pots, and neatly stacked wine bottles along the walls.

# The Sea Grill

Seafood XX

D2

19 W. 49 St. (bet. Fifth & Sixth Aves.)

**Subway:** 47-50 Sts - Rockefeller Ctr Lunch Mon – Fri
**Phone:** 212-332-7610 Dinner Mon – Sat
**Web:** www.rapatina.com/seaGrill
**Prices:** **$$$**

It's hard to tell who is in the fishbowl at this unique seafood grill overlooking Rockefeller Center's ice skating rink—the skater's whizzing by your window, or the NBC big shots trading business cards over elegant place settings. Not surprisingly, winter bookings start early at The Sea Grill, but summertime—when the doors swing open and diners can enjoy an alfresco feel overlooking the Rink Bar—holds its own charm.

Probably because of its tourist-driven locale, the fare is solid, if not terrifically surprising, with jumbo lump crab cake appetizers, served over grainy mustard sauce; or yellowfin tuna, cooked a la plancha and served with silky mounds of spinach. Save room for the house dessert, a perfectly tart and creamy key lime pie.

# Seäsonal ✿

A3 **Austrian** XX

## 132 W. 58th St. (bet. Sixth & Seventh Aves.)

**Subway:** 59 St - Columbus Circle — Lunch & dinner Mon – Sat
**Phone:** 212-957-5550
**Web:** www.seasonalnyc.com
**Prices:** **$$$**

Seäsonal Restaurant & Weinbar

This lovely new Austrian addition to a food-starved strip in Midtown West arrives courtesy of two graduates of the Vienna Culinary Institute, Wolfgang Ban and Eduard Frauneder—chefs who share a common taste for turning their staid hometown recipes on their conventional little bums.

Located behind the Jumeirah Essex House, the restaurant is small but elegant, dressed in a striking neutral palette dotted with elegant table settings. Settle in and let the warm, but polished staff walk you through tough menu names like *topfennockerl* (which turns out to be a feather-light trio of sugary cheese dumplings rolled in a fine ground of sesame and almond and served over a strawberry rhubarb compote). Kick things off with a plate of gorgeous white asparagus bathing in a perfect hollandaise accompanied by paper thin slices of speck and steamed baby potatoes laced with parsley and butter; and then move on to seared Colorado spring lamb, served over an elegant parsley root purée with roasted hen of the woods mushrooms.

The bar menu offers a great small plates menu—the perfect place to nurse a glass of wine from the restaurant's impressive by-the-glass selection of Austrian vintages.

# Shelly's

Italian XX

B3

41 W. 57th St. (bet. Fifth & Sixth Aves.)

**Subway:** 57 St — Lunch & dinner Mon – Sat
**Phone:** 212-245-2422
**Web:** www.shellysnewyork.com
**Prices:** $$

This modern, pleasant, buzzing neighborhood favorite has all the charm of a coastal trattoria, conveniently located in midtown. Still, the Italian menu offers something for everyone, from thin crust pizzas and toothsome seafood risotto, to a dry-aged Porterhouse steak for two and, of course, a selection of *pesce* flown in daily from the Mediterranean. The raw bar displays sparkling offerings, and is cleverly set up near the entrance to tempt arriving diners and passersby alike.
The prix-fixe business lunch special tempts with the likes of a balsamic glazed yellowfin tuna kissed with *fregola* and carmelized onions. The amiable staff ensures a fulfilling experience in this slender, attractive room featuring burgundy banquettes and polished wood accents.

# South Gate

Contemporary XXX

A3

154 Central Park South (bet. Sixth & Seventh Aves.)

**Subway:** 57 St — Lunch & dinner daily
**Phone:** 212-484-5120
**Web:** www.154southgate.com
**Prices:** $$$

Located in the refurbished art deco jewel that is the Jumeirah Essex House, the hotel's dining room is spectacular in its own right. A sexy vibe permeates the light and airy space, furnished with buff-colored swivel chairs, leather padded tables, and a wall clad in facetted panels of mirrored glass. The sleek bar area is accented with see-through columns displaying spirits, and offers plenty of counter space for a comfortable solo meal or canoodling couple. Inspired by its posh Central Park location, the menu follows suit with an urbane take on seasonal cuisine in such dishes as flan of spring peas with morels and prosciutto; butter-poached lobster with kimchi; and cider-roasted apple crumble.
Genuinely gracious service ensures a gratifying experience.

# Staghorn Steakhouse

**B3** — Steakhouse XX

315 W. 36th St. (bet. Eighth & Ninth Aves.)

**Subway:** 34 St - Penn Station
**Phone:** 212-239-4390
**Web:** www.staghornsteakhouse.com
**Prices:** $$$

Lunch Mon – Fri
Dinner Mon – Sat

Tucked into a gloomy, rather nondescript block in the Garment District, a steakhouse rises above the competition. Why the hullabaloo over yet another red meat joint in a city packed with them? For starters, Staghorn Steakhouse dresses a bit differently than her sisters, eschewing the usual clubby aesthetic in favor of a warm, sophisticated Japanese design.
And while the menu reads as common-as-they-come—think shrimp cocktail, aged prime steaks, and onion rings—the kitchen has such an exacting eye for detail, you'll think you've died and gone to cow heaven. Witness a simple bone-in T-Bone, cooked to just-charred, medium-rare perfection, tenderly sliced, and then paired with chive-studded mashed potatoes and a silky scoop of creamed spinach.

# Sugiyama

**C1** — Japanese X

251 W. 55th St. (bet. Broadway & Eighth Ave.)

**Subway:** 57 St - 7 Av
**Phone:** 212-956-0670
**Web:** www.sugiyama-nyc.com
**Prices:** $$$

Dinner Tue – Sat

Enter Sugiyama and you will immediately see and smell the enticing plumes of smoke rising from the red-hot stones on tabletops, where beef or seafood is cooking. Welcome to the world of *kaiseki*, a traditional Japanese dining experience that ignites taste buds with a parade of varied courses showing an amazing richness and depth of flavor. Waiters explain the dishes and the concept, and you decide how much your appetite or wallet can accommodate. Choose from a range of omakase to place yourself in Chef Nao Sugiyama's hands and fully appreciate his talent.
Reserve a space at the counter—unquestionably the best seat in the house—to interact with the charming, personable chef, and take in all the action at this very special and authentic place.

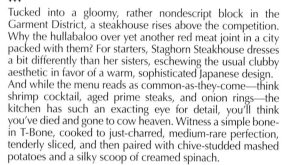

# Sushi Jun

Japanese

C2

302 W. 50th St. (at Eighth Ave.)

**Subway:** 50 St (Eighth Ave.)
**Phone:** 212-315-4800
**Web:** N/A
**Prices:** $$

Lunch Mon – Fri
Dinner Mon – Sat

Blink and you'll miss the entrance to Sushi Jun—but that would be a shame, for good things come in small packages at this unassuming sushi den, nestled into the bottom of midtown's Worldwide Plaza. Settle into one of the few available seats (there's only a small bar and a handful of tables), and indulge in the warm hospitality of the Japanese staff while they slide plate after plate of pristine sushi and sashimi—sliced into thick, abundant ribbons—your way.

Worker bees looking to dine and dash shouldn't overlook starters like the plump, briny Hama Hama oysters, topped with fresh grated radish; or the ruby-red tuna tartare, paired with a delicate quail egg. And save five minutes for a show-stopping dessert of charred sweet white potato.

# Sushi of Gari 46

Japanese

C2

347 W. 46th St. (bet. Eighth & Ninth Aves.)

**Subway:** Times Sq - 42 St
**Phone:** 212-957-0046
**Web:** www.sushiofgari.com
**Prices:** $$$$

Lunch Mon – Fri
Dinner nightly

Sushi of Gari 46 doesn't quite stack up to the near-surreal omakase experience that happens at Chef Masatoshi "Gari" Sugio's Upper Eastside prodigy, but most New Yorkers would argue that coming this close to sushi perfection in the increasingly commercial Theater District is close enough.

Not surprisingly, the action seats are at the mile-a-minute bar, where you can watch the staff slice and dice their way through gorgeous-looking Japanese fare like tender snow crab, touched with yuzu oil; or marinated big eye snapper wrapped around crunchy seaweed; or Gari's signature salmon with tomato. The full omakase show will put a heavy, albeit worthy, dent in your wallet, but those on a budget can always hit the reasonably-priced regular menu.

# Sushi Zen

Japanese

C3

108 W. 44th St. (bet. Broadway & Sixth Ave.)

**Subway:** 42 St - Bryant Pk — Lunch Mon – Fri
**Phone:** 212-302-0707 — Dinner Mon – Sat
**Web:** www.sushizen-ny.com
**Prices:** $$$

Sushi Zen's soothing and peaceful interior is a pleasant contrast to its high-traffic, albeit convenient, midtown locale. High ceilings, lots of natural light, and a sidewalk dining area made private by potted greenery and fabric panels are sure to create a sense of calm in this immaculate, well-run sushi-ya. Sit, take a breath, and let Chef/owner Toshio Suzuki stimulate your senses with his artfully prepared sushi and sashimi. Also discover a host of rolls; some traditional, like plum paste with *shiso*; and some original, like the Connecticut roll with eel and avocado. To best experience the chef's handiwork, order the omakase, which is based on the number of dishes you prefer.

Accompany meals with a selection from the impressive sake collection.

# Szechuan Gourmet

Chinese

C3

21 W. 39th St. (bet. Fifth & Sixth Aves.)

**Subway:** 42 St - Bryant Pk — Lunch & dinner daily
**Phone:** 212-921-0233
**Web:** N/A
**Prices:** $$

Timid palates and spice levels get shelved at Szechuan Gourmet, where the intrepid cooks are not afraid to bring the heat to a tear-inducing level. This is not just solid eats—this is fire-alarm, ring-the-bell, devilishly authentic Sichuan cuisine. And the throngs of people waiting for a table prove that New York is ready to accept the challenge.

Don't miss the smoky lamb filets, dusted with chili and cumin and flash-fried with garlic; or silky fish filets swimming under a nest of translucent cellophane noodles, crunchy Napa cabbage, and bamboo, all in a fantastically complex oil-slicked broth. Bring backup to sample specialties like the ribbons of crunchy conch in citrusy chili oil; or smoky wok-tossed chilies, an incendiary jumble of emerald jewels.

# Taboon

Middle Eastern XX

C1

773 Tenth Ave. (at 52nd St.)

**Subway:** 50 St (Eighth Ave.)
**Phone:** 212-713-0271
**Web:** N/A
**Prices:** $$

Lunch Sun
Dinner nightly

This inviting Middle Eastern restaurant, named for its crackling wood-burning brick oven (*taboon* in Arabic), adds character and culinary merit to an otherwise barren, somewhat industrial strip of Hell's Kitchen.

Taboon is that rare, welcoming restaurant ideal for those dining alone at the bar or as a group in the warm dining room, attentively served, and illuminated by the oven's appetizing glow. Meals begin with heavenly flatbreads, slathered with olive oil, sprinkled with rosemary and sea salt, and brought to the table still warm from the oven; fresh *tzatziki* serves as a sparkling accompaniment. Middle Eastern accents enliven delicious dishes, as in the perfectly seasoned lamb kebabs, served with creamy tahini sauce and toasted pistachios.

# Toloache

Mexican XX

C2

251 W. 50th St. (bet. Broadway & Eighth Ave.)

**Subway:** 50 St (Broadway)
**Phone:** 212-581-1818
**Web:** www.toloachenyc.com
**Prices:** $$

Lunch & dinner daily

Mexican dining is at its hottest in New York, and is further elevated at Toloache, a sophisticated yet festive two-story restaurant decked out in brightly painted tiles, tawny wood-beam ceilings, and punched-metal chandeliers.

A pleasure from start to finish, try the *tacos de pastor*, tender *guajillo*-marinated pork tacos stuffed with grilled pineapple salsa, white onion, and bright green cilantro; or the wonderfully smoky house chicken served over boldly flavored corn *pico de gallo* with a fried cheese-and-pinto bean dumpling. A spongy Meyer lemon *tres leches* cake is perfectly paired with deeply floral hibiscus coulis.

A serious list of tequilas is on offer and a worthy follow-up to one of the eight refreshing margaritas poured nightly.

# Trattoria Dell'Arte

A3 **Italian** XX

900 Seventh Ave. (bet. 56th & 57th Sts.)

**Subway:** 57 St - 7 Av
**Phone:** 212-245-9800
**Web:** www.trattoriadellarte.com
**Prices:** $$$

Lunch & dinner daily

There's a downright contagious exuberance to Shelly Firemen's always-packed Carnegie Hall classic, Trattoria Dell'Arte. It might be the smart, confident service staff, or the overflowing, recession-be-damned antipasto bar. Maybe it's the cheeky welcome motto ("What's Italian for Carnegie Hall? Trattoria Dell'Arte."), or the pretty Tuscan-villa styled rooms, lined with mahogany wine racks and dripping candles.
You'll have to pay—perhaps a bit too steeply—for this kind of *je ne sais quoi*, but the flaky, thin crust pizzas and heady dishes of finely-sauced pastas won't leave anyone disappointed. Don't miss the irresistible Italian desserts, like an airy cheesecake wrapped in chocolate sponge cake, then shot with piping-hot chocolate ganache.

# 21 Club

A4 **American** XX

21 W. 52nd St. (bet. Fifth & Sixth Aves.)

**Subway:** 5 Av - 53 St
**Phone:** 212-582-7200
**Web:** www.21club.com
**Prices:** $$$

Lunch Mon – Fri
Dinner Mon – Sat

A dowager among the city's restaurants, 21 Club started as a speakeasy during Prohibition. In the 1950s, the club debuted in its first film, *All About Eve*. Since then, the restaurant has starred in several movies, as well as playing host to a galaxy of stars, including Humphrey Bogart, Frank Sinatra, and Helen Hayes.
With its dim lighting and once-secret wine cellar (in a basement vault in the building next door), 21 Club still exudes a clandestine air. It's a place for power brokers, and the presence of a Bloomberg terminal in the lounge reminds guests that, in New York, money is big business.
Cuisine sticks to the tried and true; 21 Classics, including the burger favored by Ari Onassis, provide the best traditional experience.

# Utsav

Indian XX

C2

1185 Sixth Ave. (enter on 46th St.)

**Subway:** 47-50 Sts - Rockefeller Ctr
Lunch & dinner daily
**Phone:** 212-575-2525
**Web:** www.utsavny.com
**Prices:** 

Push past the humdrum bar seating downstairs, and make your way up the carpeted steps for a lovely surprise. This is Utsav—a unique, upscale little hideaway perched high above the hustle and bustle of 46th street, on an elevated bridge between two midtown office buildings. Besides the killer views, the restaurant has a light, simple air to it—with billowing fabrics and leafy green plants.

The gorgeous, overflowing lunch buffet brings office workers in by the droves, but the à la carte and evening menus are can't-miss as well, with soft piles of blistered, piping hot naan bread; plump, juicy garlic chicken, slathered in a tangy chili sauce, paired with a bright green salad; and spicy, tender lamb stir-fried with coconut and curry leaves.

# ViceVersa

Italian XX

C1

325 W. 51st St. (bet. Eighth & Ninth Aves.)

**Subway:** 50 St (Eighth Ave.)
Lunch Mon – Fri
**Phone:** 212-399-9291
Dinner Mon – Sat
**Web:** www.viceversarestaurant.com
**Prices:** $$

This urbane, sophisticated restaurant is the brainchild of three Italian gentlemen who met while working at the legendary (now closed) San Domenico on Central Park South. Lucky for us, all that elegant taste rubbed off on them, because ViceVersa (pronounced VEE-chay versa) is one classy joint, with a haze of muted earth tones throughout the dining room, a long, wide bar that begs to be lingered at, and a pretty enclosed garden area that opens up in back when the weather's right.

Though presented artfully, the menu is as Italian as they come, with bold, saucy plates of pasta like creamy fusilli, pocked with smoky chunks of speck and dotted with bright green peas; or plump pockets of veal, tossed with nut-brown butter, sage, and pancetta.

# West Bank Café

B2 — American XX

407 W. 42nd St. (bet. Ninth & Tenth Aves.)

**Subway:** 42 St - Port Authority Bus Terminal — Lunch & dinner daily
**Phone:** 212-695-6909
**Web:** www.westbankcafe.com
**Prices:** $$

This beloved Theater District mainstay has kept its head above the all-too-choppy waters of Manhattan's dining scene since 1978 by offering delicious, progressive American food at honest prices. To prove it, you'll have to elbow out the flock of regulars that squeeze into this simply adorned bistro most nights of the week.

The vibe is always right on cue at the West Bank Café, so settle into one of the leather banquettes, let the pleasant hum of jazz music fill your senses, and allow yourself to soak in the energy of the lively crowd. If on the menu, try the creamy puréed carrot-ginger soup, sweetened by a dash of rich coconut milk; followed by a tender skirt steak, charred just so, and flanked by a salty tower of beer-battered onion rings.

# Yakitori Totto

C1 — Japanese X

251 W. 55th St. (bet. Seventh & Eighth Aves.)

**Subway:** 59 St - Columbus Circle — Dinner nightly
**Phone:** 212-245-4555
**Web:** N/A
**Prices:** $$$

Enjoy the sounds of Japanese pop and sultry jazz while discovering this hip, urban Tokyo treasure, right here in Manhattan. Its namesake "yakitori" refers to a style of grilled meat, mainly chicken, that is marinated in a soy-based sauce and then cooked on a smoky charcoal grill, perhaps the most popular street food of Japan. The results are tender, juicy, and tasty morsels, cooked and presented on skewers. For the true yakitori gourmet, house specialties, like chicken knees or necks, reflect the menu's traditional cuisine and are often sold out early in the evening.

To complement the restaurant's authenticity, the efficient Japanese service staff does not typically disturb their guests' meals, as their cultural norm (a simple wave will do).

# SoHo & Nolita

SoHo (South of Houston) and Nolita (North of Little Italy) prove not only that New York has a penchant for portmanteaus, but that the downtown "scene" lives on now more than ever. What remains new and ever-changing are the subtle transformations that redefine these neighborhoods block by block.

Despite the retail invasion that has taken over some of SoHo's eastern corners, it remains true to its promise of sun-drenched restaurants and open-air cafés filled with European sophisticates of a certain age and supermodels lingering over salads. There are also plenty of tourists to admire them.

## Shopping in SoHo

Those fortunate enough to live in what were once artists' lofts (now multimillion dollar condos) know that there are still a few foodie gems in this area heavily focused on restaurant dining. For your at-home tapas needs, **Despana** offers Spanish foods and ingredients from oil-packed tuna to mouth-watering *bocadillos*; they will even prepare a traditional tortilla Española with advance notice. A visit to the original **Dean and Deluca**, filled with some of the cities favorite cakes and coffees, is another gourmet treat, but be forewarned that its steep prices match the sleek location. Less retouched and perhaps more focused is **Joe's Dairy**; this tiny storefront overflows with SoHo history and arguably the best Italian cheeses in town (their smoked mozzarella is to die for).

## Sleepy Nolita

Farther east is Nolita—a neighborhood as cool as its name. This is where a slightly hipper and hungrier downtown set flock (judging by its many offerings). These locals aren't living the typical midtown nine-to-five life and shun the *je ne sais quoi* of SoHo in favor of smallish spots that begin with the word "café."

At the top of this list is **Café Habana**, offering its casual crowds a gritty diner vibe and amazing Mexico City-style corn on the cob (also available for take-out next door at **Café Habana To Go**). Equally hip hangouts can be found at **Café Gitane**, serving French-Morrocan, or **Café Colonial** for Brazilian food.

The ethos in Nolita is focused: Do a single thing very well. This may have been inspired by **Lombardi's**, which claims to be America's very first pizzeria (founded in 1905) and still has lines out the door. **Hoomos Asli** may not be attractive and its service is "brisk," but they clearly put effort into the outstanding hummus, fluffy pitas, and falafels to accompany those tart, fresh lemonades whose memory will keep you cool for summers to come. For the best fish tacos this side of California, head to **Pinche Taqueria**. However, if whiling

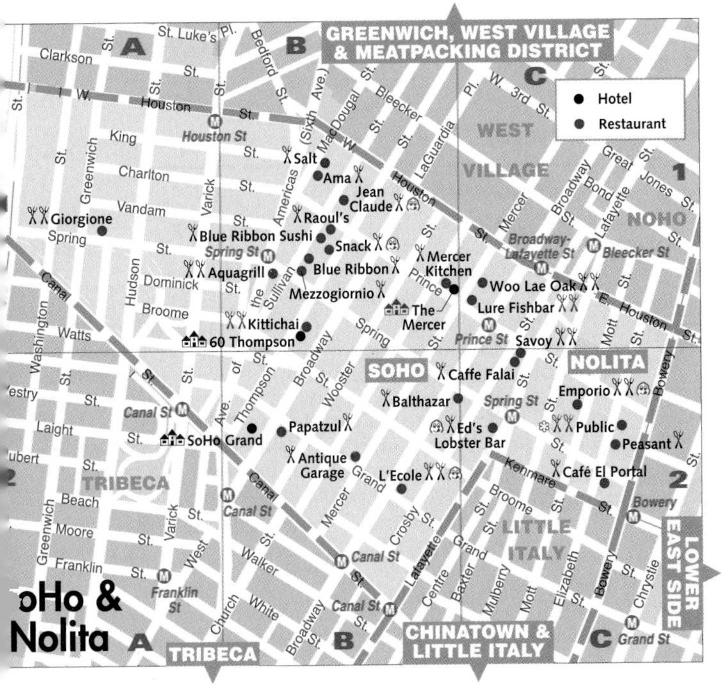


away the afternoon in one of Manhattan's most idyllic outdoor gardens suits your mood, then visit **Le Jardin Bistro**.

Even satisfying a sweet tooth is done with elevated style at **Pappabubble**, whose candies are crafted with an eye-popping sense of design. With equal ingenuity and old-school flair, **Rice to Riches** serves its celebrated bowls of rice pudding with creatively named toppings, like "Mischief" (buttery graham crackers) or "Nudge" (chilled espresso and cocoa). Cheesecake connoisseurs take note that **Eileen's Cheesecake** and its mind-boggling array of flavors has been chasing those Junior's fanatics back to Brooklyn.

Even between feedings, this area promises to nurture your inner epicurean with a visit to the Bowery. The unrefined kitchen supply stores that line the neighborhood's eastern border are technically wholesale only...but some will still sell to you for cash. Come here to stock up on sheet pans, rubber spatulas, and pu pu platters all at an outstanding discount.

One of the greater challenges Nolita poses is the decision of where to end the day, as this is when it is liveliest. Tucked into these streets are lovely little bars, each with its own stylish, NY feel, sans the masses besetting other neighborhoods. Dark and date-like places, such as **Pravda** with its assortment of vodkas or **Sweet and Vicious** for expert cocktails, are a fitting finale.

# Ama

B1 **Italian**

48 MacDougal St. (bet. Houston & Prince Sts.)

**Subway:** Spring St (Sixth Ave.)
**Phone:** 212-358-1707
**Web:** www.amanyc.com
**Prices:** $$

Lunch Fri – Sun
Dinner daily

Soft contrasts create a subtle and romantic atmosphere apropos to a restaurant which derives its name from the Italian word for love. A rustic yet sophisticated charm is enhanced with warm white walls; antique white wood floors; white paper covered tabletops; simple blonde wood chairs and paneling; and amber track lights reflecting off a mirror lining one wall. Close set tables and two long banquettes along either wall further enhance the intimate feel in the narrow dining room. A ceiling fresco of pink blossoms and bushy green arrangements sitting atop the bar and in the cozy lounge area near the picture window, adds welcome touches of the outdoors.

Fresh, Puglian influences reign on a menu offering house-made pasta dishes, antipasti, and secondi.

# Antique Garage

B2 **Turkish**

41 Mercer St. (bet. Broome & Grand Sts.)

**Subway:** Canal St (Broadway)
**Phone:** 212-219-1019
**Web:** www.antiquegaragesoho.com
**Prices:** $$

Lunch & dinner daily

It sounds ridiculous, but here goes: Imagine an adorable restaurant tucked into a renovated auto repair garage in SoHo. It's homey, *how-did-we-not-know-about-this-place*? vibe is fitted out with beautiful rugs, dripping chandeliers, and a bunch of cool antiques that you can actually purchase. As for the food, how does mouthwatering, off-the-hook Turkish meze sound?

As the saying goes: Only in New York. By day, the Antique Garage offers a quiet reprieve for SoHo shoppers; at night, couples pile in to revel in the intimacy of the close-knit tables and flickering candles. Though the menu leans decidedly Turkish—think eggplant salads and chicken shish kebabs—more general Mediterranean influences rear their head in desserts like a creamy tiramisu.

# Aquagrill

Seafood XX

B1

210 Spring St. (at Sixth Ave.)

**Subway:** Spring St (Sixth Ave.) Lunch & dinner daily
**Phone:** 212-274-0505
**Web:** www.aquagrill.com
**Prices:** $$

From the staggering selection of oysters at the raw bar to simple grilled fish, Jeremy and Jennifer Marshall's establishment aims to please all seafood lovers. The husband-and-wife team divides up the work here: Chef Jeremy watches over the kitchen while Jennifer oversees the dining room—decorated with lamps made of seashells.

The chef treats his fresh supplies with due deference, sometimes adding subtle Asian accents to enhance the preparations. Clever combinations, like falafel-crusted salmon are a hallmark of Aquagrill. Brunch is a real treat on weekends and lunch is always busy; but it's at dinner that the kitchen staff really struts their stuff. Service is smoothly choreographed, and an air of New York ambience pervades the whole operation.

# Balthazar

French X

B2

80 Spring St. (bet. Broadway & Crosby St.)

**Subway:** Spring St (Lafayette St.) Lunch & dinner daily
**Phone:** 212-965-1414
**Web:** www.balthazarny.com
**Prices:** $$$

Has an aging downtown darling ever held onto her crown as successfully as Balthazar? Nope—for this Keith McNally bistro, with its legendary red awning and brassy bistro good looks, has been a joyous zoo ever since it opened its doors in 1997.

All of which means you'll need reservations, though there are a few ways to dodge the busy bullet: The bar tables are open to walk-ins; the breakfast hours are lovely; and the bakery next door serves scrumptious salads, sandwiches, and pastries to go (not to mention a killer hot chocolate). Back at the restaurant, you'll want to ride the coattails of Balthazar's steadies, like heaping towers of glistening shellfish; and perfectly-charred steak, laid to rest under a golden stack of crunchy, salty frites.

# Blue Ribbon

B1 **Contemporary**

97 Sullivan St. (bet. Prince & Spring Sts.)

**Subway:** Spring St (Sixth Ave.) Dinner nightly
**Phone:** 212-274-0404
**Web:** www.blueribbonrestaurants.com
**Prices:** $$$

It's for good reason that the Blue Ribbon family is now liberally fanned out across the city. Meet the catalyst for it all—Blue Ribbon brasserie, a New York classic tucked into SoHo's Sullivan Street. The restaurant's welcoming and engaging staff is a luxury in a neighborhood more inclined to make you feel plain than cherished—which is quite interesting, considering Blue Ribbon has its own celebrity following.

Namely, the city's chef circuit, that regularly swings through the doors post-shift (the kitchen serves until 4:00 A.M.) come to indulge in a a selection of rawbar delights, and flavor-rich comfort classics like the playful *pu pu* platter or gourmet fried chicken, or the decadent bone marrow with oxtail marmalade.

# Blue Ribbon Sushi

B1 **Japanese**

119 Sullivan St. (bet. Prince & Spring Sts.)

**Subway:** Spring St (Sixth Ave.) Lunch & dinner daily
**Phone:** 212-343-0404
**Web:** www.blueribbonrestaurants.com
**Prices:** $$$

There's a reason you keep bumping into Blue Ribbon joints all across this city. Those Bromberg brothers sprinkle their fairy dust, and poof—delicious, casually hip eateries appear. As the name of this discrete little sushi den implies, the restaurateurs here turn their attention to the sea, where the talented Chef Toshi Ueki has one all-important question for his customers: Are you a Pacific or Atlantic man?

That's how he likes to divvy up his killer sashimi and fresh-off-the-boat (or plane) daily specials, although the spicy tuna set can tread safer waters with dishes like the crispy rock shrimp tempura. They don't take reservations and the space is itty-bitty, so aim for off-hours or lunchtime, when you can command a booth for an afternoon feast.

# Café el Portal

Mexican

C2

174 Elizabeth St. (bet. Kenmare & Spring Sts.)

**Subway:** Spring St (Lafayette St.) — Lunch & dinner Mon – Sat
**Phone:** 212-226-4642
**Web:** N/A
**Prices:** ⊜

There is something comforting about a place that doesn't try to compete with its fancy neighbors. In an area known for being a fashionista's Mecca, Cafe el Portal defies Nolita's hipper-than-thou vibe with its low-key design and casual ambience. Despite its less than impressive digs, this restaurant serves up some of the most authentic Mexican dishes in the city. Everything is made in-house at the tiny family-run place, from the fantastic tortillas to the piquant salsas.
The tiny bar boasts a tequila collection with more bottles than the restaurant has seats, and the cocktail menu goes well beyond your run-of-the-mill margarita. Reasonable prices and flavorful, fun food are just a couple more reasons why locals love El Portal.

# Caffe Falai

Italian

C2

265 Lafayette St. (bet. Prince & Spring Sts.)

**Subway:** Spring St (Lafayette St.) — Lunch & dinner daily
**Phone:** 212-274-8615
**Web:** www.falainyc.com
**Prices:** $$

The elements come together to make for a delicious meal in Caffe Falai's delicate little jewel box interior, where white-framed mirrors hang from pure white walls, and the pretty round mosaic floor tiles light up under ornate glass chandeliers. All the more reason to linger over one—or two—of former Le Cirque pastry chef, Iacopo Falai's, to-die-for pastries, lovingly displayed in the glass counter by his kitchen.
The dinner menu entices just as much, with a comforting lineup of oldies but goodies from all over Italy, like a gorgeously authentic bowl of minestrone, its heavenly scent delivering all the freshness of spring; or the quickly-becoming-legendary *gnudi*; or a spot-on risotto dancing in a mushroom purée laced with aromatic truffle.

# Ed's Lobster Bar

C2 — Seafood

222 Lafayette St. (bet. Kenmare & Spring Sts.)

**Subway:** Spring St (Lafayette St.) — Lunch & dinner daily
**Phone:** 212-343-3236
**Web:** www.lobsterbarnyc.com
**Prices:** **$$**

Finally, East Siders have a simply great seafood spot to call their own. Though not quite a beach shack, it is casually comfortable yet elegant with its New England-style décor, white wainscoting, and inviting marble bar.

An alumna of Pearl Oyster Bar, Chef Ed McFarland threw his hat in the "best lobster roll" ring, where his version deftly competes, and post-lawsuit drama, the place has finally settled. Yet beyond this cult-inducing staple, the very skilled kitchen offers a variety of excellent daily specials, salads, and an unbeatable potato galette with lobster. Wines and beers harmonize well with the saltwater menu.

Extended hours may ease the droves of the devotees queuing for tables; if you opt for takeout, don't forget Ed's pickles to go.

# Emporio

C2 — Italian

231 Mott St. (bet. Prince & Spring Sts.)

**Subway:** Spring St (Lafayette St.) — Lunch & dinner daily
**Phone:** 212-966-1234
**Web:** www.auroraristorante.com
**Prices:** **$$**

This bright new Roman trattoria arrives courtesy of Riccardo Buitoni, the man behind the beloved Aurora restaurants in Williamsburg, Brooklyn, and SoHo. Like his other two ventures, Emporio has loads of rustic charm, with a close-knit interior meant to invoke a twenties-era grocery.

The menu offers lots of roads to go down, each more delicious than the next—so cut your losses and opt to share one of the killer pizzas before digging into light-as-air squash blossoms, stuffed with cheese and anchovies; crunchy *crostini del giorno* bursting with ricotta, rhubarb, and honey; or tender, succulent lamb chops. Grapehounds should look twice at the wine list, where some Italian vintages rarely seen in the U.S. quietly lurk among the classics.

# Giorgione

Italian XX

A1

307 Spring St. (bet. Greenwich & Hudson Sts.)

**Subway:** Spring St (Sixth Ave.) — Lunch Mon – Fri
**Phone:** 212-352-2269 — Dinner nightly
**Web:** www.giorgionenyc.com
**Prices:** $$

Located on the quieter western outskirts of SoHo, this lively and stylish Italian standby glows with unpretentious, authentic cuisine, courtesy of Giorgio DeLuca (co-founder of Dean & DeLuca). Beyond the sleek bar, the narrow space is lined with chrome tables, white-leather seats, and ice-blue walls that contribute to the cool vibe. The staff may be young and hip but the focus here is on efficient, professional service.

The menu is simple, casual, and honestly delicious, with fantastic pizzas from the wood-burning oven. A raw bar, perfectly prepared salads, and pastas are among the simple Italian highlights at this rare gem that manages to be at once modern and comfortable. After dinner, remember to order a perfectly brewed espresso.

# Jean Claude

French X

B1

137 Sullivan St. (bet. Houston & Prince Sts.)

**Subway:** Spring St (Sixth Ave.) — Dinner nightly
**Phone:** 212-475-9232
**Web:** N/A
**Prices:** $$

With its tight-knit tables, lived-in good looks, and soft French music quietly thrumming in the background, this romantic little bistro could be straight off of Paris' Left Bank. Luckily for Manhattan, though, the infinitely charming Jean Claude is smack in the middle of SoHo.

In winter, the room is decidedly cozy; while summer finds the front windows thrown open and couples lingering over the reasonably-priced wine list, which boasts a nice carafe and half-carafe list. The French cooking is straightforward and delicious, with a solid lineup of bistro staples like tender *moules marinieres* and frites; seared hangar steak in a thyme, red wine and shallot reduction, paired with a sinful *gratin dauphinois*; and a spot-on rendition of crème brulée.

# Kittichai

B1 — Thai XX

60 Thompson St. (bet. Broome & Spring Sts.)

**Subway:** Spring St (Sixth Ave.) — Lunch & dinner daily
**Phone:** 212-219-2000
**Web:** www.kittichairestaurant.com
**Prices:** **$$$**

Bangkok has never looked so sexy. Dark and sultry restaurants in trendy urban hotels abound these days, but Kittichai is the real deal—with a jaw-dropping interior (replete with silk swaths, suspended orchids, and floating candles) fit to woo the beautiful people checking into the 60 Thompson hotel that houses it.

There are more authentic Thai places in the city, but Kittichai romances you with its setting and elegant cuisine that sings as much European as Thai. Try the crispy whole fish, laced with a sweet ginger curry; or pineapple-braised short ribs in green curry, paired with baby eggplant. The best route here is to try one of the chefs tasting menus, where you get a sampling of the signature dishes at terrific value, served family style.

# L'Ecole

B2 — French XX

462 Broadway (at Grand St.)

**Subway:** Canal St (Broadway) — Lunch daily
**Phone:** 212-219-3300 — Dinner Mon – Sat
**Web:** www.frenchculinary.com
**Prices:** **$$**

This fun, virtual classroom (courtesy of the French Culinary Institute) provides students their first opportunity to show their expertise, love, and respect for the tenants of traditional French cooking—just know that since this is a "learning experience" there may be a few mistakes alongside a treasured moment of brilliance. Regardless, it is clear the students here have mastered the use of top ingredients, allowing them to shine in simple preparations.

The regional French menu, which changes every six weeks, offers four- or five-course dinners, as well as an inexpensive prix-fixe lunch.

A conscientious student waitstaff caters to guests in an ambient, very "SoHo" space, with lofty windows overlooking Broadway, and images of a bustling restaurant kitchen.

# Lure Fishbar

**Seafood** ✗✗

**C1**

142 Mercer St. (bet. Houston & Prince Sts.)

**Subway:** Prince St

Lunch & dinner daily

**Phone:** 212-431-7676

**Web:** www.lurefishbar.com

**Prices:** $$$

If your credit card's not maxed out from visiting the Prada shop above this restaurant, Lure Fishbar makes a great place to drop anchor. It's decked out in a fantastic tiki-trendy style with angular porthole windows; semi-circular booths; teak paneling; and tropical-print fabrics, reminiscent of a luxury ocean liner. The only thing missing from the maritime motif is the sound of waves crashing and the feel of sand between your toes.

Have a seat at the sushi bar and order a sushi-sashimi combo, or sit at the raw bar to share a shellfish plateau (in sizes small, medium, and large). In the main dining room, you can net one of the fresh catches, which are as pleasing to the eye as they are to the palate. Just one visit and you'll be hooked.

# Mercer Kitchen

**Contemporary** ✗

**B1**

99 Prince St. (at Mercer St.)

**Subway:** Prince St

Lunch & dinner daily

**Phone:** 212-966-5454

**Web:** www.jean-georges.com

**Prices:** $$

When it opened in the basement of SoHo's Mercer Hotel, Mercer Kitchen took a position at the head of the culinary new wave. Today the restaurant, which owes its existence to wunderkind Jean-Georges Vongerichten, remains fashionable among the downtown crowd, amid chic décor, and hip staff serving highly enjoyable contemporary dishes. Its basement location feels romantic during evenings and a hidden refuge during the day.

The menu appeals with raw-bar selections, salads, sandwiches, and entrées that have roots in France but travel to faraway locales for inspiration. Raw tuna and wasabi deck pizza and lamb shanks are glazed with soy. Take a seat at the bar for a glass of rosé or a cool draft, and drink in the ambience.

# Mezzogiorno

B1

**Italian**

195 Spring St. (at Sullivan St.)

**Subway:** Spring St (Sixth Ave.) Lunch & dinner daily
**Phone:** 212-334-2112
**Web:** www.mezzogiorno.com
**Prices:** $$

The big, bright blue awnings of this Italian veteran are a fixture on the SoHo scene, and its 100 interior collages by local artists (each one a unique interpretation of the restaurant's logo) a lovely reminder of when the neighborhood was more artists than agents.

The real star of the show, of course, is the beautiful wood-burning oven, which pushes out delicious, thin-crust pies. If you're not in the mood for pizza, no problem—the pasta list goes on for days and there's an extensive list of seasonal Italian specialties like the *carciofi saltati*, a plate of tender artichoke hearts paired with crunchy pistachio, and laced with lemon and parsley—the perfect thing to pick on when spring hits and the raised terrace opens up for people watching.

# Papatzul

B2

**Mexican**

55 Grand St. (bet. West Broadway & Wooster St.)

**Subway:** Canal St (Sixth Ave.) Lunch & dinner daily
**Phone:** 212-274-8225
**Web:** www. papatzul.com
**Prices:** $$

SoHo's sleeper hit. The Mexican restaurant, Papatzul, is a refreshing addition to the model-festooned neighborhood, with a vibe that's festive, but not so festive you can't linger over your conversation. Cool, but not so cool you get slapped with attitude. Laid-back service, genial prices, and old-school ambience—need we go on? Head past the lively bar and you'll find a clump of closely-spaced tables with couples nursing pitchers of margaritas.

Kick off your meal with a fresh shrimp, scallop, and fish ceviche, dressed in a dense lime-tomato sauce and studded with avocado, jalapeño, and cilantro. An entrée of rich, layered tortilla casserole with tender shredded chicken, is dressed in rich *pasilla chile* sauce, and then laced with a cool shot of crema.

# Peasant

Italian

C2

194 Elizabeth St. (bet. Prince & Spring Sts.)

**Subway:** Spring St (Lafayette St.) Dinner Tue – Sun
**Phone:** 212-965-9511
**Web:** www.peasantnyc.com
**Prices:** $$

The emphasis at this beautiful little Nolita restaurant is honest Italian country fare—more often than not, carefully sourced and expertly prepared dishes that find their way into Chef Frank DeCarlo's beloved wood-burning brick oven.

Dimly lit and romantic, with lots of exposed brick walls and flickering candles, Peasant practically purrs date night. And a more languorous evening could not be found than one spent dawdling over a melt-in-your-mouth pizza pie, or lovely rustic dishes like four plump sardines, baked head-on in a terracotta clay pot and dusted with toasted breadcrumbs and a shake of grated lemon zest; or perfectly al dente, hand-cut *malfatti* in a hearty lamb ragù; or tender slices of lamb, dancing in a fluffy, delicate polenta.

# Raoul's

French

B1

180 Prince St. (bet. Sullivan & Thompson Sts.)

**Subway:** Spring St (Sixth Ave.) Dinner nightly
**Phone:** 212-966-3518
**Web:** www.raouls.com
**Prices:** $$$

Call it *je ne sais quoi*, Manhattan magic, or simply talent, but this well-loved classic bistro has survived 30 years in this fickle business, somehow remaining popular, sophisticated, and stylish. The authentic French food is prepared simply, but remains impressive with top ingredients and delicious flavors—as in the steak tartare with quail egg, or seared foie gras with Concord grape purée. The energetic atmosphere in the dimly lit main room is intoxicating, but those seeking a calmer spot for quiet conversation should try the bright upstairs space or tiny covered garden room.

Raoul's boasts amiable service, charm, character, authenticity, and even 15 minutes of fame when it appeared in Martin Scorcese's film, *The Departed*.

# Public ✿

Fusion XX

C2

210 Elizabeth St. (bet. Prince & Spring Sts.)

**Subway:** Spring St (Lafayette St.)
**Phone:** 212-343-7011
**Web:** www.public-nyc.com
**Prices:** $$$

Lunch Sat – Sun
Dinner nightly

Michael Weber

Set along a tree-lined Nolita street studded with girlie boutiques, Public has all the requisite trappings of downtown chic—nook-and-cranny seating, irreverent decor (public buildings are the inspiration for the industrial aesthetic), and a minor celebrity or two in the corner. It's enough to make you wonder if the food can hold up to this clever ambience.

It can, and does quite consistently—mostly due to Chef Brad Farmerie's lovely gifts with fusion food (some call it *Australasian*), but also due to a polished, professional staff intent on making sure you stay relaxed and informed. In between dishes like marinated white anchovies with saffron aïoli; mahi mahi puddled in Asian gazpacho; rosy-pink lamb stacked between thin layers of crispy fried polenta dabbed with harissa-spiked aïoli; and warm sticky toffee puddings with armagnac ice cream, be sure to check out the wine list, which boasts a sweet list of down under vintages from Australia and New Zealand.

Should you make your way next door, you'll find the Monday Room—a cool little wine bar (though there is no actual bar, just sexy leather banquettes) featuring a delightfully quirky selection of wines and a revolving canapé menu.

# Salt

B1 American

58 MacDougal St. (bet. Houston & Prince Sts.)

**Subway:** Spring St (Sixth Ave.) Lunch & dinner daily
**Phone:** 212-674-4968
**Web:** www.saltnyc.com
**Prices:** $$

The expression "neighborhood restaurant" is bandied about on a too casual basis nowadays, but Salt genuinely deserves the moniker. Diners are invited to sit at one of three communal tables in the middle of the simply furnished dining room. Here, you can rub elbows with other locals and catch up on some SoHo gossip. Or sit at a table near the large shop front windows.

Long Island duck breast, Alaskan King salmon, and New Zealand rack of lamb are some of the highlights from the brief menu that is a showcase in modern cuisine. Under the section "Protein + 2," select any two sides to accompany the main dish—a classic American mealtime formula. The menu makes fair use of fresh and flavorful combinations, incorporating seasonal and local meats and produce.

# Savoy

C1 American

70 Prince St. (at Crosby St.)

**Subway:** Prince St Lunch Mon – Sat
**Phone:** 212-219-8570 Dinner nightly
**Web:** www.savoynyc.com
**Prices:** $$

Savoy puts the sexy back in being nice—with a rustic upstairs dining room (replete with crackling fireplace) so steeped in country charm it could convince a city slicker to settle down for good. But that fuzzy-sweater interior belies a menu that's always been way ahead of its time, where the chefs let the exceptional ingredients do the work, focusing on pure flavors and seasonal ingredients from local growers.

Savoy's genius lies both in its good value as well as in its parade of scrumptious dishes like a bright dandelion salad, laced with lemon-anchovy vinaigrette and topped with a breadcrumb-crusted fried egg; or a lovely seasonal chilled nettle soup kissed with yogurt; or a smooth lemon tart topped with fluffy meringue and a dollop of lemon sorbet.

# Snack ☺

**B1**                                  Greek ✗

### 105 Thompson St. (bet. Prince & Spring Sts.)

**Subway:** Spring St (Sixth Ave.)                  Lunch & dinner daily
**Phone:** 212-925-1040
**Web:** N/A
**Prices:** ⊜⊜

Quaint, laid-back Santorini taverna, Snack is not. But you'll find so much to love in this bustling slip of a restaurant tucked into SoHo's quiet, leafy Thompson Street, you'll hardly mind the slightly clinical interior—for though the old black and white photos and selection of Greek grocery items only hint at far-off lands, those lucky enough to snag one of the four dining room tables will find Hellenic fare authentic enough to transport them at first bite.

Despite the moniker, most of the portions here are hearty, including a generously-sized shredded lamb sandwich, laced with ripe tomatoes, roasted red onions, a smear of aïoli, and a shake of fresh arugula; or a Greek salad bursting with creamy feta, kalamata olives, and fresh oregano.

# Woo Lae Oak

**C1**                               Korean ✗✗

### 148 Mercer St. (bet. Houston & Prince Sts.)

**Subway:** Prince St                        Lunch & dinner daily
**Phone:** 212-925-8200
**Web:** www.woolaeoaksoho.com
**Prices:** $$

This fresh, attractive, and trendy dining space features a roomy, open floor plan, stylish downtown crowd, and most importantly, marble-top tables outfitted with built-in grills. Here, the SoHo set learns to barbecue their own plates of black tiger prawns, thinly sliced ribeye, or Long Island duck breast. Less participatory options include traditional *bin dae duk* (mung bean pancakes), and garlicky *kal bi jim* (beef short ribs) prepared with innovation and a flair for deep yet simple flavors. Modern preparations and presentations enhance dishes ranging from fresh tofu to the wonderfully comforting classic, *bi bim baps*.

A great value, the fixed-price *bann sang* individual lunch set includes some of the restaurant's most popular dishes.

Sprint

# TriBeCa

Catering to its local clientele of creative types, trendy TriBeCa is, quite simply, a cool place to eat. Here, splurge on meals in pricey restaurants whose reputations and namesake celebrity chefs precede them, or go for more modest gastropub fare. On sunny days, snag an umbrella-shaded table outside—TriBeCa's wide sidewalks are famously accommodating and among the city's top spots for star-gazing.

This wedge of cobblestoned streets, galleries, design stores, and historic warehouses converted to multi-million-dollar lofts was named in the 1970s by a real-estate agent hoping to create a hip identity for the area. The acronym—which stands for Triangle Below Canal—describes an area that is not a triangle at all, but a trapezoid bounded by Canal Street, Broadway, Murray Street, and the Hudson River. Greenwich and Hudson streets are its main thoroughfares for dining and nightlife.

In keeping with its independence and artistry, TriBeCa offers a gourmet experience for any palate (or pricetag). On Hudson Square, **City Winery** gives urban wine enthusiasts a place to make their own private-label wine by providing the grapes (a selection of varietals from international vineyards), the barrels, the storage, and the expertise. Those looking for something to enjoy with their wine will rejoice in the monthly events sponsored by **New York Vintners**, which may include free cheese tastings or lessons on making mozzarella.

The neighborhood is loaded with wonderful bakeries, the most famed of which is Chef David Bouley's eponymous **Bakery and Market**, now back in its original location. Here, the mouth-watering selection of Viennoiserie lists everything from meringues to warm madeleines that only Proust could describe. Other venues to sate a sweet tooth include the **Duane Park Patisserie** for pastries, and seasonal specialties; or **Tribeca Treats** for scrumptious chocolates. Since 1886, venerable **Bazzini** has occupied the building where company founder, Anthony Bazzini, first opened the business in 1886. Drop by to pick up some gourmet groceries or prepared foods for dinner, and don't leave without a bag of nuts or a jar of their old-fashioned cashew butter.

**Puffy's Tavern** is a friendly neighborhood bar boasting five plasma-screen TVs for sports fans, happy-hour drinks, and hearty lunchtime signature Italian sandwiches. Speaking of local faves, **Bubby's** will cater to your homestyle food cravings.

Like every New York neighborhood, TriBeCa claims its own great pizza joints, as in the Roman-style *pizza al taglio* at newcomer **Farinella**. Owner Alberto Polo Cretara is a Neapolitan hip-hop artist who honed his pizza-making skills at the legendary Il Forno in Rome. Round up some friends

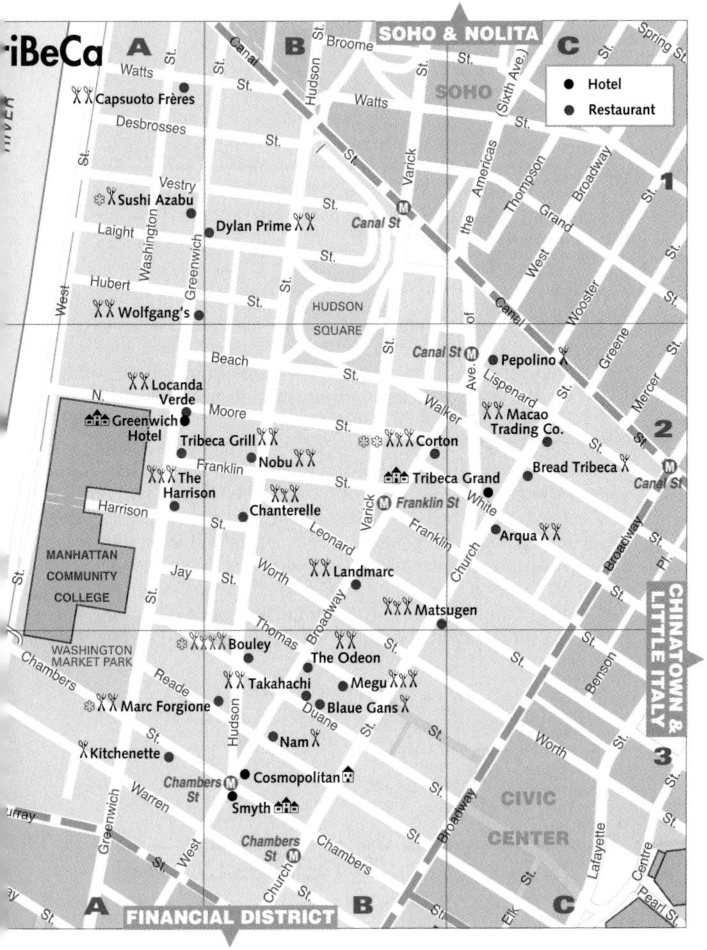


to sample his tasty four-foot-long pies.

Under the "dinner and a movie" category, the 2001 film *Dinner Rush* used TriBeCa as a stage. In fact, director Bob Giraldi shot this Mafia- and food-themed movie in his own eatery, **Gigino Trattoria**. The plot tells the story of a night in the life of a chic TriBeCa restaurant, delving into sidelines such as food critics and ambitious chefs.

Today this area is still associated with films of many stripes, thanks to the annual Tribeca Film Festival, created in 2002 by Robert DeNiro and others to revitalize the area after 9/11. This world-famous springtime event hosts twelve days of great films, special events, and community camaraderie. Throngs of folks flock downtown during this time to see the movies and experience TriBeCa's many wonderful restaurants.

# Arqua

C2 — Italian XX

281 Church St. (at White St.)

**Subway:** Canal St (Sixth Ave.) — Dinner Mon – Sat
**Phone:** 212-334-1888
**Web:** www.arquaristorante.com
**Prices:** $$

Located in a classic TriBeCa ex-industrial space, this sophisticated eatery celebrates Northern Italy in its sun-colored, light-filled space. The dining room is both subdued and tasteful, adorned with oversized windows and modern chandeliers.

Thanks to Chef/owner Leonard Pulito, who named his restaurant after the Italian town where he and his family raised their own livestock and grew their own produce, the food at Arqua is executed with an eye for excellence. House-made thin spaghetti may be bathed in an earthy wild mushroom sauce; salmon is served in a sweet and sour sauce with poppy seeds; and *branzino alla griglia* is served simply grilled and lacquered with lemon and olive oil.

Desserts may include a selection of gelati and *sorbetti* made on-site.

# Blaue Gans

B3 — Austrian X

139 Duane St. (bet. Church St. & West Broadway)

**Subway:** Chambers St (West Broadway) — Lunch & dinner daily
**Phone:** 212-571-8880
**Web:** www.wallse.com
**Prices:** $$

Taking over the space formerly occupied by Le Zinc, chef Kurt Gutenbrunner (also of Wallsé) may have saved the zinc bar and the vintage art posters of the former tenant, but he has turned the menu upside-down with his Austro-German cooking.

Open for two meals as well as late-night noshing, the restaurant focuses on Austrian specialties, including an entire section devoted to sausages. The kitchen eschews the heavy hand often used in this style of cooking and instead offers light preparations of Austrian classics like Wiener Schnitzel, with each ingredient perfectly represented—down to the fresh-grated horseradish.

For dessert, the likes of cherry strudel, homemade ice cream coupes, and *Salzburger nockerl* will leave you smacking your lips.

# Bouley ✿

Contemporary XXXX

B3

163 Duane St. (at Hudson St.)

**Subway:** Chambers St (West Broadway) — Lunch & dinner daily
**Phone:** 212-964-2525
**Web:** www.davidbouley.com
**Prices:** **$$$$**

Nicole Bartelme

Straddling a corner of Duane and Hudson, a few steps from sister restaurant, Bouley Bakery, Chef David Bouley's namesake restaurant may be discreetly marked—but one look inside and you'll soon realize this is nobody's schlub.

With its posh, jewelry box interior impeccably detailed in gorgeous linens, expensive flower arrangements, and stone basement featuring a private dining room and positively palatial bathrooms, its hard not to feel like a European princess on her wedding day. Which makes it even more remarkable, of course, that you can settle in for a lavish four-course lunch for a very reasonable $48 (six courses at dinner runs $95).

Bouley has a penchant for infusing seasonal ingredients into classic preparations like a perfectly roasted Pennsylvania chicken served over creamy green almond-buttermilk purée, paired with sautéed organic crosnes, shaved black truffles, and a buttery potato purée; a golden brown wing of skate, served over creamy celery root purée; or crispy golden duck breast dusted with Balinese black pepper in a white truffle honey jus, flanked by a romanesco broccoli purée, julienned snow peas, and a single baby turnip glazed with vanilla bean.

# Bread Tribeca

**C2**                                                 Italian ✗

301 Church St. (at Walker St.)

**Subway:** Canal St (Sixth Ave.)                    Lunch & dinner daily
**Phone:** 212-334-8282
**Web:** www.breadtribeca.com
**Prices:** $$

How downtown chow aficionados do lunch: crusty, overstuffed Italian sandwiches; a clean, cool, industrial layout; and a few famous actors chilling in the corner. With its long, wooden communal table and free WiFi—Bread Tribeca delivers the sort of bang-bang lunch that busy New Yorkers dream about, although the rustic Italian menu includes enough tempting pastas, pizzas, soups, and such, that it would be a shame not to linger longer and enjoy the chefs' myriad creations. Dip your spoon into a creamy, piping hot zucchini soup laced with a cool swirl of crème fraîche and a generous crush of black pepper.

A luscious, creamy pumpkin cheesecake, served at room temperature and carrying hints of clove and cardamom, also delivers.

# Capsouto Frères

**A1**                                               French ✗✗

451 Washington St. (at Watts St.)

**Subway:** Canal St (Sixth Ave.)                    Lunch Tue – Sun
**Phone:** 212-966-4900                              Dinner nightly
**Web:** www.capsoutofreres.com
**Prices:** $$

First, admire the stunning architectural details of the landmark 1891 building the restaurant has called home since 1980. Then, forget the slightly off-the-path location while you enjoy the view. Inside, howling steam pipes echo against carved wainscoting, dark wooden floors, and large jacquard-lined windows.

Enduring vision and commitment to providing great food and service are the hallmarks of this restaurant's sustained viability, and its place in New York culture. The honest and well-made menu may highlight a perfectly tender bœuf Bourguignon as well as sweet and savory soufflés—some of the best offered in the city. The restaurant serves as a friendly, intimate, and unpretentious foil to the hectic mega-restaurants found nearby.

# Chanterelle

French XXX

B2

2 Harrison St. (at Hudson St.)

**Subway:** Franklin St — Lunch Thu – Sat
**Phone:** 212-966-6960 — Dinner Tue – Sun
**Web:** www.chanterellenyc.com
**Prices:** $$$$

Chanterelle commemorates its 30th anniversary this year and what better way to celebrate than with a major makeover. From paint to carpet, from the menu to the kitchen, everything is up for a mid-life overhaul.

David and Karen Waltuck have been devoted to this restaurant over the decades, and an update is surely essential to ensure the longevity of a place that has many loyal followers and devotees. One thing is certain; the location remains the same on a quintessential corner of TriBeCa, well-located for the expense-account crowd that fills Chanterelle nightly.

The restaurant has been so successful, three cookbooks have come out of its kitchen over the years allowing you to recreate a little bit of the magic in your own home.

# Dylan Prime

Contemporary XX

B1

62 Laight St. (at Greenwich St.)

**Subway:** Franklin St — Lunch Mon – Fri
**Phone:** 212-334-4783 — Dinner nightly
**Web:** www.dylanprime.com
**Prices:** $$$

Dylan Prime is kind of like the ideal man. With a menu that boasts a parade of masculine cuts like Porterhouse, filet mignon, or aged prime rib, it's undeniably a steakhouse. But unlike some of the more insecure shank shacks in town, this menu isn't afraid to show its softer side with delicate diver scallops, soft fried artichokes, and silky salmon tartare. Dylan Prime's split personality doesn't end there, either. The service is swift, but relaxed—and though the mood is dark, sultry, and romantic—thanks to low lighting, cozy banquettes, and flickering votives, there's plenty of leg room.

The lunch set will find a nice deal in the $14 Dylan Prime Burger—a thick, juicy item on a warm, toasted brioche, stuffed with ruby-red tomatoes and homemade sauce.

# Corton ✿✿

Contemporary XXX

B2

239 West Broadway (bet. Walker & White Sts.)

**Subway:** Franklin St — Dinner Mon – Sat
**Phone:** 212-219-2777
**Web:** www.cortonnyc.com
**Prices:** $$$$

Richard Pare/Myriad Restaurant Group

Hot, hot, hot. Despite opening on the cusp of an economic meltdown, Drew Nieporent and Paul Liebrandt's new venture, Corton, opened to a thunderclap of critical praise in the fall of 2008, and hasn't looked back since.

Over a year later, it's still living up to the hype, and you can expect lots of bang for your bite when you settle in for Liebrandt's modern French fare, which can be sampled à la carte, as a three course prix-fixe or as an extensive, multi-course tasting menu. The sleek TriBeCa haunt is effortlessly elegant—with an airy downtown vibe washed in soft lighting and sleek, modern lines, tended to by a perfectly warm and polished staff.

But good looks aside, what really sets the foodies hearts afire is the food, which rotates daily but might include dishes like the popular "from the garden" series, a mind-blowing composition of at least 20 different vegetables, each deftly prepared using an entirely different, albeit equally complex, execution; a plate of vibrantly fresh shrimp and scallops paired with silky sea urchin; or a stunning rendition of crayfish *vol-au-vent,* laced with morel mushrooms, wood sorrel, decadent foams, and crispy circles of *pâte feuilletée.*

# The Harrison

American

A2

355 Greenwich St. (at Harrison St.)

**Subway:** Franklin St — Dinner nightly
**Phone:** 212-274-9310
**Web:** www.theharrison.com
**Prices:** $$

Almost a decade into its tenure, The Harrison is still getting it right. It's cool, but not too cool. It's casual, but not too casual. Much of the credit goes to Chef/owner Jimmy Bradley, a seasoned master of downtown hip and homey who doesn't stop at the surface goods, but digs deeper to bring in talented chefs like Amanda Freitag to seal the deal.

Grab a seat in the sexy, amber-soaked dining room and treat yourself to a spread of Freitag's seasonal fare, like fresh arctic char spooned with lemon gastrique, and laid over tender slices of cauliflower and earthy chanterelles; or jumbo crispy shrimp, served with a lemon-caper aïoli; or pan-seared hake, served in a summer corn ragout studded with favas, pearl onions, saffron, and chervil.

# Kitchenette

American

A3

156 Chambers St. (bet. Greenwich St. & West Broadway)

**Subway:** Chambers St (West Broadway) — Lunch & dinner daily
**Phone:** 212-267-6740
**Web:** N/A
**Prices:** ©©

Kitchenette brings a taste of home to TriBeCa, where a formica counter, swiveling barstools, and black-and-white floor tiles imbue this casual café with the nostalgic air of an old-fashioned luncheonette. The menu celebrates Americana, from freshly made cornbread to a tuna melt. Served on whimsical tables made from wooden doors, dishes such as moist, delicate turkey meatloaf with buttery mashed potatoes and silky-smooth gravy epitomize American comfort food. Kitchenette appeals to a wide array of diners, who love the retro feel and homey cuisine—since so many of them have children in tow, the next generation may appreciate this place just as much.

Sibling Kitchenette Uptown (*1272 Amsterdam Ave.*) is a favorite with the Columbia University crowd.

# Landmarc

B2 — French XX

179 West Broadway (bet. Leonard & Worth Sts.)

**Subway:** Franklin St — Lunch & dinner daily
**Phone:** 212-343-3883
**Web:** www.landmarc-restaurant.com
**Prices:** $$

Simple, modern bistro fare is made with flair here, largely thanks to the open grill, boldly placed just a few feet from the bar, bustling with patrons and cheery servers. This not only acts as a festive focal point for the dining room, but also transforms straightforward dishes like grilled salmon into expertly charred, juicy centerpieces. Plated alongside ratatouille and black olive tapenade, the result is divine.

The vibe at the TriBeCa space (another location is in the Time Warner Center) is relaxed but trendy, and features exposed brick walls, and a narrow second-floor balcony opens up to the street in warm weather. The frugal oenophile will be happy to know that Landmarc's famed half-bottle list is still well-chosen, and gloriously within budget.

# Locanda Verde

A2 — Italian XX

379 Greenwich St. (at N. Moore St.)

**Subway:** Franklin St — Lunch & dinner daily
**Phone:** 212-925-3797
**Web:** www.locandaverdenyc.com
**Prices:** $$$

A trip to Locanda Verde might send you reeling back to that perfect trattoria you discovered on your last day in sunny Italy—and that's a very good thing considering you're in see-and-be-seen TriBeCa. This rustic new cutie arrives courtesy of the team (Robert DeNiro is one of the partners) behind Ago, the sceney joint that formerly occupied this space. The toned down Locanda, featuring lots of wood, streaming light, and way less attitude, is an improvement.

But the biggest change is importing popular chef, Andrew Carmellini, whose lovely new menu feature all kinds of delicious rustic staples, including the chef's beloved sheep's milk ricotta (which he refined at A Voce), and an entire section dedicated to *Piccolini* (Italian small plates).

# Macao Trading Co.

Portuguese XX

C2

311 Church St. (bet. Lispenard & Walker Sts.)

**Subway:** Canal St (Sixth Ave.)
**Phone:** 212-431-8642
**Web:** www.macaonyc.com
**Prices:** $$$

Lunch Sat – Sun
Dinner nightly

Gorgeous Chinese and Portuguese fare meets a sexy, clubby ambience at the new Macao Trading Co., where there is no sign to mark the entrance—just a red light over a door on a fairly boring TriBeCa block. It's a wild difference from what lies within—a packed, opium-den like setting open till 4:00 A.M., where as much attention is given to the libations as to the beautiful dishes.

The region of Macao (often spelled Macau) belonged to the Portuguese before they handed the island over to the Chinese in 1999, and the two cultures are given equal play time, but never fused, on the restaurant's menu. Save room for a mind-blowing trio of silky flans—including mandarin, *dulce de leche*, and espresso—all topped in a decadent layer of caramel.

# Matsugen

Japanese XXX

B2

241 Church St. (at Leonard St.)

**Subway:** Chambers St (Church St.)
**Phone:** 212-925-0202
**Web:** www.jean-georges.com
**Prices:** $$$

Lunch & dinner daily

They're hardly dorm room ramen noodles, but the soba noodle—a thin noodle made from buckwheat flour served chilled or in hot broth—usually makes for a cheap date in New York. That's a big leap to the $12-$36 bowls at Matsugen—the brainchild of Jean-Georges Vongerichten and Japanese restaurateurs, the Matsushita brothers.

Good thing it's a spectacularly beautiful bowl of soba. Sure, you could get this kind of soba for less if you followed the underground Japanese food circuit, but then you wouldn't get to kick it in as stylish a space as Matsugen's, decked to the nines in black Eames chairs and runway-length communal tables. Though fresh soba—served hot or cold in three textures—is the focus, the menu also offers an omakase plus salads and sushi galore.

# Marc Forgione ✿

**B3** American XX

134 Reade St. (bet. Greenwich & Hudson Sts.)

**Subway:** Chambers St (West Broadway) — Lunch Sun
**Phone:** 212-941-9401 — Dinner nightly
**Web:** www.forgenyc.com
**Prices:** $$$

Daniel Krieger

The farmhouse-chic that permeates Manhattan's restaurant scene isn't going to find relief anytime soon if the designers here have a say in the matter. But only the most jaded critic could deny the rustic, lived-in good looks on display here: this is reclaimed flooring and moody glass lanterns at its finest. In fact, it ought to be the blueprint for like-minded interior endeavors.

The food's no slouch either, with the young, much-hyped Marc Forgione at the wheel. Even if he hadn't cut his teeth in the kitchens of famed chefs, Patricia Yeo and Laurent Tourondel, he's got excellent foodie stock in famed locavore Dad, Larry Forgione—a pedigree on full display when he elevates a humdrum corn cake to decadent new heights in his peach upside-down cake, an otherwordly concoction paired with corn ice cream and caramel corn.

A spin through the rest of his short, but impressive menu might start with theatrically-presented, divine potato rolls; a bright Kona Kampachi tartare shot with avocado and American caviar; a tender leg of suckling pig, sided with Anson Mills grits and a smattering of seasonal veg; or potato-wrapped fluke, draped in a golden-raisin-and-caper brown butter sauce.

# Megu

Japanese

B3

62 Thomas St. (bet. Church St. & West Broadway)

**Subway:** Chambers St (West Broadway) — Dinner nightly
**Phone:** 212-964-7777
**Web:** www.megunyc.com
**Prices:** $$$

Sleek, gorgeous, and sexy—Megu takes sweet advantage of TriBeCa's notoriously lofty digs. After a short descent down a row of stairs, visitors uncover a jaw-dropping décor, replete with a carved ice Buddha hovering over a pool strewn with rose petals. Above it, hangs a dramatic replica of a Japanese temple bell. Can the cuisine live up to this grand-scale design? Megu's kitchen thinks so—sourcing only the highest-quality ingredients, and turning out plates of bright, inventive Japanese delicacies, touched with influences farther afield.
Micro-greens wrapped in sheets of *yuba* are topped with a delicate mound of sashimi, and then drizzled with a sweet, spicy dressing. A midtown location provides an elegant Zen setting for the diplomat crowd (*845 UN Plaza*).

# Nam

Vietnamese

B3

110 Reade St. (bet. Church St. & West Broadway)

**Subway:** Chambers St (West Broadway) — Lunch Mon – Fri
**Phone:** 212-267-1777 — Dinner nightly
**Web:** www.namnyc.com
**Prices:** $$

Nam strives to please—and it does, bringing diners bounding back for the attentive service and alluring ambience. Slowly turning ceiling fans, backlit Vietnamese portraits, a wall lined with bamboo reeds, and natural light pouring in through the generously sized front windows all add to the appeal of this small, charming restaurant.
The food here may appear a bit scripted and the menu certainly contains no surprises, but there's something to be said for tried and true. Vietnamese standards such as *ca hap* made with perfectly steamed sea bass, bean-thread noodles, earthy yet sweet shiitake mushrooms, ginger, and scallions are rendered with good quality ingredients and a careful, if somewhat restrained, hand in the kitchen.

# Nobu

B2 Japanese XX

105 Hudson St. (at Franklin St.)

**Subway:** Franklin St
**Phone:** 212-219-0500
**Web:** www.myriadrestaurantgroup.com
**Prices:** $$$$

Lunch Mon – Fri
Dinner nightly

A kitchen that exemplifies the care, skill, and true excellence of celebrity chef, Nobu Matsuhisa, combined with business partners, actor Robert DeNiro and Drew Nieporent, has made Nobu a formula for success.

Since 1994, lines out the door have been testament to this contemporary Japanese fusion cuisine; reserving is highly recommended (or try one of Nobu's other excellent New York locations). Inside, architect David Rockwell recreates the Japanese countryside, with stylized birch trees and wall of black river stones.

While best known for its seductive sushi and sashimi, the appealing specialties like miso-glazed black cod or perfectly tender squid pasta must not be overlooked. Sharing multiple dishes may provide the best, authentic "Nobu" experience.

# The Odeon

B3 American XX

145 West Broadway (at Thomas St.)

**Subway:** Chambers St (West Broadway)
**Phone:** 212-233-0507
**Web:** www.theodeonrestaurant.com
**Prices:** $$

Lunch & dinner daily

The story of The Odeon's longevity is a study in miracles. Opening in 1980, it has survived well past its own "15 minutes of fame," typical of the city's dining scene.

Perched from a bar stool, one can take in the art deco architectural details—from the dark hardwood bar and wall panels lining the dining room, to globe lights and lazy fans hanging from the ceiling. The warm tones and lighting set the tone of an otherwise lively room.

This lovely setting enhances the very enjoyable food. Items may include Eden Brook trout, blending almond purée-butter, briny capers, and sweet tomato confit to create a depth of textural dimensions. The lunch special is a great deal for this neighborhood but, judging from the full dining room, it is no secret.

# Pepolino

Italian

C2

281 West Broadway (bet. Canal & Lispenard Sts.)

**Subway:** Canal St (Sixth Ave.) Lunch & dinner daily
**Phone:** 212-966-9983
**Web:** www.pepolino.com
**Prices:** $$

Named for a variety of wild thyme found in Tuscany, Pepolino and its original chef, Enzo Pezone, have been a TriBeCa fixture since 1999—this in itself is an accomplishment, considering this city's fickle restaurant scene.

Simple Tuscan specialties, neither stripped down nor re-imagined, bring enthusiastic visitors back for more. The menu may feature the fresh and light bread soup, *ribollita*, teeming with *cavolo nero*, root vegetables, tomatoes, beans, and sprinkled with fragrant herbs. The heartier *fettucine al coniglio* is loaded with meaty morsels of tender stewed rabbit. Although the kitchen staff sometimes lacks focus, they nonetheless excel at creative fare such as the tomato-basil pâté that may be presented with bread at the beginning of the meal.

# Takahachi

Japanese

B3

145 Duane St. (bet. Church St. & West Broadway)

**Subway:** Chambers St (West Broadway) Lunch Mon – Fri
**Phone:** 212-571-1830 Dinner nightly
**Web:** www.takahachi.net
**Prices:** $$

In a neighborhood dominated by Japanese behemoths like Nobu, Megu, and the recently opened Matsugen, the unassuming Takahachi is a welcome reprieve for nouveau Japanese fare in TriBeCa—minus the fuss, high-flying theatrics, and exorbitant price tags. And for those willing to forgo the sexy ambience, there's even a little romantic lighting from the skylights in Takahachi's dining room come sunset.

The menu is a mish-mash of the country's offerings, with a lineup that might include a bright, velvety plate of sashimi; a fresh tangle of sesame-dressed buckwheat soba noodles studded with shiitake mushrooms and avocado; or a hot appetizer of creamy black cod marinated in miso so nutty and irresistible it might give Mr. Taro Aso himself pause.

# Sushi Azabu ✿

A1 — Japanese

428 Greenwich St. (at Laight St.)

**Subway:** Franklin St — Dinner nightly
**Phone:** 212-274-0428
**Web:** www.greenwichgrill.com
**Prices:** $$$

Greenwich Grill

There are three different omakase styles to choose from at this TriBeCa sushi den: sushi, sashimi-and-sushi, or traditional. The last one is far from disappointing, but there's no contest which two reign supreme given the title of the restaurant.

Nestled into the basement of the Greenwich Grill, there's a bit of a speakeasy vibe as you make your way through the bustling grill (owned by the same group) and down to Sushi Azabu, a neatly-appointed sushi den fitted out in classic Japanese décor and a smattering of contemporary round booths. It's a particularly pleasing aesthetic to enjoy early in the night, before the super-hip TriBeCa crowd descends on the scene, sending the sometimes too-small service staff into a slightly harried state.

Still, even at the restaurant's craziest weekend hour, its hard to deny the show-stopping lineup, which might include pristine Kumamoto oysters in ponzu sauce, accented with a tiny bit of grated radish; a bright array of sashimi that might feature wildly fresh toro, tairagai, or uni dancing in sea water; grilled, miso-glazed amberjack touched with ginger root; mozuku seaweed in vinegar; or a killer maki featuring fresh salmon roe.

# Tribeca Grill

Contemporary XX

A2

375 Greenwich St. (at Franklin St.)

**Subway:** Franklin St
**Phone:** 212-941-3900
**Web:** www.myriadrestaurantgroup.com
**Prices:** $$$

Lunch Sun – Fri
Dinner nightly

Two decades ago, Drew Nieporent and Robert DeNiro turned a 1905 downtown warehouse into a New York classic. Exposed pipes and brick walls preserve the building's industrial past and set the architectural standard for many modern TriBeCa eateries.

Beautiful and powerful people comprise a large part of the clientele, along with moneyed neighborhood residents. The contemporary menu highlights dishes using well-sourced ingredients, such as the grilled Long Island duck breast with duck confit, mustard greens, shiitake mushrooms, and cashews.

The staff is efficient, well paced, and happy to bring the sommelier if guests should have questions on the very impressive wine list. For a savory dessert treat, pair this with a sampling of extensive selections of artisanal cheeses.

# Wolfgang's

Steakhouse XX

A1

409 Greenwich St. (bet. Beach & Hubert Sts.)

**Subway:** Franklin St
**Phone:** 212-925-0350
**Web:** www.wolfgangssteakhouse.com
**Prices:** $$$$

Lunch Mon – Fri
Dinner nightly

Wolfgang Zweiner's Park Avenue steakhouse adds a baby brother to the mix, and it would appear that the TriBeCa outpost is not only more chill (don't leave without chatting up the charming floor manager, Arnie), but might be turning out even better food as well.

Zwiener clocked in four decades waiting tables at Brooklyn's esteemed Peter Luger before venturing across the river with wacky ideas about improving the legendary steakhouse's recipe. A bold move, but it worked. Sure, you can dabble with a fresh house salad sporting French beans and pink shrimp or the velvety key lime pie, but the undisputed star of this show is the beautifully aged steak, cooked to crispy-outside-rosy-pink-inside perfection and ladled with lip-smacking sizzling pan juices.

# Upper East Side

The Upper East Side is a vast, mainly residential neighborhood with many faces ranging from prominent New York families to fresh from college prepsters. Closest to the park are posh spots catering to the Euro crowd and ladies who lunch. Walk further east to find young families filling the latest, casual sushi-ya or artisanal pizzeria. Along First and Second avenues, pubs are packed with raucous post-grads keeping the party alive.

The most upper and eastern reaches were originally developed by renowned families of German descent who built country estates in what has become Yorkville. **Schaller & Weber** is one of the few remaining butchers carrying traditional Austro-German products including fantastic wursts for winter steaming or summer grilling and the pungent mustards to accompany them.

The Upper East Side has a greater concentration of gourmet markets than any other neighborhood in the city, most with a European feel. Each shop may be more packed than the next, yet has made processing long lines an art of inspired efficiency. **Agata & Valentina** specializes in everything Italian with a considerable regional cheese selection. **Citarella** pumps its mouthwatering aroma of rotisserie chickens out the storefront to entice passersby, but the seafood selection is where they find nirvana. **Grace's Marketplace** is a longtime favorite, loved for its cramped corners and cascading displays. Insiders frequent their trattoria, showcasing quality ingredients carried in the store. However, the true champion of everything uptown and gourmet is Eli Zabar and his ever-expanding empire. **E.A.T.** has been a Madison Avenue darling since 1973, selling baked goods and takeout foods alongside its casual café. Later branches include his **Vinegar Factory** and newer mega-mart **Eli's**.

Still, there are plenty of smaller purveyors to patronize. **Lobel's** and **Ottomanelli** are among the cities best remaining classic butcher shops, both offering the best meats and pragmatic cooking advice. **William Greenberg Jr.** bakes New York's favorite cookie, the black-and-white, along with to-die-for babka. **Glaser's** looks and tastes of everything Old World. On the high end, **Lady M's** stylish boutique and couture cakes blend right in with its chic Madison Avenue neighbors.

For any foodie, Kitchen Arts & Letters has the largest stock of food and wine publications in the country...and owner Nach Waxman is as good a source of industry insight as any book or blog.

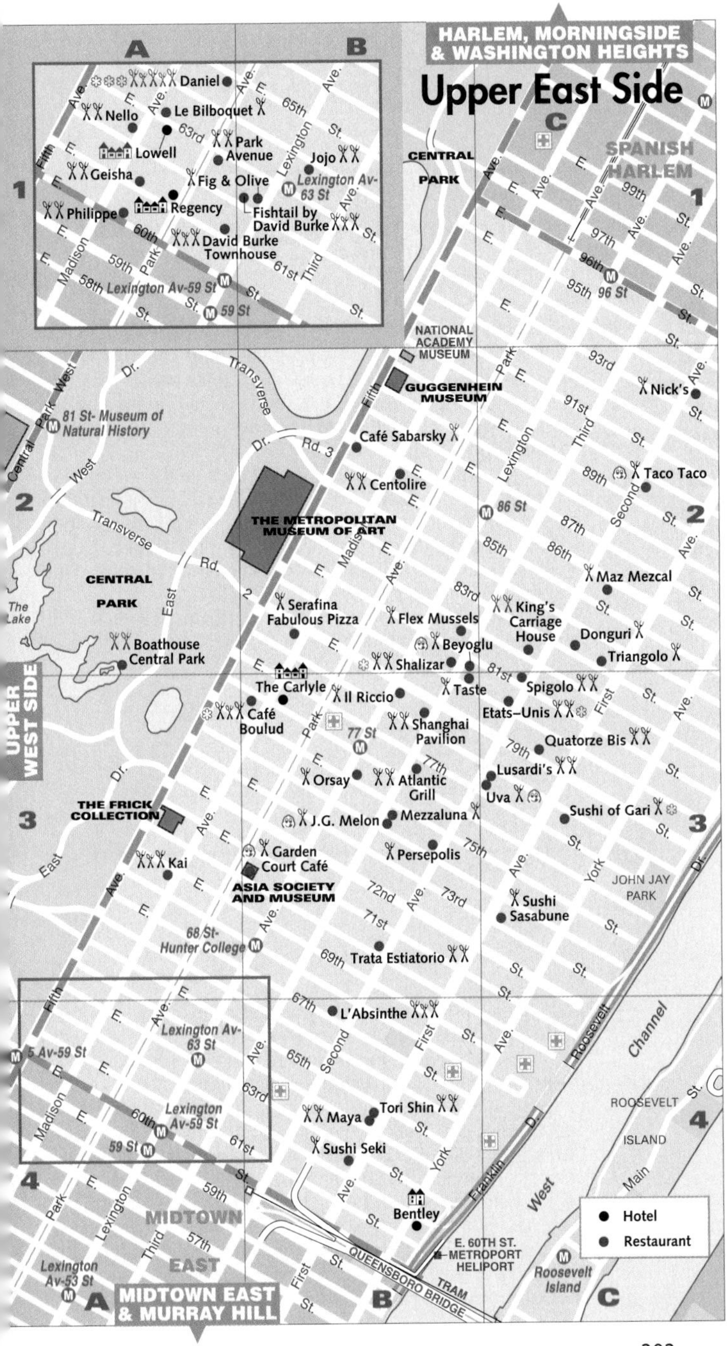

Upper East Side
HARLEM, MORNINGSIDE & WASHINGTON HEIGHTS
MIDTOWN EAST & MURRAY HILL
UPPER WEST SIDE
CENTRAL PARK
SPANISH HARLEM
MIDTOWN EAST
THE METROPOLITAN MUSEUM OF ART
GUGGENHEIN MUSEUM
NATIONAL ACADEMY MUSEUM
THE FRICK COLLECTION
ASIA SOCIETY AND MUSEUM
JOHN JAY PARK
ROOSEVELT ISLAND
E. 60TH ST. METROPORT HELIPORT
QUEENSBORO BRIDGE
TRAM
Daniel
Nello
Le Bilboquet
Lowell
Park Avenue
Jojo
Geisha
Fig & Olive
Philippe
Regency
Fishtail by David Burke
David Burke Townhouse
Nick's
Café Sabarsky
Centolire
Taco Taco
Maz Mezcal
Serafina Fabulous Pizza
Flex Mussels
King's Carriage House
Donguri
Beyoglu
Triangolo
Boathouse Central Park
Shalizar
The Carlyle
Il Riccio
Taste
Spigolo
Café Boulud
Etats-Unis
Shanghai Pavilion
Quatorze Bis
Orsay
Atlantic Grill
Lusardi's
Uva
J.G. Melon
Mezzaluna
Sushi of Gari
Garden Court Café
Persepolis
Kai
Sushi Sasabune
Trata Estiatorio
L'Absinthe
Tori Shin
Maya
Sushi Seki
Bentley
Hotel
Restaurant

# Atlantic Grill

B3 — Seafood XX

1341 Third Ave. (bet. 76th & 77th Sts.)

**Subway:** 77 St — Lunch & dinner daily
**Phone:** 212-988-9200
**Web:** www.brguestrestaurants.com
**Prices:** $$

Swimmingly similar to its downtown sibling Blue Water Grill, Atlantic Grill hooks a very Upper East Side clientele with a vast, globally-accented menu focused on the sea. A selection of sushi (from both the Atlantic and Pacific) and a raw bar are still beloved, while other offerings remember to satisfy fish-free appetites.

The large, luring space is frequented by a well-dressed, fun-loving crowd occupying two rooms—one features a nautical blue and white theme; and the other has a sunny disposition with a terrazzo floor, wicker seating, and potted palms. Sidewalk seating is in high demand when the sun comes out, and the place booms at weekend brunch.

The splendidly intent service team perfectly completes the offerings at this long-time crowd-pleaser.

# Beyoglu

B2 — Turkish X

1431 Third Ave. (at 81st St.)

**Subway:** 77 St — Lunch & dinner daily
**Phone:** 212-650-0850
**Web:** N/A
**Prices:** $$

Sharing may not come naturally to everyone; but when dining at Beyoglu, it is the best course of action. This way, one can fully experience the delicious range of Mediterranean meze that earns this establishment praise. Most of the recipes—and some wine and beer offerings—come from Turkey, though Greek and Lebanese accents can be found throughout. Warm and tender pita bread makes a delightful accompaniment to anything on the menu. Thick homemade yogurt with spinach and garlic; pan-fried cubes of eggplant with sautéed fresh tomato; grilled shrimp; and marinated octopus are a short sampling of the wide selection.

If grazing doesn't satisfy, choose from a list of larger daily specials, including meat kebabs and grilled fish.

# Boathouse Central Park

American

A2

The Lake at Central Park (E. 72nd St. & Park Dr. North)

**Subway:** 68 St - Hunter College — Lunch & dinner daily
**Phone:** 212-517-2233
**Web:** www.thecentralparkboathouse.com
**Prices:** $$

You couldn't dream up a more romantic setting for a first date or a special occasion. Nestled on the shore of the lake in the middle of Central Park, the Boathouse features peaceful water views through its floor-to-ceiling windows. Built in the 1950s, Loeb Boathouse replaced the original two-story Victorian structure designed by architect Calvert Vaux in the 1870s.
Today, the Boathouse is the only place in Manhattan for a lakeside meal. And the American fare such as jumbo lump crab cakes and pan-roasted Florida snapper with melted cabbage, scallions, and lemongrass vinaigrette makes it all the more worthwhile.
On a sunny day, sit out on the deck and watch the boats float by. After lunch, why not hit the water with a gondola ride, or a rowboat rental?

# Café Sabarsky

Austrian

B2

1048 Fifth Ave. (at 86th St.)

**Subway:** 86 St (Lexington Ave.) — Lunch & dinner Wed – Mon
**Phone:** 212-288-0665
**Web:** www.wallse.com
**Prices:** $$

In addition to the great art on view at the intimately scaled Neue Galerie, one will also find Chef Kurt Gutenbrunner's charming café modeled after a late 19th century Viennese *kaffehause*; complete with dark wood paneled walls and formally attired servers. The museum, housed in a 1914 Beaux Arts mansion, was founded by cosmetic mogul Ronald Lauder to display his collection of early 20th century Austrian and German art, as well as the collection of his friend, art dealer Serge Sabarsky.
Savory fare like hearty beef goulash and *spätzle* with cream and wild mushrooms will vie for your attention, along with an indulgent listing of classic sweets that include *sachertorte* glazed with homemade apricot jam, *linzertorte*, and quark cheese-filled strudel.

# Café Boulud ✿

French XXX

B3

20 E. 76th St. (bet. Fifth & Madison Aves.)

**Subway:** 77 St
**Phone:** 212-772-2600
**Web:** www.danielnyc.com
**Prices:** $$$$

Lunch Tue – Sun
Dinner nightly

Gabriel Viteri

Rising chef and all-around dreamy new it-boy, Gavin Kaysen, offers four roads to travel down the Café Boulud menu: traditional, seasonal, market-driven, and far-flung exotic flavors. The good news is that in Daniel Boulud's lovely little country café, there are no roads too traveled by—each and every lane of this mix-and-match menu offers up delicious possibility.

Tucked into the first floor of the elegant Surrey Hotel, the inspiration for the restaurant was the Boulud family's old farm café back in France, located just outside of Lyon, in Saint-Pierre de Chandieu. A series of white-clothed tables pepper the muted earth tones of the soothing, if somewhat plain, dining room; and springtime finds a fresh clutch of tables dotting the sidewalk.

Diners can opt for the seasonal prix-fixe or float between the menu's columns, where you might find a dish of plump ravioli filled with succulent braised beef, on a vibrant tangle of magenta cabbage; two gorgeous slivers of seared arctic char, partnered with an irresistibly crunchy falafel boasting a bright green interior and a sweet-and-sour side of eggplant; or a perfectly creamy Meyer lemon tart, shot with a silky pistachio pastry cream.

# Centolire

**Italian** XX

B2

## 1167 Madison Ave. (bet. 85th & 86th Sts.)

**Subway:** 86 St (Lexington Ave.) Lunch & dinner daily
**Phone:** 212-734-7711
**Web:** www.pinoluongo.com
**Prices:** $$$

Tuscan-born restaurateur, Pino Luongo, opened Centolire to honor those Italians who, like himself, came to America to start a new life. This establishment has a pleasantly elegant air to its second floor dining room accessed via glass enclosed elevator. The spacious setting is sunlit by large windows overlooking Madison Avenue and is attractively appointed with colorful fabrics and antique kitchen tools. The smartly attired service team graciously attends to diners and prepares Caesar salad tableside—a luscious starting point from which to enjoy the classically infused menu of housemade pastas and entrées that include farm-raised rabbit *"cacciatora."*
Centolire's ground floor dining room features an all-day café menu of salads and panini.

# David Burke Townhouse

**Contemporary** XXX

A1

## 133 E. 61st St. (bet. Lexington & Park Aves.)

**Subway:** Lexington Av - 59 St Lunch & dinner daily
**Phone:** 212-813-2121
**Web:** www.davidburketownhouse.com
**Prices:** $$$

Following the dissolution of his very public partnership with Donatella Arpaia, Chef/owner David Burke is now calling the shots at this contemporary American. Although changes are clear, much still feels familiar here, from the elegantly themed décor to the attentive service team.
The chef's bold style and unique spin is just as whimsical and quote-worthy as ever. Dinner features such creations as Hudson Valley foie gras "PB&J" with macadamia nut butter and strawberry-vanilla jam; halibut T-bone "au poivre" with lobster bordelaise; and "Bronx-style" filet mignon of veal. The lunchtime prix-fixe menu represents notable value and offers wine by-the-glass specials. This red-bricked townhouse is a popular setting for weekend brunch.

# Daniel ✿✿✿

French

A1

60 E. 65th St. (bet. Madison & Park Aves.)

**Subway:** 68 St - Hunter College

Dinner Mon – Sat

**Phone:** 212-288-0033

**Web:** www.danielnyc.com

**Prices:** $$$$

Eric Laignel

Quick, before you think: What's the best restaurant in New York? Ask many Manhattanites that, and Daniel Boulud's New York flagship, Daniel, immediately comes to mind. Even those who wouldn't rank it supreme tend to agree on one thing—it at least makes the dream team.

Those who found the former interior overbearing will probably instantly warm to the new face-lift, masterminded in 2008 by designer Adam D. Tihany. It reads more effortlessly sophisticated than stuffy, though jackets are still required, thank you very much. The main dining room gets a fresh, contemporary spin with lots of creamy whites broken up by bright Spanish paintings, and the regal custom-made chandeliers (sporting beautiful Limoge porcelain tiles) lend the room a warm, romantic glow.

The exquisite food, however, remains gloriously the same—unapologetically French, and carefully executed by Chef Jean-François Bruel. Dinner spins to the season but may include a fresh blood orange ceviche, studded with plump Nantucket bay scallops, crystal-clear Winter Point oysters and silky uni; or a tender fillet of black sea bass laced with syrah sauce, and paired with leeks royale and a perfect square of *pommes lyonnaise*.

# Donguri

Japanese

C2

309 E. 83rd St. (bet. First & Second Aves.)

**Subway:** 86 St (Lexington Ave.) Dinner Tue – Sun
**Phone:** 212-737-5656
**Web:** www.dongurinyc.com
**Prices:** $$$

Owned by Ito En, the Japanese tea company that also runs upscale *kaiseki* sibling Kai, Donguri offers an extensive menu of authentic Japanese cuisine in a very simple and cozy setting. With only 24 seats, the few tables in this tiny spot fill up quickly with a loyal and sophisticated crowd who can afford the prices and appreciate the subtle, delicate, authentically-prepared Japanese food.

Casual yet steeped in tradition, a beautifully presented assortment of classic courses can be chosen à la carte, including a number of dishes to share, with daily and seasonal specialties augmenting the menu. However, to best appreciate the selection of impeccably fresh fish flown in daily and other delicacies, call a day in advance to order the chef's omakase.

# Fig & Olive

Mediterranean

B1

808 Lexington Ave. (bet. 62nd & 63rd Sts.)

**Subway:** Lexington Av - 63 St Lunch & dinner daily
**Phone:** 212-207-4555
**Web:** www.figandolive.com
**Prices:** $$$

The bounty of the Mediterranean's olive groves is not only featured on the menu of this casually elegant Upper East (as well as two additional locations) spot, but is also available for purchase in the form of gift worthy packaging. Each dish—from seafood salad to grilled *branzino* with fig and balsamic—is accented with a specific extra virgin oil, and at dinner each meal begins with an olive oil trio to sample.

Fig & Olive makes a soothing shoppers respite. Re-fuel on light Mediterranean plates such as zucchini carpaccio; seared sea scallops with truffle tapenade; and Cote d'Azur bouillabaisse, and your strength will be renewed! The wine list echoes the same regions of origin as the fragrant oils, with many selections available by the glass.

# Etats-Unis ✿

C3 — Contemporary XX

242 E. 81st St. (bet. Second & Third Aves.)

**Subway:** 77 St — Dinner nightly
**Phone:** 212-517-8826
**Web:** www.etatsunisrestaurant.com
**Prices:** $$$

Luca Pecora/Etats-Unis

Cozy, urban, and casual, this understated little neighborhood bistro packs enormous charm into its small space. Sunlight streams through windows on summer evenings, while in winter months, the low lighting casts an intimate glow. A dining counter offers a peek into the tiny kitchen, where the staff keeps an eye on the tables and times the courses accordingly.

The menu offers wide appeal and shows seasonal focus in the likes of a crab and haricots verts salad over slices of garden-fresh tomatoes, bursting with flavor. A grilled leg of lamb brightened by mint pesto is pleasantly retro in culinary style, and delicious alongside perfectly roasted tomatoes and grilled asparagus.

The chef's signature sweet, freshly steamed date pudding, is a menu highlight. This divinely decadent cousin of sticky toffee pudding, prepared with painstaking accuracy, swims in a shallow pool of caramelized rum sauce and is crowned with a dollop of whipped cream.The restaurant's owner has carefully selected the wine list to include a nice choice by the glass, all of which are also offered by the bottle at affordable prices. As for the rest, prices climb to reflect the fine selection of international varietals.

# Fishtail by David Burke

Seafood XXX

B1

135 E. 62nd St. (bet. Lexington & Park Aves.)

**Subway:** Lexington Av - 63 St — Dinner nightly
**Phone:** 212-754-1300
**Web:** www.fishtaildb.com
**Prices:** $$$

This new concept from Chef David Burke serves up a bounty of sustainable seafood harvested by the restaurant's very own fishing boat. The preparations are stamped with the chef's unique touch as in the fish tartare, playfully presented as a trio of vibrant tuna, buttery salmon, and refreshing crab salad-filled tacos. The rare-seared loin of bigeye tuna topped with silky pan-fried foie gras and a truffled sherry reduction show the touch of a skilled kitchen.

This fitting addition to the chef's oeuvre features a sophisticated setting spread out on two levels of a cozy townhouse. The first floor is a popular lounge/oyster bar, while the upstairs dining room is wrapped in deep red and bedecked with accents that colorfully convey the fishy theme.

# Flex Mussels

Seafood X

B2

174 E. 82nd St. (bet. Lexington & Third Aves.)

**Subway:** 86 St (Lexington Ave.) — Dinner nightly
**Phone:** 212-717-7772
**Web:** www.flexmussels.com
**Prices:** $$

Despite its strong name, Flex Mussels is actually a fun, casual, and intimate seafood shack with uptown polish. Usually packed to the gills, the slim bar area features pretty touches like flowers, slender mirrors, and long-legged aluminum chairs against a dining counter. The back dining room is spare, contemporary, and more subdued.

The menu features the namesake bi-valve, hailing from Prince Edward Island, steamed in more than twenty globally-inspired guises, like the "Tokyo" with miso and seaweed. The mussels are priced by the pound and are best accompanied by sides of piping-hot, hand-cut skinny fries. The menu also features non-mussel options such as an impressive lobster roll, the likes of which would normally require a trip downtown.

# Garden Court Café

B3 — Asian

725 Park Ave. (at 70th St.)

**Subway:** 68 St - Hunter College — Lunch Tue – Sun
**Phone:** 212-570-5202
**Web:** www.asiasociety.org
**Prices:** **$$**

Flooded by natural light in the glass-enclosed, plant-filled lobby of the Asia Society, this café is a far cry from your garden-variety museum restaurant. Though it doesn't generate much fanfare, it is worth seeking out, not only for its quiet ambience, but for the Asian dishes that expertly fuse east and west.

Serving lunch Tuesday through Sunday, the menu draws inspiration from the east in its offerings that may include roasted chicken glazed with sweet chili sauce and black bean cakes with mango chutney. The bento box features two chef selections along with rice and salad.

It's a quality show, right down to the careful presentation and good service—and the museum's entry fee is not required. Don't miss the museum gift shop for its wonderful wares.

Look for our new category, small plates.

# Geisha

Japanese XX

A1

33 E. 61st St. (bet. Madison & Park Aves.)

**Subway:** Lexington Av - 59 St
**Phone:** 212-813-1112
**Web:** www.geisharestaurant.com
**Prices:** $$$

Lunch Mon – Fri
Dinner Mon – Sat

Vittorio Assaf and Fabio Granato, the duo who brought Serafina to the Upper Eastside, strike again with Geisha—though this geisha den is more polished cool than bowing modesty. Decked out in origami and cherry blossom light fixtures, Geisha's vibrant two-floor space hums with the stylish, sophisticated crowd that pours in nightly—as often for the well-rounded cocktail list as for the food. The Asian-influenced menu, originally developed by Chef Eric Ripert of Le Bernardin, rounds the usual Japanese bases—sushi, sashimi, and maki—but regulars may find themselves migrating to Geisha's sizable and creative salads.

For example, a rare duck breast with crackling skin gets a shot of texture from frisée, yellow raisins, and crunchy roasted pistachios.

# Il Riccio

Italian X

B3

152 E. 79th St. (bet. Lexington & Third Aves.)

**Subway:** 77 St
**Phone:** 212-639-9111
**Web:** www.ilriccionyc.com
**Prices:** $$

Lunch & dinner daily

♿

This low-key Italian, and its smiling cadre of charming staff, is just the right spot to recharge after an afternoon perusing the fabulous neighborhood boutiques or meandering through the nearby Metropolitan Museum of Art.

The likes of a refreshing arugula and roasted red pepper salad with marinated fresh anchovies; grilled grouper dressed simply with olive oil and fresh lemon; and a straightforward selection of dessert pastries indicates the fuss-free approach to cooking offered at Riccio, which focuses on the cuisine of the Amalfi coast. Regulars know to enjoy these dishes in the back, enclosed garden.

Inside, the space offers a cozy feel with warm ochre walls, simple furnishings, and an assemblage of photographs strewn throughout.

# J.G. Melon

B3 — American

1291 Third Ave. (at 74th St.)

**Subway:** 77 St — Lunch & dinner daily
**Phone:** 212-744-0585
**Web:** N/A
**Prices:**

J.G. Melon is the kind of place parents tell their children they used to frequent when they were young in the city. In fact in many cases, this is still the norm. It's a multi-generational watering hole for the masses, feeding Upper East Siders burgers and beers in a convivial setting that hasn't changed over the generations.

The key here is the burger. Griddled and served on a toasted bun with or without cheese, it's one of the best in the city. Add a bowl of the crispy round fries, a cool draft, and a savory chili or spinach salad starter and you've got the essence of what's been packing this place all these years.

Sure tables are tight and the waits can be long, but the service is jovial and it's come-as-your-are and, did we mention the burger?

# JoJo

B1 — Contemporary

160 E. 64th St. (bet. Lexington & Third Aves.)

**Subway:** Lexington Av - 63 St — Lunch & dinner daily
**Phone:** 212-223-5656
**Web:** www.jean-georges.com
**Prices:** **$$$**

Tucked into a lovely little red townhouse in Manhattan's tony 10021 zip code, Jean-Georges Vongerichten's first-born New York restaurant holds a special place in many Upper East Sider's hearts. With its intimate jewel box interior, filled with snug velvet banquettes, tapestry-framed archways, and seductively low lighting, the interior is less stuffy than its neighbors, with a romantic, bordello-like charm.

The compact à la carte menu is surprisingly reasonable (given the address), and might include plump half-moon rounds of ravioli with spinach and ricotta, gliding in a brown butter sauce with basil, pine nuts, and Parmesan; or tender medallions of duck breast, paired with a scoop of braised fennel and a mushroom-and-duck-sausage filled pastry.

# Kai

Japanese XXX

A3

## 822 Madison Ave. (bet. 68th & 69th Sts.)

**Subway:** 68 St - Hunter College — Lunch & dinner Tue – Sat
**Phone:** 212-988-7277
**Web:** www.itoen.com
**Prices:** **$$$**

Secreted away above the Ito En tea shop, Kai occupies a hushed, Zen space. In front, diners are invited to tables looking over Madison Avenue, while the back counter affords a ringside view of the disciplined chefs at work.

The cuisine at Kai is unquestionably refined and though an a la carte menu offers quality choices, the talent lies in the tasting menus. The *kaiseki* menu (book in advance) displays brilliance and skill as the chefs craft seasonal Japanese ingredients into meticulous preparations. As an alternative, the seasonal menu displays many of the same products with no less precision served graciously by the thoughtful staff.

Seasonal sake pairings make a pleasant coupling and share distinctive sips at a nice price.

# Kings' Carriage House

American XX

C2

## 251 E. 82nd St. (bet. Second & Third Aves.)

**Subway:** 86 St (Lexington Ave.) — Lunch & dinner daily
**Phone:** 212-734-5490
**Web:** N/A
**Prices:** **$$**

Picture the mist rolling in when dining at this bona fide facsimile of an Irish manor. The elegantly countrified setting, warmly run by Elizabeth King and husband Paul Farrell (of Dublin), features creaky wooden floors and goldenrod walls mounted with a plethora of crockery, chinoiserie, and framed portraits. White-linen tables are draped with lacy overlays and set with vintage silverware. A collection of china teapots is even available for purchase.

The nightly prix-fixe menu offers an updated take on classically prepared cuisine with items like grilled quail with carrot and parsnip hashbrowns; potato-crusted halibut with tomato-caper butter; and crème brûlée with caramelized banana. Afternoon tea is quite popular, so be sure to reserve in advance.

# L'Absinthe

B4 — French XXX

227 E. 67th St. (bet. Second & Third Aves.)

**Subway:** 68 St - Hunter College — Lunch & dinner daily
**Phone:** 212-794-4950
**Web:** www.labsinthe.com
**Prices:** $$$

Like a fine wine, L'Absinthe has improved with age. This upscale charmer has matured into a warm and amiable bistro with a soupçon of grace that raises it above similar restaurants. The remarkably accommodating staff caters to an understated, sophisticated clientele that one would expect to find in this quietly elegant setting.

The well-made menu highlights "brasserie classics," some offering modern touches, in addition to changing seasonal specials. A traditional steak tartare is quite good, served with mâche, and excellent frites. Separate menus are designed for holidays; this is truly a lovely spot for a celebration. For romance or dinner with the parents, it has the graciousness to impress—perhaps even more so after all these years.

# Le Bilboquet

A1 — French X

25 E. 63rd St. (bet. Madison & Park Aves.)

**Subway:** Lexington Av - 63 St — Lunch & dinner daily
**Phone:** 212-751-3036
**Web:** N/A
**Prices:** $$

With no sign to mark its location, beautiful young things that seem to know each other, and English lost among a host of other languages, this fun spot named after a 16th century game, will feel like a private social club. But fret not, the swank atmosphere can be enjoyed by all, unless a quiet conversation is the purpose of your visit.

The kitchen turns out confident French bistro cuisine, leaving new-fangled interpretations and fussy presentations to others. Steak tartare, roasted chicken, *moules frites*, and salade Niçoise are among the menu's greatest hits.

Add to the solid cuisine, tight quarters, and loud music, and it's no wonder why Le Bilboquet is consistently abuzz. During warmer months, the scene spills out onto the small sidewalk dining area.

# Lusardi's

Italian XX

C3

## 1494 Second Ave. (bet. 77th & 78th Sts.)

**Subway:** 77 St
**Phone:** 212-249-2020
**Web:** www.lusardis.com
**Prices:** $$$

Lunch Mon – Fri
Dinner nightly

After 25 years, Lusardi's still proves its commitment to running a great restaurant. Since Luigi and Mauro Lusardi first opened this neighborhood favorite in 1982, a loyal, well-heeled clientele has been indulging in delicious Italian cuisine. Fresh ingredients and careful preparation go into authentic fare such as their superb *tortelli*, where delicate pasta envelops spinach, mushrooms, and fontina, blanketed in creamy truffle sauce. Even a humble salad shines here.

Relish a quiet midday lunch or watch the room come alive in the evening hours, when packed with a coterie of devotees. Tiny, round, white-clothed tables lie in cozy rows down the elegant dining room; its classic, European décor continues to stand the test of time.

# Maya

Mexican XX

B4

## 1191 First Ave. (bet. 64th & 65th Sts.)

**Subway:** 68 St - Hunter College
**Phone:** 212-585-1818
**Web:** www.modernmexican.com
**Prices:** $$

Dinner nightly

Maya practically defines casual elegance. Few restaurants are able to carry off being informal enough for a weeknight while being upscale enough for a weekend, but Maya expertly straddles that line. This spirited Mexican restaurant's pastel walls and vibrant artwork make it feel like an elegant private home, and its lively scene lures the right mix of a crowd.

Far from the burrito-laden menus of the competition, Richard Sandoval's menu reads like a love letter to Mexico. Time-honored culinary traditions are updated with a contemporary twist in many of the dishes, and a seemingly limitless margarita menu complements the elegant yet zesty creations from the devoted chef. Bursting with powerful flavors, meals here go well beyond fajita fare.

# Maz Mezcal

C2 — **Mexican**

316 E. 86th St. (bet. First & Second Aves.)

**Subway:** 86 St (Lexington Ave.) — Lunch Sat – Sun
**Phone:** 212-472-1599 — Dinner nightly
**Web:** www.mazmezcal.com
**Prices:** $$

Simple Mexican food—and lots of it—leaves locals eager to return to Maz Mezcal, located on a busy stretch of 86th Street. Eduardo Silva hosts at his family's eastside stalwart and the low-key party goes on almost every night, spilling out into the street in warm weather.

The flavorful fare includes an assortment of enchiladas, flautas, tostadas, and burritos for design-your-own Tex-Mex-style combination platters; as well as house specialties that include mesquite-grilled sea bass in a rich, beer based sauce, or a tender filet mignon smothered with chipotles, onions, tomatillos, and melted cheese.

Dishes are tailored to mild palates in this family-friendly place, but if you prefer your food *picante*, the kitchen will be happy to spice things up.

# Mezzaluna

B3 — **Italian**

1295 Third Ave. (bet. 74th & 75th Sts.)

**Subway:** 77 St — Lunch & dinner daily
**Phone:** 212-535-9600
**Web:** www.mezzalunany.com
**Prices:** $$

Named after the crescent-shaped chopping knife, Mezzaluna's walls are decorated with 77 depictions of the kitchen tool created by artists, who were paid with fine Italian meals.

The dining room feels timeless with its terra-cotta floor, pink marble-topped tables, and yellow painted walls hung with rustic crockery. A wood-burning pizza oven beckons from the cozy space. The fact that Mezzaluna uses ingredients such as flour, tomatoes, and mozzarella that are only imported from Italy, make them a beloved destination for pizza. Delicately fried vegetable croquettes; homemade black linguine with shrimp and spicy tomato sauce; and pistachio *semifreddo* with bittersweet chocolate sauce are a few examples of why this institution has been going strong since 1984.

# Nello

A1 **Italian** XX

## 696 Madison Ave. (bet. 62nd & 63rd Sts.)

**Subway:** 5 Av - 59 St — Lunch & dinner daily
**Phone:** 212-980-9099
**Web:** N/A
**Prices:** **$$$$**

Nello offers a chic and polished Italian dining experience, fashionably perched among pricy boutiques and astronomical real estate. The bright and airy room, overseen by a well-orchestrated, suit-clad service team, radiates privilege and optimism—resplendent with white marble, ivory walls hung with black and white safari scenes, and thick linen-covered tables dressed with white flowers. Even the menu's typeface appears elegant... and expensive.

While high prices do not ensure an enjoyable meal, the flavorful *fegatini balsamico* (slightly rosy chicken livers sautéed with aged balsamic), and *taglioni limonello* (neat mounds of perfectly cooked house-made pasta sauced with a luxurious lemon-flavored velouté) will help ease the potential sticker shock.

# Nick's

C2 **Pizza** X

## 1814 Second Ave. (at 94th St.)

**Subway:** 96 St (Lexington Ave.) — Lunch & dinner daily
**Phone:** 212-987-5700
**Web:** www.nicksnyc.com
**Prices:** ⓢ

This Manhattan location of the Forest Hills original is everything you could want from a neighborhood pizza place. The dining room is pleasant and cozy, the service is jovial and efficient, and you can watch the *pizzaiolos* hand-tossing balls of dough and firing your pizza in the wood-burning oven.

Pizzas here are thin and crusty, spread with a good balance of tomato sauce, herbs, and your choice of toppings. Not to be outdone by the excellent pies, is the list of pasta referred to as "macaroni" and main courses that includes linguine with Nick's scampi sauce and veal baked with eggplant and mozzarella. Nick's accommodates all sizes of appetites with pizzas available in small and large and pastas and meat entrees served as half portions.

# Orsay

B3 — **French** ✗

1057 Lexington Ave. (at 75th St.)

**Subway:** 77 St — Lunch & dinner daily
**Phone:** 212-517-6400
**Web:** www.orsayrestaurant.com
**Prices:** $$

Commanding a prime corner of *cher* Manhattan real estate, Orsay is fronted with elegant wood paneling and crowned with a deep awning to protect its well-dressed clientele as they sip, sup, and socialize on this fashionable stretch of Lexington Ave. Inside, the art nouveau dining room has an impressive air of authenticity accented by a mosaic-tiled floor, lacy café curtains, and a zinc-topped bar.

Orsay's French-accented staff underscores the richly atmospheric setting. Though French at heart, the menu displays the intriguing elements of a creative kitchen. Escargots with parsley and garlic butter, or truffle-scented cheese soufflé may be offered alongside lobster ravioli made with vanilla pasta, or barbecued lamb shank with chorizo risotto.

# Park Avenue

A1 — **Contemporary** ✗✗

100 E. 63rd St. (at Park Ave.)

**Subway:** 59 St — Lunch & dinner daily
**Phone:** 212-644-1900
**Web:** www.parkavenyc.com
**Prices:** $$$

While many restaurants pay the utmost attention to seasonality on the plate, Park Avenue brings it to the entire restaurant. Every three months, the café shutters for 48 hours to re-emerge as a celebration of the season, be it spring, summer, fall, or winter. In a sort of architectural trompe l'oeil, a series of panels were devised to frame the dining room and create a fresh backdrop that changes throughout the year.

The menu displays the same determined playfulness with boosts from ingredients such as a beautifully prepared, savory pumpkin pie paired with roasted chicken in autumn; while summer beans with heirloom tomatoes adorn yellowfin tuna in warmer weather.

One constant: the decadent and shareable "chocolate cube" is a dessert menu fixture.

# Persepolis

Persian ✗

**B3**

### 1407 Second Ave. (bet. 73rd & 74th Sts.)

**Subway:** 77 St
**Phone:** 212-535-1100
**Web:** www.persepolisnyc.com
**Prices:** $$

Lunch & dinner daily

This savory Persian cuisine piques both interest and appetite, offering dishes fragrant with parsley, lemon, and saffron served with hospitality in an attractive setting. The large selection of salads and appetizers includes a trio of homemade yogurt seasoned with cucumber and dried mint, aged, dried shallots, and spinach with garlic. After a medley of starters, move on to flavorful meats such as marinated rack of lamb with eggplant purée; skewers of ground steak kebab; and saffron-marinated chicken. In lieu of the meat-focused entrées, there is a mildly spiced, satisfying vegetarian stew. Each entrée is accompanied by your choice of sour cherry-studded, almond-flecked, or dill-flavored rice.

Takeout and delivery are popular options for locals.

# Philippe

Chinese ✗✗

**A1**

### 33 E. 60th St. (bet. Madison & Park Aves.)

**Subway:** Lexington Av - 59 St
**Phone:** 212-644-8885
**Web:** www.philippechow.com
**Prices:** $$$

Lunch Mon – Sat
Dinner nightly

This luxe Chinese from former Mr Chow chef, Philippe Chow (no relation), showcases linen-draped tables set with Wedgwood flatware, chopsticks neatly stored in wooden boxes, and celebrity sightings. The support staff pairs white jackets and mandarin collar uniforms with red canvas sneakers—this whimsical departure from formality is juxtaposed by the stately monochromatic color scheme of deep brown with light accents that flows throughout the multi-room space.

The satisfying menu carries dumplings, satays, and lettuce wraps, alongside main courses that are sized for sharing. Lunchtime is a good chance to experience Philippe solo, when the popular prix-fixe is available.

Philippe Chow Express in the West Village offers casual dining and takeout.

# Quatorze Bis

French XX

C3

323 E. 79th St. (bet. First & Second Aves.)

**Subway:** 77 St
**Phone:** 212-535-1414
**Web:** N/A
**Prices:** $$

Lunch Tue – Sun
Dinner nightly

An Upper East Side favorite since 1989, Quatorze Bis now qualifies as a neighborhood institution. Dreams of Paris come to mind when drinking in this brasserie, with its marble-topped bar, French posters, and cozy banquettes; the décor is almost as delicious and authentic as the food.

French classics are executed with *savoir faire*, starting with the rustic *pâté de canard* served with cornichons, toast points, and a perfectly dressed salad. Other fine renditions of time-honored bistro favorites include juicy, tender steaks, drizzled with deglazed pan juices, accompanied by light, crispy frites. Even the hottest day of summer is the perfect occasion to indulge in the comforting and delicious warm apple tart—happily, that's how it is always served.

# Serafina Fabulous Pizza

Italian X

B2

1022 Madison Ave. (bet. 78th & 79th Sts.)

**Subway:** 77 St
**Phone:** 212-734-1425
**Web:** www.serafinarestaurant.com
**Prices:** $$

Lunch & dinner daily

Set among Madison Avenue's chic boutiques and populated by a steady stream of lovelies looking for a good meal and a good time, the mood is always fabulous at this trendy Italian spot. Getting a seat may sometimes prove difficult but specialties cooked in the hand-built, cherrywood-burning oven make the wait worthwhile. Great pizzas, homemade pastas, simple grills, and fresh salads are the crux of the menu here.

The second floor dining room has a lively and energetic feel, while the third level boasts a retractable roof for alfresco dining in warmer months. The gracious staff encourages those who wish to linger to sit back and enjoy a glass of the house sangria.

Several other Serafina locations in Manhattan ensure the party never ends.

# Shalizar ✿

Persian XX

B2

1420 Third Ave. (bet. 80th & 81st Sts.)

**Subway:** 77 St — Lunch & dinner daily
**Phone:** 212-288-0012
**Web:** www.shalizarnyc.com
**Prices:** $$

Shalizar

On a warm night, when the weather is just so and Shalizar swings open its French doors, you can almost forget you're on a busy stretch of Third Avenue in the Upper East Side—and get whisked away to a more enticing Persian locale.

The space has a minimalist appeal, with light wood floors and pale walls accented with exposed brick—up front tends to read bright and sassy, while couples retreat to the back for more intimate conversation. Either way, you're in good hands with Shalizar's knowledgeable, friendly service staff, always willing to patiently walk newbies through the traditional Persian menu.

You'll need it to comb through the menu's impossibly long dish titles, but rest assured—all of them translate deliciously. Kick things off with a platter of bright spreads boasting mint-flecked eggplant purée, rich hummus and bulgar-wheat stuffed grape leaves; a generous stew of tender chicken suspended in a rich brown sauce humming with pomegranate molasses and ground walnuts, paired with a neat mound of fluffy, dill-infused basmati garnished with tender fava beans; or a fragrant rose-infused ice cream paired with a citrus granité topped with crisp rice noodles and preserved cherries.

# Shanghai Pavilion

B3 Chinese XX

1378 Third Ave. (bet. 78th & 79th Sts.)

**Subway:** 77 St — Lunch & dinner daily
**Phone:** 212-585-3388
**Web:** N/A
**Prices:** ⊜

Service with a smile by a smartly attired staff, an attractively appointed dining room with silk curtains and apricot walls, and a menu that features a list of celebration-worthy, order-in-advance specialties give Shanghai Pavilion an upscale ambience that continually attracts a devoted following of well-heeled neighborhood residents.

Shanghai and Cantonese specialties abound, as with the slurp-inducing steamed juicy buns. While enjoying these toothsome treats, the efficient servers stealthily restock your soup spoon with the next bun from the tabletop bamboo steamer. Velvet sea bass, Grand Marnier lobster, and crispy baby chicken with bronzed skin, glazed with sweet and spicy brown sauce, are just a few of the chef's tempting specialties.

# Spigolo

C3 Italian XX

1561 Second Ave. (at 81st St.)

**Subway:** 86 St (Lexington Ave.) — Lunch Sat – Sun
**Phone:** 212-744-1100 — Dinner nightly
**Web:** N/A
**Prices:** **$$**

With less than 25 seats, a copper-topped bar, an adeptly contrived menu marked by bold flavors, and siren service, Spigolo is a place wistfully wished to be a trusted secret. However, crowds hungry for a sophisticated meal know all to well of this impressive Italian, owned and operated by husband-and-wife team Scott and Heather Fratangelo.

Clams and oysters on the half shell, or fresh Arctic char tartare studded with capers and roasted tomato, make for a bracing start; perhaps followed by excellent pastas or rustic entrées of roasted halibut with *cipollini* marmalade and Tuscan-style grilled strip steak.

The dessert selection may prove irresistible, especially when faced with divine choices like warm quince pound cake with cream cheese gelato.

# Sushi of Gari ✿

C3 — Japanese

402 E. 78th St. (bet. First & York Aves.)

**Subway:** 77 St — Dinner nightly
**Phone:** 212-517-5340
**Web:** http://sushiofgari.com
**Prices:** **$$$**

Sushi of Gari

Scores of sushi geeks can't be wrong. Ignore Sushi of Gari's arid location, workaday awning, and staccato-sounding name—there's a very good reason sushiphiles across the city pile into this place night after night. *Omakase, please*: Such a simple pair of words, and yet they begin a most extraordinary odyssey into the world of avant sushi chef, Masatoshi "Gari" Sugio.

Once inside, you'll find a warm reception from the staff, happy to attend to your every need in this contemporary, simply-appointed restaurant. With such a plain-Jane décor, regulars jockey for a seat at the sushi bar, where a culinary walk with the master may include a small plate of just-warm squid, topped with creamy strips of sea urchin; a perfectly-seared lobe of foie gras, dusted with crunchy salt in a sweet miso sauce, and paired with chopped glass noodles and a cool, pickled slice of daikon; or a delicately marinated sliver of mackerel, wrapped around nori, and filled with *shiso*, cucumber, and ginger.

The simplicity of the restaurant won't alert you to the cost, so be prepared to pay a bit for the omakase. The good news is that in Gari's house, you call the shots—and they won't stop serving until you buckle.

# Sushi Sasabune

C3 — Japanese

401 E. 73rd St. (at First Ave.)

**Subway:** 77 St — Lunch Tue – Fri
**Phone:** 212-249-8583 — Dinner Tue – Sat
**Web:** N/A
**Prices:** $$$

Nestled in the Upper East Side, the third outpost of the Sasabune family is paradise for devoted followers who appreciate premium quality fish with a palatable price tag.
The style of rice preparation is unique here, with more assertive vinegar and a warmer temperature.
Since Sasabune just serves sushi and sashimi omakase, it's not the place for newbies or picky eaters. In fact, the restaurants motto clearly states: "No Spicy Tuna. No California Roll. TRUST ME." So, those hankering for tempura should steer clear.
However, the piscine parade—starting with yellowtail sashimi and finishing with the blue crab hand roll with its toasted nori juxtaposed with a creamy filling—is wholly gratifying and justifies the cult status of this modest spot.

# Sushi Seki

B4 — Japanese

1143 First Ave. (bet. 62nd & 63rd Sts.)

**Subway:** Lexington Av - 59 St — Dinner Mon – Sat
**Phone:** 212-371-0238
**Web:** N/A
**Prices:** $$$

Seki is all about sushi and the impressive quality has anchored its popularity among the devoted neighborhood regulars. It can be tough to get a reservation at this casual establishment, so it's best to book in advance to sample creations of the namesake chef, who once worked in the kitchen of the esteemed Sushi of Gari.
In the modest dining nooks, the waitstaff keeps up a steady tempo, while at the cramped counter, chef's craft fresh-from-the-boat products into tasty morsels. Those in the know will ask about the chef's signature sushi and daily specials that aren't written on the menu, but even the spicy tuna set is well-fed here.
Late hours are a plus for night-owls, and Seki's first-rate sushi is available for takeout.

# Taco Taco

Mexican

C2

1726 Second Ave. (bet. 89th & 90th Sts.)

**Subway:** 86 St (Lexington Ave.) Lunch & dinner daily
**Phone:** 212-289-8226
**Web:** N/A
**Prices:**

With prices as palatable as the food, the reputation of this neighborhood darling extends far beyond its Upper East enclave. The tacos alone are worth a visit—picture soft corn tortillas abundantly filled with the likes of *puerco enchilado* or *pollo asado*, simply adorned with chopped onion and cilantro. Tacos aside, this colorful spot offers much more than its namesake. The authentically Mexican and Tex-Mex menu also offers burritos, *tortas*, and house specials like *chiles rellenos*, or sautéed shrimp with lemon and garlic.
The bar stocks a full variety of tequilas, but a *michelada* (beer seasoned with lime and Tabasco, served on the rocks with a salted rim) makes for a refreshing thirst quencher.
Downtown sister Mole shares a similar menu.

# Taste

American

B3

1411 Third Ave. (at 80th St.)

**Subway:** 77 St Lunch & dinner daily
**Phone:** 212-717-9798
**Web:** www.elizabar.com
**Prices:** $$

Located on what may as well be known as "Eli's block", Taste is part of Eli Zabar's vast operation that includes a sprawling market, wine store, flower shop, and even an ice-cream stand. This attractive dining room is appointed with a striking inlaid tile floor, tobacco-brown walls, and mocha-hued furnishings. At night, the rich colors are lightened by tables dressed in orange Frette linens.
The impressive menu focuses on seasonality and simplicity in offerings like peekytoe crab salad with honeydew purée; olive-oil poached salmon with greenmarket string beans; and for dessert, peach and fig tart baked in the wood-burning oven, served with vanilla ice cream.
Breakfast and lunch is self-service, with a wide variety of items priced by the pound.

# Tori Shin

B4 — Japanese XX

1193 First Ave. (bet. 64th & 65th Sts.)

**Subway:** 68 St — Dinner Mon – Sat
**Phone:** 212-988-8408
**Web:** N/A
**Prices:** **$$$**

From its unassuming façade to its mostly Japanese clientele, Tori Shin feels like a downtown speakeasy. But this is not some Asian hipster den—in fact, don't even look for sushi on the menu. This is a top-flight yakitori restaurant that elevates the charcoal culture to a whole new level.

Grab a seat at the bar, where you can watch the chefs work the grill (shipped in from Tokyo), skewering the fresh, organic chicken (raised especially for Tori Shin by a local farm in Pennsylvania) into mouthwatering concoctions laced with the restaurant's inimitable sauce. Every chicken part is used—order the omakase, and sooner or later you'll be sinking your teeth into heart, liver, or soft knee bone. Rookies, fear not: 127 million Japanese people can't be wrong.

# Trata Estiatorio

B3 — Greek XX

1331 Second Ave. (bet. 70th & 71st Sts.)

**Subway:** 68 St - Hunter College — Lunch & dinner daily
**Phone:** 212-535-3800
**Web:** www.trata.com
**Prices:** **$$$**

Everything about this bright trattoria will remind you of the sea, from the crisp blue-and-white façade to the white-washed stone walls and the colorful mosaics of ocean life above the bar. The design lures a fashionable clientele who also frequent its sister in the Hamptons.

With the Greek Islands as a theme and fresh seafood displayed on ice by the open kitchen, what else would you expect but a daily changing list of fruits of the sea? Whole fish from around the globe are the house specialty; fresh catches like grilled Alaskan halibut with crab salad and fig balsamic drizzle are nicely done. Go for lunch if you want a bargain.

Don't overlook the wine list here; many Greek varietals are cited with descriptions of their characteristics.

# Triangolo

C2 — Italian

345 E. 83rd St. (bet. First & Second Aves.)

**Subway:** 86 St (Lexington Ave.) — Dinner nightly
**Phone:** 212-472-4488
**Web:** www.triangolorestaurant.com
**Prices:** $$

Genuinely warm service keeps a devoted following returning to this neighborhood favorite, painted peach and decorated with an art deco touch; a charming outdoor dining area adorns its tree-lined sidewalk. However, the real reason to dine here is its enticing, home-style Italian cooking.

A generous menu of pastas topped with hearty homemade sauces are highlights, like farfalle with crushed tomatoes, roasted cubes of eggplant, and morsels of creamy, smoked mozzarella. In addition to these are numerous antipasti, as in grilled radicchio filled with luscious goat cheese, along with a few meat preparations.

Triangolo keeps pricing reasonable, so a glass of wine and your own dessert is sensible—that cool and creamy block of tiramisu is a must.

# Uva

C3 — Italian

1486 Second Ave. (bet. 77th & 78th Sts.)

**Subway:** 77 St — Lunch Sat – Sun
**Phone:** 212-472-4552 — Dinner nightly
**Web:** www.uvawinebar.com
**Prices:** $$

Bathed in an amber glow, this rustic wine bar features brick wall mounted sconces, votive-topped wooden tables, and a copper clad bar. The lived-in décor is complemented by an upbeat vibe, especially when dining in the charming back garden, weather permitting.

The well selected wine list includes more than 30 wines by the glass; while the substantial menu teases with Emilian-style focaccia, Sardinian flatbread, and heaping cheeses and cured meats. The kitchen is equally adept in preparing more elegant edibles, as in *polenta tartufata*—soft polenta stuffed with robiola cheese and sauced with black truffle cream. Desserts are wonderfully simple and include a special composition of orange pound cake with vanilla ice cream and dark caramel sauce.

# Upper West Side

Proudly situated between two of Manhattan's most celebrated parks, home to venerable Lincoln Center, and the beloved Natural History Museum, the family-friendly Upper West Side is one of this city's most distinct neighborhoods. It has a near-cultish belief in its own way of doing things—whether this is because they boast the world's best bagels at **H&H** or that life here means constantly tripping through the set of *Law and Order*—these residents cannot imagine being elsewhere.

First and foremost, the Upper West is a neighborhood for strolling. Its sidewalks are lined with quaint brownstones, as well as more daunting architectural feats, like the Dakota (where *Rosemary's Baby* was filmed). Imagine rambling apartments filled with bookish locals arguing with equal gusto over the future of opera, or whether the best sturgeon is at **Murray's** or **Barney Greengrass**. If a scene from *Hannah and Her Sisters* comes to mind, you are beginning to understand this neighborhood.

This enthusiasm extends to all aspects of life—particularly food. For shopping, the **Tucker Square Greenmarket** is popular and anchored on West 66th Street ("Peter Jennings Way"). Equally celebrated is the original **Fairway**, filled with reasonably priced gourmet treats. Intrepid shoppers should brave its famously cramped elevator to visit the exclusively organic second floor. No visit to the Upper West is complete without **Zabar's**—home of all things gourmet and kosher—to ogle the barrels of olives and grab a few knishes.

If in need of refreshment, stop by **Soutine Bakery**, a quiet little storefront with jaw-dropping cakes; or opt for the legendary chocolate chip cookies from **Levain**. Of course, **Magnolia's** newest outpost is sure to gain a quick cupcake following. For a more savory snack, grab a "Recession Special" at **Gray's Papaya**—the politically outspoken (check the window slogans) and quintessentially Upper West hot dog chain.

Marvelously steeped in history, two of Manhattan's longstanding restaurants are perched at the edge of Central Park. **Tavern on the Green** is acknowledged as one of the city's most romantic venues, dazzling even the weariest NYers with its evening tableau of twinkling lights and horse-drawn carriages. Yet the Upper West would not be what it is today without the old-world ambience and mythic wood nymph murals at **Café des Artistes**, which has been serving Manhattan's more colorful figures since 1919. With patrons ranging from Isadora Duncan to Itzhak Perlman, it could not be more perfectly located.

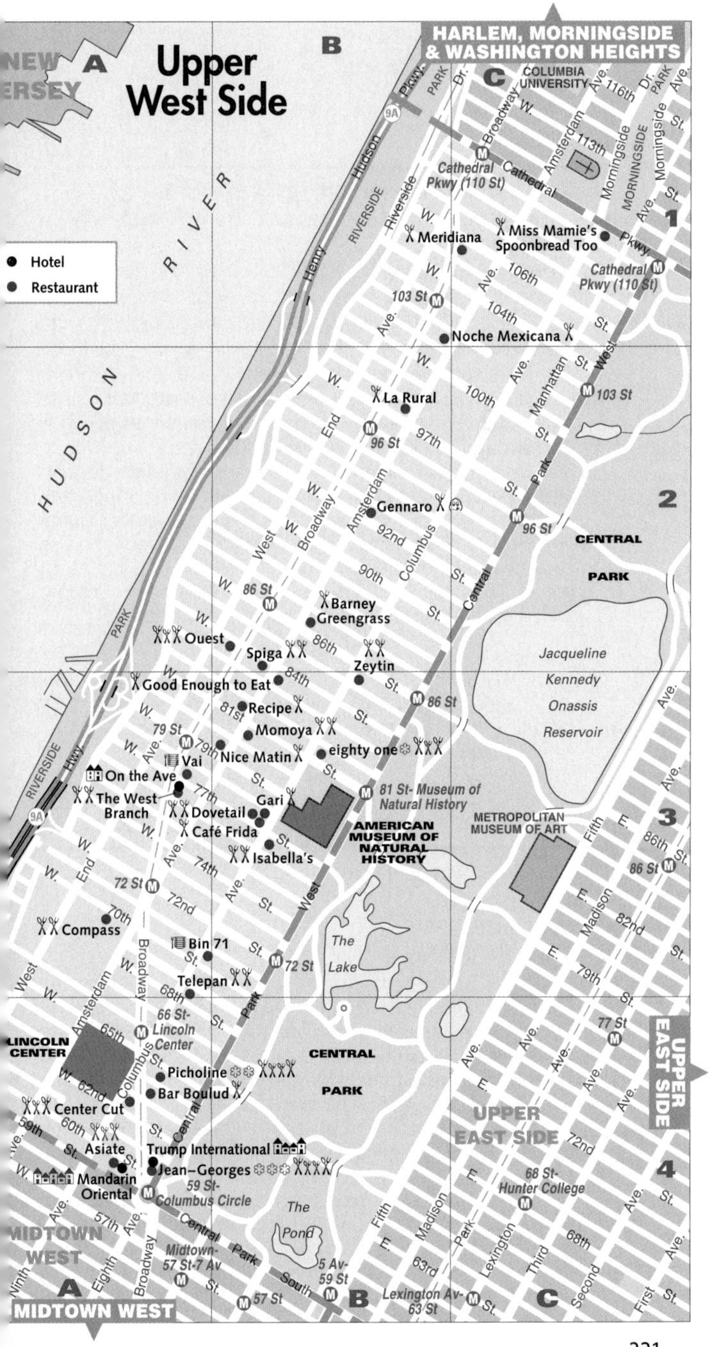
Upper West Side
Hotel
Restaurant
HARLEM, MORNINGSIDE & WASHINGTON HEIGHTS
NEW JERSEY
HUDSON RIVER
COLUMBIA UNIVERSITY
Cathedral Pkwy (110 St)
Meridiana
Miss Mamie's Spoonbread Too
103 St
Noche Mexicana
La Rural
96 St
Gennaro
Barney Greengrass
Ouest
Spiga
Zeytin
Good Enough to Eat
Recipe
Momoya
Nice Matin
eighty one
79 St
Vai
On the Ave
The West Branch
Dovetail
Café Frida
Gari
Isabella's
86 St
81 St- Museum of Natural History
AMERICAN MUSEUM OF NATURAL HISTORY
CENTRAL PARK
Jacqueline Kennedy Onassis Reservoir
METROPOLITAN MUSEUM OF ART
72 St
Compass
Bin 71
Telepan
The Lake
66 St- Lincoln Center
LINCOLN CENTER
Picholine
Bar Boulud
Center Cut
Asiate
Trump International
Jean-Georges
Mandarin Oriental
59 St- Columbus Circle
The Pond
77 St
UPPER EAST SIDE
68 St- Hunter College
Midtown-57 St-7 Av
57 St
5 Av-59 St
Lexington Av-63 St
MIDTOWN WEST

# Asiate

A4 — Fusion XXX

80 Columbus Circle (at 60th St.)

**Subway:** 59 St - Columbus Circle — Lunch & dinner daily
**Phone:** 212-805-8881
**Web:** www.mandarinoriental.com
**Prices:** **$$$$**

It's hard to imagine a finer view of Central Park than the jaw-dropping ones on display at Asiate, an elegant fusion restaurant perched on the 35th floor of the Mandarin Oriental hotel. The park, unfurled like a lush green carpet under New York's legendary skyline, is on full display from the surrounding floor-to-ceiling windows.

But views alone do not merit a restaurant, and Asiate does not miss a beat—from the masterful wait staff to the impeccably trained kitchen, pushing out dishes like red snapper sashimi, set atop daikon, and rimmed with avocado mousse, cucumber-melon gelée, and black seaweed; or a moist clay pot of Japanese brown rice, fragrant with white sesame, grilled abalone mushrooms, edamame, and tempura.

# Bar Boulud

A4 — French X

1900 Broadway (bet. 63rd & 64th Sts.)

**Subway:** 66 St - Lincoln Center — Lunch & dinner daily
**Phone:** 212-595-0303
**Web:** www.danielnyc.com
**Prices:** **$$$**

The fourth addition to Chef Daniel Boulud's New York brood isn't quite as fussy as older siblings Daniel, DB Bistro Moderne, and Café Boulud. Maybe it's because Bar Boulud likes to kick back a few now and then, as indicated by the wine barrel that marks the entrance. Inside the deep and narrow space, you'll find an ample grape list, divided into four whimsical categories:

Discoveries, Classics, Legends, and Heartthrobs. The food doesn't stray too far from the classically-trained Boulud's wheelhouse, though—upscale French comfort food, with wine-friendly nibblers like charcuterie, pâtés, and terrines dominate the menu. Don't miss the luscious desserts, like a mocha tart churned with creamy swirls of chocolate and coffee.

# Barney Greengrass

Deli

B2

541 Amsterdam Ave. (at 86th St.)

**Subway:** 86 St (Broadway) Lunch Tue – Sun
**Phone:** 212-724-4707
**Web:** www.barneygreengrass.com
**Prices:** ©©

New York's venerable "Sturgeon King" has earned its title and position as an Upper West Side institution.
In addition to serving breakfast and lunch until 5:00 P.M., they do double duty as a vibrant carry-out business and now take internet orders. The place is darling, whether eating in or taking out; the deli sandwiches—piled high with pastrami, tongue, house-cured gravlax, or homemade egg salad, and served with a big, bright, crunchy pickle—are among the best in the city.
Order a heaping plate of sturgeon with scrambled eggs and onions at this formica-clad jewel and take a trip back in time; this food is the real thing. Service without ceremony but unique NY attitude makes a trip to Barney Greengrass an authentic and essential experience.

# Bin 71

American

A3

237 Columbus Ave. (at 71st St.)

**Subway:** 72 St Lunch Wed – Sun
**Phone:** 212-362-5446 Dinner nightly
**Web:** www.bin71.com
**Prices:** $$

To call Bin 71 a wine (or espresso or panini) bar is a bit of an understatement. They have wine—a lot of it, in fact, with over thirty varieties available by the glass and bottles from as far reaching places as Slovenia. But the place walks and talks more like a charming Italian tapas joint, with a low-slung ceiling and pretty marble bar packed with an endless stream of happy, buzzing patrons.
Pick from a delicious roster of small plates, all quick and easy enough to get you in and out in time to make a show at nearby Lincoln Center, like a nutmeg-scented naked agnolotti stuffed with ricotta and swiss chard, and topped with sage, butter, and Parmesan; or three large, plump, moist meatballs bouncing in a smooth and tangy lemon and white wine sauce.

# Café Frida

Mexican

B3

368 Columbus Ave. (bet. 77th & 78th Sts.)

**Subway:** 81 St - Museum of Natural History
Lunch & dinner daily
**Phone:** 212-712-2929
**Web:** www.cafefrida.com
**Prices:** $$

This rustic, prettified hacienda has shaken its former run-for-the-border persona (the space used to house the raucous Tequila's) in favor of a warm, sophisticated design with deep red stucco walls, wrought iron chandeliers, and cozy wooden tables. Those who yearn for a little of the old café's Tex-Mex flavor will find solace in the fajitas, but Café Frida has mostly decided to trade up in favor of an authentic menu featuring handmade tortillas; bright, organic produce; and intricate Mexican specialties.

Kick things off with the crispy corn masa empanadas, crackling with salty chorizo and paired with a roasted tomato salsa; and move on to a plate of sweet and smoky enchiladas rolled with *chile pasilla* and shrimp, then dusted with *cotija* cheese.

# Center Cut

Steakhouse

A4

44 W. 63rd St. (at Broadway)

**Subway:** 66 St - Lincoln Center
Dinner nightly
**Phone:** 212-956-1288
**Web:** www.chinagrillmgt.com
**Prices:** $$$$

Tucked into the second floor of the freshly renovated Empire Hotel, Jeffrey Chodorow's new baby is a welcome addition to the Lincoln Center dining scene—a forward-thinking steakhouse with a surprisingly soft vintage atmosphere, where gracious mirrors line the walls and fragrant flowers dot the landscape.

If you're looking for serenity, its best to shoot for what would otherwise constitute prime time—8:00-10:00 P.M., when the Lincoln Center crowd is being held captive at the theater, and you can take your time with dishes like the Steak Diane, a house-aged, melt-in-your-mouth Brandt Beef filet served with fried oyster mushrooms; or a creamy spinach and artichoke pie in puff pastry, a nice addition to the usual steak-and-spuds side dish scene.

# Compass

Seafood XX

A3

208 W. 70th St. (bet. Amsterdam & West End Aves.)

**Subway:** 72 St (Broadway) — Lunch Sun
**Phone:** 212-875-8600 — Dinner nightly
**Web:** www.compassrestaurant.com
**Prices:** $$$

With a spanking new menu divvied up into categories like *fish, shellfish, vegetable* and *non fish,* it doesn't take a gumshoe to figure out Compass' new direction. Seafood is the name of the game now, and the face-lift has done this polished Upper West Side restaurant good. Guests can opt for a seat under the sleek, mosaic-patched ceiling in the dining room, or head up to the café for a quick bite and some ace people-watching.

Compass still has a few kinks to smooth out—the service can be uneven and the menu's super-trendy—but those details fade as your fork dips into tender lamb medallions, fanned over root vegetables and touched with mint purée and pine nut foam; or a sinfully dense chocolate cheesecake streaked with an Earl Grey-caramel sauce.

# Dovetail

Contemporary XX

B3

103 W. 77th St. (at Columbus Ave.)

**Subway:** 81 St - Museum of Natural History — Lunch Wed – Sun
**Phone:** 212-362-3800 — Dinner nightly
**Web:** www.dovetailnyc.com
**Prices:** $$$

It's official. The Upper West Side's culinary revival is on fire, and Dovetail is the proverbial match on the gasoline—a cozy, exposed brick charmer whose adorable factor probably outshines the food itself, but at this point only Woody Allen would kill the party.

The man fanning the flames is Chef John Fraser, who honed his craft at some of the most venerable restaurants in the world—The French Laundry, in Napa Valley, and Taillevent, in Paris—before packing up his suitcase for Manhattan. With Dovetail, the talented chef seems to have arrived home, deftly mixing ingredients in dishes like a muffuletta re-envisioned with lamb's tongue, and pressed with olives and capers; or fresh Atlantic cod served with coco beans and crab-stuffed *agnolotti*.

# eighty one ✿

**B3** Contemporary XXX

**45 W. 81st St. (bet. Central Park West & Columbus Ave.)**

**Subway:** 81 St - Museum of Natural History — Lunch Sun
**Phone:** 212-873-8181 — Dinner nightly
**Web:** www.81nyc.com
**Prices:** **$$$**

Lucy Schaeffer

Located at the base of the Hotel Excelsior, this gorgeous Upper West Side restaurant is named for the street it resides on—an impressive block that also houses the Museum of Natural History's Hayden Planetarium.

It's a good fit for Chef Ed Brown's elegant lair, where the warm staff leads you past a long, polished walnut bar, and into the vast dining room fitted out with crimson banquettes and bright flower arrangements. Farm junkies will have a field day perusing Brown's menu, a heavily seasonal affair that may include paper-thin ricotta ravioli floating in a delicate sweet pea broth fragrant with spring greens, fava beans, sweet petite peas, and pea shoots; a velvety, juicy squab dressed in seasonal sauces, served over chopped wild mushrooms and paired with cheese-topped Anson Mills polenta; or a warm strawberry crumble, accompanied by a scoop of rhubarb-ricotta gelato and a smear of strawberry jam.

Theatergoers looking to get in and out should jump at the economy special while it lasts—a delicious two course number for under $31—but don't miss a quick chat with the incredibly knowledgeable sommelier as she floats across the room: a pre-theater show in and of itself.

# Gari

**Japanese** ✗

**B3**

### 370 Columbus Ave. (bet. 77th & 78th Sts.)

**Subway:** 81 St - Museum of Natural History
**Phone:** 212-362-4816
**Web:** N/A
**Prices:** $$$

Lunch Sat – Sun
Dinner nightly

The Upper West Side outpost of Sushi of Gari (there are now three in Manhattan) fosters a hip aesthetic with its contemporary Asian décor and large glass windows facing the sidewalk.

While ingredients are top quality and everything is made to order, there is more focus on mass appeal here, with more guests appearing to choose à la carte rather than put themselves in the skillful hands of the sushi chefs, where the true beauty of Gari lies. A fine mix of sushi including signatures by Chef Masatoshi "Gari" Sugio, and cooked dishes are all prepared with a modern touch. European influences are evident in items such as the foie gras and short ribs.

Offering a well-chosen list of sake and wine, plus professional service, Gari is packed nightly.

# Gennaro

**Italian** ✗

**B2**

### 665 Amsterdam Ave. (bet. 92nd & 93rd Sts.)

**Subway:** 96 St (Broadway)
**Phone:** 212-665-5348
**Web:** www.gennarorestaurant.com
**Prices:** ⊜⊜

Dinner nightly

There might be a wait at this bright, boisterous trattoria, because the throngs of regulars who flood the place know that it can't be beat for a delicious neighborhood Italian meal. The lovely, unpretentious space, filled with colorful hanging ceramic plates, helps to pass the time until you can settle into one of the snug tables (the roomy ones seem to go to the regulars), but the food payout is worth it.

Try the perfectly tender *bucatini*, dusted with fresh cracked pepper and cheese; or a tender-to-the-fork pair of monkfish fillets licked with lemon, oregano, and capers. The daily specials list is nearly as long as the regular menu and filled with goodies; but be sure to ask about prices, which can be considerably steeper than their everyday offerings.

# Good Enough to Eat

American ✗

**B3**

### 483 Amsterdam Ave. (bet. 83rd & 84th Sts.)

**Subway:** 79 St
**Phone:** 212-496-0163
**Web:** www.goodenoughtoeat.com
**Prices:** $$

Lunch & dinner daily

Serving breakfast, lunch, dinner, and takeout, Good Enough to Eat is an affordable neighborhood gem in an area quickly pricing such establishments out of reach. The décor is oddly endearing with its kitschy folk art and cows, cows, everywhere.

Chef/owner Carrie Levin has been serving the likes of old-fashioned grilled cheese sandwiches and organic roast chicken with mashed potatoes to repeat audiences since opening in 1981. Other creations may include a moist and buttery fish sandwich with tangy watercress and "funky" slaw. Join the masses in bringing the whole family; this children's menu has been taste-tested by young and picky palates.

Out front, the wide sidewalk accommodates outdoor seating, fittingly enclosed by a white picket fence.

# Isabella's

Mediterranean ✗✗

**B3**

### 359 Columbus Ave. (at 77th St.)

**Subway:** 81 St - Museum of Natural History
**Phone:** 212-724-2100
**Web:** www.brguestrestaurants.com
**Prices:** $$

Lunch & dinner daily

For over two decades, this Upper West Side institution has boasted some of the best sidewalk real estate in the area. Lovely interiors adorned with greenery, good service, and flavorful Mediterranean food make Isabella's a worthwhile legacy. However, bi-level dining and outdoor seating (weather permitting) does nothing to ameliorate long waits for tables, especially during weekend brunch while guests enjoy a variety of Benedicts, from eggs and crabs to filet mignon.

Music keeps tempo with the bustling activity, while the charming and professional staff tends to diners relishing the likes of pumpkin ravioli with brown butter and crispy sage. Regulars know two things: for a small corkage fee, they may BYOB; and always save room for the generous desserts.

# Jean Georges ✿✿✿

**Contemporary** XXXX

A4

## 1 Central Park West (bet. 60th & 61st Sts.)

**Subway:** 59 St - Columbus Circle — Lunch & dinner Mon – Sat
**Phone:** 212-299-3900
**Web:** www.jean-georges.com
**Prices:** $$$$

Thomas Loof/Jean Georges

Sporting the legendary chef's first name, this swank, formal beauty is indisputably Jean-Georges Vongerichten's cherished flagship. Located just off the ground floor lobby of the Trump International Hotel, guests pass through the Nougatine Café (which serves an elegant breakfast, lunch, and dinner without the pomp or price tag), before finding their way into this sophisticated lair.

With a minimalist geometric motif sculpted by design guru, Adam Tihany, and soft chandelier light dancing off the cream walls, gilded ceiling, and glossy floor-to-ceiling windows, Jean Georges looks every bit the part—this is New York fine dining at its grandest.

The food is equally decadent, with a gorgeous open kitchen deftly marrying Vongerichten's passion for flavor and texture into dishes like a bowl of silky tuna ribbons with spicy radish, dressed in soy-ginger vinaigrette and laid over a small bed of mashed avocado; juicy roasted veal ladled with liquid Parmesan, served over a bed of firm artichoke hearts, and garnished with lavender flower; or a decadent dessert featuring caramel in myriad applications, like a caramel-strewn custard ribbon, or chocolate-dipped coffee-cardamom ice cream pop.

# La Rural

Argentinian

B2

768 Amsterdam Ave. (bet. 97th & 98th Sts.)

**Subway:** 96 St (Broadway)
**Phone:** 212-749-2929
**Web:** N/A
**Prices:** **$$**

Lunch Sat – Sun
Dinner nightly

From the owners of Café Frida comes this Argentinian-inspired restaurant, tucked into the space that was home to Pampa. The environs may look gritty, but once you step inside the long, narrow room, the 'hood melts away in favor of a cozy den decorated with framed mirrors, wood-covered columns, and exposed brick walls. Out back, a charming patio adds outdoor seating, weather permitting.

Focused, not fussy, the cuisine dishes up good value as well as good flavor. Excellent-quality meats star at La Rural, named for the annual livestock show in Buenos Aires. *Parrillada* amounts to a carnivore's feast, sized for two. Theatrically served at table on a portable grill, the combination of different cuts of steak, short ribs, sweetbreads, and Argentinian sausages are all perfectly juicy and cooked to order.

# Meridiana

Italian

C1

2756 Broadway (bet. 105th & 106th Sts.)

**Subway:** 103 St (Broadway)
**Phone:** 212-222-4453
**Web:** N/A
**Prices:** **$$**

Dinner nightly

Welcoming and convivial, Meridiana is the kind of place just right for gathering with friends, chatting, and getting to know people while tucking into a plate of delicious Italian food. Chef/owner Gianni "Johnny" Nicolosi and his wife, Pilar, have clearly come up with a formula for success. At the helm of this place since 1994, the couple still cossets diners in an inviting columned room painted with frescoes depicting a villa in Pompeii. Television screens are thankfully missing from the bar area.

Gifted hands in the kitchen make stalwarts such as *spaghetti con salsa di seppie al nero* new again, the al dente pasta caressed by a thick silky sauce tossed with diced calamari, fresh basil, tomato, and squid ink. Before you order, be sure to review the tempting list of nightly specials.

# Miss Mamie's Spoonbread Too

C1 Southern

366 W. 110th St./Cathedral Pkwy.
(bet. Columbus & Manhattan Aves.)

**Subway:** Cathedral Pkwy/110 St (Central Park West) Lunch & dinner daily
**Phone:** 212-865-6744
**Web:** www.spoonbreadinc.com
**Prices:** ⊜

The warm, welcoming atmosphere and service evokes an easygoing country setting—smack dab in the middle of the city. Homey, rustic touches, like kitchen implements hanging on the walls, mix well with retro red and yellow tile floors and formica-top tables. The dining room floods with natural light, while pure, raw soul music plays in the background.

The menu is a celebration of Southern classics and does not veer much from this trajectory. However, this should not stop anyone from reviewing the daily boards for specials. Food this appealing, genuine, and satisfying can only be topped with perfectly sweet homemade ice tea and red velvet cake (a dark, moist, indulgent specimen of this classic dessert). Finish with the best coffee a dollar can buy.

# Momoya

B3 Japanese

427 Amsterdam Ave. (bet. 80th & 81st Sts.)

**Subway:** 79 St Lunch Sat – Sun
**Phone:** 212-580-0007 Dinner nightly
**Web:** www.themomoya.com
**Prices:** $$$

A welcome newcomer to this (until recently) restaurant-starved stretch of the Upper West, Momoya's new uptown location appears more sophisticated than its Chelsea sibling, celebrated for its sleek setting and made-to-please sushi offerings. Curvaceous wood-textured walls disappear into the grey ceiling, leather booths, and slate floors. The marble sushi counter is complemented by sexy lighting, pulsating music, and a relaxed staff pacing service at a fine tempo.

Much care is taken with selection and preparation of ingredients—toro melts in your mouth, served alongside sweet sea urchin, spiked with a drop of soy. Desserts offer surprises that straddle East-meets-West cuisine with aplomb, as in the delicate *mille* crêpes with green tea and crème anglaise.

# Nice Matin

Mediterranean

B3

201 W. 79th St. (at Amsterdam Ave.)

**Subway:** 79 St
Lunch & dinner daily
**Phone:** 212-873-6423
**Web:** www.nicematinnyc.com
**Prices:** $$

Named after the daily newspaper published in a major city on France's Côte d'Azur, Nice Matin transports diners to the sun-drenched Mediterranean coast.

*Niçoise* dishes here exhibit as many vibrant flavors and colors as appear in the room's luminous décor. Fashioned as a coastal brasserie, Nice Matin asserts its unique personality by avoiding all the decorative clichés found in many Gallic-style restaurants; lights dangle from the tops of high pillars that spread umbrella-like against the ceiling, and tables are topped in formica.

The menu wanders the wider Mediterranean region seeking its inspiration, from a perfectly cooked risotto, delicately flavored with ginger cream, to a traditional, crisp *tarte aux pommes*, layered with sweet caramelized apples.

# Noche Mexicana

Mexican

B1

852 Amsterdam Ave. (bet. 101st & 102nd Sts.)

**Subway:** 103 St (Broadway)
Lunch & dinner daily
**Phone:** 212-662-6900
**Web:** www.noche-mexicana.com
**Prices:** ₠

Squeezed between a bunch of no-name cafés and run-down bodegas on a grungy strip of Amsterdam Avenue, Noche Mexicana certainly doesn't woo its regulars with fancy digs. Rather, it's the friendly staff and deliciously authentic Mexican fare that keep this little hole-in-the-wall jumping.

Though the menu is teeming with real-deal enchiladas and *chile rellenos*, Noche's star ticket is undoubtedly the house made tamales, which you can see being made by hand if you score a seat toward the back of the house. The soft green tamale arrives tenderly wrapped in a banana leaf, packed with sweet shredded pork and a smoky, tart green mole sauce. It's enough to make you order a second one for dessert, but a smooth caramel and vanilla-scented flan draws you back.

# Ouest

Contemporary XXX

B2

2315 Broadway (bet. 83rd & 84th Sts.)

**Subway:** 86 St (Broadway) — Lunch Sun
**Phone:** 212-580-8700 — Dinner nightly
**Web:** www.ouestny.com
**Prices:** $$$

Having been accused of arriving late to New York's food party, the Upper West Side is fighting back. The last few years have seen a slew of serious eateries marching into the hood—quite notably this popular outpost from trailblazing chef, Thomas Valenti.

As with his other ventures, Chef Valenti's top priority is his kitchen, which spins out delicious, edgy riffs on American comfort foods like plump, perfectly-grilled quail, stuffed with fresh bread crumbs, sausage, and spinach—but it would be a shame to ignore the movie star good looks of Ouest's dining room. Solo diners can grab a seat at the gorgeous mahogany bar; while bigger groups can slide into beautiful, circular red leather banquettes guaranteed to keep conversation intimate.

# Recipe

American X

B3

452 Amsterdam Ave. (bet. 81st & 82nd Sts.)

**Subway:** 79 St — Lunch & dinner daily
**Phone:** 212-501-7755
**Web:** www.recipenyc.com
**Prices:** $$

This sweet little sliver of a restaurant arrives courtesy of the team behind Land, a beloved Thai restaurant located next door to the new digs. With Recipe, they turn their well-focused attention to contemporary American fare—and the result is yet another reason to deem the Upper West Side the city's fastest rising food corridor.

In a simple space dressed in white-washed walls, reclaimed knick-knacks, and industrial light fixtures, you'll find a straightforward menu touting a rustic lineup that might include an exceptionally fresh pike mackerel, grilled whole and topped with a lively caper radish; a fresh tangle of pappardelle primavera studded with plump Gulf shrimp; or a downright sultry chocolate pignoli tart, topped with creamy caramel.

# Picholine ✿✿

Mediterranean XXXX

A4

35 W. 64th St. (bet. Broadway & Central Park West)

**Subway:** 66 St - Lincoln Center — Dinner Tue – Sat
**Phone:** 212-724-8585
**Web:** www.picholinenyc.com
**Prices:** **$$$**

Picholine

To fully understand Terrance Brennan's elegant, consistently triumphant first lady, it's best to head back to 1993, when a bright-eyed and bushy-tailed Picholine swung open her doors to a city that—faced with a recent recession—had just begun to question the validity of fine dining.

Luckily, Picholine had the goods to back up her price tag then, and still does. The menu has moved with the times, with Brennan's Provençal touches informing a simple, seasonal menu divvied into sections like Day Boats and the Land. Recently in the bar, they added a *menu d'economie*, featuring small plates for $15.

And while a series of face-lifts over the years has left her highness with an elegant yet fussy lavender and cream motif, the food remains as exquisite as ever—with dishes like a plate of silky Nantucket bay scallops, kissed with a splash of citrus and bright radish sprout; or tender, rosy-pink slices of venison laid over a bed of Brussels sprouts studded with crunchy bits of bacon. Paired with moist, parsnip-crusted French toast laced in huckleberry sauce, it's almost enough to convince you to skip dessert, but a warm apple brioche in a bright, luscious caramel sauce convinces you otherwise.

# Spiga

Italian

B2

200 W. 84th St. (bet. Amsterdam Ave. & Broadway)

**Subway:** 86 St (Broadway) — Dinner nightly
**Phone:** 212-362-5506
**Web:** www.spiganyc.com
**Prices:** $$$

Tucked away on an Upper West Side block, this delightful restaurant nestles tables into every available nook of its attractive dining room. Banquettes by the front windows, overlook the street from their raised perch, and are lined with colorful silk pillows. Sheaves of wheat in cylindrical vases add to the rustic tone set by exposed brick walls and rough-hewn wood paneling. With the arrival of Chef Stefano Bosetti, there have been few changes to the menu. Regulars can still enjoy their favorite dishes including homemade pastas followed by *secondi* that are split between meat and fish dishes. Look for good offerings by the glass on the all-Italian wine list.

Service goes smoothly, and the spirited owner manages the small space with efficiency and grace.

# Telepan

American

A3

72 W. 69th St. (bet. Central Park West & Columbus Ave.)

**Subway:** 66 St - Lincoln Center — Lunch Wed – Sun
**Phone:** 212-580-4300 — Dinner nightly
**Web:** www.telepan-ny.com
**Prices:** $$$

Chef/owner Bill Telepan keeps a careful eye on this Upper West Side favorite, where a plain green awning belies a pretty, pecan-wood interior crackling with fireplaces. The much-loved Telepan, who rose to popularity with his former restaurant, JUdson Grill, is stone serious about sustainability and organic products—and the result of all that diligence is deliciously evident in starters like house-smoked trout, laid over a fluffy corn blini and laced with springy green onion and a dollop of sour cream; or a spongy, 4-layer box cake, fitted out with fresh raspberry purée and rimmed with basil oil.

The man also takes his grapes seriously—the restaurant's hefty but unpretentious list is flooded with fantastic American, French, and New World selections.

# Vai

Italian

A3

225 W. 77th St. (bet. Amsterdam Ave. & Broadway)

**Subway:** 79 St — Dinner nightly
**Phone:** 212-362-4500
**Web:** www.vairestaurant.com
**Prices:** $$

Two wooden benches flanked by lush potted plants grace an entrance that opens into a sultry, fresh dining space softly lit by glass-encased votives atop bare, dark-wood tables.

Italian for "go", Vai is one of the newer restaurant/wine bars on the block, and a welcoming, warm spot to share a bottle of wine and *assaggi*—small plates. A long communal table reinforces this attitude at which strangers nosh side by side on *pizzette* and grilled calamari. Chef/owner Vincent Chirico (formerly of Jean-Georges) offers a straightforward, high quality menu where fluffy shavings of *ricotta salata* top tender stalks of green and white asparagus, delicately finished with truffle essence. Small plates can add up in price, so grab your favorite foodie friends and *vai*.

# The West Branch

American

A3

2178 Broadway (at 77th St.)

**Subway:** 79 St — Lunch & dinner daily
**Phone:** 212-777-6764
**Web:** www.thewestbranchnyc.com
**Prices:** $$

Tom Valenti's highly anticipated new restaurant—named after a branch of the Delaware River—aims to bring the haute American cuisine that put him on the map at nearby Ouest down a notch in both price and intricacy. Joyfully, his superb quality remains—for even when working in the realm of comfort food, Valenti's style and grace radiate through the dark, sophisticated dining space.

The menu rarely misses, skating effortlessly between simple, ground-to-order hamburgers and more upscale fare like pan-roasted quail. A tender *bucatini all'amatriciana* is coated in a rich plum tomato sauce spiked with rich pancetta, and studded with bits of egg white; while a pan-seared cod gets a kick in the pants from sweet and smoky slices of grilled zucchini.

# Zeytin

Turkish XX

B3

519 Columbus Ave. (at 85th St.)

**Subway:** 86 St (Central Park West) Lunch & dinner daily
**Phone:** 212-579-1145
**Web:** www.zeytinny.com
**Prices:** **$$**

Visitors making their way from the Museum of Natural History would do well to bypass the turn-and-burn restaurants that plague this bustling section of Columbus Avenue, and set their sights on the more exotic offerings scattered around the hood. Namely Zeytin—a lovely, upscale Turkish restaurant with supple leather chairs, polished slate floors, and great big people-watching windows.

The restaurant's name means "olive" in Turkish, but the menu easily surpasses the implied simplicity. Elaborate dishes like *harem sarmasi* and *hunkar begendi* share menu space with simple kebab fare; and the traditional, but mouthwatering, baklava dessert—perfectly rendered with tissue-thin sheets of phyllo dough, soft golden honey and crushed, syrup-soaked pistachios.

Couverts (X... XXXXX) indicate the level of comfort found at a restaurant. The more X's, the more upscale a restaurant will be.

John Peden/The New York Botanical Garden

# The Bronx

# The Bronx

The only borough attached to the mainland, the Bronx is marked by contrasts. Although abandoned apartment buildings and massive housing projects once overran the borough's south section, private foundations and grassroots movements are successfully revitalizing these areas. As always, grand mansions and lush gardens still characterize the northern areas of Riverdale and Fieldston.

Hispanics, African-Americans, Irish-Americans, West Indians, and Albanians comprise much of the current population. Though a host of Italians once settled in the Belmont area, today they only reside as proprietors of booming shops.

Thanks to 19th century journalist John Mullaly, who led a movement in the late 1800s to buy and preserve inexpensive parcels of land, 25 percent of the Bronx today consists of parkland. This includes Pelham Bay Park, with its sandy Orchard Beach. Here, step into pizza paradise—**Louie and Ernie's**—and bite into a slice of heaven. Beyond, City Island is a gem of a coastal community, much like New England with its charming inns and seafood spots. During the summer, stroll down City Island Ave., and into **Lickety Split** for a scoop of divine ice cream.

Belmont's most renowned street and Italian food Mecca, Arthur Avenue, lures from far and wide. Tear into warm, freshly baked breads from **Terranova**, **Madonia**, or **Addeo**—the choices are plenty. The pistachio-studded mortadella from **Teitel Brothers** or *salumi* from **Calabria Pork Store** are perfect salt licks for tigers on the prowl. Check out **The Arthur Avenue Retail Market**, a covered oasis built by Mayor LaGuardia to prevent pushcart vendors from crowding busy streets. The dwindling vendors inside sell quality Italian pasta, homemade sausage, olive oil, notorious heroes (up to six feet), heirloom seeds, and even hand-rolled cigars.

Although the Belmont section is now mainly known as Little Mexico and Ecuador, it happens to have a world of eastern European offerings. With this in mind, visit **Tony & Tina's** Pizza, but skip the Italian stuff. Instead, devour Albanian or Kosovar *burek*—these flaky rolls are packed with pumpkin purée and are *sine qua non*.

Take yourself out to a ball game at the new Yankee Stadium and snack from the **Lobel's** cart or if you're lucky enough to have premium seats, enjoy one of their expertly dry aged steaks.

The Eastchester, Wakefield, and Williamsbridge sections of the Bronx cradle a number of communities and their tasty eats. The spicy, smoky tidbits of the Caribbean have become a local staple. Visit Vernon's **New Jerk House** for mouthwatering jerk chicken, and end with something sweet from **Kingston Tropical Bakery**. Or for Italian, drop by tiny **G & R Deli** on

Williamsbridge Road for big flavors in their homemade sausages or rich meaty sauce sold by the quart. End at **Sal & Dom's** for some *sfogliatelle*.

Asia comes alive at **World of Taste Seafood**; peek in and discover that authentic Vietnamese food has officially arrived in the Bronx. For a flurry of Cambodian delights, step into the **Phnom Penh-Nha Trang Market** across the street.

A unique blend of Latin American spots populate the South Bronx, with the largest concentration hailing from Puerto Rico. On Willis Avenue, Mott Haven's main drag, bright awnings designate Honduran diners, Mexican bodegas, and Puerto Rican takeout; fenced off empty lots allow for older folks to chat, play cards, and linger over authentic dishes from their homeland.

Vital to New York's food business is the **Hunts Point Food Distribution Center**, a 329-acre complex containing a mass of food wholesalers, distributors, and food processing businesses. The mega complex includes **The Hunts Point Meat Market, Hunts Point Terminal Produce Market,** and **The Fulton Fish Market**, a wholesale triumvirate where the city's restaurateurs and market owners come to pick their goods.

Riverdale may not be widely known for its dining culture and culinary treasures, but **Liebman's** is still considered one of the finest kosher delis in the Bronx. They comfort local masses with dishes like steamy soups, hot dogs, and brisket. At the primped **Mother's Bake Shop**, stop to savor the traditional **babkas** and challahs; and **Skyview Wines** carries a unique selection of Kosher wines, completing your culinary journey with a touch of meat, sweet, and spirit.

Julie Larsen Maher ©WCS

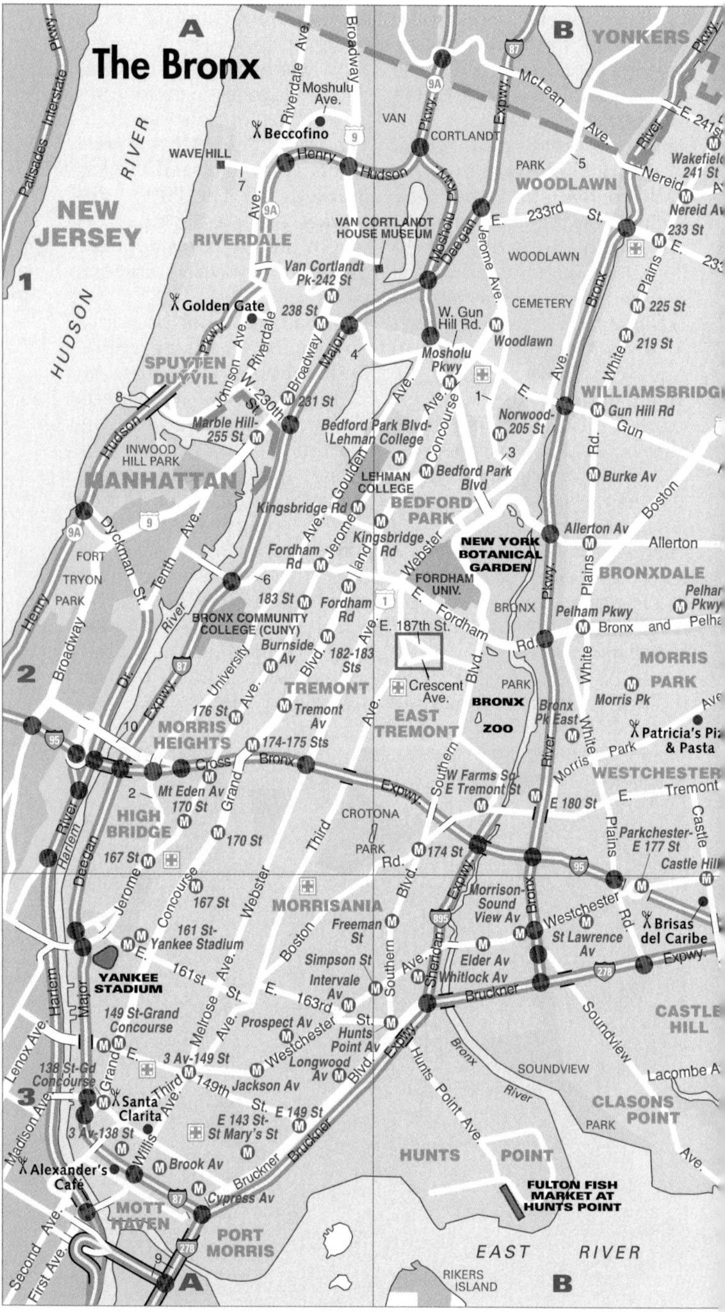
The Bronx
A
B
1
2
3
YONKERS
NEW JERSEY
HUDSON RIVER
Palisades Interstate Pkwy.
RIVERDALE
WAVE HILL
Beccofino
Golden Gate
Moshulu Ave.
Riverdale Ave.
Broadway
Henry Hudson Pkwy.
VAN CORTLANDT PARK
VAN CORTLANDT HOUSE MUSEUM
Van Cortlandt Pk-242 St
238 St
231 St
Marble Hill-255 St
SPUYTEN DUYVIL
Johnson Ave.
W. 230th St
INWOOD HILL PARK
MANHATTAN
FORT TRYON PARK
Dyckman St.
Tenth Ave.
Henry Hudson Pkwy.
McLean Ave.
Mosholu Pkwy
Major Deegan Expwy.
Jerome Ave.
WOODLAWN
WOODLAWN CEMETERY
E. 233rd St.
E. 241st
Wakefield 241 St
Nereid Av
233 St
225 St
219 St
White Plains Rd.
Bronx River Pkwy.
W. Gun Hill Rd.
Woodlawn
Mosholu Pkwy
Norwood-205 St
WILLIAMSBRIDGE
Gun Hill Rd
Burke Av
Bedford Park Blvd-Lehman College
Bedford Park Blvd
LEHMAN COLLEGE
BEDFORD PARK
Kingsbridge Rd
Goulden Ave.
Concourse
Webster Ave.
NEW YORK BOTANICAL GARDEN
Allerton Av
Allerton
Boston
BRONXDALE
Pelham Pkwy
Bronx and Pelham
MORRIS PARK
Morris Pk
Patricia's Pizza & Pasta
FORDHAM UNIV.
Fordham Rd
E. Fordham Rd.
E. 187th St.
Crescent Ave.
BRONX PARK
BRONX ZOO
Bronx Pk East
183 St
BRONX COMMUNITY COLLEGE (CUNY)
Burnside Av
182-183 Sts
University Ave.
TREMONT
Tremont Av
EAST TREMONT
176 St
174-175 Sts
MORRIS HEIGHTS
Cross Bronx Expwy.
Mt Eden Av
170 St
HIGH BRIDGE
167 St
Harlem River Dr.
W Farms Sq-E Tremont Av
E 180 St
WESTCHESTER
Tremont
Parkchester-E 177 St
Castle Hill
CROTONA PARK
174 St
Third Ave.
Southern Blvd.
MORRISANIA
Freeman St
Simpson St
Intervale Av
Morrison-Sound View Av
St Lawrence Av
Elder Av
Whitlock Av
Westchester Ave.
Brisas del Caribe
Sheridan Expwy.
Bruckner Expwy.
161 St-Yankee Stadium
YANKEE STADIUM
E. 161st St.
E. 163rd St.
149 St-Grand Concourse
Prospect Av
Hunts Point Av
Longwood Av
3 Av-149 St
E. 149th St.
Jackson Av
E 149 St
138 St-Gd Concourse
Santa Clarita
3 Av-138 St
E 143 St-St Mary's St
Melrose Ave.
Willis Ave.
Brook Av
Cypress Av
Alexander's Café
MOTT HAVEN
PORT MORRIS
Lenox Ave.
Madison Ave.
Second Ave.
First Ave.
Soundview
SOUNDVIEW
Bronx River
Hunts Point Ave.
HUNTS POINT
FULTON FISH MARKET AT HUNTS POINT
CASTLE HILL
Lacombe Ave.
CLASONS POINT PARK
EAST RIVER
RIKERS ISLAND

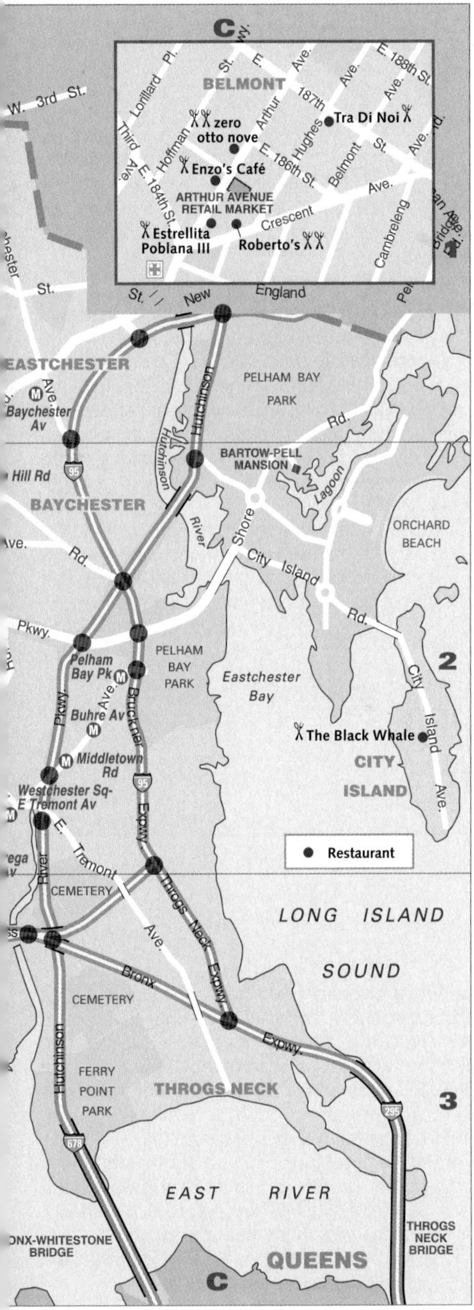


| | |
|---|---|
| Allerton Ave. | BC2 |
| Bainbridge Ave. | 1 B1 |
| Baychester Ave. | C1 |
| Boston Rd. | A3C1 |
| Broadway | A1 |
| Bronx and Pelham Pkwy. | BC2 |
| Bronx River Pkwy. | B1 3 |
| Bruckner Blvd. | A3 |
| Bruckner Expwy. | A3C2 |
| Castle Hill Ave. | B2 3 |
| City Island Ave. | C2 |
| City Island Rd. | C2 |
| Crescent Ave. | B2 |
| Cross Bronx Expwy. | A2C3 |
| Edward L. Grant Hwy. | 2 A2 |
| E. Gun Hill Rd. | B1C2 |
| E. Fordham Rd. | AB2 |
| E. Tremont Ave. | B2C3 |
| E. 149th St. | A3 |
| E. 161st St. | A3 |
| E. 163rd St. | A3 |
| E. 204th St. | 3 B2 |
| E. 233rd St. | BC1 |
| E. 241st St. | B1 |
| Goulden Ave. | A2B1 |
| Grand Blvd. and Concourse | A1B3 |
| Henry Hudson Pkwy. | A1B2 |
| Hunts Point Ave. | B3 |
| Hutchinson River Pkwy. | C1 3 |
| Jerome Ave. | A3B1 |
| Major Deegan Expwy. | A3B1 |
| Melrose Ave. | A3 |
| Mosholu Pkwy. | B1 |
| Nereid Ave. | B1 |
| New England Thruway | C1 |
| Pelham Bridge Rd. | C1 |
| Riverdale Ave. | A1 |
| Sheridan Expwy. | B3 2 |
| Shore Rd. | C1 2 |
| Soundview Ave. | B 3 |
| Southern Blvd. | B2 3 |
| Third Ave. | A2B3 |
| Throgs Neck Expwy. | C3 |
| University Ave. | A2 |
| Van Cortlandt Park South | 4 AB1 |
| Van Cortlandt Park East | 5 B1 |
| Webster Ave. | A1B3 |
| Westchester Ave. | A3C2 |
| W. Fordham Rd. | 6 A2 |
| W. 230th St. | A1 |
| W.252nd St. | 7 A1 |
| W. Gun Hill Rd. | B1 |
| White Plains Rd. | BX3 |
| Willis Ave. | A3 |

**BRIDGES**

| | |
|---|---|
| Bronx-Whitestone Bridge | C3 |
| Henry Hudson Bridge | 8 A1 |
| Robert F. Kennedy Bridge | 9 A3 |
| Throgs Neck Bridge | C3 |
| Washington Bridge | 10 A2 |

# Alexander's Cafe

American

A3

129 Alexander Ave. (at Bruckner Blvd.)

**Subway:** 3 Av - 138 St
**Phone:** 718-993-5281
**Web:** www.alexanderstogo.com
**Prices:** ⊜

Lunch daily
Dinner Mon – Sat

Situated amidst an array of vintage shops, this affable eatery is the perfect end to an afternoon of ardent antiquing. Opened in July 2007, this cozy café sports a sleek and modern décor defined by dark wood tables, black leather chairs, soft lighting, and fresh flowers, which style an inviting atmosphere. In addition to a fixed menu, there's an affordable lunch buffet, and at least five daily specials; creative, quick-thinking cooks are dared to devise delicious eats from the owner's high-quality market picks of the day.

Locals love the ever-changing selections, which could be grilled marlin steaks with buttery yellow squash and spinach, served with a savory avocado and pickle guacamole. Pair your meal with one of over a dozen unique beers offered.

# Beccofino

Italian

A1

5704 Mosholu Ave. (at Fieldston Rd.)

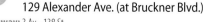

**Subway:** 231 St (& bus BX9)
**Phone:** 718-432-2604
**Web:** N/A
**Prices:** **$$**

Dinner nightly

Laughter abounds at unpretentious Beccofino, as locals sit and chat with family and friends—that is, until their plates arrive. At that point, conversation grinds to a halt as everyone digs into their dishes with gusto. Waitresses go the extra mile catering to diners' whims and smilingly field any questions about the menu. From starters such as stuffed eggplant, diners move on to gargantuan dishes of spaghetti *con scampi*, featuring an abundant amount of jumbo shrimp in a well balanced, garlic-butter sauce; or plates overflowing with specialties such as the delicately flavored veal *Sorrentino*. This Riverdale charmer sends them all home satisfied.

Exposed brick walls, terra-cotta floors, soft lighting, and warm service enhance the pleasant rustic aura.

# The Black Whale

American

C2

279 City Island Ave. (at Hawkins St.)

**Subway:** Pelham Bay Park (& bus BX12) Lunch Sat – Sun
**Phone:** 718-885-3657 Dinner nightly
**Web:** www.dineatblackwhale.com
**Prices:** $$

Squirreled away on the eastern edge of the Bronx, across a 120-year old bridge, City Island is a charming little "town" off the tourist radar—and for daytrippers short on time, the island is a godsend, with a cute, walkable main street lined with Victorian homes and kick-knack shops.

With Le Refuge no longer on the scene, Black Whale is among one of the better meals on the island, even if its eclectic shoreline charm (think mismatched tables and cozy backyard replete with birdbaths and a JFK bust) outweighs the actual food. Still, you'll find a few menu standouts like a bowl of plump, garlicky New Zealand mussels bobbing in white wine broth; Maryland crab cakes paired with a zippy red pepper coulis; or an old school apple crisp with vanilla ice cream.

# Brisas Del Caribe

Puerto Rican

B3

1207 Castle Hill Ave. (bet. Ellis & Gleason Aves.)

**Subway:** Castle Hill Av Lunch & dinner daily
**Phone:** 718-794-9710
**Web:** N/A
**Prices:** ☺☺

Bring your appetite and group of friends to tackle the bounty of delicious Latin and Puerto Rican-influenced food for bargain prices.

This mostly bilingual staff is welcoming and generous, attracting a regular clientele of families as well as food adventurers, seeking "the borough's all too familiar" flavors. The restaurant is also a favorite late night spot for Cuban roast pork sandwiches, accompanied by *morir sonando* (orange juice and milk), or a glass of Mateus wine. If available, be sure to savor the tender, flavorful, slow-cooked dishes of oxtail stew, or *pernil* served with yellow rice.

The restaurant does not take reservations, so expect a wait. The steady take-out business is testament to this restaurant's quality and earned place in the community.

# Enzo's Café

C1 — Italian

## 2339 Arthur Ave. (bet. Crescent Ave. & 187th St.)

**Subway:** Fordham Rd (Grand Concourse)
**Phone:** 718-733-4455
**Web:** N/A
**Prices:** **$$**

Lunch Mon – Sat
Dinner nightly

How the old-school Bronx Italians kick it locavore—with fresh bread whisked in from the local bakeries, cured meats sourced from the local pork store, and vanilla-scented cheesecake baked around the corner. Owner Enzo DiRende's tendency to keep things local is most likely a family tradition: his father co-founded Arthur Avenue's legendary Dominick's.

But though it's a new generation at play, the regulars who frequent this intimate, brick-lined café (as well as the recently renovated original location at *1998 Williamsbridge Rd.*) don't come looking for new-fangled Italian. Rather, it's the time-honored staples like steaming plates of fresh pasta and seasoned whole fish—perfectly rendered, and served with a shot of hospitality.

# Estrellita Poblana III

C1 — Mexican

## 2328 Arthur Ave. (bet. Crescent Ave. & 186th St.)

**Subway:** Fordham Rd (Grand Concourse)
**Phone:** 718-220-7641
**Web:** N/A
**Prices:** ⊜

Lunch & dinner daily

New Yorkers may be surprised to find Mexican food in the Bronx's Little Italy, but this jewel box of a restaurant delivers the extraordinary. Powder-blue walls, wainscoting, hand-cut flowers, and the helpful staff set the scene for quality, authentic Mexican fare.

Specials such as flavorful *budin* Azteca—a layered chicken tortilla pie with cheese—features a complex mole that is at once nutty, spicy, creamy, and thoroughly delicious. Tamales are only available on weekends, but there are numerous items—from empanadas to *camarones Cancun*—on the extensive menu. Fresh juices, *aquas frescas*, and *batidas* are sure to quench thirst and complement the wide range of mild to fiery fare. Of Estrellita's three Bronx locations, this is the most tranquil.

# Golden Gate

Chinese

A1

3550 Johnson Ave. (bet. 235th & 236th Sts.)

**Subway:** 231 St (& bus BX 7, 10, 20) — Lunch & dinner daily
**Phone:** 718-549-6206
**Web:** N/A
**Prices:** $$

The recent expansion of this beloved 50 year-old Bronx mainstay marks the enduring popularity of a certain kind of Chinese-American restaurant—one where New Yorkers of all ages rub elbows over exotic Chinese cocktails and safe, no-miss fare like chop suey, egg foo young, and pupu platters. Those lucky enough to call Golden Gate their local Chinese joint have seen the place morph into a large, deep space with new trimmings, lots of leg room, and a big, welcoming bar area that fills up most nights with loyal regulars.

Don't miss the surprisingly tender lobster with (intentionally) burnt pork; crispy barbecued spareribs, slathered with a finger-licking sweet-and-salty coating; or an old-school chicken chow mein that manages to raise the bar.

# Patricia's Pizza & Pasta

Italian

B2

1080 Morris Park Ave. (bet. Haight & Lurting Aves.)

**Subway:** Morris Park (& bus BX8) — Lunch & dinner daily
**Phone:** 718-409-9069
**Web:** N/A
**Prices:** $$

This casual eatery is perpetually filled with a devoted following who truly love this place as if home. Patricia's is the kind of nostalgic spot where one can count on finding the same comfort foods year after year, perhaps served by the same, warm Bronx waitresses-cum-sages who tell it like it is. It's a familial experience in a setting that lacks pretense.

Generous portions of hearty Italian-American classics, like linguini with white clam sauce, are sure to satisfy—and don't be shy about asking for cheese if that is your preference. Patricia's is as celebrated for its accommodating disposition as much as the delicious cuisine, which is at once familiar yet memorable.

It also does a healthy take-out business and offers a second location in Throgs Neck.

# Roberto's

C1 Italian XX

603 Crescent Ave. (at Hughes Ave.)

**Subway:** Fordham Rd (Grand Concourse)
**Phone:** 718-733-9503
**Web:** www.robertobronx.com
**Prices:** $$

Lunch Mon – Fri
Dinner Mon – Sat

Widely recognized as one of the best in the Bronx, this Southern Italian institution has more than earned its red, white, and green stripes. All that's left to do is not muck up the hype—something owner Roberto Paciullo is unlikely to let happen with his keen attention to décor (think rustic farmhouse tables and marvelous ceramic urns), detail-oriented service staff, and sigh-inducing fare.

Tuck into soft, plump pillows of agnolotti, filled with tender, braised short ribs and folded into a creamy sauce of sweet corn-butter and sage; or indulge in a traditional Neapolitan *pastiera*, lovingly crafted with a perfect little lattice hat. The daily specials are divine, but those on a budget should ask about prices—which can climb steeply when no one's looking.

# Santa Clarita

A3 Mexican X

237 Willis Ave. (bet. 138th & 139th Sts.)

**Subway:** 3 Av - 138 St
**Phone:** 718-292-9399
**Web:** N/A
**Prices:** ¢¢

Lunch & dinner daily

Make your way past the Honduran and Puerto Rican restaurants that flank Willis Avenue in the Mott Haven section of the Bronx, and you'll find a lovely little taste of Mexico. Santa Clarita's theatrical façade (replete with a rosary-draped statue of the restaurant's namesake) belies a charming interior with small wooden tables, a visible kitchen where women tend to smoking stoves, and a jukebox stocked with vibrant music.

Chef/owner Conrado Ramos (affectionately known as El Chile) likes to cue it up himself on occasion. Don't miss the appetizers like the *carnitas estilo Michoacán*, a small tortilla triple-stacked with tender, juicy *carnita*; or a soft quesadilla filled with fragrant mushrooms, zucchini flowers, and a creamy Mexican cheese.

# Tra Di Noi

Italian

C1

622 E. 187th St. (bet. Belmont & Hughes Aves.)

**Subway:** Fordham Rd (Grand Concourse) Lunch & dinner Tue – Sun
**Phone:** 718-295-1784
**Web:** N/A
**Prices:** $$

Set in a neighborhood filled with bustling large and small Italian markets and real-deal restaurants, Tra Di Noi sets itself apart with killer versions of the Italian classics. The man to thank is talented Chef/owner Marco Coletta, who has the presence of mind to stay in his kitchen most nights, while his charming wife works the dining room, showering the guests with attention.

Settle into the simply-appointed dining room and twirl your spikes around plump strands of linguine dancing in a sweet, creamy pesto; or dig into a spot-on *trippa alla Romana* in a sweet sauce laced with carrots and celery. The delicious *pizzaiola* rotates on and off the menu, but don't panic if it's m.i.a.—this friendly house has been known to accommodate emergency requests.

# zero otto nove

Italian

C1

2357 Arthur Ave. (at 186th St.)

**Subway:** Fordham Rd (Grand Concourse) Lunch & dinner Tue – Sun
**Phone:** 718-220-1027
**Web:** www.roberto089.com
**Prices:** $$

Here on Arthur Avenue, locals know that the name refers to the area code of Roberto Paciullo's beloved Salerno province. Sibling to the wildly popular Roberto's, this hot spot is also styled as an historic Italian piazza, in a casual space that rises to a skylit mezzanine.

Inside, an amiable staff serves dishes arriving hot from the magnificent wood-burning oven that anchors the space. Robust pastas baked in deliciously simple sauces are prepared alongside sophisticated versions of impeccably rustic entrées. The famed pizzas may be creatively decked with butternut squash, smoked mozzarella, and pancetta. In typical New York style, the restaurant lures magnates and the like, sitting side-by-side, finishing their meals with a perfect espresso.

Peter L. Wrenn/MICHELIN

# Brooklyn

# Brooklyn

Forage Brooklyn's trellis of neighborhoods and discover an exciting dining destination characterized by mom and pop stores, ethnic eateries, and trendy hotspots. Credit the influx of enterprising young chefs—many trained at Manhattan's top restaurants—for ushering in a new level of dining, while sedate establishments maintain the borough's rugged authenticity. The sustainable food movement has taken root as eco-conscious communities expand, and local artisans gain popularity for their high quality, handcrafted goods.

Williamsburg, traditionally an Italian, Hispanic, and Hasidic neighborhood, is now home to hipsters and artists; its streets rife with music venues, bars, and secondhand shops. Here in "Billyburg," artistic food endeavors abound: find upscale eateries in former factories, an artisan chocolate line handcrafted from bean to bar (**Mast Brothers Chocolate**), and an online cooking show dedicated to making meals and mates (*Feed Me: The Brooklyn Cooking Dating Show*). If interested in learning how to pickle, bake a great pie, or ferment kombucha, sign up for a cooking class at the **Brooklyn Kitchen**.

Besides DUMBO's breathtaking views, stroll down cobblestoned Water Street and step into **Jacques Torres** for a taste of chocolate heaven. Bordering Prospect Park, verdant Park Slope boasts blocks of tony trattorias, catering to an army of stroller-rolling parents. The **Park Slope Food Coop** is a member operated and owned cooperative selling locally farmed produce, fair trade products, grass-fed meat, free-range poultry, and more. Founded in 1973, the co-op is the largest of its kind in the country; membership is offered to anyone willing to pay a small fee and work a shift of less than three hours each month.

Carroll Gardens, a historically Italian neighborhood, offers shoppers a bevy of family-owned butchers and bakeries along Court Street. **G. Esposito and Sons** (otherwise known as the pork store) has gamey *sopressata* while **Da'Mico** is a coffee-lovers nirvana. **Caputo's** has sandwiches worth the wait but don't forget to grab a ball of their incredible mozzarella. As Court Street blends into the tree-lined blocks of upmarket, family-friendly Cobble Hill, find **Staubitz Market**, the friendliest butcher around. Continue the stroll to Atlantic Avenue with its Middle Eastern goodies at **Sahadi's** and **Damascus Bakery**.

On Brooklyn's waterfront rests Red Hook, attracting action with its large spaces and low rents. These industrious craftspeople are transforming the neighborhood's aged piers and warehouses into cool breweries, bakeries, and bistros. Royalty reigns with the Queen Mary 2 docked here. In the mood for a sweet treat; head to **Baked**; or follow the signs to **Steve's Authentic Key Lime Pie**. **The Red Hook Farmer's Market,** features produce grown on Red Hook Community Farm. Both ventures are operated by Added Value, a mentoring organization dedicated to teaching urban youth how to till, sow, and harvest. If hankering for south of the border eats, turn to the ever-popular **Red Hook Ball Field Vendors.** Catering to hordes of New Yorkers in the know, trucks and tents selling homemade Latin American and Caribbean street foods edge the soccer fields on weekends from May through October.

Saunter to Fort Greene for a taste of African delicacies: Ethiopian at **Bati's** and South African at **Madiba**, where the sidewalk offers some great alfresco dining. Land at Sunset Park, and the vivid Mexican foods and flavors will tantalize your senses. Throw caution to the wind and bite into a *pambazo* from **Tacos Xochimilco**. Rows of grocery stores carry authentic ingredients; butcher shops offer unique meats, whilst bakeries carry sweets 'n treats. Slightly south, Mexico meets China, and this fusion is best expressed in diverse culinary offerings. Sidewalks teem with vendors steaming fresh tofu; fishmongers selling offbeat provisions... bullfrog anyone? Chinatown encroaches into Bay Ridge where dim sum is delicious and Asian markets aplenty. Bay Ridge is also home to a large Middle Eastern population whose finest eats can be relished at **Tanoreen**.

In a flock of Kosher restaurants, **Di Fara** is an unorthodox pizzeria and has called Midwood home for decades. And at the end of Brooklyn, Brighton Beach is best known for its borscht and blintzes; **Café Ghechik** is a Ukranian *bijou*.

Jeanine C. Hart/MICHELIN

**Inset I**

A
- Silent H ✕
- ✕✕ Zenkichi
- ✕ Sea
- ✕ Egg
- Ⓜ Bedford Av
- Ⓜ ✕ Brooklyn Star ●
- Ⓜ ✕ Baci & Abracci
- ✕ La Superior
- Ⓜ ✕ Marlow & Sons
- ✕ Vutera
- ✕ Rye
- Dressler ✕✕
- ✕ Diner
- Peter Luger ✕

B
- MANHATTAN
- ✕ Karczma
- *Greenpoint*
- GREENPOINT
- *Nassau*
- **See inset**
- *Bedford*
- Ⓜ
- *Metropolitan*
- *Grand* Ⓜ

**See inset II**

2

3

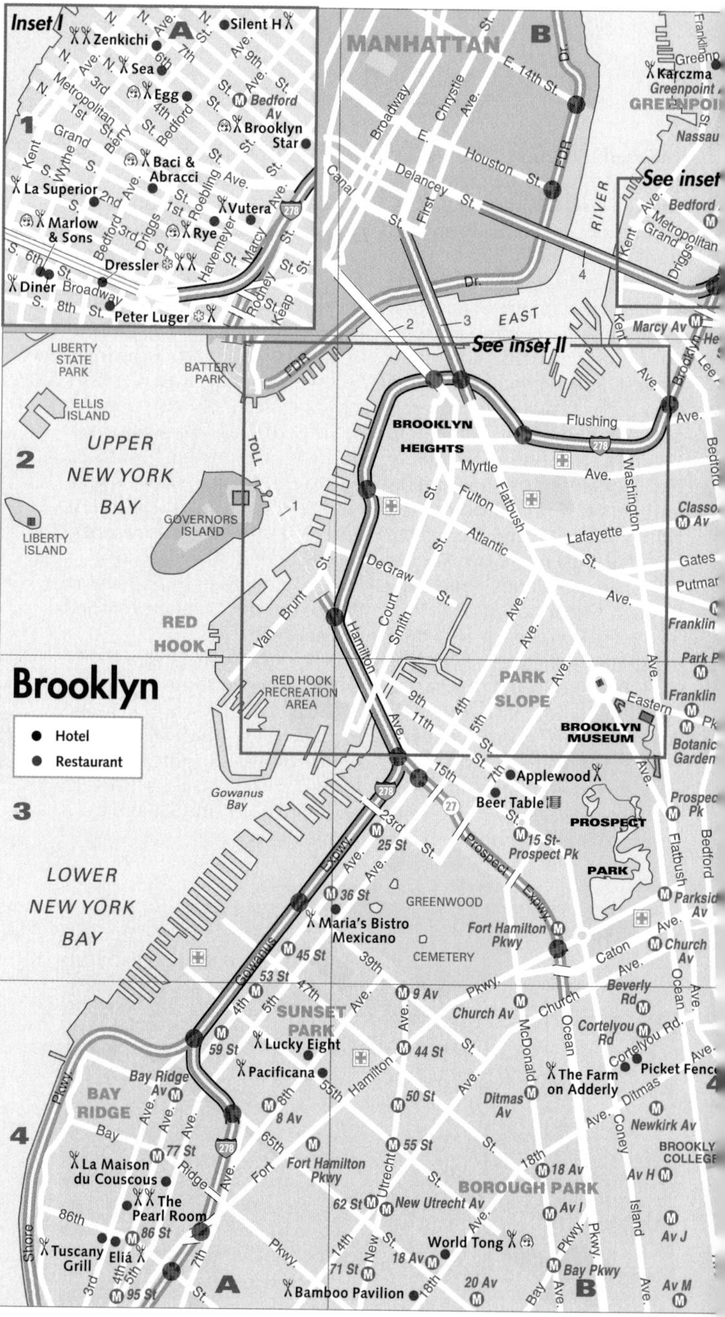

**Brooklyn**

- ● Hotel
- ● Restaurant

LIBERTY STATE PARK

ELLIS ISLAND

**UPPER NEW YORK BAY**

LIBERTY ISLAND

BATTERY PARK

GOVERNORS ISLAND

**RED HOOK**

RED HOOK RECREATION AREA

**LOWER NEW YORK BAY**

**BROOKLYN HEIGHTS**

Myrtle Ave.
Fulton St.
Flatbush
Atlantic
Lafayette
Gates Ave.
Putman
Franklin

**PARK SLOPE**

**BROOKLYN MUSEUM**

Eastern
**PROSPECT PARK**

Botanic Garden

- ● Applewood ✕
- Beer Table ▤
- Ⓜ 15 St-Prospect Pk

**PROSPECT PARK**

Gowanus Bay

Ⓜ 36 St
✕ Maria's Bistro Mexicano

GREENWOOD CEMETERY

Fort Hamilton Pkwy

Ⓜ 45 St
Ⓜ 53 St

**SUNSET PARK**

Ⓜ 59 St
✕ Lucky Eight
✕ Pacificana

Ⓜ 9 Av
Church Av
Ⓜ 44 St
Ⓜ 50 St
Ⓜ 55 St

Beverly Rd
Cortelyou Rd
✕ The Farm on Adderly
Picket Fence ✕
Ⓜ Church Av

**BAY RIDGE**

Ⓜ 77 St
Ⓜ 8 Av
Ⓜ 65 St

✕ La Maison du Couscous
✕✕ The Pearl Room
✕ Tuscany Grill   Elià ✕

Ⓜ 86 St
Ⓜ 95 St

Fort Hamilton Pkwy
Ⓜ 62 St   New Utrecht Av
Ⓜ 71 St
Ⓜ 18 Av

**BOROUGH PARK**

Ⓜ 18 Av
Ⓜ Av I
World Tong ✕
Ⓜ Bay Pkwy
Ⓜ 20 Av
Ⓜ Av M

✕ Bamboo Pavilion

**BROOKLYN COLLEGE**
Av H Ⓜ
Ⓜ Av J

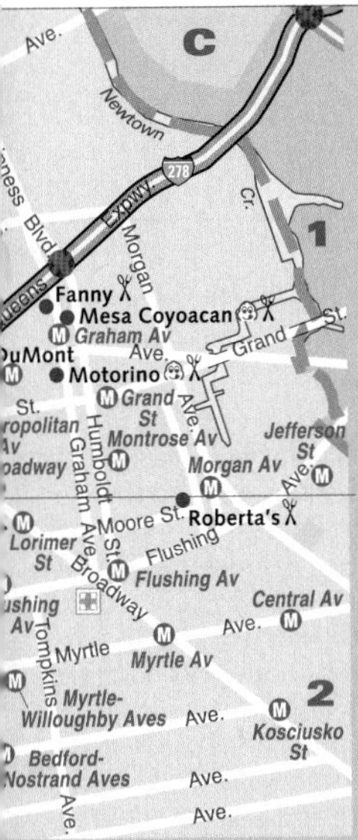


| | |
|---|---|
| Atlantic Ave. | B2 |
| Bay Pkwy. | B4 |
| Bay Ridge Pkwy. | A4 |
| Bedford Ave. | B1C4 |
| Broadway | B1C2 |
| Brooklyn-Queens Expwy. | B2C1 |
| Caton Ave. | B3 |
| Church Ave. | B3 4 |
| Coney Island Ave. | B4 |
| Cortelyou Rd. | B4 |
| Court St. | B2 3 |
| DeGraw St. | AB2 |
| Ditmas Ave. | B4 |
| Driggs Ave. | BC1 |
| Eastern Pkwy. | B3 |
| Flatbush Ave. | B2 4 |
| Flushing Ave. | B2C1 |
| Fort Hamilton Pkwy. | A4B3 |
| Franklin St. | B1 |
| Fulton St. | B2 |
| Gates Ave. | BC2 |
| Gowanus Expwy. | A4B2 |
| Graham Ave. | C1 2 |
| Grand St. | BC1 |
| Greenpoint Ave. | BC1 |
| Hamilton Ave. | B2 3 |
| Humboldt St. | C1 2 |
| Kent Ave. | B1 2 |
| Lafayette Ave. | BC2 |
| McDonald Ave. | B3 4 |
| McGuinness Blvd. | C1 |
| Metropolitan Ave. | BC1 |
| Moore St. | C2 |
| Morgan Ave. | C1 |
| Myrtle Ave. | B2C2 |
| New Utrecht Ave. | B4 |
| Nostrand Ave. | C2 |
| Ocean Ave. | B3 4 |
| Ocean Pkwy. | B4 |
| Prospect Expwy. | B3 |
| Putman Ave. | BC2 |
| Shore Pkwy. | A4 |
| Smith St. | B2 |
| Tompkins Ave. | C2 |
| Union Ave. | C1 |
| Van Brunt St. | A2 |
| Washington Ave. | B2 3 |
| 3rd Ave. | A4 |
| 4th Ave. | A4B2 |
| 5th Ave. | A4B2 |
| 7th Ave. | A4, B2 3 |
| 8th Ave. | A4B3 |
| 9th St. | B3 |
| 11th St. | B3 |
| 14th Ave. | AB3 |
| 15th St. | B3 |
| 18th Ave. | B4 |
| 23rd St. | B3 |
| 39th St. | A3B4 |
| 47th St. | A3B4 |
| 55th St. | A3B4 |
| 65th St. | AB4 |
| 86th St. | A4 |

**BRIDGES AND TUNNELS**

| | |
|---|---|
| Brooklyn-Battery Tunnel | 1 A2 |
| Brooklyn Bridge | 2 B1 2 |
| Manhattan Bridge | 3 B1 2 |
| Williamsburg Bridge | 4 B1 |

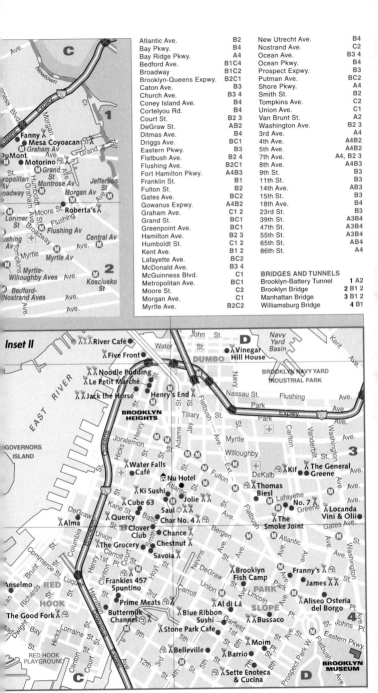

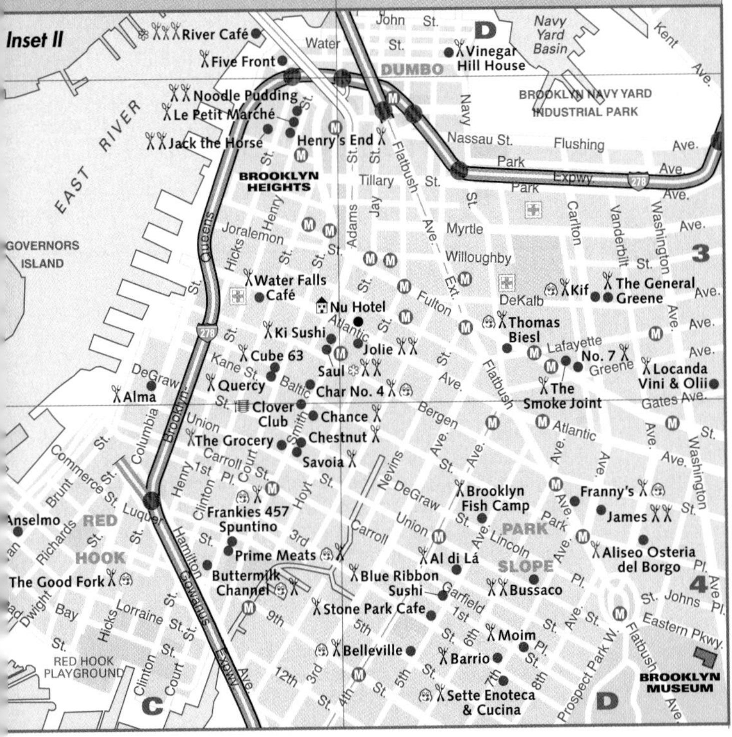

# Al di Là

D4 — Italian

248 Fifth Ave. (at Carroll St.)

**Subway:** Union St
**Phone:** 718-783-4565
**Web:** www.aldilatrattoria.com
**Prices:** $$

Lunch Wed – Sun
Dinner Wed – Mon

With its mouth-watering Northern Italian cuisine and a charming atmosphere, it's no wonder this neighborhood fixture run by husband-and-wife team Emiliano Coppa and Anna Klinger continues to be a first choice dining option for both nearby residents and foodies from afar.

The high-ceilinged room boasts a faded chic, with its church-pew seats, and eccentric touches, such as coffee pots hanging from the wall and a blown glass chandelier.

Al di La now serves a lunch menu, which is pared down from the evening offerings. The perfect seasonal salad of young spinach with favas, fennel, and pecorino; and lasagna *al forno*, richly layered with meat and tomato ragù and béchamel are not only delicious, but priced at what can simply be called "a great deal."

# Aliseo Osteria del Borgo

D4 — Italian

665 Vanderbilt Ave. (bet. Park & Prospect Pls. )

**Subway:** 7 Av
**Phone:** 718-783-3400
**Web:** N/A
**Prices:** $$

Dinner Tue – Sun

Just a few blocks north of Prospect Park, a tiny sliver of a restaurant pokes a delightful hole in the fabric of low-end joints that line the neighborhood. The quaint interior of Aliseo Osteria del Borgo is decidedly romantic, from the rustic tables to the porcelain lights to the cute garden out back. And if you sidle up to the counter with a minute to spare, the charming owner will tell you all about his labor of love.

Mercifully, the food is just as lovely, with a scrumptious lineup of Italian specialties that might include a zippy plate of baby beef meatballs; juicy, pan-roasted *trota di mare*, laid over a bundle of mushrooms in spring onion sauce; or a wicked dark chocolate tart laced with orange sauce and a lick of sweet and salty caramel.

# Alma

Mexican

C3

187 Columbia St. (at Degraw St.)

**Subway:** Carroll St
**Phone:** 718-643-5400
**Web:** www.almarestaurant.com
**Prices:** $$

Lunch Sat – Sun
Dinner nightly

Featuring an energetic, welcoming, niño-friendly first floor bar, popular billiards lounge, charming upstairs dining room, and roof-top belvedere with views of lower Manhattan and the shipyards below, Alma thrives where others have failed. This local favorite knows its clientele-appealing to hip, young families seeking occasional live bluegrass and consistently good food in a casual environment.

The contemporary Mexican fare comes in portions suitable to share, and often features subdued spices (friendly to younger or pickier palates), as in the generous bowls of creamy guacamole. Brooklyn's own Steve's Authentic Key Lime pies are showcased as dessert.

Rooftop reservations are only taken during winter months when it is enclosed and heated.

# Anselmo

Pizza

C4

354 Van Brunt St. (at Sullivan St.)

**Subway:** Smith - 9 Sts. (& bus B77)
**Phone:** 718-313-0169
**Web:** www.anselmosbakery.com
**Prices:** ⓢⓢ

Lunch & dinner Wed – Mon

The owners of Anselmo may have intended to open a bakery/café, but then they discovered the working coal-burning oven in the building's basement. They dismantled it, rebuilt it upstairs, and realized that they simply had to make takeout pizza. In the dining area, pressed tin ceilings and a 1920s cash register complete the simple and authentic scene. Now, they serve pizzas with cracker-thin crusts puffy rims, deliciously blistered from the intense heat. Try the simple margherita pie, slathered with a sauce made from San Marzano tomatoes, and topped with creamy mozzarella, basil, and a drizzle of olive oil.

This much-talked-about place is helping to revive the lonely Red Hook area, which may be catching up to more gentrified areas of Brooklyn.

# Applewood

B3 **Contemporary**

501 11th St. (bet. Seventh & Eighth Aves.)

**Subway:** 7 Av
**Phone:** 718-788-1810
**Web:** www.applewoodny.com
**Prices:** $$

Lunch Sat – Sun
Dinner Tue – Sat

Skillfully prepared cuisine and a dainty setting reflect the seriousness of Applewood's owners David and Laura Shea. The pair is committed to promoting the work of organic and local farmers in a changing menu of small plates and entrées dedicated to reflecting the seasons.

The spare yet comfortable dining room, set in a century-old townhouse on a tree-lined street, is furnished with honey-toned wood tables and spindle-back chairs. When in use, a working fireplace warms the light-colored room, accented by the work of local artists.

Thick slices of fresh bread set the tone for an enjoyable meal of wild fish and hormone-free meats in delectable offerings such as lobster risotto with mascarpone and chili oil, or pan-seared bass with tomatillo jam.

# Baci & Abbracci

A1 **Italian**

204 Grand St. (bet. Bedford & Driggs Sts.)

**Subway:** Bedford Av
**Phone:** 718-599-6599
**Web:** www.baciny.com
**Prices:** $$

Lunch Sat – Sun
Dinner nightly

This intimate, contemporary spot in the heart of the Williamsburg leaves guests giving kisses and hugs all around. The authenitic Italian kitchen excels in creating enticing, rustic courses of antipasti, pasta, *cestini*, and secondi, with decisions further complicated by the appealing daily specials.

Pizzas are the true standout, with perfectly thin crusts and toppings like smoked mozzarella, pancetta, and onion. The restaurant also serves a lovely brunch of savory frittatas or focaccia baked with Nutella. In warmer weather, meals may be best enjoyed in the charming garden behind the restaurant.

Inside, the lighting is soft, service is warm, and ambience inviting. Locals may choose to have these affectionate flavors delivered right to their doors.

# Bamboo Pavilion

Chinese

B4

6920 Eighteenth Ave. (bet. Bay Ridge Ave. & 70th St.)

**Subway:** 18 Av
Lunch & dinner Mon – Sat
**Phone:** 718-236-8088
**Web:** N/A
**Prices:** $$

How did this hot pot joint find its way onto Bensonhurst's predominantly Sicilian 18th Avenue, the one made famous by the movie Saturday Night Fever? The times they are a' changin'—for this area is now home to a growing Chinese population and enough authentic Sichuan joints to warrant some critics stating it has become the city's next Chinatown. A meal at Bamboo Pavilion might convince you, for these fiery delights don't fool around. The restaurant itself is nondescript, with bamboo-etched wallpapered walls, bright lighting, and jumbo round tables for big parties. All the more reason to set your eyes to the center of each table—where piles of soft noodles, succulent raw meats, and leafy vegetables surround fragrant pots of bubbling broth.

# Barrio

Mexican

D4

210 Seventh Ave. (at 3rd St.)

**Subway:** 7 Av
Lunch Thu – Sun
Dinner daily
**Phone:** 718-965-4000
**Web:** www.barriofoods.com
**Prices:** $$

This cozy new neighborhood fave doubles its capacity in warmer weather with a covered outdoor dining space cheerfully decorated with strings of colored lights overhead. The blithe yet beautiful spot displays a glazed ceramic tile floor, with pink and orange embellishments.

Even beyond this setting is the impressive cooking of Mexico City native and Chef/partner Adrian Leon, whose skills have been honed in some of Manhattan's most popular Mexican kitchens. Excellent tortilla chips accompanied by red and green salsa begin what is sure to be an enjoyable meal.

Parents take note: the assortment of soft *taquitos*, enticing entrées, and *"platos del dia"* is accompanied by a kid's menu offering tidbits such as miniature short rib soft tacos and the like.

# Beer Table

B3 **Gastropub**

427 B Seventh Ave. (bet. 14th & 15th Sts.)

**Subway:** 7 Av
**Phone:** 718-965-1196
**Web:** www.beertable.com
**Prices:** $$

Lunch Sat – Sun
Dinner nightly

With a listing of more than 25 bottled beers, some priced on par with fine wine, Beer Table gives the typical neighborhood pub a sophisticated new angle. Three communal tables are tucked into a pleasant setting accented with shelves of sparkling stemware and jars of housemade pickles.

Most evenings, snacks like spicy fish soup and sausage plates are offered to accompany their artisanal beer selections; but on Tuesdays the small plate format switches to a not-to-be-missed fixed menu, with optional beer pairings. Seasonal ingredients are showcased in meals that may feature baby arugula and cucumber salad with herbed yogurt, striped bass on a bed of *fregola* spiked with roasted garlic and preserved lemon, or warm strawberry *amaretti* crumble.

# Belleville

D4 **French**

330 5th St. (at Fifth Ave.)

**Subway:** 4 Av - 9 St
**Phone:** 718-832-9777
**Web:** www.bellevillebistro.com
**Prices:** $$

Lunch Sat – Sun
Dinner Wed – Mon

From décor to ambience to food, Belleville (named for the Parisian neighborhood) fashions the perfectly French bistro here in Park Slope. Designed to appear lovingly well-worn, Belleville is at once comfortable, with mosaic floors, mirrored walls displaying the wine list, rows of wood-paneled banquettes, and tables nuzzled close together. In fair weather, windows open out onto Brooklyn's bustling Fifth Avenue and sidewalk seating.

The reasonably priced menu features very good bistro fare from croques madames to steak frites. There's even a kids menu for little gourmands-in-training. This is a welcoming neighborhood place for a romantic dinner, weekend brunch, or small bites and a glass of wine in the recently opened lounge.

# Blue Ribbon Sushi

Japanese

D4

278 Fifth Ave. (bet. 1st St. & Garfield Pl. )

**Subway:** Union St — Dinner nightly
**Phone:** 718-840-0408
**Web:** www.blueribbonrestaurants.com
**Prices:** $$

Consistent excellence has made this Brooklyn location of the Bromberg brother's notable restaurant line-up worthy of bearing the Blue Ribbon name. Slats of warmly polished wood and a cool grey palette lends a chic finish to this popular spot—filled with Park Slope parents towing along the next generation of sushi connoisseurs.

Classified according to ocean of origin (Atlantic or Pacific), the sushi here is delightful and is shored up by a creative menu of maki, such as the Blue Ribbon roll which lavishly combines lobster, caviar, and *shiso*. The lengthy list of appetizers and salads may include *yasei kinoko* (broiled wild mushrooms with tamari butter).

Complement your meal with a selection from the well chosen sake list or a Japanese boutique beer.

# Brooklyn Fish Camp

Seafood

D4

162 Fifth Ave. (bet. De Graw & Douglass Sts. )

**Subway:** Union St — Lunch & dinner Tue – Sun
**Phone:** 718-783-3264
**Web:** www.brooklynfishcamp.com
**Prices:** $$

Inspired by the simplicity of rural Southern fish shacks, the menu at this Brooklyn offshoot of Mary's Fish Camp displays a reverence for seriously prepared seafood.

The welcoming bar upfront leads to a simple dining room furnished with warm-hued wood tables, topped with brown paper mats and bags of oyster crackers. Out back, picnic tables and folding chairs make a fine setting for a summertime meal, accompanied by movies shown on a whitewashed wall.

The excellent lobster roll, oyster Po' boy, and shrimp tacos are all fun favorites; but do not overlook more inspired entrées like roasted monkfish with horseradish-bacon beurre blanc. Tempting home-style desserts, like banana pudding and peach cobbler, are listed on the wall-mounted blackboard.

# Brooklyn Star 😊

**A1**

Southern ✗

### 33 Havemeyer St. (bet. N. 7th & N. 8th Sts.)

**Subway:** Bedford Av
**Phone:** 718-599-9899
**Web:** www.thebrooklynstar.com
**Prices:** 💰💰

Dinner nightly

Moving on from his partnership with Chef David Chang and leaving Manhattan behind, Chef Joaquin Baca now has a place to call his own, located in a former pizzeria that he painstakingly renovated himself. The cozy yet masculine appeal is undeniable at Brooklyn Star, with pine-lined walls, slate-topped tables, and an open kitchen preparing Southern specialties that revolve around a century-old wood burning oven.

To start, the down-home menu offers cornbread baked to-order, and light, crumbly, golden-brown biscuits served with a squeeze-bottle of honey. The hearty selection of small plates and entrées may include an awesomely crisp, battered country-fried steak with chunky mashed potatoes all boldly sauced with creamy, black-pepper spiked gravy.

# Bussaco

**D4**

Contemporary ✗✗

### 833 Union St. (bet. Sixth & Seventh Aves.)

**Subway:** Union St
**Phone:** 718-857-8828
**Web:** www.bussacobklyn.com
**Prices:** $$

Lunch Sat – Sun
Dinner Tue – Sun

The outside of this charming new eatery welcomes diners with potted flowers arranged on an arched brick entrance. Inside, the spacious setting is clean and spare, with white-washed brick walls, dark-wood furnishings, pastel landscapes, and bar area outfitted with a communal table fashioned from a fallen oak tree.

Bussaco's succinct, contemporary menu indicates a skilled hand, with the likes of fresh housemade mozzarella on a bed of herb and hazelnut-flecked quinoa; duck breast with pan-fried spaetzle in foie gras butter; and lemon-thyme pound cake topped with olive oil gelato.

The service team is effectively overseen by the establishment's owner who is also a sommelier—his interesting, global wine list includes many bottles priced under $40.

# Buttermilk Channel

American

C4

524 Court St. (at Huntington St.)

**Subway:** Smith - 9 Sts.
**Phone:** 718-852-8490
**Web:** www.buttermilkchannelnyc.com
**Prices:** $$

Lunch Sun
Dinner Tue – Sun

A fresh coat of glossy, dark paint and large windows emanating a warm glow give this establishment an inviting, turn-of-the-century maritime feel. This befits its name, which references the (once crossable) strait separating Brooklyn from Governor's Island. The butter-yellow dining room attracts a lively and diverse crowd; regardless of one's tastes, the menu is bound to please.

A listing of small bites like house-made pickles, charcuterie, and greenmarket cheeses are perfect to nibble along with a local brew and make a lovely prelude. The full offering of seasonal comfort food may include winter squash tart with homemade buttermilk ricotta; or duck meatloaf with creamy spinach purée, with a separate (equally impressive) menu devoted to vegetarians.

# Chance

Asian

C4

223 Smith St. (bet. Baltic & Butler Sts.)

**Subway:** Bergen St
**Phone:** 718-242-1515
**Web:** www.chancecuisine.com
**Prices:**

Lunch & dinner daily

Sporting a freshened décor, Chance continues to beautifully present a luscious, unique selection of Pan-Asian delights. The menu celebrates these varied influences, and even includes an occasional nod to France. Inside, ivory leather seating and dark glossy tables give the space a modern look, and attractive red lanterns suspended over the bar allude to the Asian theme.

The dim sum assortment makes a fine starting point, followed by impressive and enjoyable dishes like black pepper chicken, coated in crisp *panko* and topped with flavorful ground pork. While the carte du jour is reasonably priced, quality is not sacrificed. Savor the dinner prixe-fixe for less than $20, with decadent dessert choices such as smooth and rich vanilla ice cream brûlée.

# Char No. 4

C3 **Gastropub**

196 Smith St. (bet. Baltic & Warren Sts.)

**Subway:** Bergen St
**Phone:** 718-643-2106
**Web:** www.charno4.com
**Prices:** $$

Lunch Sat – Sun
Dinner nightly

More shrine than pub, this new Smith Street watering hole offers an encyclopedic listing of whiskey, half of which are devoted to bourbon and all are available in one or two ounce pours—allowing for a civilized examination of the elixir's varied styles.

The comfortable front bar radiates warmth with its wall of amber-filled bottles; the slender dining room in the back is decorated in shades of brown.

The Southern-inspired menu of crispy cheddar nuggets with pimento sauce; shrimp and grits; and smoked honey-glazed chicken accentuates the sweet, spicy, and charred essences, which in turn marry well with the stack of smoky bourbons. Finish it all with a lick of house-made butter pecan ice cream, drizzled with a shot of bourbon, of course.

# Chestnut

C4 **Contemporary**

271 Smith St. (bet. De Graw & Sackett Sts.)

**Subway:** Carroll St
**Phone:** 718-243-0049
**Web:** www.chestnutonsmith.com
**Prices:** $$

Lunch Sun
Dinner Tue – Sun

This Carroll Gardens eatery is the kind of place every neighborhood should have. Like its moniker, the philosophy here is comforting and seasonal. Chestnut's farm-reared chef spends time sourcing the best ingredients and then lets them shine in a menu reminding diners that the best supermarket is nature itself. The simple décor has just the right amount of personality, and the laid-back staff delivers genuinely warm service, starting your meal with fresh-baked bread and homemade pickles.

Come on Tuesday or Wednesday nights to take advantage of the three-course, prix-fixe value menus. Or, order à la carte any night to dine on skillfully-prepared items that may include salt cod *brandade*, roasted chicken breast with sausage filling, or chocolate *budino*.

# Clover Club

American

C3.4

210 Smith St. (bet. Baltic & Butler Sts.)

**Subway:** Bergen St
**Phone:** 718-855-7939
**Web:** www.cloverclubny.com
**Prices:** $$

Lunch Sat – Sun
Dinner nightly

A former shoe store is now an atmospheric new Smith Street watering hole that fashions a spot-on vintage vibe with mosaic tiled floors, glove-soft leather banquettes, and pressed-tin ceilings dangling etched-glass pendants that create a glow warmer than single malt. The rear mahogany bar is overseen by a skillful, natty bartender vigorously shaking and artfully pouring a noteworthy selection of libations, like the "improved whiskey cocktail" (rye whiskey, maraschino, absinthe, and bitters served in a frosted glass with a single block of ice).
An excellent menu of savory bites is just as impressively prepared and includes treats such as deviled eggs four ways; shrimp roll sliders; and brioche bread pudding with bourbon caramel sauce.

# Cube 63

Japanese

C3

234 Court St. (at Baltic St.)

**Subway:** Bergen St
**Phone:** 718-243-2208
**Web:** N/A
**Prices:** $$

Lunch & dinner daily

Located in charming Cobble Hill, Cube 63 is the little sister of the original Lower East Side location, yet offers superior dining. The understated dining room pleasantly features dark-wood furnishings, pale blue walls, chic lighting, and a sushi counter complemented by a back patio and two small lounge spaces.
Cooked appetizers, noodles, and raw offerings are consistently well made and attractively presented. The large selection of sushi rolls feature firm, rich fish, and include curiosity-inducing house specials with names like the Tahiti roll (shrimp tempura, eel, cream cheese, avocado, and caviar), and the electric roll (tempura fried roll with salmon, whitefish, and crabmeat). Lunchtime offers reasonably priced specials with soup or salad.

# Diner

A1 American

## 85 Broadway (at Berry St.)

**Subway:** Marcy Av Lunch & dinner daily
**Phone:** 718-486-3077
**Web:** www.dinernyc.com
**Prices:** $$

Williamsburg may be the epicenter of all that is hip, but this simple little corner spot is a longtime favorite and welcomed foil to this trendy neighborhood. In 1998, Mark Firth and Andrew Tarlow (also of Marlow & Sons) painstakingly renovated the 1920s Kullman Diner, and though the result may now seem well-worn, its casual warmth brings regulars back time and time again.

Since then, Chef Caroline Fidanza has prepared a deliciously concise menu, that may include a juicy grassfed burger or shaved asparagus salad. Abundant daily specials are also offered; imagine seasonal dishes and innovative comfort food. Although the prices are reasonable and service is informal, this is no ordinary diner—they even publish a quarterly, aptly named, *Diner Journal*.

# DuMont

C1 American

## 432 Union Ave. (bet. Devoe St. & Metropolitan Ave. )

**Subway:** Lorimer St - Metropolitan Av Lunch & dinner daily
**Phone:** 718-486-7717
**Web:** www.dumontrestaurant.com
**Prices:** $$

DuMont espouses its neighborhood's relaxed, edgy, and creative vibe. The multi-room space is warm and comfortably worn, furnished with dark-wood tables topped in brown paper, vintage tile floor, and cool leather seating handmade by the owner. There is also a lovely backyard with elevated seating called "the treehouse". Executive Chef Polo Dobkin draws crowds who clamor for the comforting and impressively prepared menu items. Favorites may include pan-roasted quail with cheddar polenta; NY strip steak with green peppercorn sauce; and of course, the DuMac and cheese (with *radiatore* pasta, a blend of cheeses, and studded with bits of bacon). Brunch keeps things rocking on weekends.

For a quick burger and a beer, try nearby DuMont Burger.

# Dressler ✿

American ✗✗

A1

149 Broadway (bet. Bedford & Driggs Aves.)

**Subway:** Marcy Av — Lunch Sat – Sun
**Phone:** 718-384-6343 — Dinner nightly
**Web:** www.dresslernyc.com
**Prices:** **$$**

Jason Joseph/Dressler

Oh, Williamsburg. You with your skinny cords and disheveled beards—how you've matured into a thriving culinary hotbed before thine very eyes. Leading this neighborhood's endless brigade of hip hot spots dabbling in refined cuisine is Colin Devlin's critically-acclaimed Dressler—a sophisticated sibling to Devlin's more casual neighborhood staples, Dumont and Dumont Burger.

Possibly thinking of the long-term game plan, Dressler occupies the same hallowed block as the legendary steakhouse, Peter Luger's—a wide, truck-rumbling street that, despite its growing list of big name eateries, has an air of remoteness. Thankfully, it's a mood that the sleek, polished Dressler—a cavernous old printer's shop redesigned with mosaic tiles, polished mahogany, and a zinc-topped bar—manages to wash away with its devotion to detail.

Chef Polo Dobkin also has an eye for minutia, and his finely-tuned American cuisine gets a contemporary polish in dishes like hand-rolled pasta, laced with a luscious rabbit ragout; or monkfish wrapped in thick, crispy bacon, and garnished with a creamy spring pea risotto; or a buttermilk panna cotta surrounded by roasted pineapple and shortbread cookies.

# Egg

A1 — American

135 N. 5th St. (bet. Bedford Ave. & Berry St.)

**Subway:** Bedford Av — Lunch & dinner daily
**Phone:** 718-302-5151
**Web:** www.pigandegg.com
**Prices:** $

Offering daily breakfast well into the afternoon, Egg's slender dining room seems to serve as a remote office for Williamsburg's work-from-home set. We may never know how many bestsellers were conceived here, while downing cups of sustainably grown coffee or doodling with crayons provided on the paper-topped tables. On weekends, the wait for a table can be lengthy—jot your name on the flipchart stationed outside and be patient.

Southern-accented preparations like fresh-baked buttermilk biscuits layered with country ham, cheddar, and fig jam are popular, but also find homemade granola served with local yogurt and griddle fare accompanied by Vermont maple syrup. Dinner hour brings the likes of deviled eggs and fried chicken with collard greens.

# Eliá

A4 — Greek

8611 Third Ave. (bet. 86th & 87th Sts.)

**Subway:** 86 St — Dinner Tue – Sun
**Phone:** 718-748-9891
**Web:** www.eliarestaurant.org
**Prices:** **$$**

Long known to Bay Ridge residents, this little gem is no longer a secret. Now, regulars share their favorite Greek restaurant with diners from Manhattan. That said, everyone is treated like family at this affable and spotless taverna.

The chef sometimes steers the menu into uncharted waters with elaborate creations and mixed results. Hold steady with the simple, traditional dishes at which the kitchen excels, like classic *spanakopita* of spinach, leeks, and feta cheese layered in flakey, buttery phyllo dough, or baklava topped with nuts and a spiced citrus-infused syrup. Generous portions assure value for money.

In the dining room, white-washed brick walls and marine blues evoke sun-washed stucco buildings and the color of the Aegean Sea.

# Fanny

Mediterranean

C1

425 Graham Ave. (bet. Frost & Withers Sts.)

**Subway:** Graham Av — Lunch & dinner daily
**Phone:** 718-389-2060
**Web:** www.fannyfood.com
**Prices:** $$

Building the perfect neighborhood bistro is a delicate thing. It should be intimate and cozy, but lively when the mood fits; it should traffic in the kind of delicious, straightforward fare regulars won't tire of easily; and the owners ought to be the kind of folks you'd want to share a drink with.

Fanny, a romantic, low-lit charmer tucked into East Williamsburg's Graham Avenue, has the formula in spades—with rustic country house good looks, two French ex-pat owners, Julie Eck and Stephane Alix, who know all their regulars' names, and a spot-on Southern French menu featuring mussels in white wine; juicy rack of lamb; silky lavender blancmange; and that final test of any bistro worth its salt—a perfect stack of crunchy frites with garlicky aïoli.

# The Farm on Adderley

American

B4

1108 Cortelyou Rd. (bet. 12th St. & Stratford Rd.)

**Subway:** Cortelyou Rd — Lunch & dinner daily
**Phone:** 718-287-3101
**Web:** www.thefarmonadderley.com
**Prices:** $$

Only a small bench and a swinging sign alert you to The Farm on Adderley's discreet storefront, tucked into a slowly improving pocket of Ditmas Park. But once inside, you'll find a super welcoming space, with a long, cozy bar that stays open until 1:00 A.M., and a softly lit dining room cast in a romantic glow.

The crowd is the usual mix of New Brooklyn—yuppies with kids in tow, catching up with friends and noshing on Chef Tom Kearney's (of Blue Hill and Jean Georges) simple, seasonal fare like country pâté dressed with cornichons, mustard, olives, and torn chicory; smoky Amish chicken roasted over alfalfa hay, quinoa, farmers cheese, and shelled peas; or an apple crisp with vanilla ice cream.

A few doors down is Sycamore, the owner's new florist/bar.

# Five Front

C2 **Contemporary**

5 Front St. (bet. Dock & Old Fulton Sts.)

**Subway:** High St
**Phone:** 718-625-5559
**Web:** www.fivefrontrestaurant.com
**Prices:** $$

Lunch Sat – Sun
Dinner Tue – Sun

Small and lovely, Five Front is located in an historic building in the desirable DUMBO neighborhood. On the walk from the High Street subway station, marvel at the magnificent Brooklyn and Manhattan Bridges that hover just overhead. Bossa nova music, butcher paper on tables, and glimmering city lights make shadows dance on the walls, all creating a warm atmosphere. The snug dining space is divided into a front bar, a second small room with exposed brick, and a back room suited for groups. A bamboo garden is a delight in warmer weather.

Contemporary dishes are prepared using fresh ingredients and may include innovative takes on classics, such as bucatini served with pistachio-basil pesto. Service is attentive, professional, and warm.

# Frankies 457 Spuntino

C4 **Italian**

457 Court St. (bet. 4th Pl. & Luquer St.)

**Subway:** Carroll St
**Phone:** 718-403-0033
**Web:** www.frankiesspuntino.com
**Prices:** 

Lunch & dinner daily

Although *spuntino* loosely translates as "snack," Frankie's offers richly satisfying cuisine to serious foodies, young newcomers, and old-school Brooklynites in a cozy setting. While food is initially prepared in the basement kitchen, the rustic meals are assembled in the casual dining room, behind a counter stacked with charcuterie and crusty breads. This practice entices guests with mouth-watering aromas of tender homemade *cavatelli* with spicy sausage and fried sage leaves; or visions of warm prunes, plumped with wine, served over generous dollops of creamy mascarapone.

Weather permitting, the best spot to dine is the inviting back garden, illuminated by strings of tiny lights. Visit the Manhattan location on the Lower East Side.

# Franny's

Italian

D4

295 Flatbush Ave. (bet. Prospect Pl. & St. Marks Ave.)

**Subway:** Bergen St
**Phone:** 718-230-0221
**Web:** www.frannysbrooklyn.com
**Prices:** $$

Lunch Sat – Sun
Dinner nightly

Run by husband-and-wife team Franny Stephens and Andrew Feinberg, who share a passion for sustainable agriculture, Franny's is an inviting spot. A comfortable bar up front and a stack of highchairs for seating little ones imply all ages are welcome here.

The centerpiece of the open kitchen is the wood-burning brick oven from whose confines the individual-size pizzas emerge puffed and crispy. Affable servers will likely tempt you with at least one of the daily specials, but remember that the chef's selection of house-cured meats and small plates is also worth considering.

Decorated with greenery, strings of white lights, and a neatly arranged pile of wood to feed the pizza oven, the patio out back is the place to be on a warm evening.

# The General Greene

American

D3

229 DeKalb Ave. (at Clermont Ave.)

**Subway:** Lafayette Av
**Phone:** 718-222-1510
**Web:** www.thegeneralgreene.com
**Prices:** $$

Lunch & dinner daily

The rustic American revolution marches on with The General Greene, a highly anticipated Fort Greene restaurant that taps the talents of acclaimed city boy chef, Nicholas Morgenstern and his accomplished staff. Together, they have cooked up a creative Southern-inflected menu guaranteed to steal the hearts of the upscale Bohemian crowd that floods this neighborhood—its simple diner good looks and coolio wait staff only seal the deal.

The seasonal menu may include a silky chicken liver pâté, dusted with sea salt; or grilled prawns, licked with an herb-infused olive oil. Save room for one of their more clever savory dishes like a thick slab of moist bread pudding, loaded with ham and gruyere, and paired with a tangle of pig's feet-studded collard greens.

# The Good Fork

Contemporary

C4

391 Van Brunt St. (bet. Coffey & Van Dyke Sts. )

**Subway:** Smith - 9 Sts (& bus B77) Dinner Tue – Sun
**Phone:** 718-643-6636
**Web:** www.goodfork.com
**Prices:** $$

It's literally a pain in the neck to get to Good Fork's far-flung Red Hook location (even if you spring for a cab, the potholes will kill you), but this is one little restaurant worth the hump. Guests can either duck into the quaint dining room, reminiscent of a train car from a bygone era, or head back to a small patio surrounded by an iron gazebo and trees wrapped in twinkling lights.

Storybook, yes—but the lovingly prepared dishes seal the deal. Run by Ben Schneider and his classically-trained Korean-American wife, Sohui Kim, The Good Fork's menu gleefully trots the globe, showcasing Kim's ethnic background—try the Korean-style steak and eggs over kimchi rice—and then switching gears to bang out a spot-on burger and salty stack of onion rings.

# The Grocery

Contemporary

C4

288 Smith St. (bet. Sackett & Union Sts.)

**Subway:** Carroll St Dinner Tue – Sat
**Phone:** 718-596-3335
**Web:** www.thegroceryrestaurant.com
**Prices:** $$

Opened in 1999, this Smith Street charmer helped put fine dining on the Brooklyn map. Today it continues to please a devoted following in a quaint space simply furnished with white paper-topped tables, whimsically accented with seasonal fruit. The verdant backyard is prized on warmer evenings, but be aware that these precious tables are offered as first-come-first-serve. Chefs and co-owners Sharon Pachter and Charles Kiely run their operation with passion and a genuine regard for their guests satisfaction.

The concise menu lists items that reflect the best of the season and local farmers' markets, such as roasted beets with goat cheese ravioli, stuffed whole boneless trout, and steamed spicy-sweet gingerbread pudding with roasted pineapple.

# Henry's End

American

C3

44 Henry St. (bet. Cranberry & Middagh Sts.)

**Subway:** High St — Dinner nightly
**Phone:** 718-834-1776
**Web:** www.henrysend.com
**Prices:** $$

For three decades, Henry's End has garnered respect from patrons who return again and again for casual and affordable American cuisine. The simple storefront features wood paneling, exposed brick, and amber lighting, lending a very old NY ambience well-suited to this area of Brooklyn. Service is friendly and professional, with the chef popping out of the semi-open kitchen to greet and hug many of the arriving regulars. Families, couples on dates, and business types comprise the jovial crowd filling the narrow room.

More ambitious menu selections may highlight game meats, such as penne with aromatic, tender, and sweet rabbit sausage, bathed in robust and spicy tomato sauce. Good flavors and unique presentations come together in this solid comfort food.

# Jack the Horse

American

C3

66 Hicks St. (at Cranberrry St.)

**Subway:** High St — Lunch Sun, Dinner nightly
**Phone:** 718-852-5084
**Web:** www.jackthehorse.com
**Prices:** $$

This adorable, exposed brick tavern has been kept under wraps by the Brooklyn Heights locals who frequent it—and no wonder. The few great restaurants that call this lovely historical district home have quickly become flooded with tourists.

One step into Jack the Horse, and you won't want to share either. Between the bright, window-lined walls and the deadly serious cocktail list, this place would not be a hit without Chef Tim Oltmans' pitch-perfect American bistro fare. Try a grilled tangle of octopus, resting on frisée salad studded with salty bits of grilled bacon, radish, fennel, and succulent tangerine; or a creamy, pan-seared hake pocked with sweet red peppers, zucchini, chorizo, and plantains bathed in a tomato-cilantro-lime broth.

# James

D4 — Contemporary XX

605 Carlton Ave. (at St. Marks Ave.)

**Subway:** 7 Av — Lunch Sun
**Phone:** 718-942-4255 — Dinner Tue – Sun
**Web:** www.jamesrestaurantny.com
**Prices:** $$

The concise menu at James first may appear simple and straightforward, like the establishment's moniker. However, plump, roasted quail stuffed with homemade duck sausage; crispy, seared salmon served on a bed of leek stew; and grilled lemon-almond pound cake accompanied by a scoop of blueberry-streaked ice cream, are all the proof one needs to see the level of sophistication and skill at work in the kitchen.

Likewise, the dining room housed on a tree-lined corner of Prospect Heights displays signs of refinement with a space accented in whitewashed brick walls and espresso-dark leather and wood furnishings. Warm lighting adds a flattering glow throughout, and the comfortable bar is nicely appointed by a vintage mirror and floral arrangements.

# Jolie

D3 — French XX

320 Atlantic Ave. (bet. Smith & Hoyt Sts. )

**Subway:** Bergen St — Lunch & dinner daily
**Phone:** 718-488-0777
**Web:** www.jolierestaurant.com
**Prices:** $$

Set on a rather nondescript stretch of Atlantic Avenue, Jolie beckons diners in Boerum Hill with its planters of greenery that decorate the sidewalk out front. Inside, a semi-circular marble-topped bar dominates the front of the restaurant, while the large dining room is in back. Walls do double duty as an art gallery; changing exhibits fill the space, lending an élan and sophistication to this *petit* bistro. As pleasant as the place is, the pièce de résistance is the walled garden area, *très jolie* indeed with its shade trees, flowering vines, and market umbrellas.

Classic bistro fare fills the menu with such French favorites as roasted chicken breast stuffed with ricotta and fresh herbs; *escargots de Bourgogne;* and steak tartare *au Cognac.*

# Karczma

Polish

B1

136 Greenpoint Ave. (bet. Franklin St. & Manhattan Ave.)

**Subway:** Greenpoint Av

Lunch & dinner daily

**Phone:** 718-349-1744

**Web:** www.karczmabrooklyn.com

**Prices:** ©©

Located in a section of Greenpoint that still boasts a sizeable Polish population, Karczma offers a lovely old-world ambience that fits perfectly with its lengthy menu boasting hearty servings of traditional specialties. The pierogis, offered in three varieties, can be steamed but are even better fried, topped with sliced onions and drizzled with butter—the lean, chopped-meat filling is ethereal. A generous listing of main courses feature grilled platters for two or three; soul-satisfying stews; and an excellent (if outrageously large) paprika-dusted pork shank braised in beer, with fluffy mashed potatoes and caraway-scented cabbage.

The charmingly rustic space is efficiently staffed by smiling servers in floral skirts and embroidered vests.

# Kif

Moroccan

D3

219 DeKalb Ave. (bet. Adelphi St.& Clermont Ave.)

**Subway:** Lafayette Av

Lunch Sat – Sun

**Phone:** 718-852-7273

Dinner nightly

**Web:** www.kifbrooklyn.com

**Prices:** $$

Wanted: adorable bohemian spot in Brooklyn with sexy velvet banquettes, billowing linens draped from the ceiling, and a leafy outdoor garden. Food should be creative, exotic, and fresh—authenticity a plus.

Kif, a clever new Moroccan spot in Fort Greene, fits the bill perfectly—mostly because the Algerian owner keeps his standards a mile high by having a completely open kitchen, where diners can watch the chefs work delicious amounts of imported spices and oils into lip-smacking good small plates like a spot-on *zaalouk*; a plate of smoky roasted eggplant purée with roasted red peppers and flecks of bright green parsley; or a plate of moist, tender grilled merguez sausages dusted with cumin and chili, and set atop a thick and smoky *harissa* sauce.

# Ki Sushi

C3 — **Japanese**

122 Smith St. (bet. Dean & Pacific Sts.)

**Subway:** Bergen St
**Phone:** 718-935-0575
**Web:** www.ki-sushi.com
**Prices:** $$

Lunch Mon – Sat
Dinner nightly

Count sushi among Smith Street's wealth of dining options. At Ki, the impressive quality and talent continue to satisfy a devoted clientele relishing the raw and the cooked in a Zen-chic space complete with a gently flowing wall of water and potted flowers.

The smiling sushi team works from a long counter stocked with a tempting array of pristine fish. The sushi and sashimi are excellent, as is the whimsical and visually appealing maki, like the Fashion Roll of chopped tuna, jalapeño, and yuzu *tobiko* wrapped in slices of raw scallop. Preparations such as rock shrimp tempura drizzled with spiced mayonnaise emerge from the small kitchen located in back.

The genuinely friendly and attentive service adds to the charm of this Cobble Hill favorite.

# La Maison du Couscous

A4 — **Moroccan**

484 77th St. (bet. Fourth & Fifth Aves. )

**Subway:** 77 St
**Phone:** 718-921-2400
**Web:** www.lamaisonducouscous.com
**Prices:** $$

Lunch & dinner Wed – Mon

Tucked just off of Bay Ridge's bustling Fifth Avenue, this teeny-tiny French-Moroccan restaurant—with its exotic mix of bright silk pillows, Moroccan ceramics, and festive lanterns—packs a mighty big flavor punch.

In addition to the traditional tagines and kebabs (all delicious in their own right), the menu offers up a savory rotation of dishes like plump, cinnamon-dusted phyllo cigars, filled with spicy chicken; or a sublime house paella of fresh shellfish and tender cuttlefish rings, tossed with chickpeas and served over a fluffy pile of couscous simmering in a heady, thyme-studded seafood broth. Save room for a sliver of flaky, baklava made from scratch, paired with a glass of wine from the restaurant's long-awaited beer and wine list.

# La Superior

A1 — **Mexican**

## 295 Berry St. (bet. S. 2nd & S. 3rd Sts.)

**Subway:** Bedford Av — Lunch & dinner daily
**Phone:** 718-388-5988
**Web:** www.lasuperiornyc.com
**Prices:** ©©

La Superior offers a fun and authentically delicious south of the border dining experience that even the city's West Coast transplants should find impressive. The restaurant's name is scrawled tattoo-like across the front of its painted brick façade, alluding to the simplistic décor: chile-red walls, vintage Mexican movie posters, and food served on colorful plastic plates.

Liquor is not available, but Mexican sodas and *aguas frescas* are offered to wash down the inexpensive fare. Highlights may include crispy flautas dressed with excellent salsa verde; *panuchos de cochinita* (slow cooked pork and mashed black beans atop a thick tortilla); and tacos like the surprisingly decadent *rajas*, filled with strips of roasted poblanos and tangy *crema*.

# Le Petit Marché

C3 — **French**

## 46 Henry St. (bet. Cranberry & Middagh Sts.)

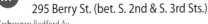

**Subway:** High St — Dinner Tue – Sun
**Phone:** 718-858-9605
**Web:** www.bkBistro.com
**Prices:** $$

This quintessential bistro styles a cozy atmosphere of exposed brick walls, dark woods, lusty red and gold wallpaper, with paper-topped tables. More intimate than many of its neighbors, the "little market" fosters romance with candlelit tables nestling close together.

The husband-and-wife duo that own this spot manage the dining room with true hospitality; she is happy to assist with selections from the fairly-priced wine list. Gallic comfort food comes in combinations like pan-seared *magret* of duck set atop luscious chestnut purée, plated with plump cherries; or country pâté served atop mesclun salad with fig compote.

This charming *boîte* opened the day after Christmas in 2006, and from the looks of things, will be celebrating many holidays yet to come.

# Locanda Vini & Olii

D3

Italian

129 Gates Ave. (at Cambridge Pl.)

**Subway:** Clinton - Washington Avs
Dinner Tue – Sun
**Phone:** 718-622-9202
**Web:** www.locandany.com
**Prices:** $$

With its enchanting atmosphere, well-prepared rustic Italian cuisine, and personalized service, Locanda Vini & Olii merits a trip out to Brooklyn. François Louy, who owns the restaurant with his wife, Catherine, warmly greets guests to this Clinton Hill eatery. Housed in a century-old drugstore, the cozy dining room employs the former apothecary shelves and drawers to display cookbooks, wine bottles, and vintage kitchen equipment.

The cuisine, deeply rooted in Tuscan tradition, is often reinterpreted. Thus mildly sweet chestnut-flavored lasagna noodles might be layered with ground pork sausage, caramelized onions, and chickpeas; and grilled duck breast served simply with pan juices and a dollop of shallot marmalade.

If you're dining with a party of four or more, call ahead to request a tasting menu.

# Lucky Eight

A4

Chinese

5204 Eighth Ave. (bet. 52nd & 53rd Sts. )

**Subway:** 8 Av
Lunch & dinner daily
**Phone:** 718-851-8862
**Web:** N/A
**Prices:** ⊜

With its plethora of dim sum spots, Chinese bakeries, and markets hawking everything from live bull frogs to fresh silky tofu, Sunset Park has emerged as Brooklyn's prominent Chinatown. From this, Lucky Eight's excellent food, good service, and pristine setting is an authentic and rewarding find.

Until late afternoon, pick from a list of some 40 items priced at 80 cents each. The laminated dinner menu is crammed with pages illustrating unique, regional Chinese fare. The aptly named signature dish, Pride of Lucky Eight, offers a sumptuous stir-fry of chives, celery, shiitake, and meaty abalone.

The highlight of the no-frills décor is the red-lacquer case at the back of the room, displaying shark fins and other artifacts.

# Maria's Bistro Mexicano

B3 Mexican

886 Fifth Ave. (bet. 37th & 38th Sts.)

**Subway:** 36 St Lunch & dinner daily
**Phone:** 718-438-1608
**Web:** www.mariasbistromexicano.com
**Prices:** $$

Instantly amiable, with good food, excellent service, and no pretensions, dining at Maria's is akin to enjoying a meal with a dear friend. The bright-orange awning and open door invite customers from this industrial area of Sunset Park into Maria's cocoon-like space, where low lighting balances the vibrant wall colors.

At the back, a display of perfectly ripe, creamy avocados entices guests to begin with made-to-order guacamole. Menu items may include a chile relleno oozing with three cheeses, paired with a lusty chile sauce, at once creamy and smoky. Specials laud the kitchen's abilities; the lusciously flavored pork loin stuffed with zucchini blossoms and roasted poblanos is presented as an alluring package on its colorful earthenware plate.

# Marlow & Sons

A1 Gastropub

81 Broadway (bet. Berry St. &Wythe Ave. )

**Subway:** Marcy Av Lunch & dinner daily
**Phone:** 718-384-1441
**Web:** www.marlowandsons.com
**Prices:** $$

By day, Marlow & Sons offers sandwiches and pastries in an urbane country store setting where shelves are chock-full of provisions that include artisanal cheeses, gourmet pickles, and local honey. But at night, the back room becomes a jovial setting for dinner with its shabby-chic furnishings, sexy lighting, and lively crowd. The unassuming blackboard listing of specials may be difficult to read, but items like polenta soup, dressed with Parmesan and olive oil; or a salted caramel tart topped with chocolate ganache makes the effort quite rewarding. Know that behind this simply stated menu is a sophisticated kitchen.

To enhance the spirited atmosphere, there is a selection of boutique sparkling wines on the well-chosen list.

# Mesa Coyoacan

Mexican

C1

372 Graham Ave. (bet. Conselyea St. & Skillman Ave.)

**Subway:** Graham Av
**Phone:** 718-782-8171
**Web:** www.mesacoyoacan.com
**Prices:** $$

Lunch Sat – Sun
Dinner nightly

Who knows what possessed the talented Ivan Garcia, the Mexican-born chef who banged out menus for Barrio Chino and Mercadito, to cross the bridge and set up his first solo venture in East Williamsburg's infamous glass tower—but every Brooklynite within spitting distance of this sexy new joint is thanking their sweet fedoras he did.

It's not just the swank interior, fitted out in richly-patterned wallpapers, snug banquettes and two long communal tables, but the mouthwatering Mexican food: tender little tacos stuffed with fragrant *birria*; chicken enchiladas in Garcia's family's *mole poblano* recipe; or *chiles en nogada*, a roasted poblano pepper stuffed with shredded pork, almonds, and fruit, laced with creamy walnut sauce and pomegranate seeds.

# Moim

Korean

D4

206 Garfield Pl. (at Seventh Ave.)

**Subway:** Grand Army Plaza
**Phone:** 718-499-8092
**Web:** www.moimrestaurant.com
**Prices:** $$

Lunch & dinner Tue – Sun

Well-known for its dining diversity, Park Slope now adds Korean as one more worldly option with Moim, tucked away on a charming brownstone-lined street. The slender space mixes a chic palette of dark wood, cement grey, and green apple, with a small front bar where guests wait for tables while sipping lime and ginger *shojutinis*.

Moim translates as "gathering," and the sizeable tables encourage sharing of the menu's polished yet inspired takes on Korean classics. The Korean "tapas" are a fine start, followed by delish *pa jun*—thick, smooth-textured pancakes copiously filled with tender scallion greens, squid, and shrimp; while hearty portions of meaty spare ribs in sweet-smoky sauce are creatively accompanied by caramelized chunks of diced sweet potatoes.

# Motorino

Pizza

C1

319 Graham Ave. (at Devoe St.)

**Subway:** Graham Av — Lunch & dinner daily
**Phone:** 718-599-8899
**Web:** www.motorinopizza.com
**Prices:**

This upscale pizzeria draws in a steady flow of passers-by with its seductive aroma of wood-oven baked pies. Embracing Neapolitan tradition, Mototrino's Belgian-born chef/owner trained in Italy and is certified by the *Verace Pizza Napoletana*. These impressive pizzas feature San Marzano tomatoes, *fior di latte* (upgrade to *mozzarella di bufala* for a nominal charge), and seasonal toppings in combinations like fresh artichoke hearts, smoked pancetta, and black olives. A simple selection of antipasti such as fire-roasted mortadella and a few sweets like *bombolini* (fresh donuts filled with the likes of crème anglaise), round out the menu.
The pleasant space is furnished with white marble-topped tables, pressed tin ceiling, and an open kitchen in back.

# Noodle Pudding

Italian

C3

38 Henry St. (bet. Cranberry & Middagh Sts.)

**Subway:** High St — Dinner Tue – Sun
**Phone:** 718-625-3737
**Web:** N/A
**Prices:** $$

Named after a savory pudding baked with noodles and traditionally served on the Sabbath, Noodle Pudding embodies all the essential qualities that make up a beloved neighborhood restaurant.
For starters, there's no sign on the door; Brooklyn Heights' cognoscenti know where to come for good, honest Italian food. Servers are helpful and well-versed about the food and wine. An air of relaxation pervades the room, with its well-spaced bistro tables, terra-cotta floor, and soundtrack of American crooners.
Uniformly wonderful, top-quality meats, fish, and produce fill a menu that lists everything from inexpensive daily specials (rabbit marinated in red wine, then slowly braised and plated with polenta) to pasta and roasted prime rib.

# No. 7

American

D3

7 Greene Ave. (bet. Cumberland & Fulton Sts.)

**Subway:** Lafayette Av
**Phone:** 718-522-6370
**Web:** www.no7restaurant.com
**Prices:** $$

Lunch Sun
Dinner Tue – Sun

Fort Greene gets a significant notch on its foodie belt with the highly-anticipated No. 7. Perched just above the C train, the unique, sunken space is anchored by an energetic bar scene up front; and a clean, white-washed dining room in back, that dims into a lovely muted palette with candles.

Chef Tyler Kord, who used to work at Jean-Georges Vongerichten's Perry Street, heads up the talented young team—and the limited, but well-executed, menu reflects his former boss' eye for detail. Try the soft, melt-in-your-mouth, crimson-red lamb carpaccio; or a tight *ballotine* of succulent roasted chicken. And save room for one of the surprising desserts, like an apple tart kicked up with a smear of goat cheese mousse and drops of heat-spiked honey.

# Pacificana

Chinese

A4

813 55th St. (at Eighth Ave.)

**Subway:** 8 Av
**Phone:** 718-871-2880
**Web:** N/A
**Prices:** $$

Lunch & dinner daily

Sunset Park has become New York City's newest spot for Chinese food, thanks largely to its fast-growing, uniquely diverse Asian population. This immaculate second-floor space, with crimson walls, vaulted ceilings, and semi-open kitchen framed by floor-to-ceiling fish tanks, is an elegant alternative to the bustle of Flushing's Chinatown. The mammoth size and efficient service make this an ideal venue for groups.

Sit back and relax while the smiling staff parades dim sum carts, overflowing with a tempting array of fresh fare, like tender steamed shrimp dumplings, or crispy cold pork on a bed of jelly fish and daikon. A full regular menu offers house specialties like south China duck casserole, or an extensive offering of traditional favorites.

# The Pearl Room

Contemporary XX

A4

## 8201 Third Ave. (at 82nd St.)

**Subway:** 86 St

Lunch & dinner daily

**Phone:** 718-833-6666

**Web:** www.thepearlroom.com

**Prices:** $$

With its jumbo garden and bright, sun-streaked dining room, this Brooklyn steady is a solid choice year-round. Most days, you'll catch a glimpse of the charming Chef/owner Anthony Rinaldi floating around, working his magic back in the kitchen and out in the dining room.

The Pearl Room is known for its vast seafood spread, and Rinaldi's wheelhouse is intricately designed fish plates like a lemon sole, coated in golden breading and pine nuts, and then tossed in a perfectly balanced lemongrass-kiwi sauce. But don't discount his other offerings—the menu boasts a wealth of vegetarian and meat dishes, many of them ample enough to split, as well as a few tongue-wagging desserts like a trio of luscious chocolate truffles rolled in bright green pistachios.

# Picket Fence

American X

B4

## 1310 Cortelyou Rd. (at Argyle Rd.)

**Subway:** Cortelyou Rd

Lunch & dinner daily

**Phone:** 718-282-6661

**Web:** www.picketfencebrooklyn.com

**Prices:** $$

Nestled into Ditmas Park, a slowly gentrifying Brooklyn neighborhood lined with Victorian homes and (gasp) real live trees, Picket Fence is pure comfort. In spring, the wide doors swing open to the sidewalk, flooding light into the beautiful, sunny dining room, lined with rattan chairs and cozy banquettes. Out back, a cheerful little garden offers waddle space for the hood's growing baby scene.

The no-fuss food does what it does simply and deliciously—with a broad menu that might include a scrumptious turkey meatloaf sandwich, the tender slices of meat studded with carrots, onions, and spices, and loaded onto a brioche bun with gravy, caramelized onions, and cheddar cheese; or a walnut-crusted sliver of cheesecake laced with strawberry compote.

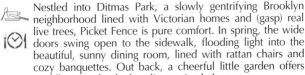

# Peter Luger ✿

A1 — Steakhouse

178 Broadway (at Driggs Ave.)

**Subway:** Marcy Av — Lunch & dinner daily
**Phone:** 718-387-7400
**Web:** www.peterluger.com
**Prices:** **$$$**

Peter Luger

Only rookies open the menu at Luger's. The loyal-as-sin clientele doesn't even crack one at this iconic Brooklyn steakhouse, tucked into an industrial street beside the Williamsburg Bridge. Sure, there are a few things in there to divert your attention, like the killer cheesecake or the freshly ground burger (served at lunch only), which is quickly developing cult status amongst the city's burger hounds.

But the star of this show is indisputably the Porterhouse—and the pros order it by number for the table ("porterhouse for 2, 3, or 4"), assign a temperature, and then tack on a few delicious sides like garlicky creamed spinach, crispy hash browns, or the thick, and irresistible, bacon.

But about that steak: prepare thyself. It's liable to be some of the best—if not the best—you'll ever sink your fangs into: dry-aged to perfection, lovingly charred and sliced into juicy pink ribbons of beefy splendor. The all-male waitstaff is knowingly gruff, but it seems to fit the bright, clanking beer hall atmosphere. If they give you too much lip, remind them that the women—not the men—hold Luger's illustrious buyer position, choosing the steaks best fit to be served in this den of macho.

# Prime Meats

Gastropub

C4

465 Court St. (at Luquer St.)

**Subway:** Smith - 9 Sts.
**Phone:** 718-254-0327
**Web:** www.frankspm.com
**Prices:** $$

Lunch & dinner daily

From the Franks (of Frankies 457 Spuntino) comes this new neighborhood fave that was inspired by a vintage sign purchased prior to the restaurant's inception. Exposed brick, dark wood furnishings, and filament-bulbs set an almost too perfect scene for throngs of Brooklyn's food cognoscenti who line the seat-less bar sipping expertly crafted libations.

Once seated, the personable staff and friendly vibe relegates any memory of a wait time to the past, especially once a selection of small plates and house specials arrives. Simplicity reigns supreme as in a celery salad of stalks, leaves, and root dressed with cider vinaigrette; grilled rib-eye of grass-fed beef, and a dessert option that can include a linzer tart, filled with homemade raspberry jam.

# Quercy

French

C3

242 Court St. (bet. Baltic & Kane Sts.)

**Subway:** Bergen St
**Phone:** 718-243-2151
**Web:** N/A
**Prices:** $$

Lunch Sat – Sun
Dinner nightly

Named for the chef's hometown in southern France, Quercy is a truly satisfying destination for authentic bistro fare. With its cobalt blue façade, checkerboard-tile floor, and a chalkboard scrawled *carte*, this Cobble Hill charmer emanates a comforting aura. The blue and white color scheme is nicely accented with touches of red, and the small art deco bar is a cozy spot to sip an aperitif prior to sitting at one of the dining room's white-paper-topped tables, tended by a cordial staff.

As one would hope and expect, the menu serves up heartwarming classics like *escargot au Cognac*; fork-tender bœuf Bourguignon; and tarte Tatin dressed with a dollop of crème fraîche, along with a wine list that highlights the varietals of southwestern France.

# River Café ✿

Contemporary XXX

C2

1 Water St. (bet. Furman & Old Fulton Sts.)

**Subway:** High St — Lunch & dinner daily
**Phone:** 718-522-5200
**Web:** www.rivercafe.com
**Prices:** **$$$$**

Noah Kalina/The River Café

When Michael "Buzzy" O'Keefe first opened the doors to his now-celebrated River Café back in 1977, the choice of location probably struck most as odd. Tucked into a sketchy slice of abandoned waterfront underneath the towering Brooklyn Bridge, the street had the kind of face only a Mother—or O'Keefe—could love.

But it did have that view—and now, over thirty years later, the area is gorgeously restored, and a history-filled walk across the bridge and into this Brooklyn neighborhood, with its cobblestoned streets and small-town vibe, is a must-do afternoon for any self-respecting New Yorker.

Resting at the foot of Water Street, along the water, you'll find a perfect cap to the day in River Café—where guests can meander through gorgeous gardens, soak in mind-boggling views of the Manhattan skyline and bridge, and dig into delicious contemporary fare like a plate of vibrant, fruitwood-smoked salmon, plated over a creamy streak of chive sauce and paired with a sesame waffle crisp piped with silky crème fraîche and thumped with a dollop of wild Sturgeon caviar; or tender fillets of lemon sole, packed with silky poached artichoke hearts, and laced with a *verjus* beurre blanc sauce.

# Roberta's

Pizza

C2

261 Moore St. (bet. Bogart & White Sts.)

**Subway:** Morgan Av

Lunch & dinner daily

**Phone:** 718-417-1118

**Web:** www.robertaspizza.com

**Prices:** ⊗⊗

A hip new pizza joint moves into an up-and-coming Brooklyn neighborhood—and the buzz begins. Roberta's made a big splash in 2008 when it opened in super-industrial Bushwick, potentially the next Williamsburg. Surrounded by warehouses and deserted lots, there's not a lot to welcome you in, but once inside you'll find a cozy little spot with communal tables and stacks of fire wood.

The star of this show is Roberta's reclaimed brick oven, which pushes out beautifully bubbling pies both classical, like the Margherita loaded with creamy mozzarella and fresh basil; and creative, like the one sporting egg and *guanciale*. A more extensive dinner menu reveals a bevy of rustic plates as well, like wood-roasted chicken and pappardelle with lamb ragù.

# Rye

American

A1

247 S. 1st St. (bet. Havemeyer and Roebling Sts.)

**Subway:** Marcy Av

Dinner Tue – Sun

**Phone:** 718-218-8047

**Web:** www.ryerestaurant.com

**Prices:** $$

Chef/owner Cal Elliott's new solo venture is housed in a non-descript section of south Williamsburg that coolly lacks any signage to promote its existence. The former bodega is outfitted with rough hewn wood flooring, zinc-topped tables, and exposed filament bulbs. The hefty bar, restored by the chef, dominates the intimate room; arched, mirror-backed shelving is stocked with a collection of brown liquors.

The succinct menu of snacks and grilled items boasts classic touches that reflect the kitchen's talents and skill. Offerings may include housemade gnocchi, topped with shreds of meltingly tender duck confit; golden and crisped, pan-roasted halibut drizzled with herb-flecked beurre blanc; or warm and fudgy chocolate cake with vanilla ice cream.

# Saul ✿

C3 **Contemporary** XX

140 Smith St. (bet. Bergen & Dean Sts.)

**Subway:** Bergen St — Dinner nightly
**Phone:** 718-935-9844
**Web:** www.saulrestaurant.com
**Prices:** $$$

Tyson Reist

Tucked into Boerum Hill's Smith Street—with its bustling sidewalks, adorable storefronts, and hip boutiques—Saul operates on a higher plane than the neighborhood's considerable other restaurant talent.

It could be the quaint brick-lined interior, splashed with artwork; or the perfect timing of the precise, but warm, staff; or even simply the good vibes set forth by the happy buzz of friends catching up after a hard day in the city. But none of that is what really earns this restaurant a seat at the big table. As your Uncle Saul might tell you with a slap to the noggin—it's the food, stupid.

Blame this delicious elitism on co-owner and chef, Saul Bolton, who cut his teeth with the legendary Eric Ripert—and clearly brought his master's penchant for intricate technique and pristine seafood across the river with him. A seasonal amuse, like a creamy lentil soup chock-full with root vegetables, sets the stage for carefully sourced fare like fresh mackerel, cut into a silky diamond and paired with a sweet and savory eggplant caponata; or a thick wedge of swordfish, topped with crispy kale fronds and spicy rounds of chorizo slices, set atop a rosemary-dusted white bean purée.

# Savoia

Italian

C4

277 Smith St. (bet. De Graw & Sackett Sts. )

**Subway:** Carroll St
Lunch & dinner daily
**Phone:** 718-797-2727
**Web:** N/A
**Prices:** $$

Whether young at-home moms, lunching construction crews, or savvy foreign visitors, all walks of life are drawn to this Smith Street charmer, pastorally furnished with wooden tables and straw-seat chairs. Exposed brick and colorful tiles complement the two-room setting, equipped with a wood-burning pizza oven. Fittingly, Savoia devotes a large portion of its menu to manifold pizza offerings made in the Neopolitan tradition. Not in the mood for pizza? There is also an ample selection of gratifying pastas, like the linguine with clams (heightened here with ground *soppressata*); as well as heartier items like the roasted pork chop with eggplant caponata and grilled *orata* with sun dried tomatoes.
Affable service adds to Savoia's casual vibe.

# Sea

Thai

A1

114 N. 6th St. (bet. Berry St. & Wythe Ave.)

**Subway:** Bedford Av
Lunch & dinner daily
**Phone:** 718-384-8850
**Web:** www.spicethainyc.com
**Prices:**

Resembling a trendy Manhattan lounge yet serving fresh, well-made Thai cuisine, Sea is an exotic bird among the small hipster bars of Williamsburg. The cavernous space pulsates with energy, and its popularity is enjoyed by a diverse clientele, from young families to large after-work groups. The dining room, flanked by two bars, has an industrial-chic vibe with its concrete floor and cement walls complemented by a section of seating around a reflecting pool crowned by a life-size Buddha. Considering the festive environs, the staff is impressively gracious and attentive.
The Thai-focused menu is reasonably priced and extensive in its offerings of dumplings, spring rolls, and salads, along with curries and sautéed dishes available with a choice of protein.

# Sette Enoteca & Cucina

D4 — Italian

207 Seventh Ave. (at 3rd St.)

**Subway:** 7 Av — Lunch & dinner daily
**Phone:** 718-499-7767
**Web:** www.setteparkslope.com
**Prices:** $$

This consistently excellent Park Slope Italian is popular with most everyone—from cool couples lingering over shared plates of light, crispy *fritto misto*, to hip moms twirling pappardelle with braised rabbit and wild mushrooms, alongside their offspring sharing pizzas. Rustic entrées offer the likes of grilled salmon over fava beans; these skillful preparations can be observed from the open kitchen.

Complement meals with selections from the all-Italian wine list, a range of bottles priced under $20, and many labels available by the glass or *quartino*.

This bustling corner location features covered outdoor dining, a bar, and a contemporary dining room with chunky, blonde wooden tables, and metallic-fabric-covered banquettes.

# Silent H

A1 — Vietnamese

79 Berry St. (at 9th St.)

**Subway:** Bedford Av — Lunch & dinner Tue – Sun
**Phone:** 718-218-7063
**Web:** www.silenthbrooklyn.com
**Prices:** ⊜

Chef/owner Vinh Nguyen struggled to find a Vietnamese restaurant to impress his visiting family, so he decided to open his own. Located on a quiet "Billyburg" corner, the pleasant room has a comfortable bar area and black-and-white photos of Vietnamese street scenes beneath ceiling fans with leaf-shaped blades.

The concise menu is composed of unique and flavorful dishes that are based on the cooking of Nguyen's family. The likes of wok-fried cubes of "shaken beef" and sautéed lemongrass chicken highlight the kitchen's use of of top-quality ingredients. A selection of "Viet-Tapas" may feature various rolls, shrimp toast, and beef carpaccio. Lunchtime offers the celebrated *banh mi*—crusty baguettes filled with meat and pickled vegetables.

# The Smoke Joint

Barbecue

D3

87 S. Elliot Pl. (bet. Fulton St & Lafayette Ave. )

**Subway:** Lafayette Av — Lunch & dinner daily
**Phone:** 718-797-1011
**Web:** www.thesmokejoint.com
**Prices:** ⚭

You may leave smelling of hickory smoke, but the taste left in your mouth from this fantastic barbecue joint is worth the stares. Settle down, grab a beer, and dig into seriously smoky ribs coated with "jointrub"—a secret house recipe—and sandwiches, all served with a variety of sauces, including the lip-smacking-good "jointsmoke" and the spicy "hollapeno" varieties. Sides include the usual suspects, but the cayenne-spiked mac and cheese and the smoky, molasses-flavored barbecued beans are perfect.

Steps away from the esteemed BAM, the setting is laid-back, and the staff is energetic, smiling, and just plain fun. Great prices leave an even better taste in your mouth. For Bed-Stuy residents, owners Craig and Ben have opened up a Southern spot, Peaches.

# Stone Park Cafe

Contemporary

D4

324 Fifth Ave. (at 3rd St.)

**Subway:** Union St — Lunch Tue – Sun, Dinner nightly
**Phone:** 718-369-0082
**Web:** www.stoneparkcafe.com
**Prices:** $$

At this corner location, large windows peer onto Park Slope's vibrant Fifth Avenue thoroughfare and small park that is its namesake. Approaching five years in the area, Stone Park Cafe remains popular with neighborhood couples and families seeking seasonally inspired, creative fare. Offerings may range from smoked salmon cheesecake to lamb cassoulet. The $30 prix-fixe menu option is a very good value for such quality.

The light and airy interior is simply accented with exposed brick, light wood, and pale sage walls. A long bar near the entrance is a welcome spot for a pre-dinner cocktail. In the sunken dining room, tables are covered with white linens, brown paper, and clear glass votives. Weather permitting, alfresco sidewalk seating is available.

# Thomas Beisl

D3 — Austrian

25 Lafayette Ave. (bet. Ashland Pl. & St. Felix St.)

**Subway:** Atlantic Ave - Pacific St — Lunch Tue – Sun
**Phone:** 718-222-5800 — Dinner nightly
**Web:** N/A
**Prices:**

This Austrian *beisl* (bistro) brings Fort Greene to life with Viennese charm, thanks to Chef/owner Thomas Ferlesch, former executive chef of Café des Artistes.

Located across from the Brooklyn Academy of Music, Thomas Beisl conjures the quintessential bistro, with its white-paper-topped tables, terrazzo floor, and blackboard scrawled with the daily specials. The engaging and attentive staff complete this picture.

The menu is a culinary homage to old-world Vienna, with traditional wiener schnitzel (or innovative versions, prepared with celeriac or cod); beef goulash; and homemade bratwurst rounding out the selections. While this is a great spot to meet for a beer, concertgoers also drop by for a perfect post-performance slice of linzer torte.

# Tuscany Grill

A4 — Italian

8620 Third Ave. (bet. 86th & 87th Sts. )

**Subway:** 86 St — Dinner nightly
**Phone:** 718-921-5633
**Web:** N/A
**Prices:** $$

Bay Ridge's ever-changing demographic does not deter this charismatic, quintessential neighborhood restaurant from serving Italian-American favorites to a loyal cadre of locals who come for dishes that burst with flavor as well as to share their latest adventures with the waitstaff.

The menu offers hefty portions of honest, good food, such as homey Hunter-style *farfalle* pasta baked in tomatoes, mushrooms, cheese, with sweet and hot sausage. Crostini of fresh, milky ricotta, roasted red bell pepper, and basil leaf over toast brushed with quality olive oil makes a wonderful prelude to any meal. Save room for decadent house-made desserts such as the pignoli tart—lemony and piney—served in a crust that is truly worth every buttery calorie.

# Vinegar Hill House

American

D2

72 Hudson Ave. (near Water St.)

**Subway:** York St — Lunch Sat – Sun
**Phone:** 718-522-1018 — Dinner Tue – Sun
**Web:** www.vinegarhillhouse.com
**Prices:** $$

Which came first, the neighborhood or the restaurant? It's hard to tell in the case of Vinegar Hill House, a popular new restaurant named for the up-and-coming neighborhood it resides in. And for the hip new occupants of this lonely stretch between DUMBO and the Brooklyn Navy Yards, Sam Buffa and Jean Adamson's cozy little restaurant couldn't have arrived at a more ideal moment.

Anyone familiar with Brooklyn's new uniform will recognize the homey, hodge-podge interior and claims of sustainable fish. What sets this place apart is its wood burning oven, which might produce perfectly-charred sourdough bread, served with a creamy smear of liver pâté; or a savory lamb, mushroom, and root vegetable ragù on a soft pile of fresh pappardelle.

# Vutera

Mediterranean

A1

345 Grand St. (bet. Havemeyer St. & Marcy Ave. )

**Subway:** Bedford Av — Dinner nightly
**Phone:** 718-388-8451
**Web:** N/A
**Prices:** $$

Head to the Rose Live Music performance space, bypass the lounge's tattooed bartender, and descend a small flight of stairs to reach this basement restaurant replete with a charmingly rough-hewn cellar look that will have you wondering if you've fallen down a rabbit hole. Bathed in candlelight, the setting is cloaked in exposed brick and stone, and furnished with flower-topped tables set with a mix-and-match collection of chairs.

The menu's sunny flavors are abundant in small plates like the fresh Spanish mackerel *escabeche* with ruby grapefruit; or entrées of tender, pan-fried parsnip gnocchi with a pesto of beet greens and blue cheese sauce. The honey-drizzled cannoli filled with Salvatore Brooklyn ricotta thinks globally and acts locally.

# Water Falls Café

C3 — Middle Eastern

144 Atlantic Ave. (bet. Clinton & Henry Sts. )

**Subway:** Atlantic Av — Lunch & dinner daily
**Phone:** 718-488-8886
**Web:** www.waterfallscafe.com
**Prices:** $$

In contrast to its simple white walls and minimal décor, this family-run favorite dishes up terrific food, excellent value, brims with hospitality, and rises well above the smattering of Middle Eastern restaurants on Brooklyn's Atlantic Avenue.

Feisty and good-humored, the owner makes sure diners are well accommodated; her mothering encourages guests to eat every last bite—or at least take any leftovers home. The menu features outstanding Middle Eastern fare, such as perfectly prepared hummus, shish kabob, *kibbeh*, and some of the best *fattoush* this side of the Arabian Sea.

An extensive list of freshly squeezed juices along with strong Arabic coffee and sweet mint tea compensate for the lack of alcohol here, and takeout is a terrific option.

# World Tong

B4 — Chinese

6202 Eighteenth Ave. (at 62nd St.)

**Subway:** 18 Av — Lunch & dinner daily
**Phone:** 718-236-8118
**Web:** N/A
**Prices:** $$

With its bland dining room and unadorned interior, this monochromatic Bensonhurst gem gets right down to business by putting its money where its customers mouths would like to be—wrapped around some killer dim sum. And judging from the flood of locals who patron the joint, this no-nonsense approach appears to be right on cue.

Dreamy carts wheeling past showcase an endless array of tiny delights, like sticky-rice dumplings wrapped in lotus leaves; golden shrimp balls; or spare ribs with black bean sauce and taro. Don't miss the phenomenal parade of tender soup dumplings, a variety of soft pouches bursting with spice-infused broths, including star anise, clove, and ginger; or the strange-smelling, but oddly addictive, durian pastries.

# Zenkichi

Japanese XX

A1

77 N. 6th St. (at Wythe Ave.)

**Subway:** Bedford Av  Dinner Wed – Sun
**Phone:** 718-388-8985
**Web:** www.zenkichi.com
**Prices:** $$

Beyond a rather forbidding wood-armored exterior, Zenkichi's small entryway is practically camouflaged. Once inside however, warm greetings ensue as you and your party are escorted through the dim, three-level space to a private dining booth. When ready to order, summon a server with the tabletop call button.

The *izakaya* menu features an assortment of snacks designed to be enjoyed with sake. Going à la carte is fine, but more impressive is the reasonably priced omakase: an eight-course seasonal feast that may feature chilled edamame soup; remarkably sweet blue shrimp tempura; rice cooked in dashi and topped with soy-marinated sea bream; or sake-infused cheesecake.

A return visit here is inevitable—just be sure to call ahead for a reservation.

Your opinions are important to us. Please write to us at: michelin.guides@us.michelin.com

Brooklyn

Jeanine C. Hart/MICHELIN

# Queens

# Queens



Nearly as large as Manhattan, the Bronx, and Staten Island combined, the borough of Queens covers 120 square miles on the western end of Long Island. Thousands of immigrants arriving here each year make Queens the most culturally diverse county in the country. They are drawn to the relatively affordable housing, a familial quality of life, and the tight-knit cultural communities formed by extended immigrant families. Such a unique convergence results in the borough's international flavor, drawing throngs of New Yorkers eager to dine on affordable, ethnic eats.

A seven mile span along The International Express (the 7 train) passes through the global smorgasbord that Queens offers. Restaurants off each stop along the way reflect the borough's ever-changing diversity. It's a microcosm of our immigrant-driven nation's culinary explosion.

Stroll through Astoria, a charming quarter of brick row houses and Mediterranean groceries. Discover grilled octopus and baklava at one of the many terrific Greek restaurants; make your way to Little Egypt on Steinway Street for a juicy kebab; or chow on Czech kielbasas at the local *biergarten*.

Flushing still reigns as Queens' most vibrant Asian neighborhood; drop in for dim sum or slurp an avocado shake and a savory bowl of piping hot *pho* like you'd find street side in Saigon. Food vendors at Flushing's mini-malls are a feast for the ravenous that's light on pockets with delights from every corner of China. You'll find anything at these stalls including hand pulled noodles, fiery Sichuan chili-oil dishes, peking duck pancakes, *bings*, and buns in a bustling setting that's right out of a Hong Kong alley. Flushing is also home the Mets' new digs, **Citi Field**. Here stadium food has gotten serious: Famed Union Square Hospitality Group dishes out many concessions.

Vivacity and diversity personify Elmhurst, the thriving hearth to immigrants primarily from China, Southeast Asia, and Latin America. The Royal Kathin, a celebration that occurs at the end of Thailand's rainy season, pays homage to the spirit of the monks. The Elmhurst adaptation may lack the floods, but offers a bounty of faithful Thai foods. Whitney Avenue hosts a blossoming restaurant row, with a range of tiny Southeast Asian storefronts. Indulge your *gado gado* craving at **Minangasli** or **Upi Jaya** and get your *laksa* on at **Taste Good**. Elmhurst spans the globe so if the powerful and pungent flavors of Southeast Asia aren't your thing, dive into an Argentinean *parilla* for a shift from Asia to the Americas.

Jackson Heights is home to a distinct South Asian community. Take in the *bhangra* beats blaring from cars rolling along 74th Street, a dynamic commercial stretch of Indian markets, Bengali sweet shops, and Himalayan-style eateries. Some faves include Indian *tandoor* specialties and Tibetan *momos* (beef dumplings). Latin Americans from Colombia, Ecuador, Argentina, Uruguay, Peru, and Mexico also make up a large part of the demographic here. Catering to their tastes, Roosevelt Avenue sizzles with a sampling of taquerias, Colombian coffee shops, and Argentinean bakeries. The bustling thoroughfare connects several neighborhoods, shape shifting from country to country.

Follow the Avenue west to Woodside, where Irish bars commingle with fiery Thai spots. Once home to a large Irish population, Woodside now shares its blocks with a small Thai and Philippine population. The kelly green awnings of decade-old pubs dot the streets and clover-covered doors advertise in Gaelic. Here **Donovan's** has one of the best burgers in all the five boroughs. Alongside is Little Manila, an eight-block stretch of Roosevelt Avenue. Here you can find Filipino groceries and restaurants galore. The recent opening of **Jollibee**, the ultra-popular fast-food chain, has folks lined up for a taste of home.

On Queens Boulevard in Sunnyside (one of the most divergent 'hoods), eat your way through Korea, Columbia, Mexico, Romania, China, and Turkey. Of course, not in one day!

May through October, head over to Water Taxi Beach at Hunters Point to soak in views of the Manhattan skyline over burgers and beers. In late June, check out The New York City Food Film Festival where food and film lovers gather to view screenings of food films while noshing on a range of scrumptious nibbles.

Courtesy of The Noguchi Museum, NY – Photo by Bill Taylor

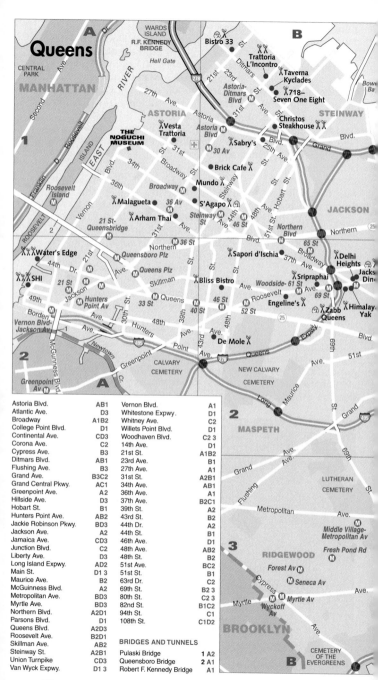

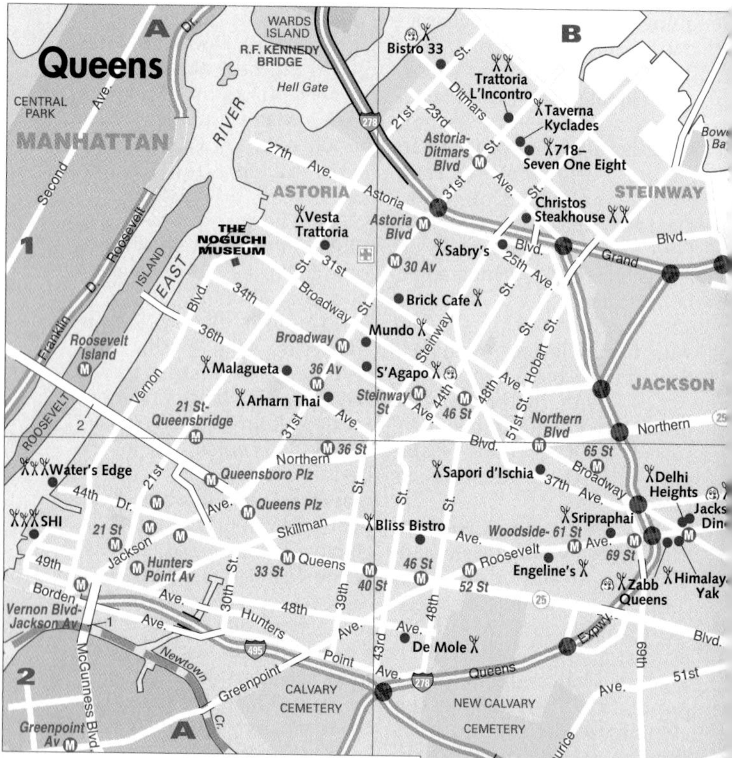


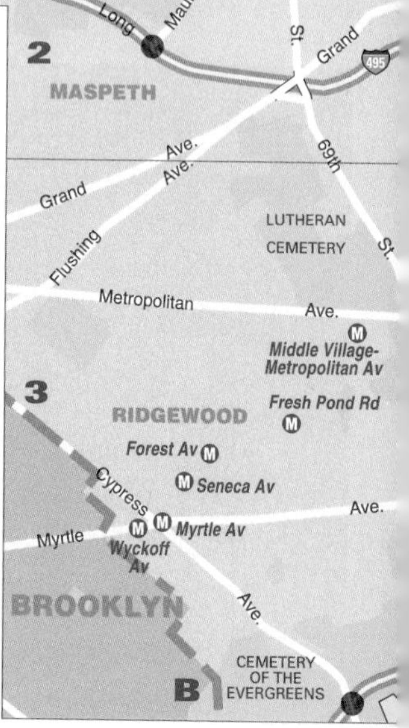

| | | | |
|---|---|---|---|
| Astoria Blvd. | AB1 | Vernon Blvd. | A1 |
| Atlantic Ave. | D3 | Whitestone Expwy. | D1 |
| Broadway | A1B2 | Whitney Ave. | C2 |
| College Point Blvd. | D1 | Willets Point Blvd. | D1 |
| Continental Ave. | CD3 | Woodhaven Blvd. | C2 3 |
| Corona Ave. | C2 | 14th Ave. | D1 |
| Cypress Ave. | B3 | 21st St. | A1B2 |
| Ditmars Blvd. | AB1 | 23rd Ave. | B1 |
| Flushing Ave. | B3 | 27th Ave. | A1 |
| Grand Ave. | B3C2 | 31st St. | A2B1 |
| Grand Central Pkwy. | AC1 | 34th Ave. | AB1 |
| Greenpoint Ave. | A2 | 36th Ave. | A1 |
| Hillside Ave. | D3 | 37th Ave. | B2C1 |
| Hobart St. | B1 | 39th St. | A2 |
| Hunters Point Ave. | AB2 | 43rd St. | B2 |
| Jackie Robinson Pkwy. | BD3 | 44th Dr. | A2 |
| Jackson Ave. | A2 | 44th St. | B1 |
| Jamaica Ave. | CD3 | 46th Ave. | D1 |
| Junction Blvd. | C2 | 48th Ave. | AB2 |
| Liberty Ave. | D3 | 48th St. | B2 |
| Long Island Expwy. | AD2 | 51st Ave. | BC2 |
| Main St. | D1 3 | 51st St. | B1 |
| Maurice Ave. | B2 | 63rd Dr. | C2 |
| McGuinness Blvd. | A2 | 69th St. | B2 3 |
| Metropolitan Ave. | BD3 | 80th St. | C2 3 |
| Myrtle Ave. | BD3 | 82nd St. | B1C2 |
| Northern Blvd. | A2D1 | 94th St. | C1 |
| Parsons Blvd. | D1 | 108th St. | C1D2 |
| Queens Blvd. | A2D3 | | |
| Roosevelt Ave. | B2D1 | | |
| Skillman Ave. | AB2 | **BRIDGES AND TUNNELS** | |
| Steinway St. | A2B1 | Pulaski Bridge | 1 A2 |
| Union Turnpike | CD3 | Queensboro Bridge | 2 A1 |
| Van Wyck Expwy. | D1 3 | Robert F. Kennedy Bridge | A1 |

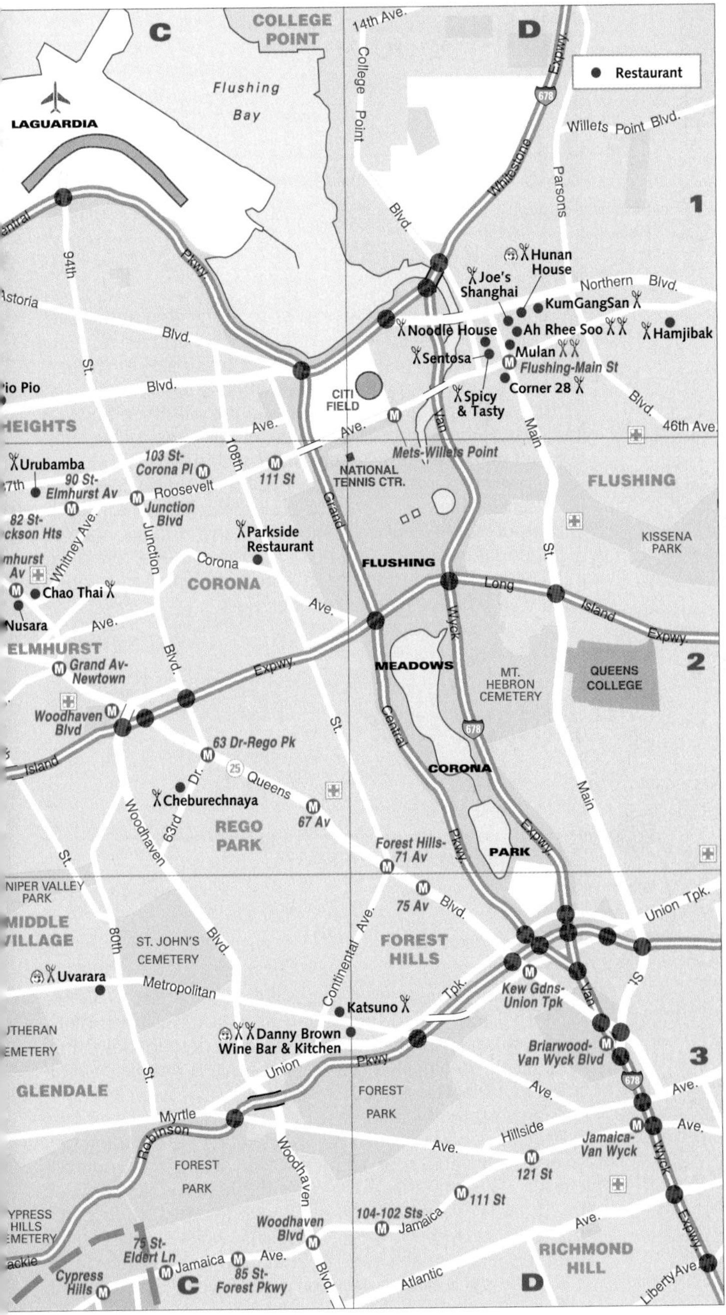
Restaurant
LAGUARDIA
COLLEGE POINT
Flushing Bay
C
D
1
2
3
Hunan House
Joe's Shanghai
KumGangSan
Noodle House
Ah Rhee Soo
Hamjibak
Sentosa
Mulan
Flushing-Main St
Corner 28
Spicy & Tasty
CITI FIELD
Mets-Willets Point
NATIONAL TENNIS CTR.
FLUSHING
KISSENA PARK
Urubamba
90 St-Elmhurst Av
103 St-Corona Pl
111 St
Junction Blvd
82 St-Jackson Hts
Parkside Restaurant
CORONA
Chao Thai
Nusara
ELMHURST
Grand Av-Newtown
Woodhaven Blvd
FLUSHING MEADOWS CORONA PARK
MT. HEBRON CEMETERY
QUEENS COLLEGE
63 Dr-Rego Pk
Cheburechnaya
REGO PARK
67 Av
Forest Hills-71 Av
75 Av
MIDDLE VILLAGE
ST. JOHN'S CEMETERY
Uvarara
FOREST HILLS
Katsuno
Kew Gdns-Union Tpk
Danny Brown Wine Bar & Kitchen
Briarwood-Van Wyck Blvd
GLENDALE
FOREST PARK
Jamaica-Van Wyck
121 St
111 St
104-102 Sts
Woodhaven Blvd
75 St-Elderts Ln
85 St-Forest Pkwy
Cypress Hills
RICHMOND HILL
Pio Pio
HEIGHTS
Northern Blvd.
Astoria Blvd.
Grand Central Pkwy.
Long Island Expwy.
Van Wyck Expwy.
Whitestone Expwy.
Union Tpk.
Jamaica Ave.
Atlantic Ave.
Hillside Ave.
Liberty Ave.
Queens Blvd.
Woodhaven Blvd.
Metropolitan Ave.
Myrtle Ave.
Roosevelt Ave.
Main St.
Parsons Blvd.
Willets Point Blvd.
College Point Blvd.
14th Ave.
46th Ave.
94th St.
108th St.
80th St.
Junction Blvd.
Corona Ave.
Whitney Ave.
63rd Dr.
Continental Ave.
Union Pkwy.
Robinson Pkwy.

# Ah Rhee Soo

Korean XX

D1

38-10 138th St. (at 38th Ave.)

**Subway:** Flushing - Main St
**Phone:** 718-713-0308
**Web:** www.ahrheesoo.com
**Prices:** $$

Lunch & dinner daily

Korean barbecue gets a sweep of sophistication at this slick and spacious restaurant tucked into the upscale Queens Crossing mall in Flushing. The place bills itself as Korean-Japanese, but only a complete sushiphile could resist the call of those multiple grills flanking the tables: Ah Rhee Soo was built for barbecue and big parties. (In fact, the menu offers four set menus for just such occasions, starting at $500.)

The good news is that you only need bring yourself to indulge in a tender plate of sweet beef ribs, freckled with radish, mushrooms, chestnuts, and jujubes; baby octopus, sautéed with tender pork belly in a hearty red sauce; or a soft tangle of cold buckwheat noodles in a heat-packing garlic sauce, spiked with boiled egg and pressed pork.

# Arharn Thai

Thai X

A1

32-05 36th Ave. (bet. 32nd & 33rd Sts.)

**Subway:** 36 Av
**Phone:** 718-728-5563
**Web:** N/A
**Prices:** ⊛

Lunch & dinner daily

Astoria takes a break from its usual souvlaki scene to dabble with Thai food—and the results are delicious. Just a block off the N train, Arharn Thai is a fairly non-descript operation, with clean, minimally-dressed tables and a couple of Thai-inspired artifacts dotting the walls.

Breaking up the blandness of the room are the vibrant Thai specialties—each dish deftly incorporating the contradictory sweet, salty, and sour elements that define the country's cuisine. The only thing missing is the heat—which is given the usual Western taming—but you won't miss it too much in plates like *Yum Ma Kear Yao*, a silky white eggplant salad with roasted vegetables and dried shrimp; or *Gaeng Ped Yen*, a roasted duck dish in red curry and sweet, cool coconut milk.

# Bistro 33

Contemporary

B1

19-33 Ditmars Blvd. (at 21st St.)

**Subway:** Astoria - Ditmars Blvd
**Phone:** 718-721-1933
**Web:** www.bistro33nyc.com
**Prices:** $$

Lunch Sat – Sun
Dinner nightly

French Culinary Institute alumnus and all-around sushi guru, Gary Anza, knifed the maki at prestigious Bond Street and Bao 111, before crossing the river to open this fantastic French-Asian fusion bistro in Astoria. Located a few blocks from scenic Shore Blvd., Bistro 33's menu effortlessly combines Anza's classical training with a bevy of Asian-influenced dishes, not to mention a foray into the deep South with alligator fritters and New Orleans gumbo.

Don't miss a dish of cool, perfectly-seared yellowfin tuna, set atop a sweet Asian pear chutney, and paired with a pristine lobe of seared Hudson Valley foie gras, sour cherries, spicy cashews, and wildflower honey. Washed down with one of Anza's seasonal, fruit-infused sakes, this is fusion done right.

# Bliss Bistro

French

B2

45-20 Skillman Ave. (at 46th (Bliss) St.)

**Subway:** 46 St - Bliss St
**Phone:** 718-729-0778
**Web:** www.blissbistro.com
**Prices:** $$

Lunch Sun
Dinner nightly

Just a fifteen minute subway ride from midtown Manhattan, Sunnyside Gardens is a pretty little pocket of Queens with shady residential streets and lush courtyards. The commute must have looked pretty good to Alim Maruf, who packed his bags at Manhattan's Park Bistro in order to transform the old American Bliss restaurant into this upscale bistro.

With its lovely garden and intimate dining room dressed in creamy whites and tables set for two, Bliss Bistro is as romantic as they come. The food matches, with glorious dishes like a frisée salad, tossed with silky duck confit and crunchy bacon; or fork-tender coq au vin, paired with a fluffy stack of mashed potatoes; or pillowy profiteroles, stuffed with vanilla ice cream bathed in rich chocolate.

# Brick Cafe

B1 — Mediterranean

30-95 33rd St. (at 31st Ave.)

**Subway:** Broadway
**Phone:** 718-267-2735
**Web:** www.brickcafe.com
**Prices:** $$

Lunch Sat – Sun
Dinner nightly

The food is simple and the service sweet at Brick Cafe, where locals rave about the brunch and the outdoor area is flooded come summer. With its chunky wood tables, reclaimed flooring, and farm bric-a-brac, the interior will transport you straight back to that little restaurant you can never remember the name of in Montmartre—and who couldn't use a little rustic romance on a corner of Queens usually reserved for Greek diners and thumping Euro clubs?
Best not to fight this kind of momentum and join the crowds digging into Southern French-and-Italian style dishes like grilled Maya shrimp, zucchini, and Portobello mushroom caps tossed in a cilantro-garlic olive oil. The brunch menu carries the usual omelets and French toast, but also octopus carpaccio.

# Chao Thai

C2 — Thai

85-03 Whitney Ave. (at Broadway)

**Subway:** Elmhurst Av
**Phone:** 718-424-4999
**Web:** N/A
**Prices:** ⊜

Lunch & dinner daily

One of the best Thai restaurants in all five boroughs, this tiny, unadorned spot in the heart of Elmhurst, sandwiched between Asian markets and restaurants, is worth every step of the trip.
To sample the kitchen's true talent, skip the regular menu in favor of the printed page of specials, keeping in mind that prices are low enough to order an extra dish or two. These offerings are closer in style to Bangkok than New York, and reflect the restaurant's commitment to properly feeding a typically Thai clientele. Heat levels can also be fantastically authentic (and raised beyond Western expectation). The house-made coconut ice cream is a sweet ending to a fiery meal.
This popular place has limited seating and is bustling during peak hours, so plan ahead.

# Cheburechnaya

Uzbek

C2

92-09 63rd Dr. (at Austin St.)

**Subway:** 63 Dr - Rego Park
**Phone:** 718-897-9080
**Web:** www.cheburechnaya.com
**Prices:** ⊖⊖

Lunch Sun – Thu
Dinner Sat – Thu

Make no mistake: the service can be halting, the halogen lighting is brutal, and the blaring Russian music videos don't exactly scream date night. But this boisterous Rego Park restaurant's inconveniences fade when the dining room's open grill lights up—crackling and sizzling with succulent kebabs—and gorgeous plates of food start flying out of the kitchen (sometimes all at once).

It's hard to miss with Cheburechnaya's gorgeous kosher food, which caters to the neighborhood's Bukharan Jewish population, but keep an eye peeled for the carrot salad, cut into noodle-thin strips and humming with chili, paprika, and cilantro; and the *Noni Toki* bread, a charred beauty that reads something like a cross between cumin seed-studded flat bread and matzo.

# Christos Steakhouse

Steakhouse

B1

41-08 23rd Ave. (at 41st St.)

**Subway:** Ditmars Blvd
**Phone:** 718-777-8400
**Web:** www.christossteakhouse.com
**Prices:** **$$$**

Dinner nightly

A dark red awning dips down over windows promising hearty portions of dry-aged beef while neat hedges line the entrance to this beloved Astoria institution. Inside, a front area serves as both bar and butcher shop, beautifully displaying their range of house-aged chops. Hardwood floors, warm tones, and mahogany tables draped in white linens complete the traditional setting.

But what sets Christo's apart from its chophouse brethren is the uniquely Greek influence of the food: *taramosalata* and salads of Greek sausage over *gigante* beans share the menu with standards like roast chicken, lobster, and ribeye. Expertly prepared sides like tart and tender dandelion greens (*horta*) tossed in lemon juice and olive oil bring fresh flavors to steakhouse dining.

# Corner 28

D1 — Chinese

40-28 Main St. (at 40th Rd.)

**Subway:** Flushing - Main St — Lunch & dinner daily
**Phone:** 718-886-6628
**Web:** N/A
**Prices:** $$

Straddling a busy corner of Flushing is the bright, double-decker goliath, Corner 28. Choose from two entrances for different—albeit tasty—experiences. The left door leads to a chaotic take-out joint, where you can score a 75¢ Peking duck from early morning until 2:00 A.M. The right door leads guests up to the second floor, where a sunlight-flooded room finds diners flipping through glossy menus while friendly servers hustle to and fro with heaping plates of Chinese food.

The space can get crowded quickly and the Chinese music can jangle the nerves, but oh-how-soothing it is to finally tuck your chopsticks into a heat-packing dish of soft, shredded pork, bathed in ruby-colored garlic sauce; or meltingly tender lamb chops, fragrant with herbs and spices.

# Danny Brown Wine Bar & Kitchen

C-D3 — Mediterranean

104-02 Metropolitan Ave. (at 71st Dr.)

**Subway:** Forest Hills - 71 Av — Dinner Tue – Sun
**Phone:** 718-261-2144
**Web:** www.dannybrownwinekitchen.com
**Prices:** $$

Poor Queens. Stuck in the shadow of culinary giants, Manhattan and Brooklyn, this little borough has always had to rely on its far-flung exotic pockets to carry its foodie clout. No more, says Danny Brown—who has packed up some SoHo chic from his days at the Cub Room, and delivered it to an otherwise dull corner of Forest Hills.

Despite its subdued location, this little gem personifies high caliber, both in its design and cuisine. Warm and sophisticated, the room is filled with sultry music and a masterful staff pushing out gorgeous plates of thick, buttery risotto pancakes, studded with toasted pecans; or moist slabs of roasted Scottish salmon. Save room for the spicy rum raisin carrot cake— irresistible when paired with a frothy cream cheese mousse.

# De Mole

Mexican

B2

45-02 48th Ave. (at 45th St.)

**Subway:** 46 St

Lunch & dinner daily

**Phone:** 718-392-2161
**Web:** N/A
**Prices:** ⊜

Sunnyside locals prize this charming Mexican bistro for its flavorful food and cozy brick-walled setting that echoes a European sense.

The reasonably priced menu—supplemented by inviting daily specials—brings forth the best of authentic Mexico dishes, featuring an impressive mole. Fajitas, nachos, and taco salad are a nod to Mexican-American tastes. Even chips and salsa are offered with flair, as freshly fried tortillas are presented SoHo-style in a paper bag and served with a rich, smoky salsa. Quench your thirst with their range of made-to-order juices or *aqua de Jamaica* (hibiscus water) freshly brewed from the dried flowers.

The warm and efficient staff here could not be more accommodating and complementary to the restaurant's family-fun feel.

# Delhi Heights

Indian

B2

37-66 74th St. (at 37th Rd.)

**Subway:** Jackson Hts - Roosevelt Av

Lunch & dinner daily

**Phone:** 718-507-1111
**Web:** www.delhiheights.us
**Prices:** $$

Gone are the ticky-tacky Christmas lights and reclaimed banquet chairs that afflict so many Indian restaurants—newcomer Delhi Heights, which occupies a prominent corner near Queens' bustling Roosevelt Avenue, aims to be a cut above, with a modern, good-looking interior and a clever menu divided into three sections: South Indian, Indian, and Indian-Chinese.

The kitchen, which offers dozens of breads, noodles, and vegetarian options, isn't afraid to kick the heat up in dishes like *keema mutter*, spicy ground lamb in a fragrant, tomato-based sauce with onions and shelled peas; and then cool you down with dishes like the *dahi vada*, a cluster of crispy lentil flour doughnuts smothered in a thick, tangy yogurt and studded with crunchy cardamom seeds.

# Engeline's

B2 Filipino

58-28 Roosevelt Ave. (bet. 58th & 59th Sts.)

**Subway:** Woodside - 61 St
Lunch & dinner daily
**Phone:** 718-898-7878
**Web:** N/A
**Prices:** 🙂

Sometimes you wake up and think—man, I would love some deep fried pork knuckles for breakfast. The good people at Engeline's won't judge you. In fact, this sweet little bakery-cum-restaurant, which doubles as a local hangout for the neighborhood's Filipino ex-pat scene, will serve it to you with a smile.

The bakery makes a mean pastry any way you slice it, but it's worth grabbing a seat at one of the simple wooden tables and plunking down some change for a full meal, for this kind of authentic Filipino comfort food doesn't come easy—try the *kare-kare*, a sweet, peanut-butter stew of oxtail and tender honeycomb tripe, kicked up with a pungent, salty fish sauce; or *menudo*, a traditional peasant stew with addictive little cubes of spicy, perfumed pork.

# Hamjibak

D1 Korean

41-08 149th Pl. (bet. Barclay & 41st Aves.)

**Subway:** Flushing - Main St
Lunch & dinner daily
**Phone:** 718-460-9289
**Web:** N/A
**Prices:** $$

A healthy assortment of *banchan* (small plates, such as kimchi or spicy mackerel) is usually a good indicator of a serious Korean restaurant, and you'll find no shortage of them at Hamjibak—a delicious Korean barbecue restaurant buried down a nondescript side street in the blossoming K-town that's sprung up near Queens' Murray Hill LIRR station.

The unassuming Hamjibak won't woo you with it's plain-Jane décor, but scores major points for the patient, oh-so-knowledgable wait staff service, and masterful Korean specialties like *daeji bulgogi*, a plate of marinated pork ribs in chili-garlic sauce sprinkled with bright green scallions; or *boyang jeongol*, a traditional hot pot of lamb, dumplings, and vegetables swimming in a rich, spicy beef broth.

# Himalayan Yak

Tibetan

B2

72-20 Roosevelt Ave. (bet. 72nd & 73rd Sts.)

**Subway:** 74 St - Broadway
Lunch & dinner daily
**Phone:** 718-779-1119
**Web:** N/A
**Prices:** ⚭

The slick, revamped Himalayan Yak is not too far from its former digs, but a change of scenery has served it well. The new location boasts sultry sienna walls and handsome exposed brick, lined with carved masks and little black and white Yaks.

The food, on the other hand, remains deliciously the same. Perhaps best described as Indian light, this hybrid restaurant draws specialties from several cuisines, including Nepalese, Tibetan, Himalayan, and Indian. Take a culinary tour with *tsam thuk*, a thick, porridge-like soup served at room temperature, and bobbing with yak milk; or gigantic beef dumplings in a rich, savory soup of tender greens and diced carrots; or a vegetarian tray which includes pickled mango strips and Indian pepper paper bread.

# Hunan House

Chinese

D1

137-40 Northern Blvd. (bet. Main & Union Sts.)

**Subway:** Flushing - Main St
Lunch & dinner daily
**Phone:** 718-353-1808
**Web:** N/A
**Prices:** ⚭

Sweet Flushing! Does New York's rising (and slowly reigning) Chinatown ever cease to delight those willing to trek out to its far-flung environs? Not if Hunan House has anything to say about it—a plain, but tidy, little joint pushing out authentic, hard-to-find Hunanese fare.

The province's name means "south of the lake," and Hunan kitchens typically use more seafood than those of neighboring Sichuan—though they certainly share their neighbor's affinity for chili peppers. Witness a braised fish head in a spicy broth, topped with pickled chilies and cool cilantro; a fragrant, delicately preserved beef with pickled peppers and "white chili" (which turns out to be fried bean curd skin); or Hunan-style spare ribs laced with red chili sauce.

# Jackson Diner

B2

Indian

## 37-47 74th St. (bet. Roosevelt & 37th Aves.)

**Subway:** Jackson Hts - Roosevelt Av
Lunch & dinner daily
**Phone:** 718-672-1232
**Web:** www.jacksondiner.com
**Prices:**

Gone are Jackson Diner's budget chandeliers and gaudy seating—thoughtful sconces now grace the wall, and the tables sparkle in clean, tidy little rows. What hasn't changed, thank goodness, is the scrumptious Indian food. This Queens steady bills itself as "A Culinary Passage to India"—a promise it delivers on, though it has lost some substantial heat with the arrival of more and more Western faces.

Easy enough to get over when you sink your teeth into crispy samosas filled with spicy peas and potatoes; tangy lamb vindaloo simmered in a thick ginger and tamarind-chili sauce; or jumbo dumplings served with three bright dipping sauces of creamy burnt-orange tamarind, chunky coconut and black mustard seed, and bright green coriander.

# Joe's Shanghai

D1

Chinese

## 136-21 37th Ave. (bet. Main & Union Sts.)

**Subway:** Flushing - Main St
Lunch & dinner daily
**Phone:** 718-539-3838
**Web:** www.joeshanghairestaurants.com
**Prices:** $$

City kids that have given up on the banal kitchen at the Pell Street outpost of this popular soup dumpling house ought to take a little jaunt out to the original in Flushing, Queens. Because the doughy little pouches sure earn their pleated stripes at this location, thank you very much.

Kick things off with an order of the pork and crab soup dumplings—for the uninitiated, these are thin, soft purses of dough filled with a rich, lip-smacking-good hot broth. If you don't end up ordering back-to-back rounds of these heavenly dumplings, you might try any number of dishes like a trio of sweet and salty wine chicken, jellyfish strips, and duck's web feet; or tender sautéed pork, diced with minced jalapeño, diced squid, and dried tofu.

# Katsuno

Japanese

C3

## 103-01 Metropolitan Ave. (at 71st Rd.)

**Subway:** Forest Hills - 71 Av — Lunch Tue – Fri
**Phone:** 718-575-4033 — Dinner Tue – Sun
**Web:** www.katsunorestaurant.com
**Prices:** $$

Authentic Japanese food has finally crossed the bridge to Queens, and not a moment too soon, but blink and you'll miss this tiny new gem. There is no sign to mark the entrance, only a small white lantern and the traditional Japanese *noren* curtains to usher you into a beautiful plain little space with a smattering of tables. While his wife runs the front room, the talented Katsuyuki Seo crafts every plate, and the chef's flawless technique is evident right from the first slice.

The seasonal menu employs fish flown in from Japan daily, and might include a translucent tangle of fresh squid noodles, topped with needle-thin yuzu zest; or a bowl of toothsome soba, bobbing in a fragrant broth with grilled scallion, silky tofu, and tender slices of duck breast.

# KumGangSan

Korean

D1

## 138-28 Northern Blvd. (bet. Bowne & Union Sts.)

**Subway:** Flushing - Main St — Lunch & dinner daily
**Phone:** 718-461-0909
**Web:** www.kumgangsan.net
**Prices:** $$

This establishment focuses on pleasure, with an attractively sprawling interior, lovely terrace with a burbling fountain, lush greenery, and a voluminous menu, as well as a sushi bar. Named for a range of mountains (translated as "Diamond Mountains") in North Korea, this local favorite perpetually buzzes with throngs of diners who partake in the well-made and satisfying fare. The large selection of steaming noodles, bubbling casseroles with chili-spiced broth, and barbecued meats are all made with authentic seasonings imported from Korea. To spark the taste buds, each table receives a generous selection of small dishes (*banchan*) at the start of the meal. Another location in Midtown West is open 24/7 as well.

# Malagueta

Brazilian

A1

25-35 36th Ave. (at 28th St.)

**Subway:** 36 Av
**Phone:** 718-937-4821
**Web:** N/A
**Prices:** ㊂

Lunch Sat – Sun
Dinner Tue – Sun

Chef/owner Herbet Gomes and his wife, Alda Teixeire, have created an intimate and unassuming Brazilian bistro, offering a culinary homage to their culturally rich and brilliantly diverse homeland. Inside, olive green and deep red walls are judiciously covered with oil paintings, surrounding tables dressed with white linen and fresh flowers.

Well-composed and authentic specialties like *peito de pato* (sautéed duck breast) or *moqueca de camarao* (shrimp stew with palm oil and coconut milk) tend towards the hot, salty, smoky, and sour ends of the flavor spectrum. Saturday diners should indulge in the hearty, flavorful, and rustic Brazilian clay-pot black bean stew, *feijoada compela*. Service is personable, well-informed, and dedicated to your enjoyment.

# Mulan

Asian

D1

136-17 39th Ave. (at Main St.)

**Subway:** Flushing - Main St
**Phone:** 718-886-8526
**Web:** www.mulan-restaurant.com
**Prices:** **$$$**

Lunch & dinner daily

Just a short walk from Flushing's bustling main drag, sits the Queens Crossing mall—a Time Warner Center for the borough's Chinatown, if you will. And like its Manhattan counterpart, there are a few upscale restaurants worth checking out, should you find yourself in this neck of the woods.

One of them is the gorgeous Mulan—a modern Asian restaurant filled with cherry blossom silk panels and creamy leather chairs that's making a quick name for itself with polished service and a respectable wine list (for Flushing, that is). Not to mention continental Cantonese fare like the char-grilled salmon, varnished with a honey-tinged miso sauce and topped with sweet mango; or bone-in chicken, puddled in a dark, aromatic sauce pocked with creamy whole chestnuts.

# Mundo

International

A1

31-18 Broadway (at 32nd St.)

**Subway:** Broadway — Dinner nightly
**Phone:** 718-777-2829
**Web:** www.mundoastoria.com
**Prices:** $$

Located off of a busy Astoria thoroughfare, Mundo attracts crowds of hungry locals happy to have this little gem to call their own. The simple interior features a changing display of artwork and in warmer months, tables spill out onto the sidewalk giving the cozy space a quaint European atmosphere. The cuisine, much like the neighborhood, offers an array of global representation. Appetizers like grilled *halloumi* cheese, empanadas, and edamame tastefully coexist with chicken Milanesa and beef-filled Ottoman dumplings.

Vegetarians will be pleased with the variety of meat-less items. Mundo's co-owners have put together an establishment that is sure to please—"Willie" Lucerofabbi warmly attends to the front-of-the-house while "John" Caner runs the kitchen.

# Noodle House

Chinese

D1

38-12 Prince St. (bet. 38th & 39th Aves. )

**Subway:** Flushing - Main St — Lunch & dinner daily
**Phone:** 718-321-3838
**Web:** N/A
**Prices:** 

Also known as Nan Shian Dumpling House, it is easily found among a strip of restaurants reflecting the diversity of Flushing's dominant Asian population. Simply decorated, the comfortable dining room features rows of closely set tables and a mirrored wall that successfully gives the illusion of space.

This enjoyable and interesting menu focuses on noodle-filled soups, toothsome stir-fried rice cakes, and the house specialty, steamed pork buns. These are made in-house and have a delicate, silky wrapper encasing a flavorful meatball of ground pork or crab and rich tasting broth. Eating these may take some practice, but take your cue from the slurping crowd: puncture the casing on your spoon to cool the dumplings and avoid burning your mouth.

# Nusara

C2

Thai

82-80 Broadway (at Whitney Ave.)

**Subway:** Elmhurst Av

Lunch & dinner daily

**Phone:** 718-898-7996

**Web:** www.nusarathaikitchen.com

**Prices:** **$$**

Tucked into an Elmhurst strip mall teeming with enough Asian food to send Asiaphiles into a coma, Nusara is indisputably the belle of the ball. Its edge? Ace Thai food, a pretty, softly lit dining room, and a staff willing to bend over backwards for their customers.

Newbies to authentic Thai will rejoice in Nusara's snappy, well-organized menu with its detailed explanations, but the spice-shy should proceed slowly. For all the sweetness of the staff, Nusara isn't afraid to bring the heat in dishes like whole red snapper, tossed in garlic and pepper; or mouthwatering, seasonal Chinese watercress, sautéed with ginger, red chili, and garlic. Cool your heels with a roasted duck salad, loaded with pineapple and cashews in a chili and lime vinaigrette.

# Parkside Restaurant

C2

Italian

107-01 Corona Ave. (bet. 108th St. & 51st Ave. )

**Subway:** 103 St - Corona Plaza

Lunch & dinner daily

**Phone:** 718-271-9871

**Web:** N/A

**Prices:** **$$$**

Enter this warm, convivial Corona landmark and immediately feel welcomed by all—from hostess and bartender, to server and chef. A contagious, celebratory spirit fills the enthusiastic diners enjoying old-fashioned, Italian-American dishes in a perennially packed, multi-room space. Its brick arches, twinkling white lights, wicker chairs, and hanging foliage conjure an upscale greenhouse, staffed by tuxedo-clad waiters.

Take a seat among the family-friendly patrons and order a plate of perfectly prepared *rigatoni all'amatriciana*, served in a fresh tomato sauce with pancetta and basil; or thin cutlets of *veal piccata*, glazed in a luscious lemon-caper sauce. When the dessert tray rolls by, make sure you've saved room for biscotti or the beloved cannoli.

# Pio Pio

Peruvian

C1

84-13 Northern Blvd. (at 84th St.)

**Subway:** 82 St - Jackson Hts — Lunch & dinner daily
**Phone:** 718-426-1010
**Web:** www.piopionyc.com
**Prices:** ©©

Spanish for "chirp chirp", this charming eatery serves up authentic Peruvian fare in a colorful, casual atmosphere; vibrant hues tint the walls while bright Peruvian paintings hang on exposed brick. True to its signature sound, Pio Pio calls attention to the chicken; exquisitely marinated, cooked rotisserie style, and served with a garlicky green sauce, this bird will have your taste buds tweeting in ecstasy. The sides are also something to sing about: try a generous plate of *tostones* (fried unripe plantains) or the zesty avocado salad. The combos—best shared—are a great value, offering a whole chicken plus two or more sides at a bargain price.
On a sunny day, grab a table in the garden and cool off with a refreshing pitcher of sangria.

# Sabry's

Seafood

B1

24-25 Steinway St. (bet. Astoria Blvd. & 25th Ave.)

**Subway:** Astoria Blvd — Lunch & dinner daily
**Phone:** 718-721-9010
**Web:** N/A
**Prices:** $$

Located in an area of Astoria that has recently become Little Egypt, Sabry's uses Egyptian accents in preparing an array of seafood—a large ice-filled case displays the day's fresh catch at the entrance. Prepared in the style of many Mediterranean eateries, fish from this case are grilled or baked whole, permeated with Middle Eastern flavorings like garlic, cumin, cardamom, and red pepper. Aromatic tagines, including a shellfish version cooked in a rich and heady tomato sauce, are equally delicious. Baba ghanoush is packed with flavor, and the freshly made pita bread makes a fantastic accompaniment.
Be aware that the restaurant does not serve alcohol, nor is BYO permitted. However, there are other interesting options, including a tasty mint tea.

# S'Agapo

A1 — Greek

## 34-21 34th Ave. (at 35th St.)

**Subway:** Steinway St — Lunch & dinner daily
**Phone:** 718-626-0303
**Web:** N/A
**Prices:** **$$**

When in Astoria, go where the Greeks go, and in the case of S'Agapo ("I love you" in Greek), you'll quickly discover why this place is always crammed with Greeks, locals, and Manhattanites sipping ouzo or a great bottle of wine.

Located on a quiet residential block bordering Astoria and Long Island City, S'Agapo is owned and managed by a charming couple from Crete. The taverna focuses on providing authentic food at palatable prices, with personal service.

Rustic preparations of perfectly grilled fish, lamb, and an extensive assortment of cold and hot appetizers mean that no diner goes away hungry. A number of Cretan specialties (house-made lamb sausage, Cretan cheese dumplings), as well as the quiet outdoor terrace, set S'Agapo apart.

# Sapori d'Ischia

B2 — Italian

## 55-15 37th Ave. (at 56th St.)

**Subway:** Northern Blvd — Lunch Tue – Sat
**Phone:** 718-446-1500 — Dinner Tue – Sun
**Web:** N/A
**Prices:** **$$**

If you're looking for red-checkered tablecloth Italian-American, its best to keep on trucking past this little Woodside gem, because the house rules posted at the bar spell it out clear as mud—they don't grate cheese on seafood, they don't serve butter, and you can forget the lemon peel in your espresso.

So what do Frank and Antonio Galano, the father-son team who runs this adorable little restaurant and grocery, do? How about flat-out delicious Southern Italian seafood, a little live piano on occasion, and darn reasonable prices. Don't miss the killer housemade black linguine in an intricate white wine sauce pocked with juicy clams, *peperoncino*, and roasted garlic; or a delicate chocolate and hazelnut torte paired with a scoop of pistachio ice cream.

# Sentosa

Malaysian

D1

39-07 Prince St. (at 39th Ave.)

**Subway:** Flushing - Main St — Lunch & dinner daily
**Phone:** 718-886-6331
**Web:** N/A
**Prices:** ⓢⓢ

Sentosa, the Malay word for tranquility, celebrates an agreeable intermingling of the mainly Chinese and Indian influences of Malaysia's multi-ethnic descendants. This very enjoyable restaurant features a contemporary setting with warm lighting, polished teak, and stone tiles. Meals here may begin with thin, crisp, and chewy pancakes of *roti canai*, attractively served with a chicken curry dipping sauce.

Other flavorful offerings may include *rendang*, a rich stew of tender beef simmered in coconut milk, perfectly heated with chili paste; alongside a large selection of rice and noodle dishes. Just remember to save room for your vegetables, like the halved okra pods, sautéed with alluring *belacan*, made from fermented, ground shrimp.

# 718 - Seven One Eight

Mediterranean

B1

35-01 Ditmars Blvd. (at 35th St.)

**Subway:** Astoria - Ditmars Blvd — Lunch & dinner daily
**Phone:** 718-204-5553
**Web:** www.718restaurant.com
**Prices:** $$

With its lovely sienna hues, silky fabrics, and flickering red votive candles, this elegant little Astoria charmer brings a dose of warmth to this section of Astoria. Named for the Queens area code it resides in, 718's menu fiddles with Mediterranean fare quite deftly—dinner might include a tender roasted duck with crispy skin, lovingly fanned out over a fluffy potato purée studded with earthy mushrooms and a lick of tart passion-coriander sauce; or a decadent molten chocolate cake that turns sinful and oozing when the fork delivers the first blow.

The regularly packed happy hour bar is a fantastic place to take a peek at the restaurant's ample tapas menu, and on Friday nights you may soak up the *caliente* Latin beats to your hearts content.

# SHI

Asian

A2

47-20 Center Blvd. (bet. 47th & 48th Aves. )

**Subway:** Vernon Blvd - Jackson Av
Dinner nightly
**Phone:** 347-242-2450
**Web:** www.shilic.com
**Prices:** $$

Tucked into the base of a gorgeous high-rise building along the East River, SHI is the stamp Long Island City's been waiting for: Consider this upscale hipster hub signed, sealed, and delivered.

Developers have poured millions into the new buildings that dot this area of the waterfront, and SHI is appropriately stunning—with floor-to-ceiling windows offering breathtaking views of the Manhattan skyline; sexy white leather plush chairs flanking the beautiful bar area; and a dining room dripping in crystal chandeliers. So how does the food fit into all this? Solidly, with simple, well-crafted Chinese-American and Japanese specialties like tender shrimp, wrapped in smoky bacon; and crispy popcorn beef, topped with chilies and bright cilantro.

# Spicy & Tasty

Chinese

D1

39-07 Prince St. (at 39th Ave.)

**Subway:** Flushing - Main St
Lunch & dinner daily
**Phone:** 718-359-1601
**Web:** N/A
**Prices:**

This bustling pocket of Queens is home to a dizzying array of restaurants, bakeries, and stores, all jockeying to win the love of Flushing's booming Asian population. Spicy & Tasty has not only captured their hearts, but a few critics' steely tickers in the process. The result of which can now be seen in the diverse ethnicities scattered across the spacious dining room, and in the food—which seems to use less of that punchy Sichuan heat lest they scare the newbies.

But food this good still makes the cut, and its fun to watch the warm, knowledgeable staff walk first-timers through steaming plates of dumplings, plump with a fiery red chili sauce and tender minced meat; or broad noodles in a rich, meaty sauce dancing with scallions and chili peppers.

# Sripraphai

Thai

B2

64-13 39th Ave. (bet. 64th & 65th Sts.)

**Subway:** Woodside - 61 St
Lunch & dinner Thu – Tue
**Phone:** 718-899-9599
**Web:** N/A
**Prices:** $$

A few years ago, this local favorite set off a critical firestorm for delivering killer, authentic-as-it-gets Thai food, then smartly expanded into roomier digs. In the current space, you'll find a large, elegant dining room with an enormous backyard garden, replete with gurgling fountain.

But with the flood of Westerners hovering like wolves outside the front door, has this beloved Woodside restaurant tamed her fiery ways? She has, but the bland food still remains quite popular regardless of diminished quality. The menu may feature bright green papaya salads; tender roasted duck over a bed of greens; fluffy Thai-style frittatas studded with ground pork; or fresh soft shell crab, lightly fried and pooled in delicious coconut-laced green curry.

# Taverna Kyclades

Greek

B1

33-07 Ditmars Blvd. (bet. 33rd & 35th Sts. )

**Subway:** Astoria - Ditmars Blvd
Lunch & dinner daily
**Phone:** 718-545-8666
**Web:** www.tavernakyclades.com
**Prices:** $$

This classic and beloved Greek taverna, helmed by a dedicated chef/owner and staff, continues to serve fresh fish daily, grilled or fried (available for inspection in a showcase refrigerator in the semi-open kitchen), along with heaping portions of side dishes. It is a perfect spot to dine family style.

Years of non-stop service to a loyal and diverse clientele has not diminished the classic patina of the small, but warm and boisterous dining room. The setting here is no frills. Diners are seated on simple wood chairs elbow to elbow. Meals can also be enjoyed year-round in the enclosed garden area. The surrounding space is crowded with back-to-back stores and restaurants. Service here is cool, helpful, and without attitude. *Opa*!

# Trattoria l'Incontro

Italian XX

B1

21-76 31st St. (at Ditmars Blvd.)

**Subway:** Astoria - Ditmars Blvd — Lunch & dinner Tue – Sun
**Phone:** 718-721-3532
**Web:** www.trattorialincontro.com
**Prices:** **$$**

When you're in the mood for feel-good Italian, hop the N train and take it straight out to the last stop to track down this convivial Astoria mainstay. A new expansion and wine bar still might not be enough room to hold the throngs of serious eaters that flood this place nightly, but no matter how busy they get, Abruzzi native Tina Sacramone and her son, Rocco, always find time to pour on the hospitality.

A brick oven in back churns out a host of savory pies (including a chocolate-stuffed one for sweethounds), or you can choose from a dizzying array of specials. A small plate of fresh, grilled sardines is garnished with white bean and red onion salad; and a heaping portion of fresh *bucatini* arrives loaded with shiitakes and crisp pancetta.

# Urubamba

Peruvian X

C2

86-20 37th Ave. (at 86th St.)

**Subway:** 82 St - Jackson Hts — Lunch & dinner daily
**Phone:** 718-672-2224
**Web:** www.urubambarestaurant.com
**Prices:** **$$**

This new Jackson Heights restaurant claims it has been serving traditional Peruvian food since 1976, albeit not at this location. The owner used to run Inti Raymi, a restaurant up the street, but closed it to open the handsome little Urubamba—a long, narrow space lined with Peruvian artifacts, indigenous paintings, and brick-lined walls.

Don't miss the proper Peruvian breakfast served on weekends, where diners can feast on *chanfainita*, a mouthwatering traditional beef stew, or *sopa de gallina*, a fragrant chicken noodle soup. At night, diners tuck into moist, golden tamales filled with chicken, hard boiled eggs, and black olives; light-as-air shrimp chowders, topped with bright green cilantro; and towering platters of fresh, lime-poached ceviche.

# Uvarara

C3 — Italian

79-28 Metropolitan Ave. (at 80th St.)

**Subway:** Middle Village - Metropolitan Av (& bus Q54) — Lunch & dinner Tue – Sun
**Phone:** 718-894-0052
**Web:** www.uvararany.com
**Prices:** $$

The "location is everything" memo must have missed the convivial Italian family behind Uvarara, who plunked down their new Italian wine bar between two cemeteries on a gloomy stretch of Metropolitan Avenue. But thank goodness, because this kind of cozy Bohemian charmer—with its killer wine list and deliciously honest cooking—wouldn't be nearly as cool in the city.

Housed in what was once a showroom for headstones, the sultry interior is all sex appeal now, with low, flickering candles, mismatched chairs, and beaded curtains made of wine bottle corks. The menu rolls with the seasons, but might include a puffy Naples-style *pizzetta* stuffed with creamy buffalo mozzarella, ripe tomatoes, and basil; or baked gnocchi, tossed in butter and fresh sage.

# Vesta Trattoria

A1 — Italian

21-02 30th Ave. (at 21st St.)

**Subway:** 30 Av — Lunch & dinner daily
**Phone:** 718-545-5550
**Web:** www.vestavino.com
**Prices:** $$

Named for the virgin god of the hearth in Roman mythology, the adorable new Vesta is already popular with the local Astoria set. You can blame the low-lit, brick-lined interior, which offers the kind of easygoing weeknight meal the neighborhood was begging for, but our money's on the greenmarket-inspired Italian menu—where it's as easy to indulge in celebrated old-world steadies as it is to head into more intricate culinary territory. Add to that a slew of vegetarian options, and a small, but clever, wine list—and you've got a sleeper.

Don't miss the delicious *minestra* soup; the fresh, hand-rolled pastas; or the Baby Jesus cake, a fluffy spice cake with a crispy, toffee-like crust covered in a caramel sauce and a fluffy dollop of whip cream.

# Water's Edge

A2 — American XXX

4-01 44th Dr. (at the East River)

**Subway:** 23 St - Ely Av — Lunch Mon – Sat
**Phone:** 718-482-0033 — Dinner nightly
**Web:** www.watersedgenyc.com
**Prices:** $$$

A complimentary boat shuttles guests with reservations from Manhattan's 35th Street pier to this well-known Queens institution—a fine dining establishment that owes most of its clout to its stellar location rather than to its stuffy ambience. So how good can one location be? How about river-front, in a city starved for waterfront space—with an entire wall of windows offering up jaw-dropping views of the East River and Manhattan skyline. And at sunset, that's pretty enough to sit back in your slightly dated Louis XV-style chairs, soak in the live piano, and sink your teeth into predictable-but-solid fare like lump crab with creamy avocado and charred asparagus; or caramelized pan-seared diver scallops, paired with Israeli cous-cous and long beans.

# Zabb Queens

B2 — Thai X

71-28 Roosevelt Ave. (bet. 70th & 72nd Sts.)

**Subway:** 74 St - Broadway — Dinner nightly
**Phone:** 718-426-7992
**Web:** www.zabbqueens.com
**Prices:** ©©

Surrender to your adventurous palate and expect the unexpected at Zabb Queens, famed for its scrumptious Thai food. Showcasing the cuisine of the Issan region of northeastern Thailand, this family-run restaurant aims to please with unique specialties such as crispy catfish *larb* with mango, cashews, chile, and lime juice; or delicious bowls of drunken noodles, evenly sautéed in sweet sauce with broccoli, beef, and tomatoes. Homemade coconut ice cream made rich with coconut meat and milk—is a delightful highlight that demonstrates the kitchen's dedication to quality. The staff is friendly and eager to assist in this well-maintained but unimpressive setting.

East Village sibling, Zabb City, also offers an exquisite Thai meal.

Jeanine C. Hart/MICHELIN

# Staten Island

# Staten Island

Unless you live there, chances are that Staten Island is different from the perception. Think of ports, shores, and waterfronts perched at the gateway to New York Harbor. Then, consider that, in some ways, much of what enters the city has first passed through this most secluded borough.

It is only fitting that the bridge which opened it up and may have ended its previously bucolic existence be named for Giovanni da Verrazano, the Italian explorer who first arrived here in 1524. This is particularly apt, because one of the strongest and most accurate generalizations of Staten Island is that it is home to a large Italian-American population. No self-respecting foodie would consider a visit here without picking up a scungilli pizza from **Joe and Pat's**, or at least a slice from **Nunzio**...and maybe **Denino's**, too.

Beyond this, Staten Island continues to surprise with its ethnically diverse neighborhoods. Take a virtual tour of the eastern Mediterranean at **Dinora's Market** in Stapleton for imported olives, cheeses, and freshly butchered halal meat. Or, visit the old-world Polish delis, many of which seem to comfortably survive based on their large take-out business...and those delicious home-made jams. Sri Lankan devotees can rejoice in the area surrounding Victory Boulevard for its storefront eateries and restaurants serving an impressive range of this spicy and fragrant cuisine, with perhaps a stop at **Lakruwana** or **Lakshmi's**. Close by these newcomers are a few authentic taquerias as well as the **St. George Greemarket**, where one can find produce grown locally on Staten Island's own Decker Farm. Historic Richmond Town also organizes the family-focused festival *Uncorked!*, featuring the best in professional and homemade wine and food, offering select recipes of traditional favorites.

With all this in mind, it should be no surprise to learn that the Staten Island of the future includes plans for a floating farmer's market, aquarium, and revamped waterfronts. So sit back and have a drink at one of the vibrant bars along Bay Street, and lament the world's myopic view of this much maligned borough. Drive through some of the city's wealthiest zip codes, boasting superb views of Manhattan and beyond. Whether here for the Sri Lankan fish buns from **New Asha**; to glimpse the world's only complete collection of rattlesnakes at the S.I. Zoo; or to seek out the birthplaces of Christina Aguilera and Joan Baez, a visit to Staten Island is sure to surprise.

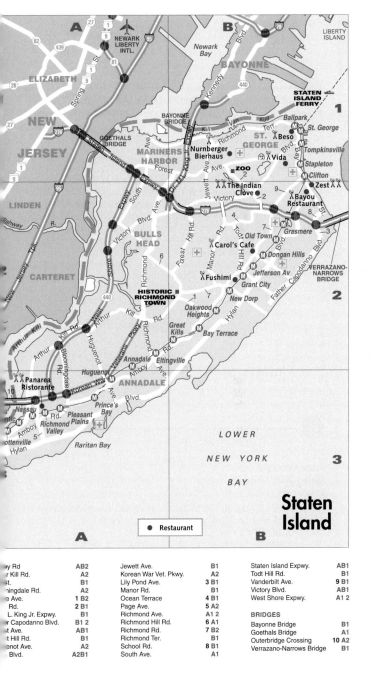

| | | | | | |
|---|---|---|---|---|---|
| ·y Rd | AB2 | Jewett Ave. | B1 | Staten Island Expwy. | AB1 |
| r Kill Rd. | A2 | Korean War Vet. Pkwy. | A2 | Todt Hill Rd. | B1 |
| it. | B1 | Lily Pond Ave. | 3 B1 | Vanderbilt Ave. | 9 B1 |
| ningdale Rd. | A2 | Manor Rd. | B1 | Victory Blvd. | AB1 |
| e Ave. | 1 B2 | Ocean Terrace | 4 B1 | West Shore Expwy. | A1 2 |
| Rd. | 2 B1 | Page Ave. | 5 A2 | | |
| L. King Jr. Expwy. | B1 | Richmond Ave. | A1 2 | **BRIDGES** | |
| r Capodanno Blvd. | B1 2 | Richmond Hill Rd. | 6 A1 | Bayonne Bridge | B1 |
| t Ave. | AB1 | Richmond Rd. | 7 B2 | Goethals Bridge | A1 |
| t Hill Rd. | B1 | Richmond Ter. | B1 | Outerbridge Crossing | 10 A2 |
| enot Ave. | A2 | School Rd. | 8 B1 | Verrazano-Narrows Bridge | B1 |
| Blvd. | A2B1 | South Ave. | A1 | | |

# Bayou Restaurant

**B2** — Cajun

1072 Bay St. (bet. Chestnut & St. Marys Aves.)

**Bus:** 51, 81 — Lunch & dinner daily
**Phone:** 718-273-4383
**Web:** www.bayoustatenisland.com
**Prices:** **$$**

Just a ferry hop from Manhattan and you are on your way to Cajun Country. Make sure you land at Bayou Restaurant, Staten Island's very own slice of the French Quarter. Despite its location in a somewhat nondescript neighborhood, close your eyes, prepare your palate, and step inside this faithfully recreated New Orleans bistro. Exposed brick walls make a gallery for trumpets, banjos, Mardi Gras beads, and portraits of Louisiana's favorite son, Louie Armstrong.

Here, the menu showcases the delicious basics of what N'awlins does best, offering red beans and rice, simmered in beer with just the right splash of heat; or skillets generously filled with seafood jambalaya in rich, spicy sauce. For dessert, the very popular fried cheesecake with raspberry sauce deserves every mouthful of praise it receives.

# Beso

**B1** — Spanish

11 Schuyler St. (bet. Richmond Terrace & Stuyvesant Pl.)

**Bus:** N/A — Lunch & dinner daily
**Phone:** 718-816-8162
**Web:** www.besonyc.com
**Prices:** **$$**

A free ride on the Staten Island Ferry from Manhattan will deliver you right across the street from this new addition to the island's dining lineup. Bring some friends to Beso ("kiss" in Spanish) to enjoy a fun night out without spending a fortune. Inside this lovely space, shawls double as window treatments, an antique Spanish sideboard forms part of the bar, and a white adobe fireplace is studded with colorful tiles. Locals love the grazing menu of vibrant tapas, which can include anything from *guajillo*-crusted tuna to *fundito* (broiled chorizo served in a green-chile and tomatillo sauce topped with melted Mahon cheese). And that's not all: entrées will pique your interest with the likes of a grilled ancho-crusted salmon fillet and a roasted duck breast glazed with honey and smoked chile.

# Carol's Cafe

American

B2

1571 Richmond Rd. (at Four Corners Rd. & Seaview Ave.)

**Bus:** 74, 76, 84, 86 — Dinner Wed – Sat
**Phone:** 718-979-5600
**Web:** www.carolscafe.com
**Prices:** $$$

Well-known on Staten Island for the cooking school she operates above her restaurant, owner Carol Frazzetta presides over the kitchen here. Frazzetta graduated from Le Cordon Bleu and studied at the Culinary Institute of America before opening Carol's Cuisine (the cooking school) in 1972. It was only natural that she would follow suit with her own café.

Decorated with a feminine touch, evident in the pink linen napkins, fresh flowers, and hanging plants that decorate the interior, Carol's only serves dinner. The seasonal menu travels through the U.S. and Europe for inspiration, fixing on the chef's favorite dishes. With entrées like oven-roasted beef brisket and pancetta- and mushroom-stuffed veal chop, homework never tasted quite so good.

# Fushimi

Fusion

B2

2110 Richmond Rd. (bet. Colfax & Lincoln Aves.)

**Bus:** 51, 81 — Lunch & dinner daily
**Phone:** 718-980-5300
**Web:** www.fushimi-us.com
**Prices:** $$$

Fushimi is one of the better Japanese-leaning restaurants on Staten Island. In a league of its own, the fare here is quite imaginative and inclines towards fusion. While the product may not be blue-ribbon, the presentation will certainly lure you—large white platters are elaborately decorated with fronds, tepees of bamboo, and the like. Despite its trite location, the expansive *mise en scéne* puts diners in a convivial mood, and is an ideal setting for the local crowd. The tiled foyer meanders into two areas: a bar packed with revelers sipping on drinks served in blue-tinged stemware; and a warm, whispery dining room/sushi bar filled with music and animated diners.

With its charming outdoor space (parking is available on premises), Fushimi is a magnet for visitors in the mood to lunch and lounge.

# The Indian Clove

Indian XX

B2

1180 Victory Blvd. (at Clove Rd.)

**Bus:** 61, 62, 66 — Lunch & dinner daily
**Phone:** 718-442-5100
**Web:** www.indianclove.com
**Prices:** $$

Poor Staten Island. With its spaghetti-and-meatballs reputation, New York City's oft-ignored borough has always been treated like a bit of a culinary stepchild. But change is in the air with The Indian Clove, a clever new Indian restaurant with a fresh, modern interior soaked in beautiful, natural light, and a serious talent for Indian fare.

Try the orange and fig salad, a gorgeous minimalist number with skinless orange segments and crispy greens; or the *tandoori jhinga*, a perfectly-cooked plate of plump, tender shrimp in fragrant spices; or a silky, bone-in lamb chop curry, spiked with chili and garlic, then carpeted in fresh coriander. Non-meat eaters should head next door to Victory Bhavan—a vegetarian, kosher restaurant by the same owners.

# Nurnberger Bierhaus

German X

B1

817 Castleton Ave. (at Davis Ave.)

**Bus:** 46, 96 — Lunch & dinner daily
**Phone:** 718-816-7461
**Web:** www.nurnbergerbierhaus.com
**Prices:** $$

A warm *willkomen* awaits patrons at this cozy Bavarian *biergarten* in the mostly residential neighborhood of West Brighton. The comfy, kitschy surroundings summon an old-world charm: waitresses don traditional frocks, peppy German folksongs pipe through the air, steins and knickknacks line shelves, and a suit of armor stands at the door.

A dark-wood bar with well-worn spouts supplies guests with a splendid, albeit dizzying, selection of imported brews; while the kitchen cooks up an authentic array of rich regional specials, like wursts and schnitzels alongside sauerkraut and mashed potatoes. The Black Forest Cake—moist and chocolaty, studded with black cherries tucked in layers of light buttercream—is the perfect end to a day of unabashed comfort seeking.

# Panarea Ristorante

Italian XX

A3

35 Page Ave. (bet. Boscombe Ave. & Richmond Valley Rd.)

**Bus:** 74 — Lunch & dinner daily
**Phone:** 718-227-8582
**Web:** www.panarearistorante.com
**Prices:** $$

Named after one of the most beautiful Aeolian Islands, this delightful spot with a lovely, accommodating staff lies in the midst of a strip mall; its cheery exterior belies the unlikely surroundings. Inside, elegant mahogany furnishings offset soft yellow walls, colorful ceramic vases display bright flowers, and low lighting casts a warm glow. A cozy banquette and ornate wine wall enhance the dark-wood bar area, which offers seating in addition to the two spacious dining rooms.

The Italian menu presents a selection of hearty entrées and house-made pastas (also available in half-orders). Linguini with fresh clams and sautéed zucchini can be ordered with whole wheat pasta for a healthier version, perhaps to offset the Italian cheesecake for dessert.

# Vida

American X

B1

381 Van Duzer St. (bet. Beach & Wright Sts.)

**Bus:** 78 — Lunch Fri – Sat
**Phone:** 718-720-1501 — Dinner Tue – Sat
**Web:** N/A
**Prices:** $$

Festooned with braids of dried poblanos, this entryway opens to a luminous, immaculate room dressed in sunny shades of yellow, serving food that further brightens this Staten Island find. Vida indeed breathes new life into its dishes, many of which tip their hats to a Southwestern culinary heritage, like the hefty Mexican duo of corn tortillas filled with flavorful Chimayo chicken or juicy pulled pork.

Accompaniments are also perfectly cooked, such as the black beans that arrive heady with thyme and fired up with chili. Tempting as the menu is, innovative daily specials display care, creativity, and are not to be missed. Desserts, such as a dense, creamy pumpkin cheesecake perfumed with cinnamon and clove, showcase the best of each season.

# Zest

B2 **French** XX

977 Bay St. (bet. Lynhurst & Willow Sts.)

**Bus:** 51, 81
**Phone:** 718-390-8477
**Web:** N/A
**Prices:** **$$**

Lunch Tue – Fri
Dinner Tue – Sun

Inside this area's new and welcome French bistro, dark wood paneling, handsome wainscoting, and jazzy red portraits reinforce a "supper club meets the Mediterranean" aura. Lighting emits a romantic golden hue to warm the cozy dining room, where close tables are set with clean, crisp linens, and topped with a votive candle and fresh flowers. A semi-private room is a great option for larger parties. The restaurant also offers outdoor seating (weather permitting) and a top-floor lounge.

The French menu features familiar favorites such as hearty and aromatic cassoulet of white beans, tender lamb, and rich duck sausage, or a traditional tarte Tatin. Though prices may be pricey by neighborhood standards, the dishes are of surprisingly fine quality.

Good food without spending a fortune? Look for the Bib Gourmand.

NY WATERWAY
FRANK SINATRA

# Where to Stay

# The Maritime

B3

363 W. 16th St. (at Ninth Ave.)

**Subway:** 14 St - 8 Av
**Phone:** 212-242-4300 or 800-466-9092
**Web:** www.themaritimehotel.com
**Prices:** $$$

121 Rooms
4 Suites

The Maritime Hotel

Polka-dotted with porthole windows, The Maritime Hotel is a 2003 reincarnation of the truly unique, 12-story white-tile edifice designed by Albert C. Ledner in 1966 to house the National Maritime Union. The location, amid Chelsea's art galleries and the Meatpacking District's hip nightlife, assures the property a clientele encompassing artists and fashionistas as well as business travelers.

A complimentary bottle of wine and a personalized note welcome guests to the cabin-like rooms, each echoing the nautical feel with its five-foot porthole window and palette of sea blues and greens. All include a CD player and a flat-screen LCD TV. Marble baths and 500-thread-count bed linens add the luxury of an ocean-liner state room. A warning to guests seeking peace and quiet: request a room on a higher floor rather than try and engineer the noise-reducing "window plugs" in the middle of the night.

Dining options include La Bottega, an Italian trattoria with a large outdoor terrace; and chic Matsuri for Japanese cuisine. Between Cabanas rooftop bar and Hiro Ballroom, opportunities abound to drink in the Chelsea scene.

# The Bowery Hotel

A2

335 Bowery (at 3rd St.)

**Subway:** Astor Pl
**Phone:** 212-505-9100 or 866-726-9379
**Web:** www.theboweryhotel.com
**Prices:** $$$$

135 Rooms
7 Suites

Gregory Goode/The Bowery Hotel

This nondescript block of what was once known as Skid Row might seem an unlikely location for a trendy boutique hotel, but Eric Goode and Sean MacPherson (who brought you the Maritime in Chelsea) are betting that their new East Village property will draw hordes of hipsters and Europeans. Though the block can be dodgy late at night, it's within easy walking distance of New York's coolest 'hoods (East Village, SoHo, Nolita, Greenwich Village, Lower East Side).

From the outside, the hotel's new redbrick façade towers castle-like above neighboring structures. Giant black-paned windows give the building a pre-war charm. Step inside and you'll be engulfed in the dim, sultry lobby, where dark woods, fireplaces, velvet couches and mosaic mirrors create a distinctly Old World air.

Those huge, sound-proofed windows afford great city views, and paired with whitewashed brick walls, make the rooms seem larger. A mix of period and contemporary pieces add to the Art Deco-meets-21st-century design, while 500-thread-count bed linens, hi-def TV, and rainfall showerheads add luxury.

The outdoor courtyard bar and restaurant Gemma are popular with the in-crowd.

# Cooper Square Hotel

A2

25 Cooper Square (bet. 4th & 5th Sts.)

**Subway:** Astor Pl
**Phone:** 212-475-5700 or 888-251-7979
**Web:** www.thecoopersquarehotel.com
**Prices:** $$$$

139 Rooms
6 Suites

The Cooper Square Hotel

What's different about the Bowery these days? Well, besides the appearance of chic boutiques and restaurants, the curving 21-story glass and aluminum tower that rises above Cooper Square. Designed by Carlos Zapata Studio and opened in fall 2008, this hotel adds a sleek note to a once-gritty East Village neighborhood.

Unlike its façade, the lodging's intimate interior spaces take their cues from the 19th century tenement building around which the hotel is built. Check-in is not your standard experience. When guests walk through the huge wooden doors, they are escorted not to the front desk (there isn't one), but to the Library, a book-lined lounge area set up with an honor bar and warmed by a fireplace in winter. Here room keys are issued and a more personalized version of the check-in process is accomplished.

Guests are escorted to rooms that command striking views of the city and feature a warm minimalist décor courtesy of furnishings by B & B Italia. An eclectic collection of books is on hand in each room. Downstairs, Table 8 restaurant brings the market-driven cuisine of Chef Govind Armstrong from L.A. to Gotham.

# Best Western Seaport Inn

C2

33 Peck Slip (at Front St.)

**Subway:** Fulton St
**Phone:** 212-766-6600 or 800-937-8376
**Web:** www.seaportinn.com
**Prices:** $$

72 Rooms

Best Western Seaport Inn

This pleasant and welcoming Best Western hotel in Manhattan's Financial District is the perfect perch for history buffs seeking old New York with modern amenities to make any guest feel at home while traveling. Cobblestoned streets and Federal-style structures on the surrounding blocks transport visitors back in time to the 17th century, when the settlement known as Nieuw Amsterdam was taking shape. This hotel is steps from the historic ships docked at South Street Seaport.

Tidy, well-kept rooms have recently been refreshed; all come equipped with comforts including a safe and complimentary wireless high-speed Internet access (available throughout the hotel). Rooms on the 6th and 7th floors offer private balconies overlooking the Brooklyn Bridge—a glittering sight after dark. The upgraded chambers also offer flat-screen TVs and whirlpool soaking tubs. Other perks include a complimentary continental breakfast each morning and fresh-baked cookies in the afternoon.

For shoppers, the mall at Pier 17 is a short walk away (where one can also catch a water taxi to Brooklyn). Also nearby are the skyscrapers of Wall Street and the greensward of Battery Park, which borders New York Harbor.

# Gild Hall

B2

15 Gold St. (enter on Platt St.)

**Subway:** Fulton St
**Phone:** 212-232-7700 or 800-268-0700
**Web:** www.thompsonhotels.com
**Prices:** $$$

126 Rooms

Thompson Hotels

A magnet for a young, hip, moneyed crowd, Gild Hall is a new member of the Thompson Hotel group. Located just steps from Wall Street, South Street Seaport, and some of downtown's best bars, this fashionable roost was conceived by interior-design guru Jim Walrod. The boutique property's style brings to mind a European gentlemen's club in the wood paneling, leather furniture, antler-shaped chandeliers, and shelves of fine literature. Yet there's nothing stodgy here; the leather furnishings sport sleek modern lines, and the chandeliers are crafted of chrome.

This clubby feel continues down the cranberry-colored hallways to the tranquil masculine-style guestrooms, where oversize leather-covered headboards, custom designed wood furnishings, and plaid throw blankets team with contemporary touches such as Sferra linens, mini-bar selections courtesy of Dean and DeLuca, and tinted glass tiles in the baths.

On the ground floor, Libertine does an ultra-modern take on an English tavern, spotlighting pub fare. Visit the Library Bar upstairs (2nd floor) if you're looking to sip on drinks and pump up the party vibe.

# The Ritz-Carlton, Battery Park

A2

2 West St. (at Battery Pl.)

**Subway:** Bowling Green
**Phone:** 212-344-0800 or 800-241-3333
**Web:** www.ritzcarlton.com
**Prices:** **$$$$**

259 Rooms
39 Suites

Spa

The Ritz-Carlton New York, Battery Park

If unique art deco furnishings, top-notch service, and stunning views of New York Harbor, the Statue of Liberty, and Ellis Island sound like your idea of a hotel, put on this Ritz. Occupying floors 3 to 14 of a 39-story glass and brick tower, the Ritz-Carlton, Battery Park lords it over a neighborhood that includes several museums as well as the greensward that defines the southwestern tip of Manhattan.

Guests nest here in spacious rooms and suites outfitted with Frette linens, featherbeds, and down duvets and pillows. Accommodations with harbor views have telescopes for checking out the dramatic waterscapes. All rooms provide classic Ritz luxury enhanced by plush robes, Bulgari bath amenities, and deep soaking tubs.

Of course, the hotel offers 24-hour room service, but you can dine on prime Angus beef on-site at 2 West; or lull over some classic cocktails in the lounge before retiring to your glorious room. Before you turn in, hand over your city-worn shoes for a complimentary overnight shine.

After a day of high-end shopping and sightseeing, return for a solid workout at the fitenss center, followed by luxurious pampering at the top-of-the-line Prada spa.

# Wall Street Inn

B3

9 S. William St. (bet. Beaver & Broad Sts.)

**Subway:** Wall St (William St.)
**Phone:** 212-747-1500 or 877-747-1500
**Web:** www.thewallstreetinn.com
**Prices:** $$

46 Rooms

The Wall Street Inn

Although it's not actually on the street that traces the wood-plank wall erected by Dutch colonists in 1653, this charming inn is nonetheless a good option for travelers with business on Wall Street. Tucked away off Williams Street, the Wall Street Inn fills two landmark buildings that date back to 1895 and 1920.

Early American period reproductions, floral prints, and marble baths decorate the two classes (superior and deluxe) of tasteful rooms; and with in-room refrigerators, high-speed Internet access, a small basement exercise room, and complimentary continental breakfast, this low-key hotel offers good value for money. A small business center offers a full range of services. The back of the inn overlooks cobbled Stone Street, one of the narrow 17th century byways, which boasts some of the city's more renowned watering holes, namely Ulysses and Brouwers.

While party-loving guests appreciate the ability to stumble back to the hotel, there is a downside. Despite the soundproofed windows, lower rooms on this side of the property are privy to the noise made by other revelers on a nightly basis.

# The Carlton

B1

88 Madison Ave. (at 29th St.)

**Subway:** 28 St (Park Ave. South)
**Phone:** 212-532-4100 or 800-601-8500
**Web:** www.carltonhotelny.com
**Prices:** $$$

293 Rooms
23 Suites

The Carlton Hotel

New and old dovetail seamlessly in this Beaux-Arts property, which premiered in 1904 as the Hotel Seville. The attractive property has gracefully entered the 21st century courtesty of a $60 million renovation led by starchitect, David Rockwell. The project's showpiece is the grand three-story lobby. With its new entrance on Madison Avenue, this space synthesizes early-20th century style with sleek seating and crystal chandeliers shrouded in cylindrical metal-mesh covers—a Rockwell signature. A sepia-toned portrait of the Hotel Seville, the lobby's focal point, glitters like a rainy scene through the three-story waterfall that envelops it.

All 316 rooms have a modern aspect and include geometric-print fabrics, 42-inch flat-screen TVs, and large work desks. Streamlined furnishings now complement such amenities as Frette linens, in-room wireless Internet access, plush robes, and Apple iHome sound systems.

Off the lobby, the casual-chic Café serves breakfast, lunch, and dinner, and its bar does a brisk happy-hour business.

# Gramercy Park Hotel

B2

2 Lexington Ave. (at 21st St.)

**Subway:** 23 St (Park Ave. South)
**Phone:** 212-920-3300 or 866-784-1300
**Web:** www.gramercyparkhotel.com
**Prices:** **$$$$**

140 Rooms
45 Suites

Gramercy Park Hotel

Reinvented by hip hotelier Ian Schrager and artist Julian Schnabel, the lobby of this 1925 Renaissance Revival-style edifice could be an artist's home with its juxtaposition of true antiques and contemporary pieces. A custom-made Venetian glass chandelier hangs from the coffered ceiling, illuminating periodically changing works by modern masters such as Andy Warhol, Keith Haring, and Schnabel himself.

Velvet draperies in deep-rose hues with royal blue accents, tapestry-print fabrics, and louvered wood blinds lend a masculine feel to the rooms. Original photography and paintings adorn the walls. In keeping with its history of hosting artists, actors, and other glitterati, the hotel still pampers its guests. A landscaped private rooftop garden for dining (accessible only via a special key); a key to adjacent Gramercy Park—impossible to access unless you live on the square overlooking the gated greensward; personal trainers at the on-site Aerospace gym; and a "best of" room-service menu from famous area restaurants will give you the idea. Meanwhile, the celebutante scene at the Rose and Jade bars begs you to don your best Manolos.

# Inn at Irving Place

B3

56 Irving Pl. (bet 17th & 18th Sts.)

**Subway:** 14 St - Union Sq
**Phone:** 212-533-4600 or 800-685-1447
**Web:** www.innatirving.com
**Prices:** $$$$

12 Rooms

Roy Wright

Infused with a 19th-century charm not often found in Manhattan hotels, this inn takes up two single-family brownstones built in 1834. To find it, look for the street number; the inn is unmarked. Walk inside and you'll be enveloped in a cozy parlor furnished with antique settees and armchairs covered in floral-patterned silk. If it's cold out, chances are the fireplace will be roaring.

A glass of champagne and a plate of cookies welcome you to your room. Decked out with hardwood floors and period furniture, each of the 12 guestrooms offers a work desk, a well-stocked minibar and a Sony CD/radio. Pedestal sinks, antique mirrors, and black and white tile decorate the large bathrooms.

In the morning, a continental breakfast including fresh-baked croissants and sliced fruit is served in the parlor or delivered to your room—whichever you prefer. For a civilized afternoon break, make reservations for the five-course high tea at Lady Mendl's tea salon. Cibar Lounge, also on-site, is a clubby place for a martini and light fare.

One caveat: If you're traveling with heavy luggage in tow, note that there's a steep flight of stairs at the inn's entrance.

# W - Union Square

B3

201 Park Ave. South (at 17th St.)

**Subway:** 14 St - Union Sq
**Phone:** 212-253-9119 or 877-782-0027
**Web:** www.whotels.com
**Prices:** **$$$$**

257 Rooms
13 Suites

W New York - Union Square

Since its launch in New York City in 1998, the W brand has come to signify sophistication in its minimalist contemporary design and stylish comfort. This member of the Starwood group is no exception. Designed by David Rockwell, it recalls the grand gathering places of the early 20th century inside the landmark 1911 granite and limestone Guardian Life Building, but with a modern twist. In the two-story lobby, the Living Room provides a chic place to meet and greet under tall arched windows, while up the striking staircase, the Beaux-Arts-style Great Room preserves the past. Now used for conferences, this grand chamber is framed by splendid marble columns and original plasterwork on the coffered ceiling.

Rooms and suites each come in three sizes and even the least-expensive rooms are large by New York City standards. All see to your comfort with luxurious velvet armchairs, massive work desks, goose-down duvets and pillows, and beaming windows with an incredible view of Union Square.

The neighborhood's hip frequent the swank basement club, Underbar; while Olives caters to gourmands with a Mediterranean menu designed by Chef Todd English.

# Gansevoort

B1

18 Ninth Ave. (at 13th St.)

**Subway:** 14 St - 8 Av
**Phone:** 212-206-6700 or 877-462-7386
**Web:** www.hotelgansevoort.com
**Prices:** $$$$

166 Rooms
21 Suites

Hotel Gansevoort

In the Dutch language, the name "Gansevoort" refers to the goose (*gans*) at the head (*voort*) of a flock of geese, and indeed, this swanky hotel rises above; its 14 stories tower over the burgeoning hip-dom of the Meatpacking District.

As you step into the ultra-chic lobby, you'll be launched into the 21st century through a 14-foot-high revolving door. Inside, the building seems to be supported by light, thanks to internally illuminated glass columns. Lofty rooms with 9-foot ceilings dress in dusky hues with splashes of blackberry; beds wear 400-thread-count Egyptian cotton sheets, and large lavish bathrooms are equipped with sleek steel sinks. On the high floors, huge windows command fabulous views of the Hudson River and surrounding city. Downstairs, Ono seats 300 for Japanese food.

Speaking of views, check out the hotel's rooftop. The neighborhood hot spot and the Gansevoort's signature, the rooftop holds the hip Plunge Bar and a heated swimming pool that pipes in underwater music. Special events are made even more so in the rooftop loft, where a landscaped garden can't quite compete with the 360-degree cityscape.

# The Standard

B1

848 Washington St. (at 13th St.)

**Subway:** 14 St - 8 Av
**Phone:** 212-645-4646
**Web:** www.standardhotels.com
**Prices:** $$$

337 Rooms

Nikolas Koenig

Setting the standard for accommodations in the Meatpacking District, this modern slab of concrete and glass stands on concrete stilts above an area filled with low-rise warehouses. The structure's lofty position insures that the hotel lords it over the neighborhood, drinking in every inch of this spectacular city. As if that weren't enough, the building is literally suspended above the High Line, the city's much-anticipated new greensward that is revamping an abandoned freight railway into a public park.

The lobby sets the sexy tone with its mirrored ceiling, sleek furnishings, and light-diffusing walls. Rooms are small, the décor funky and retro. Baths are open to the rest of the space, so privacy is in short supply. Hands-down, the floor-to-ceiling windows win the prize for their breathtaking panoramas of the Hudson River and the Manhattan skyline. Ask for a corner room to optimize your view.

Off the lobby, the Living Room cocktail lounge overlooks the grand plaza and spins tunes by live DJs on Friday and Saturday nights. Planned for the near future is a rooftop that will house a hip lounge and a giant Jacuzzi.

# The Hotel on Rivington

B2

107 Rivington St. (bet. Essex & Ludlow Sts.)

**Subway:** Delancey St
**Phone:** 212-475-2600 or 800-915-1537
**Web:** www.hotelonrivington.com
**Prices:** $$$

89 Rooms
21 Suites

© Hotel on Rivington

Grit and glamour collide on the Lower East Side, a neighborhood that has come into its own while retaining its diversity and refreshing lack of attitude. A great example of the area's newfound glamour, the Hotel on Rivington towers 21 stories above low-rise brick buildings. Floor-to-ceiling glass walls offer magnificent unobstructed views of Manhattan.

The remarkable result of a collaboration of cutting-edge architects, designers, decorators, and artists from around the world, this hotel combines sleek minimalist décor with ultramodern amenities, and, yes, comfort. If you notice anything else besides the view, you'll appreciate the Swedish sleep system that conforms to your every curve by sensing your body temperature and weight, as well as the Italian mosaic bathrooms decked out with heated floors, steam showers, and two-person Japanese-style soaking tubs. An on-site fitness facility, a DVD library of rare films, and a restaurant serving global fare round out the amenities.

Largely populated by guests who work in the fashion, music, and media industries, the Rivington appeals to an artsy clientele who prefers not to stay in mainstream midtown.

# The Benjamin

B3

125 E. 50th St. (bet. Lexington & Third Aves.)

**Subway:** 51 St
**Phone:** 212-715-2500 or 866-222-2365
**Web:** www.thebenjamin.com
**Prices:** $$$$

112 Rooms
79 Suites

Spa

The Benjamin

From its ECOTEL certification to the cheerful and efficient staff who greet guests by name and care for them, The Benjamin ensures the comfort of its visitors. Before you arrive, just call the Sleep Concierge, who will help outfit your room with your preferred pillow (from a menu of 12 different types), aromatherapy fragrance, and relaxing lullaby. Then settle into the custom-designed mattress, wrap yourself in the fluffy duvet, and drift off to sleep. Argon-gas-filled windows should filter out any unwanted sounds. Canine guests can expect equally sweet dreams thanks to customized pet beds, puppy bathrobes, and gourmet food.

Rooms are designed as executive suites, encompassing all the technological amenities to facilitate working on-site. Many of the accommodations also have galley kitchens with state-of-the-art appliances. Given advance notice, the hotel will even stock your fridge with your favorite foods and beverages. Don't care to cook? The Restaurant at The Benjamin and the Emery Bar are right downstairs.

In the public spaces, marble floors, upholstered walls, and Venetian mirrors reflect the spirit of this 1927 structure, which owes its elegant style to architect Emery Roth.

# Elysée

B2

60 E. 54th St. (bet. Madison & Park Aves.)

**Subway:** 5 Av - 53 St
**Phone:** 212-753-1066 or 800-535-9733
**Web:** www.elyseehotel.com
**Prices:** $$$

89 Rooms
12 Suites

Hotel Elysée

Low-key, intimate, and discreet, the Elysée has weathered the decades with grace since its opening in 1926. A timeless quality pervades the black and white marble flooring and gold-fabric-covered walls of the lobby, as well as the French-influenced old-world style in the guestrooms where cut-glass and polished brass sconces cast a warm glow. In its early days, this hotel was a haven for writers, actors, and musicians. Vladimir Horowitz once lived in the suite where his piano still stands; Tennessee Williams lived and died here (in the Sunset Suite); and Ava Gardner once made this her New York home.

The property's soft residential ambience appeals to a range of patrons. Moneyed or not, they appreciate the complimentary breakfast and evening wine and hors d'oeuvres, served in the second-floor Club Room; as well as the computer located there for guest use. Guests may also request a complimentary pass for nearby NY Sports Club including their daily fitness classes.

The Elysée is known and loved for its premier location, just steps away from 5th Avenue with its shopping galore, MoMa, St. Patrick's, Rockefeller Center, and many other midtown gems.

# Four Seasons New York

B1

57 E. 57th St. (bet. Madison & Park Aves.)

**Subway:** 59 St
**Phone:** 212-758-5700 or 800-487-3769
**Web:** www.fourseasons.com
**Prices:** **$$$$**

305 Rooms
63 Suites

Spa

Peter Vitale

Noted architect I.M. Pei designed the monumentally elegant Four Seasons New York in 1993. Nothing is small about this property. The tallest hotel in the city, the limestone-clad tower soars 52 stories in a Postmodern style inspired by the 1920s. Inside the 57th Street entrance, you'll walk into a grand foyer decorated with temple-like pillars, marble floors and a 33-foot backlit onyx ceiling.

The hotel also boasts some of the city's largest rooms, which, at 600 square feet, are doubtless among the most luxurious as well. A recent refurbishment installed plasma-screen TVs in the opulent bathrooms, which also feature marble soaking tubs that fill in just 60 seconds. Top-drawer service includes a 24-hour concierge, perks for pets and children, and a fabulous newly redesigned spa offering a full spectrum of massages, facials, and body treatments. You'll find state-of-the-art exercise equipment, along with a whirlpool, steam room, and sauna in the fitness facility.

When you're ready to kick back with a martini, stop by The Bar, with its soaring ceilings and cozy curving banquettes. The intimate lounge called Ty serves afternoon tea as well as evening cocktails.

# Library

A4

299 Madison Ave. (enter on 41st St.)

**Subway:** Grand Central - 42 St
**Phone:** 212-983-4500 or 877-793-7323
**Web:** www.libraryhotel.com
**Prices:** $$$

60 Rooms

HK Hotels

A welcoming inn well-located in Midtown, The Library keeps to a literary theme with its collection of 6,000 volumes (if that's not enough books for you, the New York Public and the Pierpont Morgan libraries are just minutes away). Each floor is numbered after a category in the Dewey Decimal System, and rooms contain books on a particular subject. Math maven? Request a room on the fifth floor. Literature your thing? Head to the 8th floor.

Rooms, though small, are comfortable, and manage to squeeze a basic desk, an all-inclusive entertainment center (containing bookshelves, drawers, a small closet, a mini bar, and a flat-screen TV) into the cramped quarters. Modern bathrooms come equipped with a hairdryer, magnifying mirror, and scale.

On the second floor, the Reading Room is where you'll find the complimentary continental breakfast laid out in the morning, snacks throughout the day, and the wine and cheese reception each evening. The comfy Writer's Den and the terrace Poetry Garden are perfect for—what else?—reading.

When it's warm outside, head up to the rooftop bar—Bookmarks—for a cocktail and snack.

# New York Palace

A3

455 Madison Ave. (enter on 50th St.)

**Subway:** 51 St
**Phone:** 212-888-7000 or 800-697-2522
**Web:** www.newyorkpalace.com
**Prices:** $$$$

808 Rooms
86 Suites

Spa

The New York Palace

Best recognized by its lovely gated courtyard—formerly a carriage entrance—on Madison Avenue at 50th Street, The Palace serves up New York City on a silver platter. Enter through these gates and you'll be immersed in the old-world opulence that fills the 1882 Villard Houses, a U-shaped group of brownstones designed in the Italian Renaissance style by the firm of McKim, Mead and White.

Today the property blends the town houses with a 55-story tower added in 1980. Here, you'll find 808 guest rooms, 86 suites, a vast spa and fitness center, and 22,000 square feet of conference facilities. Guests in the modern tower rooms have access to a private lounge and concierge, as well as personal butler services. More modest deluxe rooms feature no less comfort, however, with their warm tones, new bedding, and oversize marble baths.

If you can tear yourself away from this palace be sure to check out the neighboring sights and sounds. Come back for afternoon tea in the lobby, or to experience cutting-edge cuisine in Gilt's sexy walnut-paneled space. Sophisticated cocktails abound in the contemporary Gilt Bar, which spills into the opulent courtyard terrace during warmer weather.

# Roger Williams

A6

131 Madison Ave. (at 31st St.)

**Subway:** 33 St
**Phone:** 212-448-7000 or 888-448-7788
**Web:** www.hotelrogerwilliams.com
**Prices:** **$$$**

191 Rooms
2 Suites

Hotel Roger Williams

Just blocks from the Empire State Building, this stylish boutique hotel makes a bright impression with its clean lines and pure colors. The "living room," as the lobby is called, is adorned with light wood paneling, soaring ceilings, and 20-foot-high windows creating an airy, cosmopolitan feel. Comfy contemporary furniture scattered throughout the lobby provide contemporary spaces to meet and greet.

Though on the small side, rooms at "the Roger" all feature flat-screen plasma TVs, mini bars, Aveda bath products, and wireless high-speed Internet access. Splashes of tangerine, lime green, cobalt blue, and red illuminate each room. The peppy colors aren't noisy and neither are the accommodations, thanks to well-insulated windows that help dampen the hustle and bustle of Midtown. Japanese-inspired double rooms add shoji screens and sliding-glass bathroom doors, while 15 garden terrace rooms enjoy private patios and stirring cityscapes.

A help-yourself European style breakfast—ranging from fresh croissants, to smoked salmon and prosciutto—is available in the mezzanine lounge each morning, and it's a sunny spot for an afternoon espresso as well.

# 70 Park Avenue

A5

70 Park Ave. (at 38th St.)

**Subway:** Grand Central - 42 St
**Phone:** 212-973-2400 or 877-707-2752
**Web:** www.70parkave.com
**Prices:** $$$

201 Rooms
4 Suites

David Phelps

For sophisticated Midtown digs located mere minutes away by foot from Grand Central Terminal, 70 Park can't be beat. This Murray Hill property embodies the Kimpton Group's signature elements: care, comfort, style, flavor, and fun.

Care highlights thoughtful amenities such as the pet-friendly policy, and a dedicated yoga channel on your flat-screen TV. In-room comfort surrounds you in the down comforters and pillows, terrycloth robes, and luxury bath products. Designed by Jeffrey Bilhuber in neutral hues of limestone gray, shimming bronze, and light cocoa brown, the hotel's contemporary style speaks for itself. The complimentary wine reception held around the limestone fireplace on weeknights affords guests an opportunity for fun, as does the lively bar scene at the Silverleaf Tavern. You'll taste the 70 Park flavor in the tavern's limited menu of pub fare.

Other reasons to stay here? An easy walk to midtown offices and shopping, 24-hour room service, in-room spa services, and guest privileges at the NY Sports Club—a couple of blocks away. Strollers, cribs, and connecting rooms accommodate families.

# The St. Regis

A2

2 E. 55th St. (at Fifth Ave.)

**Subway:** 5 Av - 53 St
**Phone:** 212-753-4500 or 800-759-7550
**Web:** www.stregis.com/newyork
**Prices:** $$$$

186 Rooms
70 Suites

Spa

Bruce Buck

Stylish and elegant, and with service close to perfection, the St. Regis reigns among the city's finest hotels. Commissioned by John Jacob Astor in 1904, this Beaux-Arts confection at the corner of Fifth Avenue is located just blocks from Central Park, MoMA, and other Midtown attractions. Its public spaces and lobby, from the painted ceilings to the marble staircase, are steeped in Gilded Age opulence.

Rooms fitted with elegant guestrooms are lined with silk wall coverings and custom-made furniture. Guests in the spacious suites (the smallest is 600 square feet and range up to 3,400 square feet) are cosseted with extra luxuries, such as a bouquet of fresh roses delivered daily. Unparalleled service includes a butler you can call on 24 hours a day, an on-site florist, complimentary garment pressing when you arrive, and the exclusive Remède spa. Their signature massage calms jangled nerves with a mix of Shiatsu, Swedish, deep-tissue, and reflexology.

Be sure to stop in the King Cole Bar to peek at Maxfield Parrish's famous mural, and to sip a Bloody Mary, which was introduced here in the 1920s.

# The Vincci Avalon

A6

16 E. 32nd St. (bet. Fifth & Madison Aves.)

**Subway:** 33 St
**Phone:** 212-299-7000 or 888-442-8256
**Web:** www.theavalonny.com
**Prices:** **$$**

80 Rooms
20 Suites

VINCCI HOTELES

Right around the corner from the Empire State Building, this boutique property indulges business travelers with six meeting rooms and complimentary high-speed Internet access in each guestroom. Leisure travelers and theater lovers profit from The Avalon's setting, a short walk from Times Square and the bright lights of Broadway.

All appreciate large "Superior" rooms, each of which flaunt 27-inch flat-screen TVs, ample closet space, velour robes, and Irish cotton linens. Dark hardwood floors, earth tones (soft green, brown, and rust), and Italian marble baths accentuate the décor. At the top tier of room types, the 20 executive suites average 450 square feet and come with Jacuzzi tubs, Fax machines, sofa beds, and Bose Wave radios.

Just off the elegant lobby, which is set about with pillars and paneling, the Library/Club room is a den-like area with free access to WiFi and a personal computer. Guests here will enjoy thoughtful and warm service from the affable staff, as well as discounted passes to the nearby Boom gym. The Avalon Bar & Grill serves a buffet breakfast each morning and American fare for lunch and dinner.

# The Waldorf=Astoria

B3

301 Park Ave. (bet. 49th & 50th Sts.)

**Subway:** 51 St
**Phone:** 212-355-3000 or 800-925-3673
**Web:** www.waldorfastoria.com
**Prices:** $$$$

1235 Rooms
208 Suites

The Waldorf=Astoria

Nothing says New York high society like the Waldorf=Astoria. Built in 1931, the hotel blends exquisite art deco ornamentation and lavish Second Empire furnishings. The original Waldorf, built in 1893, was demolished along with its companion, the Astoria, to make room for the Empire State Building. The huge "new" hotel (including its boutique counterpart with a private entrance, the Waldorf Towers) occupies the entire block between Park and Lexington avenues. Its lobby features a striking inlaid-tile mosaic and art deco chandelier, and emanates a generally palatial feel.

A $400-million renovation refreshed the grand dame; and deluxe fabrics as well as classic furniture dress the richly appointed and beautifully maintained rooms and suites, all outfitted with sumptuous marble baths.

Long a Midtown power scene, the mahogany-paneled Bull and Bear teems with brokers and finance types who come for the signature martinis, the dry-aged prime Angus beef, and the men's-club ambience. Also among the property's four restaurants, Peacock Alley (in the center of the main lobby) is worth seeking out for its elegant cuisine.

# W - The Tuscany

A5

120 E. 39th St. (bet. Lexington & Park Aves.)

**Subway:** Grand Central - 42 St
**Phone:** 212-686-1600 or 888-627-7189
**Web:** www.whotels.com
**Prices:** **$$$**

113 Rooms
7 Suites

W New York - The Tuscany

Tucked away on tree-lined 39th Street, not far from Grand Central Station, The Tuscany (not to be confused with its sister spot, W New York - The Court, located on the same block cultivates a sensual, relaxed atmosphere. It begins in the cozy lobby (or "living room" in W speak) done up in luxuriant purples, greens, and browns. Velvets and satins, rich woods and supple leather add to the lush feeling of the space, which beckons as a comfortable spot for a drink or a private conversation.

Spacious rooms, highlighted by bold, deep colors and textures, feature original contemporary furnishings in the typical W style. Pillow-top mattresses, goose-down duvets, and spa robes make for a comfy stay. Bathrooms, however, are on the small side, but at least feature fun Bliss products. In-room electronics include access to a CD/DVD library. W's signature "Whatever, whenever" service is available 24/7 by pressing "0" on your cordless, dual-line phone.

Athletic types will want to visit Sweat, the on-site fitness center. Before or after your workout, you can grab a quick bite at the Audrey Cafe.

# Algonquin

C3

59 W. 44th St. (bet. Fifth & Sixth Aves.)

**Subway:** 42 St - Bryant Pk
**Phone:** 212-840-6800
**Web:** www.algonquinhotel.com
**Prices:** $$$

150 Rooms
24 Suites

Algonquin Hotel

New York's oldest operating hotel remains true to its classically elegant roots and timeless aura. Best known for the the circle of literati, including Dorothy Parker and Robert Benchley, who lunched in the Round Table Room in the years after World War I, the Algonquin preserves the feel and look of a fine Edwardian club.

Rooms have been smartly upgraded to include all modern amenities (tastefully hidden); top-quality fabrics and fittings lend rich jewel tones to the accommodations. You may not want to rise from your pillow-top mattress, 350-thread-count linen sheets, down pillows, and the famous "Algonquin Bed." (Order one for home, if you like.) Each of the suites adds a fully stocked refrigerator.

For a taste of 1930s café society, step into the Oak Room, the legendary cabaret where famous audiences and performers (crooners Harry Connick Jr. and Diana Krall got their starts here) made merry. The mood lingers, and the shows still go on, with such talent as Andrea Marcovicci and Jack Jones. In the intimate Blue Bar, you'll find artwork by the late Al Hirschfeld, who was a regular.

# Casablanca

C3

147 W. 43rd St. (bet. Broadway & Sixth Ave.)

**Subway:** 42 St - Bryant Pk
**Phone:** 212-869-1212 or 888-922-7225
**Web:** www.casablancahotel.com
**Prices:** $$

43 Rooms
5 Suites

Christopher Ottaunick/HKHotels

Exotic tilework, warm wood paneling, and wrought-iron details greet guests at this European-style family-owned hotel. Convenient to Times Square and its many attractions, the Casablanca takes on the theme of the 1942 film starring Humphrey Bogart and Ingrid Bergman—without being kitschy. All the elements are here, from the pastel mural of the city of Casablanca that decorates the lobby stairway to the second-floor cafe called—you guessed it—Rick's.

With its tiled fireplace and bentwood chairs, Rick's Café is where you can wake up to a complimentary continental breakfast. In the afternoon, a selection of tea, coffee drinks, and cookies will tide you over until the wine-and-cheese reception at 5 P.M. Room service is provided by Tony's de Napoli restaurant, next door to the hotel.

The Moroccan ambience extends to the rooms, furnished with wooden headboards, damask linens, ceiling fans, and bathrobes. Guests enjoy free passes to the New York Sports Club, and a DVD library of films starring New York City.

No matter where you go when you leave this oasis, one thing's for sure: you'll always have Casablanca.

# Chambers

B4

15 W. 56th St. (bet. Fifth & Sixth Aves.)

**Subway:** 57 St
**Phone:** 212-974-5656 or 866-204-5656
**Web:** www.chambershotel.com
**Prices:** $$$$

72 Rooms
5 Suites

Scott G. Morris/SGM Photography

Ideal for doing serious business or serious shopping (Bendel's is around the corner; Norma Kamali is next door; Bergdorf's is one block up), Chambers exudes a downtown feel despite its midtown location. It all begins with the two-story lobby where plenty of open space and a flickering fireplace provide a welcome cozy space. Sequestered seating on the mezzanine level above is the place to sneak away to with your laptop or a glass of wine—perhaps both.

The hotel's commitment to contemporary artists shows beautifully in the well-curated collection of more than 500 original pieces of art that is displayed throughout the public spaces, with different installations on each floor. Rooms continue the modern mood in SoHo-like appointments such as a plate-glass desktop balanced on a sawhorse-style base, and a poured concrete floor in the bathroom. Despite the cool aspect of the front-desk staff, service is very warm and accommodating.

Whether you're visiting for business or pleasure, one thing is for sure, the hotel will envelop you with their creativity and luxury.

# City Club

C3

55 W. 44th St. (bet. Fifth & Sixth Aves.)

**Subway:** 42 St - Bryant Pk
**Phone:** 212-921-5500
**Web:** www.cityclubhotel.com
**Prices:** **$$$**

62 Rooms
3 Suites

Matt Hranek

Originally conceived as an elite social club opened in 1904, the City Club now opens its doors to all. Located on 44th Street, the intimately scaled hotel is situated among a number of still active private clubs and has a sophisticated and exclusive ambiance with a petite lobby that feels more like the entryway of a private residence than a hotel. The rooms are attractively designed to maximize square footage with a handsome beige and brown color scheme dominating. Marble bathrooms are outfitted with bidets and Waterworks showers.

All guests enjoy complimentary high-speed Internet access as well as in-room DVD players, and electronic safe-deposit boxes. In the evening, turndown service includes a plate of freshly baked cookies. Truly spectacular are the hotel's three duplex suites, decked out with private terraces and circular stairways that lead up to the sleeping room from a well-appointed sitting room below. Room Service is provided by Daniel Boulud's DB Bistro Moderne (*see restaurant listing*) which connects to the lobby via a panelled wine bar.

# Jumeirah Essex House

A3

160 Central Park South (bet. Sixth & Seventh Aves.)

**Subway:** 57 St - 7 Av
**Phone:** 212-247-0300 or 888-645-5697
**Web:** www.jumeirahessexhouse.com
**Prices:** $$$$

428 Rooms
81 Suites

Jumeirah Group

Operated by the Dubai-based Jumeirah hospitality group, the venerable Essex House flaunts its enviable location at the foot of Central Park, with the shops and restaurants of 5th Avenue and the Time Warner Center right outside its door. This art deco gem, which opened its doors the same year as the Empire State Building (1931), underwent a $90-million facelift after its new owners took over. Public spaces, outfitted with the likes of Macassar ebony chairs, and red wood carpets hand-knotted in Nepal, now pay homage to the hotel's vintage.

Why wouldn't you feel coddled in a room fitted with custom-designed furnishings, a glass-vessel sink, a touch-screen control pad, and lights underneath the nightstands to prevent stumbling in the dark? Access to the in-house spa and 24-hour health club are added perks.

Newest on the roster of renovations is the 2,500-square-foot two-bedroom Presidential Suite, indeed fit for royalty with magnificent park views, original artwork, sumptuous fabrics, and bathrooms lined in marble and rosewood.

Tony Chi designed the dining room at South Gate, where contemporary cuisine takes on an urbane twist.

# Le Parker Meridien

A3

118 W. 57th St. (bet. Sixth & Seventh Aves.)

**Subway:** 57 St
**Phone:** 212-245-5000 or 800-543-4300
**Web:** www.parkermeridien.com
**Prices:** **$$$$**

510 Rooms
221 Suites

Andrew Bordwin/Le Parker Meridien

To reach the lobby here, guests must pass through a columned, two-story hallway lined with marble, which sets the tone for Le Parker Meridien experience. The hotel, just steps away from Carnegie Hall, Central Park, and Fifth Avenue shops, divides its accommodations between the upper and lower tower—each has their own elevator bank.

Expect ergonomically designed rooms and suites to tout contemporary chic with platform beds, warm woods, 32-inch TVs, and CD/DVD players. There's a business center on-site, but if you wish to work in your room, a large desk, high-speed Internet access, and a halogen reading lamp provide all the necessities.

In the morning, fuel up on tasty breakfast dishes at Norma's. Then get in a workout at Gravity—the 15,000-square-foot fitness facility—or take a dip in the enclosed and heated rooftop pool that overlooks Central Park. For dinner, choose between French bistro fare at Seppi's or a simple burger at the rough-and-ready burger joint, arguably the best in the city.

Whimsical touches, like a "do not disturb" sign that reads "fuhgetaboudit," and vintage cartoons broadcast in the guest elevators, set this place apart from your standard midtown business hotel.

# The London NYC

A3

151 W. 54th St. (bet. Sixth & Seventh Aves.)

**Subway:** 57 St
**Phone:** 212-307-5000 or 866-690-2029
**Web:** www.thelondonnyc.com
**Prices:** $$$$

549 Rooms
13 Suites

The London NYC

The London NYC is like a hop across the Pond without the guilt of those pesky carbon emissions. Formerly the Righa Royal Hotel, The London with its ivy-covered façade rises 54 stories above Midtown.

Guest suites epitomize modern sophistication with Italian linens, limed oak flooring, sectional sofas, and embossed-leather desks. Tones of soft gray, plum, sky-blue, and crisp white dominate. Styled by Waterworks, bathrooms have the last word in luxury, with white marble mosaic-tile floors, double rain showerheads, and sumptuous towels and bathrobes.

Since service is a hallmark of The London, the expert concierge services of Quintessentially are on hand to assist you with any business or personal requests. Novel extras include complimentary cleaning of your workout wear, and an iPod docking station in each room.

The London is also known as the New York home of celebrity chef Gordon Ramsay. He may be infamous for his cantankerous spirit, but Gordon Ramsay at The London *(see restaurant listing)* impresses with its polished service and contemporary cuisine. For a casual alternative, try Maze for Ramsay's menu of small plates served in a sleek brasserie setting.

# Metro

C4

45 W. 35th St. (bet. Fifth & Sixth Aves.)

**Subway:** 34 St - Herald Sq
**Phone:** 212-947-2500 or 800-356-3870
**Web:** www.hotelmetronyc.com
**Prices:** **$$**

179 Rooms
3 Suites

Linda Davis/Hotel Metro

Though not hip or stylish, the Hotel Metro is nonetheless a good stay for the money. Located in the heart of the Garment District, near Penn Station (light sleepers take note that the hotel's location is not a quiet one), the building was constructed in 1901. An art deco-inspired lobby leads into a spacious breakfast room/lounge where tea and coffee are available throughout the day.

Guest rooms have been recently refurbished and are equipped with mini-bars, and upgraded "plush-top" mattresses. Many of the marble bathrooms benefit from natural light, and the overall standard of housekeeping is good. The hotel offers high-speed wireless Internet access, as well as a small business center. Room rates include a complimentary continental breakfast served in the lounge area.

From the large rooftop bar which has become quite popular, you can enjoy stunning views of the Empire State Building and the surrounding neighborhood, which includes Macy's, for all you hard-core shoppers.

# The Michelangelo

A4

152 W. 51st St. (at Seventh Ave.)

**Subway:** 50 St (Broadway)
**Phone:** 212-765-1900 or 800-237-0990
**Web:** www.michelangelohotel.com
**Prices:** **$$$**

163 Rooms
15 Suites

The Michelangelo

Steps from Times Square, the Theater District, Rockefeller Center, and midtown offices, The Michelangelo caters to both leisure and business travelers. A recent renovation has polished the two-story lobby, regal in its liberal use of marble, rich fabric panels, and crystal chandeliers.

Winding hallways have been freshened with new paint and carpeting; shelves of books add a homey touch. Attractively appointed with marble foyers, small sitting areas, down pillows, and Bose radio/CD players, guest rooms are generous for Manhattan, with a standard king measuring about 325 square feet (upgrades get bigger from there). Marble bathrooms come equipped with hair dryers, make-up mirrors, deep soaking tubs, terrycloth robes, and even a small TV. Part of the Starhotels group, The Michelangelo interprets hospitality with *gusto di vivere italiano*. Turndown service, a complimentary continental breakfast, a small fitness center, and limo service to Wall Street on weekday mornings number among the amenities.

Chef/partner Marco Canora Canora (also of Hearth) has added a touch of urbane flair to the hotel's erstwhile dining room with Insieme, and its duet of classic and contemporary Italian dishes.

# The Peninsula New York

B4

700 Fifth Ave. (at 55th St.)

**Subway:** 5 Av - 53 St
**Phone:** 212-956-2888 or 800-262-9467
**Web:** www.peninsula.com
**Prices:** $$$$

185 Rooms
54 Suites

The Peninsula New York

When this magnificent 1905 hotel was built as The Gotham, it was the city's tallest skyscraper, towering 23 stories. Today the property still sparkles as the Peninsula group's U.S. flagship.

Plush rooms exude a timeless elegance, and art nouveau accents complement their rich colors and appointments. Ample in size and well-conceived for business travelers, each guest room provides a silent fax machine, and a bottled-water bar (with a choice of still or sparkling water). Service is a strong suit at The Peninsula, and the smartly liveried staff effortlessly executes your every request.

You could spend hours on the rooftop, site of the new ESPA, the state-of-the-art fitness center, and the glass-enclosed pool. Asian, European, and Ayurvedic philosophies inspire the spa treatments; check in early and relax in the Asian tea lounge, then loosen up those muscles in the steam room or sauna before your massage. Sharing this lofty perch, the new rooftop bar, Salon de Ning, wows patrons with its Fifth Avenue views and vivid Shanghai style. In addition to the interior bar, there are two large outdoor terraces furnished with Chinese-style day beds—perfect for a romantic liaison.

# The Plaza

B3

768 Fifth Ave. (at Central Park South)

**Subway:** 5 Av - 59 St
**Phone:** 212-759-3000
**Web:** www.theplaza.com
**Prices:** $$$$

180 Rooms
102 Suites

The Plaza

This storied beaux-arts masterpiece once again ushers the well-heeled and well-traveled through its gilded doors. Opened in 1907 and now managed by Fairmont Hotels & Resorts, this historic landmark has been lavishly renovated to restore the past and embrace the future. The hotel's Fifth Avenue lobby has an ethereal feel with gleaming marble flooring, Baccarat chandeliers, and picture windows framing the Pulitzer fountain in Grand Army Plaza.

Generously sized accommodations mix elegant appointments with a touch-screen monitor that dims the lighting, adjusts the temperature, and contacts guest services. You won't want to leave the mosaic stone-tiled bathroom complete with 24-karat-gold fixtures. And with each guest floor staffed by a team of affable butlers, the service is as impressive as the surroundings.

Purveyors of all things luxurious await at the Shops at the Plaza, where the best place for *kaffee und kuchen* is Demel Viennese pastry shop on the lower level. For prime pampering, treatments at Caudalíe Vinothérapie Spa use beneficial polyphenols extracted from grapes. End your day with a Manhattan at the Oak Bar followed by a scrumptious dinner at the spiffed-up Oak Room.

# The Ritz-Carlton, Central Park

B3

50 Central Park South (at Sixth Ave.)

**Subway:** 5 Av - 59 St
**Phone:** 212-308-9100 or 800-826-8129
**Web:** www.ritzcarlton.com
**Prices:** **$$$$**

213 Rooms
47 Suites

Spa

The Ritz-Carlton New York, Central Park

Built in 1929 as the St. Moritz, the Ritz holds its place at the vanguard of luxury and graceful service among Manhattan's hotels. While the marble-floored reception lobby remains intimate, it opens into a grand two-story gathering space.

Sumptuous guestrooms are generously sized, beginning at 425 square feet and topping out at 1,900 square feet for the Central Park Suite. Steeped in Old World elegance, rooms dress up in rich fabrics, crisp, white 400-thread-count linens, and a plethora of fluffy pillows. Gleaming, luxurious, and oversized marble baths are stocked with spacious vanities, hairdryers, and Frédéric Fekkai products.

If stress has sapped your energy, a visit to the on-site La Prairie spa is in order. The massage menu tailors treatments to most every ailment of upscale urban life, including jet lag, shopping fatigue, and executive stress.

The addition of BLT Market brings a frequently changing menu of market-fresh breakfast and dinner fare designed by Chef Laurent Tourondel. For afternoon tea or a well-shaken martini, stop by the clubby Star Lounge, or relax in the lobby over an expertly-prepared and served refreshment.

# 6 Columbus

D1

6 Columbus Circle (at 58th St.)

**Subway:** 59 St - Columbus Circle
**Phone:** 212-204-3000
**Web:** www.sixcolumbus.com
**Prices:** $$

88 Rooms

Thompson Hotels

This new addition to the Thompson Hotels collection (which includes 60 Thompson in SoHo) sparkles with a hip vibe. You can't beat the location, across the street from the Time Warner Center and Central Park. Despite its ritzy setting, the urban retreat is casual in style and surprisingly reasonable in price.

Sixties-mod describes the décor, which dresses the public spaces with teak paneling, molded chairs, and leather sofas in a palette of earthy tones. The same spirit—and teak paneling—infuses the sleek rooms, where custom-made furniture and chrome accents abound. Walls are decorated with artwork by fashion photographer Guy Bourdin. Frette linens, soft lighting, iPod docking stations, and complimentary WiFi Internet access round out the amenities. Bath products are by Fresh.

Adjacent to the lobby, Blue Ribbon Sushi Bar and Grill adds a new concept by the well-known Blue Ribbon Restaurants group. Japanese fare here runs the gamut from hamachi to hanger steak. As for the young staff, they're friendly and helpful, catering to a clientele largely made up of savvy urban professionals and international visitors.

# Sofitel

D3

45 W. 44th St. (bet. Fifth & Sixth Aves.)

**Subway:** 47-50 Sts - Rockefeller Ctr
**Phone:** 212-354-8844 or 877-565-9240
**Web:** www.sofitel-newyork.com
**Prices:** $$$$

346 Rooms
52 Suites

William Huber

Located mid-block on 44th Street, this 30-story glass and limestone tower couldn't be more convenient to Fifth Avenue shopping, Times Square, and the Theater District. It's an easy walk from here to Grand Central Station too. Owned by the French hotel group— Accor—the Sofitel New York maintains a European feel throughout.

The art deco-style lobby is as welcoming as it is elegant, set about with blond wood paneling, green marble, and groups of sleek leather club chairs arranged on a colorful floral-patterned carpet. Off the lobby, Gaby Bar offers a stylish lounge in which to sip a cocktail, while its sister restaurant—also called Gaby—features flavorful French classics along with more contemporary fare for lunch and dinner.

Honey-colored velvet drapes, red chenille armchairs, sumptuous damask linens, and marble baths outfit the attractive and well-maintained guest rooms. The glass-topped blond wood desk paired with a cushioned leather chair caters to business travelers; WiFi Internet access is available for a fee. A thoughtful touch for European guests, a voltage adaptor is included in each room.

# Warwick

A4

65 W. 54th St. (at Sixth Ave.)

**Subway:** 57 St
**Phone:** 212-247-2700 or 800-203-3232
**Web:** www.warwickhotelny.com
**Prices:** **$$$**

359 Rooms
67 Suites

Bruce Katz/Warwick New York Hotel

Newspaper magnate William Randolph Hearst built the Warwick New York Hotel in 1926 so that his lady friend, Marion Davies, could host their merrymaking band of Hollywood and theatrical friends in style. Convenient to MoMA and the Theater District, the 33-story hotel underwent a facelift, and the smart guest rooms haven't lost their traditional feeling. Larger than many city hotel quarters, rooms here incorporate slick modern touches such as temperature controls that sense your presence. Go for broke and book the Suite of the Stars, where Cary Grant lived for 12 years; it boasts 1,200 square feet of space and its own wrap-around terrace.

For business travelers, high-speed Internet access is available throughout the hotel, and the business center in the lobby offers 24-hour fax and copying services. There's also an on-site fitness facility.

After working, or working out, treat yourself to a meal at Murals on 54, in full view of Dean Cornwall's wonderful murals depicting the history of Sir Walter Raleigh. Commissioned by Hearst in 1937 for the hotel's former Raleigh Room, these paintings have now been restored to their original luster.

# Washington Jefferson Hotel

C2

318 W. 51st St. (bet. Eighth & Ninth Aves.)

**Subway:** 50 St (Eighth Ave.)
**Phone:** 212-246-7550 or 888-567-7550
**Web:** www.wjhotel.com
**Prices:** $

135
Rooms

Washington Jefferson Hotel

Fresh, contemporary design at a decent price in Manhattan was once a pipe dream, but the Washington Jefferson Hotel delivers style without a high price tag. Located in the up-and-coming neighborhood of Hell's Kitchen, the hotel is close to the bright lights of the Theater District.

The lobby is warm and welcoming, and the staff ensures that all guests feel at home from the moment they step inside the doors. Rooms are somewhat spartan, with platform beds dressed in crisp white linens, yet provide all the necessary amenities (TV with premium channels, radio/CD player). Clean lines extend to the bathrooms, outfitted with slate flooring and slate-tiled tubs. While standard rooms are on the small side, comfort is never sacrificed. Guests have 24-hour access to a small exercise room on-site, while serious athletes can take advantage of the reduced-price daily pass to Gold's Gym, available at the hotel's front desk.

Although there is no room service, you can enjoy lunch and dinner at the hotel's restaurant, Shimuzu. Sushi is a popular component here, but for those who prefer their fish cooked, the restaurant offers a delightful array of traditional Japanese dishes.

# The Mercer

B1

147 Mercer St. (at Prince St.)

**Subway:** Prince St
**Phone:** 212-966-6060
**Web:** www.mercerhotel.com
**Prices:** $$$$

67 Rooms
8 Suites

Thomas Loof/The Mercer

Even if your name isn't Leonardo DiCaprio, Cher, or Calvin Klein, you'll be equally welcome at The Mercer. Housed in a striking Romanesque Revival-style building erected in 1890, the hotel caters to the glitterati with discreet, personalized service, and intimate elegance. The modern lobby feels like your stylish friend's living room, complete with comfy seating, appealing coffee-table books, and an Apple for guests' use.

A Zen vibe pervades the guestrooms, fashioned by Parisian interior designer Christian Liaigre with high, loft-like ceilings, large European-style windows that open, soothing neutral palettes, and Asian decorative touches. Don't fret if you get a room facing the street; soundproofing filters out the noise. You'll find everything you need for business or leisure travel in your room, right down to scented candles and oversize FACE Stockholm bath products. Forgot something? The hotel's warm staff will gladly accommodate you with a laptop, a cell phone, or a fax machine in your room.

Sure, the hotel offers 24-hour room service, but in this case the food comes from Jean-Georges Vongerichten's Mercer Kitchen, located in the basement.

# 60 Thompson

B1

60 Thompson St. (bet. Broome & Spring Sts.)

**Subway:** Spring St (Sixth Ave.)
**Phone:** 212-431-0400 or 877-431-0400
**Web:** www.60thompson.com
**Prices:** $$$$

85 Rooms
13 Suites

Thompson Hotels

With its spare 1940s look inspired by French designer Jean-Michel Frank, 60 Thompson absolutely oozes SoHo style. The lobby, decorated in gray, brown, and moss-green tones, is accented by bouquets of fresh flowers, and natural light floods in from floor-to-ceiling windows.

Room sizes vary, but all sport a minimalist look, with crisp, white Frette linens standing out against a wall of dark, paneled leather. Business travelers take note that 60 Thompson has replaced the requisite in-room desk with a sitting area in its standard rooms. Bathrooms are tiled with chocolate-colored marble and stocked with spa products by Fresh. For those who don't appreciate the smell of cigarette smoke in their room, the hotel devotes two entire floors to non-smoking chambers.

Check out the rooftop bar on the 12th floor, where you can sip a cocktail and drink in the great city views. In good weather, the rooftop scene is a hot one, whereas the lobby bar bustles year-round with a cool crowd. Downstairs, Kittichai puts out modern Thai cuisine in an Asian-chic setting. The small bar here mixes fantastic and creative cocktails.

# Soho Grand

B2

310 West Broadway (bet. Canal & Grand Sts.)

**Subway:** Canal St (Sixth Ave.)
**Phone:** 212-965-3000 or 800-965-3000
**Web:** www.sohogrand.com
**Prices:** **$$$$**

361 Rooms
2 Suites

Soho Grand

Cutting-edge fashion, fine art, and delicious dining beckon in the blocks right outside this hip hotel (whose equally chic sister, the Tribeca Grand, lies a short walk to the south). Inside, designer William Sofield calls to mind the neighborhood's industrial roots in the lobby's clean lines, concrete pillars, and cast-iron details.

Rooms are swathed in neutral tones, with leather headboards, Egyptian cotton sheets, and a host of modern amenities. Bose Wave CD/radios, DVD players, and in-room CD selections come in every room; iPods and docking stations are available on request. For true grandeur, reserve one of the penthouse lofts. In these spacious custom-designed suites, you will have the luxury of two bedrooms, as well as a 1,200-square-foot wrap-around furnished terrace on which to entertain or simply to take in the killer view of the Manhattan skyline.

Bicycles are on hand for complimentary guest use when the weather permits; and the hotel's "grandlife" website provides a wealth of information about goings-on in the city. Families are welcomed with signature programs for babies and children, not to mention the hotel's pet-friendly policy. Ain't life grand?

# Cosmopolitan

B3

95 West Broadway (at Chambers St.)

**Subway:** Chambers St (West Broadway)
**Phone:** 212-566-1900 or 888-895-9400
**Web:** www.cosmohotel.com
**Prices:** $

125 Rooms

Cosmopolitan Hotel

This privately owned seven-story hotel enjoys a valuable location in the heart of TriBeCa, while catering to more budget-conscious visitors to the city. Just a few steps away from Wall Street, SoHo, and Chinatown, the Cosmopolitan pulls in a steady clientele of business travelers and European tourists, who may appreciate the hotel's low prices, convenient setting, and cigarette-friendly policy.

The Cosmopolitan may lack the frills of some grander city hostelries, but guests can use the money saved on a room here to splurge on a show or dinner in a fine restaurant. Basic rooms are well-maintained, fairly spacious, and they all have private baths. Scant in-room amenities include a hair dryer, cable TV, a ceiling fan, and free wireless Internet access. Ask for a room on the back side of the hotel if worried about the street noise. Despite the fact that the entire hotel is smoking-friendly, the halls and the rooms seems absent of cigarettes traces.

The hotel does not offer room service, but the Cosmopolitan Café is right next door. This tiny eatery, with its rustic country style, makes a good spot for a light breakfast or to catch a quick sandwich at midday.

# Greenwich Hotel

A2

377 Greenwich St. (at N. Moore St.)

**Subway:** Franklin St
**Phone:** 212-941-8900
**Web:** www.thegreenwichhotel.com
**Prices:** $$$$

75 Rooms
13 Suites

The Greenwich Hotel

Spanning the worlds of classic elegance and city chic, this TriBeCa recent addition was unceremoniously unveiled in spring 2008. Though the hoopla was kept to a minimum—despite the fact that Robert DeNiro and his son are partners—the Greenwich is a hotel to crow about. Attention to detail is evident here from the construction materials to the organic bath amenities, all reflecting au courant Italian sensibilities.

Among the 88 rooms, no two are alike. Carved pine doors open into refined chambers boasting Duxiana beds, custom-designed settees, and hardwood floors. Ten-foot-high ceilings create an airy feel. The same care is taken in the design of the bathrooms, with their brass hardware, Frette towels, and mosaic tiled showers. All the modern electronic amenities apply as well.

An on-site fitness center and a lantern-lit indoor swimming pool will take care of your exercise needs, while the Japanese-inspired Shibui spa spotlights relaxation with a shiatsu room and a room for traditional bathing rituals. Italian fare takes top billing at Locanda Verde by Chef Andrew Carmellini.

# Smyth

B3

85 West Broadway

**Subway:** Chambers St (West Broadway)
**Phone:** 212-587-7000 or 888-587-6984
**Web:** www.thompsonhotels.com
**Prices:** **$$$**

96 Rooms
4 Suites

Michael Weber

The latest in the Thompson Hotel Group's string of boutique properties around Manhattan, the Smyth is a 13-story condominium/hotel hybrid; the top four floors are dedicated to Smyth Upstairs, consisting of 15 luxurious apartments. Designer Yabu Pushelberg decked out the stunning public spaces in a modern mélange of marble, onyx, leather, and textured wall coverings. It all combines to create a playful sense and a sexy vibe—with attitude to spare.

Room décor reflects a mid-20th century sensibility, illustrated by clean lines, white walls, velvet fabrics, Sferra linens, and lots of wood. Despite the hotel's location right off busy Chambers Street, the windows do a surprisingly good job of blocking out noise from the street below. Suite upgrades add the likes of a wet bar, two full bathrooms, and perhaps a terrace with seating for six. In the bathrooms, gray-and-white marble subway tiles create a sparkling facing on the walls.

Promised for the future are a high-end restaurant, a private cellar bar, and amenities such as in-room massage, valet parking, and a personal shopper. The jury is still out, but the Smyth may be destined as the new TriBeCa hot spot for the hip traveling set.

# Tribeca Grand

C2

2 Sixth Ave. (at Church St.)

**Subway:** Canal St (Sixth Ave.)
**Phone:** 212-519-6600 or 877-519-6600
**Web:** www.tribecagrand.com
**Prices:** $$$

196 Rooms
7 Suites

Tribeca Grand

Frequented by celebrities and the oh-so-hip Euro-set, the Tribeca Grand gives every guest the star treatment. Sister to the Soho Grand, this hotel greets guests in its airy, vaulted atrium lobby—often used as a movie backdrop—whose clean lines evoke the Prairie style of architect Frank Lloyd Wright. In the evening, the lobby's swanky Church Lounge becomes a destination in itself, as it fills with the hot and hip music- and film-industry set. In summer, the party spills out to sidewalk seating along Sixth Avenue.

Deep earth tones, with bright sparks of orange and yellow, color the comfortable guest rooms, which are equally well-equipped for business and leisure travelers. Movie mavens may want to reserve an iStudio room, furnished with a video camera and a computer loaded with every program an amateur film buff could want.

Paris Hilton may feel perfectly at home here, but so would her pup. Owned by Leonard and Emanuel Stern, members of the family that founded Hartz Mountain Industries, the Tribeca Grand accommodates pets in equally high style. Had to leave your four-footed friend at home? Request a goldfish to keep you company in your room.

# Bentley

B4

500 E. 62nd St. (at York Ave.)

**Subway:** Lexington Av - 59 St
**Phone:** 212-644-6000 or 888-664-6835
**Web:** www.nychotels.com
**Prices:** **$$**

161 Rooms
36 Suites

Bentley Hotel

It may be a little bit of a walk to the subway, Central Park, and the shops, but sitting right on the East River, with easy access to-and-from the airports, it's worth the extra blocks for the value and accessibility. The Bentley may not be new or trendy, but it makes a fashionable first impression. Floor-to-ceiling windows, geometric-patterned carpets, marble flooring, and contemporary furnishings fill the Art Deco lobby of this 21-story glass-and-steel office building, which was converted into a hotel in 1998.

By New York City standard, rooms are surprisingly spacious. A bit the worse for wear, furnishings and carpeting adhere to a neutral color scheme. Seating nooks by the windows take in views of the East River and the Queensboro Bridge. Families favor the extra space offered in the 36 suites, complete with pull-out sofas or futons. Given the location and moderate prices, this hotel is a good find.

The Bentley doesn't serve breakfast, but guests have complimentary access to a cappuccino bar 24 hours a day. If you don't feel up to dining out, the rooftop restaurant serves up panoramic city views with its limited menu. Valet parking, free daily newspapers, and concierge service count among other amenities provided.

# The Carlyle

B3

35 E. 76th St. (at Madison Ave.)

**Subway:** 77 St
**Phone:** 212-744-1600 or 800-227-5737
**Web:** www.thecarlyle.com
**Prices:** $$$$

123 Rooms
58 Suites

Spa

Masterson

Named for British historian Thomas Carlyle, this hotel epitomizes opulence with its fine artwork, Baccarat crystal light fixtures, and marble baths. Individually decorated Classic aka "standard" rooms are dressed in Louis XVI-style with original Audubon prints, 440-thread-count Italian linens, and elegant area rugs over wood floors. A select few of the Carlyle's roomy suites feature a baby-grand piano for the musically inclined.

Since it opened across from Central Park in 1930, The Carlyle has hosted every American president since Truman, along with a roster of foreign dignitaries from Prime Minister Nehru to Princess Diana—how's that for an A-list?

For entertainment, there's Café Carlyle, where Woody Allen regularly jams with the Eddie Davis New Orleans jazz band. Legendary Bemelmans Bar, renowned for its whimsical mural of characters from artist Ludwig Bemelmans' famous Madeline series of children's books, is a popular place for a cocktail.

With a contemporary menu almost as classy as the crowd it draws, the handsome Carlyle Restaurant proves a perfect complement to the hotel's sophistication. The hotel's new Sense Spa offers weary guests 4,000 square feet of soothing indulgence.

# The Lowell

A1

28 E. 63rd St. (bet. Madison & Park Aves.)

**Subway:** Lexington Av - 63 St
**Phone:** 212-838-1400 or 800-221-4444
**Web:** www.lowellhotel.com
**Prices:** **$$$$**

23 Rooms
47 Suites

The Lowell

From the moment you step inside the silk-paneled lobby, you'll sense the European elegance that defines The Lowell. Intimate and sumptuous, this place appeals to those who value discretion, in both the size of the property and the attitude of the staff.

With suites outnumbering rooms 47 to 23, the emphasis here is on residential luxury. Indeed, this art deco brick and glazed terra-cotta structure was completed in 1926 as an apartment hotel. While lavish suites boast wood-burning fireplaces, private terraces, kitchens, and more, all rooms are individually decorated with marble baths and original art and antiques.

In 2008, the Lowell unveiled new healthful-living options in response to requests from its sophisticated travelers. Guests need not forsake their daily exercise when the hotel's fully equipped fitness center offers personal trainers and Pilates instructors, in addition to Cybex equipment and free weights. Maps of nearby Central Park are available for those who prefer to exercise outdoors. Come mealtime, menus for the Pembroke Room and in-room dining are now stocked with nutritious, low-calorie, and low-carb choices—so there's no excuse for cheating on your diet.

# The Regency

A1

540 Park Ave. (at 61st St.)

**Subway:** Lexington Av - 59 St
**Phone:** 212-759-4100 or 800-233-2356
**Web:** www.loewshotels.com
**Prices:** $$$$

267 Rooms
86 Suites

Spa

Thibault Jeanson/Lowes Hotels

Public spaces ooze personality at the Loews flagship, sitting right on Park Avenue. Accommodations are bland in comparison, but large by New York standards, with abundant closet space and enough room to stay comfortably for several days (as long as you don't mind that the mattresses and bathrooms could use upgrading). The pleasant team offers a high level of service, and if your pup is traveling with you, the hotel offers dog-walking services as well as a separate room-service menu for pets.

For good dining and entertainment options, you don't have to leave the hotel. The upscale restaurant, 540 Park, is always packed in the evening, attracting as much of a local following as it does hotel guests. At breakfast, this place shakes with major players brokering deals over bacon and eggs. The Library lounge is a cozy—and popular—spot for a cocktail any night of the week. Its menu runs to comfort food such as chicken pot pie and braised lamb shank.

Last but not least, there's Feinsteins at the Regency, named for its owner—pop vocalist and songwriter Michael Feinstein. This blast from the past still packs 'em in for cabaret headliners six nights a week.

# Mandarin Oriental

A4

80 Columbus Circle (at 60th St.)

**Subway:** 59 St - Columbus Circle
**Phone:** 212-805-8800 or 866-801-8880
**Web:** www.mandarinoriental.com
**Prices:** $$$$

202 Rooms
46 Suites

Mandarin Oriental, New York

Everything you could desire in New York City lies literally at the doorstep of the Mandarin Oriental. Occupying floors 35 to 54 in the north tower of the Time Warner Center, this hotel flaunts its enviable location overlooking Central Park. Also the site of such stellar restaurants as Per Se and Masa (*see restaurant listing for both*), hotel guests have direct access to the shops located inside the Time Warner Center at Columbus Circle. And don't pass up the contemporary Asian cuisine on-site at Asiate.

From the moment you enter to the moment you leave, the hotel's top-drawer service will make you feel like a VIP. Masculine yet delicate, modern yet timeless, guestrooms incorporate soigné touches such as cherry woods, silvery silks, and Fili D'oro linens. The view's the thing here; and the scenery is played up to full advantage with a wall of floor-to-ceiling windows in each room.

No visit to this unforgettable place is complete without a trip to the 36th-floor spa, which offers a customized "journey for the senses," booked in blocks of time rather than by treatment. The lobby lounge is an elegant spot to sip on a modern cocktail while taking in the panoramic view.

# On the Ave

A3

2178 Broadway (at 77th St.)

**Subway:** 79 St
**Phone:** 212-362-1100 or 800-497-6028
**Web:** www.ontheave.com
**Prices:** $$

242 Rooms
27 Suites

On The Ave

Broadway without the buzz is what awaits you On the Ave. Guests here get a respite from the bustle of midtown in this quiet upper west side neighborhood, where many of the city's natural and man-made treasures can be found. Fancy a walk in Central Park or a visit to the Museum of Natural History? Both are less than three blocks away. If you wish to explore farther afield, the subway station is just a two-block walk.

Shades of gray, ecru, and pewter color the restrained contemporary room décor, while baths sport brushed stainless-steel sinks and marble tiles. If you're not afraid of heights, rooms on the top three floors boast balconies with panoramas of the Hudson River and Central Park. Don't have a view? Take the elevator to the 16th floor, where you can relax and look out over uptown from the furnished and landscaped balcony. Backlit black-and-white photographs of Gotham City adorn the lobby and hallways of this hotel.

Exhausted and ravenous after a day flooded with shopping and sightseeing? Stay cozy in your room and call for room service from The West Branch for a slew of comforting and contemporary American delights.

# Trump International
## Hotel & Tower

A4

1 Central Park West (at Columbus Circle)

**Subway:** 59 St - Columbus Circle
**Phone:** 212-299-1000 or 888-448-7867
**Web:** www.trumpintl.com
**Prices:** $$$$

38 Rooms
129 Suites

Trump Hotel Collection

An icon for its association with its flamboyant owner, this 52-story tower does Donald Trump proud. The location is ideal, with upscale shopping at the Time Warner Center and the attractions of Central Park right outside the door.

More than two-thirds of the accommodations—located on the 3rd through 17th floors—are spacious one- or- two-bedroom suites boasting custom-designed furniture and great city and park views. A blissful night's sleep awaits in lodgings that range from 460 square feet for a junior suite to 1,350 square feet for a two-bedroom unit. All have kitchens stocked with china and crystal; if you don't feel like cooking, you can arrange for a member of the staff from the stellar chef—Jean Georges' restaurant—to prepare a gourmet meal in your room.

The 55-foot-long indoor pool is perfect for swimming laps, and the Techno-Gym equipment at the fitness center supplies a challenging workout (personal training and one-on-one yoga sessions are available).

Offering everything from complimentary business cards to free local phone calls, Trump's signature Attaché service caters to The Donald in everyone.

# Nu Hotel

D3

85 Smith St. (bet. Atlantic Ave. & State St.)

**Subway:** Hoyt - Schermerhorn
**Phone:** 718-852-8585
**Web:** www.nuhotelbrooklyn.com
**Prices:** $

90
Rooms
3
Suites

Gridley & Graves Photography

Housed in a condominium tower near the quaint residential neighborhood of Cobble Hill, Nu Hotel opened in July 2008 and caters to the budget-conscious with contemporary style for reasonable rates. Located steps away from the government offices of downtown Brooklyn, the hotel is as ideally situated for those with business in the area as it is for guests visiting nearby family and friends.

Wide hallways lead to eco-friendly rooms dressed in organic white linens and modern light wood furnishings against a cool palette swathed in lead-free paint. White-tiled bathrooms incorporate a whimsical touch: a chalkboard wall for doodling or leaving messages for housekeeping. Inspired by urban lofts, suites may add a hammock or bunk beds as inventive sleeping spaces for extra guests.

The hotel has no restaurant, but does offer a complimentary daily buffet continental breakfast downstairs at Nu Bar.

And, sure, you can take the subway into Manhattan-there are a multitude of lines nearby-for shopping and dining, but why bother when the chic boutiques and culinary enticements of Smith Street are such an easy walk away?

# Indexes

## Where to **Eat**

# Alphabetical List of Restaurants

## C

## N



## O



## P



## Q



## R

## T



## U



## V



## W



## X



## Y



## Z

# Restaurants by Cuisine

## American

| | | |
|---|---|---|
| Alexander's Cafe | ✗ | 354 |
| Barbuto | ✗✗ | 113 |
| Beacon | ✗✗ | 228 |
| BG | ✗✗ | 230 |
| Bin 71 | 🍴 | 333 |
| Black Whale (The) | ✗ | 355 |
| BLT Market | ✗✗ | 231 |
| Blue Hill ✿ | ✗✗ | 115 |
| Blue Smoke 😊 | ✗ | 85 |
| Boathouse Central Park | ✗✗ | 305 |
| Braeburn | ✗✗ | 117 |
| Bridge Cafe | ✗ | 72 |
| Buttermilk Channel 😊 ✗ | | 373 |
| Cafe Cluny | ✗ | 118 |
| Carol's Cafe | ✗ | 439 |
| Casellula | 🍴 | 234 |
| Clover Club | 🍴 | 375 |
| Cookshop | ✗✗ | 17 |
| Craft | ✗✗✗ | 88 |
| Diner | ✗ | 376 |
| Dressler ✿ | ✗✗ | 377 |
| DuMont | ✗ | 376 |
| Egg 😊 | ✗ | 378 |
| Farm on Adderley (The) | ✗ | 379 |
| Five Points | ✗✗ | 123 |
| 44 & X Hell's Kitchen | ✗✗ | 240 |
| Four Seasons (The) | ✗✗✗✗ | 193 |
| General Greene (The) | ✗ | 381 |
| Good | ✗ | 124 |
| Good Enough to Eat | ✗ | 338 |
| Harrison (The) | ✗✗✗ | 293 |
| Harry's Steak & Cafe | ✗ | 73 |
| Henry's End | ✗ | 383 |
| Hudson River Cafe | ✗✗ | 157 |
| Jack the Horse | ✗✗ | 383 |
| J. G. Melon 😊 | ✗ | 314 |
| Kings' Carriage House | ✗✗ | 315 |
| Kitchenette | ✗ | 293 |
| Landmark Tavern | ✗✗ | 246 |
| Maloney & Porcelli | ✗✗✗ | 199 |
| Marc Forgione ✿ | ✗✗ | 296 |
| Market Table | ✗ | 132 |
| Métrazur | ✗✗ | 200 |
| New Leaf Café | ✗ | 158 |
| No. 7 | ✗ | 392 |
| Odeon (The) | ✗✗ | 298 |
| Picket Fence | ✗ | 393 |
| Recipe | ✗ | 343 |
| The Red Cat | ✗✗ | 24 |
| Rye 😊 | ✗ | 397 |
| Salt | ✗ | 283 |
| Savoy | ✗✗ | 283 |
| Taste | ✗ | 327 |
| Telepan | ✗✗ | 345 |
| 21 Club | ✗✗ | 266 |
| Union Square Cafe | ✗✗ | 103 |
| Vida 😊 | ✗ | 441 |
| Vinegar Hill House | ✗ | 403 |
| Water's Edge | ✗✗✗ | 432 |
| West Bank Café | ✗✗ | 268 |
| West Branch (The) | ✗✗ | 346 |

## Argentinian

| | | |
|---|---|---|
| La Rural | ✗ | 340 |

## Asian

| | | |
|---|---|---|
| Aja | ✗✗ | 178 |
| Chance | ✗ | 373 |
| China Grill | ✗✗ | 235 |
| Garden Court Café 😊 | ✗ | 312 |
| Kampuchea 😊 | ✗ | 167 |
| Kuma Inn | 🍴 | 168 |
| Momofuku Noodle Bar 😊 | ✗ | 63 |
| Mulan | ✗✗ | 422 |
| Pranna | ✗✗ | 98 |
| SHI | ✗✗✗ | 428 |

## Deli



## Eastern European



## Ethiopian



## European



## Filipino

## French



## Fusion



## Gastropub



## German



## Greek



## Indian

## International



## Italian

## Moroccan

| | | |
|---|---|---|
| Café Mogador | ℵ | 47 |
| Kif 🍴 | ℵ | 385 |
| La Maison du Couscous | ℵ | 386 |

## New Zealand

| | | |
|---|---|---|
| Nelson Blue | ℵ | 75 |

## Persian

| | | |
|---|---|---|
| Persepolis | ℵ | 321 |
| Shalizar 🌸 | ℵℵ | 323 |

## Peruvian

| | | |
|---|---|---|
| Panca | ℵ | 137 |
| Pio Pio | ℵ | 425 |
| Urubamba | ℵ | 430 |

## Pizza

| | | |
|---|---|---|
| Adrienne's Pizzabar | ℵ | 72 |
| Anselmo | ℵ | 367 |
| Keste Pizza & Vino | ℵ | 128 |
| Luzzo's | ℵ | 61 |
| Motorino 🍴 | ℵ | 391 |
| Nick's | ℵ | 319 |
| Roberta's | ℵ | 397 |

## Polish

| | | |
|---|---|---|
| Karczma | ℵ | 385 |

## Portuguese

| | | |
|---|---|---|
| Macao Trading Co. | ℵℵ | 295 |

## Puerto Rican

| | | |
|---|---|---|
| Brisas Del Caribe | ℵ | 355 |

## Russian

| | | |
|---|---|---|
| Firebird | ℵℵℵ | 239 |
| Russian Samovar | ℵ | 258 |

## Scandinavian

| | | |
|---|---|---|
| Aquavit | ℵℵℵ | 182 |

## Seafood

| | | |
|---|---|---|
| Aquagrill | ℵℵ | 273 |
| Atlantic Grill | ℵℵ | 304 |
| BLT Fish | ℵℵ | 84 |
| Blue Fin | ℵℵ | 231 |
| Brooklyn Fish Camp | ℵ | 371 |
| Compass | ℵℵ | 335 |
| Ed's Lobster Bar 🍴 | ℵ | 276 |
| Esca | ℵℵℵ | 238 |
| Fishtail by David Burke | ℵℵℵ | 311 |
| Flex Mussels | ℵ | 311 |
| Jack's Luxury Oyster Bar | ℵ | 53 |
| Le Bernardin 🌸🌸🌸 | ℵℵℵℵ | 247 |
| Lure Fishbar | ℵℵ | 279 |
| Marea 🌸 | ℵℵℵℵ | 248 |
| Mary's Fish Camp | ℵ | 132 |
| The Mermaid Inn | ℵ | 61 |
| Oceana 🌸 | ℵℵℵ | 203 |
| Pearl Oyster Bar | ℵ | 138 |
| Sabry's | ℵ | 425 |
| Sea Grill (The) | ℵℵ | 259 |
| Water Club (The) | ℵℵℵ | 216 |
| Wild Edibles | ℵ | 216 |

## South African

| | | |
|---|---|---|
| Braai | ℵℵ | 232 |

## Southern

| | | |
|---|---|---|
| Amy Ruth's 🍴 | ℵ | 155 |
| Brooklyn Star 🍴 | ℵ | 372 |
| Dizzy's Club Coca-Cola | ℵ | 237 |
| Melba's | ℵ | 158 |
| Miss Mamie's Spoonbread Too | ℵ | 341 |
| The River Room | ℵ | 159 |

## Southwestern

| | | |
|---|---|---|
| Mesa Grill | ℵℵ | 95 |

## Spanish

| | | |
|---|---|---|
| Alcala | ℵℵ | 180 |
| Bar Carrera | 🍽 | 45 |
| Bar Jamón | 🍽 | 83 |

## Sri Lankan



## Steakhouse



## Thai



## Tibetan



## Turkish



## Uzbek



## Vegan



## Vegetarian



## Vietnamese

# Cuisines by Neighborhood

## MANHATTAN

### Chelsea

*American*

| | | |
|---|---|---|
| Cookshop | ✗✗ | 17 |
| The Red Cat | ✗✗ | 24 |

*Contemporary*

| | | |
|---|---|---|
| Klee Brasserie | ✗✗ | 20 |
| 202 ⊙ | ✗ | 25 |

*Fusion*

| | | |
|---|---|---|
| Morimoto | ✗✗✗ | 23 |

*Indian*

| | | |
|---|---|---|
| Bombay Talkie | ✗ | 16 |

*Italian*

| | | |
|---|---|---|
| da Umberto | ✗✗ | 18 |
| Del Posto ✿ | ✗✗✗✗ | 19 |
| Le Zie 2000 | ✗✗ | 22 |

*Japanese*

| | | |
|---|---|---|
| Matsuri | ✗✗ | 22 |
| Naka Naka | ✗ | 23 |

*Mexican*

| | | |
|---|---|---|
| Crema | ✗ | 18 |
| Rocking Horse Cafe | ✗ | 24 |
| Sueños | ✗ | 25 |

*Spanish*

| | | |
|---|---|---|
| El Quinto Pino | 🍺 | 20 |
| Tia Pol | 🍺 | 26 |
| Txikito | 🍺 | 26 |

*Steakhouse*

| | | |
|---|---|---|
| Craftsteak | ✗✗✗ | 17 |

*Vegan*

| | | |
|---|---|---|
| Blossom | ✗ | 16 |

### Chinatown & Little Italy

*Chinese*

| | | |
|---|---|---|
| Chatham Square | ✗ | 30 |
| Dim Sum Go Go ⊙ | ✗ | 31 |
| Fuleen Seafood | ✗ | 31 |
| Golden Unicorn ⊙ | ✗ | 32 |
| Great N.Y. Noodletown ⊙ | ✗ | 32 |
| Mandarin Court | ✗ | 35 |
| New Yeah Shanghai | ✗ | 36 |
| Oriental Garden | ✗✗ | 37 |
| Peking Duck House | ✗ | 38 |
| Red Egg ⊙ | ✗ | 39 |
| Shanghai Café | ✗ | 39 |

*French*

| | | |
|---|---|---|
| Parigot | ✗ | 37 |

*Italian*

| | | |
|---|---|---|
| Da Nico | ✗ | 30 |
| Il Cortile | ✗✗ | 33 |
| Il Palazzo | ✗✗ | 33 |
| Pellegrino's | ✗ | 38 |

*Korean*

| | | |
|---|---|---|
| Júp Shē | ✗ | 34 |

*Malaysian*

| | | |
|---|---|---|
| New Malaysia | ✗ | 35 |
| Nyonya ⊙ | ✗ | 36 |

*Mexican*

| | | |
|---|---|---|
| La Esquina | ✗ | 34 |

*Vietnamese*

| | | |
|---|---|---|
| Thai So'n | ✗ | 40 |
| Xe Lua | ✗ | 40 |

### East Village

*Asian*

| | | |
|---|---|---|
| Momofuku Noodle Bar ⊙ | ✗ | 63 |

*Basque*

| | | |
|---|---|---|
| Euzkadi | ✗ | 50 |

*Contemporary*

| | | |
|---|---|---|
| Apiary | ✗✗ | 44 |
| Back Forty | ✗ | 44 |
| ChikaLicious Dessert Bar | 🍺 | 48 |
| Joe Doe | ✗ | 55 |
| Momofuku Ko ✿✿ | ✗ | 62 |
| Momofuku Ssäm Bar ⊙ | ✗ | 63 |

## Greenwich, West Village & Meatpacking District

## Harlem, Morningside & Washington Heights

## Midtown West

## Upper East Side



## Upper West Side

# Starred Restaurants

*Within the selection we offer you, some restaurants deserve to be highlighted for their particularly good cuisine. When giving one, two, or three Michelin stars, there are a number of elements that we consider including the quality of the ingredients, the technical skill and flair that goes into their preparation, the blend and clarity of flavours, and the balance of the menu. Just as important is the ability to produce excellent cooking time and again. We make as many visits as we need, so that our readers may be assured of quality and consistency.*

*A two or three-star restaurant has to offer something very special in its cuisine; a real element of creativity, originality, or "personality" that sets it apart from the rest. Three stars – our highest award – are given to the choicest restaurants, where the whole dining experience is superb.*

*Cuisine in any style, modern or traditional, may be eligible for a star. Due to the fact we apply the same independent standards everywhere, the awards have become benchmarks of reliability and excellence in over 20 countries in Europe and Asia, particularly in France, where we have awarded stars for 100 years, and where the phrase "Now that's real three-star quality!" has entered into the language.*

**The awarding of a star is based solely on the quality of the cuisine.**

✿✿✿

## Exceptional cuisine, worth a special journey.

One always eats here extremely well, sometimes superbly. Distinctive dishes are precisely executed, using superlative ingredients.



✿✿

## Excellent cuisine, worth a detour.

Skillfully and carefully crafted dishes of outsanding quality.



✿

## A very good restaurant in its category.

A place offering cuisine prepared to a consistently high standard.

# Bib Gourmand

This symbol indicates our inspector's favorites for good value. For $40 or less, you can enjoy two courses and a glass of wine or a dessert (not including tax or gratuity).

# Under $25

# Brunch

# Late Dining



## MANHATTAN

### Chelsea



### Chinatown & Little Italy



### East Village



### Financial District



### Gramercy, Flatiron & Union Square

## Greenwich, West Village & Meatpacking District



## Harlem, Morningside & Washington Heights



## Lower East Side

## QUEENS



## STATEN ISLAND

# Indexes

## Where to **Stay**

# Alphabetical List of Hotels

# Notes

Michelin

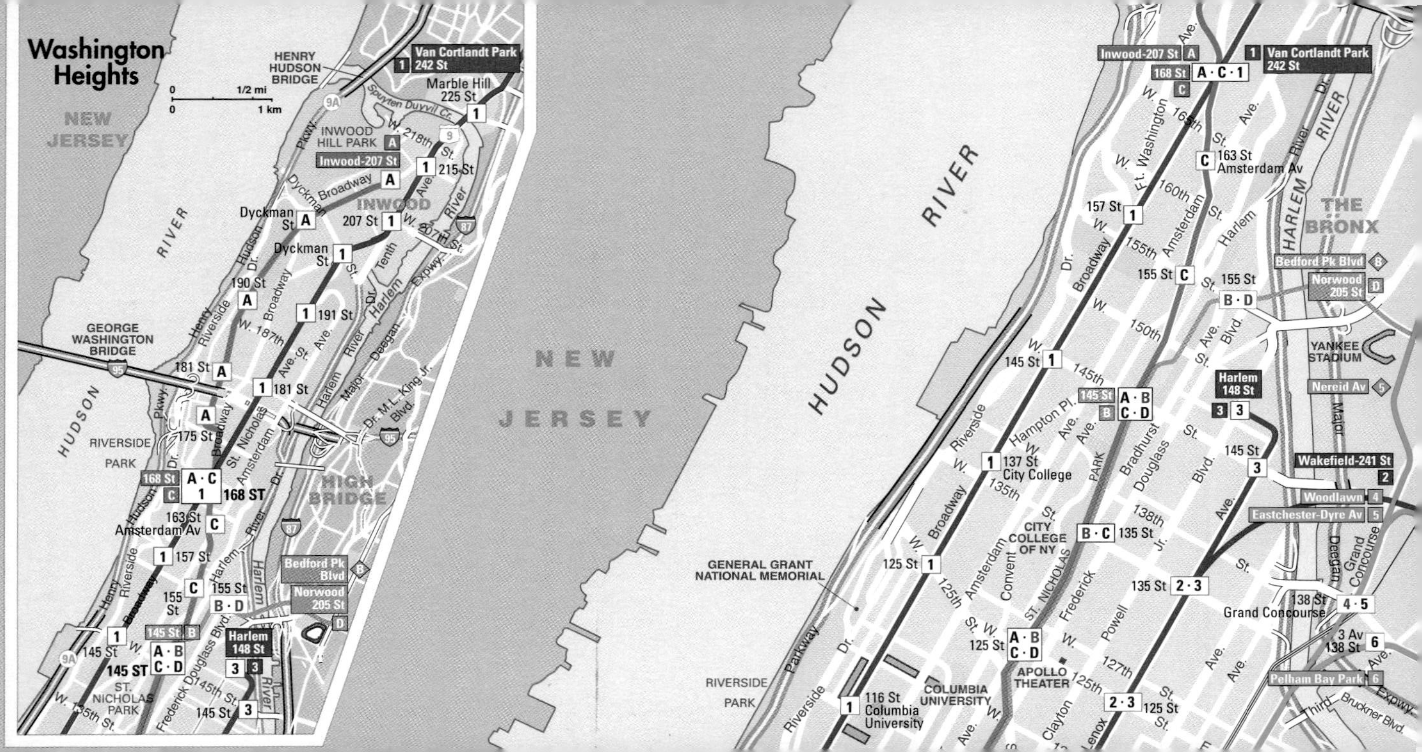
Washington Heights
0 1/2 mi
0 1 km
NEW JERSEY
HENRY HUDSON BRIDGE
Van Cortlandt Park 242 St
Marble Hill 225 St
INWOOD HILL PARK
Inwood-207 St
215 St
INWOOD
Dyckman St
207 St
190 St
191 St
GEORGE WASHINGTON BRIDGE
181 St
175 St
RIVERSIDE PARK
168 St
168 ST
163 St Amsterdam Av
157 St
155 St
Bedford Pk Blvd
Norwood 205 St
Harlem 148 St
145 St
145 ST
ST. NICHOLAS PARK
HIGH BRIDGE
HUDSON RIVER
NEW JERSEY
THE BRONX
HARLEM RIVER
YANKEE STADIUM
Nereid Av
Wakefield-241 St
Woodlawn
Eastchester-Dyre Av
137 St City College
CITY COLLEGE OF NY
135 St
125 St
GENERAL GRANT NATIONAL MEMORIAL
Grand Concourse
138 St
3 Av 138 St
Pelham Bay Park
APOLLO THEATER
COLUMBIA UNIVERSITY
116 St Columbia University
RIVERSIDE PARK